ST. PETERSBURG

A CULTURAL HISTORY

OTHER BOOKS BY SOLOMON VOLKOV

Young Composers of Leningrad
(*Leningrad and Moscow, 1971*)

Testimony: The Memoirs of Dmitri Shostakovich
(*New York, 1979*)

Balanchine's Tchaikovsky:
Conversations with Balanchine on His Life, Ballet and Music
(*New York, 1985*)

From Russia to the West:
The Music Memoirs and Reminiscences of Nathan Milstein
(*New York, 1990*)

Joseph Brodsky in New York
(*New York, 1990*)

Remembering Anna Akhmatova:
Conversations with Joseph Brodsky
(*Moscow, 1992*)

ST. PETERSBURG

A CULTURAL HISTORY

SOLOMON VOLKOV

Translated by Antonina W. Bouis

THE FREE PRESS

New York · London · Toronto · Sydney · Tokyo · Singapore

THE FREE PRESS
A Division of Simon & Schuster Inc.
1230 Avenue of the Americas
New York, N.Y. 10020

Printed in the United States of America

Designed by REM Studio, Inc.

printing number
1 3 5 7 9 10 8 6 4 2

Library of Congress Cataloging-in-Publication Data

Volkov, Solomon.

   St. Petersburg: a cultural history/ Solomon Volkov;

[translator] Antonina W. Bouis.

      p.   cm.

   Includes index.

   ISBN 0-02-874052-1

   1. Saint Petersburg (Russia)—Civilization.   I. Title.

DK557.V65   1995

947'.453—dc20   95-24116

                                                   CIP

To Erwin A. Glikes

(1937–1994)

For eighteen years my publisher, mentor, friend

CONTENTS

its status as capital of Russia and, almost dead of hunger and cold, tried to remain faithful to itself. This is the Petersburg of Anna Akhmatova.

PREFACE

*... absence is the best medicine
for forgetting ... but the best way
to forget forever is to see daily ...*
ANNA AKHMATOVA[1]

On May 16, 1965, a string quartet of young musicians with their instruments in cases and their folding music stands boarded a cold and uninviting commuter train on the outskirts of Leningrad en route to the northern shore of the Gulf of Finland. It was a Sunday, and they were off to visit the poet Anna Akhmatova, who every spring spent her time in the dacha settlement of Komarovo, the former Kellomäki, some forty kilometers from Leningrad.

I was twenty-one and first violinist of the ensemble, made up of students from the Leningrad Conservatory. Since my youth, I had known by heart many of Akhmatova's poems, for I considered her the greatest Russian poet alive, as did a multitude of other literature lovers, and I had long wanted to express my delight and deepest respect to her. Finally, I learned Akhmatova's telephone number, called her, introduced myself, and offered to play whatever she liked. After some reflection, she named Shostakovich, a very fortunate choice for us, because just recently we had been the first ensemble in Leningrad to have learned his latest quartet, the Ninth, and performed it at the Shostakovich Festival in Leningrad with the composer present.

And this work, a half-hour piece not yet published, we performed for Akhmatova at her green dacha, which she called "a booth." It was probably the most unusual concert performance of my life—for an audience of one, a seventy-five-year-old grande dame in a black kimono worn over a festive pink dress, who sat majestically in a deep armchair, her eyes half shut. She seemed to be absorbing the bitterness, alienation, and tragic intensity of Shostakovich's music, so compatible with her own late poetry. The dramatic fates of Akhmatova and Shostakovich, closely tied to Petersburg, had crossed more than once. They had both been criticized by the Soviet authorities; they had addressed each other in their works, and in the book of poetry she gave the composer, Akhmatova had written: "To Dmitri Dmitrievich Shostakovich, in whose era I live on earth."

While we played, the unpredictable Baltic weather, probably in unison with the music, went crazy; a terrible wind was followed by hail and then snow. But when we finished, the sun was shining. Akhmatova sighed, "I was afraid only that the music would come to an end." Then Akhmatova and I went out on the porch. And nature—perhaps continuing its competition with the music—tried to prove that it always had the last word if it wanted it: above snow-covered Komarovo a brilliant rainbow filled the sky.

Enjoying the rainbow, Akhmatova noted portentously in her throaty, hypnotic voice, "The weather was like this, I recall, in May 1916" and proceeded to recite her poem "May Snow," written almost half a century earlier.

> *A translucent veil covers*
> *The fresh turf and melts unobserved.*

Was there a lover of Russian poetry who did not know that languorous, magnificently realized poem, which ended with the lines,

> *In me reposes the sadness which King David*
> *Regally bestowed upon the millennia.*

I was struck by Akhmatova's uncanny ability, which I later learned was very characteristic of her, to combine seemingly incompatible historic periods and events and make complex parallels between them, showing, in Akhmatova's opinion, a predestination and repetition of the apparently most unexpected and unpredictable turns of fate. For this witness to and participant in the cataclysms of the twentieth century, who had survived immeasurable suffering and trials, the times were out of joint, and setting them right was the most natural undertaking, her daily duty. Akhmatova extended with ease an instantaneous but sturdy thread between the snows of 1916 and 1965, at the same time conscious of the significance of such a union, only superficially random, which inevitably took on a profound cultural and philosophical meaning. For me, this calm imperiousness in dealing with time and space was one of the most significant lessons I took away from my encounters with Akhmatova. That is why I trace to that extraordinary May day in Komarovo, filled with transcendent music and illuminated by the marvelous rainbow, the impulse realized almost thirty years later in this book.

Whenever I visited the Russian Museum in Leningrad—to my mind the best collection of Russian art in the country—I often stopped in the section devoted to early-twentieth-century painting by the enormous decorative panel created in 1908 by Leon Bakst, a leading figure in the artistic association *Mir iskusstva* (World of Art) and famous in the West as the art director of Diaghilev's Ballets Russes. Entitled *Terror Antiquus* (Ancient Terror), that imposing painting depicted the destruction of ancient Atlantis, the mythical civilization that flourished, according to Plato, on an enormous island in the Atlantic Ocean. The island's inhabitants had achieved incredible cultural and spiritual heights but the gods punished them for their excessive pride. Atlantis was swallowed up forever by the churning ocean.

Bakst's painting, with its bird's-eye view of the violent storm, the ancient temples slipping into the ocean, and the theatrical flash of lightning crossing the canvas, made a striking impression on me. I was particularly struck by the statue in the center of the composition, a goddess who accepted with a calm smile the destruction of the civilization that had given birth to her. The goddess was isolated from the chaos around her by a higher wisdom, a higher knowledge that protected her.

I was a teenager then and found out only later that Bakst, a passionate devotee of the ancients, had depicted in *Terror Antiquus* the goddess Aphrodite, who symbolized for him the victory of love and art over blind destruction. And still later that painting seemed to me the almost perfect visual metaphor for the Atlantis of the twentieth century—the glorious culture of the city in which I lived.

Founded in 1703 as Sankt-Peterburg by Peter the Great on the eastern shore of the Gulf of Finland, the capital of the Russian Empire, this city, twice willfully and unwisely renamed (it became Petrograd in 1914 and Leningrad in 1924), was world famous as an architectural gem, with resplendent palaces proudly lining the banks of the spectral Neva.

The beauty of Petersburg's historic buildings is obvious. Erected with unparalleled sweep, luxury, artistry, and refinement, they exude an almost mystical enchantment, particularly during the white nights of early summer, which plunge the classical architecture into an atmosphere of fantasy.

But I was always more attracted and mystified by the great works of literature and music created in that magical city or inspired by it: the works of Pushkin, Glinka, Gogol, Dostoyevsky, Mussorgsky, Tchaikovsky—speaking of the nineteenth century alone. In Petersburg, the inanimate excitingly came to life, palaces and monuments moved onto the pages of prose and poetry or were reflected in the spellbinding music, only to freeze once again on the granite banks of the river and along the open squares but now enriched and elevated, like magically enticing symbols.

The classic, and perhaps greatest, example of this symbiosis is the legendary fate of the equestrian statue of Emperor Peter by Etienne Maurice Falconet, unveiled in 1782 in the center of the Russian capital on the orders of Catherine the Great. Onlookers were struck by its power and by the strength with which the sculptor had realized his idea—the emperor, dressed in a Roman toga and crowned with a laurel wreath, imperiously extending his hand while proudly looking down from his rearing steed on the city that he created and that personifies Russia. But this bronze monument did not acquire its true symbolic significance for Petersburg's fate and its status as the capital's most famous silhouette until the publication in 1837 of *The Bronze Horseman,* the narrative poem written four years earlier by Alexander Pushkin.

The poet Prince Peter Vyazemsky maintained that he was the first to point out to Pushkin the visual ambiguity of the statue. "Peter seems to have made Russia rear back rather than urge it forward."[2] Pushkin placed Falconet's sculpture at the center of his poem and "revived" it, creating a masterpiece in which that ambiguity was transformed into a philosophical puzzle about the country's destiny and the fate of its capital—both of which were irrevocably tied in Pushkin's mind. And for over a century and a half Russia's best minds have been trying to solve that puzzle, offering ever more convoluted solutions, examining from different angles the poem and the statue, which would be known forever after as the Bronze Horseman.

Poets, writers, philosophers, and historians were constantly interpreting the general idea, the imagery, and even the details of Pushkin's *Bronze Horseman* and Falconet's statue. Here are two samples. For our contemporary Abram Tertz (Andrei Sinyavsky), the steed beneath the imperious rider is "Poetry itself, rushing in a frenzy toward the heavens, and frozen in a storm of water, fire, and metal." And in the early twentieth century the sharp eye of the subtle and gloomy Innokentii Annensky, Akhmatova's poetry teacher, fastened on the symbolic serpent, which is hard to notice in the general composition—the impatient horseman tramples it and leaves it behind:

> *The tsar did not manage to kill the snake,*
> *And it survived to be our idol.*

With his poetic genius, Pushkin transformed a "merely" brilliant monument to the awesome emperor into the emblem of Petersburg, a sign of its majesty and endurance, and also into the symbol of the awful fate and terrible suffering that was to befall the city. However, the significance of his *Bronze Horseman* is even greater: in essence, it is the start of the Petersburg mythos.

Earlier one could speak of the existence of the Petersburg legend, which arose and was cultivated almost from the moment of the capital's establishment. That is astonishing enough, for legends usually form much after the event that gives rise to them. But the miracle of the almost instantaneous appearance of the capital of a huge empire on inhospitable northern soil was so striking, and the cost of that miracle in human lives was so high, and the personality of its creator so extraordinary that Petersburg quickly inspired both praise and condemnation of a mystical character.

Fully formed in the second half of the nineteenth century, the Petersburg mythos included the official legends of the miraculous appearance of the lovely city in a marsh and the folklore predictions of its imminent demise. It also had absorbed the so-called Petersburg text, which consisted of the literary works, paintings and drawings, music, and theatrical productions devoted to it, the marvelous buildings but also the complex of philosophical and moral ideas connected with Petersburg's special place on Russian soil and in Russian history. Another component of the mythos was its creators themselves, both authors of works inspired and dedicated to Petersburg and historical and political figures.

The Petersburg mythos would not have existed without Peter

the Great and Pushkin. The emperor forced Petersburg into the vast body of the Russian state, and the granite city acted as an irritant—the grain of sand in the mollusk's shell that became the nucleus of a pearl. Thanks to Peter, the mysterious manifestation of the new capital incorporated the cosmogonic element into the mythos, and Peter himself appears as the traditional mythological cultural hero. Subsequently, he is joined by the figure of the man-myth Pushkin in the same capacity.

But the legendary image of Petersburg's founder was always doubled, reminding us of the fairy-tale twins endowed by opposite traits, one who does good and the other evil. This fundamental duality of the Petersburg mythos was first inculcated into the Russian cultural consciousness by Pushkin. After Pushkin, it became ever clearer that, as Vladimir Toporov put it,

> The inner meaning of Petersburg is in that antithesis and antimony that cannot be reduced to unity, which death itself makes the basis of new life, and understood as the answer to death and as its expiation, as the achievement of a higher level of spirituality. The inhumanity of Petersburg is organically tied to that type of humanity, esteemed highly in Russia and almost religious, which is the only one that can comprehend inhumanity, always remember it, and with that knowledge and memory build a new spiritual ideal.[3]

Pushkin gave the subtitle "A Petersburg Tale" to his *Bronze Horseman*. As we know, one of the meanings of the ancient Greek word *mythos* is "narrative." The Petersburg texts picked up the duality of the city and of its founder and began to depict the capital not as the paradise Peter had envisioned but as a hell.

That fateful transformation was inspired by Nikolai Gogol, who saw Petersburg as a virtual kingdom of the dead, "where everything is wet, smooth, even, pale, gray, and foggy." For Gogol, Petersburg was a bacchanalia of demonic forces hostile to humans, where the soil was always shifting, threatening to suck up the majestic edifices, the soulless government offices, and the multitudes of petty clerks within them.

Soon the theme of the city's destruction blocks out all others in the Petersburg mythos. Foreboding and prophecies of doom took on unprecedented power in the works of Fyodor Dostoyevsky. Pushkin had interpreted the threatening Baltic waters as a terrible force or a cleansing substance akin to the mythological World Ocean.

Dostoyevsky doomed Petersburg, "that rotten, slimy city," to vanishing along with the fog, like smoke.

The Petersburg mythos, according to a modern scholar, "reflects the quintessence of life on the edge, over the abyss, on the brink of death."[4] A watershed in its existence arose in late-nineteenth-century music, when Peter Tchaikovsky in his ballets and particularly in his "Petersburg" opera, *The Queen of Spades* (based on Pushkin), combined that sense of life over the abyss with a premonition of his own tragic end and injected a searing nostalgia into the Petersburg mythos.

Never before had music played such a decisive role in the drastic transformation of a great city's image. Under the influence of Tchaikovsky's music, *Mir iskusstva*, led by Alexander Benois and Sergei Diaghilev, began resurrecting the idea of Petersburg as a providential and vitally necessary cultural and spiritual leader of Russia. They shared Tchaikovsky's foreboding of cataclysms threatening the city. This was the genesis of Bakst's *Terror Antiquus*.

The premonitions of sensitive creative artists proved to be prophetic. From the moment of its establishment, Petersburg was subjected to destructive floods. And in the twentieth century its culture and the city itself were in fact in danger of disappearing. It was ravaged by terror and hunger, underwent three revolutions, and suffered a siege unparalleled in modern history. It ceased to be the capital of the country and lost its best people, its self-respect, its money and power, and, finally, its glory.

By the middle of the twentieth century the Petersburg mythos was submerged. One could only surmise its existence, as if the city had become another Atlantis.

Of course, even in Stalinist Russia the works of Pushkin and Gogol were studied, but Dostoyevsky was under deep suspicion. Tchaikovsky's role in the renaissance of the Petersburg mythos was not mentioned, and Boris Asafyev's early pioneering works on the subject were banned. There was no possibility of openly discussing the Petersburg texts of the twentieth century—they had vanished into a historical black hole.

Russian modernist movements were branded "decadent" in the Soviet Union. The Silver Age—the brilliant flowering of Russian culture after 1910, or as Akhmatova put it, "The time of Stravinsky and Blok, Anna Pavlova and Scriabin, Rostovtsev and Chaliapin, Meyerhold and Diaghilev," was officially termed "the most shameful and most mediocre" period in the history of the Russian intelligentsia.

The Party verdict on Akhmatova declared, "Akhmatova's work belongs to the distant past; it is alien to contemporary Soviet reality and cannot be tolerated on the pages of our magazines."[5] This was the attitude toward almost all Petersburg culture of the early twentieth century, with the exception of two or three figures retouched beyond recognition.

It was not simply a question of aesthetics but of politics as well. Both Lenin, who moved the capital back to Moscow from Petrograd in 1918, and Stalin, who subjected Leningrad to terrible suffering, felt nothing but suspicion and hostility for the city, fearing the development there of a hotbed of political and cultural opposition. This unwillingness to tolerate the city in his empire was shared by another notorious dictator of the century, Adolf Hitler.

The assassination in 1934 of Party boss Sergei Kirov in Leningrad, sometimes called in Russia "the murder of the century," gave Stalin (now believed to be its real perpetrator) the excuse to unleash a squall of terror on the city. After the war Stalin fabricated the "Leningrad Affair," which put the city back on the political blacklist. As a result, according to the writer Daniil Granin, "the name 'Leningrader' was used more and more infrequently. After the Leningrad Affair it sounded suspicious."[6]

During my youth, it was impossible to talk about any of this in public. Even the complete truth about the city's incredible suffering during the 900-day German siege was suppressed by the Soviet authorities. We all lived with the impression that the city had a gigantic gag down its throat. Its past was being destroyed, its present humiliated, and its hopes for the future torn out by the roots.

The French Enlightenment philosopher Denis Diderot had this to say about the move of the Russian capital from Moscow to Petersburg: "It is extremely unwise to place the heart on the fingertip." In the Soviet era, authorities kept cutting off the oxygen to Russia's former "heart"; it shriveled and almost stopped beating, for it was dying, but no one was allowed to sound the alarm. When I started writing in Russia about art, and particularly when I was preparing my book *Young Composers of Leningrad* (1971) for publication, I had to deal with this over and over. The very concept of Petersburg or Leningrad culture was being quashed. "What's so special about this culture? We have only one culture—the Soviet one!"

The Petersburg Atlantis sank to the bottom of the Soviet political ocean. But it stubbornly continued its submerged existence there—in the form of bizarre but beautiful ruins, under terrible atmospheric pressure, in darkness and muteness. To behold these marvelous ruins, one had to dive deep and stay underwater for a long time. Nevertheless, many people in Leningrad did just that, despite the danger. A new Petersburg mythos was ripening in the underground.

Its central figure, and to a great degree its creator, was Anna Akhmatova, the courageous voice of the city on the Neva. In her youth, Akhmatova had a reputation as a Cassandra, prophesying and mourning the destruction of Troy. As early as 1915 she saw Petrograd as a "granite city of glory and misfortune." Later she wrote,

> I brought on death to my dear ones
> And they died one after another.
> O my grief! Those graves
> Were foretold by my word.

In the popular imagination Akhmatova turned into a symbolic "poetic widow," the keeper of the sacred flame, the mourner for the victims of the revolution, for Petersburg's lost grandeur. She molded the new Petersburg mythos from one poem to another, and her stiff mixture was bound by blood—living, steaming moisture, without which no sacrifice or prophesy can endure.

Petersburg as a city rose on the bones of its nameless builders. Those victims were part of the legend of the monster capital that stifled the little man. The blood of the new innocent victims, poured out under Stalin's ruthless terror, gave birth to a new mythos that it also confirmed and strengthened, the Petersburg as martyr, the symbol of Russia's tragic fate and of its hopes for a phoenixlike rebirth. This metamorphosis had never occurred in history—a radical change in the mythos of a city.

Every mythos has "exoteric" elements, which are comprehensible to many, and "esoteric" elements, which are known only to the initiated. In the Stalin years, Akhmatova created the esoteric mythos of Petersburg the martyr in her works, particularly in *Requiem*, the poetic distillation of the horrible pictures of mass repressions by their witness. Her *Requiem*, which was too subversive to commit to writing, was known at first only to a few of Akhmatova's closest friends, who memorized it, thus turning themselves into living depositories of banned truth.

In contrast, Shostakovich's Fifth and Seventh ("Leningrad") Symphonies, even though they revealed essentially the same banned theme, were allowed to resound openly, and they quickly became widely known not only in the Soviet Union but throughout the world. That was one of the paradoxes of the situation: modern symphonic music, in its language seemingly more elitist than descriptive poetry, turned out to be the bearer of the public message of Leningrad's tragic fate.

Beleaguered but unbroken, Shostakovich continued this Petersburg line in his picturesque Eleventh Symphony, and also in his late quartets, while Akhmatova moved from prophesying a terrible future to the re-creation of the legendary past ("Just as the future ripens in the past,/So the past smolders in the future") and crowned her construction of the new Petersburg mythos with the monumental *Poem Without a Hero*, whose true hero was, of course, her beloved Northern Palmyra.

Akhmatova did not live to see either *Requiem* or *Poem Without a Hero* published in full in the Soviet Union. They were clandestinely copied by hand or typed and received with growing enthusiasm, even as the Soviet cultural apparatus not only ignored but tried to stamp out and destroy the unofficial Petersburg mythos that stubbornly grew stronger. One of the most notorious post-Stalinist acts of government repression was the show trial in 1964 of the young Leningrad poet Joseph Brodsky, a protégé of Akhmatova's, charged with "parasitism."

Exiled to the north and later expelled to the West in 1972, Brodsky settled in the United States, where with his talent and powerful intellect he became an heir to the "American branch" of Petersburg modernism. I use this term to unite a group of creative giants who had never declared their membership in any artistic school. Nevertheless, there was much to link Igor Stravinsky, Vladimir Nabokov, and George Balanchine. All three came from Petersburg, and after years in Europe they settled in the United States, where they had an enormous influence on American culture and created their "nostalgic" version of the Petersburg mythos, which attracted the attention of the Western intellectual elite when that mythos was being persecuted ruthlessly in the Soviet Union.

Brodsky picked up that tradition, thereby creating a link between the two great strata of Petersburg culture, sundered by the inexorable historical forces of the turbulent twentieth century.

I first met Brodsky in Leningrad in the early 1970s, but paradoxically I became truly acquainted with him only in New York, where I moved in 1976, having emigrated from the Soviet Union. In

1979 I published *Testimony*, the memoirs of Dmitri Shostakovich, written in collaboration with the composer while we were both in the USSR. Several other collaborative projects followed: *Balanchine's Tchaikovsky* (with George Balanchine, 1985), *From Russia to the West* (with violinist Nathan Milstein, 1990), *Joseph Brodsky in New York* (conversations with the poet, 1990), and also with him a book of dialogues about Akhmatova, published in 1992 in Moscow. But for all those years I was working on a book devoted to Petersburg culture and the Petersburg mythos—an idea that had flashed through my mind on the unforgettable day in May 1965 with its snow and its rainbow, when my friends and I played the Shostakovich Ninth Quartet for Akhmatova in her dacha near Leningrad.

The need for such a book seemed even greater since neither in the Soviet Union nor anywhere else was there a comprehensive cultural history of the city that included literature, music, theater, ballet, and the arts. Paris, Vienna, Berlin, and New York were firmly established in the world's consciousness as important cultural centers, where revolutionary aesthetic concepts were born and the clash of brilliant personalities created the greatness of modern art. People were fascinated by the "nervous splendor," energy, and vitality of those grand cities.

But Petersburg did not join this distinguished group, which seemed grossly unfair to me. This was the city where Diaghilev's artistic ideas were formed, where Meyerhold realized many of his most daring theatrical experiments, where the young Stravinsky composed his amazing music, where Matiushin and Malevich held the premiere of their epochal futurist opera, *Victory Over the Sun*; this was the city where one could find the roots of the literature and the theater of the absurd, of the New Criticism and of contemporary structuralism, of plotless ballet and the modern symphony. But through a fateful combination of cultural and political reasons, all these splendid accomplishments and famous names floated in some kind of space and time vacuum and remained strangely unconnected.

I began collecting the material for documenting this era in the early 1960s, meeting in Leningrad (and later in Moscow) with remarkable people, survivors of the Silver Age, the creators, participants, and observers of the flowering of Petersburg culture in the early twentieth century. Some of them held prominent social positions; others, often beset by terrible hardships and chastened by bitter experience, tried to live out quiet lives.

But they all wanted to recall those glorious years that were buried under a historical avalanche and about which they felt the new, indoctrinated generation knew nothing nor cared to know. That is why these people responded gratefully to any well-meaning interest in their past.

Another unique cross section of Petersburg culture and an invaluable source of information about the era was revealed to me when I moved to the West. Here I had the good fortune to meet with some quintessential Petersburgers, who managed to preserve despite the tribulations of exile and their advanced years a clear memory of the events of their youth. These gentle souls met me sympathetically, in large part because they were pleased by my enthusiasm for the city that they themselves continued to consider the greatest and most beautiful in the world. A part was also played by the fact that they at last had an opportunity to discuss and savor with a new arrival from Russia the details of their precious impressions of the distant past—in their native tongue! I was very touched by one interlocutor who had described in all particulars a performance he had seen in prerevolutionary Petersburg and suddenly admitted that he had not discussed that topic for about sixty years.

Then, in the late 1970s, the old émigrés and I, a new one, knew that the barbarous, artificial division of Russian culture into "Soviet" or "metropolitan," on the one hand, and "abroad" or "émigré," on the other, which began with the Communist regime in Russia and was propagated with great ferocity, would continue if not forever then for an unbearably long time. We feared we would not live to witness the reunification of Petersburg culture or the recognition in Russia of the greatness of the Petersburg mythos.

In predicting the fate of the Soviet empire, we were not the only ones to be mistaken: almost the entire world was wrong. Few had expected the suddenness and speed with which the empire collapsed and the startling changes that would occur in Russia in the late 1980s. Unprecedented political, economic, social, and cultural shifts shook the country and turned it upside down. For the city on the Neva they meant, among other things, an almost inconceivable salvaging of the Petersburg mythos from beneath the sea, as if the legendary Atlantis had reemerged before the very eyes of its descendants. The names of vilified individuals and artistic phenomena returned from oblivion; authors whose works it had been a punishable offense to distribute just a few years earlier were declared overnight to be classics and were printed in great numbers; and the canvases long hidden in dusty ware-

houses were once again glowing with their vivid colors at festive exhibitions.

The culmination of this dizzying process was the return on September 6, 1991, of the city's historic name—St. Petersburg. Petersburg
culture celebrated its unexpected and thus all the more satisfying triumph.

I thought about this gift from fate as I strolled along the streets
of Petersburg in the fall of 1993: how fleeting it had been, like a
mirage, and how important it was to preserve it in my heart—for
myself and in memory of those old Petersburgers, native and émigré,
who had not lived to see the changes for which they had desperately
hoped.

Joseph Brodsky liked to say, "You cannot enter the same river
twice, even if it is the Neva River." In vain I whispered to myself a line
from Mandelstam's poem, "I have returned to my city, familiar to the
point of tears." I did not recognize the city; rather, I recognized it with
difficulty, gradually—like a slowly developing photograph. Many
years ago I had left Leningrad, where I had studied, fallen in love,
played the violin, and started writing; now I had returned—albeit very
briefly—to Saint Petersburg.

Yes, the changes were striking. There wasn't a single state-
owned store or café on the legendary Nevsky Prospect, and its glorious panorama brought the poems of Nikolai Zabolotsky to mind:
"There the Nevsky is in glitter and dreariness, changing its skin in the
night." The street names familiar from my youth were gone—their
original names had been reinstated. Now, ironically, the constructions, monuments, and heroes of the Soviet era were swiftly receding
into history.

The city clearly wanted to part as quickly as possible from its
recent humiliating existence, and a writer, yesterday a Leningrad and
today a Petersburg writer, observed, "In moments of acute historical
changes we fall under the influence of ideas, brilliant in their simplicity and obviousness—ideas of a symbolic revenge on the past. *They*
brought Lenin into the Mausoleum—*we* will take him out; *they* blew
up the church—*we* will build it again; *they* called the city their way
and *we* will return its former name."[7]

Sometimes it seemed to me that the only constant of the city
was its visual symbol, the Bronze Horseman, that only at its pedestal
could I understand the multitude of doubts, questions, regrets, and
recollections that assailed me. The physical and spiritual dynamism
that animates this sculpture could lift the spirits of the most hidebound

pessimist. The Bronze Horseman is in an eternal leap, connecting Petersburg soil with the Baltic sky above it.

For me the Bronze Horseman personified the vitality of the Petersburg mythos, its eternal ambivalence, its ascent to the heights of the human spirit, but also the constant threat—from without and within—to the equilibrium, to the very existence of that mythos. Before the Bronze Horseman you unwittingly forget about the zigzags of current politics, about economic problems, and are left alone with time, with the mythos that will live and thrive for a long time to come, I hope.

Here, at the foot of the statue, I recalled with gratitude all those—there were several hundred of them—whose testimony, stories, advice, materials, documents, and photographs helped me prepare this book. Particularly inspiring was my personal contact with the book's four protagonists—Anna Akhmatova, George Balanchine, Dmitri Shostakovich, and Joseph Brodsky—who in the contemporary world stand as paragons of artistic, intellectual, and ethical standards. Meeting those artists shaped my life and was one of its greatest blessings. For each of those four giants, Petersburg always remained the leading creative symbol and impulse, and each has inimitably played a pivotal role in the creation of the new Petersburg mythos.

I want also to name here some of my interlocutors and correspondents over the last three decades, both in Russia and in the West, many of whom are major figures in Petersburg and Russian culture. They are Iogann Admoni, Nikolai Akimov, Grigory Alexandrov, Nathan Altman, Boris Arapov, Leo Arnshtam, Gennady Banshchikov, Alexander Beniaminov, Olga Berggolts, Andrei Bitov, Valerian Bogdanov-Berezovsky, Isaiah Braudo, Lili Brik, Nina Bruni-Balmont, Semyon Bychkov, Mihail Chemiakin, Alexandra Danilova, Anatoly Dmitriev, Leonid Dolgopolov, Sergei Dovlatov, Sofia Dubnova, Mikhail Dudin, Orest Evlakhov, Kurt Fridrikhson, Valery Gavrilin, Valery Gergiev, Tamara Geva, Evdokia Glebova, Gleb Gorbovsky, Lazar Gozman, Irina Graham, Daniil Granin, Boris Grebenshikov, Yuri Grigorovich, Lev Gumilyov, Pavel Gusev, Vladimir Horowitz, Anatoly Kaplan, Vasily Katanyan, Aram Khachaturyan, Nikolai Khardzhiev, Andrei Khrzhanovsky, Alexander Knaifel, Georgy Kochevitsky, Yuri Kochnev, Leonid Kogan, Kirill Kondrashin, Maria Konisskaya, Zinovy Korogodsky, Gidon Kremer, Alexander Kushner, Konstantin Kuzminsky, Viktor Liberman, Fyodor Lopukhov, Lev Loseff, Berthe Malko, Mikhail Matveyev, Yakov Milkis, Nathan Milstein, Alexander Mintz, Yevgeny Mravinsky, Anatoly Nayman, Ernst Neizvestny, Yevgeny Nesterenko, Rudolf Nureyev, David Oistrakh, Alexandra Orlova, Boris Paramonov, Nadezhda Pavlovich, Maya Plisetskaya, Boris Pokrovsky, David Pritsker, Lina Prokofiev, Lev Raaben, Rita Rait, Yevgeny Rein, Mstislav Rostropovich, Gennady Rozhdestvensky, Vadim Salmanov, Dmitri Shagin, Marietta Shaginyan, Veniamin Sher, Vladimir Shinkarev, Viktor Shklovsky, Maxim Shostakovich, Iosif Shvarts, Sergei Sigitov, Yuri Simonov, Sergei Slonimsky, Gennady Smakov, Arnold Sokhor, Vladimir Solovyev, Viktor Sosnora, Vladimir Spivakov, Vera Stravinsky, Georgy Sviridov, Alexander Tcherepnine, Yuri Temirkanov, Boris Tishchenko, Alexander Tyshler, Yulian Vainkop, Mikhail Verbov, Pavel Vulfius, Leonid Yakobson, Roman Yakobson, Mariss Yansons, Maria Yudina, Sergei Yursky, Sergei Yutkevich, Vyacheslav Zavalishin, Kurt Zanderling, Irina Zegzhda, Lydia Zhukova, and Yevgeny Zubkov. I am forever grateful to them for their attention, forbearance, responsiveness, and patience.

Some aspects of my work I also discussed with Peter Vail, Alexander Genis, Roman Timenchik, Lazar Fleishman, and Mikhail Yampolsky. These consultations were of great help.

I thank Adam Bellow and Loretta Denner for their wholehearted support of this project, and my wife, Marianna, for her enormous help as a researcher and photographer.

In 1922 a book was published in Petrograd, *The Soul of Petersburg*, by Nikolai Antsiferov, a pioneering student of local lore. The author, unlike traditional travel guide writers, did not dwell on dates and details but concentrated instead on the genius loci of Petersburg, a city of "tragic imperialism," as he put it. Antsiferov's vivid *Soul of Petersburg* was the work not of an academic observer with pretensions to covering everything and being "objective," but a passionate testimony of a participant in Petersburg's tragedy. Antsiferov's own fate was unhappy (he was arrested and exiled several times), as was that of his book, which was suppressed soon after publication and reprinted only seventy years later. A precious first edition is one of the items dearest to my heart in my private library.

Another important creative stimulus and model for me was the work of several art and music critics, who worked in Petersburg-Petrograd in the first decades of the twentieth century. Alexander Benois, Nikolai Punin, and Igor Glebov (the pseudonym of Boris Asafyev) were very popular in their time; they were published in high-brow journals and mass circulation newspapers, playing a dual and equally outstanding role—as creators of revolutionary concepts of modern culture and as its influential interpreters for the Russian educated classes. Their contribution to the comprehension of the city's grandeur and mystical significance is invaluable. For many decades their most perceptive works were deemed too controversial for Soviet readers and were not reprinted. Only now are they coming out of the shadows. Their passionate desire to enlighten their audience, to make available the highest achievements of the human spirit, in conjunction with their erudition and cosmopolitanism, makes these authors timely and necessary today in Petersburg.

My book is to a great degree a tribute to these writers. In addition, for the more than seven years needed to complete my work, a constant source of intellectual sustenance was James H. Billington's interpretative study of the development of Russian culture, *The Icon and the Axe*. Reading it strengthened me in my resolve to write this book, not as an encyclopedia of Petersburg culture but as an elaborated conceptual history of the development, over several centuries, of the Petersburg legend and the Petersburg mythos.

C H A P T E R

1

describing how the great city of St. Petersburg was built, how the mythos of this wonder was created, and how classical Russian literature from Pushkin to Dostoyevsky boldly and brilliantly interpreted the image of the city and, in the end, profoundly changed it.

Alexander Pushkin was nervous and angry. The poet was in the second week of his self-imposed exile in Boldino, the small steppe estate of his father some six hundred miles from Petersburg. Pushkin's purpose in coming here was to write poetry, in solitude and peace, far from the bustle of the capital. But the verse, spitefully, wouldn't come. His head ached, his stomach hurt; could it be the heavy Russian diet—potatoes and buckwheat groats?

He was worried about his substantial debts. The only way to get rid of them was to hope for inspiration from God, to produce something significant, and then sell that "something" profitably to his Petersburg publisher. But it was difficult for Pushkin to concentrate on poetry; he was tormented by jealousy, obsessed with worry about his young wife, who remained in Petersburg. The famous beauty, Natalya, was flattered by the attentions of the social lions, while the temperamental Pushkin naturally climbed the walls. He crudely berated his wife in a letter from Boldino: "You're pleased that studs chase after you like a bitch, their tails stiff up in the air and sniffing your ass; nothing to be happy about! . . . *If you have a trough, the pigs will come.*"[1]

The dreary autumn weather would have plunged anyone into deep depression. But Pushkin, despite his African ancestry, loved the northern clime. He hoped that the Russian autumn would bring him inspiration, as it always had. It tormented him first, then paid off; verse finally came. The happy poet awoke at seven in the morning, worked in bed until three in the afternoon, then rode horseback in the mud for two hours, cooling off his head, overheated with ideas.

"I started writing and have already written tons,"[2] he announced proudly to his wife in a letter to Petersburg dated October 30, 1833. The next day at dawn, in his quick but beautiful hand, he finished the fair copy of his narrative poem, *The Bronze Horseman*. We know that because of the notation on the final page: "five after five a.m." (that is, contrary to his habit, the poet had worked all night).

Pushkin rarely documented his work with such accuracy. Apparently, even he, who never underestimated his genius, understood that in those twenty-six October days he had achieved something unique and extraordinary. (Which may also be why he asked five thousand rubles from his publisher upon returning to Petersburg, an unheard of sum in those days.) The poet's intuition did not fail him: *The Bronze Horseman* is still the greatest narrative poem written in Russian. It is also the beginning and at the same time the peak of the literary mythos about St. Petersburg.

The Bronze Horseman, subtitled by the author "A Petersburg Tale," is set during the flood of 1824, one of the worst of many that has regularly befallen the city. But the poem begins with a grand and solemn ode honoring Peter the Great and the city he founded, "the beauty and marvel" of the north. Then Pushkin warns, "Sorrowful will be my tale," though previously he had treated the flood of 1824 frivolously, noting in a letter to his younger brother, Lev, *"Voilà une belle occasion à vos dames de faire bidet."*[3]

Then there is a sharp change in the protagonist, point of view, and mood. From Peter the Great and the early eighteenth century the action of Pushkin's poem jumps to his contemporary Petersburg, where the poor clerk Yevgeny dreams of happiness with his beloved Parasha. A storm begins and rages into a flood. Caught in the center of the city, in Senate Square, Yevgeny saves himself by climbing onto a marble lion. Before him, towering above the "outraged Neva," is the statue of Peter, "an idol on a bronze steed," the Bronze Horseman himself.

The waves that cannot reach Peter, "the powerful master of fate," who had founded the city in such a dangerous location, threaten to engulf Yevgeny. But he is more worried about the fate of his Parasha. The storm recedes and Yevgeny hurries to her little house. Alas, the house has been washed away and Parasha is missing. Her death is unbearable to Yevgeny, who loses his mind and becomes one of Petersburg's homeless, living on handouts.

It is a plot typical of many a romantic tale. If Pushkin had ended it there, *The Bronze Horseman*, imbued with resounding verse that is at once ecstatic and precise—to date no translation has fully captured its brilliance—would not have risen to the philosophical heights at which it still serves as the most powerful expression of the ambiguity and eternal mystery of St. Petersburg's mythos.

No, the culmination of this "Petersburg Tale" is still ahead. Pushkin brings his hero back to Senate Square. Yevengy once again faces the bronze "idol with outstretched hand / The one, whose fatal will founded the city beneath the sea." So Peter the Great is at fault for Parasha's death. And Yevgeny threatens the "miracle-working builder." But the madman's attempted rebellion against the statue of the absolute monarch on his rearing steed is short-lived. Yevgeny runs away imagining that the Bronze Horseman has come down from his pedestal to pursue him. No matter where the panicked Yevgeny turns, the cruel statue keeps gaining on him, and the terrible chase continues through the night under the pale Petersburg moon.

Thereafter, ever since that night, whenever Yevgeny makes his way through Senate Square, he proceeds cautiously; he dares not look up at the triumphant Bronze Horseman. In imperial Petersburg no one may rise up against even a statue of the monarch; that would be blasphemy. The life of the now completely humiliated Yevgeny has lost all meaning. In his wanderings he comes across Parasha's ruined little house, washed up on a small island, and he dies on its doorstep.

This brief retelling of the comparatively short poem (481 octosyllabic lines) might create the impression that Pushkin's sympathies are fully with poor Yevgeny, who became the prototype for an endless line of "little people" in Russian literature. But then the mystery of *The Bronze Horseman* would not have puzzled Slavic scholars the world over for the last one hundred fifty years and given rise to the hundreds of works approaching it from literary, philosophical, historical, sociological, and political points of view.

The mystery lies in the fact that while the reader's first emotion is acute pity for the poor Petersburger, the perception of the poem does not end with that; new emotions and sensations wash over the reader. Gradually one understands that the author's position is much more complex than it might at first have seemed.

The Bronze Horseman in Pushkin's poem obviously represents not only Peter the Great and the city he founded but also the state it-self and just about any form of authority—and, even more broadly, the creative will and force, upon which the society depends, but which also clash inevitably with the simple dreams and desires of its mem-bers, the insignificant Yevgenys and Parashas. What is more impor-tant—the individual's fate or the city's and the state's triumph? It is Pushkin's genius that he does not present a clear-cut answer. In fact, the text of his poem is open to opposing interpretations and so com-pels each reader to resolve its moral dilemma anew.

The opening lines of *The Bronze Horseman*, depicting Peter the Great as he decides to found Petersburg, are perhaps the most popular in Russian poetry. Every year millions of Russian schoolchildren mem-orize them: "On the shore of empty waves *He* stood, filled with great thoughts, and stared out."

This is a mythologized image, of course. But almost everything having to do with the founding of Petersburg is surrounded by leg-ends, great and small. According to one of them, on May 16, 1703, on an island (which was called Zayachy, "Hare") in the estuary of the Neva River, chosen because of its access to the Baltic Sea, Peter tore a halberd from a soldier's hands, cut out two sections of peat, laid them crosswise, and announced: "The city will be here!"[4] Then, toss-ing the halberd aside, Peter picked up a shovel and work began. This was the start of the six-towered fortress with the Dutch name Sankt Piterburkh, named by the tsar not after himself, as the popular mis-conception has it, but after his patron saint, Apostle Peter.

Another legendary image recorded in the manuscript entitled "On the conception and construction of the Ruling city of St. Peters-burg," which appeared shortly after Peter's death, presents the eagle that suddenly appeared over Peter's head as the foundation of the fortress was being laid. The anonymous author stressed that this was exactly what had happened when Constantinople was founded by the first Christian emperor, Constantine the Great. Peter buried in the foundation a golden ark with a piece of the remains of Holy Apostle Andrew, the first to bring Christianity to Russia.

Contemporary historians are skeptical about these legends,

justly noting their propagandistic character. In 1703 Peter already was planning to proclaim the Russian Empire, which he did in 1721, taking the title "Great" along with Russian Orthodox Emperor. So imperial symbols and parallels, particularly the traditional Russian historical analogy with the "New Rome"—Constantinople—were very important to him.

In fact, Peter was not even on Zayachy Island that fateful day when the city was founded. The initial work on the small piece of land—about 750 meters long and 360 wide—was directed by Alexander Menshikov, one of Peter's most trusted lieutenants and the future first governor of Petersburg. Prosaic facts also contradict Pushkin's grand lines cited earlier: the area wasn't all that "empty." The Swedish fort of Nienschanz stood nearby and a populous fishing village was situated on the opposite shore.

One thing is absolutely clear, though—Zayachy itself was uninhabited, a miserable swampy place that would never have become the site of the future imperial capital if not for the will and vision of Tsar Peter.

What moved him? What led to that strangest of choices, later resented and dismissed by hordes of critics? And their argument was sound—that for geographical, climatic, strategic, commercial, and nationalistic reasons, the mouth of the Neva was no place for the new capital of Russia or any large city.

The answer is probably rooted as much in Tsar Peter's psychology as in the complex political and economic reality of early-eighteenth-century Russia. Peter was born in 1672, the fourteenth child of Tsar Alexei of the Romanov dynasty, and was eventually crowned in 1696 in Moscow, then the capital of all Russia, inheriting an enormous, relatively backward country. He believed it needed radical *perestroika* or "restructuring" and, therefore, maximal increase in contacts and trade with the West. In many ways, Russia was already prepared for the rule of a reform-minded tsar. It simply did not expect that the new autocrat would be a person with Peter's extraordinary character and habits.[5]

Peter grew up to be tall (over six feet seven inches) and strong. He could easily roll up a silver plate or cut a bolt of cloth in the air. He was tireless in all his pursuits, businesslike, with an insatiable thirst for knowledge. He longed for sea air. This was exactly what Russia needed as well. Let's not forget it had long struggled to gain access to the sea, with its tempting promises of lucrative trade with foreigners.

But few of the Russian boyars—mostly the old noble councillors who surrounded the young tsar—expected Peter to take up the work of *perestroika* with such passion, demolishing along the way all the proprieties and customs of his ancestors. Muscovite tsars were supposed to sit enthroned majestically in the Kremlin, not imitate—as Peter soon began doing—the crude manners and habits of Dutch or German skippers and craftsmen.

Peter turned out to be an amazing monarch, and not only by Russian standards. He seemed to know everything and be able to do anything. As a young man he had mastered fourteen trades, including woodworking, carpentry, and shoemaking. He considered himself a good surgeon. They say Peter left a whole sack of teeth he had pulled; he loved to practice dentistry, terrorizing his courtiers. But the tsar prided himself particularly on being the best shipbuilder in the land. The launching of every new ship was also an excuse for a great drinking bout. Usually stingy, Peter spared no expense on these occasions.

As no Russian monarch before or after him, Peter was full of contradictions and paradoxes. On occasion he could be merry, gentle, and kind. But more often he was horrible in his wrath, frighteningly unpredictable, and needlessly cruel, personally torturing his enemies in hidden chambers. Of course, he had to fight for power and sometimes for his life. Barbaric incidents like the Moscow uprising of the Russian irregular army in 1682, when soldiers with fearsome pikes speared many of Peter's relatives and tore them apart before his eyes, must have greatly influenced his character and behavior. Still, his dominant trait was unlimited confidence in his own righteousness. As a true Russian autocrat, he considered himself the absolute sovereign whose subjects were deprived of every right. By providential design, he could not be wrong; therefore his every wish had to be obeyed, no matter what the cost.

At times Peter seemed to be a simple, sincere, and accessible man. But he also perceived himself as a demiurge, a kind of divine actor whose stage was not only Russia but all Europe and more. Not for nothing did the chancellor, Count Golovkin, upon bestowing the honorific "the Great" on Peter speak glowingly of a Russia that had "come out of the Darkness of Ignorance onto the Theater of Glory of the whole world" under the emperor's leadership. Peter was challenging, demanding, deliberately outrageous. This love of the grand gesture marked all his actions. A dramatic change of form was no less important than a change of content as far as Peter—the actor on the world stage—was concerned. In fact, he was apparently convinced that the form often determined the content. This conviction of Peter's was to become an integral part of the entire future Petersburgian culture.

Despite the opinion of many later historians Peter loved Russia, its talented people, its colorful language, the country's rituals and its food, particularly *shchi* (cabbage soup). But he hated Russian filth, indolence, thievery, and the fat, bearded boyars in their heavy clothes. He hated Moscow, too, the ancient Russian capital where he was almost murdered, and its rebellious soldiers, whom he constantly suspected of conspiracies against him.

So Peter started with a vengeance to change Russia's traditions and symbols. He ordered the boyars' beards to be cut (and at the same time the beards of the rest of the population, save the clergy and the peasants) and forced them to dance minuets at the Parisian-style "assemblies" he instituted. He gave his army a new uniform (and, of course, new weaponry) of the Western type, a new banner, and new orders, and he modernized the Russian alphabet. All these mostly symbolic transformations signaled in no uncertain terms the coming of the new age for Russia.

But the greatest expression of Peter's sovereign willfulness, his Russian maximalism, and his addiction to the supersymbolic gesture was, ultimately, the founding of St. Petersburg. Retrospectively, this feat became loaded with a multitude of interpretations and explanations; but the idea of establishing a new city just then and on just that spot seemed in fact to be no more or less than the act of an incredibly rich, reckless, and sometimes lucky gambler risking it all in one supreme wager. Peter wanted to astonish Russia and the entire civilized world, and he succeeded.

In fact, this seemingly crazy idea had developed gradually. The first impulse toward a concept of a city that would be completely novel, even avant-garde, for Russia came to young Peter back in Moscow. There he would sneak off into the foreign settlement, where German, Dutch, Scots, and French craftsmen, merchants, and mercenary soldiers lived, to enjoy their company and friendship.

A clearer image of his ideal city, one that had nothing in common with the muddy, dangerous Moscow, where Peter's enemies could hide in the crooked streets, formed during the young tsar's trips to Europe, particularly to Holland. First Peter started to fantasize about a place like Amsterdam: clean, neat, easily observable and therefore controllable, on the water, with rows of trees reflected in the city's canals. Then Peter's vision grew much grander: *His* city would soar like an eagle: it would be a fortress, a port, an enormous wharf, a model for all Russia, and at the same time a shopwindow on the West.

Yes, a shopwindow, and not an ordinary one. The comparison of Petersburg with a window into Europe belongs not to Peter but the Italian traveler Count Francesco Algarotti, who used it in his *Lettera sulla Russia* in 1739. Peter would not have come up with this metaphor, if only because his attitude toward the West, like everything else with him, was ambivalent. Peter often repeated, "We need Europe for a few decades, and then we must show it our ass." The proud autocrat probably would have preferred the way Pushkin put it a hundred years later: "Russia entered Europe like a launched battleship— accompanied by the hammering of axes and the thunder of cannons." This desire to speak with Europe on equal terms, even if accompanied by cannon fire, is also very typical for subsequent generations of Russian writers, including the more Western-oriented like Nikolai Gumilyov.

A great Russian historian, Vassily Klyuchevsky, always insisted that "moving toward Europe was only a means toward an end in Peter's eyes and not the end itself."[6] He pointed out that the goal of Peter's legendary trips to western Europe was always to steal the latest know-how and to lure highly qualified European specialists to Russia. All that helps explain why, once he wrested access to the Baltic Sea from the Swedes, Peter did not use the important centers already established there—like Riga, Libava (Liepājā), or Revel (Tallinn)—as a base, even though their locations, not to mention their climate, were much more conducive for regular contacts with the West.

Peter wanted a clean break with the past, but he wanted to make that break on his own terms. He didn't need a test site already "spoiled" by existing ties with western Europe. Only the island in the mouth of the Neva seemed like a suitable laboratory for the tsar's grand experiment.

The first house in Petersburg—for Peter himself, two rooms and a storeroom that doubled as bedroom—was built of fir logs by the tsar with the help of soldiers in three days, in May 1703. Its walls were painted to resemble brick, the better to remind Peter of his beloved Amsterdam. The city plan was small-scale at first. But since with every day the tsar's appetite increased, the plan became more elaborate. The Amsterdam model was soon abandoned. Peter was now going after no less than a northern Paris or Rome. Instead of naturally developing on high ground, Petersburg was begun on lowland, below sea level—a risky and fateful decision, resulting in much danger for its future inhabitants. The tsar plotted the city with ruler in hand as a system of islands, canals, and broad, straight *pershpektivy* (prospects, from the Latin *pro-specto*, to look into the distance), so that it would present a clear geometrical pattern. The main *pershpektiva*, the nearly three-mile-long Nevsky Prospect, was built in 1715.

To realize all these constantly changing plans, tens of thousands of workers from all over the country were herded to the Neva delta. It was a motley crew—peasants, soldiers, convicts, captured Swedes and Tatars. There was no housing, no food, no tools for them; they transported excavated dirt in their clothing. Drenched by pouring rains, attacked by swarms of mosquitoes, the wretches pounded wooden pilings into the swampy ground. How many died of starvation, disease, and exhaustion? Probably hundreds of thousands. Peter did not care, so no one kept track.

Later, the official court historian, Nikolai Karamzin, would sigh, "Les grands hommes ne voyent que le tout," explaining, "Petersburg is founded on tears and corpses." The severe Klyuchevsky seconds this conclusion: "I doubt one could find a battle in military history that led to the death of more soldiers than the number of laborers who died in Petersburg. . . . Peter called his new capital his 'paradise'; but it turned into a big cemetery for the people."[7] Not only the humble builders of Petersburg were terrorized by Peter. The celebrated French architect Alexandre Jean-Baptiste LeBlond, who designed the general plan for the city's construction, was, according to a historian, "beaten by the tsar and soon after died." Other foreigners who worked on "the New Rome"—Italians, Germans, Dutch—feared Peter as they had never feared their own rulers. "Everything trembled, everything submitted wordlessly," commented Pushkin.

Peter's muzzled and stunned subjects were showered with dozens of harshly worded ukases calling for more speed and more order in erecting the tsar's ideal city: decrees on more recruits; decrees on the highly regulated model houses for "noble," "wealthy," and "common" people; decrees ordering all Russian stonemasons to Petersburg and banning the construction of stone buildings in all other cities of the country; decrees on the obligatory delivery of stones by ship and land for paving the streets of his "paradise," with the exact number of stones necessary (there were enormous fines for each un-delivered stone).*

Pushkin, who thought that Peter "despised humanity perhaps more than did Napoleon," was puzzled: "It is worth pondering: the difference between Peter the Great's state accomplishments and his temporary ukases. The former are the fruit of a broad mind, imbued with good will and wisdom, the latter *are often cruel, willful, and, it seems, written with the knout.*"

The tsar's knout whistled mercilessly and constantly, so the city grew at incredible speed. Declared the new capital of Russia in 1717, it had over forty thousand residents by 1725, toward the end of Pe-ter's reign—an eighth of the country's urban population. The emperor had succeeded in building a unique monument: not a pyramid, or a cathedral, but an entire city that quickly overshadowed the former capital, Moscow.

Under the jealous and impatient eye of Peter—which usually led to one architect beginning some building or other, a second one continuing it, and a third completing it—were built the Peter and Paul Fortress and the Admiralty, with their proud spires, the Twelve Col-legia (ministries established by Peter on the European model), and the most famous and beloved of Petersburg's beautiful public parks, the Summer Gardens, creating the stylish rectangle that for the next one hundred fifty years set the tone for the construction of Petersburg.

State establishments had to be built with a pomp worthy of a great empire, although the emperor personally still preferred simple rooms for himself, where everything was functional. His house in the Summer Gardens had a carpentry workshop, with a sign the tsar put on the door: "No one without orders or who has not been called in-side may enter, be he stranger or a servant of this house, so that at least here the master may have a quiet place. Peter."

To amuse himself, Peter went to the most luxurious house in Petersburg—the stone palace of the capital's first governor, Men-shikov. It is characteristic of Peter's upwardly mobile Russia that Men-shikov, a man without a noble lineage but hardworking, sneaky,

---

* A typical ukase intended to protect the wooden streets of Petersburg and signed by Peter read, "from this time on all clamps and nails used on men's and women's shoes may no longer be sold and no one may have any; just as no one, no matter his rank, may wear shoes or boots shod this way; and if someone does have shoes or boots shod this way, he will be fined harshly, and the merchants who keep such clamps and nails will be sent to hard labor and their prop-erty confiscated."

merry, and brilliant, went from being a hot-pastry vendor to the tsar's batman and then to the highest positions in the empire. Light and air poured into the huge windows of the palace, which stood on Vasilyevsky Island, on the banks of the Neva. The large main dining room had tables along the walls each of which could hold a whole roasted bull.

Peter and Menshikov's other guests ate a lot and drank even more. A fat court jester rode the room on a small horse and shot a pistol every time the tsar drained his goblet. That was the signal for deafening cannon fire on the embankment which overpowered even the roars of Peter's inebriated entourage. A foreign visitor noted that on such occasions more gunpowder was used up than for the storming of some fortresses.

Peter himself sliced the enormous pies that were brought in one after another. One time a beautiful female midget jumped out of a pie completely naked except for some red ribbons. The tsar and his guests were delighted, for Peter loved dwarves, jesters, and all kinds of monsters, and the imperial court had dozens of them.

Once the guests had stuffed themselves, they danced until two in the morning. The physically inexhaustible Peter adored the energetic Western dances and forced his overweight boyars to jig, too; this was an obligatory part of his "civilizing" program for Russian society. The emperor particularly insisted that old men with gout dance; he was amused by their suffering. Once they caught their breath they went back to the table to continue the party till dawn. No one dared go home or even leave the room without Peter's permission. Foreign ambassadors fell to the floor and instantly fell asleep. Guests urinated on them, while Peter held the candle.

The tsar was not known for his fastidiousness. Pushkin relates, in the historical notes he collected under the English title *Table Talk*, the following story:

> Once a little Negro servant who accompanied Peter I on a walk stopped to relieve himself and suddenly shouted in terror: "Sire! Sire! My intestine is coming out!" Peter came over to him, looked, and said, "Liar: that's not an intestine, it's a tapeworm!"—and he pulled the tapeworm out with his fingers.

Pushkin concludes, " The anecdote is rather dirty, but it depicts Peter's customs. " The morning after such a party, they took a hair of the dog and then went to one of Petersburg's thirty or so bathhouses. The men's and women's baths were next to each other on the riverbank. They undressed right in the street and went inside to steam. When the heat became too much for them, they ran out and jumped into the river. In winter, when the river froze, the lobster-red giant of a tsar and his entourage could be seen frolicking naked in the snow.

And always after a relaxing drinking interlude came more stressful, exhausting work. Peter once described himself as a man pulling uphill while millions pulled downward. But those passive and obedient slaves considered themselves innocent victims of the tsar's whims, the most trying of which was the creation of St. Petersburg. The underlying hostility toward the new city was expressed in folk legends and prophecies that crystallized simultaneously with the construction of Petersburg even before it was completed.

According to one such instant legend, perhaps the most popular, Eudoxia, Peter's first wife, whom the tsar forcibly exiled to a convent, cursed the new city: "Sankt-Peterburg will stand empty!"[8] This pronouncement clashes head-on with Peter's no less famous "The city will be here!" Word of mouth spread about the kikimora, a dreadful mythic creature that hopped into the bell tower of the Trinity Church (Petersburg was founded on the day of the Trinity).[9] This was also supposed to foretell the quick destruction of the city, and nature itself suggested the source: the almost annual floods repeatedly wreaked havoc in the city.

The grim "underground" mythology about Petersburg persisted in spite of the official imperial mythology, which was sparkling and optimistic. In the official hierarchy, Peter the Great was a demiurge and his creation, Petersburg, stood as a result of nothing less than divine inspiration. In the folk consciousness, every change Peter wrought on Russia, and especially the new, rootless capital that had devoured so many Russian lives, was the result of the devil's machinations. So the masses nicknamed Peter the "Antichrist tsar." The belief in the imminent end of Petersburg, which would also bring the end of the world, was widespread in Russia at that time. Resentful comments overheard about the "cursed city" or the "Antichrist tsar" brought complainers swiftly before the dreaded Secret Chancellery both during Peter's lifetime and after his death in 1725. They were then beaten mercilessly with the knout, burned with hot irons, broken on the rack, or had their tongues torn out. But the anti-Petersburg talk didn't cease. Although it was suppressed, it created a constant accompaniment for the continuing expansion and beautification of the capital.

□   □   □

In the sixty years after Peter's reign, Russia had six rulers, the result of early deaths and palace coups. Of them, if we omit Peter's niece, the tall and heavy Anna Ioannovna (during whose reign, 1730–1740, Petersburg was twice desolated by suspicious fires, which greatly simplified the official policy to transform the city from wooden buildings to stone), only one consistently pursued Peter's dream of a modern "New Rome"—his daughter the Empress Elizabeth, who came to the throne with the support of the palace guards in 1741.

The blonde beauty Elizabeth, merry, "voluptuous" (according to Pushkin), physically strong like her father but, unlike him, uninterested in affairs of state, gave the Italian architect Francesco Rastrelli, her favorite, a free hand to fulfill his exquisite architectural projects. Temperamental and capricious, Rastrelli built luxurious royal residences in a lacy Baroque style outside Petersburg—in Peterhof and Tsarskoe Selo, later celebrated in the poetry of Pushkin, who lived there, and in the twentieth century by Anna Akhmatova.

In twenty years, Rastrelli, who did not hesitate to spend Elizabeth's treasure, managed to change the face of Petersburg: he added a dose of southern fantasy to its northern European solidity. Rastrelli's triumph was his project for the Winter Palace—the imperial residence on the Neva. Begun in 1754 and completed in 1817, after the architect's death, this grand building does not seem bulky or pretentious despite its more than one thousand rooms and almost two thousand doors and enormous windows.

The light blue walls of the Winter Palace seemed to dissolve in the generous sculptural order. It glowed against the pale northern sky and steel gray river. The white columns were arranged in a syncopated rhythm that created an unexpected effect of motion. When one looked at the Winter Palace, it appeared to be flying, an impression compounded by its shimmering reflection in the Neva.

The Winter Palace cost two and a half million rubles, equal to the value of forty-five tons of silver. This expense and others like it had to be glorified in prose and poetry and captured in engravings and paintings. The first members of the Russian intelligentsia, created by Peter, gladly accepted their commission: to describe his Petersburg. Hadn't Petersburg opened the way for talented people, no matter what their origin? they argued. Hadn't Peter founded the Academy of Sciences, the first Russian newspaper, the first public museum and library—all in Petersburg? Pushkin expressed this attitude succinctly: "the government is ahead of the people; it likes foreigners and cares about the sciences." Hurrying after the government, the intelligentsia in its widening rift with the masses did not simply reproduce the smart facade of Petersburg; it improved on it. This imperial "socialist realism" was probably begun by the engraver Aleksei Zubov, whose enormous work *Panorama of Petersburg* (1716) depicts with punctilious naturalism not only actual buildings but those that were only in the planning stage at the time.

Peter the Great, having eradicated much of the old Russian culture, quickly scattered new seeds into the soil, and the young shoots took root in Petersburg. The writers of that period delighted in the newness of their capital, relished its rapid growth, and took pride in its lush palaces and brimming cultural life. The dark current of anti-Petersburg folklore apparently did not reach them or was rejected as "barbaric."

These writers identified with Petersburg to the point of dissolving into it. Even if they were bought off by the government, they didn't feel it—their enthusiasm was unadulterated. Their service to the state, which for them was identified with imperial power and symbolized by Petersburg, was devoid of cynicism.

In the verses of Antioch Kantemir, Vassily Trediakovsky, Mikhail Lomonosov, or Alexander Sumarokov describing Petersburg, archaic in style now but still full of energy and feeling, the tendency to find parallels with mythological gods and goddesses is striking. Even in his lifetime Peter was compared to God. So only one more step was needed for the city of St. Peter to be forever identified by his descendants as the city of Emperor Peter. This remarkable shift in stress exists to this day.

That is why eighteenth-century odes to the tsar and his new capital are imbued with the themes of "divine law," or Providence, whose power brought about the city's foundation. Also, there is the sense of almost childlike wonder at the miracle of the instantaneous appearance of Petersburg in an inhospitable setting. It was the early bards of the capital who started referring to Peter as "miracle-working builder," an image that Pushkin used masterfully and from a completely different vantage in *The Bronze Horseman*.

Peter the Great did not need flattery while alive and even less when dead. His heirs were not so self-confident. So the emotional tone of our sincere court writers rose higher and higher until it reached its limit—at least for prerevolutionary Russian literature—in its praise of the Empress Catherine II, who, like Elizabeth, was brought to power by court guards inspired by gifts and champagne.

Catherine, who reigned thirty-four years (1762–1796), is the best-known Russian ruler in the West after Peter.[10] Her notoriety is based primarily on innumerable romantic escapades and the extravagant favors she showered on her lovers, including the talented Grigory Potemkin, the propaganda genius after whom the inglorious "Potemkin villages" were named. As hardworking as Peter and endlessly vain, Catherine was also pronounced the Great. And as with Peter, the evaluation of her significance in Russian history depends on the historian.

The opinion of twenty-three-year-old Pushkin—as much a historian as a poet—is aphoristically sarcastic:

> If ruling means knowing human weakness and using it, then in that case Catherine deserves the awe of posterity. Her brilliance blinded, her friendliness attracted, and her generosity attached. The very voluptuousness of this clever woman confirmed her majesty. Creating only a weak resentment among the people, who were used to respecting the vices of their rulers, it caused vile competition in highest circles, for one needed neither intelligence, nor achievements, nor talents to obtain the second place in the government.

Catherine brought a new style of architecture to Petersburg. From fanciful baroque, so beloved by lighthearted Elizabeth, it switched to an imitation of antiquity and started to acquire its now famous neoclassical look, somewhat analogous to European architectural fashion but undeniably Russian, with drama and grandeur. Catherine, herself German, spoke Russian with a thick accent. Her architects were French, Italian, and Russian; but Petersburg already had obtained its own set of stylistic rules, filtering and transforming foreign influences. We could even say the city did not really change but that its successive builders had to adjust to it somehow, as clever servants adjust to the caprices of a haughty master.

Under Catherine, twenty-four miles of the Neva's banks were "dressed in granite" (Pushkin) from Finland. These severe monumental walls with their numerous stairs leading down to the water became as important a symbol of Petersburg as the stone bridges that spanned the Neva and the city's canals at the same time.

Vainglorious Catherine wanted to be popular not only in Russia but in Europe as well. Ten days after ascending the throne she proposed to Denis Diderot and other French *philosophes* that their epic *Grande Encyclopédia* be printed in Petersburg. Having declared that Russia had entered a new era and was now a superpower, Catherine was prepared to do everything to prove it. In particular, even though she understood nothing of art by her own admission, Catherine began assembling the collection that was to transform the Hermitage into one of the great art museums of the world. At Paris auctions she bought paintings by Raphael, Giorgione, Titian, Tintoretto, Rubens, and Rembrandt. From the collection of Sir Robert Walpole alone, Catherine selected fifteen Van Dykes at once.

These extravagant purchases and the other bold and generous acts of the new empress quickly became the talk of Europe, as she had intended. Invited by the publicity-hungry Catherine, the first fellow travelers, mostly French, came to Petersburg to learn—under the gaze of the empress's keen gray eyes—more about this progressive city and then to relate to the civilized world the thrilling news: Russia had every right to call itself a European state. Following Voltaire's example—unlike Diderot, he never reached Petersburg but, for a generous fee, wrote *L'Histoire de l'empire de Russie sous Pierre le Grand*—they proclaimed Catherine the Northern Semiramyde and Petersburg the Northern Palmyra. Catherine's policy of controlled cultural exchanges met with considerable success.

One of Catherine's wisest cultural decisions was to invite to Petersburg—at the suggestion of Diderot—Etienne Falconet, the Parisian sculptor, to erect an enormous equestrian monument to Peter I. Fifty-year-old Falconet arrived in the Russian capital in 1766 with his seventeen-year-old student, Maria Callot, and twenty-five pieces of luggage, to spend the next very difficult twelve years there. Falconet's voluminous correspondence with Catherine—though they were both living in the same city!—contains ample evidence of the obstacles he encountered: the nervous and touchy sculptor constantly complained, expressing outrage and disgust over countless problems—red tape, sloppy workers, the absence of supplies and materials—faced by any foreigner trying to build something in the Russian capital. The empress, in typical Russian fashion, tried to reason with him and calm him down.

From faraway Paris, Diderot advised Falconet how to approach his task. The sculptor, Diderot suggested, ought to surround the statue of Peter, in the spirit of the era, with symbolic figures of Barbarism (dressed in fur skins and gazing fiercely at the emperor), Love of the People (extending her arms to Peter), and the Nation (enjoying tranquillity while comfortably reclining on the ground). Understandably irritated, Falconet shot back from Petersburg, "The monument will be realized with utmost simplicity. It will not have Barbarism, Love of the People, or the symbol of the Nation."[11] The sculptor's own model of a horseman who had just galloped up on a cliff, his right hand extended, had already been approved by Catherine.

Curious Petersburgers flocked to Falconet's studio in droves. Accustomed to the critical reactions of Parisians, the sculptor could not understand why the Russians would scrutinize the model of the statue, then leave without a word. Did their silent attentiveness indicate disapproval? He calmed down only after long-term foreign residents of Petersburg explained that restraint was the main characteristic of the capital's populace. The city, which had recently celebrated its fiftieth anniversary, had already developed a particular psychological type: "all buttons buttoned," unsentimental, tending to irony and sarcasm—characteristics that remain valid to this day.

All the while, Falconet's tribulations continued. He could not get the laurel-crowned head of the horseman right. At last it was completed by Callot, and, they say, all in one night. The only known woman sculptor of the period created what is generally acknowledged to be a very good likeness of Peter the Great. The face is comparatively small but broad, with jowls, a slightly pointed nose, and a sharp, willful jaw; the raised brows shade the fanatical gaze of the protruding eyes. Peter seemed to be both staring transfixed into the distance and at the same time angrily squinting at the viewer, something Pushkin noted later.

Nothing about this monument was simple, and every detail of the sculpture elicited arguments and nagging doubts in the sculptor and his clients. How should the horseman be dressed? What kind of horse? Lengthy discussion was provoked by Falconet's idea of having a snake—allegory of evil and envy—under the horse's hoofs. Catherine, who was to make the final decision on this issue, was unsure: "The allegorical snake neither pleases nor displeases me."[12] The question was resolved only after a flattering letter from Falconet to Catherine: every great person—Peter and, of course, the Empress Catherine—courageously overcame the envy of ungrateful contemporaries, insisted the sculptor; thus the snake could not be left out. Catherine, sensitive to every flattering comparison with Peter, agreed: "There is an ancient song which says, if it is necessary, then it is necessary. That is my answer regarding the snake."[13]

It took four years to find a site for the monument. Even more dramatic was the search for and delivery of a huge hunk of granite for the pedestal. The stone was located twelve miles from the capital and even after initial carving weighed over fifteen hundred tons. It took thousands of people to move it and the process lasted over three years. The court poet, Vassily Ruban, sang its praises in verse typical of the epoch:

> Colossus of Rhodes, tame your fiery gaze,
> And the tall Pyramids along the Nile
> Can stop considering themselves miracles!
> You are made by mortal hands,
> But this is a Russian mountain untouched by human hands,
> Which heard the voice of God from Catherine's lips
> And came to the city of Peter through the Neva's depths,
> And fell beneath the feet of Peter the Great!

On August 7, 1782, on the hundredth anniversary of Peter's ascension to the throne and sixteen years after Falconet began his work, the monument was at last unveiled. The sculptor himself was not there to see it. After an especially nasty argument with Catherine and accusations by courtiers that he had squandered money, Falconet fled to Paris. His last contribution to the monument was the text of the laconic inscription, which was to be engraved on the pedestal: "For Peter the First erected by Catherine the Second." The final version of the inscription, edited by Catherine, read, "For Peter the First from Catherine the Second." An accomplished writer, Catherine achieved much simply by removing the predicate. In Falconet's draft, the accent was on "erected," that is, on the monument. Catherine brought the "First-Second" continuity closer, thereby stressing, and legitimizing, her status as heir to the great monarch.

Petersburgers of various estates—from aristocrat to peasant—gathered at Senate Square on the banks of the Neva. The monument was covered with special curtains that opened when Catherine appeared; cannons were fired and military music resounded. The guards passed in review before the monument with their banners lowered.

On the occasion, Catherine declared an amnesty for criminals and debtors in jail. During a special liturgy celebrated by Peter's tomb in the Cathedral of Peter and Paul, the metropolitan struck the tomb with his staff and cried, "Arise ye now, great monarch, and behold your pleasing invention: it has not withered in time nor has its glory dimmed!" This call to Peter was pronounced with such passion and bathos that the heir to the throne, little Paul, became afraid that "grandpa would get out of the coffin." An aristocrat standing nearby quietly remarked to his neighbors, in an exercise of low-key Petersburg humor, "Why is he calling him? Once he gets up, we'll all get it!"[14]

Even though almost everyone immediately appreciated the more obvious virtues of Falconet's monument, it is unlikely that the first viewers really understood they were present at the unveiling of one of the great European sculptures of the eighteenth century. And as they circled the statue of Peter, discovering ever new aspects of the emperor's depiction—wise and determined lawmaker, fearless military leader, unbending monarch who would not be stopped—the gratified Petersburgers could not foresee that Falconet's work would become the most important and most popular representation of their city, and that the tortuous process, fraught with cultural and political overtones, of elevating this statue to an enduring symbol would be started by a yet unborn Russian poet.

Senate Square was a most appropriate site for the monument, because the Senate itself had been decreed by Peter; the Admiralty stood nearby and the square was situated in the busiest part of the city. The monument was always surrounded by curious admirers. It was here that revolutionary guardsmen gathered in 1825 in an attempt to prevent Nicholas I from taking the throne. Since this took place on a morning in December, the rebels were called "Decembrists."

A massive artillery round scattered the revolutionaries. "Between shots you could hear blood streaming along the street, melting the snow and then freezing, red on white," one of them recalled later. By evening the hundreds of corpses had been cleared away and the blood covered with fresh snow. But the blood was never wiped away from the marmoreal face of Petersburg—the city's history would continue as it had begun.

And yet what idyllic harmony had preceded it. By the early nineteenth century, in the reign of Alexander I, people managed to forget completely about the bones on which this Northern Palmyra had been built. They tried not to recall the grim interlude of 1796–1801, the reign of Catherine II's extravagant son, the tyrant Paul I.

Paul's own courtiers killed the "snubnosed villain" on a chilly March night. Unhappy with his unpredictable and sometimes bizarre edicts, they rushed into his bedroom in the new residence, the Mikhailovsky Palace, in the heart of Petersburg, just painted his favorite shade of red, and strangled their master. When the news reached the emperor's son, Alexander, a sentimental dreamer who had known about the conspiracy, he burst into tears. His hysterics were swiftly cut short by one of the conspirators, who ordered, "Stop playing the child and go rule!"

The majestic Mikhailovsky Palace with its golden spire still stands as a haunting symbol of regicide—not the first or the last in Russian history. In 1838, a sixteen-year-old freshman named Fyodor Dostoyevsky would cross the doorstep of the castle, which by then had been converted to the engineering school. He didn't excel as an engineer, but he did become one of the most visionary and influential builders of the Petersburg mythos.

The early years of the new emperor, Alexander I, blue-eyed and nearsighted (both literally and metaphorically), could be characterized by a single line from Pushkin's poem—"The marvelous beginning of Alexander's days"—a nostalgic line that would become extremely popular in early-twentieth-century Petersburg. The war of 1812 with Napoleon, called the Patriotic War in Russia, united the entire society—peasants, intelligentsia, nobility—around its liberal monarch in nationalistic fervor.

In 1814 the pensive tsar rode a white horse into Paris, accompanied by victorious Russian troops (among whom were the future Decembrists). Triumphant Petersburg celebrated this providential union of Russia and Europe in a brilliant new architectural style: the Russian Empire. Created with the participation of domestic masters, it was the refined apotheosis of neoclassicism. Petersburg's main features, ordered and severe, took the shape we know today. St. Isaac's Cathedral was begun; Palace Square was completed.

Educated Russians of the first decades of the nineteenth century regarded their capital with special love and attachment. It was a city that inspired wonder and admiration. For in Petersburg their enormous country, so backward a mere century ago, appeared ennobled, disciplined, and directed—under the enlightened leadership of Emperor Alexander—to become a rightful member of a common Europe.

For these poets, writers, artists, and patrons Petersburg was not simply the symbol of Russia's political triumph and military ascension; it was also the embodiment of its flowering culture. Willpower had overcome savage nature, and refined Petersburgers enjoyed the fruits of civilization as did the inhabitants of other important European capitals.

The city was extolled in this manner—perhaps for the last time with such sincerity and harmony—by the impressionable and feckless poet Konstantin Batyushkov, later elevated to the rank of "Columbus of Russian Art Criticism," in his article "A Stroll to the Academy of Arts" (1814):

> Marvelous buildings, gilded by the morning sun, were reflected brightly in the clean mirror of the Neva, and we both exclaimed unanimously, "What a city! What a river!" "The only city!" the young man repeated. "So many subjects for the artist's brush! . . . I must leave Petersburg," he continued, "I must leave it for a bit, I must see the ancient capitals: old Paris, sooty London, in order to appreciate Petersburg's worth. Look—what unity! how all the parts respond to the whole! what beauty in the buildings, what taste, and what variety from the mixture of water with buildings."

Having put Paris and London in their place, Batyushkov finished with a toast:

> How many wonders we see before us, wonders created in such a short period, in a century, just one century! Glory and honor to the great founder of this city! Glory and honor to his successors, who completed what he had barely begun, in the course of wars, internal and foreign discord! Glory and honor to Alexander, who more than anyone, during his reign made beautiful the capital of the North!

Such a classic speech would have been impossible for the Decembrists, who in their own words "no longer believed in the good intentions of the government." Their favorite aphorism, "The world is beginning to learn that nations do not exist for tsars but the tsars for nations," was previously unthinkable in Russia, where the concept of monarchy was traditionally viewed as sacred.

In 1825 these first modern Russian dissidents marched boldly into Senate Square, their weapons drawn. The crowd looked on speechless. These armed men were no longer loyal subjects but claimed to be intellectually and morally free citizens of Russia—not classicists at all but revolutionary romantics. It was the first crack in the facade of Petersburg's neoclassical Empire.

Pushkin's *Bronze Horseman* further opened this first crack. The poem was interpreted by many as an allegory and requiem for the failed Decembrist uprising, which had threatened to flood Petersburg just as the elements had a year earlier. On the day of the uprising Pushkin was two hundred miles away, in the village of Mikhailovskoe, serving his five-year exile for his nonconformist thinking, by the order of

Alexander. Now Nicholas I was on the throne, succeeding his elder brother Alexander, who had died in 1825—under somewhat mysterious circumstances—far away from Petersburg, in the southern city of Taganrog. Soon Nicholas recalled Pushkin to Petersburg for a private audience.

Deemed extraordinary by contemporaries, this meeting between tsar and poet in 1826 immediately became the stuff of legend. It was said that Nicholas I and Pushkin spoke for two and a half hours, an audience no minister was granted at the time. What did the imposingly handsome, thirty-year-old emperor with blond hair and hypnotizing, cold gray eyes talk about with the poet, who was three years younger, of medium build, with abrupt movements, curly hair, and a dark complexion? Pushkin, deeply touched, ran from Nicholas's study with tears in his eyes. "How I would like to hate him! But what can I do? For what can I hate him?" In his turn, Nicholas announced to his stunned courtiers that he had just talked with "the wisest man in Russia."

The emperor's question to the poet was, "Pushkin, would you have taken part in the rebellion on December 14th, if you had been in Petersburg?" Pushkin replied honestly and boldly that without any doubt he would have been in Senate Square with the revolutionaries. "All my friends were there."

As we know, Pushkin was forgiven by Nicholas, who appreciated directness and honesty. Then the conversation turned to Nicholas's intended far-reaching reforms; the emperor asked Pushkin for advice and support. The tone and content of the conversation brought to Pushkin's mind the illustrious reformer, Peter the Great. A virtuoso manipulator, Nicholas had undoubtedly been striving for that very effect.

At that moment a spiritual triangle was created: Peter I–Nicholas I–Pushkin. This must be kept in mind when reading *The Bronze Horseman*, which was completed eight years after the Decembrists were defeated. The potential readership for almost everything Pushkin wrote in those years was divided in two: Nicholas and everyone else. Nevertheless, even though Pushkin began his "Petersburg tale" with a panegyric, he quickly gave it a tragic character.

Pushkin was prepared to agree with Nicholas, who maintained with hypnotic willfulness that Russia needed an absolute sovereignty, that without a strong ruler the country would perish. At the same time Pushkin feared and hated tyranny.

Before Pushkin, Petersburg had known only praise. But

Pushkin's vision of the city was dualistic. His evaluation of the role of Peter and his reforms, of the civilizing effect of the city, and of the future of autocratic rule (that is, the past, present, and future of all Russia) seems in *The Bronze Horseman* to rest in balance. Neither took precedence. But their equilibrium was not clearly fixed: the scales trembled and vibrated.*

Nicholas I did not live up to Pushkin's hopes. Later Anna Akhmatova even felt that the tsar had tricked the poet consciously. Outraged, she told me that Nicholas "did not keep his word, and *that* is unforgivable for an emperor."[15]

More important, he also tricked the country, which had expected reforms from the young, energetic tsar. Gifted in many ways—he knew several languages, was a brilliant orator, and played the flute—Nicholas was fixated on order.[16] He pictured Russia as a gigantic mechanism that had to function exactly as he (wisely) set it. An echo of Peter's mania could be seen in that, and at first, the people, hypnotized, blindly obeyed the new emperor. But Nicholas lacked his predecessor's monumental vision, and the times were quite different too. The tsar's unwavering confidence in his own infallibility was no longer enough to drag Russia forward.

Nicholas was called by one ironic observer the "Don Quixote of autocracy." But this peculiarly Russian Don Quixote tried fanatically to turn his capital into an army barracks, with no room for disobedience or any flash of independent thought. For only in the army, the emperor believed, could be found "order, strict, unconditional legality, where there are no 'know-it-alls' or the passion of contradiction. . . . everyone is subordinate in a single, definite goal, everything has its designation." Nicholas often repeated, "I regard all human life as service," and also, "I need people who are obedient, not wise."

With this attitude, the emperor obviously began to regard Pushkin and other leading intellectuals expendable. Nicholas was not particularly upset by Pushkin's death in 1837, at the age of thirty-seven, in a Petersburg duel. (By contrast, this tragic event would later be considered, by all literate Russians, one of the greatest catastrophes in Russia's cultural history.) When another brilliant Russian poet, twenty-six-year-old Mikhail Lermontov, was killed in a duel in 1841, Nicholas is supposed to have said disdainfully, "A cur's death for a cur."

* As Russia's most popular poet after Pushkin, Alexander Blok wrote in 1910, underlining the nervous instability that transfixes the reader, "*The Bronze Horseman*—we all exist in the vibrations of its bronze."

In the three decades of his austere reign (1825–1855), Nicholas I froze Petersburg and all Russia. Already in the era of Alexander I, the poet Vassily Zhukovsky complained that the residents of Petersburg "were mummies, surrounded by majestic pyramids, whose grandeur exists not for them." Nicholas succeeded brilliantly in bringing Petersburg's image even closer to his beloved barracks. The splenetic and wise friend of the late Pushkin, Prince Vyazemsky, noted sadly, "straight, correct, evened out, symmetrical, monotonous, and complete, Petersburg can serve as an emblem of our life. . . . In people, you can't tell Ivan from Peter; in time, today from tomorrow: everything is the same."

So it was in December 1828 that nineteen-year-old Nikolai Gogol came to this disciplined, haughty, cold city from the bright, gentle, warm Ukraine. The ambitious provincial—skinny, sickly, and big-nosed—arrived in Petersburg with radiant dreams, confident of conquering the capital instantly. As with most young men, even those with talent, these dreams proved somewhat difficult to realize.

In one of his first letters home to his mother, young Gogol shared his impressions of the capital, revealing the sharp eye of its future vivisector:

> Petersburg is a rather large city. * If you want to stroll its streets, with squares and islands in various directions, you will probably walk more than 100 versts, and despite its size, you can have anything you might need without sending far, even in the same building. . . . The house in which I live contains two tailors, one *marchand de mode,* a shoemaker, a hosiery manufacturer, a repairer of broken dishes, a plasterer and house painter, a pastry shop, a notions shop, a cold storage for winter clothing, a tobacco shop, and finally, a midwife for the privileged. Naturally, this building has to be plastered all over with gold signs. I live on the fourth floor.[17]

Walking through the streets in the daytime, Gogol eagerly plunged into the bustling life of the capital. He spent hours peering into shop windows on Nevsky Prospect, which displayed such exotic fruits brought from overseas as oranges, pineapples, and bananas.

Unable to resist, Gogol ate in one French pastry shop after another. He visited the Academy of Arts, praised by Batyushkov, where

---

*At this time the population of St. Petersburg was rapidly approaching a half-million.

the works of the professors and the best students were on display; Gogol formed close friendships with some of the latter.

In the popular newspaper *Severnaya pchela* (*Northern Bee*), Gogol could read about literary news, in which he was desperately interested, as well as about government postings, robberies, and suicides. The paper allotted a lot of space to reports and discussion of fires—a subject always topical in Petersburg. And, of course, there were constant predictions of another feature of life in the capital—floods.

In politics, both foreign and domestic, *Severnaya pchela* cultivated the greatest caution and unbounded loyalty to the emperor. The careerist editor, Faddei Bulgarin, who did not mind stooping to denounce his colleagues to the secret police, strictly obeyed the orders given him from above by the chief of the gendarmerie, who was also chief censor: "Theater, exhibitions, shopping mall, flea market, inns, pastry shops—that's your field and don't take a single step beyond it."

In the evenings foppish Gogol headed for the theater, "my best pleasure." The streets of Petersburg were illuminated by thousands of oil lamps and the recent innovation, gaslights. The combination of light, darkness, and fog gave the city a spectral appearance. Expensive carriages pulled by teams of six horses drove up to theater entrances. Dandies escorted well-dressed ladies, mysterious and, to the young provincial, seemingly inaccessible; laughter and bits of gallant compliments in French melted into the damp air. Mounted police helped the drivers park the numerous coaches blocking the square.

On the stage of the Imperial Alexandrinsky Theater Vassily Karatygin, a six-foot giant with a roaring baritone and majestic gestures, stunned audiences with his Hamlet. Like all authors in Russia, Shakespeare was subjected to strict censorship. Nicholas personally made sure that no political allusions or even curse words as gentle as "devil take it" were spoken on stage.

Gogol was delighted by Karatygin's acting. Later he recalled that the great actor "grabs you up in a heap and carries you off, so that you don't have time to realize what's happening."[18] Nicholas, too, was well disposed toward the actor, who resembled him physically. Once the emperor, accompanied by an aide, dropped by the actor's dressing room.

"They tell me you portray me well," he said to the actor. "Show me."

"I don't dare, Your Imperial Majesty!"

"I'm ordering you!"

Karatygin pulled himself together, grew visibly taller, his eyes took on a steely, hypnotizing hue, and he barked at the adjutant, "Listen, dear boy, make sure that actor fellow Karatygin receives a case of champagne!"

Nicholas burst out laughing and the next morning a case of champagne was delivered to the actor's house.

With stories like these, it is no wonder Gogol began to set his sights on a great Petersburg career including an attempt to join the imperial theater as an actor. A calamity. Then he tried to become a painter, then a bureaucrat, and, finally, a teacher. Gogol thought he was ascending the ladder of success and wealth, but he was stuck every time on the bottom rung. Petersburg persistently refused to recognize him; and Gogol, in turn, came to hate Petersburg. The city would remain forever alien to him: inviting but hostile, a world he could never conquer. And when Gogol began writing, the grotesque and alienated image of Petersburg quickly became the center of his prose.

Gogol's first Petersburg novellas appeared in 1835—*Nevsky Prospect, Diary of a Madman,* and *Portrait;* then came *The Nose,* which Pushkin published in 1836, shortly before his death, in his journal *Sovremennik;* and then in 1842, the most famous work of this cycle was published, *The Overcoat.*

Gogol, and through him all later imagery of Petersburg, was heavily influenced by E. T. A. Hoffmann; even a hundred years later, in her *Poem Without a Hero,* Akhmatova curses the "Petersburg devils" and calls them "midnight Hoffmanniana."

Like Hoffmann, Gogol combines the oppressively quotidian with unrestrained fantasy. A beautiful stranger met on Nevsky Prospect turns out to be a cheap prostitute. A mysterious portrait has fatal powers. A smug bureaucrat's nose escapes from his face and assumes an independent personality.

These incredible events could take place only in Gogol's Petersburg—a terrifying and demonically captivating city, seen through the wide eyes of a young southern provincial, scared of life. Gogol's early febrile impressions of the city, stirred by the pen of a literary genius, pour out in a passionate kaleidoscope of romantic monologue, a colorful phantasmagoric picture worthy of Chagall, describing the central and most famous street in the capital:

> O, don't trust that Nevsky Prospect! . . . It's all deceit, all dreams, it's all not what it seems! . . . For God's sake, get away from the street lamp! And walk by as fast as you can. You'll be lucky if it does noth-

ing more than spill its noisome oil on your elegant coat. Everything else besides the street lamp breathes deceit. It lies all the time, that Nevsky Prospect, but especially when night thickens upon it, separating the white and pale walls of the houses, when the entire city turns into thunder and sparkle, myriads of carriages falling from the bridges, postilions shouting and leaping on horses, and when the demon himself lights the lamps only so that he can show things in their not real form.

As a beginning writer, Gogol roamed the clean, orderly streets of Petersburg—the emperor was fixated on cleanliness and hygiene—which were filled with grand ceremonial proceedings of all kinds. In his personal life Nicholas I was ascetic and moderate, rising at dawn and working eighteen hours a day. But he understood the need for public rituals that underscored the solidity of the empire and of his divine right to rule.

Petersburg was the city of the court and of an enormous garrison. It was filled with a multitude of clerks; ordinary people did not jam its streets. The rabble, as it was called then, behaved with care when they came to Petersburg. With a vigilant eye, the capital's self-important police (immortalized by Gogol in *The Nose*) interfered in every trifle. On New Year's Day, the emperor opened the Winter Palace to all; thirty thousand and more came. Food and drink were provided in abundance for the common folk. Quietly and in awe, the solemn crowd awaited the appearance of Nicholas and his wife.

They would arrive to the strains of a polonaise followed by his retinue in full dress, as the light from thousands of candles flooded the huge reception room. Nicholas kindly but coolly spoke with "his" people, as he walked among these coachmen, servants, and craftsmen. At the end, the guests left satisfied and sober. Nothing was stolen— not a dish or a utensil. The law and order so dear to the emperor's heart prevailed.

For high society the balls at the Winter Palace were naturally much more luxurious, with succulent dinners for a thousand guests seated in the shade of orange trees. The empress adored masquerades and wanted the women of the court to appear there in their fanciest dresses—velvet and lace, gold, pearls, and diamonds. "The empress would rest her gaze on a beautiful new gown, having turned her disappointed eyes from a less fashionable dress. And as the empress's gaze was law, the women dressed up, and the men grew bankrupt, and sometimes stole, in order to dress their wives," a rather puritanical lady of the court indignantly fumed in reminiscence. At these masquerade balls, Nicholas I paid especial attention to lovely young debutantes.

It was the persistent demands of the court entourage that led to Pushkin's death. Pushkin's wife, the beautiful Natalie, who was so much in demand at these balls, was the hub of love affairs, gossip, and intrigues. This atmosphere of real and imagined affairs led to the poet's tragic duel. One can easily see how Pushkin's ambivalence toward the court and the emperor caused him a lot of pain. But Gogol, the untitled, poor, and extremely ambitious outsider, did not interest Nicholas in the least, and so suffered even more.

That gave even greater passion to Gogol's alternative mythos of Petersburg. In literature he justifiably felt like a mighty monarch, not simply juggling verbal worlds with blinding virtuosity, but, as he truly believed, influencing the course of life itself through his writer's magic. Gogol juxtaposed the brilliant balls and posh receptions that were beyond his reach to his own obsessive vision of the capital. In revenge, he built a monster Petersburg inhabited by caricatures, a mirage Petersburg, and finally, a deserted, ghostly Petersburg. Balzac wrote about Paris this way and Dickens about London. But Gogol's mystical Petersburg is much more the fruit of his fevered imagination, far removed from the reality of the city.

The constant themes of Gogol's eccentric, intriguing, highly comic, sentimental, wildly romantic, distorted, and ultimately overpowering Petersburg tales are fog, darkness, cold reflecting surfaces, and fear of vast open spaces. Every one of these themes is totally exaggerated and taken to extremes. Gogol's Petersburg, in the words of his delighted fan Vladimir Nabokov, is turned into "a reflection in a blurred mirror, an eerie medley of objects put to the wrong use, things going backwards the faster they moved forward, pale gray nights instead of ordinary black ones, and black days."[19]

In his influential *Overcoat,* Gogol places the petty clerk, a direct descendant of Yevgeny from Pushkin's *Bronze Horseman,* in the middle of an endless Petersburg square, "which looked like a terrifying desert." It is here that robbers seize the overcoat, which the clerk had acquired with such painstaking labor, even though a square is far from the best place for a mugging.

Deprived of his metaphorical overcoat, Gogol's hapless hero is left naked to face his main enemy—the city, where, according to Gogol, there is eternal winter, where even "the wind, in accordance with Petersburg custom, blew at him from all four quarters" (again impossible in reality) and where the white snow whipped up by the cutting wind is identified with the useless deadly paper snow that falls on the helpless individual from anonymous ministries and offices—a Kafkaesque image forty-one years before Kafka's birth. Of course, the poor clerk dies and indifferent Petersburg, according to Gogol, goes on without him as if he had never existed.

In a similar situation Pushkin would probably hesitate to bring a final judgment. But Gogol has no doubts: the culprit is Petersburg, ruthlessly destroying the personality, a soulless heap "of houses tumbled one upon the other, roaring streets, seething mercantilism, that ugly pile of fashions, parades, clerks, wild northern nights, specious glitter, and base colorlessness."

Gogol's image of a demonic Petersburg became mystical. The city of his imagination is not really a city at all anymore but a land of the living dead: a black hole that sucks people into it, the Great Nothing. "The idea of the city," Gogol wrote, is "emptiness taken to the highest degree." The deep-seated rejection of Petersburg so typical of the common people rose to the surface in his writing, slowly but inexorably becoming part of the social and philosophical discourse of the educated classes.

Gogol was the first (1837) to publish an extended literary comparison of the old and new capitals—Moscow and Petersburg— starting a long line of such essays, right up to Yevgeny Zamyatin's *Moscow-Petersburg* (1933). In the popular consciousness Moscow symbolized everything national, truly Russian, and familiar. Moscow was a city whose roots went back to religious tradition, making it the rightful heir of Constantinople, and thus the Third Rome, as the Orthodox monks of the sixteenth century taught. ("There can be no Fourth Rome," they added.)

Peter the Great subordinated the church to the state. Petersburg, despite certain external religious attributes fixed to official legends, was planned and built as a secular city. Moscow's silhouette was determined by the "forty times forty" churches and their belfries. Petersburg's silhouette is made of dominating spires.

The people perceived the godless, foreign-looking Petersburg as alien, a gigantic squid sucking the lifeblood out of Russia. Gogol legitimized that view by formulating the people's vague doubts into the famous line, "Russia needs Moscow; Petersburg needs Russia."

Gogol's verdict became a catchphrase for the Slavophiles, the influential nationalistic literary, philosophical, and—as much as the post-Decembrist climate allowed—political movement of the times, which called for a special path of development for Russia, eschewing Western models. They considered the entire "Petersburg" period of Russian history to be a tragic mistake and saw salvation in a return to pre-Petrine, patriarchal norms and forms of social life. "Long live Moscow and down with Petersburg!" was their battle cry.

Almost every utterance by Gogol—who considered himself to be a divinely endowed person, prophet, and spiritual adviser—was law to the Slavophiles. But even the so-called Westernizers, who dreamed of a Russian constitution and European-style parliament, recognized Gogol's importance, especially after his early death in 1852. Gogol's mystical picture and negative assessment of Petersburg's significance reigned in the minds of his contemporaries, easily outweighing the preponderant hundred years of praise for the capital.

This was an extremely rare instance when the writing of a single man, albeit a recognized literary genius, could change so drastically the established perception among the educated classes of a great city. But this is the way literature works in Russia. Hence the Petersburg mythos changed from Peter's version to Gogol's.

Gogol had a powerful ally in this unprecedented achievement—Nicholas I. For the Russian intelligentsia of the mid-nineteenth century, haughty, autocratic Petersburg grew completely confused with the monumental, neoclassical Nicholas. Finally, the two blended into one. Neither had lived up to the expectations of the intelligentsia.

People had counted on reforms from Nicholas, but he tightened the screws instead; they had expected mercy, but he vengefully hanged five leaders of the Decembrist uprising. After Pushkin, many other major writers including Gogol had offered to become enlightened allies of the Russian autocracy. Their civic aspirations were rejected and Nicholas created the "Third Division of His Imperial Highness's Own Chancellery," the precursor of the Soviet ideological secret service.

Nicholas's role in forming the image of Petersburg can be compared negatively to that of Peter the Great. Peter reached out to the young Russian intelligentsia. Under Nicholas, Petersburg stopped being a city in which a principled intellectual could have an honest career. Even writers who sold out were rewarded unenthusiastically. The days of Catherine the Great, when a successful poem in praise of the empress and her capital could receive a royal recompense, say, a gold snuffbox sprinkled with diamonds, were gone for good. A touring

Italian singer like the famous tenor Giovanni Rubini was more likely to be so rewarded.

A contemporary complained that under Nicholas I, "little attention was paid to Russian literature"; the government had based its strength "on a million bayonets instead of a philosophical dream. There was no profit in being considered an archmonarchical essayist."[20] On the contrary, in intellectual circles it had become quite fashionable to abuse the Petersburg so beloved of Nicholas: cruel, bureaucratic, officious, where even the streets were attention-straight, as if on parade. "That granite, those bridges with chains, that neverending drumming, all that has a depressing and overwhelming effect," a hotheaded Slavophile summed up in disgust.

Following in the footsteps of Gogol, hurling a challenge and waving a fist at the capital, since one couldn't threaten the emperor, was considered a sign of artistry and freethinking. These temperamental and amusing attacks on Nicholas's Petersburg would make a wonderful anthology. And the prose and poetry of Apollon Grigoryev (1822–1864) are among the most inspired of the lot.

A great fan of Grigoryev's, the symbolist poet Alexander Blok later characterized him as a stormy and tormented youth with the soul of Dmitri Karamazov. Grigoryev moved from patriarchal Moscow at the age of twenty-one to Petersburg, supported by Freemason friends. He said he "was transported to another world. This was the world of Gogol's Petersburg, the Petersburg in the era of its miragelike originality. . . . a strange and *poshly* world."

I believe Grigoryev was the first to apply the many-meaninged Russian word *poshly* to Petersburg, a word Nabokov, a Petersburger in exile, tried to explain to his American students a hundred years later. "Russians have, or had, a special name for smug philistinism—*poshlust. Poshlism* is not only the obviously trashy but mainly the falsely important, the falsely beautiful, the falsely clever, the falsely attractive. To apply the deadly label of *poshlism* to something is not only an aesthetic judgment but also a moral indictment."[21]

Even in Russia, which loves its poets, Grigoryev is not very popular. He was too bohemian: he drank wildly with Gypsies (when he didn't have enough money for vodka, he drank cologne and kerosene, a habit that remains among Russian alcoholics today), married a prostitute, and died in Petersburg—a few days after release from debtors' prison—from a stroke following a violent argument with his publisher.

I remember the fascination with which I opened a volume of

Grigoryev's poems. It was in 1959; I was fifteen, in my second year in Leningrad, where I had moved from Riga to study. Like multitudes before me, I was enchanted by the beauty and magic of Leningrad's white nights. They begin in May, and it was wonderful on a night like that to stop with a sweetheart on the bridge aptly called Bridge of Kisses, and declaim from *The Bronze Horseman*: ". . . the transparent twilight of dreamy nights, the moonless glow . . ."

What a shock it was to come across a demonic picture of a white night, stylistically similar to the invective of Grigoryev's peer Charles Baudelaire:

> *And in those hours when my proud city*
> *Is covered by night without dark or shadow,*
> *When everything is transparent, then a swarm of disgusting visions*
> *Flickers before me . . .*
> *Let the night be as clear as day, let everything be still,*
> *Let everything be transparent and calm—*
> *In that calm an evil illness lurks—*
> *And that is the transparency of a suppurating ulcer.*

It's hard to imagine that this Masonic exposé, which Grigoryev called "The City," was published in 1845, twelve years before *Les Fleurs du Mal*. And it appeared in the popular and fully loyal Petersburg journal with the pompous title *Repertoire of the Russian and the Pantheon of All European Theaters*, controlled by the ambition-driven government spy Faddei Bulgarin. And then this virulently anti-Petersburg work by Grigoryev was praised ("a marvelous poem") by the liberal guru of that period, the leading literary critic, Vissarion Belinsky. That's how wide the gamut of anti-Petersburg moods ranged then in Russian culture—from the extreme right to the extreme left. . . .

The irony of subsequent events led to the situation a bit more than a century later in Khrushchev's Leningrad, when I could not bring this poem of Grigoryev's into school to discuss it with my literature teacher because its spirit, aesthetics, and symbolism would have seemed subversive and I could have provoked serious trouble.

Naturally, I debated "The City" fiercely (though not very loudly) with my best friend. And, of course, we immediately sensed the viciousness of its attack: the mystical and democratic Grigoryev denied the image of the white nights painted by the rationalistic and aristocratic Pushkin in *The Bronze Horseman*.

In the second half of the nineteenth century it became possible to denigrate not only Pushkin and his idealized Petersburg of the introduction to *The Bronze Horseman* but also Falconet's equestrian statue of Peter I, which had inspired Pushkin. Typical is the impromptu verse of the cynical and sharp-tongued epigrammist Nikolai Shcherbina (1821–69). Shcherbina had the snake under the horse's hoofs of Petersburg's founder elicit associations that were directly the opposite of the noble imagery of the eighteenth century:

> *No, it wasn't a snake the Bronze Horseman*
> *Trampled, galloping forward,*
> *He trampled our poor people,*
> *He trampled the simple folk.*

And this was not written by someone from the opposition but a major government official! In folktales Falconet's monument had long been compared to one of the horsemen of the apocalypse. It was clear that the people's view of Peter and his reforms, so long stifled and suppressed, had become firmly rooted in public cultural life, that oral tradition had been transformed into the literary tradition, and the opinion from "below" and from "above" on Petersburg had merged and almost coincided.

"Sankt-Peterburg will stand empty!" That legendary curse was now discussed in the salons of Moscow and Petersburg, but it also became the topic of popular poems such as "Underwater City" (1847) by Mikhail Dmitriev, which predicted with unsuppressed glee the coming inexorable flooding of the capital, unimaginable not only in Pushkin but even in Gogol.

> *Now the belfry spire*
> *Is alone visible from the sea.*

The government tried to stop the anti-Petersburg literary flood. The head of the vicious Third Division and the chief of the gendarmerie, Count Alexander Benkendorf, issued guidelines, eerily similar to the ones proclaimed a hundred years later by Stalin's ideology chief, Andrei Zhdanov: "Russia's past was amazing, its present is more than marvelous, and as for the future, it is greater than anything the wildest imagination could picture; that is the point of view for examining and writing Russian history."

The hack writer Alexander Bashutsky, fulfilling the commission from the literary police, issued an idealized "Panorama of Saint-

Petersburg": incredible descriptions of a lovely city in which cleanliness and order reigned, without brawls, fights, drunkards, prostitutes, or beggars. Planning a luxurious edition, Bashutsky ordered special engravings from London, but the ship delivering them sank. So did the Panorama: no one bought it and Bashutsky lost a lot of money. The sophisticated public in the capital did not accept descriptions of Petersburg cooked up from recipes by the gendarme chief.

However, the *Physiology of Petersburg*, a two-volume anthology published in 1845, became extremely popular. Belinsky participated in it under the editorship of young Nikolai Nekrasov, the poet, gambler, and entrepreneurial publisher. Nekrasov saw that the foreign bookstores in Petersburg were selling many copies of small, elegant books from Paris titled *Physiologie de l'amoureux* or *Physiologie du flaneur*, with amusing descriptions of all Parisian types. So Nekrasov collected articles by his friends about Petersburg mores and personages. He wanted to make money, and he needed something sensational. The book he put together gave the stunned reader a picture of the Russian capital that had nothing to do with Bashutsky's cloying Panorama.

Even though Nekrasov's collection contained Belinsky's brilliant thoughts on the popular theme Petersburg and Moscow, as well as articles about the Imperial Alexandrinsky Theater and the typical clerk and journalist of the capital, most of the space was devoted to the city's outskirts and lower depths—coachmen, organ grinders, tramps, drunkards, and prostitutes, huddled in filthy attics or stinking cellars.

Gogol's style and ideas clearly influenced this collection. The authors were not embarrassed by their dependence on him; on the contrary, they flaunted it. For instance, the illustration for Nekrasov's satiric poem "The Clerk" was a funny wood engraving of the hero of the poem angrily reading Gogol's *Overcoat*.

Establishment reviewers were outraged: "How could people with unspoiled, much less with refined taste find interesting caricatured descriptions of the dirtiest sides of the lives of a janitor, lackey, coachman, cook, store keeper, evening butterfly or dolly?" As usual, the reading public responded vigorously to this rhetorical question: the entire press run of *Physiology of Petersburg* sold out immediately. Its success was promoted by two rave reviews. Each appeared anonymously but were written by the anthology's two main contributors—Belinsky and Nekrasov. Obviously, in the increasing competition for readership, journalistic ethics did not count for much.

Inspired by his success, Nekrasov quickly prepared a new edition, *Petersburg Anthology*, which came out in early 1846. Once
again, Nekrasov, Belinsky, and other leading writers took part, but
what really put this publication on the historical map was the debut
of twenty-four-year-old Fyodor Dostoyevsky, with his novel significantly titled *Poor Folk*.

Dostoyevsky wrote *Poor Folk* in a little over nine months in a
narrow furnished room in an apartment house near St. Vladimir's
Cathedral in Petersburg, the result of an intensive psychological insight the author later called "the vision on the Neva." He had seen a
Petersburg story taking place in dark corners, a pure and honest petty
clerk, a humiliated and sad girl. . . .

Gogol's *Overcoat*, the quintessential Petersburg parable of a
clerk, had been published only two years earlier. "We all came out of
The Overcoat," Dostoyevsky is alleged to have said. But the beginning writer, borrowing much from Gogol, had rejected his cruel irony.
His hero is no grotesque marionette but a living, suffering, thinking
man, described with warmth and lyric grace. He loves and is loved,
but that love ends tragically, for there can be no happiness in a city
where there is "wet granite underfoot, around you tall buildings,
black, and sooty; fog underfoot, fog around your head."

Gogol read and generally liked *Poor Folk* but he failed to appreciate the originality of Dostoyevsky's style. He found the work too
wordy and "talky."

Dostoyevsky himself did not realize at first that *Poor Folk* was
sounding a completely new note in Petersburg literature. He worked
on the novel another half year after it was finished—Dostoyevsky
never again polished his work this thoroughly. His roommate, the
young dandy Dmitri Grigorovich, who had already published a story,
full of bravura, about organ grinders in *Physiology of Petersburg*,
took the manuscript to his friend Nekrasov. Grigorovich and
Nekrasov started reading the novel aloud, in turn, and stayed up all
night. When they got to the last page, Nekrasov wept unashamedly.

And in a typically Russian burst of spontaneity now called
"Dostoyevskian," they decided to visit Dostoyevsky. It was a warm
white night in May. Dostoyevsky was back from a nocturnal walk and
sitting in the window, too excited to sleep, when Grigorovich and
Nekrasov burst in. All three began an agitated, exalted conversation
with outbursts, quick leaps from topic to topic, and copious quotations from the shared idol, Gogol. The scene could have been a page
from some future novel of Dostoyevsky's.

Later that same day, early in the morning, Nekrasov appeared on Belinsky's doorstep, exclaiming "A new Gogol has appeared!" The critic remarked dryly, "You have Gogols growing like mushrooms." But once he had read the manuscript, Belinsky had to see Dostoyevsky immediately. "Bring him here, bring him quickly!"

Once he met the sickly, pale, freckled, blond, and very nervous Dostoyevsky, the critic was even more touched. Indicating a space about two feet from the floor, he kept telling his friends, "He's little, just this tall." When they later met Dostoyevsky, they were very surprised: the young writer was taller than Belinsky.

Dostoyevsky admitted once to his brother, "I have a horrible flaw: unlimited pride and ambition." The raves from Belinsky, Nekrasov, and their friends convinced him he was a genius. Wanting to be distinguished in some way from the other participants in the *Petersburg Anthology,* he approached Nekrasov and demanded that every page of *Poor Folk* be outlined with a special black border.

Poor Folk was published without any borders. But that did not interfere with the sensational and unprecedented reception given Dostoyevsky's novel and the whole anthology. Several hundred copies were sold in the first few days. Nekrasov's edition became one of the three great best-sellers of Russian literature of that period, the other two being Gogol's *Dead Souls* and Count Vladimir Sollogub's satirical travelogue, *Tarantas.*

Count Sollogub, a fashionable writer close to court circles, ran around Petersburg and pestered the other writers in the anthology. "Who is this Dostoyevsky? For God's sake, show him to me, introduce us!"[22] Terrified of the competition, the cynical Bulgarin attacked the anthology in his newspaper, *Severnaya pchela.* He accused the authors of slavish imitation of Gogol and called the movement the "natural school" for its attention to the darker side of life. In his reports to the secret police, he went much further: "Nekrasov is the most abandoned communist: you need only to read his poetry and prose to be assured of that. He keeps singing the praises of revolution."[23]

We all know that attacks can help a book's popularity. Belinsky immediately expropriated the derogatory label, which has so often happened—from ancient Gothic to later impressionism—in world culture. In his next article, Belinsky announced that the "natural school" was a good name for new voices in literature: all the old ones were not natural, that is, artificial and false. And the term "natural" remained for Russian literature of the Gogol era.

The young Dostoyevsky, though he gave Gogol his due in allusion and associations in his later writings, was actually moving further away from his idol. His bold new novella, *The Double* (subtitled "A Petersburg Poem"), irritated Belinsky, who was ever changeable in his moods and opinions.

A Petersburg clerk who is losing his mind and is pursued by his double seems a typical Gogolian subject. But Dostoyevsky, who was suffering from as yet undiagnosed epilepsy, described his hero's madness with clinical precision. This was the beginning of Dostoyevsky's fearless immersion into the depths of the subconscious.

Belinsky justly saw this as a betrayal of the idea of the social novel, which was so close to the critic's heart. Dostoyevsky's "sentimental novel" *White Nights* made Belinsky no happier, for it was a touching fantasy that grew out of the writer's wanderings through the suburbs and back alleys of Petersburg. In a letter to a friend, the critic complained, "Each new work of his is a new fall. . . . We were tricked, my friend, by 'the genius' Dostoyevsky!"

Breaking with Belinsky, Dostoyevsky began attending meetings of young people in the home of the nobleman Mikhail Petrashevsky, one of the first Russian socialists, who resembled a stage villain and behaved with great impudence. For instance, one day Petrashevsky came to the Kazan Cathedral on Nevsky Prospect dressed as a woman. He stood on the women's side of the church and prayed loudly. His thick black beard, which he did not bother to shave or even cover up, upset the women. They summoned a policeman, who addressed the disturber of the peace with the words, "Kind lady, I believe you are a man in disguise." To which Petrashevsky replied without hesitation, "Kind sir, I believe that you are a woman in disguise." The policeman was stunned; Petrashevsky slipped out of the church, leaped into his carriage, and rushed home.

Every Friday Petrashevsky, the well-educated eccentric whom we would now describe as "a character out of Dostoyevsky," hosted fifteen to twenty young people, the cream of the capital's intelligentsia: clerks, officers, teachers, musicians, artists, scholars, and writers, among them Apollon Grigoryev. In the lively, companionable atmosphere, they read lectures, discussed the ideas of the French utopian socialists Count Henri de St.-Simon and Charles Fourier, and current issues like censorship and emancipation. Petrashevsky's "Project for Emancipation of the Serfs" was one of the most daring political documents of the time. Several members of the circle openly called for revolution in Russia. Worried by the birth of socialist society in the capital, the secret police placed an agent provocateur in Petrashevsky's circle.

On February 22, 1848, a ball given by the tsarevich was interrupted by the unexpected arrival of Emperor Nicholas, who announced to the astonished guests, "Gentlemen, saddle your horses! A republic has been proclaimed in France!" The tsar really had planned to send troops to aid the dethroned Louis-Philippe but changed his mind and instead tightened the controls in his already choking capital.

Nicholas and his entourage were in a panic and feared the worst. Once, the empress returned from a walk and related happily that the residents of Petersburg still raised their hats to her. "They're bowing! They're bowing!" she exclaimed delightedly. Traumatized for life by the Decembrist uprising of 1825, Nicholas assiduously sought and snuffed out conspiracies. The Petrashevsky circle was an ideal target for him.

On the night of April 22, 1849, after a regular Friday night meeting at Petrashevsky's house, the members were arrested on orders written by the tsar: "Begin arrests. . . . God speed! May His will be done!" They were driven in special black carriages to the Third Division. (Stalin's victims were brought to the Lubyanka Prison in cars dubbed Black Marias.) Among the thirty-four "conspirators" arrested was a constant visitor to Petrashevsky's home, Fyodor Dostoyevsky. Next to his name on the list were the words "One of the most important."

Dostoyevsky and the others in the case were kept in solitary confinement in the Peter and Paul Fortress. Nicholas was furious: "Let them arrest half the residents of the capital, but they must find the threads of the conspiracy." Dostoyevsky was interrogated and the investigator promised, "I am empowered by the Tsar to pardon you if you tell me everything." Dostoyevsky said nothing. The sentence, pronounced by a military court, read, "Death penalty by firing squad." In the case of the "state criminal" Petrashevsky, twenty-one other people were also condemned to death.

Nicholas worked out the ceremony of the execution himself. A lover of military maneuvers and parades, he selected the square of the Semyonovsky Life Guards Regiment as the site. In the 1960s, when I attended plays at the Leningrad Theater for Young Audiences and crossed the vast square now named Young Pioneer, I had no idea that it was there that Dostoyevsky and his comrades were brought under gendarme convoy on December 22, 1849.

They were made to stand on a wooden platform erected in the middle of the square. Dostoyevsky managed to tell his neighbor the plot of a new novella he had written in the Peter and Paul Fortress. A young, frightened priest gave the condemned men a last sermon. Dostoyevsky later said, "I didn't believe it, I didn't understand, until I saw the cross. . . . A priest . . . We refused to confess, but then we kissed the cross. They wouldn't joke with the cross!"

Dostoyevsky and the others were dressed in white canvas robes with long sleeves that reached almost to the ground, and pointed hoods that fell over their eyes. Petrashevsky laughed hysterically and said, "Gentlemen! We must look ridiculous in these rags!" He and two others were tied to three stakes hammered into the ground in front of the platform. The orders rang out: "Pull the hoods over their eyes!" The squad aimed their rifles at the men. "I was in the second row, and I had less than a minute to live," Dostoyevsky later recalled in horror.

But instead of gunfire there was a drum roll: retreat! A general rode up to the platform and read Nicholas's decree reducing the death penalty to hard labor. One of the men tied to the stake went mad. Another cried out angrily, "Who asked him?" No one felt any gratitude to the emperor, who had come up with this sadistic ritual. Dostoyevsky never forgave Nicholas for the "tragicomedy" of his mock execution. "Why such mockery, so ugly, unnecessary, useless?"

Sent to Siberia to the Omsk Fortress, which served as prison, Dostoyevsky spent four years in heavy shackles, day and night. He didn't take up a pen for almost ten years.

Here, in the Omsk Fortress, Dostoyevsky learned in 1853 about the start of the Crimean War, in which the Russian Army fought against the Turks and then the British and French, who had joined them. Things did not go so well for Russia. Nicholas had expected a triumph. Despite the emperor's endless stream of orders, bureaucratic inertia and embezzlement prevailed. It became clear that decades of military parades on the squares of Petersburg were no substitute for technological progress. The Russian Army was backward and poorly equipped. The loss in the Crimea turned into a cruel and absolutely unforeseen humiliation for Nicholas's Petersburg.

The sharp-tongued poet Fyodor Tyutchev authored a typical Petersburg bon mot: "Nicholas has the facade of a great man." Under the pressure of the fateful events in the Crimea, the facade crumbled, and according to people close to the emperor, the huge and haughty fifty-year-old man "wept like a baby every time he heard more bad news."

In February 1855 Nicholas got the flu and died within a few days, according to the official version. (Some historians think it was suicide.) He called his elder son, Alexander, to his private apartments in the Winter Palace and confessed, "I'm turning my command over to you in disorder." His last advice to his heir was "Hold on to everything," and he gave an energetic shake of his fist, despite swiftly approaching death. Even on his deathbed—an iron cot with a gray soldier's overcoat instead of a blanket—Nicholas remained true to himself.

Petersburgers, awed by the thirty-year reign of the "Don Quixote of autocracy," refused at first to believe the news of his death. "I always thought, and I wasn't alone, that Emperor Nicholas would outlive us, and our children, and maybe our grandchildren," wrote one in his diary.

The writer Ivan Turgenev, a curious and sociable man, headed for the Winter Palace to check out the rumors and approached a guard. "Is it true that our Sovereign has died?" The soldier grimaced and said nothing. But Turgenev persisted stubbornly until the soldier barked, "It's true, move along." Seeing that Turgenev still didn't believe him, he added, "If I said that and it weren't true, I'd be hanged." He turned away. Only then did Turgenev believe it.

Fate and his personal qualities made Nicholas play a unique role in the development of Petersburg culture. He both encouraged and stifled it. "They chase us toward enlightenment with the whip, and with the whip they punish the overly educated," noted Alexander Herzen. Nicholas, like Stalin one hundred years later, personally interfered in all areas of culture: literature, music, painting, theater, opera, ballet, and architecture. In every field he considered himself a specialist.

During the reign of Nicholas and under his personal supervision, the majestic ensembles of the Palace and Senate Squares, the magnificent St. Isaac's Cathedral, and other impressive architectural complexes like the famous Teatralny and Mikhailovskaya Streets were built. A good measure of the importance Nicholas attributed to architecture can be seen in an order he gave forbidding residents of Petersburg from building houses over seventy-seven feet high, that is, higher than the cornice of the Winter Palace. The majority of these projects were executed by Nicholas's favorite architect, Carlo Rossi, born in 1777 in Petersburg to an Italian ballerina. Nicholas valued Rossi's artistic genius and his honesty, determination, and responsibility for his work.

Rossi, in planning the construction of the Imperial Alexandrinsky Theater, proposed covering the enormous hall with a special system of metal girders—a risky idea for those times. Nicholas doubted their strength and ordered construction stopped. His vanity stung, Rossi wrote the tsar a letter stating that should anything happen to his roof, he should be immediately hanged on one of the theater's trusses, as an example to other architects. Such arguments always worked with Nicholas, and he allowed the building to be completed. Performances continue to this day in the theater, one of the city's most beautiful. Nothing has gone wrong with the roof yet.

People were not as durable as girders, and one after another broke during the emperor's reign. The critic Kornei Chukovsky used to proclaim, "A writer in Russia must live a long time," but Pushkin, Lermontov, and Gogol did not live up to this maxim. Nicholas did not care. Even though he had begun his reign with an audience for Pushkin, he ended it by keeping Dostoyevsky from writing. Such was the evolution of the emperor's attitude toward Russian culture.

Konstantin Kavelin, a professor at Petersburg University, wrote to a Moscow friend on March 4, 1855, "That Kalmyk demigod, that fiend of clerical-uniform enlightenment, who had cut out the face of thought, who had destroyed thousands of characters and minds, has kicked the bucket." He added, as if echoing the formula of Benkendorf, chief of the secret police, on Russia's "past, present, and future": "If the present were not so horrible and grim, and the future so mysterious and enigmatic, one could go mad with joy."[24] Petersburg's residents feared that things would be even worse under the new emperor, Alexander II.

Alexander, tall like his father, was handsome and blue-eyed. Despite Tyutchev's crack that when the emperor spoke with an intelligent person, he looked like a rheumatic standing in a draft, he gradually loosened the reins. It began with trifles. Under Nicholas, beards were definitely frowned upon. Now, when the clerks of a ministry asked for permission to grow at least mustaches, the new emperor replied, "Let them wear beards, as long as they don't steal."

Tyutchev called the new period "a thaw," one hundred years before Ilya Ehrenburg used the same term for Khrushchev's reforms after Stalin's death. Alexander II pardoned the surviving Decembrists and members of the Petrashevsky circle, including Dostoyevsky. The writer returned to Petersburg wearing a martyr's halo. He quickly published the novel *The Insulted and the Injured*, which he had planned in exile, yet another variation of his old best-seller, *Poor Folk*.

It presents the same picture of the capital, viewed by an attentive observer, with the familiar, almost stereotypical details: the inky black vault of the northern sky, beneath which grim, angry, and soaked passersby vanish in the foggy distance of a Petersburg street, illuminated by weakly flickering lights.

The reading public greeted *The Insulted and the Injured* with enthusiasm. Meanwhile, Dostoyevsky continued wandering around Petersburg, greedily peering into the city's rapidly changing features. This process of change was greatly influenced by the decree of February 19, 1861, whereby Alexander II emancipated the serfs.

The historic and far-reaching decision to repeal serfdom was taken against the advice of most of Alexander's entourage. Gendarmes on horseback patrolled Nevsky Prospect from early morning on the day of the announcement, expecting agitation and possibly rebellion.

The capital was unusually excited, but happily so: people gathered in all parts of the city, discussing the staggering news, embracing and weeping in joy. Someone would start reading the proclamation aloud, and others would chime in with cries of "Long live the Emperor!" and sing the national anthem, "God Save the Tsar." A relieved Alexander II recorded in his diary, "The day was absolutely calm, despite all anxieties."[25]

Waves of freed serfs invaded the capital to earn a living. In 1858, with a population of almost half a million, Petersburg was the fourth-largest city in Europe after London, Paris, and Constantinople. In 1862, Petersburg had 532,000 residents, and in 1869, according to the first major census, 667,000.[26] Factories and plants were mushrooming outside the city and the capital's new residents settled there. Drinking, brawling, crime, and prostitution flourished in these neighborhoods. Taverns and brothels popped up all over the city. *Golos* (The Voice), a Petersburg newspaper, complained in 1865, "Drunkenness of late has taken on such horrifying proportions that it forces us to think about it as a social catastrophe."[27]

Another newspaper described the "mecca" of the Petersburg alcoholics thus: "Stolyarny Alley has 16 houses (8 on each side of the street). These 16 houses have 18 drinking establishments, so that those wishing to enjoy merry-making liquids and who come to Stolyarny Alley do not even need to look at the signs: come into any house, even any porch—and you'll find wine." On neighboring Voznesensky Prospect there were six taverns, 19 bars, 11 beer halls, and 16 wine cellars.[28]

Cheap prostitutes, drunk and heavily made up, patrolled the

streets. These were the loners, the most worn and derelict of the lot. Their more successful young colleagues worked on Ligovsky and Nevsky Prospects, while the most enterprising joined the more respectable of the city's 150 brothels.

Nicholas I, with his mania for order in all areas, tried to control prostitution as well. In 1843 he created a system of police and medical supervision of the oldest profession, twenty years before England did. In Dostoyevsky's day around two thousand prostitutes were registered in Petersburg, more than in Berlin or Marseilles, but fewer than in Paris or New York.[29] Naturally, there were many more unregistered prostitutes, without the official "yellow" passports.

Prostitutes were recruited primarily among peasant girls who came to Petersburg; many were the wives and daughters of soldiers; others belonged to the bourgeoisie. But the ranks of prostitutes were also filled with women from bankrupt noble families and impoverished clerks—in the words of a newspaper writer of those days, "women who have nothing to eat, who have been desiccated by need, jabbed by the needle that gives pathetic pennies for painstaking labor."

Often in the families of retired clerks, the Petersburg journalist wrote, "even mothers sell their daughters into depravity, out of oppressive poverty." The lot of most was poverty, drunkenness, death from disease, usually venereal, primarily from syphilis, which spread quickly in Petersburg despite police-medical actions.

Wandering through the city, Dostoyevsky would come out from "drunken" Stolyarny Alley, onto nearby infamous Haymarket Square, where quite recently executioners had publicly whipped serfs from the provinces. I always shudder when I read Nekrasov's poem that draws a parallel between the fate of oppressed serfs and of literature in Nicholas's Russia:

> Yesterday, around six,
> I dropped by Haymarket;
> They were beating a woman with a knout,
> A young peasant woman,
> Not a sound from her breast,
> Only the whistling whip . . .
> And I said to the Muse, "Look!
> It's your own sister!"

Haymarket was the "belly" of Petersburg. Crowds bustled there from morning till night, buying up food piled high on counters under light awnings. Noise, mud, and a strong rotten smell ruled there.

Lusty pie men bustled around the counters with their hot wares. Like their "patron," Menshikov, who was Peter's friend and the first governor of Petersburg, they were a thieving, brazen lot—if a buyer complained that the filling contained a piece of rag, they replied haughtily, "What did you expect for three kopecks, velvet?"

The city became a melting pot for the many ethnic groups of the Russian Empire. Depending upon the year, 10 to 20 percent of the capital's residents were non-Russian, a motley mix of sixty groups. The biggest were Germans, Poles, Belorussians and Ukrainians, Finns and Swedes, Jews, Balts, and Tatars. Some, particularly the Germans, occupied a prominent place in the capital's bureaucratic machine. Others became tradesmen and craftsmen.[30] Thousands huddled on the outskirts in rude huts and barracks.

For them the city was not Petersburg but "Piter"—a nickname that indicated familiarity, a certain irony, cynicism, affection—a complicated mixture that characterized the newcomers' attitude to the capital that took them in. This attitude was reflected in the rhymed proverb *"Piter boka povyter"* (Piter wore them out), which many years later found its way into *Poem without a Hero,* by Akhmatova, herself intensely fascinated by Dostoyevsky's Petersburg.

Even as Petersburg exploited, humiliated, and unified its new residents, it challenged, urged on, and refined them. Vistas for all kinds of activities opened up for the hardest-working and cleverest. You could buy or sell anything in Petersburg.

For instance, Stock Exchange Square was the place to buy exotic shells, huge tortoises, monkeys, and talking parrots. A parrot that could chatter in Italian went for one hundred rubles—a huge sum in those days. A vendor immediately offered a big rooster, also for a hundred rubles. "But for that price I could buy a parrot that talks," a potential purchaser argued. "Mine doesn't talk but he's a terrific thinker," was the immediate rejoinder.

Naturally, the capital's seething commercial activity, coupled with the sharp increase in population, fed a growing crime rate. According to official statistics, close to ten thousand crimes took place each year in Petersburg. But there were few serious cases, thanks to the extraordinary police controls: around one hundred murders and attempted murders, around fifty rapes, about forty passed counterfeit bills, and about a dozen cases of arson.

Petersburg had two mortal enemies—water and fire—which emptied the city many times. The two most memorable floods were in 1777 and 1824. (The flood of 1924 later joined their number.) The

fire of 1862 was remembered longest, for most of the commercial section—Gostiny Dvor, Apraksin Dvor, Shchukin Dvor, and Tolkuchy
Market—burned to the ground during several weeks of May and June
of that year. Even the Ministry of Foreign Affairs and numerous private homes were destroyed; losses were in the millions of rubles. A
stunned eyewitness described an apocalyptic scene: black clouds of
smoke, a fiery sky, and columns of flame showering huge sparks. A
strong wind tossed burning embers to the roofs of distant houses, even
across the Fontanka River, which burst into flames like torches.[31]

The populace, horrified at the sight, panicked. Dostoyevsky
too shared these feelings. In the extremely tense atmosphere of such
substantial reforms, where opposition to the emancipation arose on
both right and left, even the fires became political events.

In late 1861 Petersburg was shaken by the first serious student
unrest in the country's history. According to a hostile observer, the students, in demanding more autonomy, "very artfully achieved the greatest scandal possible. The authorities were forced to arrest them two or
three times a day, in the streets, in huge crowds. To the students' great
delight, they were detained in the Peter and Paul Fortress."[32]

The reaction of Petersburg society was sharply divided along
political lines, as had become habitual: some, primarily the intellectuals, supported the rebellious students; the rest attacked them fiercely.
The term "nihilist," first used by Turgenev, became commonplace.
The author had used it to describe Bazarov, the hero of his novel *Fathers and Sons*—a young antisocial positivist with anarchist overtones. One of the most famous revolutionaries of the period, the
theoretician of terror Sergei Stepnyak-Kravchinsky, explained the
essence of "nihilism" this way: "The basis of this movement was un-
encumbered individualism. It was the negation, in the name of personal freedom, of any restraints placed on man by society, family, or
religion."

All this situation needed to explode was a lit match. First it
happened figuratively: on May 14, 1862, a radical proclamation
spread throughout Petersburg. "Young Russia," as it was titled, called
on the people to kill the tsar and destroy the ruling classes. If that were
not enough, it also mocked religion, family, and marriage. Like "a
thunderclap over the capital,"[33] the leaflets taught the stunned and
outraged residents that revolutions go hand in hand with national dis-
asters. The mysterious and threatening Young Russia (nihilists?) ad-
vocated mass arson to provoke a not-so-natural disaster of their own.

Two days later, mass fires did break out in Petersburg. Was it coincidence or accident? Was it really arson, and if so, by whom? A desperate act by nihilists or a coldly calculated provocation by the authorities, attempting to discredit the young revolutionaries?

Even today, historians still cannot answer these questions. It is important that back then, in stifling, charred, smoke-blanketed Petersburg, public opinion, aided by official newspapers, blamed the long-haired, bespectacled student "nihilists" and Poles rebelling against Russia's suppression of their homeland's independence.

A rumor that the city was being torched on all sides by three hundred villains spread among the masses. Witnesses were found who had seen "nihilists" smearing fences and walls with special flammable mixtures. Students were afraid to walk around in the streets in uniform because of the many attempts at mob justice. Even in educated circles people said that Petrashevsky and his group were behind the fires. As one politically engaged woman wrote to another, "all the exiles in that case have been pardoned; and perhaps this is how they are expressing their gratitude. I don't know how one can be merciful anymore."[34]

Clearly Dostoyevsky, as one of the pardoned Petrashevsky circle, had reason to feel uncomfortable during that period. He desperately begged Nikolai Chernyshevsky, the idol and mouthpiece of young radicals, to keep his followers from committing arson.

The calm and ironic Chernyshevsky later described with cold mockery Dostoyevsky's arrival as a visit from a madman: "Seeing that the mental state of the poor patient was one in which doctors forbid any disagreement with the sufferer, I replied, 'All right, Fyodor Mikhailovich, I will obey your wishes!' "

Almost in total panic, Dostoyevsky rapidly scribbled a magazine article demanding "the widest openness (*glasnost*)" from the government in investigating the causes of the fires. The writer was upset: "Without a doubt, fewer houses and streets would have burned down if people had not been taught by blows to the face and other forcible measures to forget their own active role in keeping the public and social order." Dostoyevsky's unsigned article was promptly banned by the preliminary censors, and Alexander II himself added a wrathful "Who wrote this?" to his copy.[36]

Petersburg was no longer the same. Surrounded by a ring of grim, sooty factories, littered with hovels and ugly tenements, the great city was threatening to become a nightmare, far worse than the most horrible fantasies of Gogol or Apollon Grigoryev.

This new, lugubrious Petersburg—new not only to Dostoyevsky but also to the unsettled native Petersburgers—gave the writer a powerful inspiration for the most famous murderer in Russian literature—the former student Rodion Raskolnikov, the protagonist of the novel *Crime and Punishment.*

This novel is the quintessential Petersburg work. The city is an important character, as important as Raskolnikov. Outside of Petersburg, the student fallen on hard times was unthinkable; he was the creation of the new Petersburg. According to Dostoyevsky this "most fantastic city in the world" "was invented" (also Dostoyevsky's expression) by Peter the Great and his heirs. In the same spirit the writer's imagination had invented the delirious vision of the Petersburg superman / nihilist, stalking an old woman pawnbroker with ax concealed beneath his overcoat.

Raskolnikov's "ugly dream" of murder for profit was also, according to Dostoyevsky, the specific emanation of the Petersburg atmosphere. In that sense Petersburg, with its historic pride as a city pretending to have conquered nature, is a co-conspirator in the ideological crime of the impoverished student, who with devilish pride breaks "natural" social boundaries. Joseph Brodsky, with a subtle feeling for the stylistics and poetics of Dostoyevsky, even maintained in our conversation that "Raskolnikov's idea about killing the old pawnbroker is definitely a personal one," meaning that Dostoyevsky himself had considered robbery, and even murder for gain. And Brodsky added, half in jest, "Considering what society does to an author, he has every right to think this way."

Raskolnikov loves people and despises them; "two contradictory personalities alternate in him," Dostoyevsky says. Parallel to his double personality, a double image of Petersburg develops in *Crime and Punishment*: on the one hand, "the marvelous panorama" of the Neva (even though it makes a "grim and mysterious impression"); on the other hand, the depressing sketches of an urban hell with their "disgusting and sad colors."

"This is a city for the half-mad. . . . There are few more grim, harsh, and strange influences on a man's soul than in Petersburg. Just think of the climatic influences!" the investigator mockingly reminds Raskolnikov, and the author the reader. The picture of Petersburg is painted with broad strokes, brief descriptions (in the style of stage directions), and a multitude of exact, concrete details.

The color yellow, which Dostoyevsky hated, dominates the picture. Yellow was associated with the capital, where many houses were traditionally painted that color. In *Crime and Punishment,* yellow wallpaper and furniture persecutes the heroes, who seem to be placed inside a whirling painting by van Gogh.

The book's first sentence calls our attention to the extreme heat of those two weeks during which the novel's action takes place. Dostoyevsky stresses the heat and humidity and unbearable stench later on—they form a counterpoint to Raskolnikov's feverish, overheated state.

Raskolnikov lives on that "drunken" Stolyarny Alley, next to the Haymarket Square described earlier. Dostoyevsky uses the grotesque ensemble of that part of Petersburg for full effect, down to the tiniest detail: the tenements filled with pathetic renters in their coffinlike rooms; the bars, brothels, pawnshops, police offices.

In the novel thirteen steps lead to the top floor of Raskolnikov's building, to his room; curious tourists can count them today in Petersburg. From the gate of Raskolnikov's house to the house of the moneylender he intends to kill are 730 steps, by Dostoyevsky's count, and that is also correct.* Even the stone under which Raskolnikov hid the stolen goods was real. Dostoyevsky once pointed it out to his wife while on a walk, and when she asked how he had ever ended up in that deserted courtyard, he replied, "For the reason that brings pedestrians to out-of-the-way spots."

Dostoyevsky's Petersburg is an "invented" city, which nevertheless has all the signs of reality. That is why in Germany, where Dostoyevsky's European (and worldwide) fame began, *Crime and Punishment* was admired both by the naturalists of the 1880s and the neoromantics and expressionists of the early twentieth century. Raskolnikov, swinging his ax at the moneylender's head, is incomparably more real than Gogol's Nose praying in the Kazan Cathedral. But at the same time, it is an unreal, symbolic figure, and just as unreal, in Dostoyevsky's oft-proclaimed conviction, is the Petersburg that gave rise to Raskolnikov.

The writer's pen had turned the spectral city of his imagination into "Dostoyevsky's Petersburg," something solid and familiar to all of us. It happened thanks to his virtuoso manipulation of exact details and the unity and power of the book's mood. When *Crime and Punishment* was first published, the apparent accuracy of its description confused the critics, even the hostile ones: "Before you is the real city with familiar streets and alleys."[37] Naive people! Of course, more

---

* Dostoyevsky also selected the victim's profession with great care, paying attention to the circumstances of contemporary Petersburg. Usury became a widespread phenomenon in the capital during the 1860s.

perceptive readers immediately suspected that Dostoyevsky was not simply depicting naturalistically the difficult life of the capital's "lower depths," but was creating his own mythos about Petersburg.

The leading radical critic, Dmitri Pisarev, defending Dostoyevsky against accusations of slandering "the whole body of Russian students," used this very point: how can one speak of slander if the action takes place in a mysterious and strange city; according to the perceptive Pisarev, the reader of *Crime and Punishment* experiences "the sensation of ending up in a new, special, and completely fantastical world, where everything is done inside out and where our ordinary concepts cannot be enforced."

The hypnotic effect of Dostoyevsky's vision is incomparable. His impulsive narrative, sometimes almost incoherent but always masterfully organized, is so overwhelming that it sweeps away even the fiercely resisting reader. Therefore, Dostoyevsky's Petersburg is a reality that will exist as long as there is Russian literature. For decades Dostoyevsky's interpretation of the city was the only possible one for a great majority of people in Russia and the West.

Typical of that is the confession of the writer Vladimir Korolenko, no great fan of Dostoyevsky's. When Korolenko graduated from a provincial high school in 1871 and arrived in Petersburg, he saw it through Dostoyevsky's eyes: "I liked everything here—even the Petersburg sky, because I had known it already from descriptions, even the boring brick walls blocking that sky, because I knew them from Dostoyevsky."[38]

Dostoyevsky's landscape of the city is a markedly prosaic one—the suburbs where the "poor folk" live, "the insulted and the injured." His identification with the new "plebeian" population of the capital was so strong that he rejected all the Petersburg architecture of the eighteenth and early nineteenth centuries, that is, the buildings that were considered masterpieces before and after him.

Dostoyevsky was convinced that those buildings were pathetic imitations of European styles. The writer's gaze slid scornfully along the panorama of Petersburg: "Here's the characterless church architecture of the last century, there's a pathetic copy in the Romanesque style of the turn of the century, and there's the Renaissance."

Dostoyevsky's aesthetic judgments arose from his political and social viewpoints, primarily his total rejection of Peter the Great and his reforms. According to Dostoyevsky, Peter struck a blow against the Russian Orthodox Church—the main support of the national spirit; attacked Russian traditions; and dug a chasm between the people and the educated class. Dostoyevsky considered Peter the first Russian nihilist. His wife recalled that the writer spoke passionately of Peter as if he were his worst personal enemy.

Therefore, Dostoyevsky considered Peter's founding of Petersburg a criminal act: a nihilistic gesture, a meaningless challenge to nature, traditions, and the people's spirit and well-being. In his notebook, the writer quotes Pushkin's line from *The Bronze Horseman,* "I love you, Peter's creation." As if trying to justify himself before the Pushkin he idolized, he notes, "I'm sorry, I don't love it. Windows, holes—and monuments."

This anti-Petrine position—and all of Dostoyevsky's so-called pessimistic, perverted work, alien to socialism—was condemned in Stalin's Soviet Union. The dictator did not like Petersburg, but he respected Peter the Great, even though he considered him insufficiently cruel.*

This rejection of Dostoyevsky lingered for decades after Stalin's death. The Soviet Union reluctantly published Dostoyevsky, included him stingily in school curricula, and continued to scold him for "ideological mistakes," as if he were a contemporary dissident.

The Soviet authorities' suspicion of Dostoyevsky was manifest in trifles. For instance, I merely quoted Dostoyevsky's words on Peter's despotism and his "anti-people attitude in the highest degree" in an article published in the Moscow journal *Sovetskaya muzyka.* This elicited a harsh rebuke from *Sovetskaya kultura,* a newspaper of the Central Committee of the Communist Party. This may seem funny now, but at that time neither I nor my frightened colleagues at *Sovetskaya muzyka* felt much like laughing.

The most "intentional" city in the world—that is Dostoyevsky's famous and final condemnation of Petersburg. That "intendedness," that is, artificiality, the total absence of national roots, is an intolerable flaw and sin in Dostoyevsky's eyes. That built-in lack of national sentiment in the Russian capital is, according to the writer, the cause of Petersburg's constant hostility toward the true Russian personality.

Dostoyevsky had been to London, Paris, and Berlin. Those metropolises had horrified him, and he was disgusted to find similar traits in Petersburg. He hated bourgeois Europe, and so he rejected the necessity of a "window into Europe," as Petersburg's apologists por-

---

* Stalin once expressed his concern in a heart-to-heart with a favorite actor: "Peter didn't kill enough of them."

trayed it. It was a window, Dostoyevsky said, through which the Russian elite looked at the West and saw all the wrong things.

A city like that certainly had no right to exist. It had to vanish. And here Dostoyevsky enthusiastically picked up the folklore tradition prophesying the destruction of the city that came into being unrightfully. As we recall, Petersburg was supposed to be deserted (the "curse of Tsaritsa Eudoxia"), flooded, or destroyed by fire. Dostoyevsky invented his own, more fantastic version, which at the same time seemed in its striking simplicity to be the only possible version for the disappearance of Petersburg.

Dostoyevsky let his beloved idea come from the lips of the hero of *The Adolescent,* a novel written in 1874 that holds a special place in the writer's oeuvre. This passage is the crowning moment of the Petersburg mythos in Dostoyevsky's interpretation. Characteristically, it is in this text that Dostoyevsky makes a pointed reference to Falconet's equestrian statue as depicted in Pushkin's *Bronze Horseman,* starting in fact a polemic with him and at the same time continuing the literary and cultural tradition so vital for Russian society:

> A hundred times amid the fog I had a strange but persistent dream: "What if, when this fog scatters and flies upward, the whole rotten, slimy city goes with it, rises with the fog and vanishes like smoke, leaving behind the old Finnish swamp, and in the middle of it, I suppose, for beauty's sake, the bronze horseman on the panting, whipped horse?"

Dostoyevsky's Petersburg mythos, incorporating the discoveries of French writers (Hugo, Balzac, Flaubert), the German Hoffmann, the English Dickens, and the American Poe, in its turn substantially altered the perception of Western metropolises by their residents. Raskolnikov the Petersburg student began to wander the streets of Berlin, Paris, and London. Nietzsche admitted (in *Twilight of the Gods*), "Dostoyevsky is one of the happiest discoveries of my life." For many a French writer, the image of the back streets of Paris was forever tinged by his impressions of *Crime and Punishment.* Raskolnikov's spirit hovers over Rainer Maria Rilke's *Notebook of Malte Laurids Brigge.*

Dostoyevsky's Petersburg became part of the Western cultural and spiritual experience even more than Gogol's Petersburg, because in general Dostoyevsky's novels, which were rightly labeled "ideological" by Russian critics, do not suffer significantly when their verbal tissue is transplanted to another language—unlike the virtuoso works of Gogol, often built on pure wordplay, or even more so, the works of Pushkin, whose writings are almost naked in comparison with those of both Gogol and Dostoyevsky. Western audiences accept on faith the perfection of Pushkin and his Petersburg creations. But at least part of Pushkin's renown in the West paradoxically rests on the popularity of three Russian operas based on his works: *Boris Godunov* by Modest Mussorgsky (premiered in 1874), and Peter Tchaikovsky's *Eugene Onegin* (premiered in 1879) and *Queen of Spades* (premiered in 1890).

The paradox is made all the greater by the fact that Mussorgsky and Tchaikovsky, for all their enormous respect for Pushkin, moved far from his style and emotions in their music. The artistic and psychological strivings of both composers—who differed so markedly from each other in their lives and work—coincided with the ideas and emotions of their contemporary, Dostoyevsky.

Parallels of this sort are inevitably tentative. Mussorgsky and Tchaikovsky each created his own highly idiosyncratic and enormous world with clearly marked boundaries. Nevertheless, their works are so closely entwined with Dostoyevsky's artistic ideas and produce an effect that so remarkably resembles that created by reading some of his more troubled outpourings that a comparison between the writer and the two composers becomes unavoidable. All the more so, since Mussorgsky and Tchaikovsky contributed to the Petersburg mythos—the former with a few extraordinary compositions, the latter with a long line of his principal works.

The cult of Petersburg began with poetic odes. The problem of Petersburg was first posed in a narrative poem. The dismantling of Petersburg was also performed by literature. For over one hundred thirty years literature reigned almost unchallenged there.

Opera and ballet flourished in imperial Petersburg in the early nineteenth century, but they did not have a substantial impact on the Petersburg mythos. They were exotic flowers that ornamented the grim reality of Nicholas's Petersburg but did not confront the "damned questions" the city asked its residents.

The situation gradually began to change. The way was prepared by the general upsurge in Russian culture, a revolution that took place by the middle of the nineteenth century in music and then in art. This revolution changed contemporaries' perceptions of Petersburg. For too long it had been reflected in the mirror of literature. Of course, the mirror had been held by geniuses—Pushkin, Gogol, Dostoyevsky.

The crystalline mythological image of a majestic, beautiful city, the imperial capital, was replaced in that mirror, thanks to these writers, with another reflection—phantasmagoric, with horrible but still beautiful features. Little by little even that image began shattering, fading, disappearing.

Then the mirror in which Petersburg was seen came into the hands of different people: musicians and after them, artists. Their lives were no less eccentric, mysterious, and strange than the fate of the city in whose palaces and cramped apartments they lived, on whose luxurious and beckoning prospects they strolled, lost in thought, on whose granite embankments they stood in quiet joy or in profound, black depression, and whose captivating legend they transformed decisively, irrevocably.

And this is how it happened.

CHAPTER
2

which describes how the mirror that reflected St. Petersburg for almost one hundred fifty years was passed from the hands of the writers to musicians and then artists, and in which the reader learns how a Queen of Spades, if felicitously played, could influence the charms of an imperial capital.

T hroughout Petersburg reigns an astonishingly profound and wonderful musicality,"[1] marveled Alexander Benois, an artist who in the early twentieth century played a unique role in restoring the Petersburg mythos to its glory. His younger contemporary, the musicologist Boris Asafyev, affirmed the presence of music in the St. Petersburg legend even more resolutely.

> The Petersburg culture now cannot be crossed out of the history of Russia and humanity. And music plays perhaps the dominant role in that culture. Especially the work of Tchaikovsky, inspired by the illusions of the Petersburg white nights and the stark contrasts of winter: black tree trunks, the snow cover, the oppressive weight of granite, and the precision of cast-iron fences.[2]

That passage, written by Asafyev in 1921 in a hungry, dying Petrograd, is remarkable, since it describes Tchaikovsky's music as if it were a masterly drawing by Alexander Benois, and it makes clear the collision of music and art in the creation of a new image of Petersburg. Taking the lead, in this respect nineteenth-century Petersburg music also had a powerful influence on European and world culture; the Russian visual arts of that period could not even dream of such a role.

How did it happen that music, the least descriptive of the arts, turned out to be a far more truthful, albeit troubling, mirror of life in Petersburg than poetry, painting, or the other arts? The answer lies in the uniqueness of Petersburg's existence—there, the external image and the inner content often do not coincide.

Externally Petersburg of the eighteenth and nineteenth centuries could be seen as a triumph of rationalism. Formed by the baroque and neoclassicism, the Russian capital was considered both by its inhabitants and by foreign observers the epitome of architectural harmony. Innumerable paintings, watercolors, drawings, engravings, and lithographs by such skilled artisans as Fyodor Alexeyev (1755–1824), Andrei Martynov (1768–1826), Stepan Galaktionov (1779–1854), and Vassily Sadovnikov (1800–1879) depicted it that way. Sadovnikov's fame was based upon his popular lithographic panorama of the Nevsky Prospect, advertised this way: "The buildings are copied from nature with astonishing fidelity, with not a single sign omitted."[3]

All these pictures, often notable for their mastery and accuracy, nowadays impart a sense of too many things left unsaid: meticulously drawn, solitary, somehow lost little human figures are merely props against a background of Petersburg's fabulous but emotionally neutral classicist buildings and huge squares. These works convey neither the real face of Petersburg nor its soul; neither its majesty and propriety nor its spirituality. Artists, accurately depicting the city's various sites, did not convey or explain its magical attraction or repugnant cruelty. Compared to the later *Nevsky Prospect* by Gogol, Sadovnikov's hugely successful lithographs, which were sold in two long rolls, are a mere curiosity.

Much more interesting is the *Magic Lantern;* the full title is "Magic Lantern, or A Spectacle of St. Petersburg's Traveling Sellers, Masters, and Other Folk Craftsmen, Depicted with a True Brush in Their Real Clothes and Presented Conversing with One Another, Commensurate With Each Person and Title," a monthly anthology of hand-colored lithographs with extended dialogue captions that appeared at the same time as Sadovnikov's panorama.

Leafing now through the pages of *Magic Lantern,* one is struck by the variety of wares and services offered to customers on the streets of early-nineteenth-century Petersburg. The colorfully dressed characters depicted with understanding and sympathy in the touchingly angular lithographs—besides Russians, there are Germans, Frenchmen, a Finn, a Jew, and even a man from Central Asian Bukhara—sell Dutch honey cakes, French bread, rolls, buns and *blini,* oranges, apples, nuts, prunes, baked pears, candy, hot *sbiten* (a spiced tea and honey drink), kvass (a fermented soft drink), milk, veal, beef, hot dogs, pike, perch, game, flowers, dishes, watches, combs, needles, pins, brooms, wax, shawls and scarves, magazines and newspapers, and even plaster busts of Homer, Democritus, and . . . Charlotte from Goethe's *Young Werther.*

The simplicity of both the drawings and the dialogues in *Magic Lantern* is equally appealing. But the gap between the best pages of *Physiology of Petersburg,* which came out under Nekrasov's editorship three decades later, and the engravings that accompany them is obvious and sometimes depressing. The text depicts real emotion, while the illustrations are still clumsily conventional, albeit more naturalistic than in the *Magic Lantern.* The artists were clearly lagging behind the writers, both in the discovery of the "new" Petersburg and in the radical literary change in attitude toward the "old" one.

Perhaps only one painting of that period conveys the true majesty and horror of the Petersburg mythos, and it is not overtly related to the Petersburg theme. Entitled *Last Day of Pompeii,* it is a huge canvas depicting the destruction of the ancient city by lava from Mount Vesuvius, as described by Pliny the Younger. It was begun in Rome by Karl Briullov, a Russian painter of the Petersburg-Italian school, in 1827 (that is, seven years before the publication of Lord Bulwer-Lytton's famous novel on that theme) and completed by him in 1833.

Briullov's painting, which created quite a stir in Europe, was delivered on the ship *Tsar Peter* to Petersburg, where it was "imperially approved" by Nicholas I and exhibited at the Academy of Arts. Its colossal triumph was greater than that for any other previous Russian painting. "Men of power and artists, socialites and scholars, simple folk and craftsmen—all are imbued with the desire to see Briullov's painting," records the supplement to *Severnaya pchela* for October 21, 1834. "This desire is raging throughout the capital, in all estates and classes, in the suites on the English Embankment, in the workshops and stores on Nevsky Prospect, in the shops in Gostiny and

Apraksin Dvor, in the poor quarters of clerks on the Peski and in the offices on Vasilyevsky Island."[4]

In Petersburg they called Briullov the "divine Karl." Pushkin was so excited and charmed by the *Last Day of Pompeii* that he began a poem dedicated to it (it was left unfinished):

> *Vesuvius opened its jaws—smoke rolled out—flames*
> *Spread widely, like a battle banner,*
> *The earth is agitated—from shaken pillars*
> *Idols fall! The people, chased by fear,*
> *Under rain of stones, under burning ashes*
> *In crowds, aged and young, flee the city.*

Gogol produced an ecstatic article that began, "Briullov's painting is one of the brightest phenomena of the nineteenth century. It is the resurrection of painting." The emperor granted the artist an audience and made him a cavalier of the Order of St. Anna. Nicholas liked the mastery of Briullov's work; they say he also liked the artist's young wife. The temperamental and proud Briullov, who was very short, became extremely jealous of the gigantic Nicholas. One morning his wife, standing by the window, saw the emperor in a sled pulled by a raven steed drive up to the Academy of Arts, where the Briullovs lived. She cried out, "Oh, it's the sovereign!" The furious Briullov rushed over and screamed, "So, you recognized him!" and tore an earring from her pierced ear.

The Petersburgers who flocked to see Briullov's *Last Day of Pompeii* were transfixed by his unabashedly romantic depiction of a natural disaster, which ruined a beautiful city and its inhabitants: a reminder of the precarious position of their own metropolis exposed to the merciless forces of nature. There was something operatic in the drama of Briullov's painting (Gogol was the first to note it, but he approved—such were the tastes of the period), but Petersburgers squirmed anyway. The artist had touched a deep-seated, unconscious fear.

The dissident Alexander Herzen came up with the words to describe that vague feeling in an article on the traditional "confrontational" theme about the opposites, "Moscow and Petersburg," which circulated throughout Russia in *samizdat* some twenty-five years later (and which had been read aloud at meetings of the socialistic Petrashevsky circle): "Briullov, who developed in Petersburg, selected for his brush the terrible image of a wild, irrational force, destroying people in Pompeii—that is the inspiration of Petersburg!"

Briullov's painting shone and vanished in the pale Petersburg sky like an ephemeral comet. The artist could never repeat his unparalleled success, even though he was surrounded by loyal students, a new generation of artists that, under the influence of Briullov, "a man with wild and uncontrollable passions," as a contemporary noted disapprovingly, "became enamored of effects and phrases: it shouted about the grandeur of the artist, the sacredness of art, grew beards large and small and shoulder-length hair, and dressed in eccentric costumes to distinguish itself from ordinary mortals—and to top it off, following its teacher's example, unbridled its passions and drank itself into a stupor."[5]

Briullov, who was used to the Italian atmosphere, spent the dreary Petersburg evenings and nights in the company of bohemian bachelors at the house of his friend Nestor Kukolnik, the romantic poet and debauchee. Kukolnik, a braggart and adventurer, was celebrated for his superpatriotic dramatic play (which also had received Nicholas's approval) *The Hand of the Almighty Saved the Fatherland,* which described in mystical tones the tumultuous path to the throne of the first Russian ruler from the Romanov dynasty, young Mikhail, who became tsar in 1613.

A regular member of Kukolnik's rowdy gatherings, with music and champagne, was the composer Mikhail Glinka. Thirty-two-year-old Glinka became popular after the premiere of his first opera in 1836, in which the peasant Ivan Susanin surrenders his life to save Mikhail Romanov from the invading Poles. It was a legendary subject, from the same historical period represented in Kukolnik's play. The composer called his opera *Death for the Tsar.* Nicholas I renamed it *A Life for the Tsar,* demonstrating that he was as deft an editor as his grandmother, Catherine the Great.

Russians justly consider Glinka to be the father of their national music, as Pushkin is the father of their national literature. Glinka's talent and oeuvre have much in common with Pushkin's—the same lightness and precision, naturalness and expressiveness, simplicity and harmony. Both Glinka and Pushkin possessed innate mastery, an ability to assimilate different Western influences but also an instinctive understanding and original interpretation of the Russian national psyche.

As in the case of Pushkin, the respectful attitude of the West toward Glinka is based on his reputation as a national cultural hero. His music is not understood here, or liked, or regularly performed. Mountings of Glinka's operas, which are always present on Russian stages, are rare in the West. It is even more astonishing because in music there is no real language barrier to impede comprehension, as in the case of literature.

Unconditional delight in Glinka, however, has never crossed beyond the borders of the Slavic countries, even though confident assurances that his music was just about to be accepted in Europe began to be heard in Russia during the composer's lifetime. In the West Glinka is still viewed merely as a talented imitator of European musical formulas of the time, not as an original genius.

The Russian cult of Glinka, like the cult of Pushkin, is universal, reaching its apogee in prerevolutionary years; Igor Stravinsky noted later, "poor Glinka, who was only a kind of Russian Rossini, had been Beethovenized and nationally-monumented."[6] It's curious that in the 1971 Soviet edition of the conversations between Robert Craft and Stravinsky, in which I first encountered this rather complimentary quotation (that is, in terms of Stravinsky's tastes, for at the time he much preferred Rossini to Beethoven), the word "only" was omitted by the editor because it was thought to be apparently "derogatory" toward Glinka.

Glinka's music became an intrinsic part of the childhood of most of the figures of early Russian modernism, and therefore was always wrapped for them in special memories. The family of Alexander Benois was particularly proud of an Italian great-grandfather who was "director of music" in Petersburg and Glinka's predecessor. Benois's ancestor even wrote an opera on the same legendary subject of Ivan Susanin, but twenty years earlier, and subsequently, without envy, diligently conducted the premiere of his rival's work.

Benois recalled that the young Sergei Diaghilev "idolized Glinka":[7] Glinka's operas were sung by heart at Diaghilev's house. Nikolai Roerich, later coauthor of the libretto and first designer for Stravinsky's ballet *Le Sacre du printemps,* basked in his childhood impressions of listening to Glinka's "golden" operas at the Imperial Maryinsky Theater:

> It seemed as if the musicians were playing from golden scores. There was anxiety that everybody in the box take their seats promptly. The gentleman with the baton had come!—this important information

would be delivered from the front, in fear that there would be late-comers moving their chairs and talking, while down there the musicians would already be playing magically from the golden pages.[8]

After the Bolshevik revolution of 1917, Glinka became an inconvenience because of his monarchist opera. In those years Igor Stravinsky cultivated appreciation of Glinka in the West, but it did not take here, and the pragmatic Stravinsky gradually moderated his praise. In the Soviet Union Stalin turned out to be an unexpected admirer, and Glinka was force-fed to the public aggressively and almost violently, as potatoes had been in the reign of Catherine the Great.

In the years after World War II, Soviets proclaimed Glinka the "measure of all things," the official cultural icon, and his harmonic and optimistic music was used by the authorities as an antidote (in numbing doses) to the works of "pessimists and decadents" from Wagner to Shostakovich.

I remember a venerated Soviet musicologist's heartrending tale about the persecution and attacks on his book, published in 1948, which mentioned—rather cursorily—the influence of Mozart on Glinka's compositions. The howl of outrage was unanimous, asserting Glinka to be absolutely original and free of all possible Western influences. The poor musicologist was punished for his heresy; his work was not published (nor was he paid) for many years.

Instead countless publications asserted that Glinka's operas "laid the foundation for the period of primacy of Russian music in the development of the musical culture of the entire world." One such book, published in 1951, contained quite a surrealistic image: "Glinka amongst us sings the glory of the indestructible might of our Soviet Fatherland."[9]

A result of such co-optation, using Glinka as propaganda for the Stalinist regime, was the alienation of Russia's intellectual youth from his music. In the Leningrad of the 1960s, we virtually rediscovered for ourselves Glinka's indisputably "Petersburgian" works (in terms of their beauty and purity of line and the nobility of their emotions), thanks to our "underground" idol, Stravinsky. I remember the impression the passages from the Russian edition of Stravinsky's *Chroniques de ma vie* made on us. Published in 1963, Stravinsky raved about Glinka's artistry as "a perfect monument of musical art" and his orchestration, "so intelligent . . . so distinguished and delicate."[10]

Soviet hagiographies presented Glinka as a knight without fear or reproach, antimonarchist, a virtual Decembrist who worked from morning till night creating what was peculiarly called "Russian national realistic music." The real Glinka, who appeared on the pages of his contemporaries' memoirs—small, pale, unkempt, a famous Petersburg drunkard with a glass of champagne always in his hand—seemed a curious, unorthodox creature.

In his posthumously published *Notes*, Glinka described in greatest detail the real and imaginary ills that beset him—headaches, toothaches, neck aches, bad nerves, stomachaches, liver aches, and so on, with the names and characteristics of all the doctors who attended him and the effectiveness of all the medications they prescribed, including the decoction (*"rob antisyphilitique"*) called *"eau de M-r Pollin,"* which Glinka had to stop taking because it caused "unbearable migraines."[11] With the same thoroughness he listed his numerous paramours: Russian, Polish, German, French, Italian, and Spanish women, usually "pretty and slender" but sometimes "pretty and plump."

Glinka mentions music in his *Notes* mostly in passing, as befits a spoiled Russian nobleman and dilettante composer. Where did this hypochondriac, this babied and capricious, egotistical and indolent nobleman who always felt ill find the strength to produce his great work? After *A Life for the Tsar*, Glinka composed another grand opera—*Ruslan and Lyudmila*—based on the Pushkin tale, charming in its abundance of bel canto melody and lush orchestration. He also wrote a succession of popular symphonic works, numerous compositions for the piano and other instruments, and eighty marvelous art songs; Glinka particularly valued this genre for its spontaneity and accessibility.

Glinka loved performing his own songs, among which there are numerous masterpieces, playing the piano around two in the morning at parties in Kukolnik's unruly house, where the composer spent all his time. The other guests were all talented people but they were far from Glinka's stature. They understood this and surrounded the composer with sincere adoration. Glinka found refuge here from his failing marriage to a woman who berated him for wasting too much money on music paper.

In the 1970s, Leo Arnshtam, a friend of Shostakovich's youth and a filmmaker commissioned by Stalin personally in 1946 to make a biographical film on Glinka, told me the spicy details of Glinka's closed divorce documents, giggling over the fact that his wife was accused not only of adultery but also of bigamy.

Completely frazzled, Glinka decided in 1840 to escape from Petersburg to Paris, where he composed a special work for his last fling at Kukolnik's, his only vocal cycle, of twelve songs, called *Farewell to Petersburg*. The faithful Kukolnik produced words to accompany Glinka's luscious melodies.

One of Glinka's most impressive works, *Farewell to Petersburg* is a kaleidoscope of pictures and emotions, united by a noble and expressive manner of vocal writing; it includes a passionate confession of love, sorrowful meditations, a lullaby, an attempt to capture the beauty of the Russian landscape ("The Lark," popular in Russia), and a musical depiction of a Petersburg spree among a circle of delighted and loyal friends. With typically Russian "universal responsiveness" (Dostoyevsky's expression) and Petersburgian sensibility, it uses an Italian barcarole, a Spanish bolero, and a Jewish song; the song, as well as some references to Palestine in the text, kept the cycle from being performed in full in the Soviet Union after the Arab-Israeli Six-Day War of 1967, when Brezhnev broke diplomatic ties with Israel.

One of the pieces in *Farewell to Petersburg*, "Travel Song," is of particular interest. It is probably the world's first truly artistic vocal depiction of a railroad trip. The first railroad in Russia, connecting Petersburg with suburban Tsarskoe Selo, was still considered an innovation since it had opened only a few years earlier, in October 1837.

Contemporaries perceived the introduction of railroad transport not simply as a current sensation but as a symbolic event confirming the wisdom and correctness of the historical path chosen by Peter the Great: "Fire breathes from the nostrils! And twenty carriages attached to one another roll down cast-iron tracks, like a single arrow shot from a bow! What would Peter I say and feel if by some miracle he was here among us and could fly the twenty-five versts from Petersburg to Tsarskoe Selo in twenty-five minutes! What joy would reign in his heart!"[12]

After writing *Farewell to Petersburg*, Glinka suddenly changed his mind about leaving. Instead, he published his cycle, with "extraordinary success," as the press noted: it went into three editions. The popular Petersburg journal *Library for Reading* particularly singled out "Travel Song," "in which movement defines a special life, hustle and bustle—the necessary qualities of a trip on the railroad. The external sense of the trip and inner excitement, passionate and imbued with hope and expectation, are presented with exquisite refinement. In terms of artistry, this is probably the best number in *Farewell to Petersburg.*[13]

Still, subsequent works by Glinka, especially major ones, had at best succès d'estime. Nicholas I left the theater before the end of the long-awaited and highly publicized premiere of *Ruslan and Lyudmila*. Taking that as a signal, the aristocratic audience applauded Glinka's opera mildly; some even hissed. Discouraged, Glinka sat nervously in the director's box with his friend, the chief of the gendarmes corps. Seeing Glinka hesitate over whether to come out for bows, the sympathetic but cynical gendarme pushed the composer onto the stage with the words, "Go on, Christ suffered more than you."[14]

A contemporary recalled that after the premiere of *Ruslan and Lyudmila,* "everyone went home subdued, as if after a nightmare."[15] The public rushed to the conclusion that Glinka has written himself out in his first opera, *A Life for the Tsar.* The composer, no Christ at all (his acquaintances compared Glinka to the delicate blossom *Mimosa sensitiva*), fell into a deep depression.

Glinka couldn't live without the high of adulation for his creative gifts. He blossomed only when supported and applauded. Then, in the appropriate atmosphere and after a few glasses of champagne, he would gladly perform his marvelous songs as he had in the past. He had a tenor voice, not very high but resonant and unusually flexible, and so he interpreted his works for friends to an explosion of sincere delight.

In 1849 the young Dostoyevsky heard Glinka when the composer sang before some members of the dissident Petrashevsky circle. *Ruslan and Lyudmila* was always one of Dostoyevsky's favorite operas. And hearing Glinka sing, the writer was greatly moved; that evening remained in his memory as one of the most powerful impressions of his life. Many years later Dostoyevsky described Glinka performing his art song in the novella *The Eternal Husband,* judging the performance in terms of his "realistic aesthetic" of that period: "No adept musician or some sort of salon singer could ever have achieved that effect. . . . In order to sing that small but extraordinary piece, what was needed was the truth, real, total inspiration, real passion."

In the end Glinka fled the city, which he called "vile," "hateful Petersburg." "The local climate is definitely harmful to me, or perhaps, my health is even more affected by the local gossips, each of whom has at least one drop of poison on the tip of his tongue,"[16] he complained to his beloved sister. Count Sollogub recalled visiting Glinka in those days at his Petersburg apartment, when the composer frightened him with his "martyred look and gloomy cynicism."[17]

But before leaving for Berlin (where Glinka died in 1857 at the age of fifty-two of the aftereffects of the flu, which led to paralysis of the heart), the composer left behind a work that, despite its seeming lack of pretension and its modest length, became the true model and powerful source of Petersburg music. It was the orchestral version of Glinka's old piano piece, "Valse-Fantaisie," a remembrance of "the days of love and youth," as the composer elegiacally informed the paralyzed friend to whom the score was dedicated.

This astonishing waltz, pure Pushkin in its mood and mastery, is the real inspiration behind the magical waltzes of Tchaikovsky, which later conquered the world. (There are echoes of the "Valse-Fantaisie" even in the famous "Blue Danube" waltz by Johann Strauss, Jr., who held Glinka in esteem.) Tchaikovsky said of another piece by Glinka, "Kamarinskaya," that it contained, as an acorn contains an oak, the entire Russian symphonic school. "Valse-Fantaisie," that incomparable Petersburg musical poem of love, longing, and suffering, already contains the emotional intensity, smooth melodic curves and swings, and the virtuoso "silver" orchestration of the waltz revelations of Tchaikovsky (and later of Glazunov), but in a classically pure and balanced form.

In composing this sentimental music without sentimentality, Glinka could have repeated Pushkin's line "My sorrow is radiant." "Valse-Fantaisie" is pure Petersburg erotica—passionate but controlled. In Petersburg (as in Europe) a young woman from an aristocratic home could not dance the waltz without special permission from an adult chaperone. Petersburg adapted the European waltz by "hiding" its sexual daring, and so Glinka gave the erotic longing an almost spiritual tone, as if foreshadowing by half a century the basic motif of Anna Akhmatova's early poetry.

It was probably exactly this quality that made "Valse-Fantaisie" one of the favorite musical works of George Balanchine, who had danced in *Ruslan and Lyudmila* as a child on the stage of the Maryinsky Theater. In the West, Diaghilev and Stravinsky approved and further fueled the young choreographer's cult of Glinka, urging him to ignore the coolness toward the Russian classic among European musicians.

Balanchine told me how Diaghilev, laughing at and mocking the ignorance of Western critics, showed him a clipping from a French newspaper that asserted Glinka would have been all right if he had not stolen his melodies from Tchaikovsky![18] Becoming one of Stravinsky's closest friends and collaborators, Balanchine understood the importance for the composer, unknown to many Western observers, of Glinka's oeuvre. Stravinsky's biographer, Robert Craft, recalled that as he listened with Balanchine to a recording of Stravinsky's *Perséphone* in 1982, he was astonished to hear the choreographer exclaim, "Glinka!" (and also "Tchaikovsky!") during melodies that to Craft seemed "purely French."[19]

Balanchine staged "Valse-Fantaisie" three times for the New York City Ballet, in 1953, 1967, and 1969, revealing a spectacle of nostalgic elegance. His friend and collaborator, the artist Mstislav Dobuzhinsky, always associated that work of Glinka's with the magic and poetry of the Petersburg white nights. Balanchine's ideas on the "Valse-Fantaisie" were so explicit and powerful that even John Martin, the influential ballet critic of the *New York Times,* usually not one to take note of some obscure Russian connection, turned out to be more penetrating in his review of this piece than usual: "The music, winning and melodious, with no break, no change of tempo, passes from persuasiveness to virtual hypnosis, and it is easy to realize why once the genteel waltz was considered an instrument of the devil."[20]

When he left Petersburg forever in 1856, Glinka got out of his carriage at the city limits and spat on the ground that, in his opinion, did not give his genius its due. He returned to the capital only in his coffin; fewer than thirty people attended his interment. Among them was Count Sollogub, who recorded in his memoirs that when the coffin was lowered into the grave, the composer Alexander Dargomyzhsky, standing next to him, remarked bitterly, "Look at that, please, it's as if they were burying some titular councillor."[21] On the hierarchical ladder of tsarist Russia, titular councillor was one of the lowest ranks. Perhaps Dargomyzhsky recalled those words a few years later, when he composed his famous art song, "Titular Councillor," a musical satire imbued with bitterness about the fate of "the little man" in St. Petersburg.

Sollogub felt that Glinka, who was "ambitious and proud to the extreme," had been destroyed by the lack of official recognition and status commensurate with the composer's great aspirations: "Sensing his extraordinary gift, he quite naturally dreamed of an extraordinary position, which, incidentally, in those circumstances, was impossible. Had there been a conservatory, he would have been made director, of course. But there was no conservatory."[22]

In the Petersburg of Nicholas I, the social position of music and musicians was uncertain and ambiguous. The other arts—painting, sculpture, architecture—were supervised by the Academy of Arts, founded in 1757 by Empress Elizabeth. This gave their practitioners some status and rights—great help in the severely codified and over-bureacratized state that was Russia. In particular, graduates of the Academy of Arts were given the official title "free artist," which gave them certain privileges.

The artists of the opera and ballet belonged to the system of imperial theaters and were thus considered to be in government service; the same was true of the members of the Court Singing Capella. But the profession of musician per se did not exist from the legal point of view in Russia, and for musicians this created countless unpleasant incidents.

The first Russian performer to become world famous, the pianist Anton Rubinstein, recalled encountering one such absurd situation. Rubinstein was the son of a Jew who had converted to Russian Orthodoxy, and once the pianist went to the Kazan Cathedral in Petersburg to sign up for confession. The deacon asked him, "Your name? Who are you?"

"Rubinstein, artist."

"Artist, does that mean you work in a theater? No? Perhaps, you're a teacher at some institute? Or you are in service somewhere?"

Rubinstein tried to explain to the deacon that he was a concert pianist. Finally, the deacon had the sense to ask Rubinstein about his father. Satisfied, he listed the great artist in the confession book as "son of a merchant of the second guild."[23]

Petersburg's musical life in the first sixty years of the nineteenth century was concentrated in several aristocratic salons, because until 1859 public concerts were allowed only during Lent, when the theaters were closed, that is, six weeks a year. The most famous of these salons was in the home of the wealthy Counts Vielgorsky—the brothers Mikhail and Matvei, eccentric and refined music lovers, but also clever courtiers.

The counts had, weekly, sometimes quite impressive concerts: Beethoven's Ninth Symphony was first heard in Russia at the Vielgorskys'. Three hundred or more guests would come to listen to Franz Liszt playing piano or to see Robert Schumann conduct one of his symphonies. It was there that people enjoyed the art of the Italian prima donnas visiting Petersburg and stared with curiosity at the famous European avant-garde composers of the day—Berlioz and Wagner.

Berlioz called the Vielgorsky house "a small ministry of fine arts," and for good reason: there one could regularly hear the metallic voice of Russia's main patron of the arts—His Majesty Nicholas I; frequently it was after a concert at the Vielgorskys' that the fate of a visiting European musician would be decided—whether he would leave Russia rich or without a penny. Among the accepted, Clara Schumann enthusiastically reported to her father, "Those Vielgorskys are marvelous people for artists; they live only for art and do not spare any expense."

Another concert series with a solid reputation (and a European fame) was held at the house of General Alexei Lvov, the ambitious and imperious director of the Court Singing Capella and composer of the Russian national anthem, "God Save the Tsar." Glinka had hoped passionately that the unofficial contest in 1833 would result in his monumental, joyful chorus "Glory" from A Life for the Tsar becoming the state anthem. Alas, Nicholas chose the much more formulaic work of his close friend Lvov, in whose company he liked to make music; as Sollogub explained, "the sovereign did not want to be glorified, he wanted people to pray for him."[24]

A similar situation occurred in 1943 when Stalin selected the music of his toady—also a general, but a Soviet one—Alexander Alexandrov, rejecting the entries by Shostakovich and Khachaturian. Lvov's melody is often heard in our day, whenever Tchaikovsky's popular 1812 Overture or his Slavonic March is performed, because they include the anthem. Another melody by Glinka, "Patriotic Song," was finally chosen as its anthem by the post-Soviet Russia in the 1990s.

An habitué of Lvov's aristocratic musical salon recalled, "Every educated member of Petersburg society knew that temple of musical art, attended in its time by members of the imperial family and the high society of Petersburg; a temple in which for many years (1835–1855) mingled the authorities, the artists, wealth, taste, and beauty of the capital."[25]

Lvov was a virtuoso violinist himself, but he always insisted that he was only a musical dilettante and not a professional, for a general and important bureaucrat being "merely a musician" seemed humiliating. Schumann, who heard Lvov play in Leipzig, called him a "marvelous and rare performer" and wrote, "If there are other such dilettantes in the Russian capital then many a European artist could learn there rather than teach." Still, Rubinstein was absolutely right in suggesting that music in Petersburg would not flourish without musical training being sponsored by the state.

Rubinstein was the ideal figure to accomplish this grand design. Short and stocky with a mane of hair and strongly resembling Beethoven (Rubinstein did not deny rumors that he was Beethoven's illegitimate son), the Russian pianist had, besides his talent as performer and composer, boundless energy and self-confidence. It helped that he had developed ties to the royal family necessary for the success of his endeavor. As a boy he had played in the Winter Palace, where Emperor Nicholas greeted him with, "Ah, your excellency." "I was told," Rubinstein recalled later, "that the tsar's word was law, and that had I mentioned it I would have been an 'excellency.' "[26]

Nicholas made the little boy imitate Liszt's playing (with all of Liszt's mannerisms) and laughed heartily; the amusing wunderkind was showered with precious gifts. And as Rubinstein insisted later, he had never seen anything more generous than the tsar's gifts, particularly if they were handed to him right on the spot in the Winter Palace: "the gifts that were sent the following day were not as valuable."[27]

Rubinstein became a kind of musical secretary to the Grand Duchess Elena Pavlovna, wife of Emperor Nicholas's brother, Grand Duke Mikhail. The grand duke was a boor, while Elena Pavlovna, a beautiful and smart German princess from Württemberg, strove to create a European-oriented intellectual and artistic climate for herself in Petersburg. Gradually that German lady, described even by her enemies as "highly amusing, serious, and lovely," became the main patroness of the arts in Russia. During long evening talks with Elena Pavlovna in her palace on Kamenny Island, where Rubinstein had moved, they finalized plans for a conservatory in Petersburg. The impressions of those conversations, life in the palace, and the landscapes around it were captured by Rubinstein in his charming piano pieces, collected in the cycles *Kamenny Island* (1853–1854), *The Ball* (1854), and *Soirées à St. Petersburg* (1860).

But nothing came of the plans to "Europeanize" Russian music in Nicholas's lifetime. Rubinstein wrote that when he returned from revolutionary Berlin to Petersburg in 1849, the trunk with his musical compositions was confiscated by customs agents who suspected the notes concealed some sort of seditious writings. In Petersburg the capital's governor stamped his feet at Rubinstein and shouted, "I'll have you in chains! I'll send you to Siberia!" And the

Petersburg police chief sent the artist, by then a European star, to one of his clerks with the instructions, "Play something for him, so we'll know that you really are a musician."[28]

In that atmosphere it would seem hopeless to talk about respect for musicians, but Rubinstein did not give up: in 1859, with the help of Grand Duchess Elena Pavlovna, he organized the Russian Musical Society, which subsequently added "Imperial" to its name. Elena Pavlovna became the "most august chairwoman" of the society, which inaugurated regular symphonic and chamber concerts with frequently adventurous programming. Music classes began under the society's auspices, and in 1861 they became the Petersburg Conservatory, the first in Russia.

This was an enormously significant step. The Petersburg Conservatory bred the performing and composing schools that would conquer the entire world in the twentieth century. The names Heifetz, Elman, Zimbalist, Milstein, Mravinsky, Prokofiev, and Shostakovich speak for themselves. George Balanchine also attended that conservatory, and he always recalled his musical mentors with affection and gratitude.

The flood of candidates for study at the first Russian conservatory was overwhelming, and naturally it included some oddballs; one noble lady brought her retarded son to Rubinstein "because everyone chases him away, so let him study music at least." The first students (there were 179 of them) were a motley crowd that had gathered from all corners of the empire; among them was a shy, unassuming senior clerk of a department in the Ministry of Justice, the twenty-two-year-old Peter Tchaikovsky.

The accusations, complaints, and arguments, so typically Russian, overheated and often unfair, filled the air almost immediately; the strife was about both the idea of the conservatory and about Rubinstein personally. Vladimir Stasov, the temperamental and quite influential critic, insisted that higher education could be useful in science but not in art, and so conservatories would interfere "with creativity in the most harmful way" and "serve only as a hotbed for mediocrities."[29]

Stasov, who was playfully called "Bach" by his friends and ridiculed as an ignoramus by his enemies, asserted that small-scale schools were better for the development of original Russian music. He was defending the vital tradition of intimate Petersburg musical circles, which by that time had produced remarkable artistic results.

Among them, the most curious group gathered in the late 1850s around the composer Alexander Dargomyzhsky.

The wealthy landowner Dargomyzhsky had long attracted admirers of his art, primarily young and pretty amateur female singers. Small and bewhiskered like a cat, the composer, in imitation of Glinka, spent hours at his piano illuminated by two candelabra, while accompanying his lovely students as they sang his unconventional, expressive art songs. He sang along in his strange, almost contralto voice. This is how Dargomyzhsky's *Petersburg Serenades* premiered. That cycle of refined vocal ensembles soon gained popularity among the capital's dilettantes.

After the success of his opera *Rusalka* (based on a Pushkin tale and produced in Petersburg in 1856), Dargomyzhsky started to be visited by beginning composers as well. Among them were the nineteen-year-old nobleman from Nizhni Novgorod, Mily Balakirev, and the young military engineer who graduated from the same academy as Dostoyevsky, César Cui, born in Vilno, the son of a Frenchman and a Lithuanian woman. Both were uncommonly gifted musicians whose talents Dargomyzhsky appreciated. Soon they were joined by the son of a Pskov landowner, the guardsman Modest Mussorgsky, a "very elegant little officer, as if from a picture,"[30] with aristocratic manners, who could play excerpts from *Trovatore* and *Traviata* sweetly and gracefully on the piano, and proud of the fact that at the age of thirteen he "had been granted the particularly courteous attention of the late Emperor Nicholas," according to Mussorgsky's "Autobiographical Notes" from 1880.

Dargomyzhsky blossomed in the company of these young geniuses, and his art songs became sharper and bolder. If Glinka's music can be considered congenial to the works of Pushkin, Dargomyzhsky's works were beginning to echo the Petersburg of Gogol's tales and the world of *The Physiology of Petersburg,* the collection edited by Nekrasov.

In those years the satirical chansons of the French poet Pierre-Jean Béranger, translated into Russian, were very popular. Dargomyzhsky wrote his two masterful art songs, very Petersburgian in mood and outlook, to texts by Béranger. He presented them in the form of an originally conceived ballad, almost a stage monologue, in which the Frenchman's themes, transplanted to Petersburg's soil, sounded daringly freethinking and challenging. "The Old Corporal" was a frontal attack on one of the two main institutions of Nicholas's empire, the army, and "The Worm" on the other, the bureaucracy.

From a purely artistic point of view, these are two marvelous, melodramatic musical tales, with an expressive vocal part and laconic accompaniment. The great Russian bass Fyodor Chaliapin recalled singing "The Old Corporal" for Leo Tolstoy at his home (with twenty-six-year-old Sergei Rachmaninoff at the piano): "When I tearfully spoke the last words of the soldier about to be shot: 'God grant you get home,' Tolstoy took his hand from under his belt and wiped two tears that fell from his eyes."[31]

Audiences were just as touched when Chaliapin performed with Russian passion "The Worm" and Dargomyzhsky's other song about a miserable, intimidated clerk, "The Titular Councillor." Their striking, almost caricatured depiction of these men who were so close to the heroes of Gogol's *Diary of a Madman* and *The Overcoat* provoked one hostile critic to describe the characters as "this scum of Petersburg's corners."

While he was creating these sarcastic and at the same time deeply felt sketches in the late 1850s, Dargomyzhsky practically pre-ordained the manner of performance, inserting numerous author's remarks as if in a dramatic scene by Gogol: "with a sigh," "squinting," "smiling shyly." This attention to close detail combined with his general satirical but compassionate attitude put Dargomyzhsky next to Gogol's followers in the "natural school" and brought him together with radical writers grouped around *Iskra (The Spark)*, the popular, ultraleftist Petersburg satirical journal.

It seemed that Dargomyzhsky, who was respected paradoxically by both the establishment (he had become a board member of the Imperial Russian Musical Society in 1859) and the young intellectual rebels, had positioned himself comfortably at last and could rest safely on his laurels. This hard-won security makes his last artistic leap even more amazing—a kind of swan song, the opera *The Stone Guest,* which would have far-reaching influence on the subsequent avant-garde strivings of Petersburg music. Dargomyzhsky wrote it to the almost unchanged text of one of Pushkin's *Small Tragedies,* a variation of the Don Juan theme.

Just as Pushkin had, in his day, competed with no less than the mighty shadow of Molière, Dargomyzhsky challenged Mozart. Naturally, the Russian's chamber opera was in an altogether different "weight class" from Mozart's monumental and all-encompassing *Don Giovanni*. But no less incisive a music critic than Shostakovich told me that of the two musical interpretations of the Don Juan legend, he definitely preferred Dargomyzhsky's.[32]

We may appreciate Shostakovich's point of view better if we understand that Dargomyzhsky's opera is, from start to finish, an experimental—to the point of being polemical—work, a quality which probably endeared it so to Shostakovich. It was created in accordance with his *profession de foi:* "I want sound to express the word directly. I want the truth."

Dargomyzhsky's intention was nothing more or less than a radical reform of the operatic genre. In *The Stone Guest* he rejected most traditional operatic techniques. There are no developed arias, no ensembles, no choruses in his work; instead there is only a flexible recitative that follows closely Pushkin's text. The music flows whimsically, sensitively re-creating the subtlest change in mood, but it is subordinated to the logic of speech; and it is exactly this quality, conveying to the Russian listener of Dargomyzhsky's opera an acute and almost physical pleasure, that gets in the way of the work's appreciation in the West. To Russians this work sounds astonishingly daring and bold to this day.

In writing *The Stone Guest,* the already severely ill composer relied as never before on the moral support of his talented young friends. Balakirev, Cui, and Mussorgsky were joined by the illegitimate son of a Georgian prince, the rosy-cheeked and handsome Alexander Borodin, and a young naval officer, the tall and bespectacled Nikolai Rimsky-Korsakov. This group, eventually led by the fanatical and despotic Balakirev, met almost weekly at Dargomyzhsky's to follow the progress of *The Stone Guest.* Dargomyzhsky sang Don Juan with inspiration while Mussorgsky helped with the part of Leporello. And every time the master would muse, "I'm not writing it, it's some force I do not understand."

Stasov, an eyewitness of these unforgettable Petersburg evenings, later said,

> It was delight, awe, it was an almost prayerful bowing before a mighty creative force, which had transformed that weak, bilious, sometimes petty and envious man into a powerful giant of will, energy, and inspiration. 'The Balakirev group' was overjoyed and delighted. It surrounded Dargomyzhsky with its sincere adoration, and with its profound intellectual sympathy rewarded the poor old man in the final days of his life for all the long years of his moral loneliness.[33]

After each new presentation, Dargomyzhsky usually mused that, if he died without finishing *The Stone Guest,* he wanted Cui to finish writing it and Korsakov to orchestrate it. And that's what happened. On January 17, 1869, Dargomyzhsky was found dead in his bed, the manuscript of *The Stone Guest* open on his lap. Only the last few pages of the piano score were left unfinished. Completed and arranged lovingly by his young friends in 1870, the opera was staged at the Maryinsky Theater two years later.

There was a reason for the delay. Nicholas I's decree of 1827, which had remained in force even after the emperor's death, stated that a Russian composer could receive no more than 1,143 rubles for an opera, while Dargomyzhsky's executor demanded a fee of 3,000 silver rubles. The court minister who supervised the Maryinsky Theater refused to pay that sum. (For the sake of comparison, Verdi's honorarium for an opera specially commissioned by Alexander II, *La Forza del Destino,* which the composer premiered in Petersburg in 1862, came to 22,000 rubles.) At Stasov's urging, the needed sum was collected—not by musicians but by Petersburg artists, who then offered the rights to Dargomyzhsky's opera "to the Russian theater and the Russian people" for free.

Presented to the Petersburg audience, *The Stone Guest* was met by the predictable raptures from Stasov and confusion, even hostility, among the uninitiated, who charged that Dargomyzhsky in his last years had fallen "completely under the sway of our home-grown musicoclasts."[34]

But this wonderfully "musicoclastic" opera, inspired and completely original, gave a powerful impulse to the radical strivings of the Petersburg group of composers. This group, whose members are listed here in birth order (Borodin, 1833; Cui, 1835; Balakirev, 1836; Mussorgsky, 1839; and Rimsky-Korsakov, 1844), entered music history under the "tactless" (according to Rimsky-Korsakov) name *Moguchaya Kuchka* (Mighty Handful), in the West, the Mighty Five, invented by the group's ideologue, Stasov.

The Mighty Five may be the most outstanding artistic group that ever existed in Petersburg or elsewhere in Russia. It assured the domination of Russian artistic development for years to come by a similar kind of friendly alliance: both the realistic painters known as Peredvizhniki (Wanderers) and later the members of the modernist *Mir iskusstva* started out as participants in circles that were connected not only by aesthetics but also by close personal ties. The members of the Mighty Five, musical amateurs who basically taught one another under the stern leadership and supervision of Balakirev, decisively changed the style and substance of Russian music and, in the person of their most famous representative, Mussorgsky, noticeably influenced Western culture as well.

The connection between Dargomyzhsky and Mussorgsky is unquestionable. Mussorgsky dedicated the first song of his cycle, *The Nursery*, to Dargomyzhsky, "the great teacher of musical truth." Under the influence of *The Stone Guest* and the (at first) joking suggestion of Dargomyzhsky, Mussorgsky began composing an opera to the unchanged prose text of Gogol's play *The Marriage*, that satirical, "completely unbelievable event in two acts" from the life of a bachelor Petersburg clerk. Mussorgsky explained, "This is what I would like. For my characters to speak on stage the way living people speak . . . in *The Marriage* I am crossing the Rubicon."[35] It sounded like a manifesto of musical realism, but the result was just as "unbelievable" as Gogol's Petersburgian grotesque play.

Mussorgsky's *Marriage* today is perceived as a prescient forerunner of expressionism; in its day even Dargomyzhsky, the young innovator's mentor, thought that Mussorgsky "had gone a little too far." The other circle members, delighted by early fragments of the opera, viewed *The Marriage,* presented to them in the form of the completed first act, as just a curiosity.

Mussorgsky himself was almost frightened by the audacity of his experiment and announced, "*The Marriage* is a cage in which I am kept until I become tame and then I can come out."[36] He broke off the composition and left the opera unfinished. Appreciation of *The Marriage*'s real value came only a half-century later.

Dargomyzhsky's *Stone Guest* and Mussorgsky's *Marriage* speeded the future development of Russian opera, setting off a chain reaction of experimental works created by Petersburg musicians. They are Rimsky-Korsakov's chamber opera *Mozart and Salieri* (1897, after Pushkin); Prokofiev's *The Gambler* (1916), based on the Dostoyevsky novel; and Shostakovich's *The Nose* (1928) and *The Gamblers* (1942), after Gogol.

All these works have in common the composer's persistent, almost fanatical desire to conquer new musical territory and revolutionize musical language. By "cross-breeding" music with prose, not poetic texts as had been the custom, these works produced sometimes shocking, though ultimately deeply satisfying, results. More important, the composers' very approach to their themes was refreshingly unorthodox, without reliance on traditional postromantic effects. In these respects, all these operas could count *The Stone Guest* and *The Marriage* as their forerunners.

At the same time, *The Stone Guest*'s music served as a model for Russian lyrical dramatic recitative, construed as closely as possible to cantilena (usually not the case with Italian recitative). Dargomyzhsky's opera was built as an unbroken line of miniature ariosos and monologues. This device gave a powerful impetus to structural experiments in Russian opera. As for *The Marriage*, it was the first extended work to develop satirical, grotesque musical language, with all its jolting contrasts and exaggerations, when the composer, in the best Russian-Petersburg tradition, mocks his characters but at the same time "weeps" over them. Taking into account all these aspects, we see how Stravinsky, Prokofiev, and Shostakovich are all deeply indebted to Dargomyzhsky and Mussorgsky.

The rich musical life of Petersburg in the 1860s and 1870s, attracting ever more participants and larger audiences, was defined by a strident conflict between two seemingly unequal forces. The camp of the Imperial Russian Musical Society and the Petersburg Conservatory was headed by the capricious Anton Rubinstein. To counterbalance their Western-oriented and, in the opinion of the young nationalists of the Five, decidedly anti-Russian direction, the other dictator, Balakirev, founded his own educational organization, called "Free Music School."

At Balakirev's school not only were the basics of music taught free of charge to poor students, clerks, and craftsmen, but regular concerts were given with programs consisting primarily of works by the Five. However, Balakirev and his friends had trouble competing with the Russian Musical Society, because the participation of Grand Duchess Elena Pavlovna ("the muse Euterpe," as she was called by admirers and foes alike, owing to her role as august patroness) gave Rubinstein access to a constant and generous imperial subsidy.

Trapped in the vise of an exhausting financial deficit, Balakirev and his circle found release in cursing Rubinstein along the lines of "Stupinstein." They did not eschew anti-Semitic cracks, either. The wounded Rubinstein complained, "Sad is my lot, no one considers me his own. In my homeland I am 'kike,' in Germany I am a Russian, in England, I'm Herr Rubinstein, everywhere a stranger."[37]

In his battle with the hated Russian Musical Society, Balakirev even used the advice of a Petersburg fortune-teller who was in love with him, "a real witch," according to Rimsky-Korsakov. Cui attacked the "conservatives" in his music column in *Sankt-Peterburgskie vedomosti*, an influential newspaper. The most radical member of the "Balakirev party," Mussorgsky, was mobilized to help by composing a rather mean musical parody called *Rayok* (The Peepshow), in which he mocked the enemies of the Mighty Five, including "Euterpe" Elena Pavlovna.*

The life and work of Mussorgsky is woven from paradoxes. The composer resembled one of Dostoyevsky's characters. Many of his confused views and tastes were formed by the idealism of the radical youth of the 1860s in Petersburg.

It was in Petersburg, in May 1855, right after the death of Nicholas I, that the twenty-six-year-old Nikolai Chernyshevsky published his influential booklet, "The Aesthetic Relations of Art to Reality," with its basic thesis, "the beautiful is life." This became the guiding motto of the sixties generation. According to Chernyshevsky, true art re-creates reality in the forms of life itself and at the same time is a "textbook of life." In other words, art must be "realistic" and "progressive," actively participating in the political struggle, the final goal of which is revolution and a specifically Russian socialism that somehow does not resemble the Western models.

An even more radical critic, Dmitri Pisarev, also an idol of Petersburg youth, rejected the very meaning of art. In his opinion the only thing that art might be good for was to depict "the suffering of the starving majority, to dwell on the causes of that suffering, constantly to draw society's attention to economic and social issues."

Pisarev, a confirmed nihilist, saw little use in classical art, which, in his opinion, was far removed from life. He insisted that Pushkin's work was "somniferous," hopelessly out of date. Pisarev wrote that Pushkin was merely a "frivolous versifier, shackled by petty prejudices," a useless and even harmful "parasite," a definition that would be applied a hundred years later, first by the Soviet press, then by the courts to another poet, at the time a Leningrader and future Nobel laureate, Joseph Brodsky.

The views of the energetic young literary nihilist, which found broad support among the Petersburg students of the sixties, were shared by many aspiring artists of the capital as well. Journals with articles by Chernyshevsky, Pisarev, and other radicals were greeted in

*Almost eighty years later, Shostakovich would pick up this tradition with his anti-Stalinist *Rayok*, which documented the suppressed anger of the Soviet intellectual frightened by the "anti-formalist" Zhdanov campaign of 1948.

the Petersburg art world with avid interest, circulated, and read until
the pages wore out. Many took delight in Pisarev's anarchistic call,
"What can be broken should be broken, what can take a blow is useful, what smashes to smithereens is garbage."

And so the privileged Academy of Arts, for a long time the
dominant factor in the artistic life of Petersburg and all of Russia, received its first unexpected blow from within in 1863. Fourteen of the
most talented students of the academy quit, refusing to obey what they
considered old-fashioned and meaningless rules.

"The rebellion of the fourteen" provoked a clash between the
official, ossified art of Petersburg and the young nationalist talents,
who were feeling their strength. This was an unheard-of collective—
and therefore, for the cultural establishment, an especially dangerous—protest against the bureaucratization of Russian art, which had
been turned by Nicholas I into an office department, where the re-
wards were generous and the demands severe.

The young rebels formed the Petersburg Artists' Cooperative,
headed by the charismatic twenty-six-year-old Ivan Kramskoy. In imitation of the heroes of Chernyshevsky's popular novel, *What Is to Be
Done?*, they organized a "commune," renting a large house in Petersburg where they lived, worked, and ate; the household expenses
and income were shared. There would be up to fifty guests at the inexpensive but lively dinners held at the cooperative; articles about art
were read aloud and discussed, someone would sing or play the piano, and sometimes they even held dances. The Artists' Cooperative
quickly turned into a flourishing enterprise: word of the rebels, despite the official ban on mentioning their departure from the academy
in the press, spread far and wide, and there were enough people in Petersburg who wanted to have a fresh Russian landscape, or a busy
genre scene, or a realistic portrait done by one of these young talents,
to sustain them.

After conquering Petersburg, the young rebels' next big step
was taking over the inert Russian provinces. In 1870 the cooperative
was transformed into the Brotherhood of Wandering Art Exhibits.
The idea was to move paintings all over the country that would otherwise be available only to residents of the capital. The general public would see and have an opportunity to buy original art. The
painters, besides expanding their audience and potential market for
their works, also collected the modest entrance fees to the exhibits.

The exhibits of the Wanderers, as they were called, were held annually, and each became an event that was discussed for the rest of the year. Astonished viewers crowded in front of the pictures, expressing outrage or delight that instead of the mythological, conventional heroes and idealized still lifes and landscapes they were being shown genre scenes involving clerks, merchants, or—horrors!—drunken peasants.

If the Wanderers did exhibit a historical painting, it would be from the Russian past. They rejected the tradition of Briullov, whose once-famous *Last Day of Pompeii* was now mocked by the outspoken ideologue of the Wanderers (and of the Mighty Five), Stasov, for its "superficial beauty," "melodrama," and "Italian fake declamation instead of honest feeling." Briullov's oeuvre had to wait until 1898 for its "rehabilitation," when the hundredth anniversary of his birthday was marked by opulent banquets (with some of the leading Wanderers present) and rapturous speeches.

The paintings of the most important Petersburg Wanderers—Ivan Kramskoy, Nikolai Ge, Ilya Repin, Arkhip Kuindzhi—sold like hot cakes. A rich merchant wanted to buy a landscape by Kuindzhi, and the artist told him an amusing story. When that landscape was just finished, the paint still not dry, an unassuming naval officer looked into the artist's studio: could they sell him that painting?

"It's beyond your means," the artist replied.

"How much do you want?"

"Nothing less than five thousand," the painter said, naming an incredible sum just to get rid of his uninvited guest.

The officer responded calmly, "Fine, I'll take it." It was Grand Duke Konstantin.

Rumors of such incidents spread rapidly through Petersburg, and as a result prices for the Wanderers' works rose even higher. The emerging Russian bourgeoisie had money to spend. Growing public opinion demanded art that was engaged and "realistic." The idea of collectivism in culture, of cooperatives, associations, and circles was in the air.

Mussorgsky, as befitted a man of the sixties, also considered himself a collectivist, a political radical, and a "realist." He was genuinely upset when the Balakirev circle began to come apart over personal conflicts and artistic disagreements. But for all this, Mussorgsky was indisputably the most isolated member of that circle and the hardest to understand. The grandeur, acuity, and uncompromising nature of the composer's artistry, in conjunction with the morbid intensity of his personality, doomed Mussorgsky to solitude. In this lay the roots of his creative and personal drama.

Mussorgsky's fervent desire for collective effort, including living in a "commune," so typical of the Petersburg of the sixties, was often accompanied by outbursts of the most extreme individualism. (Mussorgsky never had a family.) His naive striving for "realism" in music paradoxically led him to the grotesque, the depiction of hallucinations, and pathological characters. An atheist, he created some of the most intensely mystical pages in Russian music. And, finally, Mussorgsky's political radicalism was almost totally transformed into aesthetic radicalism. The composer's battle cry became "Forward! To new shores!"

In a list he made not long before his death of people who had especially influenced his development, Mussorgsky first entered and then crossed out Dostoyevsky. Why? One could argue endlessly, but the obvious reason is the similarity between the central personae of Mussorgsky's operas and the protagonists of Dostoyevsky's novels. In both artists' works, the aesthetic ideal was the search for a "new word."

The unbearable torment of Tsar Boris Godunov in the eponymous opera after the tragedy by Pushkin, which Mussorgsky wrote in 1869–1872, echoes the torment of Raskolnikov, the Petersburg student in *Crime and Punishment,* published a few years earlier. And Dosifei, the leader of the eighteenth-century schismatics in *Khovanshchina* (which Mussorgsky called a "national musical drama"), resembles in many ways the elder Zosima in *The Brothers Karamazov;* each was written in the late 1870s.

The similarities were not, of course, the result of conscious imitation or borrowings by Mussorgsky; rather, they stemmed from the same artistic approach. Each character—Dostoyevsky's student and monk, Mussorgsky's tsar—falls under the same artistic microscope mercilessly revealing the deepest, most contradictory, most encoded emotions and spiritual longings. Both Dostoyevsky and Mussorgsky were fascinated by the mystery of the Russian soul and its inexplicable duality. In their works, kindness and cruelty, wisdom and folly, good humor and ill can be easily combined in the same person.

To this day commentators are confounded by the character of Shaklovity, the head of the *sysknoi prikaz* (the seventeenth-century secret police) in *Khovanshchina.* Shaklovity is a patriot, a traitor, an informer, a philosopher, a killer—a mass of contradictions. Mussorgsky, who wrote the original libretto of *Khovanshchina* himself, was accused of shoddy craftsmanship, since it appeared that Shaklovity defied all the operatic clichés. Mussorgsky's Shaklovity, however, is far from poorly wrought. He is ambitious and cruel, a real political figure. Mussorgsky, like his contemporary Dostoyevsky, had succeeded in creating a complex character. We need look no further than Russia's later, terrible history to confirm yet again the genius of Mussorgsky's psychological insight.

Like Dostoyevsky, Mussorgsky's work depicts "the insulted and the injured" with all their passion and pain. Like Dostoyevsky too, he raises these pathetic characters to tragic heights until the grotesque and the majestic coexist. Mussorgsky could accomplish this not only because he had compassion for these poor people, not only because he felt a sense of guilt toward them, but because in his works he almost became them. Like Dostoyevsky's most inspired pages, Mussorgsky's music is vivid, confused, feverish, and ultimately hypnotizing.

There are other strikingly similar traits in the creative techniques of the writer and the composer as well. Mussorgsky used many of Dostoyevsky's methods and devices, among them the confessional monologue, so typical of Dostoyevsky's novels. It is Dostoyevsky's trademark, so to speak. The descriptions of hallucinations and nightmares make up some of his most memorable writing. And *Boris Godunov* employs three such Dostoyevskian monologues by Tsar Boris to hold the opera together. One of the most powerful scenes is Boris's hallucination, when he sees the ghost of the tsarevich, murdered on his orders.

The same can be said for another characteristic trait of Dostoyevsky's plots, the sudden outbursts of "scandals," which sharply delineate the motives and characters of the protagonists. Joseph Brodsky brought to my attention the extraordinary importance of these scandals in the structure of Dostoyevsky's novels.[38] Such a scandal is brilliantly drawn by Mussorgsky in the second act of *Khovanshchina*, when the princes hold a secret council to argue over Russia's political future. This is the most impressive "political" scene in the history of opera.

Paradoxically, Mussorgsky and Dostoyevsky share the same ambivalence toward open political tendentiousness and "engagement" in a work of art. For this reason both writer and composer, without collusion, criticized the popular political poetry of their contemporary Nekrasov. Of the works of the Wanderers, they preferred the ones where the social theme did not predominate, where, as Mussorgsky put it, there wasn't a "single civic theme, or a single Nekrasovian misery."

It is telling that the inspiration for one of Mussorgsky's most famous works was the visual arts. *Pictures at an Exhibition,* written for piano and later orchestrated by Ravel, was inspired not by a realistic canvas of the Wanderers but by the symbolic and grotesque drawings of the composer's friend Viktor Hartman, exhibited posthumously in Petersburg in 1874.

The figure of the *yurodivy* is typical of both Dostoyevsky and Mussorgsky. The Russian word applies to the holy fool as well as the village idiot. But it also transmits many historical, cultural, and religious notions. The phenomenon of the *yurodivy,* which dates to the fifteenth century, was a marked presence in Russian history until the eighteenth century, when it moved into Russian literature and art as a national symbol.

In the Russian tradition, the *yurodivy* is the odd man out, a social critic and prophet of apocalyptic change. Challenging trivial truths, turning them inside out and mocking them, he demonstrates their shallowness, hypocrisy, and absurdity. Using his sometimes feigned madness as a weapon, the *yurodivy* pits himself against both the rulers and the crowd.

In the opera *Boris Godunov,* the *yurodivy,* a minor character in the Pushkin tragedy, was turned into the spokesman for the oppressed and beleaguered Russian people. The confrontation between Boris and the *yurodivy,* who accuses the tsar of infanticide before the stunned crowd and the boyars, is one of the opera's climaxes. Boris's reaction is characteristic and historically accurate. He stops the guards who are about to arrest the *yurodivy.* "Don't touch him! . . . Pray for me, blessed one!" Traditionally, Russian tsars tolerated the *yurodivy*'s outspoken statements because they considered the men possessed of higher wisdom.

The final, heartbreaking moment of the opera is the *yurodivy*'s terrifying, hopeless plaint, prophesying the coming of dark times: "Weep, weep, Russian people, hungry people!"—the piercing, ageless wail of long-suffering Russia itself.

In Mussorgsky's art song to his own text, "Svetik Savishna," the *yurodivy,* suffering and gasping, vainly tries to declare his love to a beautiful woman. It is a stunning work. "A horrible scene. Shakespeare in music," exclaimed one of the first listeners. The tongue-tied laments interspersed with shrieks convey the torment of the humiliated, rejected man with such expressive power that the naturalistic musical scene turns into a symbol with countless interpretations. For me this song has always seemed to be the most perceptive of allegories for the relationship between the illiterate, suffering Russian people and its inaccessible intellectual elite.

"Svetik Savishna" was especially dear to Mussorgsky. He even signed many of his letters "Savishna," seemingly identifying with the song's *yurodivy*. This self-identification was not random: Mussorgsky was a *yurodivy* composer, whipsawed by the external dynamic of his fate and his own centrifugal psychological impulses.

Interestingly, even his closest friends called him a *yurodivy*. In their attitude toward Mussorgsky, for all the public praise of his musical gifts, there was always a note of intellectual condescension. Balakirev privately stated that Mussorgsky was "almost an idiot."[39] Stasov readily agreed: "I think he is a total idiot."[40] For Rimsky-Korsakov, the most circumspect of the group, Mussorgsky's personality was made up of two components—"on the one hand, a prideful opinion of himself and a conviction that the path he has selected in art is the only correct one; on the other, a complete downfall, alcoholism, and the resultant constantly cloudy head."[41]

The word was spoken—alcoholism! Mussorgsky drowned himself in a sea of wine, cognac, and vodka. It turned him before the very eyes of his stunned friends from a refined gentleman into an antisocial bum, a Petersburg *yurodivy*.

Of course, alcoholism was Mussorgsky's personal weakness, but at the same time it was a typical phenomenon for that part of Mussorgsky's generation that wanted to oppose the establishment and express its desperate protest through extreme forms of behavior. "An intense worship of Bacchus was considered to be almost obligatory for a writer of that period," noted a contemporary. "It was a showing off, a 'pose' for the best people of the sixties." Another commentator seconded this opinion: "Talented people in Russia who love the simple folk cannot but drink."[42]

Spending day and night in a Petersburg tavern of low repute, the Maly Yaroslavets, in the company of bohemian dropouts like himself, Mussorgsky consciously broke his ties with the "decent" circles of the Petersburg elite. He and his fellow drinkers idealized their alcoholism, raising it to a level of ethical and even aesthetic opposition. Their bravado was little more than a course toward isolation and eventual self-destruction.

On his way to the abyss, Mussorgsky expressed his doubts. Testimony to his ambivalence was his most Petersburg composition, the song cycle with its symbolic title, *Sunless* (1874, to the poetry of his close friend, Arseny Golenishchev-Kutuzov). In the six clearly autobiographical song-monologues of *Sunless,* Mussorgsky portrays himself as one who feels as if the present did not exist for him in the heart of a megalopolis. His failed love, his feeble attempts at contact and communication were all in the past, but even the past might be an illusion. A woman's brief glance in a crowd turns into a haunting memory—Mussorgsky accents that detail with surreal insistence reminiscent of Dostoyevsky.

Mussorgsky's protagonist, lacking a present, doubting the past, has no future, either. He suffers during a Petersburg white night, enclosed by the four walls of his small room, just like Raskolnikov, and sums up his lonely, joyless existence. And when the final song of the cycle is complete, lulling and enchanting, it becomes obvious that the hero, in quiet prostration, has no other way out but suicide. The city rejects the crushed individual and so he is prepared to vanish into nothingness.

Sunless is one of Mussorgsky's creative peaks and his most significant contribution to the Petersburg mythos first sketched by Dostoyevsky. This cycle has an extraordinarily flexible vocal line free of formal constraints, with bold harmonies and the freshness of its piano accompaniment, and an astonishingly laconic manner and restraint that made Mussorgsky a revelation for Claude Debussy and Maurice Ravel, and through them for later musical culture. It is a miniature encyclopedia of the composer's style and makes clear why Mussorgsky's influence, enormous in Russia, is noticeable in many vocal works of twentieth-century Western composers.

Mussorgsky's death was in fact if not in intent a suicide. After a stroke brought on by drinking, he was placed by his friends in a military hospital. Under the strict care of a sympathetic doctor, Mussorgsky's health began to improve. But feeling better, he bribed the guard with twenty-five rubles, a large sum in those days, to bring him a bottle of forbidden alcohol.

That bottle of cognac, consumed in one sitting with an apple for an hors d'oeuvre, brought on a fatal stroke. Mussorgsky had time only to cry, "It's all over! Ah, I am a wretch!" Learning of Mussorgsky's death, one of his drinking companions at the Maly Yaroslavets tavern noted philosophically, "Even a copper coffee pot burns out over a spirit flame, and a man is more fragile than a coffee pot."[43]

A powerful testimony to Mussorgsky's end is a portrait by Ilya Repin in March 1881, painted in just four days of an incredible improvisational surge, only ten days before the composer's death. Repin, a leading Wanderer, friend, and admirer of Mussorgsky (the feeling was mutual), rushed to the military hospital where the composer was a patient.

Barely known in the West, Repin is familiar to virtually every Russian through his large historical and genre canvases in a realistic style. Energetic, animated, a somewhat eccentric man and a productive painter (he left over a thousand works), Repin was always attracted to topical subjects. The art critic Abram Efros called him the greatest "political commentator" of Russian art.

Repin was also probably its greatest portraitist at a time that, in Stasov's worried words, was "not at all conducive to the development of portraiture: photography has almost killed the portrait and all Russian talent for it has quieted down, suddenly leaving the stage." Not Repin: rich and famous, he was welcome everywhere—in the Winter Palace and in a nihilist commune. Repin's portraits were psychologically penetrating and artistically masterful. In them he immortalized the tsar's family, high government officials, and the leading writers, actors and actresses, scholars, professors, jurists, and clergy of the day, as well as Russian peasants. Repin was genuinely interested in and attracted to people of all classes and convictions—the elite of Petersburg, its bureaucrats and technocrats, its conservatives, liberals, revolutionaries, and simple folk.

Repin's portrait gallery of Petersburg intellectuals and cultural figures remains the most interesting and significant of any Russian. The deathbed portrait of Mussorgsky holds a special place here. It is a unique document, capturing the artistic personality on the verge of collapse, the moment when the great composer and the *yurodivy*, the alcoholic and the lumpen coexist in one body and soul.

Mussorgsky is depicted carelessly wrapped in a green hospital gown with raspberry lapels. Sitting in the light, his figure looks particularly pathetic; the sun ruthlessly reveals his crumbling, puffy face of a bluish tint with "a red potato nose,"[44] in Repin's words, unkempt reddish-brown hair, and tangled beard. But the same light draws the viewer's attention to the composer's huge, bottomless gray-blue eyes, the magnetic center of the portrait. Those eyes, expressing hidden torment, are nevertheless pure and quiet. Mussorgsky seems to be obediently awaiting death while listening to the sounds fading in his head. It is the humility of the *yurodivy* who knows that by accepting his torment in this life and thus fulfilling his duty, he goes to meet a higher power.

Mussorgsky's corpse was still warm when Stasov brought Repin's portrait to an exhibit of the Wanderers in Petersburg, where it was attacked furiously by the reactionary press for its "cruel realism." It also elicited praise. The head of the Wanderers, the golden-tongued Kramskoy, sat down before the portrait, as if glued to his chair, and, bringing his face almost even with Mussorgsky's, devoured it with his eyes, exclaiming, "It's incredible, it's simply incredible!" And in fact, the only nineteenth-century depiction of a composer that rivals Repin's is Delacroix's portrait of Chopin.

The year 1881 began unhappily for Russian culture. In February fifty-nine-year-old Dostoyevsky died in Petersburg. After that the death of forty-two-year-old Mussorgsky deprived the country of another of its greatest creative geniuses. Petersburgers were well aware of the significance and tragedy of those irreplaceable losses. But even those deaths were overshadowed by an event perceived by most Russians as a national catastrophe. On March 1, 1881, revolutionary terrorists killed "Tsar Liberator" Alexander II.

Alexander II's basically liberal rule was distinguished by several important reforms, including the historic emancipation of the serfs in 1861, two years before the slaves were freed in the United States. Russia acquired a jury system, limited self-rule for cities and provinces, a more or less independent press (including publications of a fairly radical bent), and universities open to the lower classes. The rights of women and minorities were expanded and certain kinds of corporal punishment, such as flogging, were abolished.

But as had happened before in Russian history and would happen again, liberal reforms did not bring their initiator the deserved popularity. The country was convulsed by change. In Petersburg the attitude of many intellectuals toward Alexander II was rather condescending. Nihilist students thirsted for radical reforms. Officers and bureaucrats openly gossiped about the emperor's liaison with Princess Ekaterina Dolgorukova, his junior by twenty-eight years. Still, when the nihilist Dmitri Karakozov tried to shoot the emperor in the Summer Gardens on April 4, 1866, the news of the unsuccessful attempt rocked Russia. The newspapers reported that a peasant accidently had bumped into Karakozov, spoiling the shot; they also indicated, incorrectly, that the terrorist was Polish.

This led to numerous performances of Glinka's patriotic opera, *A Life for the Tsar,* in which a peasant also saved the first Romanov tsar from the Poles. One such performance was described by twenty-six-year-old Peter Tchaikovsky, then a budding composer:

> As soon as the Poles appeared on the stage, shouts began: 'Down with the Poles!' The choristers were confused and stopped singing, and the audience demanded the anthem, which was sung about twenty times. At the end the Sovereign's portrait was brought out, and the ensuing madness cannot be described.[45]

Karakozov was hanged and terrorist acts stopped for a while. But in January 1878 the revolutionary Vera Zasulich shot and wounded severely the Petersburg city chief, Fyodor Trepov. This began a series of successful terrorist attacks. The revolutionaries did not merely take down the highest tsarist officials, but also explained their attacks to the public and even dared to announce them beforehand. Special warnings from the revolutionaries were delivered to the chief of the gendarmes, Mezentsov (as one of the terrorists recalled, "practically in person") and to the Petersburg city prefect, Zurov. After each ensuing attack, leaflets rationalizing and defending it would appear throughout the city.

Even though the underground revolutionary cells were small, their members were dedicated to the highest degree, energetic, and intelligent; each attempt was planned carefully. When they decided to kill Mezentsov, they made up a timetable of his walks. Learning that Mezentsov was always accompanied by an adjutant and that the chief wore a protective vest, the attackers ordered an especially heavy dagger, explaining to the sword maker that they needed it for hunting bear. The journalist Sergei Stepnyak-Kravchinsky, who had been chosen to execute the death sentence that had already been pronounced publicly, got the signal from his accomplice and, concealing the dagger inside a newspaper, approached the strolling Mezentsov in front of the tsar's Mikhailovsky Palace. While another conspirator distracted the adjutant, Kravchinsky struck the gendarme with the dagger in the stomach below the vest, then leaped into a waiting carriage drawn by a prized trotter, which carried the terrorist down a planned escape route and off to safety.

The chief of the gendarmes died of the wound, and Kravchinsky described the assassination in an underground brochure called "A Death for a Death," widely distributed in Petersburg and all of Russia. Such audacious attacks carried out in broad daylight left the capital in a state of shock as the revolutionaries announced, "those who decided questions of life and death with a single flourish of the pen now see with horror that they are also subject to the death penalty." One of the leading nihilists explained the terrorist campaign, unprecedented in boldness, scope, and success, this way: "When they gag the mouth of a man who wants to speak they thereby untie his hands."[46]

In Russia the gigantic pyramid of power was topped by the tsar. The emperor was not only a symbolic figure but also a real sovereign. Therefore the liberal Alexander II was inevitably held responsible for the actions of his most reactionary bureaucrats. "It was getting strange," wrote Vera Figner, a leading terrorist, "to beat the servants for doing the bidding of their master and not touching the master."[47] The revolutionaries also wanted to shock Petersburg, so they decided at all costs to kill the tsar. Just a few dozen people with limited funds were in charge. But they were young and, most important, fanatically certain of the rightness of their cause. Alexander II could move the country along the path of reform as much as he wanted—he was doomed anyway.

In 1879 they shot once more at Alexander II, who had been told by a fortune teller that there would be seven attempts on his life. The emperor had been walking—alone as usual—on Palace Square. This time again the terrorist, like Karakozov before him, missed and was also hanged. So the revolutionaries decided to use a much more effective weapon than firearms: dynamite. But the sophisticated plan to blow up the tsar's train did not work either. Then they placed the explosive in the cellar below the Winter Palace. Another failure. The powerful explosion that killed or wounded some seventy Finnish soldiers guarding Alexander II miraculously left the emperor untouched.

Nevertheless, the social and political fallout from that explosion was extensive, leaving the capital in a panic. "All Russia can be said to be under siege,"[48] the minister of defense Dmitri Milyutin wrote in his diary. In Petersburg during the winter of 1878–1879 alone, over two thousand were arrested on suspicion of subversive activity. But for the unfettered nihilists, the hunt for Alexander, unprecedented in the annals of political terror, had turned into an obsession.

This was understood by the bewildered and frightened sovereign of a huge and powerful empire: "They are hunting me like a wild animal," he would complain. "What for? I haven't even done any personal good deed for them that they should hate me so!" Even their implacable foe, Dostoyevsky, had given the terrorist's stubbornness its due: "We say outright: these are madmen, yet these madmen have their own logic, their teaching, their code, their God even, and it's as deepset as it could be."

On March 1, 1881, Alexander II was returning to the Winter Palace from a military parade accompanied by guards in a special armored coach built in Paris. When the carriage reached the deserted embankment of the Catherine Canal, a terrorist jumped out from behind a corner and tossed a bomb at the feet of the galloping horses. Once again the emperor leaped out unharmed from the shattered carriage, although two of the guards were wounded. Alexander went up to them. A crowd gathered. The attacker had been taken away.

"Glory to God, Your Majesty, that you are safe," muttered one of the guards.

"Thank God," replied the tsar.

"It's too soon to thank God!" shouted a man in the crowd and threw a second bomb at Alexander. This time the emperor was mortally wounded, both legs torn off. After seven unsuccessful attempts, the eighth terrorist action had succeeded. Brought to the Winter Palace, the emperor died within a few minutes. Ironically, on his desk was the draft of the long-awaited constitutional reforms, which he had planned to sign that day.

Having won the battle, the revolutionaries lost the war. All the participants in the assassination of Alexander II were eventually arrested, tried, and hanged. Alexander III, Alexander's thirty-five-year-old son, ascended to the throne. A huge man, decisive and stubborn, he was a confirmed conservative whose father's death had only strengthened his conviction that Russia was not yet ready for liberal reform. The new emperor's ideal was the autocratic rule of his grandfather Nicholas I; the Russian ship of state veered sharply to the right.

Public opinion helped Alexander III. Tchaikovsky's reaction to the murder of the Tsar Liberator, expressed in a letter from Naples to his patroness, Nadezhda von Meck, was typical:

> The news shocked me so that I almost fell ill. In such horrible moments of national catastrophe, during such incidents that shame Russia, it is hard to be abroad. I would like to fly to Russia, learn the

details, be among my own people, take part in demonstrations of sympathy for the new Sovereign, and howl for revenge with the others. Will the vile ulcer of our political life not be uprooted completely this time? It is horrible to think that perhaps this recent catastrophe might not be the epilogue of the whole tragedy.[49]

Tchaikovsky even signed up for the Holy Brotherhood, a secret organization created by the Russian aristocracy to protect the new emperor and fight terrorism.[50] Interestingly, this fact has never yet been mentioned in any Russian—or, for that matter, Western—biography of the composer. Even without the help of the Holy Brotherhood, however, the police crushed the remnants of the revolutionary cells in Petersburg and the rest of Russia. The ghost of the Martyr Tsar, as the late emperor was now called, rumored to appear at night at the Kazan Cathedral, could be pacified.

Instead, the ghosts of the seemingly vanquished revolutionaries flooded Russian culture: prose (the novels and stories of Turgenev, Dostoyevsky, Leo Tolstoy, and Vsevolod Garshin); poetry (the poems of Yakov Polonsky and Semyon Nadson); painting (the works of Repin, Vassily Vereshchagin and Vladimir Makovsky). The Wanderer Nikolai Yaroshenko went so far as to show his painting *At the Lithuanian Castle,* depicting Petersburg's main prison (called the Russian Bastille) with a revolutionary young woman standing in front of it, at a Wanderers' exhibition in Petersburg the day the tsar was killed. This naturally caused a sensation. Alexander II's brother, Grand Duke Mikhail, was outraged. "What pictures he paints! The man is a socialist!" The painting was immediately removed from the show and Yaroshenko was placed under house arrest.

The Lithuanian Castle was burned down during the February Revolution of 1917. The infamous prison was replaced by an ugly apartment house, which I saw every day for four years when I lived at the dormitory of the music school of the Leningrad Conservatory.

The image of the revolutionary nihilist moved from Russia to the West, where the press gave broad coverage to Russian terrorism, the assassination of Alexander II, and the subsequent government repressions. The nihilists became a modern symbol, much like the Soviet dissidents a century later. Oscar Wilde wrote the drama *Vera, or the Nihilists* in 1881. Sarah Bernhardt and Eleonora Duse starred in Victorienne Sardoux's drama *Fedora,* based on the life of nihilists. The image of the Russian revolutionary appeared in popular works of Emile Zola, Alfonse Daudet, Guy de Maupassant, and Mark Twain.

And it was incorporated, at last, in the pages of the popular magazine *The Strand* in a Sherlock Holmes story by Sir Arthur Conan Doyle, "The Adventure of the Golden Pince-Nez" ("reformers—revolutionists—Nihilists, you understand"). This, of course, was real fame.

The murder of Alexander II also served as an impetus, however oblique, for the creation of a specifically Petersburg artifact in jewelry. It occurred as a clever court jeweler, the Russified François Fabergé, puzzled over Alexander III's commission for a pleasant Easter surprise for his wife, who could not get over the assassination of her father-in-law. Fabergé came up with a charming, quite expensive toy, which fully embodied the Russian tsar's idea of a nice Easter surprise: a golden chicken egg that could be opened to reveal a miniature golden chick.

The virtuoso work of the court jeweler so charmed the empress that the next Easter the commission was repeated, and Fabergé put a completely different surprise in the new egg. And so the imperial Fabergé Easter eggs became a tradition, interrupted only by the revolution of 1917. Of the 55 or 56 legendary eggs created by Fabergé, presumably only 43 or so survived; for many obsessed collectors they represent, perhaps along with Diaghilev's ballet productions, the most opulent and refined achievement of imperial Russia. This is, of course, a matter of personal taste. In any case, the Fabergé eggs amply demonstrate the exquisite mastery exhibited by the jewelers of Petersburg, as well as the wealth of Fabergé's august clients.

In general, however, Alexander III was a rather stingy monarch, perhaps in imitation of Peter the Great. But neither he nor, later, his son, Nicholas II, begrudged their loved ones the enormous sum of fifteen thousand rubles, the cost of each of those Easter eggs. If not for the revolution, this expense might have turned into a prudent investment, since in our day the value of the eggs is incalculable.

Many historians insist that Alexander III was an uneducated, coarse, and brutish man, albeit with a lot of common sense. But these assertions contradict some of the facts of the emperor's involvement with Russian culture. A passionate patriot, even a chauvinist (he was a pathological anti-Semite), Alexander III became one of the leading patrons of the Wanderer artists. His rich collection of Russian paintings served as the basis for his museum of visual and fine arts, open to the public in 1898 in the Mikhailovsky Palace, renamed the State Russian Museum under the Bolsheviks.

Alexander III greatly increased the subsidy to the imperial theaters. The orchestra of the Russian opera grew to 110 members and the choir to 120. The stagings of both ballet and opera were lavishly produced, with huge sums specifically allocated for costumes and scenery.

Every spring Alexander III personally approved the repertoire for the opera and ballet, often making significant changes; he did not miss a single dress rehearsal in his theaters. The emperor was involved in all the details of new productions—and not just from whim or pleasure; his motivations were also political. He knew that the imperial theaters—opera, ballet, and drama—were the mirror of the monarchy; the brilliance and opulence of their productions reflected the majesty of his reign. Therefore he correctly viewed the attacks in the liberal press, especially after the repeal in 1882 of the imperial monopoly on theater productions in Petersburg, as veiled attacks on his regime, noting once that the newspapers pounded his theaters "because they are forbidden to write about so many other things."[51]

On the emperor's personal orders, the Maryinsky Theater presented Meyerbeer's *L'Africaine,* Boito's *Mefistofele,* Massenet's *Manon,* Leoncavallo's *I Pagliacci,* Gounod's *Romeo et Juliette,* and Mascagni's *Cavalleria Rusticana.* This Italo-Franco preference reflected not only the sovereign's musical tastes but Russia's political orientation at the time. The worsening relations with Germany led to the closing of the German Theater in Petersburg in 1890; as a knowledgeable courtier commented, "This was one of the repressive measures in response to the treacherous behavior of Prince Bismarck!"[52]

Of the Russian composers, Tchaikovsky had long been a favorite of Alexander III. Knowing that, we can understand more easily why the emperor was rather hostile toward the music of the Mighty Five, a seemingly inconsistent position for a Russian nationalist. Alexander personally crossed out *Boris Godunov* from the proposed repertoire for the 1888–1889 season of the Maryinsky Theater, replacing it with an opera by Massenet. In his prejudice against Mussorgsky and his comrades, the tsar was not alone, and his allies in this matter were not all conservatives. Among the most famous opponents of the Mighty Five were the liberal novelist Ivan Turgenev and the radical satirist Mikhail Saltykov-Shchedrin.

The denunciations of the Mighty Five are among the more curious episodes in the history of Petersburg culture. They prove that purely aesthetic prejudices often make as strange bedfellows as politics. The artist Repin recalled how the staunch foe of the monarchy, Saltykov-Shchedrin, published a satirical attack on Mussorgsky and his mentor, Stasov: "All of Petersburg read that lampoon of a young talent, dying of laughter; it was a funny tale of a noisy aesthete presenting a homegrown talent to a jury of connoisseurs and how the hung-over talent grunted his new aria on a civic theme: about a coachman who had lost his whip."[53]

Mocking the "realism" in music proclaimed by Mussorgsky and supported by Stasov, Shchedrin had Stasov deliver the following absurd tirade in his article: "We must depict in sound combinations not only thoughts and sensations, but the very milieu in which they take place, not leaving out the color and shape of the uniforms."

Turgenev, who couldn't stand the music of Balakirev or Mussorgsky, scolded Stasov for supporting them: "Of all the 'young' Russian musicians there are only two with positive talent: Tchaikovsky and Rimsky-Korsakov. The rest—not as people, of course (as people they are charming) but as artists—the rest should be put in a sack and thrown in the water! The Egyptian king Ramses XXIX is not as forgotten today as they will be forgotten in 15 or 20 years."[54] Fortunately, this prophecy did not come to pass.

The relations between Tchaikovsky and the Mighty Five were extremely complex and confused. They began fatefully on that March day in 1866 when Tchaikovsky, then twenty-six, sitting in a Petersburg café, opened the influential newspaper *Sankt-Peterburgskie vedomosti* to read the first-ever review of his graduation composition. A member of the Mighty Five, Cui had an extremely negative reaction to Tchaikovsky's cantata performed at his examination: "The conservatory composer Mr. Tchaikovsky is totally without merit."

That "terrible verdict," in Tchaikovsky's words, shook the beginning composer. He saw black, his head spun, he threw down the newspaper, and "like a madman" (as he later described it) ran out of the café to wander around the city all day, repeating over and over, "I'm nothing, a mediocrity, I'll never be anything, I am talentless."[55]

Trying to overcome his hurt, Tchaikovsky one day attended a party at Balakirev's. The attitude of the Mighty Five toward Tchaikovsky becomes clear from the memoirs of Rimsky-Korsakov, who described their meeting this way: "He turned out to be a pleasant conversationalist and a nice man, who knew how to behave simply and to speak seemingly sincerely and frankly."[56] Note the sarcastic and suspicious "seemingly."

Still, Tchaikovsky persisted in befriending Balakirev; he dedicated one of his works to him and at Balakirev's suggestion wrote one of his masterpieces, the symphonic poem *Romeo and Juliet*. But in the long run, Tchaikovsky did not turn Balakirev's circle into the Mighty Six, as the eternal enthusiast Stasov had first predicted: the tastes, views, ties, preferences, goals, and finally characters of the "Mighties" and of Tchaikovsky were too different. This inevitably led to conflicts—often veiled, sometimes open.

The most hostile, almost morbid relations were between Tchaikovsky and Mussorgsky. How fine it would have been had the two greatest Russian composers of their time liked, or at least understood and respected, each other! Alas, the reality was different, and no attempts by later biographers to smooth over the situation succeeded. The temperamental Mussorgsky, sensing an enemy in Tchaikovsky, mocked him at every opportunity, never calling him anything but by his derisive nickname Sadyk-pasha. In his turn, the usually quite generous Tchaikovsky wrote to his brother after having "thoroughly studied *Boris Godunov*," "I send Mussorgsky's music to hell with all my heart; it is the tritest and basest parody of music."[57]

Tchaikovsky's confidant the critic German Laroche spilled onto the newspaper pages what the composer had reserved for private discussions; calling *Boris Godunov* a "musical defecation," he pitied "the conductor, singers and instrumentalists, brought by fate to deal with that stinking substance."[58] Besides everything else, an important issue was the struggle for the Maryinsky stage, the most influential in the empire. It is only now that we presume that the operas of Mussorgsky and Tchaikovsky could coexist peacefully on that or any other stage. Laroche did not think so, nor did Alexander III.

Laroche wrote,

> The Russian musician who leafs through the piano score of *Boris* some thirty years from now will never believe, just as no contemporary foreigner believes, that those black signs on white paper depict anything that had been actually sung and played publicly, in costumes, before large crowds that had not only gladly paid money for their seats, but had presented the composer with a laurel wreath . . . that the wild sounds and wild opinions about them were heard not in some barbarous country, but in a brilliant capital. . . . An abyss must have gaped between Petersburg and the rest of the world; consequently the patriotic feeling of people with healthy tastes was profoundly insulted.[59]

The paradox is that in his tirade Laroche combined an appeal to Western taste and judgment along with one to Russian "patriotic feeling." Such ambivalence reflected the duality of Petersburg's position as the "window on the West" and at the same time the capital of a powerful empire with a chauvinist monarch. Speaking of "healthy tastes," Tchaikovsky's close friend was wisely making a deep courtier's bow. And suddenly the emperor's cultural policy and particularly the mystery of the Russian tsar's animosity toward Mussorgsky becomes clearer.

The thirty-year reign ("too short," in the words of the artist Alexander Benois) of Alexander III solidified the return to the ideals of patriotism and nationality under the aegis of autocracy, first proclaimed by the emperor's grandfather Nicholas I. In Alexander's eyes loyalty was true patriotism, and any attempt at aesthetic radicalism smacked of subversion. The French-language *Journal de St.- Petersbourg* called the members of the Mighty Five "les pétroleurs de la république des beaux arts."

Tchaikovsky, on the contrary, was perceived by Alexander III as a loyal composer. And, in fact, the composer was personally devoted to the emperor and wrote a coronation march and cantata for him, for which he received a ring with a large diamond valued at fifteen hundred rubles from the tsar. The emperor's generosity to Tchaikovsky continued and in 1888 he granted the composer a lifetime pension of three thousand rubles a year.

Tchaikovsky may be the most popular and beloved Russian cultural figure in the West. In America, for instance, where his fame was fanned by his conducting at the opening of Carnegie Hall in 1891, it would be hard to imagine a Christmas not enveloped in the sounds of *The Nutcracker* or a Fourth of July without the cannon and fireworks accompanying the *1812 Overture*.

This unprecedented popularity is based primarily on the obvious emotional accessibility and lushness of Tchaikovsky's melodies. An intriguing element is added by the romantic and sensational aspects of Tchaikovsky's biography: his homosexuality and alleged suicide.

How did Tchaikovsky's homosexual passions affect his life and music? Did he take poison in Petersburg in 1893, in his fifty-fourth year? And did the authorities cover it up by announcing the composer had died in a cholera epidemic? As a schoolboy in Soviet Leningrad, I had heard tales from old Petersburgers about Tchaikovsky's homosexuality and his strange death. Later in New York Balanchine had discussed these issues at length with me. It is clear, however, that the full evaluation of all these rumors can be made only after a thorough and objective study by Russian and Western specialists of the materials kept in Russian archives. The participation of the latter is particularly important since the topics of homosexuality and suicide, especially relating to popular and beloved figures, touch on Russian national pride and were still taboo in the Soviet Union even at the end of the 1980s.

Both Stravinsky and particularly Balanchine insisted on calling Tchaikovsky a "Petersburg" composer. This was based not only on the facts of his life—Tchaikovsky studied in Petersburg and died there; many of his works were first performed in the capital, which he often visited and where he had many friends—but on such personality traits as nobility, reserve, and sense of moderation, and of course the effective use of the "European" forms in his compositions, so consonant with Petersburg's European architecture.

But there are even more typically Petersburgian features in Tchaikovsky's work. Music lovers look primarily for emotional agitation in it, enjoying what Laroche, who understood the composer as no one else did, called its "refined torment." But that leaves out the important part of Tchaikovsky's work so popular with the masses, which could be called "imperial," that is, the glorification of the Russian empire and the victories of Russian arms.

The imperial theme is traditional in Russian culture. The first proud note of it was sounded in Petersburg by none other than Pushkin (if we discount the rather formulaic exercises of his ode-writing predecessors).

In Pushkin's era Petersburg was already the capital of an empire that had defeated the military might of Poland and Sweden, had annexed Finland and the Baltic states—Estonia, Latvia, and Lithuania—in the West and the Tatar lands in the south, and had embarked on the conquest of Transcaucasia. All this—including the Ukraine, Belorussia, and the vast Siberian expanses, sparsely settled by pagan tribes—constituted an enormous territory, swiftly approaching in size one-sixth of the world's land area. The victory over Napoleon and the conquering march of Russian troops across Europe into Paris increased the imperial ambitions of the Petersburg elite.

The cult of the Russian soldier and his bayonet flourished. When the Poles rebelled against their Russian conquerors in 1830 and Nicholas I replied with cannons, calls for aid to the rebels resounded in France. In that moment Pushkin responded with a scintillating poem, "To the Slanderers of Russia," a blistering manifesto of impe-

rial pride and Petersburg's ambitions, formulated as a series of poetic
rhetorical questions:

> *Or is the Russian tsar's word now powerless?*
> *Or is it new to us to argue with Europe?*
> *Or has the Russian grown unaccustomed to victories?*
> *Or are there not enough of us? or from Perm to Tauris,*
> *From the cold rocks of Finland to the flaming Colchis,*
> *From the stunned Kremlin*
> *To the walls of stagnant China,*
> *Flashing its steel bristles,*
> *Will not the Russian land rise?*

These proud, iron-hard lines were very effectively used by Soviet propaganda during the war with Nazi Germany—naturally, omitting
mention of the tsar.

With the new lands, newly conquered peoples entered the Russian Empire. Some did this without particular resistance; others, for
instance, the Muslim nationalities of the Caucasus, fought ferociously
for many decades for their independence. The attitude of the Russian
cultural elite to these new imperial subjects was ambivalent.

That ambivalence was already apparent in Pushkin's narrative
poem *A Prisoner of the Caucasus* (1820–1821). Pushkin, in the spirit
of Rousseau, was enraptured by the freedom-loving rebellious Circassians, their hospitality, simplicity, and customs. But he finished the
poem with a hymn to the Russian two-headed eagle and the Russian
troops who cut through the Caucasus, destroying the freedom-loving
Circassians like "the black contagion."

As was the case with most of the continuing themes of Russian
culture, it was also Pushkin who set the tone in this instance. Attracted
by the exotic mores of the multinational subjects of the Russian Empire, Petersburg writers, artists, and composers still treated those peoples with suspicion and sometimes even outright hostility. The Tatar
and Muslim tribes of the Caucasus were depicted as barbarians to
whom the Russian sword brought civilization and the true religion,
Russian Orthodoxy. The Swedes and Germans were often described
as primitive, simpleminded, and cruel; the Poles as conceited brag-
garts; the Jews as dirty and greedy ignoramuses.

The rapid expansion of the empire, the ethnic variety of its peoples, and Petersburg's growing appetite for conquests found particular reflection in Russian music. The list of works related to the imperial
theme in one way or another is enormous. In music the Pushkin role

of founder of new paths was played, of course, by Glinka with his opera *Ruslan and Ludmila*. This mythical epic, based on Pushkin, presents the idea of a Slavic nucleus, which like a magnet attracts into its sphere of domination peripheral characters, from the mysterious Finn to the charming Persian girls.

After Glinka came Dargomyzhsky with his *Malorossiiskaya* (Ukrainian) and *Chukhonskaya* (Finnish) fantasies for orchestra. But it was the Caucasian motifs that Russian composers found the most attractive. Here the pioneer was the leader of the Mighty Five, Balakirev, who brought back notations of local folk songs and dances from his trips through Georgia. Balakirev was especially enchanted by the Georgian lezghinka: "There is no better dance. Much more passionate and graceful than the tarantella, it reaches the majesty and nobility of the mazurka."[60] The result of Balakirev's Caucasian enthusiasms were his symphonic poem *Tamara* and the piano fantasy *Islamey,* which elicited the praise of Franz Liszt, became popular with the public, and is still the touchstone for Russian piano virtuosi.

The extreme importance of Oriental motifs for the Mighty Five was underscored by Rimsky-Korsakov: "These new sounds were a sort of revelation for us then, we all were literally reborn."[61] He was the first in the group to write a major work of an Oriental character, the symphony *Antar* (1868), which was followed by his symphonic suite *Scheherazade,* still a staple of symphonic orchestras around the world.

A little-known episode in the history of Petersburg music is indicative of the importance for it of imperial themes. In 1880 the twenty-fifth anniversary of Alexander II's reign was marked with great pomp. Among other festivities *tableux vivants* were planned, depicting various significant moments of Alexander II's era, including Russia's military victories. The music for these "living pictures," commissioned by the government, was written by leading composers, including Rimsky-Korsakov, Mussorgsky, Borodin, and Tchaikovsky.

Mussorgsky's chauvinism is well known. It was second only to Balakirev's, whose religious fanaticism and anti-Semitism were legendary. The Polish characters in *Boris Godunov* are drawn with extreme antipathy; they are no less caricatures than the Poles in Glinka's *A Life for the Tsar,* which is particularly striking in the much more realistic and psychologically sophisticated opera by Mussorgsky.

Paradoxically, Mussorgsky's "Jewish" music hardly reflects his anti-Semitic feelings at all. The marvelous choruses "The Destruction of Sennacherib" and "Jesus Navin" (the musical theme for which

Mussorgsky borrowed from neighborly Jews), "Hebrew Song," as well as the famous "Two Jews, One Rich, One Poor" from *Pictures at an Exhibition* are imbued with respect for biblical Jewish figures but also with sympathy for modern Jewish people, who suddenly found themselves on the territory of the Russian Empire with the annexation of the Ukraine, Lithuania, and Poland, where millions of Jews resided.

In just the same way, Mussorgsky's orchestral march "The Capture of Kars," intended to accompany one of the living pictures in honor of the conquest of that Turkish fortress by Alexander II's army, is triumphant but by no means jingoistic. Moreover, Mussorgsky's vocal ballad "Forgotten," composed six years earlier, is one of the most powerful antiwar statements in world music. The remarkable story of its creation gives evidence of the existence inside Petersburg culture of a powerful opposition to its prevailing imperial ambitions.

In March 1874 the battle artist Vassily Vereshchagin opened an exhibit in Petersburg of his works, depicting the conquest of Turkestan by Russia. Diligently crafted, almost photographic in technique, his paintings re-created the highlights of the military actions in central Asia. A tireless laborer and flashy self-promoter, Vereshchagin knew how to present his works to best effect. They were dramatically lit, in later years with custom-built electric projectors, a recent innovation. The exhibit enjoyed a sensational success with the Petersburg public.

Astonishing in their naturalistic detail and unsettling in their fearless depiction of the horrors of war, Vereshchagin's canvases were enormously popular not only in Russia but also in Europe, where the artist was considered the best contemporary Russian painter, and in New York City, where Vereshchagin's exhibition of 1889 brought him $84,000, a large sum for those days.

To get into the Vereshchagin show in Petersburg, people spent hours in line, shivering in the cold spring wind. The Petersburg intelligentsia attended, including Stasov and Mussorgsky. The high military authorities were also there. And inevitably, a scandal broke out.

The estimable generals, deeply offended by what they saw, accused Vereshchagin of defaming the honor of the Russian military. They were particularly outraged by his painting *Forgotten*, which depicted the body of a dead Russian soldier abandoned by advancing troops. Next to the corpse lay his rifle, and a cloud of hungry vultures swirled over him. "It is impossible for Russian soldiers to be abandoned on a battlefield, unburied!" one of the generals shouted at the artist. Vereshchagin, who had gone through the entire Turkestan campaign in the front ranks of the fighting, was "half-crazed with anger and indignation," Stasov reported. The painter removed *Forgotten* and two other canvases that had provoked particular criticism and burned them.

"Vereshchagin came to me and told me what he had just done," Stasov recalled. "He was furious, pale and shaking. When I asked 'Why did you do it?' he replied that he had 'slapped those gentlemen with it.' "[62] With this gesture, unprecedented in Russian art history, the artist created a furor (as well as great publicity for his show). Meanwhile, the conservative press continued to attack with a vengeance Vereshchagin's "antipatriotic" paintings. They preferred the also extremely illusionistic but pro-imperial and promilitary war panoramas so popular in Russia in the late nineteenth century.

One of these panoramas, exhibited in a specially built round structure on the embankment of the Catherine Canal where Alexander II was soon to be assassinated, was described by Alexander Benois. The panorama depicted the capture of Kars (commemorated by Mussorgsky's orchestral march), and the boy Benois spent hours on the viewing platform, especially enjoying the "just-like-real" foreground: models of fortifications, bushes, cannons, scattered guns, and corpses of the defeated foe.[63]

Petersburg's cultural elite was involved in a fierce debate to resolve several fundamental questions that might arise in any aggressively expanding state that had not only a strong army but an independent intelligentsia. Among them were the following: what is more important, patriotism or humanism? Is the game worth playing? Do military victories only strengthen the oppressive state machine and enrich the top, or do they bring some benefits for the Russian "simple people" as well? And what about the conquered nations, their culture and customs? Should they be preserved, or is Russification inevitable and "progressive"?

The antiwar feelings among the Petersburg intellectuals was strong enough to guarantee Vereshchagin's show great success. But naturally, the pro-imperial forces were extremely active too, at the imperial court, in the newspapers, and in artistic circles. If the horrors of war must be depicted, they said, let it be the cruelty of the enemy, shown to the public for educational purposes, like, for instance, the popular painting *Turkish Atrocities*, a work of Konstantin Makovsky, a bon vivant favorite of the Petersburg aristocratic salons. They began talking about Makovsky's canvas after none other than Alexander II broke into tears upon seeing it. The artist had painted two fearsome Turks attacking a half-dressed Slavic girl. Among the small minority that did not like Makovsky's canvas was little Benois, who even as a child had rather independent tastes. As Benois later recalled, he thought the poor girl in the painting was simply drunk.[64]

Vereshchagin's burning of his antiwar paintings truly shocked the liberal segment of Petersburg society, which had great sympathy for the artist and was outraged by the military's pressure. Everyone understood that the artist had done something very important, creating a precedent and determining the positions of liberal culture vis-à-vis imperial Petersburg. Among those who reacted strongly to that symbolic act of defiance was Mussorgsky, who immediately decided to "resurrect" in sound Vereshchagin's lost painting, *Forgotten*.

That desire actually reflected some important ideals of the Mighty Five. First, they aspired to integrate music, word, and image, making them equal participants in the projected all-powerful union of the arts with literature. Mussorgsky was deeply convinced of the legitimacy of such a union. (And it was typical of the times that Vereshchagin also wrote prose and poetry, and even tried his hand at composing.) Then there was the passionate desire for music's active involvement in Russia's political and civic life. The expression of that desire was Mussorgsky's aphorism: "Art is a medium of conversing with people and not a goal."

Finally, on the part of Mussorgsky, there was the wish to preserve what a comrade in art had created. Such a brotherly impulse not to leave the work of your friends unfinished or destroyed was typical also for the other members of the Mighty Five; it became a Petersburg tradition. And so Dargomyzhsky's *Stone Guest,* several operas of Mussorgsky, and Alexander Borodin's opera *Prince Igor* were completed posthumously by the friends of the original creators.

This Petersburg ritual of preserving any creative spark dear to the heart was important for Shostakovich, too, who completed and orchestrated the opera *Rothschild's Violin,* by his student Veniamin Fleishman, fallen in the battle for Leningrad in 1941.

Composed to a specially written text by Arseny Golenishchev-Kutuzov, the author of the poems for Mussorgsky's song cycle *Sunless,* in the spirit of Dostoyevsky, Mussorgsky's "Forgotten" is striking in its lapidary expressiveness. Depicting in a mere twenty-seven measures not only a soldier's death in battle, his body devoured by vultures, but

also the sorrowful lullaby that appears and vanishes unexpectedly—
the song of the peasant woman who waits in vain for her husband—
Mussorgsky's small masterpiece of the ballad far surpasses
Vereshchagin's obvious and rhetorical painting, which we know from
reproductions. As in the case of *Pictures at an Exhibition,* the composer's tribute to an artist brought the work that served as his creative
impulse real fame and the recognition of posterity.

Mussorgsky's "Forgotten" was immediately banned by the Petersburg censors. This rare instance of a nervous reaction from the authorities to a musical ballad's political message only confirmed
Mussorgsky's ambitions regarding the civic potential of his beloved
art. So he continued to express his antiwar feelings in music by writing, three years later, "The Field Marshal," a part of his *Songs and
Dances of Death,* with words by Golenishchev-Kutuzov once again.
Here Death appears as a military leader riding in the quiet of the night
through the field after battle. Victory was Death's and not the soldiers', and he sings a wild, triumphant song to the majestic and grim
melody of a Polish anthem from the period of the anti-Russian uprising of 1862. (Its choice must have been dictated by Mussorgsky's anti-
Polish feelings.) The musical picture of Death on horseback, delivering
a mocking, cynical, howling monologue, is part of a European tradition; Albrecht Dürer's cycle of engravings or Liszt's *Totentanz,* which
appeared two decades before Mussorgsky's song, come to mind. But
Mussorgsky's song is filled with a purely Russian broad emotional-
ism and theatricality.

The piano accompaniment to "The Field Marshal" and the
other songs of that cycle achieves orchestral effects in its intensity and
drama, so it was natural for Shostakovich to orchestrate *Songs and
Dances of Death* in 1962. Seven years later, noting that he wanted to
continue Mussorgsky's "too short" cycle on death (only four pieces),
Shostakovich wrote his Fourteenth Symphony for soprano, bass, and
chamber orchestra, in which he obsessively added to the musical
gallery of death's appearances.

Mussorgsky is an interesting example of the Petersburg artist:
His vivid, nationalistic music not only lacks strong imperial traits, but,
because of its antimilitaristic tendencies, it was perceived by the authorities as being directed against the pillars of the state. For this reason Grand Duke Konstantin Nikolayevich, then the vice president of
the Imperial Russian Musical Society, stopped his son from applaud-
ing at the premiere of *Boris Godunov* and then shouted (according to
eyewitnesses), "This is a shame for all of Russia, not an opera!"[65]

　　Along with Mussorgsky, the other members of the Mighty Five, even those much more conservative in their political views, were "under suspicion." From the aesthetic point of view, they were all dangerous extremists as far as the emperor and his court were concerned. In addition, they all behaved independently, constantly coming into conflict with the official system of cultural administration. In disciplined Petersburg, and especially in the strictly regimented sphere of the imperial theaters, this was considered intolerable and could help explain why Alexander III, in reviewing the proposed repertoire for the imperial opera in 1888, not only crossed out *Boris Godunov* but put a question mark next to the planned premiere of *Prince Igor,* a most patriotic and perfectly "imperial" opera by Borodin.

Borodin, the oldest member of Balakirev's circle, was a physically hearty man almost to his last day. To everyone's surprise, he died unexpectedly in 1887 in his fifty-fourth year while at a costume ball. Fooling around and making everyone laugh, the composer suddenly leaned against a wall and fell dead to the floor. The diagnosis was a heart attack. He did not finish his major work, *Prince Igor,* on which he had worked with interruptions for eighteen years. A man of phenomenal musical gifts, Borodin had a multitude of other interests. He was an outstanding chemist and, as head of the chemistry department at the Petersburg Medical-Surgical Academy, quickly moved up the ladder, at thirty-three having a civil rank equivalent to general.

　　Chemistry constantly kept him from composing, as well as from numerous civic functions; in particular, Borodin, a staunch defender of women's rights, was one of the founders of the first medical courses for women in Russia. His colleagues at the academy found it strange that a talented scientist could be distracted by musical "trifles"; Petersburg suffragettes considered Borodin's struggle for equal rights for women to be his paramount activity. He himself seemed unable to decide which was the most important: science, civic duties, or composing.

　　Friends in the Mighty Five, who held Borodin's musical ability in high regard, were dismayed by his disregard of composition. Rimsky-Korsakov recalled bitterly his attempts to urge Borodin to work more diligently on *Prince Igor:*

> Sometimes you'd go see him and ask what he had done. And he'd show you a page or two of score or maybe nothing at all. You'd ask, "Alexander Porfiryevich, have you written?" And he'd reply, "I

have." It would turn out he's written a lot of letters. "Alexander Por-firyevich, have you at least arranged such-and-such a number?" "I have," he would reply seriously. "Thank God, at last!" "I arranged it to be moved from the piano to the table," he would continue just as seriously and calmly.[66]

After Borodin's untimely death Rimsky-Korsakov and his younger friend, Alexander Glazunov, completed and orchestrated *Prince Igor.* One of the main reasons for this noble deed was the cult of continuity that reigned in Petersburg, as well as the desire for a certain kind of art school, or at least a revolutionary circle like Balakirev's that functioned as a school, to remain intact.

In a city that seemed almost perfect in its architectural order-liness and completeness, the very idea of completeness was in the air, influencing creative people; every work, it seemed, had to be finished. This impulsive longing for order clearly affected Rimsky-Korsakov, the most Petersburgian in character and aesthetics of the Mighty Five. As the most professional of the group, Rimsky-Korsakov not only completed (with Cui) Dargomyzhsky's *Stone Guest,* completed and orchestrated Mussorgsky's *Khovanshchina,* edited and reorchestrated his *Boris Godunov,* and prepared his *Marriage* for publication, but edited (with friends) Glinka's opera scores.

Dedicated to Glinka, Borodin's *Prince Igor* continued the pa-triotic line of *A Life for the Tsar.* The plot of the opera, based on a Slavic epic text of the twelfth century, is suitably simple. The Russian Prince Igor goes on a campaign against the hostile Asiatic tribe of Polovtsians, is taken prisoner, and escapes. This spare story was de-veloped by Borodin in such a way as to make his work the most im-perial opera in the history of Russian music.

Two contrasting worlds are depicted in *Prince Igor*—the Rus-sian and the Polovtsian. Naturally, Borodin's sympathies are with the Russians, even though the composer was the illegitimate son of a Georgian (Imeretin) prince. Prince Igor is the ideal hero, first among equals, and he is supported by the boyars, the troops, and the people. He is the personification of Russian statehood as Borodin saw it: strong, just, civilizing. On the other hand, the nomadic barbarian Polovtsians, for whom the idea of the state is alien, live in a world of violence and destruction.

For Borodin the ethical superiority of Russians over Asiatics was obvious. But the composer's Caucasian roots gave him a subtle, intuitive understanding of Oriental musical material. This penchant for working with non-European motifs was earlier realized brilliantly by Borodin when he took part with other Russian composers in writing music for the *tableaux vivants* for the twenty-fifth anniversary of Alexander II's reign. Borodin's *In Central Asia* was the most successful and durable of the works composed for that official occasion. The symphonic picture with a vividness reminiscent of Vereshchagin's genre paintings from central Asia beautifully and eloquently re-created the atmosphere of Turkestan—languid but filled with a sense of hidden danger. Explaining his music, Borodin wrote in the program, "Through a vast desert comes a foreign caravan, guarded by Russian troops." In fact, *In Central Asia* is written from the point of view of the Russian soldier patrolling a vanquished Asian province; Borodin wholly identified with what he called the "Russian fighting might."

In contrast to *In Central Asia,* the music of the Polovtsians in *Prince Igor* is much more dynamic and imbued with a sensual joy approaching ecstasy. It is also militant and threatening. Borodin is clearly at home emotionally in the Polovtsian camp. He is not just an observer but practically a participant in the frenzied orgy. This is one of the obvious reasons why audiences all over the world are enchanted by the Polovtsian dances. The mind may resist their hypnotism, but they still work on the subconscious. And the impact of the music is even greater when performed out of context, as a separate symphonic or ballet number, thus severing the logical and intellectual bonds provided by the patriotic libretto.

Nevertheless, taken as a whole, *Prince Igor* is undoubtedly proclaiming the triumph of reason over emotion, and loyalty to a strong sovereign over the free-for-all of anarchy. Still, in 1888 the wary Alexander III, prejudiced against the aesthetically rebellious Mighty Five, had to be persuaded of the opera's propagandistic values.

Mitrofon Belyaev, the lumber millionaire and Petersburg patron of the arts, took on the difficult task. Following the prescribed Byzantine court procedures, he petitioned Alexander III to allow him to present the tsar with the printed score of *Prince Igor,* published at Belyaev's expense. If the sovereign accepted such a present, that would signal the rehabilitation of *Prince Igor;* the question mark hanging over the production would thus disappear. In the accompanying explanatory note the millionaire patron of the arts duly stressed the patriotic and loyal content of Borodin's opera. After some thought, Alexander III accepted the present, and the opera was restored in the repertory plans of the imperial theater.

The production of *Prince Igor* was opulent and extremely realistic; in particular, the costume and set designers studied Vereshcha-gin's central Asian paintings. The Polovtsian scenes required over two hundred people onstage. At the premiere the famous bass of the imperial stage, Fyodor Stravinsky, the father of the composer, Igor, stood out. From the opera's first performance on October 23, 1890, it was a hit with the Petersburg audience; according to contemporary accounts, the public "roared" in a surge of patriotic fervor.

Prince Igor had a profound effect on twenty-year-old Alexander Benois. Calling Borodin "a *dilettante* prophet of genius," Benois recalled later how the music of *Prince Igor* helped him cross the emotional bridge from the legendary world of ancient Russia and its "proud and noble rulers" to modern, imperial Petersburg. "Through it, Russian antiquity became close and familiar to me, a hardbitten Westernizer; this music beckoned me with its freshness, something primordial and healthy—the very things that touched me in Russian nature, in Russian speech, and in the very essence of Russian thought."[67]

The contagious patriotism of *Prince Igor* united such polar opposites as Sergei Diaghilev, the young aesthete and snob who never missed a performance of the new opera, and Alexei Suvorin, the conservative nationalist publisher of *Novoe vremya* (*New Times*), the largest newspaper in Petersburg. Suvorin, who never interfered with the music department of his quite glib publication, broke this rule to announce in print that the modern autocratic Russia is the continuation and apotheosis of the opera's central idea of the unity of people and ruler.

Borodin's music, including his three powerful symphonies, two string quartets, exquisite in beauty and inspiration, and a few lovely art songs, did not win great popularity in the West. In America, Borodin is best known through the musical *Kismet,* which was based on his melodies. *Prince Igor* is staged relatively infrequently, even though the Polovtsian dances, choreographed by Michel Fokine, which created a sensation in Diaghilev's Paris season of 1909, are familiar to lovers of ballet. But Borodin had a marked influence on Western musical professionals, especially the French impressionists. Both Debussy and Ravel were enchanted with his exotic melodies and unusual harmonic idiom. For the Western ear Borodin's Orientalism is the most significant and interesting aspect of his legacy.

But for Russian audiences, what is essential in Borodin—his opera and his symphonies, especially the second, the "Bogatyr"—is his patriotic appeal. This was confirmed yet again during World War

II, which the Russians call the Great Patriotic War. In those years the most popular opera, overshadowing both Mussorgsky and the eternal favorite, Tchaikovsky, was *Prince Igor*, along with Glinka's *A Life for the Tsar*, renamed *Ivan Susanin*, an epiclike and triumphant tale of the exploits of a Russian warrior and his passionate love of his homeland.

If Borodin can be called the leading proponent—in terms of talent and significance—of the imperial idea in Russian music, then Tchaikovsky comes immediately behind him. Such a coupling may seem unlikely only at first glance. After all, Tchaikovsky is a true child of Petersburg, the most imperial of imperial cities.

Boris Asafyev, the most perspicacious Russian specialist on Tchaikovsky, while insisting that only two great Russian cultural figures had felt at home in Petersburg—Pushkin and Dostoyevsky—would immediately add a third name: Tchaikovsky. In Petersburg the young Tchaikovsky graduated from law school with the title titular councillor, then served for over three years in the Ministry of Justice, living the typical life of a young clerk in the capital.

Like his friends, Titular Councillor Tchaikovsky spent his days properly writing draft resolutions on legal cases and his evenings strolling like a dandy along Nevsky Prospect, stopping at fashionable restaurants. He regularly attended dance halls, was an avid theatergoer, and enjoyed bachelor parties. Delighted by Petersburg society, Tchaikovsky announced, "I admit I have a great weakness for the Russian capital. What can I do? I've become too much a part of it. Everything that is dear to my heart is in Petersburg, and life without it is positively impossible for me."[68]

Tchaikovsky's career was progressing swiftly at the Ministry of Justice, and he soon became a court councillor. It came as a great surprise for many of his relatives when in 1862 Tchaikovsky's name was listed among the first students of the capital's conservatory, founded by Anton Rubinstein. Tchaikovsky's uncle, a highly proper gentleman, was embarrassed: "What a shame! To trade jurisprudence for a honker!"

His studies at the Petersburg conservatory made Tchaikovsky a real musical professional. But not only that. Introducing him to European principles and forms of organizing musical material, the conservatory training also gave the young composer a sense of belonging to world culture. This feeling became very important for Tchaikovsky's relations with Petersburg, since it saved the composer from the traditional conflicts with the city's cosmopolitan spirit, which were almost inescapable at that time in the circles of the artistic elite.

Becoming the bard of St. Petersburg was more natural and easier for the worldly Tchaikovsky than for any other Russian composer after Glinka. Petersburg was a musical melting pot. Italian tunes were whistled on Nevsky Prospect, and a few steps away one could hear an organ grinder playing a Viennese ländler. The emperor liked French operas, but there was also a tradition at the court, dating back to Empresses Elizabeth and Catherine the Great, to invite singers from the Ukraine to Petersburg.

Tchaikovsky soaked up the capital's music like a sponge: Italian arias from the stage of the imperial theater, French ditties and cancans, the solemn marches of military parades, and the sensuous waltzes that had conquered aristocratic Petersburg. The popular, melancholy Petersburg lieder called *romansy* held a special sway over Tchaikovsky's imagination. They were beautiful, darkly erotic flowers that grew in fashionable salons after a complex cross-fertilization of Russian folk tunes and Italian arias. Glinka and a group of Russian amateur composers had worked over the creation of this strange and attractive hybrid. Spicy notes of anguish and passion, borrowed from Gypsy songs that filled Petersburg at that time, were added to their refined creations.

The Petersburg *romansy,* shaded with Gypsy idiom, lost their hothouse tenderness when they boldly crossed the threshold from the fashionable salons to real life. And yet, they became the delight of the broad masses of Russian music lovers, the Russian pop music of its time. The comfortably sentimental and sad or sensually passionate formulas of the *romansy* appeared more than once—reworked and ennobled—in Tchaikovsky's music.

Musicians sometimes joke that Tchaikovsky wrote three symphonies—the Fourth, Fifth, and Sixth. In fact, his first three symphonies are rarely performed in the West or in Russia. But it is in the early symphonies that young Tchaikovsky's imperial inclinations manifest themselves most vividly.

Elevated by Tchaikovsky's genius, the whole variety of musical sounds from his St. Petersburg lives on in these first three symphonies: the sorrowful marches, the aristocratic, sultry waltzes, the *romansy* of its salons and suburbs, the ballet scenes and arias from its imperial stages, music of its folk festivities, fairs, and holidays.

The finales of Tchaikovsky's early symphonies are without exception anthems, imperial apotheoses. A Russian folk song is heard in the finale of the First Symphony; in the finale of the Second, there is a Ukrainian folk song; and a polonaise is introduced in the last movement of the Third Symphony. At the time, Poland and the Ukraine belonged to the Russian Empire. Tchaikovsky's integration of those themes into the framework of his symphonies, Petersburgian in form and content, signifies his support of the unification of various nations under the aegis of the Russian tsar, whose titles included Tsar of Kiev, of Poland, of Georgia, Lord of Lithuania, Volhynia, Podolia, and Finland, Prince of Estonia, Livonia, Karelia, Bulgaria, Lord and Sovereign of the countries of Iveria, Kabardinia and the provinces of Armenia, Lord of Turkestan, etc. Tchaikovsky also exploited the emotional and symbolic possibilities of the Russian anthem, "God Save the Tsar," to the fullest extent. It is included, with all its psychological and political overtones, in two of Tchaikovsky's popular orchestral works: *Slavonic March* (1876) and the *1812 Overture* (1880).

Tchaikovsky wrote *Slavonic March* in support of one of the most cherished ideas of imperial Russia—Pan-Slavism. Like an overwhelming majority of educated Russians, Tchaikovsky fervently hoped for the unification of all the Slavic people of southeastern Europe under Russia. When in 1876 little Serbia arose against Turkish hegemony, the atmosphere in Russia—where everyone seemed to root for the brave Serbs—became so electric that the performance of *Slavonic March* with its Serbian folk melodies inevitably elicited outbursts of patriotism and noisy political demonstrations. Tchaikovsky, who liked to conduct this work himself, was enormously pleased. His satisfaction with the propagandistic role of his music was profound and probably the most sincere of all Russian composers; it was certainly more sincere than the later cases of Prokofiev and Shostakovich.

The *1812 Overture* sang the glory of the greatest military and political victory of the ruling Romanov dynasty, in the Patriotic War against Napoleon. This dramatic and triumphant composition became (like *Slavonic March*) a warhorse in the West, but in the Soviet Union it was not performed in its original version for over seventy years. Instead, the Soviets provided a doctored version. The Soviet composer Shebalin performed a musical vivisection, removing the imperial anthem. A similar fate befell the *Slavonic March*.

Also deliberately forgotten were Tchaikovsky's sacred works for chorus (whose existence is due to Alexander III's personal commission), as well as his *Liturgy of Saint John Chrysostom* and the *Ves-*

per Service. When Balanchine was preparing his Tchaikovsky festival at the New York City Ballet in 1981, I reminded him about the composer's sacred music. Balanchine, a deeply devout man and a fanatic admirer of Tchaikovsky, was very interested and asked me to bring him a recording of the liturgy. He returned the record to me with a curt, "It's no Bach."

As is known from his letters and diaries, Tchaikovsky's attitude toward religion was ambivalent. But he considered composing sacred music as an act of loyalty and patriotism, a gift on the altar of the fatherland, so it became one of the important aspects of the imperial theme in Tchaikovsky's work.

In 1877 Russia, inspired by Pan-Slavic slogans, declared war on Turkey. Tchaikovsky, along with almost the entire Petersburg intelligentsia, followed with avid interest the actions of the Russian troops, headed by Alexander III and his sons. As never before, the composer had the sense of being an organic part, emotionally and creatively, of the great empire. For some time, the usually extremely self-centered Tchaikovsky even forgot his own, sometimes quite dramatic troubles. "It's shameful to shed tears for oneself," he confessed in a letter, "when the country is shedding blood in the name of a common cause."[69]

But in a strange way, the Fourth Symphony, which Tchaikovsky wrote during the Russo-Turkish War, turned out to be a first step away from his earlier imperial interpretation of that genre. In the Fourth the protagonist steps beyond the limits of the ritual relations of society and state. We know of a letter from Tchaikovsky to his benefactress, Nadezhda von Meck, in which he devotes a long passage to the hidden program of the Fourth, describing it as an attempt of man to avoid his fate. In the composer's melodramatic explanation, a "fateful force" hangs over the autobiographical hero "which does not allow his desire for happiness to reach its goal."

In the finale of the Fourth Symphony, Tchaikovsky puts the lone individual in conflict with society for the first time. Here this conflict is still resolved by subordinating the personal to the collective. Tchaikovsky comments, "If you can't find reason for happiness in yourself, look to other people. Go out among the people. . . . Feel the joy of others. Life is possible, after all."[70] But in the Fifth Symphony, written eleven years later (1888), such a compromise between hero and society is no longer possible. And in the finale the alienated protagonist must observe a pompous triumphal parade from the side.

(This musical philosophical idea was used with tremendous effect by Shostakovich in the finale of his Fifth Symphony, in the tragic year 1937.)

The Sixth Symphony *(Pathétique)*, written not long before Tchaikovsky's death, depicts the tragic confrontation of the individual and fate and mourns his final, total destruction. This most popular of Tchaikovsky's symphonies is perhaps his most pessimistic work. I find in it a distant conceptual echo with Richard Wagner's *Götterdämmerung*.

In the first movement of the *Pathétique* Tchaikovsky quotes the funeral chorale of the Russian Orthodox service, "Rest among the saints." In conversations with close friends Tchaikovsky readily admitted that the symphony presents the story of his life, in which the last movement plays the part of De Profundis, a prayer for the dead. But even the very first listeners, who knew nothing about its hidden program, guessed that the Pathétique might be the composer's artistic farewell to this world. After the last rehearsal of the symphony, conducted by Tchaikovsky, Grand Duke Konstantin Konstantinovich, a talented poet and fervent admirer of the composer, ran into the green room weeping and exclaiming, "What have you done, it's a requiem, a requiem!"

On October 16, 1893, the *Pathétique* was premiered in a charged atmosphere of the white-columned Assembly of the Nobility. Prolonged ovation greeted the appearance of the rather short but slender, elegant Tchaikovsky at the podium. The composer's handsome face, with still dark eyebrows and mustache framed by silvery hair and a neatly trimmed gray beard, was pale as usual, but his cheeks were flushed with excitement.

Tchaikovsky began conducting with the baton held tightly in his fist, again in his usual way. But when the final sounds of the symphony had died away and Tchaikovsky slowly lowered the baton, there was dead silence in the audience. Instead of applause, stifled sobs came from various parts of the hall. The audience was stunned and Tchaikovsky stood there, silent, motionless, his head bowed.

"The symphony is life for Tchaikovsky," Asafyev once noted. In Asafyev's flowery description the *Pathétique* "captures the very instant of the soul's parting from the body, the instant of the life force radiating into space, into eternity."[71] This is the opinion of Tchaikovsky's younger contemporary, who knew many of his friends well; so we can be certain that the Petersburg elite read Tchaikovsky's last work as a tragic novel with a sorrowful epilogue. And inevitably next to

Tchaikovsky's name arose that of Dostoyevsky. In a typical passage, another contemporary wrote of the composer and the writer, "With a hidden passion they both stop at moments of horror, total spiritual collapse, and finding acute sweetness in the cold trepidation of the heart before the abyss, they both force the reader or the listener to experience these feelings, too."[72]

Tchaikovsky and Dostoyevsky once met at a mutual friend's house in the fall of 1864; neither left any reminiscences about the meeting. But we know that Tchaikovsky read Dostoyevsky eagerly all his life, sometimes taking delight, sometimes rejecting his writings. The Brothers Karamazov captivated the composer at first, but as he continued to read, he felt depressed. "This is becoming intolerable. Every single character is crazy."[73] Tchaikovsky's final conclusion was, "Dostoyevsky is a genius, but an antipathetic writer."[74]

Yet the congeniality of Tchaikovsky and Dostoyevsky, as we have seen, was acutely felt by the composer's younger contemporaries. They equated Tchaikovsky's symphonies, beginning with the Fourth, with psychological novels in the center of which—for the first time in Russian music—was an ambivalent, suffering personality. Like Dostoyevsky's characters, Tchaikovsky's hero persisted in exploring the meaning of life while trapped in the fatal love-death-faith triangle in the best Dostoyevskian fashion.

Tchaikovsky conveyed in music this Dostoyevskian confusion about life's mysteries and contradictions using techniques characteristic of Dostoyevsky's novels, including the writer's favorite piling up of events and emotions leading to a catastrophic, climactic explosion.

The frenzied longing for love, which saturates many pages of Tchaikovsky's symphonies, also fills Dostoyevsky's novels, while the other pole of the same passion, typical of both, is the fascination with and fear of death, combined with the need to confront it.

Compare Tchaikovsky's attitude toward death with Mussorgsky's. Mussorgsky was close to Dostoyevsky in describing the tragedy of a lonely soul in the social desert of the city. But the theme of death as interpreted by Mussorgsky clearly belongs to another era. For all its expressiveness and drama, Mussorgsky's vocal cycle Songs and Dances of Death is still a series of grand romantic pictures in music. Mussorgsky observes death from offstage, as if from the sidelines.

For Mussorgsky the most perplexing mystery is life, not death. For Tchaikovsky the opposite is true, and this brings him so much closer to Dostoyevsky. For Tchaikovsky as for Dostoyevsky, fate is synonymous with death. Tchaikovsky's notes explaining the hidden

"program" of the Fifth Symphony are very significant: "The fullest sub-
mission before fate, or, which is the same thing, before the inexplicable
predestination of Providence." Reading this, one can almost feel the
pain that fatalism and pessimism bring down upon Tchaikovsky. And
he instantly adds (this note relating to the second movement of the
Fifth): "Should one throw oneself into the arms of faith???"[75]

But such a move, so profound and natural for Dostoyevsky,
and so tempting for Tchaikovsky, did not become the lever of the composer's late output. He never really threw himself into the arms of
faith, and so the theme of St. Petersburg became a kind of creative anchor for the mature Tchaikovsky. Being one of the builders of the Petersburg mythos took on special significance for Tchaikovsky: in
creating that mythos, he pushed aside the horrible images of triumphant death from his creative consciousness.

Depicting Petersburg and its themes in his symphonies, Tchaikovsky
covered a path in a quarter of a century that took the rest of Russian
culture one hundred and fifty years to traverse. In his first three symphonies the composer's delight in the brilliant atmosphere of the imperial capital with its colorful parades and opulent balls is evident.
This attitude is similar to that of the early bards of Petersburg. But
even in those first three symphonies, Tchaikovsky's pleasure is already
complicated by the intrusion of new images. They are, first of all, genre
pictures, scenes of festivities on the streets and squares of the city;
these impressions are close in spirit to the young Gogol.

Tchaikovsky also introduces here a clearly melancholy note,
which does not permit the listener to forget that the author lives in
the second half of the nineteenth century. This melancholy is sharply
on the rise in Tchaikovsky's Fourth Symphony, where the sentimental pity for a solitary soul, lost in the metropolis, makes us recall Dostoyevsky's *White Nights*. In his late symphonies, Tchaikovsky
noticeably universalizes this conflict between the individual and society. On the one hand, it seems to shoot upward, into the vistas of the
universe, presenting the individual arguing with fate. On the other
hand, the individual poses tragic questions to himself and himself
alone, in the style of Dostoyevsky.

The sense of doom permeates Tchaikovsky's *Pathétique*. This
feeling, absolutely uncharacteristic of Dostoyevsky, also betrays the
composer's attitude toward Petersburg. In mourning himself, solip-
sistic Tchaikovsky mourns the demise of the world. That is why the
Sixth Symphony can be seen not only as a requiem for the individual

but also for the city and its society. Tchaikovsky's musical soul was among the first to perceive the coming cataclysms of war and revolution. No one understood yet that the culture of Petersburg was doomed. Tchaikovsky did not understand it, either. He just felt the breath of doom's approach. This breath tinged his music, as it would a mirror, making it foggy and ambiguous. Nonetheless, it did register a recognizable picture of St. Petersburg.

Dostoyevsky, for his part, hated Peter the Great and his creation—this alien colossus, a city hostile to the Russian spirit, a foreign body forcing itself into Russian space and subjugating it to its evil will. Dostoyevsky's passionate desire was Petersburg's total obliteration. Mussorgsky, too, shared much of Dostoyevsky's attitude toward Peter and his reforms; one can find ample evidence in *Khovanshchina*, in which the anti-Petrine forces are presented with understanding and profound sympathy. Tchaikovsky, by intuitively grasping and emotionally experiencing the imaginary destruction of the empire and of Petersburg as if it were real, went beyond Mussorgsky and Dostoyevsky. Tchaikovsky felt somehow that doom was around the corner, and, being a composer, he shouted it out as loudly and clearly as he could, filling his music with hysterical warning.

In this reaction, Tchaikovsky became the first Russian composer with a profound nostalgia toward Petersburg. The nostalgic motifs of his music, intertwining with delight for Mozart and the eighteenth century, gave us *Variations on a Rococo Theme* for cello and orchestra (1876) and the *Mozartiana* suite (1887), so beloved by Balanchine. But Tchaikovsky's nostalgia, his intuitive horror before the coming revolutionary catastrophe, and his pity for Petersburg were reflected with particular power in his ballets and his opera *The Queen of Spades*. It was in these works that the transformation of the Petersburg mythos began to crystallize in the late 1870s and early 1880s.

Yet the city still stood and was reflected in the steely Neva River, apparently unperturbed by the tumult surrounding it. Its mythology had begun before its history, developed in time with it, and was transformed from the imperial to the romantic to an evil and fatalistic aura by men of genius. And still it stood, prepared for the next transformation, stately and seemingly impassive.

This new transformation was driven in tandem by music and the visual arts, a pairing which was highly unusual for Russia, where literature had always reigned supreme. Russia was and still is a logo-centric country, however strange that idea may seem to Western fans of Russian music, ballet, and the Russian pictorial avant-garde. There-fore, it was only natural that the original mythos of Petersburg em-anated from literature: first the Petersburg of Pushkin, then of Gogol, and of Dostoyevsky, each building upon, enriching and ultimately dis-placing, if not entirely replacing, the preceding. By the early 1880s, the Petersburg of Dostoyevsky, subsuming the imagery of Pushkin and Gogol, reigned unchallenged in Russian culture.

And then Tchaikovsky appeared on the scene. His music gave a new impetus to the Petersburgian theme in art, freeing it of the dic-tates of literature. Tchaikovsky's *Queen of Spades* is the prime exam-ple of this trend.

Pushkin's prose novella *The Queen of Spades* (1833) is one of his most Petersburgian works. This is a tale about Ghermann, the ob-sessed gambler trying to learn the secret of the three winning cards from the old countess; eventually he loses his fortune and his love and goes mad. Pushkin's story contains many of the motifs found in the predominantly literary mythos of Petersburg. Pushkin's narrative is restrained, dry, almost ironic; it makes the reader more willing to be-lieve that anything is possible in the city described, including the ap-pearance of a dead countess. Here, in Pushkin's characteristically laconic form, even the landscape of Petersburg foreshadows the fu-ture, much wordier depictions of Gogol and Dostoyevsky: "The weather was awful: the wind howled, wet snow fell in big flakes; the lamps glowed dimly; the streets were empty."

Fifty-seven years later, in the opera based on the Pushkin story (with the libretto by Tchaikovsky's brother, Modeste), the composer altered the hero's name minimally, from Ghermann to Gherman, but in his reinterpretation the plot and characters of *The Queen of Spades* underwent much more serious changes. Some of them are natural be-cause it was a question of creating a grand melodramatic opera from a compressed prose work. But many of the changes were derived from Tchaikovsky's completely different feelings toward Petersburg. As Asafyev colorfully reports,

> The poison of Petersburg nights, the sweet mirage of its ghostly im-ages, the fogs of autumn and the bleak joys of summer, the coziness and acute contradictions of Petersburg life, the meaningless waste of Petersburg sprees and the amorous longing of Petersburg's romantic

rendezvous, delicious meetings and secret promises, cold disdain and indifference of a man of society for superstition and ritual right up to blasphemous laughter about the other-worldly and at the same time the mystical fear of the unknown—all these moods and sensations poisoned Tchaikovsky's soul. He carried that poison with him always, and his music is imbued with it.[76]

There was none of that romantic "poison" in Pushkin. For Pushkin, the Petersburg of *The Queen of Spades* is a place with a glorious past and future and with a delightful and maybe sometimes slightly mysterious present. In this tale he does not even contemplate the possible doom of the city. Pushkin hides his love for Petersburg beneath irony and uses supernatural events as mere props.

In *The Bronze Horseman,* Pushkin is much more serious and full of pathos; there Petersburg is the symbol of Russia, and Pushkin interprets contradictions to the Petersburg existence as contradictions to the Russian historical path. Still the poet is convinced of the "unshakability" of the imperial capital, though he doubts that the horrible human price paid for that unshakability was justified.

When Tchaikovsky wrote works with an historical or heroic theme, the patriotic idea in them always prevailed; therefore, it is useless to seek psychological depth in them. But in his late works, Petersburg's ambiance is psychologized in the extreme. Here people do not think about the fate of the state but only about love, life, and death. Death triumphs in *The Queen of Spades:* the countess dies (as in Pushkin), but the main characters—Gherman and his love, Liza—die too. And their death predicts the fall of Petersburg itself. Once it is perceived, this sense of the city's doom is impossible to ignore, it so suffuses the music.

Tchaikovsky's psychological identification with Gherman, rare even for the extremely sensitive composer, is well known. The fateful scene—the appearance of the countess's ghost, who tells Gherman the secret of the three winning cards—so deeply disturbed Tchaikovsky that he feared the ghost would come to him as well. When writing Gherman's death scene, the composer wept out loud. In the diary of Tchaikovsky's manservant, there is a notation naively describing the feverish composition of *The Queen of Spades* (the opera was written in forty-four days) and Tchaikovsky's hysterical compassion for his hero: "he cried all that night, his eyes were still red, he was very exhausted. . . . He felt sorry for poor Gherman."[77]

In Pushkin, the confrontation between Ghermann and the ghost of the countess is presented rather ironically and skeptically. For Tchaikovsky this scene presented an opportunity to look into the "other world" and perhaps even to establish some kind of occult contact. Asafyev indicated that in Tchaikovsky's *Queen of Spades* the scene with the ghost sounded like a musical incantation, and he insisted that for a religious person to write it that way was blasphemous. Asafyev compared that episode with Dostoyevsky's famous story "Bobok," in which the writer tries to guess what the buried but not yet decomposed former residents of Petersburg talk about in a cemetery.

In this case, too, the difference with a work of literature is striking. In *The Queen of Spades* we do not find a trace of the cynicism inherent in "Bobok," for Tchaikovsky obviously sensed that the times when the Petersburg theme could be handled in such a way were gone. As far as the composer was concerned, the curtain was coming down. Mourning Gherman at the end of the opera with a lofty and gloomy chorale, Tchaikovsky mourned Petersburg and himself, as he would later do in the *Pathétique*. It was because Tchaikovsky tied Gherman's fate to the fate of the Russian capital (and of himself as well) that it became such a psychologically vibrant symbol of the new era of Petersburg's culture.

And as is almost inevitable in Russia, this cultural transformation could not have been achieved without the help of Pushkin's omnipresent spirit. But while Pushkin's *Bronze Horseman* dominated the "literary" stage of Petersburg's cultural history all by itself, his *Queen of Spades* could be transformed, or rather, almost completely dissolved in the waves of Tchaikovsky's music in order to take part in the fading away of the old mystique of Petersburg and the creation of a new one.

Chronicling the creation of *The Queen of Spades,* the naive but considerate manservant noted, "If, God willing, Peter Ilyich finishes composing just as well as he started, and this opera is seen and heard on the stage, then, probably, following the example of Peter Ilyich, many will shed a tear."

And in fact, many did shed tears when *The Queen of Spades* was first performed at the Maryinsky Theater, on December 5, 1890. That premiere can be considered a symbolic and, in many ways, pivotal moment. A group of young Petersburgians who tried not to miss a single performance of a Tchaikovsky opera or, for that matter, of his ballet *Sleeping Beauty,* produced at the Maryinsky earlier that year, used Tchaikovsky's music as the catalyst in the formation of the new Petersburg mythos.

The leader of the group, who dubbed themselves the Nevsky Pickwickians, was twenty-year-old Alexander Benois, the son of a wealthy and influential Petersburg architect. The Benois family had Italian, French, and German roots. Alexander's maternal great-grandfather, who came to Russia from Venice in the late eighteenth century, was named "director of music" of Petersburg by Nicholas I in 1832; his grandfather was the architect of the Maryinsky Theater. A curious detail: entering upon marriage, Benois's Catholic grandfather and Lutheran grandmother agreed, to avoid religious friction in the family, that their male descendants would be Catholic and the females Lutheran. Alexander Benois felt that this decision contributed to his family's tradition of broad-mindedness and tolerance, both religious and aesthetic.

Interested in both painting and music, Benois was sent to Karl May's private school, one of the best in Petersburg. There he befriended Dmitri Filosofov, Konstantin Somov, and Walter Nouvel, and in the best Petersburg tradition founded a circle they called the Society for Self-Education. The club members were only sixteen and seventeen years old. They usually met at the Benois apartment and took turns giving diligently prepared lectures on music, art, and philosophy, followed by lively discussions.

Soon the Pickwickians were joined by the young artist Leo Rozenberg, who later became famous under his pseudonym, Leon Bakst; elected "speaker" of the club, he moderated the debates. That they sometimes grew heated is evidenced by the fact that the bronze bell Bakst used for calling his friends to order eventually cracked.

The Nevsky Pickwickians considered themselves Petersburg cosmopolites. As Benois recalled, they "valued the idea of some sort of united humanity." In their intense dreams the young club members imagined no less a feat than bringing Russian art out of isolation and into Europe. But those dreams would have been nothing more than that if their group had not been joined by Filosofov's cousin from the provinces—a young, energetic, and self-confident charmer named Sergei Diaghilev.

The country cousin was the startling opposite of the thin, pale, and restrained Petersburger Filosofov. Benois recalled that Diaghilev astounded them with his un-Petersburgian appearance. "He had round rosy cheeks and sparkling white teeth, which showed as two even rows between his bright red lips."[78] Diaghilev, who had a re-sounding baritone, dreamed of becoming a singer; he also took lessons in composition at the Petersburg conservatory. But he was almost completely ignorant about art, and his literary tastes were equally embarrassing to his new friends.

Benois took up the education of Diaghilev, acting for many years as his mentor and, as Benois called himself, his "intellectual protector." Diaghilev amazed Benois with his uncommon abilities: "with wild leaps he went from total ignorance and indifference to a demanding and even passionate study"[79] of European and Russian culture. Benois observed in astonishment as his "beloved and most colorful student" became a specialist, almost instantly, in—say—the little-studied, arcane realm of eighteenth-century Russian art. But Benois always considered Diaghilev's main talent to be his willpower—to which he added energy, stubbornness, and a considerable understanding of human psychology: "He, who was too lazy to read a novel and who yawned while listening even to a most interesting lecture, was capable of spending a long time to study carefully the novel's author or the lecturer himself. The ensuing verdict was always acutely accurate and insightful."[80]

Even before Diaghilev arrived in Petersburg, Tchaikovsky was one of his favorite composers. But his adoration had been naive and provincial, with a preference for the more emotional melodies ("explosions of lyricism," in Benois's expression), not respect filtered through intellect and taste, as was the case among St. Petersburg's elite. Under Benois's careful tutelage Diaghilev's delight in Tchaikovsky turned into a focused admiration that was bound to have important consequences for the future of Russian culture in general and the fate of the Petersburg mythos in particular.

For Benois the Tchaikovsky cult began somewhat earlier, with the Maryinsky Theater premiere of one of Tchaikovsky's most evocative Petersburgian works, the ballet *The Sleeping Beauty*. Rather prejudiced against Russian composers at the time, the Westernizer Benois was unexpectedly struck by "something endlessly close and dear" in Tchaikovsky's music. It appeared, Benois felt, as if in response to an unconscious expectation and immediately became "his own" for Benois, infinitely and vitally important. So Benois tried not to miss a single performance of *Sleeping Beauty;* one week he went four times. For Benois and his friends, it was the perfect embodiment of their own inchoate and immature aesthetic.

The Nevsky Pickwickians were attracted to Tchaikovsky's

Western orientation, in this case the special scent of Francophilia—
the libretto was based on Charles Perrault's fairy tale *La Belle au bois
dormant*—but also the traditions of German romanticism. In *Beauty*'s
music Benois heard the echoes of the "world of captivating nightmares" of his beloved writer E. T. A. Hoffmann. Benois was drawn
to Tchaikovsky and at the same time frightened by the "mix of strange
truth and convincing invention"[81] not unlike Hoffmann's.

Another enchanting quality of Tchaikovsky's music for Benois
was what he called its "passé-ism." By this Benois meant not only
adoring the past as such or Tchaikovsky's particular talent for stylization but the vibrant sense of the past as being the present. This great
gift of Tchaikovsky's, "something like beatitude," according to
Benois, connected to an acute anticipation of death and a "real sense
of the otherworldly." Benois found a brotherly artistic soul in
Tchaikovsky, who, he thought, was, like all the Nevsky Pickwickians,
also attracted to the "kingdom of shadows," where "not only separate individuals but entire eras live on."[82] And the *Sleeping Beauty*
production itself, in which so many masters came together—the composer, the choreographer Marius Petipa, the designers, and the outstanding dancers—became for Benois an example of the endless
possibilities of ballet as a true Gesammtkunstwerk.

In those days, few people had a serious interest in ballet. In educated Petersburg circles ballet was despised, an echo of the nihilist
ideas of the 1860s. Benois, who had loved ballet in his youth, was beginning to cool toward it when his fierce passion for *The Sleeping
Beauty* turned him into an ardent balletomane once more.

So Benois, the eternal proselytizer, infected all his friends with
his fanatical enthusiasm for *The Sleeping Beauty,* first among them
Diaghilev, who moved to Petersburg a year and half after the ballet's
premiere. Without his newly kindled balletomania, claimed Benois,
there would have been none of Diaghilev's Russian Seasons in Paris,
nor his famous ballet company, nor the subsequent worldwide triumph of the Russian ballet.

After the cultural awakening caused by *The Sleeping Beauty,*
Benois and his friends awaited impatiently the premiere of *The Queen
of Spades*. Benois's circle, Diaghilev included, was present in full force
that evening at the Maryinsky Theater. The audience's reaction to the
new opera was rather restrained, but Benois was immediately "enthralled by a flame of rapture." Tchaikovsky's music, he recalled, "literally *drove me mad,* turned me into some kind of visionary for a
time. . . . it took on the force of an incantation, through which I could

penetrate into the world of shadows that had been beckoning me for such a long time."[83]

The Queen of Spade's passé-ism took on special significance for the Nevsky Pickwickians because it was directed not at Europe, so dear to their hearts yet remote, but at the city in which they lived. Benois explained:

> I instinctively adored Petersburg's charms, its unique romance, but at the same time there was much that I did not like in it, and there were even some things that offended my taste with their severity and "officiousness." Now through my delight in *The Queen of Spades* I saw the light. . . . Now I found that captivating poetry, whose presence I had only guessed at, everywhere I looked."[84]

This was one of the most startling and magical moments in the evolution of the nearly two-hundred-year-old Petersburg mythos. That mystique had begun with paeans to Peter the Great's imperial ambitions. Then Pushkin in his *Bronze Horseman* tried to weight the scales. Which would weigh more: a new capital or the fate of the pathetic clerk crushed by Peter's will? Neither Gogol nor Dostoyevsky after him ever bothered with that question. Gogol's grotesque city and Dostoyevsky's supposedly realistic cauldron of hell were both places where "little" people suffered and died. The city as mirage, as giant octopus, great and heartless deceiver, eternal foreigner on Russian soil—that was the image of Petersburg inherited from Gogol and Dostoyevsky. In Russia's literature-centered culture of the 1880s, that terrible image became almost universally accepted.

Any casual description of Petersburg in those days had to begin with Gogol and Dostoyevsky (and usually end there); crowds of imitators exploited and vulgarized the imagery of their illustrious predecessors, and Petersburg under their pens turned from a mysterious and fateful capital into a prosaic and boring place. The fantastic realism of Dostoyevsky's urban landscapes turned into dreary naturalism with his followers. The mirage dissipated. The formerly imposing Petersburg houses, no longer concealing mystical or criminal revelations, turned into gray, empty shells. Sometimes it seemed that if Petersburg were to vanish suddenly, in accordance with Dostoyevsky's feverish wish and stark prophesy, no one would notice. Even the once-commanding mystique of Petersburg was close to disappearing, because there was no longer any mystery about the city.

Benois and his friends not only reinvigorated that mythos, they managed to give it a new content. This transformation, itself miraculous and unique, had its own inner logic.

The first shifts can be seen with a close look at the universe of Dostoyevsky himself, a writer who was obsessive but not at all dogmatic. Dostoyevsky was a passionate nationalist, but he also had a trait that Osip Mandelstam would later term "a longing for world culture." In his famous speech on Pushkin, given in 1880, Dostoyevsky called for the Russian "to become brother to all men, *uniman,* if you will." The result of his musing on the "European" essence of Pushkin's work, this neologism represented Dostoyevsky's conclusion that Pushkin's works held a prophetic call to "universal unity."

Dostoyevsky's speech, hailed throughout the land with unprecedented acclaim, was the milestone from which some of his younger contemporaries marked the new period in Russian culture: they saw in it a rejection of the nationalist-isolationist path, which was leading to a dead end, and an appeal for the expansion and therefore the renewal of the Russian artistic tradition.

Dostoyevsky's ideas were particularly compelling for Tchaikovsky, who reacted morbidly to the Mighty Five's criticism that he was not "Russian" enough. In his memoirs Benois states that in "progressive" musical circles "it was considered obligatory to treat Tchaikovsky as a renegade, a master overly dependent on the West." Tchaikovsky, naturally enough, knew this. That is why in his notebook covering 1888–1889, amid addresses and other notations there is a note made by the composer before his trip to Prague, where he would have to appear frequently at various receptions in his honor: "Start speech with Dostoyevsky's *uniman.*"

Tchaikovsky was, probably, the first great Russian composer to think seriously about the place of Russian music in European culture. He regularly conducted his compositions in the West, forming close business and friendly ties with many of the leading musicians of Europe and the United States; for Russians this was also new and unusual. Typical is a letter from Paris, in which Tchaikovsky somewhat wistfully tells his patroness, Nadezhda von Meck, "How pleasant it is to be convinced firsthand of the success of our literature in France. Every book *étalage* displays translations of Tolstoy, Turgenev, and Dostoyevsky.... The newspapers are constantly printing rapturous articles about one or another of these writers. Perhaps such a time will come for Russian music as well!"[85]

This remark clearly shows Tchaikovsky's impatient anticipation of a person like Diaghilev, whose central idea would be the promotion of Russian culture in the West. Young Diaghilev's manifesto might have been his memorable words: "I want to nurture Russian painting, clean it up and, most important, present it to the West, elevate it in the West." Subsequently, Diaghilev did exactly this and, of course, for much more than just painting.

On October 26, 1892, the writer Dmitri Merezhkovsky gave a lecture in Petersburg on "The Reasons for the Decline of Russian Literature." A reporter for the mass circulation *Novoye vremya* summarized it this way: " 'We are standing on the brink of an abyss,' announced Merezhkovsky, recommending that we seek salvation from contemporary French decadents."[86] After many years of dominance by nationalistic, utilitarian, and nihilistic ideas, the Petersburg artistic elite sensed that Russian culture was in crisis. Once again, it turned to the West, wanting to be in step with the latest European cultural developments. And this is what Merezhkovsky really proclaimed. His lecture, which aroused great interest—among the respondents were Leo Tolstoy and Chekhov—actually signaled the appearance of the first fledgling modernist movement in Russia—symbolism.

Merezhkovsky called for "an expansion of artistic impressionability." This "new impressionability" ought to be learned, he lectured, from Western masters: besides the French symbolists Merezhkovsky also named the then-popular Edgar Alan Poe and Ibsen; but he also included as allies the revered classics of Russian literature. Benois immediately joined Merezhkovsky's "decadent" movement, and they were even friends for a time. Later the sober Petersburgian Benois would confess that he joined out of a mistaken desire to appear "avantgarde." "It was the time of the typical fin de siècle, whose preciousness and modernity were expressed in the cult (at least in words) of everything depraved with an admixture of all kinds of mysticism, often turning into mystification."[87]

The "anti-bohemian" Benois was particularly put off by Merezhkovsky's wife, the "decadent" poetess Zinaida Hippius. Always dressed all in white ("Like the princess of Dreams"), a tall, thin, pretty blonde with a Mona Lisa smile always playing on her lips, and never tiring of striking a pose (in Benois's opinion), Hippius stood in sharp contrast to her short, scrawny, shy husband. The very first question Hippius asked of Benois and his friends was, "And you, gentlemen students, what are you decadent about?"

Ideas for renewal and change were in the air of Petersburg, but no one knew just how to realize them. A few years later Merezhkovsky and Benois, together with Diaghilev, would found a journal, *Mir iskusstva* (World of Art) that would become the triumphant mouthpiece and at the same time the label of a new direction in Russian culture. But before a new era could start, the old one had to be put to rest. That was done by two unexpected deaths that were felt most painfully.

The first was the still-mysterious demise of Tchaikovsky in Petersburg on October 25, 1893, at the age of fifty-three. With the special permission of Alexander III the memorial service was held at the overflowing Kazan Cathedral. The emperor, though expected, did not attend but he did send an impressive wreath. There were over three hundred wreaths altogether, and the closed coffin seemed to drown in them. The funeral procession was the longest in Petersburg history: hundreds of thousands of people came out onto the streets.

The Imperial Maryinsky Theater, still the bastion of the aristocracy, had recently started to attract new patrons, particularly for performances of Tchaikovsky's operas and ballets, especially students and young professionals. Tickets were impossible to obtain, and when they tried distributing them by lottery, up to fifteen thousand people a day were among the hopefuls. A huge young audience was created for Tchaikovsky's music.

So on the day of Tchaikovsky's funeral all lectures in the city's schools were canceled to allow the students to say good-bye to their beloved composer. Crowds of students took part in the procession, since the city had dozens of gymnasiums and other schools, and over twenty colleges: the famous Petersburg University and various academies and institutes. Young professionals, the Russian intelligentsia, teachers, doctors, lawyers, engineers, and journalists, educated in Russia and in Europe and as a rule liberals, were also out in force. They mourned their idol. It seemed as if the whole of "thinking" Petersburg paid tribute to one of its greatest representatives, intuiting the role that Tchaikovsky's works would play in evolving the city's mythos.

A year after Tchaikovsky's death, on October 20, 1894, Alexander III expired unexpectedly, not yet fifty years old. The energetic and seemingly healthy tsar was suddenly brought down by an incurable case of nephritis. When Alexander III ascended the throne in 1881, he had a choice according to one of his councilors: "lose everything or oppress everything." Alexander chose to be "oppressor." Still, despite his dictatorial mien, he gained the respect of many, including Benois, who had been presented to the emperor; the young aesthete recalled that Alexander III created a "strange and awesome" impression. Benois was particularly astounded by the emperor's steely, light blue eyes; when Alexander concentrated his cold gaze on someone, it could have the effect of a blow.[88]

Benois to his final days (he died in Paris in 1960) insisted that Alexander III's reign had been "in general, extremely significant and beneficial" and had prepared the way for the flowering of Russian culture in the early twentieth century, the so-called Silver Age. In that we can believe him; after all, he was one of the leaders of that Silver Age. He was also convinced that had Alexander III reigned another twenty years, the history of the entire world would have been much more benign.

In contrast, the heir to the throne, the future Nicholas II, with his "unprepossessing and rather folksy" looks left Benois unimpressed. Nicholas reminded him of a "small-time army officer."[89] In early 1894, with the first sign of Alexander III's illness, a court general wrote in his diary, "The sovereign had the flu. . . . It is terrible to think what would happen if the tsar were to die, leaving us to the hands of the child-heir (despite his twenty-six years), knowing nothing, prepared for nothing." On the day of the emperor's death, next to his laconic notation, "The tsar passed away at two fifteen," the courtier added a prophetic phrase in English: "A leap in the dark!"[90]

A decidedly conservative ruler, Alexander III realized nevertheless the importance of rapid economic and industrial development for Russia, and he tried to create the most beneficial conditions for that purpose. The changes came in an avalanche. In Petersburg, giant factories were built and powerful new banks appeared on the scene. A reactionary political commentator wrote with horror of "the bulky figure of capital entering our modest country." The sense of insecurity was widespread, but so was the anticipation of immense riches. Petersburg was in a fever.

Right after Alexander III's death, the enormous boom prepared by his rule began, with Russian industry growing at 9 percent annually. Even the revolutionary leader Vladimir Lenin maintained that Russia in that period had "the most advanced industrial and financial capitalism."

This frantic economic activity, new for Petersburg, created numerous *nouveaux riches* who wanted to be acknowledged as the true masters of the city. They wanted to feel like generous patrons of the arts and were prepared to spend substantial sums to support national culture. The motivation was simple and logical: an economically strong Russia had to take its rightful place in the family of civilized nations. The flowering of Russian culture would undoubtedly help that process along. Therefore, Russian culture had to be Westernized, and as quickly as possible. In this quest for rapid Westernization the desires of factory owners, market speculators, and bankers coincided with the dreams of the vast majority of the Petersburg intelligentsia. This created a receptive climate in Petersburg for the ideas of Benois, Diaghilev, and other innovators. In Benois's words, they were calling for a "departure from the backwardness of Russian artistic life, getting rid of our provincialism, and approaching the cultural West," which was then realized with considerable speed and success.

In 1895, Diaghilev wrote to his stepmother, whom he loved dearly, "I am, first of all, a great charlatan, although brilliant, and secondly, a great charmer, and thirdly, very brazen, and fourthly, a man with a great amount of logic and small amount of principles, and fifthly, I believe, without talent; however, if you like, I believe I have found my true calling—patronage of the arts. For that, I have everything, except money, *mais ça viendra.*"[91]

In this remarkable attempt at self-analysis, with a certain coquetry forgivable in a man of twenty-three, there is a prediction that came to pass very quickly. Always behaving as if he had money (he had none), Diaghilev managed to find enough financial support to organize three exhibits a few years later. The last, opened in 1898—with great pomp, as Benois recalled (there was an orchestra) and with unheard of refinement (numerous hothouse plants and flowers in the hall)—served as the first manifesto of the artistic intentions of the Benois–Diaghilev group.

At last in late 1898, Diaghilev brought his and Benois's longstanding, heretofore utopian dream to life: they started an art magazine. Modeled on foreign publications of the modern style like the British *Studio,* the German *Pan* and *Die Jugend,* and the French *La Plume,* Benois and Diaghilev's brainchild was called *Mir iskusstva* (*World of Art*), which represented quite a revolutionary concept for Russia. It was the first artistic publication by a group of like-minded young people who wanted to use it as a beacon for broad cultural change in the country. It was also the first magazine in Russia's history prepared and designed as a complete artistic concept.

Mir iskusstva immediately caught the attention of the Petersburg elite with its attractive appearance: large format, excellent paper, well-designed headings, and endpapers. Each issue had wonderful reproductions, specially made in Europe, of works by modern Russian and Western painters. Diaghilev dug its delicate typeface out of the printing house of the Academy of Sciences, where it had lain since Empress Elizabeth's reign. The magazine's logo, by Bakst, was a solitary eagle on a mountaintop.

For Diaghilev and his friends this logo was a symbol of independent and free art, proudly presiding high above the mundane. But in fact *Mir iskusstva* was closely tied to the economic and cultural transformations at large in Russian society. It was no accident that the magazine was financed by Princess Maria Tenisheva, whose husband, a Russian self-made man, built the first car factory in Petersburg, or by the Moscow merchant Savva Morozov, who had grown rich by building railroads. At first Diaghilev himself felt that one of the main goals of the magazine should be the promotion of Russian art industries: the growing textile, fabric, ceramic, china, and glass enterprises. Benois earnestly insisted that "in essence so-called industrial art and so-called pure art are sisters, twins of the same mother—beauty—and resemble each other so much that sometimes it is very hard to tell them apart."[92]

In an interview in *Peterburgskaya gazeta,* Leon Bakst happily promised that each issue of the new magazine would present model designs for craftsmen and workers; special attention would be paid to designs for fabric, furniture, and pottery, ceramics, majolica, mosaics, and wrought iron. Stasov, defender of the Wanderers and realistic art, worriedly wrote to a friend about Diaghilev's feverish activity, "that shameless and brazen piglet is trying to get all kinds of merchants, traders, industrialists and so on to subscribe to his publication."[93]

Stasov, who called Diaghilev a "decadent cheerleader" in print and *Mir iskusstva* "the courtyard of the lepers" (an image borrowed from Victor Hugo's *Notre-Dame de Paris*) had ample reason for sounding the alarm. Even though eventually the young modernists' magazine did not become a catalogue and handbook for the rapidly developing Russian arts industry, and the number of its subscribers never exceeded one thousand, the influence of *Mir iskusstva*—both the magazine and the artistic circle it represented and later the whole movement that took its name—had a revolutionary effect on all spheres of Russian cultural life, including the applied arts.

Just as in the early 1860s young artists in Petersburg had passed around every issue of the radical journal *Sovremennik* with the latest article by the nihilistic guru Chernyshevsky, now they heatedly debated the innovative ideas of *Mir iskusstva*. Passions boiled. The penny press slung mud at Diaghilev, Benois, and company, and just as had happened with the Wanderers, rich buyers attracted by the scandal came to the studios of the *Mir iskusstva* artists: stockbrokers, doctors, lawyers, and big bureaucrats who wanted to be au courant and fashionable.

On the pages of his magazine, Benois tirelessly touted promising new names and exciting artistic and cultural concepts. He propagandized the artists of Art Nouveau like Beardsley, the Viennese secessionists, and later the French postimpressionists. Benois called on Russian art to free itself from the conventions of genre, from the slavish dependence on literature displayed by the Wanderers, and also from the shallow salon academism that was still influential both in Russia and the West. But he didn't proclaim the concept of art for art's sake, either. According to Benois, a broader concept of art that included music and theater should develop. This Western idea, assimilated through the writings of Wagner and Nietzsche, was taken to heart by the Petersburg modernists and was destined to play an enormous role in their future undertakings.

Benois considered the renaissance of the cult of Petersburg one of his most important goals. He always stressed that he was by no means a Russian nationalist ("I never did mature enough to become a real patriot"), but he never missed an opportunity to declare his love for Petersburg. He said he lived with the imperative "Petersburg über Alles."

In Benois's inner world the St. Petersburg of the past was always present, the city of Peter the Great and the empresses Elizabeth and Catherine the Great, a city of architectural beauty and stirring military parades, colorful carnivals, and folk festivities, but also the city of solitary dreamy walks in the Summer Garden and assignations by the Winter Canal. That is why, the artist had insisted, "I had had a presentiment since childhood of the music of *Queen of Spades* with its miraculous 'calling forth of spirits,' and when it did appear I accepted it as something long awaited."[94] Passed through the prism of Tchaikovsky's music and magical anew, Petersburg's image and destiny became paramount for Benois, Diaghilev, and their friends at *Mir iskusstva*. With a burst of proselytizing energy typical of this group, the members of *Mir iskusstva* tried to win over the Russian artistic, intellectual, and financial elite in their quest for the "rebirth" of Petersburg. The start of this cleverly conceived and effectively executed campaign can be considered the appearance in the pages of *Mir iskusstva* in 1902 of Benois's impassioned article "Picturesque Petersburg," profusely illustrated by beautiful photographs and drawings.

The article was a groundbreaking event in the transformation of the mythos of Petersburg in the twentieth century. As if issuing a manifesto Benois proclaimed, "I don't think there is a city in the whole world which enjoys less sympathy than Petersburg. What names hasn't it been called: 'rotten swamp,' 'ridiculous fancy,' 'impersonal,' 'bureaucratic department,' 'regimental office.' I could never agree with all that."[95]

Benois complained bitterly, "the opinion that Petersburg is ugly is so firmly fixed in our society that none of the artists of the last fifty years turned to the city for inspiration, disdaining this 'unpicturesque,' 'stiff,' and 'cold', place. . . . None of the major poets of the second half of the nineteenth century defended Petersburg."[96]

Aspiring to change all that, the immensely erudite Benois wrote a series of elegantly argued articles defending the city, which symbolized for him all that was great, truly spiritual, and promising in Russian culture. In some ("The Architecture of Petersburg," "The Beauty of Petersburg") he enthusiastically drew the readers' attention to the grandeur, balance, and beauty of the capital's neoclassical buildings. Asserting that "we broke the records in European architecture" in the first third of the nineteenth century, Benois maintained that there wasn't a building in Western architecture of that period that could rival the Admiralty, for instance, and that next to the monumental Triumphal Gate erected in Petersburg in 1838 to commemorate the victories in the Russo-Turkish War that ended a decade earlier, Berlin's Brandenburg Gate looked like a pathetic toy. In other articles ("The Agony of Petersburg" and "Vandals") Benois protested the uninformed renovations of many unique buildings of old Petersburg and called urgently for "a renaissance of an artistic attitude toward neglected Petersburg."

As usual, Benois's writings were supported by indefatigable Diaghilev's energetic actions. Through Diaghilev's efforts, art shows were mounted one after another, all cleverly propagandizing the old Petersburg. In 1903, for the two hundredth anniversary of the city's founding, the capital's residents beheld an important collection of lithographs of Petersburg, artfully exhibited. As one enchanted viewer recalled, "one could see how much of Petersburg's street life still remained from the old days."[97]

In the following years the number of exhibits emphasizing the beauty of the city and its art increased steadily. Many books about Pe tersburg appeared, and magazines also were devoted to it, such as *Artistic Treasures of Russia* and *Olden Years*. Contemporary architects started imitating Petersburg's neoclassical models, because the bureaucrats, bankers, and factory owners began commissioning houses in the only recently despised classical style. "The interest in art of that period is becoming widespread," a historian noted with genuine surprise. "Everyone is studying, collecting, drawing, and praising it."[98]

The resourceful artists of *Mir iskusstva* were of course leading the way. Their paintings, watercolors, drawings, engravings, once again revealing the unparalleled charm and poetry of old Petersburg, became quite popular with the public. An even more important step was taken when Benois created a series of marvelous watercolors depicting Petersburg of the eighteenth century: *The Summer Gardens under Peter the Great; The Empress Elizabeth Deigns to Stroll Through the Streets of Petersburg; The Fontanka under Catherine II; The Changing of the Guard in Front of the Winter Palace under Paul I*. These watercolors had been commissioned by the publishing house that belonged to the Society of Saint Eugenia, a Petersburg charity that supported retired nurses. The publishing house printed thousands of postcards of the highest quality. The ones with views of old Petersburg by Benois and his *Mir iskusstva* colleagues became best-sellers and could be seen in every "proper" Petersburg home. At the same time, these popular postcards brought the message of *Mir iskusstva* to a mass audience.

Carefully reconstructing historic events, costumes, and scenes, Benois's watercolors do not pretend to be authentic. They illustrate his articles about Petersburg, not the city's actual history. The artist is always present in them: attentive, loving, with a barely noticeable irony. The composition of Benois's works is usually rather theatrical; the color stresses the paper's texture. This is stylization quite typical of early modern European art.

Almost all of his friends recall Benois as a charming person. And of course, they were all enthralled by his enormous erudition and his genius for cultural propaganda. The role of that stooped, bald, and black-bearded man with the attentive brown eyes behind pince-nez in the renaissance of Russian artistic taste and the flowering of modern Russian theater and ballet cannot be overestimated. Not many contemporaries considered Benois a truly great artist, and he wasn't one. But even the most demanding Russian connoisseurs used words like "great," "astonishing," and "epochal" when describing two series of Benois's works—his illustrations for Pushkin's *Bronze Horseman* and *The Queen of Spades*. (There's obviously no escape from Pushkin and his visionary works in dealing with the fate of St. Petersburg.)

Mir iskusstva resurrected the art of the book in Russia. The pioneer here, as in much else, was Benois. He persistently propounded the idea of the book as an artistic concept. Everything in a book, Benois would explain again and again—the paper, typeface, illustrations, design elements, and, of course, jacket—had to be integrated. For Petersburg at the turn of the century this was a revolutionary idea. But it quickly gained acceptance, since the tastes of customers were becoming markedly more sophisticated.

That lofty artistic ideas almost instantly penetrated the mass market was—for Russia, at least—astonishing. The energy of Benois and his friends seemed boundless, as they found time for everything and got involved everywhere, trying to push Petersburg's cultural life to new limits. And they succeeded. Petersburg's book design and manufacture, like many other crafts that drew the attention of the *Mir iskusstva* activists—posters, interior design, porcelain, even toys—underwent a true renaissance, thanks to their pioneering efforts.

Benois's thirty-three drawings for Pushkin's *Bronze Horseman* appeared in the first issue of *Mir iskusstva* for 1904 and immediately caused a sensation. The magazine, alas, ceased publication in the same year, the victim of incompatible ideas. Between the mystic, decadent Merezhkovsky and the much more sober and practical Benois and Diaghilev, a schism developed over the literary, "philosophical" bent represented by Merezhkovsky's camp and the artists' desire to be free of unwelcome literary intrusions.

It is telling that many contemporary Russian artists considered the publication of Benois's illustrations of Pushkin—despite the fact that the impetus for them came from a literary work—to be the most significant artistic event in the five years of the magazine's existence. On the other hand, Benois's drawings delighted writers as well, especially those of modernist leanings. One of the major poets of that era, the symbolist Valery Bryusov, proclaimed, "At last we have drawings worthy of a great poet. In them the old Petersburg is alive as it is alive in the poem."[99]

Everyone was astounded by Benois's magical ability to recreate the charms of the imperial capital—in the naive words of another poet, "as if the artist had just been there, in the streets of

Petersburg of centuries past, and is now telling us what he had seen."[100] But, of course, the series of drawings was not a guidebook to old Petersburg. It was also not really illustrative of Pushkin's work. The best drawings, especially those depicting the statue come to life and pursuing its victim down the empty streets of the city at night, are truly dramatic; as one of the first reviewers noted, "It is profound, it is sometimes as horrible as a dream, with all the naïveté and simplicity of a dream."[101] Benois did not attempt to comment in his illustrations on Pushkin's grand musings on the fate of Russia, its mysterious capital, and its suffering subjects.

Rather, Pushkin and his *Bronze Horseman* strike the ideal keynote, as always, for testing the new sounds of the song about Petersburg. The music of that song in the Benois interpretation and that of his friends had little in common with the original *Bronze Horseman*. That is precisely why Benois did not get into the questions that worried Pushkin and his commentators so much, that is, who was right, who was guilty, and was the tragedy of the *Horseman*'s poor Yevgeny accidental or preordained. Benois's desire was to elicit pity and love for Petersburg, not for Yevgeny. The literary tradition of the "little man" was of no use for this purpose.

As we know, Pushkin was not quite sure about Petersburg's role in Russia's destiny. For Gogol and Dostoyevsky, the verdict in the "Petersburg case" was clear: "Guilty!" The force that initially moved Benois to try to overthrow this unjust verdict was Tchaikovsky's music. Alas, the members of *Mir iskusstva* could not find another ally in contemporary Russian culture. The disciples of the Imperial Academy of Arts continued dutifully to glorify the capital, but for them it was a matter of sheer routine, not conviction. The Wanderers, taking literature's lead, attacked Petersburg ferociously out of ideological and social hatred. The aesthetics of the city were pushed to the background and became completely irrelevant.

By forging an alliance with music unique in Russian culture, *Mir iskusstva* achieved the impossible—it turned the tide. Its members led the counterattack on a wide front, in all areas of culture. Russian culture, and in particular art, almost suffocating from the weight of strident ideology, started to reclaim its own language once again. At the same time the perception of aesthetic grandeur and the deep emotional and psychological significance of Petersburg was gradually resurrected. The mythos of the capital gained new luster, and once again one could faintly hear the clanging of hoofs under The Bronze Horseman.

□   □   □

The members of the Benois circle were called "retrospective dreamers." They looked into the future, but their hearts, as befitted real romantics, belonged to the past. And as for all romantics, music was their guiding light. In Benois's travels to the era of imperial Petersburg his constant companion became Tchaikovsky.

A great deal united the two men, who never met. Tchaikovsky and Benois both idealized the role of superman (or, rather, the superperson) in history, particularly in Russian history. For them Petersburg was not simply an incomparably beautiful city but a magical place inhabited by "living shadows": Peter the Great, the amazing Russian empresses (and for Benois, there was also mad Paul I, whose image so intrigued him). Thus the imperial longings of both Tchaikovsky and Benois had an aesthetic and personal character. They personalized their monarchist feelings, so that, for example, Alexander III, who patronized Tchaikovsky and maintained a kindly relationship with the Benois family, embodied the Russian monarchy for both of them. Imperial Petersburg of the present and the past blurred into one for composer and artist.

So both Tchaikovsky's and Benois's extraordinary interest in ballet comes as no surprise—after all, it was the most imperial of all the arts. Nicholas I, who perceived a resemblance between the order and symmetry of ballet exercises with that of the military parades he so loved, particularly enjoyed ballet. And we find echoes of the cult of parades and military music in both Tchaikovsky and Benois. Tchaikovsky and Benois were also intrigued by ballet's obsession with dolls and the dancers' doll-like aspect, the automatic and predictable movements. This was a frequent theme in E. T. A. Hoffmann, beloved by both. One of Tchaikovsky's most whimsical creations, the *Nutcracker* ballet, plays with a favorite Hoffmannesque idea of the fine line between human and doll, between a seemingly free individual and a windup mechanism. The idea of an animated doll both attracted and repelled Tchaikovsky. It was, of course, a purely balletic image that was realized brilliantly once again in a joint production of Benois and Stravinsky, the ballet *Petrouchka*.

The enchantment with ballet took on special significance in Petersburg. Besides the longing for a synthesis of the arts found in both Tchaikovsky and Benois, there was also the foreboding of an avalanche of anarchy and a subconscious wish to escape the coming destructive forces. Before Tchaikovsky's very eyes, nihilism ceased being merely a philosophy, and the composer learned along with other residents of the capital what Petersburg political terror could be. Later, Benois was fated to be present when, under the Communist regime, that terror changed from an individual to a mass basis. Ballet dolls—they were the final refuge, a haven in a windswept sea.

Tchaikovsky was the first genius of Russian culture to express the horror of coming destruction for Petersburg and the disappearance of its festive, romantic universe. Tchaikovsky exhibited immeasurably more creative power than Benois or any other member of *Mir iskusstva* could ever aspire to do. Still, Tchaikovsky was heard but not understood. The decoding and popularization of Tchaikovsky's prophetic vision was realized by Benois, who made up in energy and verve what he lacked in creative powers. Thus, on the threshold of the twentieth century the mythos of Petersburg was driven, contrary to Russian tradition, not by literature but by art.

When the capital of the empire seemed unshakable, while its very existence was perceived as a threat to the unfettered spirit, the mythos of Petersburg—in its literature-dominated, revolutionary interpretation—predicted the fall of the city. But as soon as the signs started to appear—however vague and inexplicable—of coming winds and ruinous floods, the more aesthetically and emotionally sensitive of the artistic circles sharply decreased their maledictions.

The image of the city, cleared of its nihilistic ideological associations, started to change noticeably. From sinister it was gradually transformed to benign, from dour to luminous. The artist Mstislav Dobuzhinsky, a member of *Mir iskusstva* and a friend of Benois, felt in those days that he was rediscovering Petersburg as a city "with languorous and bitter poetry." For aesthetes, Petersburg at the start of the century was once again becoming a temple. They cherished "the sensation of mystery."[102] They imagined it was the mystery of the past; actually, it was the future that was mysterious and unpredictable.

The Petersburg mythos of the early twentieth century was about to enter a completely different, terrible era. On the way the capital, its image, and its mythos had to endure unprecedented catastrophes. Petersburg's fate would change radically and with it, or rather, despite it, the symbolism of Petersburg would change, too, as would its place in the context of Russian and world culture and history.

Subsequently a number of great writers, poets, composers, artists, and choreographers would participate in the creation of a startlingly new concept of Petersburg. They would do so while surviving the destruction of many of the old city's material and spiritual values, the disappearance of its name, as well as the death of multitudes of its inhabitants.

> We thought: we are paupers, we have nothing,
> But as we started to lose one thing after another,
> So that every day became
> A memorial day—
> We began composing songs
> About God's great munificence
> And about our former wealth.

This poem by Anna Akhmatova, which she liked the most of her early poetry, was prophetic, as was so much of her writing. When it first appeared in 1915, no one fully guessed to what degree all of Petersburg's "wealth" would soon become "former."

CHAPTER
3

in which we learn how merry it was living in Petersburg in 1908, how that merriment was soon interrupted, and how the city first lost its name and then its status as capital of Russia and, almost dead of hunger and cold, tried to remain faithful to itself. This is the Petersburg of Anna Akhmatova.

I n 1908, there were published and distributed in Petersburg around seven and a half million books, describing the adventures of Nat Pinkerton, Nick Carter, and other legendary detectives. They were thin (several dozen pages) and cheap (10–12 kopeks) editions in colored cardboard covers, with titles like *Pinkerton's Trip to the Other World, The Mysterious Ice Skater, The Steel Sting,* and *The Murderous Model.* For a city 30 percent of whose population was illiterate, such sales figures, even for light fiction, could only be considered astonishing. Just twenty or thirty years earlier the most popular and inexpensive book would have found only a few tens of thousands of readers in the city. For example, *Crime and Punishment,* published in Dostoyevsky's lifetime, sold some four hundred copies *a year.*

Obviously, the primary reason for this incredible expansion of the Petersburg book market was the city's rapid growth. By 1900, almost a million and a half inhabitants swelled the city, and the number continued to increase rapidly (in 1917 there would be almost two and a half million; that is, the population grew by almost 70 percent in just seventeen years).[1] In the gigantic metropolis beautiful buildings, broad squares, granite embankments, and wide avenues filled with fashionable people lay next to ugly, poorly lit neighborhoods densely populated with workers' families.

Those were two different worlds. The modernist poet Mikhail Kuzmin described in his diary how a friend looked out the window one evening "at the dark factories with such grim fear, as if he were a guard looking down from the city tower at the Huns at the city gates." Petersburg was the leading industrial center of Russia, its technological laboratory, and its main port. Here steel was produced, steam engines, cannons, and diesel engines manufactured, oil tankers, destroyers, and submarines built. Here with ever increasing speed, powerful social forces unfolded, changing first the cultural and political face of Russia, then of the world.

It was in Petersburg that the first Russian revolution erupted in 1905. Since the turn of the century, a quiet but palpable dissatisfaction had ripened here among the urban masses directed against the young tsar, Nicholas II. The ruling elite felt that to hold off the social explosion, Russia needed a "small, victorious war." Japan was targeted for the demonstration—no match, it would seem, for the mighty Russian Army. But the war, which began in 1904, did not go the way Nicholas and his generals had planned. The Russians lost one bloody battle after another. The loss of the Russian fleet in the Tsushima Strait, between Japan and Korea, was a horrible shock for Petersburg. Wandering organ grinders lamented the tragedy in the city's courtyards, eliciting tears and contributions more generous than usual from residents.

At first the liberal intelligentsia merely "gave the finger inside its pocket," in the words of Alexander Benois, the traditional behavior of the Russian opposition. But, as Benois recalled, "following the tragedy playing in the Far East, following the shame that the nation was forced to feel, the usual 'mutterings' turned to something else. The revolution was no longer on the far horizon. Russian society felt the instability and unreliability of everything and sensed the need for radical change."[2] Zinaida Hippius wrote about the same thing: "Something was breaking in Russia, something was being left behind, and something that had been born or resurrected strove forward. . . . Where to? No one knew. . . . There was tragedy in the air. Oh, not everyone sensed it. But very many did, and in many things."[3]

In August 1905 Russia signed a humiliating peace treaty with

Japan in Portsmouth, New Hampshire. Theodore Roosevelt acted as mediator. The populace was caught up in a storm of outrage, with Petersburg at its center. They had not forgotten Bloody Sunday, the nightmarish day of January 9, 1905, when guards, cavalry units, and police attacked a peaceful demonstration by Petersburg workers. That day almost 150,000 people had marched from various parts of the city toward the Winter Palace. Their leader, Father Georgy Gapon, planned to hand Nicholas II a petition that began: "We, workers, have come to you, Sovereign, to seek truth and protection. We are impoverished, we are oppressed and burdened with unbearable work. . . . We are seeking our last salvation from you, do not refuse to help your people." The demonstrators were carrying icons, church banners, and portraits of Nicholas II; many were singing the anthem, "God Save the Tsar."

Neither Father Gapon nor the workers knew that the tsar was not in the Winter Palace that day; fearing terrorists, he was away at his country residence. His German wife kept saying, "Petersburg is a rotten town, not one atom Russian." And his supercilious generals firmly—and stupidly—decided to teach the Petersburg plebeians a lesson once and for all. When the crowd approached the Winter Palace, the order came: "Fire!" The troops attacked the unarmed demonstrators in other parts of the city, too. No one believed the government statement that around one hundred people died; rumor put the number in the thousands.

Petersburg had not seen such a massacre since the fateful December 14, 1825, when Nicholas I, the grandfather of Nicholas II, scattered the Decembrists on Senate Square with artillery fire. That irretrievably tragic day marked the appearance of the abyss between Russian tsar and intellectuals. Bloody Sunday of 1905 had even more unpredictable consequences. The words of Father Gapon echoed throughout the land: "We no longer have a tsar. A river of blood separates the tsar from the people." Anna Akhmatova, who was sixteen in 1905, used to repeat, "January 9 and Tsushima were a shock for life, and since it was the first, it was particularly terrible."[4]

In the fall of 1905, the first Russian revolution seized the country. Strikes virtually paralyzed Petersburg. Factories closed, the stock exchange was inactive, schools and pharmacies shut down. There was no electricity and the eerily deserted Nevsky Prospect was illuminated by searchlights from the Admiralty. A unique alternative form of political power arose spontaneously—the Petersburg Soviet of Workers' Deputies, with the radical Leon Trotsky as its cochairman. Unpre-

pared to use brute force further, Nicholas II on October 17, 1905, issued a Constitutional Manifesto, which promised the Russian people
freedom of speech and assembly. Too little, too late. A sarcastic ditty
rang through the streets of Petersburg: "The tsar got scared and made
a manifesto; the dead got freedom, the living got arrest-o!"

The cynics were right—the Duma, a legislative assembly created by the tsar's manifesto, never acquired real power. The rights
granted were curtailed one after another. The first political parties created in Russia led a precarious existence. But the revolutionary ferment quieted down. Life in Petersburg returned to normal. Chasing
away gloomy thoughts about politics, the residents of the capital tried
to distract themselves and have some fun again.

Petersburg's prospering commercial life had brought into full bloom
a large class of assertive, self-indulgent bourgeois whose appearance
was a relatively recent phenomenon in Russia. Their aspirations and
activities added something new to the older court traditions of wealth
and cultural style.

Once more the elegant city was shimmering and dizzying. Once
more luxurious carriages bearing arrogant and mysterious well-
dressed ladies whom Osip Mandelstam would later call "fragile Europeans" raced down Nevsky Prospect. The most impressive were the
private carriages pulled by expensive thoroughbreds with a satiny
sheen to their coats.

The horses, with battery-operated lanterns hanging from the
shafts, were no longer frightened by the recently installed trolleys, nor
by the first "taximotors," but they still snorted at the exhaust fumes.
Footmen in costumes matching the crests on the doors of the carriages
rode on the running boards. The lackeys of the palace carriages stood
out in their bright red liveries with capes trimmed in gold braid and
black eagles. The red caps of the gallant hussars repeated the striking color. The guards galloped in dashing gray coats with sword
hilts peeking out of the slit left pocket. Each regiment had its own
uniform. The colorful assortment of epaulets, orders, buttons, and
trouser stripes gladdened the eye. Nor were the military the only ones
with special uniforms—civil servants, engineers, even students all had
their own.

In Petersburg, as always, the cult of Nevsky Prospect thrived.
In an almost ritual parade, high-placed bureaucrats and lowly clerks,
naval and army officers, important gentlemen, nouveaux riches, and
bohemians sauntered along the street. Some moved with the precise

tread appropriate to capital denizens, while others gawked around,
turning to follow pretty ladies, in attempts to flirt. Many stared at the
enticing shop windows that carried expensive goods from all over the
world.

Oysters from Paris, lobsters from Ostend, flowers from Nice!
The aristocracy particularly liked the English Shop on Nevsky, where,
as Vladimir Nabokov later recalled, one could buy all sorts of com-
forting things: fruitcakes, smelling salts, Pears soap, playing cards, picture puzzles, striped blazers, talcum-white tennis balls, and football
jerseys in the color of Cambridge and Oxford.

Nevsky Prospect was also called the street of banks. Of the fifty
buildings making up the section from the Admiralty to the Fontanka,
there were banks in twenty-eight, including the Russian-British, the
Russian-French, and the Russian-Dutch branches. In the passageway
from Nevsky Prospect to Mikhailovsky Square were the jewelers: diamonds on black velvet, blinding brooches, expensive rings and necklaces. Signs, announcements, and stylish posters, many done in the
fashionable *Mir iskusstva* manner, advertised Russian and foreign
brand names: the jewelry by craftsman Fabergé and the maker of cardboard holders for Russian *papirosy* cigarettes, Viktorson Senior;
Singer sewing machines, chocolates by Georges Borman, Konradi's
cocoa, Siou perfumes and colognes, Zhukov's soap.

The capital's fashionable idlers stopped by the poster column:
where should they go tonight? Petersburg had three operas, a famous
ballet company, a lively operetta, and opulent theaters for every
taste—from the very respectable, imperially subsidized Alexandrinsky, which tended to stage serious plays, to the frivolous Nevsky Farce,
known for its topical parodies of famous contemporaries. The "decadent" Meyerhold was being parodied there. He had recently been
asked to direct at the Alexandrinsky Theater, where his premiere of a
Knut Hamsun drama had been a terrible flop. How could they have
let a thirty-four-year-old upstart, with outlandishly modernist attitudes, take charge at the imperial theater? Now, they said, he was
planning to "modernize" Wagner at the Maryinsky Opera. We'll see,
we'll see. . . .

The year 1908 brought forth Sarah Bernhardt and Eleonora
Duse on the Petersburg stages. The posters proudly announced the
appearance of a flashy conductor, Arthur Nikisch, who was a brilliant
interpreter of Tchaikovsky, though connoisseurs really preferred the
more serious conducting style of Gustav Mahler, who had recently
been a hit in the capital.

Pablo Casals was playing Bach and tickets were available. How about going to that? Especially since if you weren't a subscriber it was almost impossible to get tickets to the Maryinsky, where people lined up the night before. Students and young ladies warmed themselves by bonfires so that they could rush the box office at ten the next morning—and hope for the best. The great draw there was the incredibly popular basso Fyodor Chaliapin in the exotic opera *Judith* by the composer Alexander Serov, who had died almost forty years earlier. The young Tchaikovsky had adored this opera and it clearly influenced opera composition by such composers as Mussorgsky and Borodin.

Chaliapin was appearing in the role of the villainous Babylonian Holofernes. One habitué observed acidly that when the giant Chaliapin, moving with the grace of a panther, approached the footlights, reached out with his bare arms, and sang in his thunderingly resonant basso, "This city has many wives! Its streets are paved with gold! Beat them and trample them with horses—you'll be the city's new king!" chills ran down the spines of the beautiful ladies in full dress and the important gentlemen sitting in the light blue velvet chairs at the imperial theater. The memory of revolutionary 1905 was still fresh.

When the performance ended, Chaliapin, still in heavy makeup and his ornate "Assyrian" costume, would go up to the huge scenery workshop located over the hall at the Maryinsky Theater. The artist Alexander Golovin would work until morning on the singer's portrait in the role of Holofernes. Almost sixty years later, barely keeping up with the tireless Leningrad choreographer Leonid Yakobson, I ran up those endless, narrow stairs, which Chaliapin with his large entourage had ascended so majestically. "So this is where they all went," I thought, entering the spacious room, empty but so alive for me with its splendid ghosts. There stood the legendary Chaliapin, his guests, and Golovin, the most fashionable stage designer of Petersburg, the silver-haired darling of its high society.

It was Golovin, who had the ear of even high-placed bureaucrats, who got Meyerhold into the imperial theaters. Now, questioning the great singer casually about his recent triumph in Paris—Chaliapin had stunned the French with his Boris Godunov in the production brought to France by Diaghilev, with scenery by Golovin—the artist swiftly sketched Holofernes with charcoal on a large canvas, while his scenery for the next premiere dried in a corner beside them. In 1967, in the same place, I saw the scenery, painted in the lacquer-box style of Palekh folk artists, drying for Yakobson's forthcoming adventurous ballet, *Wonderland*. Golovin's portrait of Chaliapin as Holofernes had been hanging for many years by then in a place of honor at the Tretyakov Gallery, the country's most famous museum of Russian art.

Wednesdays and Sundays were ballet days at the Maryinsky. In 1908 Anna Pavlova and Vaslav Nijinsky starred in the productions of the twenty-eight-year-old Michel Fokine. In one night could be seen two of Fokine's most innovative works, his one-act *Egyptian Nights* and *Chopiniana,* a plotless wonder that later became famous in the West under the title *Les Sylphides.* The court balletomanes sniffed: even ballet, that holy of holies, was being taken over by the nasty modernists! They had to put up with it, for Nijinsky and Pavlova were just wonderful, air and champagne! Of course, Fokine could create a *real* dance, if he tried. Have you seen his "Dying Swan?" A lovely piece and Pavlova is incomparable in it. They say she is off on her first European tour. Petersburg won't be the same without her. . . .

But not everyone, after all, was crazy about the ballet alone. Petersburg's snobs attended the refined concerts of the avant-garde circle, called "Evenings of Contemporary Music." This association could be considered the musical branch of *Mir iskusstva;* connoisseurs met in small hallways to sample the latest musical morsel from Paris, Berlin, or some Scandinavian capital.

In December 1908, the forty-fifth concert of the Evenings of Contemporary Music, in the hall of the Reformation School, presented the debut of a seventeen-year-old student of the Petersburg Conservatory, Sergei Prokofiev. "Touchy, clumsy, and ugly" in Nathan Milstein's words,[5] Prokofiev at the piano looked even younger than he was. The reviewer of the reputable newspaper *Rech* was rather sympathetic: "The author, a young student who interpreted his own music, is undoubtedly talented, but his harmonies are often strange and even bizarre and thus go beyond the bounds of the beautiful."[6]

At that same concert the Petersburg audience, among whom was the twenty-six-year-old Igor Stravinsky, heard for the first time the music of Petersburger Nikolai Myaskovsky, another conservatory student. The know-it-alls compared Myaskovsky's three settings of the "decadent" poems of Zinaida Hippius with the vocal works of Stravinsky, who was becoming quite famous, heard at Evenings of Contemporary Music last year. Well, Myaskovsky's works were probably more refined and mature than the sweet but naive attempts of Stravin-

sky, who was much too influenced by his teacher, Nikolai Andreyevich Rimsky-Korsakov. . . .

Rimsky-Korsakov, that master of Russian music, had died recently, in June 1908, from heart paralysis. Walter Nouvel, Stravinsky's
friend and mentor in the Evenings of Contemporary Music, who was
called the arbiter of the arts by the modernists, liked to say, "I feel
that the sooner Rimsky-Korsakov dies the better for Russian music.
His enormous figure oppresses the young and keeps them from taking new paths."[7] Just in May Prokofiev had seen Rimsky-Korsakov
in the hallway of the conservatory and noted somewhat wistfully in
his diary, "I looked at him and thought—there he is, a man who has
achieved true success and fame!"[8] And in August Stravinsky was writing to Rimsky-Korsakov's widow, "If you only knew how I share your
terrible grief, how I feel the loss of the endlessly dear and beloved
Nikolai Andreyevich!"[9]

Stravinsky asked the widow of his teacher to help him have
performed his "Funeral Song" for wind instruments, op. 5, which he
wrote with incredible speed. It was dedicated to the memory of Rimsky-Korsakov. The widow pulled strings and Stravinsky's tribute
would be played in Petersburg in early 1909 in a special memorial
concert. . . .

Bookstores lined the sunny side of Nevsky Prospect. Their windows
were a true exhibit of Petersburg art, with multicolored book jackets
by artists of *Mir iskusstva* like Alexander Benois, Mstislav Dobuzhinsky, and Sergei Chekhonin. The books were poetry collections of the
leading Russian symbolists—Fyodor Sologub, Valery Bryusov, Andrei
Bely—and also the debuts of Mikhail Kuzmin, Igor Severyanin, and
Vladislav Khodasevich. *Earth in Snow,* the third book by Alexander
Blok, was getting a lot of attention: the twenty-eight-year-old poet
was probably the most intriguing figure of the symbolists by now.

You could attend a lecture by that Blok fellow at the Religious-
Philosophical Society. Its meetings took place in the hall of the Geographical Society, attracting large crowds. There you could see the
monks' cloaks and the high chic of wealthy socialites; many fashionable philosophers, writers, and artists never failed to come. The burning issues of Neo-Christianity were discussed; the Petersburg elite saw
renewed Orthodoxy as one of the important elements of the coming
new society. "These gatherings were remarkable as the first meeting
of representatives of Russian culture and literature, who were infected
by religious angst, with the members of the traditional Russian Or-

thodox Church hierarchy," the philosopher Nikolai Berdyayev, an active and passionate participant, recalled in his autobiography. "We spoke about the relationship of Christianity and culture. The central theme was that of flesh and sex."[10] The huge statue of Buddha towering over the hall was covered during those Christian debates "to avoid temptation."

The auditorium overflowed for Blok's appearance on November 13, 1908. He spoke in a monotone but hypnotically, like a true poet, saying that in Russia "the people and the intelligentsia constitute not only two different concepts but truly two realities; one hundred fifty million on one side and several hundred thousand on the other; and neither side understands the other at the most fundamental level."

The audience began to whisper, Why be so pessimistic about the current situation? Aren't literacy and culture growing among the masses? But Blok continued quietly: "Why do we feel more and more frequently two emotions: the oblivion of rapture and the oblivion of depression, despair, indifference? Soon there will be no room for other emotions. Is that not because the darkness reigns all about us?" The power of the poet's persuasion was so strong that the people in the hall shivered, anticipating the gathering gloom.

But the audience's liberal sensibility was particularly affronted by Blok's dire prophecy, pronounced almost matter-of-factly: "In turning to the people, we are throwing ourselves under the feet of a troika of wild horses, to our certain death." This grim prediction elicited a chorus of outrage but also the delight of many who were sick of the liberal orthodoxy. Even though the announced debate had been banned by the police, the audience surrounded Blok after his lecture. An enraged liberal professor denounced Blok as a reactionary. A poet friend of Blok's remarked sarcastically, "He who fears the future is neither with the people nor the intelligentsia."

Blok listened to his opponents with a barely perceptible smile, his face resembling a stone mask. His notebook soon recorded, "It is most important for me that in my theme they hear a real and terrible memento mori."[11] And not long before that Blok had written, "I must admit that the thought of suicide is often lulling and vivid. Quiet. To vanish, disappear 'having done all that I could.' "[12] In 1908 the Petersburg police registered close to fifteen hundred suicide attempts.

Blok was focusing on a new phenomenon—the urban masses, baptized "The Coming Boor" by the father of Russian symbolism, Dmitri Merezhkovsky. These new unkempt who hungered for "bread

and circuses" were frightening and incomprehensible to the elite.
"Who are they, these strange people, unknown to us, who have so
unexpectedly revealed themselves? Why hadn't we even suspected
their existence until now?" demanded the horrified influential Petersburg literary critic Kornei Chukovsky. He scoffed, "I'm afraid to sit
among these people. What if they suddenly neigh or have hooves instead of hands?" "These people" were beyond redemption as far as
Chukovsky was concerned: "No, they're not even savages. They are
not worthy of nose rings and feathers. Savages are visionaries, dreamers, they have shamans, fetishes, and curses, while this is just some
black hole of nonexistence."[13]

The main amusement for this new mass audience was motion pictures.
Petersburg was covered with a network of cinemas playing foreign
films. It was only in 1908 that the first Russian feature film was made,
about the legendary rebel and robber Stepan Razin; in 1964 Dmitri
Shostakovich would compose his monumental poem for bass, chorus,
and orchestra on this theme so beloved in Russia. But by 1909 there
were twenty-three Russian motion pictures; their number grew
tremendously and reached five hundred by 1917. Filmmaking and
movie theaters had become a profitable part of Petersburg's nascent
entertainment industry.
    "Look into the cinema auditoriums. You will be amazed by the
makeup of the audience. Everyone is here—students and gendarmes,
writers and prostitutes, officers and all kinds of intellectuals in glasses
and beards, workers, clerks, merchants, society ladies, modistes, in a
word, everyone,"[14] mused a journalist. But this was exactly what
frightened Chukovsky and his kind. They presented an apocalyptic
vision of a coming "culture market," where the goods would have to
compete and the survivors would be "only those that are the most
adapted to the tastes and whims of the consumer" (as Chukovsky formulated that "horrifying" prospect in 1908).
    For him, as for many Russian intellectuals, the thought of cul-
ture as a product was still humiliating and shameful. That ideological puritanism was curious since Chukovsky himself won fame and
fortune, appearing regularly in the popular periodical press. And at
the turn of the century the more commonsensical Russian journalists
freely admitted that "a newspaper is as much a capitalist enterprise
as coal mining or manufacturing alcohol."[15]
    The newspaper boom started in Petersburg in the late nine-
teenth century. As censorship weakened and printing costs declined,

along with the price per issue, the number of readers of periodicals increased. The real explosion occurred in 1908, when the Jewish entrepreneur Mikhail Gorodetsky founded the daily *Gazeta-Kopeika* (*Kopek Gazette*). This tabloid really did cost one kopek but managed in its four to five pages (half of which were advertising) to squeeze in some foreign news, national politics, and accounts of life in the capital, naturally with a bent for sensationalism. Each issue had a lot of photographs; the regularly featured novels in installments were accompanied by original illustrations. The publisher's motto was "Everything that interests the world," and his politics were quite liberal.

In the beginning the *Gazeta-Kopeika* printed 11,000 copies, but by 1909 its circulation had grown to 150,000 and by 1910 the street vendors and the hundreds of stores and kiosks were selling 250,000 copies a day of the tabloid. Gorodetsky turned his flourishing business into a powerful newspaper and magazine conglomerate, publishing among others *Zhurnal-Kopeika*, the humor pamphlet "Kopeika," the weekly *World Panorama*, and the illustrated magazine *Solntse Rossii* (*The Sun of Russia*), for which the avowed foe of mass culture, Chukovsky, wrote a column.

All these publications, which were aimed at the widest possible audience, allotted considerable coverage to national culture, particularly literature. For instance, Leo Tolstoy's eightieth birthday, in August 1908, was celebrated by both the liberal and the right-wing press. Typically a journalist proposed, "It would be good, in honor of Tolstoy's eightieth birthday, to give up sexual relations on that great day, and donate the money saved thereby [!] to the development of cooperatives."[16] On a more serious note, in 1917 *Gazeta-Kopeika* offered its readers as a premium the complete collected works of Leo Tolstoy in fifty-six volumes.

Comparatively little has been written about the connections between Russian mass culture and its highbrow literature, even though it was in Russia that popular newspapers and magazines regularly published the works of leading writers. Anton Chekhov began his career with humorous stories in such lowbrow publications as the Petersburg magazine *Oskolki* (*Fragments*) and the tabloid *Peterburgskaya gazeta*. In one newspaper he published a crime novel, *The Shooting Party*, in nine months of installments.

For many years, Chekhov was a prolific contributor to the monarchist, ultrachauvinist Petersburg newspaper *Novoye vremya*, which Nicholas II read thoroughly every day (they say he had a special copy on vellum made just for him). Chekhov gave them some of his best stories. The publisher of *Novoye vremya*, the spiritual heir of the Petersburg journalist and publisher Faddei Bulgarin, the owner of the infamous *Severnaya pchela*, was Alexei Suvorin, who was just as clever and unprincipled as Bulgarin. Suvorin was one of the first to recognize Chekhov's talent and paid him well. According to Chekhov, when he started working for *Novoye vremya*, "I felt I was in California."

Suvorin's group published several newspapers and magazines, the annual reference book *All Petersburg*, calendars, and the so-called Cheap Library, which flooded the country with some three hundred titles of Russian and foreign classics. He put out a special series for reading in trains. They and his other publications were sold in Suvorin's own book stores and hundreds of kiosks in railroad stations. Suvorin was often accused of greed and shameless commercialism, to which he replied with total sincerity, "I worked for Russian education and Russian youth. . . . I can go to any judgment and die peacefully."[17]

A contemporary spoke of Suvorin as a gifted editor who avidly sought new authors: "Like a fisherman, he cast a line with a lure and felt true pleasure when a large fish ended up on his hook."[18] One contributor to *Novoye vremya* described it as "an obliging chapel where you could pray any way you wanted, as long as it sounded vivid and talented."[19] That at any rate was fair with regard to the newspaper's theater section, which was considered one of the best in the capital. As for the arts, *Novoye vremya* hated the decadents and so it readily published articles by the temperamental foe of modernism, Vladimir Stasov, who occupied the ideological pole opposite Suvorin. Once Stasov explained his work in the "reactionary" newspaper this way: "When I need multitudes of the Russian public, who know only *Novoye vremya*, to read about this or that, I boldly go to Suvorin."[20]

Another colorful figure in the world of the press was Solomon Propper, an Austrian citizen who, according to popular legend, appeared in Petersburg with no money and bought the rights for thirteen rubles at auction to publish *Birzhevye novosti* (*Stock Exchange News*). It was said that Propper never did learn to speak Russian tolerably, but he certainly mastered the rules of the newspaper game. In a relatively short time he increased the paper's circulation to ninety thousand. According to one of his workers, "Propper used blackmail: firms that refused to advertise in his newspaper were soon denounced as not creditworthy. He did it cleverly, between the lines. The banks called him a revolver."[21]

Soon Propper was buying up estates and houses, received the rank of councillor of commerce, and even became a member of the city duma of Petersburg. But most important, he expanded his publishing business, sending out often as free supplements numerous magazines, including *Accessible Fashions, Family Health, Knowledge and Art,* and *Ogonyok (Little Flame). Ogonyok,* founded in 1908, was particularly popular. By 1910 its circulation had reached 150,000, and by 1914 it peaked at 700,000, surpassing all other existing Russian periodicals of the time.

All of Propper's publications covered culture extensively. There was a popular joke in Petersburg: "What's the most theatrical newspaper?" *"Stock Exchange News."* "And the most stock-oriented newspaper?" *"Theater Review."* The latter was published by the financier I. O. Abelson, patron of the young violinist Nathan Milstein.[22] Propper took into account that the Russian public devoured news about new books, plays, art, music, and movies, and reports from auctions. To woo and keep readers, the Petersburg mass media tried to inform them about every interesting event in those fields. That's how the Russian modernists came to their attention.

A pioneer here was the illustrated weekly *Niva (Cornfield),* founded in 1869 in Petersburg by Adolf Marx, from Prussia. By the beginning of the nineteenth century *Niva's* circulation had reached 275,000. Its success came in great part thanks to the magazine's steady publication of contemporary Russian prose and generous presentations of lithographs of paintings by realist Russian artists. According to a contemporary, Marx "understood a bit of art, and even less of literature."[23] But his enterprising instinct led him to select authors like Leo Tolstoy, whose novel *Resurrection* premiered in the pages of *Niva,* and Chekhov.

In 1899 Marx bought the rights to Chekhov's works from the author for 75,000 rubles, an incredible sum in those days. Marx did not read Chekhov; nevertheless, his intuition correctly told him he would not lose the advance. He paid leading writers a thousand rubles for what was called a printer's sheet (approximately six thousand words) and was justly called "the creator of literary fees." The system of patriarchal and "friendly" relations between publisher and author, by which the fee often was determined by publisher's whim and not by actual demand in the cultural marketplace, was vanishing.

Marx's personal tastes were definitely conservative. But Merezhkovsky, the father of Russian symbolism, was published in

Niva as early as 1891 and soon became a regular contributor. Other leading symbolists followed and in 1906 the magazine presented twenty-six-year-old Alexander Blok. His poetry then appeared simultaneously in other influential Petersburg publications. For instance, the serious political newspaper *Slovo* (*The Word*) published the young poet's verses four times in February and March 1906. And the popular liberal newspaper *Rus'* ran Blok's works five times in April 1907 alone.

The symbolists, who had started out a mere fourteen or fifteen years earlier as an esoteric group, despised and mocked, suddenly became fashionable. Just recently Blok's literary debut in a small religious-decadent journal, *The New Path,* led reviewers to smirk that this "new path led to an old hospital for the mentally ill." Now it was becoming clear that the symbolists had been accepted by the reading public. Weary of the naturalism and positivism of the last few decades, readers were impressed by the symbolists' demonstrative aestheticism and mysticism. They also liked the erotic motifs, which were fairly strong in the poems and prose of the symbolists, and so unusual in classical Russian literature.

Eroticism was becoming all the rage in 1908. In Petersburg two editions of Mikhail Artsybashev's novel *Sanin* caused a sensation that led to polemics in the press and the public. The novel's eponymous hero was summed up by a contemporary critic as someone who "eats a lot, drinks even more, says many mostly unnecessarily gross things, brawls hard, and artistically seduces beautiful women."[24] The prudish critic did not mention that *Sanin*'s themes included rape, suicide, and incest.

Artsybashev was officially charged with publishing a pornographic and blasphemous work. This naturally increased interest in the book: most of the reviews of 1908 were of *Sanin*; a critic wrote, "There is a new ism, Saninism." Students debated the topic, "Is Sanin right?" Saninist clubs spread throughout the city. All this reflected real market demand.

In early 1908 Chukovsky, incensed by the "wholesale lurid relishing of sexual bestiality," sounded the alarm. "Thousands of unthinkable, impossible books about sodomy, lesbian love, masochism have flooded the book stores."[25] The "serious" press wrung its hands: the book market, which offered over eighteen thousand Russian-language titles in 1908, was dominated by pornography and crime novels, "and the literature of a progressive tendency is going through a hard year." The prudish newspaper of the Russian revolutionaries, *Pravda,* saw an enemy of its political ideals in erotic literature: "In *Sanin,* Artsybashev spits on any social work and, in effect, proclaims, 'Vodka and broads!' instead of 'Proletarians of the world, unite!' "[26]

On the contrary, some of the Russian symbolists greeted Artsybashev's novel with sympathetic interest. For the exquisitely refined poet and essayist Innokenti Annensky *Sanin* was something "caricatured and metaphysical in a purely Gogolian way. Whether you like it or not is your business, but without a doubt, the caricature turned out to be *powerful.*" Blok, noting in passing that Artsybashev "has no language of his own," admitted that in the amoral Sanin he sensed at last "a real man, with an iron will, a restrained smile, ready for anything, young, strong, and free."

That is more a self-portrait of Blok than a portrait of Sanin. Freedom meant much to the Russian symbolists; freedom from the old, oppressive morality and from the traditional literary conventions. Learning first from Baudelaire, Rimbaud, Verlaine, and Verhaeren, the symbolists changed the course of Russian poetry with their bold images, metaphors, and unusual rhyme schemes. After many years of the reign of realistic prose, a new mass interest in poetry had been awakened in Russia. In those conditions Blok and his symbolist friends were not only esteemed; they had become brand names that could guarantee readership for a new newspaper or magazine.

The popularity of Blok and his cohorts—especially compared with their Western decadent brethren—was promoted by their active participation in the topical debates then raging in Petersburg. Writing of the early years of Russian symbolism, the critic D. S. Mirsky noted, "Aestheticism substituted beauty for duty, and individualism emancipated the individual from all social obligations."[27] However, the symbolists did not hold to these positions for long, and there were several reasons for that.

In Russia, literature rarely disengaged itself from society. Also, many symbolists, for all their proclaimed aesthetic interest in the contemporary West, had deep Slavophile roots. While announcing their cosmopolitanism, they still considered themselves Russian patriots. These patriotic feelings came to the fore in crises like revolution or war. The Russian symbolists had started out as solitary, misunderstood prophets, but in their hearts they really wanted to speak to and for the masses. Their dream came to pass, and the Russian public adopted the symbolists.

The political climate in Russia helped. Any literary gesture, however innocent, could be perceived as a political act. It's quite possible that the esoteric lecture Blok gave at the Religious-Philosophical Society in 1908 would not have generated a lot of interest were it not for the mindless interference of the police, who had banned the discussion. That clumsy act attracted the popular press and turned that and later appearances by Blok into events with national significance, as so often happened in early-twentieth-century Russia, where literary and religious activities were concerned.

In her final years Akhmatova often said that symbolism had been perhaps "the last great movement" in Russian literature.[28] Absorbing much of the Russian classical and Western modernist traditions, Russian symbolism became an influential and complex phenomenon. Erudite, talented, often brilliant individualists whose tangled personal relationships sometimes influenced their aesthetic standing, the symbolists were forever breaking and re-forming ranks. Any attempt to delineate concisely their ever-changing positions would be futile. But it is possible to divide them conditionally into the "elder" Russian symbolists (Dmitri Merezhkovsky, Zinaida Hippius, Valery Bryusov, Konstantin Balmont, Fyodor Sologub) and the "younger" ones (Alexander Blok, Andrei Bely, Vyacheslav Ivanov). And even here it should be noted that, for example, Ivanov was in fact older than Bryusov but debuted as a poet significantly later.

Another important distinction would be geographic. Bryusov, Balmont, and Bely were Muscovites; the Merezhkovskys, Sologub, Blok, and Ivanov lived in Petersburg. In their arguments the symbolists often defined the enemy camps as "Moscow" and "Petersburg," but the borders were very flexible, with unexpected allies and defectors. The "Muscovites" on the whole were more "decadent" and, disdaining abstract theorizing, strove for pure aestheticism. The "Petersburgers," on the other hand, readily debated religious and civic themes.

For all the acrimony of the debates between the Muscovites and the Petersburgers, the public perceived the symbolists more or less as a single group. At first the most famous among them was the Muscovite Balmont. But the audience soon focused on Blok. "Blok's poetry affected us the way the moon does lunatics,"[29] Chukovsky recalled. His poetry's lyrical expressiveness and musicality, its hypnotic, singsong quality, exalted mystical imagery, and undoubted erotic appeal attracted readers, especially women.

The appeal of Blok's poetry was compounded by his magnetism. Tens of thousands of postcards with his photograph were sold all over Russia, adorned with the refined "face of the young Apollo" (as the photo was described) in a glorious aureole of blond curls, sensual lips, an exalted look in his pale gray eyes. Blok was photographed in a black shirt with a smooth white collar, his hands folded together—the ideal image of the symbolist poet.

According to Chukovsky, Blok was "unbearably, unbelievably" handsome. "I had never before nor after ever seen a person exude magnetism so clearly, palpably, and visibly. It was hard to imagine that there was a young woman in the world who might not fall in love with him."[30] A female contemporary concurred: "In those days there wasn't a single 'thinking' young woman in Russia who wasn't in love with Blok."[31]

We learn of a typical fan's love for Blok from this reminiscence:

> Sonechka Mikhailova was a "Turgenev girl" with a long soft braid and small black eyes, who blushed easily. Once she walked behind Blok for a long time as he returned from some meeting with a friend. Blok was agitated, arguing furiously, and smoking—Sonechka picked up the butts, collected a small box of them, and probably still has them to this day. Dying of love for Blok, she would go to his house. But not daring to enter, she would stand by the door and kiss the wooden handle of the entry, weeping.[32]

Blok was showered with letters asking for a rendezvous ("It would be the greatest day of my *life!*") or demanding advice; one young writer famous in Petersburg circles told Blok that her marriage was fictitious and she wanted to have his child, who most certainly would be a genius. (She offered the same proposal to two other writers at the same time, though.) Many young poets sent their works to Blok; the fortunate ones who got a response—even negative—were undoubtedly proud for the rest of their lives. But his inaccessibility became legendary, and many who wanted to show Blok their work did not dare to do so.

One of Blok's meek admirers was Marc Chagall, a nineteen-year-old artist from the backwater town of Vitebsk and new in Petersburg. Soon after his arrival Chagall went to the premiere of Blok's play *The Fair Show Booth* directed by Meyerhold. In a long room with a small stage, a show unlike anything the Russian theater had ever known went on for forty minutes. Harlequin, Pierrot, and Columbine, the traditional characters of commedia dell'arte, appeared in Blok's play, but here they were ultramodern and typically symbolist, even decadent. The eccentric and challenging poetry interplayed with the transparent music (composed by the poet Mikhail Kuzmin, who was also an accomplished musician). For Meyerhold this was a wonderful opportunity to realize his ideas of symbolist theater. Later he would write, "The first push toward setting the path of my art was given . . . by the fortunate invention of the plan for Alexander Blok's marvelous *The Fair Show Booth*."[33]

Meyerhold himself—tall, lanky, with a hooked nose and abrupt gestures—played Pierrot. In a harsh, almost creaking voice, he shouted at the stunned audience, "Help! I'm bleeding cranberry juice!" At the end of the play Pierrot summed up the action: "I'm very sad. And you think it's funny?" He then took a flute from the pocket of his traditional white costume with big lace collar and played a simple melody, typically Kuzminian.

As the lights gradually went on, the bewildered audience sat in silence. But then a storm broke out, which another poet described, not without envy: "I had never seen before or since such implacable opposition and such delight in the fans in a theater. The vicious whistling of the foes and the thunder of friendly applause mixed with shouts and cries. This was fame."[34]

This highly eccentric spectacle made an indelible impression on the young Chagall. Like many of his peers, he wrote lyric poetry à la Blok, which he didn't dare show to Blok himself. But Chagall retained the atmosphere, symbols, and images of *The Fair Show Booth* throughout his life.

Blok societies were appearing all over the country and the cult of the poet was spreading. At parties high school students would read to one another, trying to imitate the author's monotonous-hypnotic manner, Blok's most "decadent" verse:

> In tavern, alleys, and side streets,
> In the electric dream wide awake,
> I sought the endlessly beautiful
> Who were immortally in love with fame.

Or his poem "The Unknown Woman," about the mysterious beauty, floating past the poet like a vision, in a cheap suburban restaurant filled with "rabbit-eyed drunkards"—the poem was reprinted in the popular anthology *Reader-Declaimer* and read all over Russia:

> Ancient beliefs waft
> From her heavy silks,
> And her hat with funereal feathers,
> And her narrow hand in rings.

Prostitutes on Nevsky Prospect quickly bought hats with black ostrich feathers and demonstrated they were au courant to potential clients. "I'm the Unknown Woman, would you like to get to know me?" Or even more temptingly, "We are a pair of Unknown Women. You can have the 'electric dream wide awake,' you won't regret it." The reading public gave Blok the title "poet of Nevsky Prospect." This was, in the words of a contemporary critic, "the decadence of decadence."

Despite all this, Blok remains to this day one of the most loved—and widely read—Russian poets. The lyrical power, vivid imagery, and haunting rhythm of his verse retain all the impact they had on his first readers. Today Russians may wince at some of Blok's highly charged romantic sentiments and yet, again and again, they surrender to his magical voice.

Along with the other "thinking young women of Russia," teenage Anna Gorenko read and reread Blok's "The Unknown Woman." "It is marvelous, that intertwining of trite quotidian life and the divine vivid vision," the seventeen-year-old poetess enthused, just having picked "Akhmatova" as a pseudonym. "Akhmatova" has strangely Tatar overtones for a Russian ear, but Anna decided on it anyway, since her father, a naval engineer, had forbidden her to publish poetry signed Gorenko, because "I don't want you sullying my name!" The cult of Blok, traditional for the times, reigned in young Anna's family; for instance, her sister "idolized" Blok and insisted, in the fashionable decadent way, that she had "the other half of Blok's soul."[35]

The complicated relations between Akhmatova and Blok and the legend that surrounded them would hold one of the most important places in Akhmatova's life; later she would complain that the legend "threatens to distort my poetry and even my biography." But then, in 1907, Akhmatova had no inkling of it, even though she had a high enough opinion of herself from childhood.

Born, as she liked to remind us, in the same year as Charlie Chaplin, Tolstoy's *Kreutzer Sonata,* and the Eiffel Tower, Akhmatova wrote her first poem at age eleven. But her father called her a "decadent poetess" even earlier. She began her autobiography at eleven, and at fifteen she stopped in front of the dacha where she was born and blurted out to her mother, "There will be a memorial plaque here someday."

"Mama was upset," Akhmatova later recalled. " 'God, how badly I brought you up,' she said." In this, as in many other things, Akhmatova was a prophet: her birthplace had become a tourist attraction by the end of the twentieth century. When a high school girlfriend brought Akhmatova a bouquet of lilies of the valley, she rejected it scornfully, declaring she needed at least "hyacinths from Patagonia."[36]

In high school Akhmatova attracted attention for her slender, agile figure, her face with its large, bright eyes contrasted with her dark hair, brows, and lashes; her unusual profile (her girlfriends noted her nose with the "special" bump); her pride, stubbornness, and capriciousness; and, in particular, her wide knowledge of modernist poetry.

Nikolai Gumilyov, three years her senior, fell in love with Akhmatova when she was fourteen. Like her relationship with Blok, this was to be the start of the other great Russian cultural legend of the twentieth century, another leitmotif in the Akhmatova mythology. Gumilyov, who subsequently became a famous poet, was destined for a horrible end. But in 1903 the gangling, cross-eyed, lisping seventh-grader did not make much of an impression on the supercilious, sharp girl. Poems dedicated to her did not help (Gumilyov had started writing poetry at the age of five).

Gumilyov, however, was also stubborn and persistent. He studied versification with single-minded diligence, immersed himself in Western poetry (especially the French symbolists), and continued over the next many years to offer his hand and heart to Anna. He had dedicated to her an impressive cycle of love poetry, in which he described her as a mermaid, a sorceress, and a queen, and he affirmed he had attempted suicide several times because of her. She refused him several times, then half agreed, and then refused again. At last she wrote to her best friend, "Pray for me. It can't be any worse. I want to die," and then on April 25, 1910, she married Gumilyov. As it often happens, marriage was the beginning of the end of their relationship. Suddenly Gumilyov found Akhmatova's company tiresome.

The newlyweds headed straight for Paris. As Akhmatova liked to put it later, 1910 was the year of Leo Tolstoy's death, the crisis of Russian symbolism, and her meeting with the young and unknown artist Amedeo Modigliani. But that year she saw him only once. They became close in 1911, when Akhmatova was in Paris again. Many years later Joseph Brodsky described their relationship with poetic license as "*Romeo and Juliet* performed by members of the royal house." This characterization, Brodsky told me, " vastly amused" the elderly Akhmatova.[37] In 1911 Akhmatova and Modigliani wandered in the Paris rain, went to the Louvre to look at the Egyptian mummies (thin and mysterious, Akhmatova was later called the "mummy who brings everyone bad luck"), and watched strange-looking bi-planes circle the Eiffel Tower, Akhmatova's peer.

Flying was the latest thrill in Paris and in Petersburg. Blok, who never missed an aerial show, wrote a poem entitled "Aviator," dedicated to the memory of a pilot who had died before his eyes. The pilots, who also amused themselves by innocently throwing oranges down at targets, interested everyone. They seemed dashing and sexy; a Petersburg theater ran a farce in which a lady wanting to have an affair with a pilot flies up into the clouds with him. Passionate sounds soon fill the stage and the audience watches the lady's intimate articles of clothing float down upon them, as if they were at a striptease where the stripper was invisible.

Modigliani, according to Akhmatova, was also fascinated by aviators and thought that they must be extraordinary people. She remembered meeting the famous pilot Louis Bleriot. She was having dinner with Gumilyov in a Paris restaurant; unexpectedly Bleriot came up to them. During the meal Akhmatova had slipped off her tight new shoes. When they got home, she found a note with Bleriot's address in one of them.

Modigliani did a series of drawings of Akhmatova, some of them nudes. One delicate portrait, in an Egyptian mode (Modigliani was then in his Egyptian phase), is often reproduced today on the jackets of Akhmatova's books. But in her first book, published in 1912—at her own expense with a printing of only 300 copies—under the unassuming title *Evening*, Akhmatova did not use Modigliani's portrait. Instead, *Evening* had a typically *Mir iskusstva* frontispiece by Evgeny Lanceray. (Akhmatova said Modigliani laughed openly at the art of *Mir iskusstva*.)

The critics were more than kind to *Evening*, and its small printing sold out immediately. Even the critical Gumilyov (according to Akhmatova "a man direct to the point of cruelty, judging poetry with extreme severity") approved of the book. Earlier he advised his wife to go into dancing instead: "You're so lithe." Akhmatova herself rather coquettishly referred to her first book as "the poor poems of a shallow girl." If she is to be believed, she was so upset that *Evening* was coming out that she fled to Italy and "sitting in a trolley, looked at my companions and thought. 'How fortunate they are—they don't have a book coming out.' "

Some readers seem to think now that Russia's women first found their poetic voice and cultural representative in Akhmatova, and that in that sense she made her debut on an empty stage, so to speak. This is not so. Akhmatova's creativity was the pinnacle of a long and glorious literary tradition. Akhmatova, and her younger contemporary Marina Tsvetayeva, were poets of genius (they both intensely disliked the word "poetess"), but there were quite a few successful and famous Russian women writers before them.

In fact, the first well-established Russian poetess, Anna Bunina (1774–1829), was a distant relative of Akhmatova's maternal grandfather. Princess Zinaida Volkonskaya (1792–1862) and Countess Eudoxia Rostopchina (1811–1858) were in their time compared to comets blazing across the Russian literary firmament, writing notable verse and prose. Pushkin himself published a sensational work in 1836, *From the Notes of a Maiden Cavalryman,* by Nadezhda Durova—the memoirs of the author's incredible exploits, dressed as a Cossack, in the battles against Napoleon.

As the literary and periodical market exploded in Russia, professional women's participation in it rose significantly as well. Publishing companies and magazines desperately needed translators, copy editors, copyists, and secretaries; educated Russian women gladly accepted the jobs, horrifying the authorities. In 1870 Pyotr Shuvalov, the omnipotent chief of the gendarmes, presented Emperor Alexander II with a special report that sounded the alarm: "Our woman dreams of leading an immoral life, saying that the word morality was invented by the despotism of men. . . . We must admit that a woman nihilist is much more harmful than a woman of openly indecent behavior." And the gendarme, who was known as "the head inquisitor of the empire," demanded, "Can a woman who spends half the day in an office filled with men, where certain ties and demoralization are inevitable, be a loving mother and a good housewife?"[38]

But the swift integration of women into the world of literature could not be stemmed by the police, or the emperor, or even male writers clearly worried by the growth of competition and losing influence in an area they had traditionally dominated. One leading liberal journalist of the period expressed the views of the majority of his fellow men when he charged, without any real proof, that "You women come to the manuscript marketplace—I am speaking of the manuscript market, not the idea marketplace, calm down—you come with the most horrible, the most treacherous weapon: you knock down prices impossibly. You are dooming other workers to starvation."[39]

The education level of Russian women was rising, and their economic independence was becoming stronger accordingly; this nat-

urally led to an increase in the number of women as a significant segment of the reading public. And that trend was confirmed by various
reader surveys: there were many women subscribers to public and private libraries and they were increasingly buying newspapers, journals,
and books.

In Petersburg many magazines appeared that targeted a specif-
ically female audience. Among them were *Zhenskii vestnik* (*Woman's
Herald*) and *Damskii listok* (*Ladies' Sheet*). The weekly *Zhenshchina*
(*Woman*), in content and form similar to the popular *Ogonyok* (with
the subtitle *Mother—Citizen—Wife—Housewife*), had departments
like Women in the Arts, Women's Creativity, Famous Actresses, For
Mothers About Children, Woman-Citizen, The Elegant Woman,
Women of the World, Women in New Roles, Famous Contemporary
Women, Women and Humor. The publishers may still have made sar-
castic remarks about "reading ladies," but they had to take the siz-
able group of potential customers into account.

One of the first and most striking examples of that audience's
economic power came in 1909, when *The Keys of Happiness,* a novel
by the then little-known writer Anastasia Verbitskaya, sold thirty
thousand copies in four months, creating the terms "women's genre"
and "women's novel" in Russia. Verbitskaya, who had gone all the
way from copy editor of a newspaper to author of the number-one
best-seller, now wrote novels filled with vivid adventures of passionate and talented women of the artistic milieu.

Exalted in tone, Verbitskaya's colorful potboilers, openly propagandizing leftist and feminist views, elicited extremely hostile reviews from the same critics who had patronizingly patted her on the
back before the phenomenal success of *The Keys of Happiness*. In the
newspaper *Rech* (*Speech*), the ubiquitous Chukovsky, admitting that
"our young people are crowding after Mrs. Verbitskaya," still proclaimed that this was literature "for urban savages."[40]

Such scorn did not diminish Verbitskaya's popularity—on the
contrary. Her novels continued to sell in huge quantities and spawned
numerous imitations. Verbitskaya, a socialist by conviction and a civic
activist by temperament, became chairwoman of the Society for the
Betterment of Women's Condition and energetically helped other
women writers. In the 1910s their position grew considerably stronger
and women's names ceased to be a rarity among best-selling authors.
Eudoxia Nagrodskaya's erotic novel, *Wrath of Dionysus*, with its typically "women's genre" artist heroine and advocacy of free love, went
through ten printings in just a few years. Lydia Charskaya and Klav-

dia Lukashevich (the latter became the newborn Dmitri Shostakovich's godmother in September 1906 and inculcated a love of reading in little Dmitri) were among the most popular names in contemporary fiction. In the 1940s, when Boris Pasternak was working on his novel, *Doctor Zhivago,* he said that he was "writing almost like Charskaya," because he wanted to be accessible and dreamed that his prose would be gulped down, "even by a seamstress, even by a dishwasher."[41]

Russian women poets had reached a mass audience even earlier. After the Boer War of 1899–1902, organ grinders in every Petersburg courtyard played the touching song "Transvaal, Transvaal, my dear country, you are in flames!" The words of this moving, sentimental ballad, which became a folk song, were written by Glafira Galina, a thirty-year-old poet. Even now I can't listen to it without the threat of tears. Another of her poems, "The forest is being cut down—the young, tender-green forest," an allegorical description of the tsarist repressions of students, elicited "delight and tears," Mikhail Kuzmin said, when it was read in public and prompted the authorities to exile Galina from Petersburg. So when her collection of poems, *Predawn Songs,* came out in 1906, it sold five thousand copies, a healthy sale for poetry.

Naturally, the young Akhmatova was interested in and influenced by the comparatively new female "decadent" tradition. At its beginning stands the extraordinary figure of Marie Bashkirtseff. The Russian but thoroughly Francophile Bashkirtseff, who died in Paris of tuberculosis a few days before her twenty-fourth birthday in 1884, was a successful artist who exhibited in the Salon and corresponded with Guy de Maupassant. She dreamed of great love and universal recognition. Feeling that she would not have long to live, Bashkirtseff devoured knowledge with incredible intensity, quickly turning from a precocious wunderkind into an independent-minded and assertive young woman. Her real fame came posthumously from the diary that she kept in French from the age of thirteen, published by the poet André Theuriet in 1887, three years after her death.

The emotionally and stylistically exalted diary, described by Bashkirtseff as "the life of a woman, recorded day after day, without any pretense, as if no one in the world would ever read it and at the same time with a passionate desire that it be read," touched on many popular fin-de-siècle themes. Bashkirtseff's self-image was wildly romanticized; when her diary was published in Russia, neither Leo Tolstoy nor Chekhov liked it. But it was those very qualities that endeared her to the first Russian modernists. Valery Bryusov noted in his diary that Bashkirtseff "is me, with all my thoughts, convictions, and dreams." And Velimir Khlebnikov, one of the leading Russian futurists, considered her outpourings "the exact diary of my spirit."

Independent and ambitious young women all over Russia became engrossed in Bashkirtseff's diary. Its admirers included the young Marina Tsvetayeva, who dedicated her first book, *Evening Album*, published in 1910, to "the brilliant memory of Maria Bashkirtseff." This prompted the snob Gumilyov to rebuke Tsvetayeva in his review. This sarcastic attitude toward Bashkirtseff on the part of Akhmatova's husband gives a clue to a telling detail. When Akhmatova's first book, *Evening*, is reprinted now, it has the following epigraph from Theuriet:

> *La fleur des vignes pousse*
> *Et j'ai vingt ans ce soir.*

I believe Akhmatova used those lines to establish a connection with the work or at least the image of Bashkirtseff, whose admirer and champion Theuriet was. And it is significant that the "nod" in Bashkirtseff's direction appeared for the first time in Akhmatova's collection published in 1940, when the authorities ended a fifteen-year ban on her poetry. This was her first volume of selected works, in a sense. Gumilyov had been dead for almost twenty years by then. One can speculate that Akhmatova restored the epigraph, originally intended for the book in 1912, which she had removed at the time either because of Gumilyov's opposition or from fear of being mocked by him and his friends for her "bad taste." The lesson given to Tsvetayeva was learned well by the proud and ambitious Akhmatova.

Another seminal proto-decadent figure in poetry was the famed beauty Mirra Lokhvitskaya (1869–1905), who also died young of tuberculosis. Lokhvitskaya was cheered and celebrated at her public readings and at age twenty-seven received the most coveted Russian literary award of the day, the Pushkin Prize, for her first collection. She was called the "Russian Sappho," as was Akhmatova later, because she wrote primarily of love—passionate, ecstatic, exotic. At first she was accused of "immodesty," "unchasteness," even "immorality," though Tolstoy himself defended her: "It's the young drunken wine spouting. It will quiet down and cool, and pure waters will flow."[42]

The first Russian Nobel laureate in literature, Ivan Bunin, recalled how Lokhvitskaya's public image hardly corresponded with her real life. Neither her passionate admirers nor her severe critics ever suspected that Lokhvitskaya was "the mother of several children, a homebody, and indolent in an Eastern way: she even receives guests lying in a robe on her sofa."[43] Lokhvitskaya was close to the "older" symbolists in the melodiousness of her verse, its message of emotional and erotic emancipation, and her growing interest in medieval matters, including satanic cults. Women in Lokhvitskaya's poetry resembled the ideal of the pre-Raphaelites, but in one of her popular poems of 1895 there appears a stanza strikingly similar to the themes and images of the vintage Akhmatova:

> *And if the mark of the chosen is upon you*
> *But you are doomed to wear the yoke of slave,*
> *Bear your cross with the majesty of a goddess.*
> *Know how to suffer!*

The most famous and influential of the modernist poetesses was Zinaida Hippius, the "decadent Madonna." All Petersburg was talking about the tall beauty with green eyes who dressed extravagantly and presented herself in an outlandish way. Bunin's description may help us understand why Hippius's mere appearance caused a sensation: "a heavenly vision walked in slowly, an angel of astonishing thinness in snow-white garments and golden loose hair, along whose bare arms something akin to sleeves or wings fell to the very floor."[44]

Along with her husband, Merezhkovsky, Hippius imperiously "ran" Petersburg's symbolist movement for many years by receiving a steady flow of visitors after midnight in her apartment, recumbent on a chaise longue, smoking long, scented cigarettes and unceremoniously peering at her guests through her famous lorgnette. Her opinions and declarations were epigrammatic and beyond appeal. The denizens of literary Petersburg respected, hated, and, most important, feared Hippius.

For beginning modernists a visit to the Merezhkovsky salon was mandatory, almost a ritual. But Akhmatova avoided that ritual. The reason was the reception the Merezhkovskys had given to young Gumilyov in 1906. Hippius described his visit devastatingly in a letter to Bryusov:

> Twenty years old. Deathly pallor. His sententious ideas are as old as the hat of a widow visiting the cemetery. He sniffs the ether (about time!) and says that he alone can change the world. "There were attempts before me . . . Buddha, Christ. . . . But unsuccessful."[45]

Peter the Great was challenging, demanding, deliberately outrageous, full of contradictions. His idea of establishing a new city in 1703—the future capital of the Russian Empire, St. Petersburg—appeared as the whim of an incredibly rich, reckless, and lucky gambler. Peter wanted to astonish Russia and the entire civilized world, and he succeeded.

(Top) At the unveiling of the monument to Peter the Great in 1782, the gratified Petersburgers could not foresee that Etienne Falconet's work would become the most important representation of their city.

(Above) The flooding of Petersburg in 1824 inspired the creation of Pushkin's *Bronze Horseman* in 1833. Thus nature, culture, and history collided conspicuously.

(Right) The Bronze Horseman, at once dashing into the sky and rooted in stone, gave birth to the legend that as long as the monument remained in place Petersburg would not perish.

(Right) The Petersburg mythos would not have existed without Alexander Pushkin, who transformed what had been no more than a monument to the great emperor—though an awesome one—into the very emblem of Petersburg, a sign of its majesty and endurance, and also into the symbol of the awful fate and terrible suffering that were to befall the city. Self-portrait of the poet, 1829.

(Above) The Bronze Horseman pursues poor Yevgeny: in Pushkin's poem the statue represents not only Peter the Great and the city he founded but also the state itself. What is more important—the individual's happiness or the city's and the state's triumph? Illustration by Alexander Benois for Pushkin's *Bronze Horseman*, 1916.

(Right) Mikhail Glinka, "a kind of Russian Rossini": his *Valse-Fantaisie*, in which erotic longing acquires an almost spiritual tone, was the wellspring of Petersburg music.

(Below) Imperial Petersburg in winter: view of the Neva River and St. Isaac's Cathedral. Lithograph of the mid-nineteenth century.

(Left) Nikolai Gogol shattered the image of imperial Petersburg, creating his own obsessive vision in which the capital is not really a city at all, but a land of the living dead. Drawing by Nathan Altman, 1934, for Gogol's *Petersburg Tales*.

(Below) Gogol's Nevsky Prospect: "It's all deceit, all dreams, it's all not what it seems!"

(Above left) Fyodor Dostoyevsky on St. Petersburg: "I'm sorry, I don't love it. Windows, holes—and monuments." Wood engraving by Vladimir Favorsky, 1929.

(Above right) Dostoyevsky's spectral Petersburg will exist as long as there is Russian literature. Mstislav Dobuzhinsky's illustration, 1922, for Dostoyevsky's *White Nights* creates an atmosphere of quiet despair.

(Right) Modest Mussorgsky, who created "Dostoyevskian" operas, died of acute alcoholism. This portrait was done by Ilya Repin in Petersburg's military hospital just ten days before the composer's death in 1881.

(Above) Petipa's *Sleeping Beauty*, set to Tchaikovsky's music, inspired the unprecedented re-evaluation of the Petersburg mythos: it was transformed from sinister to benign, from dour to luminous. An 1890 photograph, taken after the ballet's premiere at the Maryinsky theater.

(Left) Marius Petipa endowed his ballets with a vision of Petersburg's grandeur and sense of architectural harmony and classical purity.

(Left) Peter Tchaikovsky's music was a forewarning for Petersburgers of the coming collisions and catastrophes.

(Below) Tchaikovsky's opera *The Queen of Spades*, based on Pushkin, brought its listeners "the poison of Petersburg nights, the sweet mirage of its ghostly images." Design for the 1931 production by Vladimir Dmitriev.

After a reception like that, it's no surprise that when Akhmatova wanted to show her poems to Hippius in 1910, she was dissuaded: "Don't go, she's very nasty to young poets." Later Hippius made a point of calling Akhmatova and inviting her to her salon, but even then there was no meeting of the minds. And in the last years of her life, Akhmatova was still hostile toward Hippius, saying that she was "a clever, educated woman, but nasty and mean." Merezhkovsky also displeased Akhmatova. "Typical boulevard writer. How can you read him?"[46]

There was also the scandalous affair of the poetess Cherubina de Gabriac in 1909, which made a big impression on Akhmatova. The sensational hoax caused one of the last famous duels in the history of Russian culture. What mattered most for Akhmatova was the fact that one of the duelists was Gumilyov.

The stage on which this spectacle, so symbolic of the era, was played out was the editorial office of the new modernist journal *Apollo*. The magazine continued the work and line of *Mir iskusstva* and was organized by Gumilyov and the influential art critic Sergei Makovsky. Financing came from Mikhail Ushkov, the son of the immeasurably wealthy tea magnate.

In Petersburg Makovsky was considered an arbiter of taste. No one else in the capital had such long, starched collars or such glossy patent leather shoes. Gossip had it that the flawless part in his hair had been permanently etched by a special lotion from Paris. His waxed mustache stood out challengingly. Makovsky, a mediocre poet, considered himself the highest authority in literature as well and edited Blok's poems because they were "grammatically incorrect."

In 1965, Akhmatova characterized Makovsky flatly and quite unjustly as a "world-class philistine and a total idiot."[47] It turns out that he asked her an embarrassing question when she and Gumilyov returned from their Parisian honeymoon: "Are you satisfied with your sex life now?" After that, Akhmatova told me, she avoided being left alone with Makovsky.

In early September 1909 an elegant envelope sealed with black wax and imprinted with a coat of arms and the motto *Vae victis* arrived at the *Apollo* office on the embankment of the Moika River. Opening it, Makovsky found Russian poems and an accompanying letter written in refined French on paper with a black border signed by Cherubina de Gabriac, apparently a wealthy noblewoman. The return address was a post office box.

Makovsky was impressed by the poetry but even more so by the letter, and immediately replied, also in French, with a request that more work be sent. The next day the mysterious Cherubina called Makovsky. That was the start of their affair by phone, which the entire staff of *Apollo* followed avidly. Makovsky was certain that his new love was at least a countess and worried, "If I had forty thousand a year, I'd court her." Cherubina de Gabriac, keeping her distance, continued to intrigue Makovsky, calling him almost every day. "What an astonishing woman! I always knew how to trifle with a woman's heart, but the sword is knocked from my hands now," Makovsky mused.

A selection of twelve poems by Cherubina appeared in *Apollo*. Literary Petersburg was abuzz; a young poet wrote to a friend, "Their characteristic trait is frenzied Catholicism; the mix of sin and repentance (the hymn to Ignatius Loyola, prayers to the Virgin, etc.). At any rate, no one has ever written like this in Russian before."[48] Only a few people knew that Cherubina de Gabriac did not exist, that her fiery poems filled with "mystical eros," as Vyacheslav Ivanov put it, were a hoax.

Every literary hoax has elements of parody. In order to succeed, the hoax must reflect existing trends of the literary scene. Cherubina was invented by the young, erudite poet Maximilian Voloshin and his lover, Elizaveta Dmitrieva. The latter was a twenty-two-year-old teacher of history at a women's high school in Petersburg, earning eleven and a half rubles monthly, who wrote interesting verse. But the "modest, inelegant and lame" (as Voloshin described her) Dmitrieva had no hope of making the necessary impression on the aesthete Makovsky.

The hoax was intended to mock Petersburg's symbolist establishment, which dreamed of a new poetic female star in the image described by Marina Tsvetayeva: "Not Russian, obviously. Beautiful, obviously. Catholic, obviously. Rich, oh, incalculably rich, obviously (female Byron, without the limp), externally happy, obviously, so that she could be unhappy in her own pure and selfless way." Voloshin and Dmitrieva's Cherubina was "constructed" to those specifications, and that is why their hoax succeeded so brilliantly.

This attack on the prejudices of the symbolists was a risky one. After the game got too complex, and the besotted Makovsky was on the verge of a nervous breakdown, someone revealed Cherubina's true identity to him. Dmitrieva came to the editor of *Apollo* to apologize. Many years later Makovsky described the visit:

The door opened slowly, too slowly it seemed to me, and a woman entered, with a strong limp, rather short and plump, with dark hair and a large head and a truly horrible mouth, from which fanglike teeth protruded. She was simply ugly. Or did it seem that way to me in comparison with the image of beauty that I had envisaged all those months?[49]

A woman poet was not allowed to be ugly, poor, and truly miserable, as opposed to miserable in verse, and so Dmitrieva's poetic career was soon over. *Apollo* did run another large selection of her poetry, which it served up with great elan, with artwork by Yevgeny Lanceray. But it was the beginning of the end. The star of Cherubina de Gabriac vanished from the poetic horizon, while Voloshin, still the center of attention, continued to manipulate Cherubina's name, maintaining as late as 1917 that "to a certain extent she set the tone for modern women's poetry." Tellingly, in 1913 two other hoax images of poetesses appeared, as if to confirm the public's longing for a female voice in poetry: "Nellie," whose coy poems were written by Valery Bryusov, and the completely parodic "Angelica Safyanova."

The drama of Cherubina-Dmitrieva was not limited to literature. The sensational incident that followed upon it, never to be forgotten by either Akhmatova or Tsvetayeva, crossed the line between literary games and utter cruelty. Before her meeting with Voloshin, Dmitrieva had had an affair with Gumilyov. Such a relationship was entirely in keeping with the erotically and melodramatically charged atmosphere of the period. Dmitrieva later insisted that Gumilyov had begged her to marry him: "He twisted my fingers and then wept and kissed the hem of my dress."

But Dmitrieva, in turn, became infatuated with Voloshin, so Gumilyov's love, according to Dmitrieva, turned to hate. "He stopped me at the *Apollo* offices and said, 'I'm asking you for the last time— will you marry me?' I said, 'No!' He grew pale. 'Then you'll hear from me.' "[50] Soon both Voloshin and Dmitrieva learned that Gumilyov was denouncing her publicly, without mincing words.

On November 19, 1909, the poets of *Apollo* met in the studio of the artist Golovin (the creator of Chaliapin's portrait in his role as Holofernes), under the roof of the Maryinsky Theater. Present were Alexander Blok, Vyacheslav Ivanov, Innokenti Annensky, Mikhail Kuzmin, and Alexei Tolstoy. So were Makovsky, Gumilyov, and Voloshin. Golovin was supposed to paint a group portrait. They could hear Chaliapin downstairs on stage, singing an aria from *Faust*. When he finished, the stocky, broad-shouldered Voloshin, who weighed at least two hundred pounds, jumped up and slapped tall, pale Gumilyov in the face. After a stunned silence, the only comment came from Annensky, who never lost his Olympian calm: "Dostoyevsky is right—a slap really does have a wet sound."

Right there in the studio, Gumilyov challenged Voloshin to a duel, considering himself particularly knowledgeable about the custom. Two days were spent finding antique pistols. Voloshin insisted that if they weren't the exact ones Pushkin used in his legendary duel, they were certainly of that period; and they naturally had their duel in the same place as Pushkin's. The avalanche of jokes and mockery over the duel, in part because it had been so earnestly planned in the grand tradition, spread all over Petersburg. Every local reporter had a good laugh at the expense of Voloshin and Gumilyov.

The terms were a distance of twenty paces, one shot apiece. Luckily, both Voloshin and Gumilyov missed. The Petersburg newspapers got the story of the outcome and pounced mercilessly on the duelists. Makovsky was probably right in his supposition that the "reporters of the yellow press used this as a pretext to get their revenge on *Apollo* for its bold literary claims."

The final blow came from their own symbolist camp, when Zinaida Hippius wrote a story that ridiculed a duel "of two third-rate poets." In those days of persistent hounding by both the press and gossip-mongers, Voloshin saw Petersburg as "the main test tube of Russian psychopathy." However, both he and Gumilyov survived the scandal intact. Not so Dmitrieva. She understood the rules of the game when she told Makovsky, "Once I bury Cherubina, I bury myself, never to be resurrected."[51] And, indeed, Dmitrieva disappeared from the literary scene for a long time.

Twenty-year-old Akhmatova intently watched how the story unfolded and she never forgot those autumnal days of 1909. First of all, she was deeply wounded by the affair between her husband and Dmitrieva. But Akhmatova's professional ambitions must have been injured even more. Voloshin wrote to a friend in November 1909, "Cherubina de Gabriac's success is enormous. She is imitated, people who have nothing to do with literature learn her by heart, and the Petersburg poets hate and envy her."

In the final analysis, both the hoax and duel were in large part about literary competition. Toward the end of her life, Akhmatova spoke of Dmitrieva with undisguised scorn: "She thought that a duel of two poets over her would make her a fashionable Petersburg lady and would guarantee her place in the capital's literary circles." But, according to Akhmatova, "Something in Dmitrieva's calculations went wrong."

In the late 1950s Akhmatova summed up the whole story in comments so frank that few readers would have imagined Akhmatova had written them had they not been in her own hand: "Obviously, at the time (1909–1910) there was a kind of secret vacancy for a woman's place in Russian poetry. Cherubina tried to fill it. Either the duel or something in her poetry kept her from taking that place. Fate wanted it to be mine."[52]

To this sober evaluation of her own position in Russian poetry at the end of the century's first decade, Akhmatova adds a revealing comment: "Amazingly, this was half-understood by Marina Tsvetayeva." Any discussion of Russian poetry of the twentieth century inevitably brings up the paired names of Akhmatova and Tsvetayeva. They are juxtaposed and compared, which is understandable, since it is difficult to imagine two poets more different in temperament and technique.

Tsvetayeva, three years younger than Akhmatova, lived a tragic life and hanged herself in 1941 at age forty-nine in a small provincial town. Her complex relations with Akhmatova deserve a study of their own. I will touch here on only one aspect—their struggle for primacy in Russian women's poetry in the 1910s. The eighteen-year-old Tsvetayeva had published her first work, *Evening Album*, in the fall of 1910, that is, a year after the Cherubina de Gabriac affair and a year and a half before Akhmatova's first book came out. Tsvetayeva was published in Moscow, Akhmatova in Petersburg, and as is always the case in Russia, the difference was not simply geographical.

Akhmatova's image is inexorably tied to Petersburg for her readers and contemporaries, as Tsvetayeva's is with Moscow. Tsvetayeva wrote, "With my entire being I sense the tension—inevitable—with my every line—we are being compared (and in some situations—pitted)—not only Akhmatova and I, but Petersburg poetry and Moscow poetry, Petersburg and Moscow."

Tsvetayeva could be generous and many times, especially in her poems, she spoke of her reverence for Akhmatova and could even grant literary Petersburg primacy over Moscow, as she did in her colorful letter to Mikhail Kuzmin:

It was so cold—and there are so many monuments in Petersburg—
and the sleigh flew so fast—everything blurred—and all that was left
of Petersburg was the poetry of Pushkin and Akhmatova. Ah, no—
there were also the fireplaces. Everywhere I was taken, there were
huge marble fireplaces—entire oaken groves were burned!—and polar bears on the floor (polar bears by the fire!—monstrous!), and all
the young men parted their hair—and they all had volumes of
Pushkin in their hands. . . . Oh, how they love poetry there! In all my
life I never recited as many poems as I did there in two weeks. And
they don't sleep there at all. A call at three A.M. Can we come over?
Of course, of course, we're only starting. And it goes on like that until morning.[53]

But Tsvetayeva's sympathies for Petersburg did not ease the fierceness
of the struggle for literary supremacy either in 1910 or later, especially
because Tsvetayeva found many influential allies in this battle. In her
memoirs, she recalled Voloshin, who was already involved in creating Cherubina de Gabriac, asking Tsvetayeva to invent a few other
mythical poets as well, like "seventeen-year-old Mr. Petukhov" or
"the Kryukov twins, poetic geniuses, brother and sister." Voloshin enchanted Tsvetayeva with a picture of her total victory over her enemies' camp: "Besides you, no one will be left in Russian poetry. With
your Petukhovs and twins you, Marina, will drive them all out,
Akhmatova, and Gumilyov, and Kuzmin."

Bryusov, the master of Moscow symbolism, tellingly supported
Tsvetayeva's *Evening Album* in an important review. Speaking of the
"terrifying intimacy" of Tsvetayeva's poems, he noted, "When you
read her books, you occasionally feel uncomfortable, as if you had
peeked immodestly through a half-shut window into someone's apartment and observed a scene strangers should not see."[54] Most interestingly, Tsvetayeva's debut was hailed by Gumilyov—another
confirmation of Gumilyov's high moral scruples as a critic. Gumilyov
too stressed the extraordinary frankness of the *Evening Album*.
"Much is new in this book—the bold (sometimes excessive) intimacy;
the themes, for instance, children's crushes; the direct, almost crazed
affection for the trifles of life."[55]

Voloshin seemed to be summing up a critical consensus when,
while listing several names in late 1910 that he felt were notable in
contemporary women's poetry (Tsvetayeva was on that list, but not
Akhmatova), he stated, "In some respects this women's lyric poetry
is more interesting than the men's. It is less burdened with ideas and
is deeper and more frank."

So Akhmatova was probably correct when late in life, recalling this era, she stated, "I filled the vacancy for a woman poet, which was open." There was such a vacancy. But it's unlikely that anyone could simply fill it. It had to be taken. It had to be won.

Roman Timenchik observed that there are a variety of "masks" in Akhmatova's early poetry.[56] She seemed to be trying on one mask after another, figuring out which would be the most effective and attractive. Leafing through *Evening,* one can find Marie Bashkirtseff's decadent pose and Lokhvitskaya's duality, shifting back and forth between chastity and sin. Surely Akhmatova, who miraculously survived the tuberculosis that killed two of her sisters, must have felt a bond with both Bashkirtseff and Lokhvitskaya, who had succumbed to that disease in their youth. Undoubtedly, Akhmatova took into account the intellectual striving and technical virtuosity of Zinaida Hippius. *Evening* contains stylizations of female "naïveté," comparable to Tsvetayeva's early attempts. The frenzied religiosity of some of Akhmatova's works resembles the poetry of Cherubina de Gabriac. Many readers of the early Akhmatova pictured her, like Cherubina, as a mysterious foreigner. The list of borrowings, echoes, and outright imitations can be lengthened considerably, including the sometimes astonishing similarity of the early Akhmatova's turns of phrase with the style of popular "women's fiction."

Yes, Akhmatova borrowed shamelessly everywhere and this must be stressed to correct the mistaken but firmly rooted notion that she appeared suddenly in Russian literature, like Athena from the head of Zeus. This view of Akhmatova, which ignores her ties with the rich tradition of women's literature in Russia, was based and survives on the scorn for women's writing in the Russian literary establishment.

"Women's fiction" was held in particular contempt and still is. Verbitskaya attracted a mass audience as long as worn copies of her books were still in circulation, while she was attacked relentlessly by conservatives and revolutionaries alike. The Soviet authorities stopped publishing Verbitskaya after the revolution, just as they stopped publishing Bashkirtseff, Lokhvitskaya and Hippius. During the Soviet years, the "women's novel" disappeared completely. Until recently, even the mere mention of it could be found only in academic books, where it was routinely disparaged—in passing, without critical analysis.

Still, it is obvious that if Akhmatova's first book had offered readers only a parade of familiar "masks," it would not have garnered the attention it did. Boris Eikhenbaum documented the reaction of the poetry connoisseurs of the time: "We were surprised, amazed, delighted, we argued, and finally, felt pride."[57]

As even the first critics had immediately noted, "Akhmatova can speak in a way that makes long-familiar words sound new and sharp." They wondered about the "teasing disharmony" of her poems. They also agreed right away that her "broken rhythms express a morbid crisis of the soul" of a Petersburg lady.

Bryusov was probably one of the first to point out an important feature of *Evening*: "In a number of poems you can see an entire novel." Chukovsky observed: "Take a story of Maupassant, compress it extremely, and you will get an Akhmatova poem." But Osip Mandelstam later pointed out another and what he considered more important tradition for her:

> Akhmatova brought into Russian lyric poetry the enormous complexity and psychological wealth of the nineteenth-century Russian novel. Akhmatova would not exist if it were not for Tolstoy and his *Anna Karenina*, Turgenev with *A Nest of Gentlefolk*, all of Dostoyevsky and some Leskov. Akhmatova's genesis lies in Russian prose, not poetry.[58]

Akhmatova's first readers were intrigued by the narrative line of her poems, which was so different from the poetic generalizations of the symbolists, and, even more so by the fact that this narrative was the point of view of a contemporary woman living in Petersburg. It was like reading *Anna Karenina* retold by its heroine. Her public was also amazed by the appearance in Akhmatova's poems of ordinary, "nonpoetic" words. Her poetry is full of seemingly inconsequential items like dark veils, fluffy muffs, and gloves. In the poetry of the decadents these objects could appear as symbols, but for Akhmatova they were things in their own right. Yet she uses them to astonishing effect. The tragedy of unrequited love is expressed with a few simple props:

> *I put on my right hand*
> *The glove for my left.*

This is reminiscent of Chekhov, who expressed human drama in plain and sometimes incongruous words and acts. The dialogue of Chekhov's characters usually reveals only the tip of the iceberg. Akhmatova also uses this method. Her words appear like rocky islands in an ocean of silence.

This is why Akhmatova's first admirers all had a sense of the unusual weight and significance of each of those words. It seemed to them the narrator was losing her breath. Akhmatova spoke of love sparingly, as if with difficulty, and without pathos or hysteria. Thus, sophisticated Petersburgers could read an Akhmatova love poem aloud without embarrassment. It was their own voice, their world-view, presented with unprecedented clarity, precision, and psychological insight.

Of one such poem, Vladimir Mayakovsky observed, "This poem expresses refined and fragile feelings, but it is not fragile itself. Akhmatova's poems are monolithic and will resist the pressure of any voice, without cracking." Another prescient contemporary was Tsvetayeva: "Akhmatova writes about herself—about eternity. Akhmatova, without writing a single abstractly generalized line, gives our descendants the most profound picture of our age—by describing a feather in a hat."

When I first heard Akhmatova read her poetry in the 1960s, her presence and performance had an astonishing effect on me, but I was perceiving Akhmatova as a living classic. It turns out Akhmatova had enchanted her audiences when she was young, too. Even then she was considered an "exemplary reciter of poetry." She read with restraint, without pathos, but "every intonation was planned, tested, and calculated."[59] They said she prepared for every appearance, practicing before a large mirror. She knew one had to fight for the audience's attention, and she was prepared to put in the necessary time and effort. Akhmatova was a total professional from an early age. That is a particularly Petersburgian trait.

Akhmatova started her readings in the intimate circles of symbolist Petersburg, particularly at "the Tower," one of the most important centers of intellectual life in the city—the salon of the leading symbolist poet, Vyacheslav Ivanov. It was called the Tower because Ivanov's large apartment was situated in a building with a semicircular, towerlike section. The regulars at the Tower met on Wednesdays around midnight and parted at dawn. Their gentle, golden-curled host, moving rhythmically as if dancing, greeted the guests. His legendary erudition as well as the pince-nez and black gloves, which he seldom removed because of eczema, made Ivanov resemble one of Hoffmann's fantastic characters.

An evening at the Tower usually began with one of the guests reading a paper on a topic such as "Religion and Mysticism," "Individualism and the New Art," or "Solitude." This was followed by an involved discussion. Candles were lit in the chandeliers, red wine flowed, and by morning poetry was read.

The Tower was imbued with an intensely intellectual atmosphere. As a woman poet who participated in the meetings recalled,

> We quoted the Greeks by heart, took delight in the French Symbolists, considered Scandinavian literature our own, knew philosophy and theology, poetry and history of the whole world. In that sense we were citizens of the universe, bearers of the great cultural museum of humanity. It was Rome at the time of the fall. We did not live, but rather contemplated the most refined that there was in life. We were not afraid of any words. We were cynical and unchaste in spirit, wan and inert in life. In a certain sense we were, of course, the revolution before the revolution—so profoundly, ruthlessly, and fatally did we destroy the old tradition and build bold bridges into the future. But our depth and daring were intertwined with a lingering sense of decay, the spirit of dying, ghostliness, ephemerality. We were the last act of a tragedy.[60]

The atmosphere at the Tower was heady, thanks in great part to the host's charms. Akhmatova, who later said, "This was the only real salon I ever saw," admitted that Ivanov "knew how to manipulate people." When they were alone, Ivanov expressed delight in Akhmatova's poetry, comparing her poems with the works of Sappho. Then he forced her to read for his guests, only to subject the same poems to harsh criticism unexpectedly. Akhmatova's pride was hurt. In addition, Ivanov and company tried to break up her relationship with Gumilyov, suggesting, "He does not understand your poetry."

Ivanov was hostile to Gumilyov, and he once publicly attacked his poetry. This humiliating incident was just one in a series of conflicts that led to the open break by Gumilyov and Akhmatova with both the symbolist leaders and the movement itself. Gumilyov, according to Akhmatova, "decided that he had to organize young poets and choose his own course." He and his friend, the poet Sergei Gorodetsky, published a manifesto in the January 1913 issue of Makovsky's *Apollo,* proclaiming that a new literary school, acmeism (from the Greek *acme,* the highest degree), had come to replace obsolescent symbolism. As Akhmatova later explained, "Without a doubt, symbolism was a nineteenth-century phenomenon. We were right in our rebellion against symbolism, because we felt like people of the twentieth century."[61]

Akhmatova always insisted that in acmeism, practice preceded theory and that in particular, Gumilyov's manifesto came out of his observations of her poetry and the poetry of their friend Osip Mandelstam. Akhmatova met Mandelstam, a scrawny, thin-skinned redhead with jerky movements, at Ivanov's Tower, where Osip was very articulate, as opposed to the taciturn Akhmatova. That evening there was a heated discussion of the recent premiere of *Prométhée, le poème du feu*—a grandiose composition by Alexander Scriabin, a favorite of the capital's modernists whom Mandelstam adored.

Mandelstam may have formulated best the acmeists' objections to "professional symbolism"—"Not a single clear word, only hints and unfinished thoughts." He joked that the Russian symbolists "had sealed off all words, all images, intending them exclusively for liturgical use. It became quite inconvenient—you couldn't get around them, or get up, or sit down. . . . A man wasn't master of his own house anymore."

Acmeism attempted to stop the inflation of words inherent in "professional symbolism." No wonder Mandelstam stressed that Akhmatova's poems, contrary to those of the symbolists, seemed to be forced out between gritted teeth and insisted paradoxically that it was "the tastes and not the ideas of the acmeists that killed symbolism," which was "bloated, vanquished by the dropsy of big themes." As Akhmatova said—somewhat sarcastically—late in life, "I am an acmeist and therefore am responsible for every word. It was the symbolists who spoke all kinds of unintelligible words and assured the public that there was a great mystery behind them. But there was nothing, but nothing, behind them."

Akhmatova, Mandelstam, and Gumilyov considered themselves acmeists to the end, never renouncing, even under intense pressure in the Soviet times, the literary school they created. This intransigence of the leading acmeists may be better understood in light of Mandelstam's proud statement, "Acmeism is not only a literary but a social phenomenon in Russian history. With it a moral strength was reborn in Russian poetry."

The nucleus of the acmeist group consisted of just a half dozen young poets, but their bright talent and promise were so obvious that the symbolists met them with weapons drawn. Akhmatova once complained to me that the acmeists had no money, no millionaire patrons, and the symbolists, who had both, took all the important positions and tried to block the acmeists from all the magazines. "Everyone criticized acmeists—the right and the left."

Akhmatova should have been particularly upset by the caution and skepticism toward the acmeist circle of Alexander Blok, a poetic idol of her youth. She had met Blok in the early 1910s and saw him at Ivanov's Tower. Blok recognized her gift, but his attitude toward Akhmatova's poetry was ambivalent, especially in the beginning.

According to one memoirist, when Blok was asked to speak his mind after Akhmatova read at the Tower, he said, "She writes as if for a man, but poetry must be written for God."[62] Wrote a contemporary, "The 'Akhmatova-like' line began to dominate women's poetry in Russia."[63] This, apparently, annoyed Blok. When he once heard someone being accused of imitating Akhmatova, Blok leaned over to his companion and said in a half-whisper, "Imitate her? Her cup is empty; there is nothing to borrow."[64] The symbolist leader, Valery Bryusov, began referring sarcastically to Akhmatova as the "musical instrument with only one string."

By that time Blok, of course, had turned into a living legend whose every step was avidly watched, every word discussed, and every poem sifted for clues to his private life. For the quintessential symbolist poet, this was a natural situation, since Russian symbolism brought the traditional romantic identification of artist and person to its outer limits.

As the poet Vladislav Khodasevich observed, "Life events penetrated writing. And the reverse occurred, too—what was written by anyone became a real life event for all."[65] In Blok's case this equation reached its extreme, as confirmed by Yuri Tynyanov: "When they speak of Blok's poetry, they almost always unconsciously imagine a *human face* behind it—and everyone falls in love with the *face* and not with the *art*."[66]

In this tight interweaving of life and literature, the excitement of strong emotions, especially love, played the role of drugs that increased creativity. In turn, the "real" events behind the writing gave it an additional interest and spice. "Therefore," Khodasevich noted, "everyone was always in love—if not in fact, then they deluded themselves into thinking that they were. The smallest spark of something resembling love was blown up as much as possible."[67]

Even his family called Blok the "northern Don Juan." His affairs often "migrated" into his poems, and so awed Petersburgers followed Blok's published love poems as though they were an intimate diary made public, forever trying to connect a particular poem to its supposed inspiration. This at times created embarrassing situations for all involved. For instance, the actress Natalya Volokhova, whom

Blok courted relentlessly, was offended by some of the poems in the cycle *Snow Mask*, which was dedicated to her. "Particular phrasings," quite unambivalently stating that their affair had been consummated, did not, according to Volokhova, "correspond to the reality." The embarrassed Blok had to explain that "poetry licenses a certain exaggeration."

The rules of this rather cruel literary game were dictated by men. Women could be angry or, on the contrary, feel flattered and "immortalized," but on the whole they remained the subjects of male writers' literary manipulations.

Akhmatova became a revolutionary in this particular area too. Other female poets had published love poetry, of course, but Akhmatova was the first "to construct" a literary love affair; that is, for the first time, by force of her public readings and publications in magazines, a woman created a public perception of an affair in which, for a change, attention was focused on a man *she* selected for the purpose.

This literary "affair" of Akhmatova's caught on almost immediately with her readers because the subject of the literary charade was none other than Blok, a nationally famous person. Akhmatova had turned the tables on Blok, using his own devices.

Her first poem that was centered on Blok, the ballad "Gray-Eyed King," appeared in 1911 in *Apollo*. It became phenomenally popular and was even set to music and sung in cabarets by the fashionable chansonnier of the period, Alexander Vertinsky. (The public knew that Blok had gray-blue eyes from the popular portrait done in 1907 by Konstantin Somov, a leading member of *Mir iskusstva*.) In subsequent years the number of Akhmatova's love poems in that vein increased. They starred "my famous contemporary," bearing "a short, resounding name," a restrained, gray-eyed poet. The readers in the capital had no doubt that the poems were addressed to Blok. This implicit understanding gave these poems a sensational edge and, to their readers, the pleasure of insider's knowledge.

Blok reacted to this bold attempt to change the rules of the game with cautious interest. He must have decided not to meet Akhmatova halfway in real life. His mother, who shared the poet's most intimate secrets, commented forthrightly on his decision in a letter to a friend. "I keep waiting for my son to meet and fall in love with a woman who is anxious and profound, and therefore also tender. . . . And there is such a young poetess, Anna Akhmatova, who is reaching out to him and would be prepared to love him. But he is turning away from her, even though she is beautiful and talented. But she is sad. And he doesn't like that." Quoting the opening lines of Akhmatova's ballad,

> Glory to you, endless pain!
> The gray-eyed king died yesterday

Blok's mother concludes compassionately, "You can judge for yourself what that miserable young maiden must feel."[68]

But on a purely literary plane, Blok apparently decided to participate in Akhmatova's charade, since he wrote a madrigal and dedicated it to her. And when Akhmatova in turn replied to the madrigal with a new poem, Blok suggested—perhaps hoping to outmaneuver her—that they have both works printed in a small theatrical magazine published for the Petersburg elite by his friend the director Meyerhold. Even though the magazine's circulation was only three hundred, the impact of the publication was enormous, assuring readers in the know that there definitely was an affair between Blok and Akhmatova.

In Akhmatova's second book, *The Rosary,* published in March 1914, the Blok theme dominated. This collection established Akhmatova's reputation for readers of that era and made her a truly popular poet. In the following years *The Rosary* appeared in at least nine other editions.

A contemporary chronicled Akhmatova's ascension: "At literary evenings the young people went crazy when Akhmatova appeared on the stage. She did it skillfully, aware of her feminine charm." Another witness of Akhmatova's frequent literary appearances in Petersburg recalled, "Her success was extraordinary. Students and young women surrounded their beloved poetess. It was hard to reach her in the intermissions—the young people crowded around her in an impenetrable wall."[69]

Once Akhmatova was invited to appear at the first Russian university for women, the so-called St. Petersburg Higher Bestuzhev Courses. The leading Russian feminists were in attendance. In the green room Akhmatova saw Blok and learned that she was supposed to appear after him. Frightened by the prospect of appearing on stage after the most famous poet in Russia, she asked him to switch places with her. She was rebuffed with a polite but firm, "We're not tenors." Nevertheless, Akhmatova was a great success, prompting an esteemed feminist to comment, "Now she got equal rights for herself at least."

□   □   □

By this time postcard pictures of Akhmatova, like the ones of Blok, were available throughout Russia. And her popularity with artists as a model had even surpassed Blok's.

It's interesting to recall that exactly in those years a woman named Vera Kholodnaya became the most famous Russian movie star. Her sad beauty, cool demeanor, and expressive eyes made Kholodnaya "the queen of the Russian screen." I don't believe anyone has yet pointed out the resemblance of Kholodnaya's heroines in character and image with the "Akhmatova type."

Kholodnaya's films, like Akhmatova's poems, usually represented unrequited, duped, or humiliated love. Akhmatova spoke with irony of the fact that she had become the favorite author of "love-sick high school girls." These girls also wept at Kholodnaya's silent films. It is telling that equally talented actresses of the period with traditionally Russian looks, voluptuous and vivacious, were not as popular as Kholodnaya. The "decadent" type clearly attracted mass audiences.

Artists apparently sensed this too, and so portraits of Akhmatova appeared one after the other around town in fashionable exhibits. Some were academic, even saccharine (Akhmatova justly called one such attempt a "candy box"); others nodded in the direction of decadence. A twenty-six-year-old Jewish artist, Nathan Altman, stirred up the greatest sensation with a portrait of Akhmatova shown in the spring of 1915 at a regular *Mir iskusstva* exhibit.

Born in the Ukraine, Altman had already traveled to Paris, where he befriended other Russian Jewish artists—Marc Chagall from Vitebsk, Osip Zadkine from Smolensk, and Chaim Soutine from Minsk. There in 1911 Altman accidentally met Akhmatova in the street. He wanted to come to the Russian capital, but it wasn't possible because Jews were banned from living in Petersburg.

The only exceptions made were for wealthy merchants, people with higher education, certified craftsmen, and those who had served in the military. Altman had to go to the small town of Berdichev in the Ukraine, the birthplace of the pianist Vladimir Horowitz,[70] to get a diploma for a "sign painter," which, in fact, certified him as a highly qualified house painter. Only with that certificate could the already famous artist move to the capital.

By 1910, thirty-five thousand Jews lived in the Russian capital, where they made up less than 2 percent of the population. Many of them were educated, affluent, and influential. Among Petersburg's

Jews were prominent bankers, accomplished musicians, and leading journalists. The essayist Vassily Rozanov even asserted that "the Jews were able to 'make or break' a person in our literature, and thereby they became its 'chiefs.' "[71]

Jews were playing an increasingly important role in Petersburg's modernist circles. Among Akhmatova's closest friends, for she always considered herself a militant "anti-anti-Semite," were Mandelstam and one of the leading female avant-garde painters of the period, Alexandra Exter. Akhmatova readily agreed to pose for Altman, who had moved to a seventh-floor furnished apartment in the "New York" building, a favorite of Petersburg artists.

For a long time Altman worked persistently on the portrait. During rest periods, to amuse herself and demonstrate her famous agility, Akhmatova would climb out the window and make her way along the ledge to visit friends on the same floor. Sometimes Mandelstam would drop in and he and Akhmatova would make up funny stories, laughing like teenagers, rolling on the floor and bringing neighbors running to see what all the noise was about.

Altman had become close to the critic Nikolai Punin, Akhmatova's future third husband, and the modernist artists around Punin— Lev Bruni, Pyotr Miturich, and Vladimir Lebedev. Punin later wrote, "Altman had the face of an Asian, quick movements, and wide cheekbones. He always brought in the bustle of life, he had a practical mind, but an amusing and cheerful one."[72]

When I came to see the seventy-seven-year-old Altman in Leningrad in the fall of 1966, his conversation was ironic but to the point. He was reluctant to speak of Akhmatova, who had died recently—perhaps because lately they had not been particularly close. But more likely, it was because Akhmatova had been ambivalent in her last years toward his painting of her. She found it too "stylized," preferring instead a portrait by Alexander Tyshler, another Jewish artist she considered a genius; perhaps she was influenced by Mandelstam's praise of Tyshler.

But in 1915, when Altman's portrait of her was exhibited in Petersburg, it made a tremendous impression. Punin, an influential and insightful critic, always considered it the best of Altman's works. Thin and angular, Akhmatova was depicted seated in a piercingly blue dress and a bright yellow shawl. Instantly that image of the fashionable poetess, shown at a fashionable exhibit by an artist coming into fashion, took on the significance of a symbol. First, it was beyond doubt a portrait not only of Akhmatova but also of an idealized image of the modern female poet, a fact well understood by the viewers and Akhmatova. Second, it was a symbol of the times—according to Roman Timenchik, "the embodiment of the general spiritual unease."

Altman's painting became a kind of an aesthetic manifesto for the "Punin group." As Punin later wrote, "This portrait rejected the traditions of impressionism and introduced the problem of constructivist forms. We were particularly interested in forms then."[73] Contemporaries found cubist influences in Altman's portrait, but in a conversation with me in 1966 Altman denied that vehemently: "They decided that I was a Cubist, and a bad one at that. First they christen a brunet a redhead, and then they say that he's a false redhead. But I never was a Cubist." I remember well how his small gray brush of a mustache curled mockingly as he spoke. Georges Braque, whose photo had been cut out of a French Communist newspaper and was attached to Altman's easel, looked somewhat uncomfortable listening along with me.

Punin avoided the word "cubism" in his review of Altman's portrait in *Apollo* in 1916. "It's significant that in this work Altman did not seem to have the desire to show beauty (at least the beauty of Akhmatova's eyes), character, give expression—all that is typical of the impressionist. His sole aim was to reveal form—the form of the body (in particular, the kneecap, collarbone, foot, phalanxes, and so on), the bench, stool, flowers, and shawl."[74]

Describing the portrait later, the poet Benedikt Livshits also mentioned "the imperial folds of blue silk" and directly tied Altman's painting to the acmeist experiments in literature: "Acmeism is feeling around for heavyweight correlates to itself in painting."[75] Obviously, acmeists were flirting with cubism, selecting and noting works close to them, usually the ones that used cubist techniques. Besides Altman's cubist-like portraits, landscapes, and still lifes, this wing of Petersburg art was distinguished by the sharp, angular portraits by his friends Lev Bruni and Boris Grigoryev and, in a later period, Yuri Annenkov, as well as by some of the cubistically constructed still lifes by Kuzma Petrov-Vodkin.

A true union of Russian cubism and acmeism did not take place, however, because in Russia cubism tied itself to literary futurism. At the same exhibit of *Mir iskusstva* in 1915 where Altman's Akhmatova portrait appeared, there was a portrait by Miturich of the modernist composer and later intimate friend of Akhmatova, Arthur Lourié. Punin wrote that Miturich's brush strokes were "unique and error-free. Their loveliness lies in their distinctively feminine yet dry manner. I would not call Miturich a lyric poet, but there is a tender poetry nevertheless in his works."[76] One might have thought Punin was writing about Akhmatova's poems.

There was a clear correlation between the ideas of the Punin group and the aesthetics of the acmeists. Just as the acmeists "overcame" symbolism, the young artists of Petersburg were "overcoming" impressionism. They were still tied by personal relations to the older members of *Mir iskusstva* and exhibited together with them, but they were attracted by more radical ideas. But the decisive move toward the more avant-garde happened a bit later, and for the time being, in Punin's words, the young rebels were all "entwined in their specifically Petersburg, *Mir iskusstva* 'graphic' attitudes toward their material."[77]

Altman told me that when he arrived in Petersburg from Paris, he encountered Akhmatova once again at the artistic cabaret The Stray Dog.[78] Now a legendary establishment, which opened on New Year's Eve 1912 and survived until spring 1915, it was a favorite hangout for the artistic elite of Petersburg in that period.

The role of The Stray Dog for Russian culture is comparable to that of the Left Bank cafés in Paris. But The Stray Dog was more elitist and refined than La Coupole, Les Deux Magots, or Closerie des Lilas. After all, they functioned as ordinary cafés, distinguished by their colorful clientele. To get into The Stray Dog, located deep in the cellar of a house on the corner of Italyanskaya Street and Mikhailovskaya Square that had once belonged to the Jesuits, guests had to sign a thick volume bound in pigskin before entering. This ritual in itself turned The Stray Dog, which had no waiters, into a private club. Serious lectures and futurist poems were read there, clever plays were performed, and avant-garde exhibitions mounted.

For example, when the actor Boris Pronin, the manager of The Stray Dog (also known as the "Hund-direktor") announced "Caucasus Week," the cellar featured talks describing trips to the Caucasus, an exhibit of Persian miniatures, and evenings of Oriental music and dance. In the same manner, the establishment had a "Marinetti Week," with the participation of the famous visiting Italian futurist, and a "Paul Fort Week" for the Parisian poet who in 1912 was elected "Prince of Poets" by his contemporaries.

As the tall, elegant poet Benedikt Livshits, whose admirers claimed that the nine muses always danced around him, recalled, "The basic premise of The Stray Dog existence was the division of humanity into two unequal categories—representatives of the arts and 'pharmacists,' with the latter label covering all other people, no matter what they did and what their professions were." Writers and artists were admitted free of charge, while the "pharmacists" had to pay a hefty admission, up to 25 rubles per head. They were glad to pay—where else could they see the prima ballerina Tamara Karsavina on a giant mirror performing numbers choreographed by Michel Fokine, or watch the poet Vladimir Mayakovsky in the pose of a wounded gladiator, lying in his famous striped shirt on a huge Turkish drum and triumphantly striking it at the appearance of each bizarrely arrayed comrade in futurism?

The futurists and their shocking behavior got a lot of press in Petersburg. Thus a prospering "pharmacist"—lawyer, stockbroker, or dentist—could show how up-to-date he was by recounting his "personal" meeting at The Stray Dog with those "horrible modernists"— but of course he might then add, "Maxim Gorky himself said, 'There's something to them!' "

The futurist Vasilisk Gnedov was notorious for his *Poem of the End*, which consisted of a single, sharp circular movement of the arm. There were no words in the *Poem of the End* and thus this experimental "poetry of silence" could be regarded as a precursor forty years earlier of the aesthetically analogous "music of silence" by the American composer John Cage.

But the tone at The Stray Dog was set nevertheless not by the futurists but by the acmeists and their friends. They usually gathered after midnight and left around dawn. In that little cellar they lived "for the audience," playing the role of the bohemians of the imperial capital. Livshits left a seemingly sarcastic but actually affectionate description of that "intimate parade," at which the poets transformed themselves into stage actors, and the audience took a voyeuristic ride.

> Wrapped in black silk, with a large oval cameo at her waist, Akhmatova floated in, stopping at the entrance so as to write her latest poem in the "pigskin book" at the request of Pronin, who was rushing to greet her, with the unsophisticated "pharmacists," their curiosity piqued, wildly guessing who's who in the poem.
> Attired in a long frock coat, not leaving a single beautiful woman without his attention, Gumilyov retreated, moving backward among the tables, either to observe court etiquette or to avoid "dagger" looks at his back.

Under the vaults of The Stray Dog, painted with flowers and birds by the artist Sergei Sudeikin, what Diaghilev called "intimate art" was made nightly. "Pianists, poets, and artists who were present were simply invited on stage. Voices would call, 'We want so-and-so,' and almost no one refused."[79] Musical improvisation took on great importance here. Cultural Russia of that era lived under the strong impression of Alexander Scriabin's grandiloquent musical statements. His ecstatic works were consonant with the poetry of the symbolists. In the casual ambiance of The Stray Dog several people worked on music they considered alternative to Scriabin's overheated visions.

One of them, Arthur Lourié, was a composer of enormous potential that was partially realized later, when he fled Soviet Russia for France and then to the United States. But only one other man from that informal association that I would call the musical circle of The Stray Dog was a professional composer. Ilya Sats was renowned for his music for the plays at the Stanislavsky Art Theater.

Sats was apparently the first to experiment with the "prepared" piano, again anticipating similar experiments by John Cage, which were conducted thirty years later. Sats placed sheets of metal and other objects on piano strings to change the sound. The traditional "sound palette" was not enough for him, and Sats sought new timbers and techniques of producing sound as well as new untempered sounds, similar to what would later be called *la musique concrète*. Insisting that he spoke for "an entire group of seekers," Sats wrote, "Music is the wind, and rustling, and speech, and banging, and crunching, and squalling. That is the symphony of sounds which makes my soul cringe and weep and which I long for. Why is there no register called 'Wind,' which intones in microtones?"[80]

Lourié was in solidarity with Sats and proposed a theory that he grandly called the "theater of reality." Its essence was that everything in the world was proclaimed art, including the sound made by every object. Lourié also experimented with quarter-tone music and proposed a new type of piano with two settings of strings and a double (three-color) keyboard. But for lack of such a new instrument, Lourié had to settle for playing at The Stray Dog, where he "extended his hands, nails chewed down to the half moon, with a suffering look toward the Bechstein, smiling like Sarasate might, having been offered a three-string balalaika."[81]

Arthur—he took the name in honor of his favorite philosopher, Schopenhauer, adding a second name, Vincent, in honor of van Gogh—Lourié, who had converted to Roman Catholicism as a teenager at the

Petersburg Maltese Chapel, once gave an influential lecture at The Stray Dog, calling for "overcoming impressionism" and achieving synthesis by using the primitive. The esteemed Petersburg music critic Vyacheslav Karatygin, also a regular at The Stray Dog, explained, "The more certainly and energetically the process of 'specification' and 'purification' of particular art forms proceeds, the more acutely do we sometimes feel a strange longing for the possibility of their 'synthesis.' Such synthesis is realizable only with the help of an artificial primitivization of the main elements of those being synthesized."[82]

This program resembled the ideas of the French composer Eric Satie, propounded at about the same time, which were later realized in the works of Les Six and in what Satie called *la musique d'ameublement*. Satie himself wrote laconic piano pieces in the 1910s and also little waltz songs that were popular in Parisian cafés.

Independently of Satie, and in some ways preceding him, Stray Dog regular Mikhail Kuzmin, called "the greatest of minor poets" in Petersburg, made similar experiments. Akhmatova asked Kuzmin to write the introduction to her first book. Kuzmin was a great poseur, and there were many contradictory legends about him in Petersburg, summed up by a female contemporary this way:

> Kuzmin is the king of aesthetes, the arbiter of fashion and taste. He is the Russian Beau Brummell. He has three hundred sixty-five vests. In the morning high school students, lawyers, and young Guardsmen come to his "petit lever." He is an Old Believer. His grandmother is Jewish. He studied with the Jesuits. He was an apprentice in a corn-chandler's shop. In Paris he danced the cancan with the models of Toulouse-Lautrec. He wore an ascetic's chains and spent two years as a penitent in an Italian monastery. Kuzmin has supernatural "Byzantine eyes." Kuzmin is a monster.[83]

Kuzmin was the first to introduce an openly homosexual theme into Russian poetry and prose. His novella *Wings,* which appeared in 1906, was attacked as pornographic. But characteristically for the Petersburg of that period, the leading modernists immediately came to Kuzmin's defense. Blok published an article that announced, "Kuzmin's name, surrounded now by such coarse, barbarically trivial talk, is for us a charming name."

Kuzmin had spent several years at the Petersburg Conservatory in Rimsky-Korsakov's composition class, but did not graduate; he explained his transformation into a poet this way: "It's easier and simpler. Poetry falls ready-made from the sky, like manna into the mouths of the Israelites in the desert. I never rewrite a single line."[84]

But Kuzmin didn't drop music. He was the much discussed composer for Meyerhold's memorable production of Blok's pioneering drama, *The Fair Show Booth*. Kuzmin's songs became popular among the Petersburg elite. He sang them, accompanying himself on the piano, first in various salons, including Ivanov's Tower, and then at The Stray Dog. Kuzmin liked to say of his work that "it's only little music, but it has its poison." One visitor to The Stray Dog confirmed the charming impression Kuzmin's songs created:

> Cloyingly sweet, wanton, and breathtaking languor overtakes the audience. In a joke you hear sadness, in laughter, tears—
>
> *Child, do not reach for the rose in springtime,*
> *You can pick the rose in summer, too.*
> *In early spring you must pick violets,*
> *Remember, there are no violets in summer.*
>
> The banal modulations blend with the velvety tremolo voice and it's not clear how and why, but the simple, childish words take on a mysterious significance.[85]

The director Nikolai Evreinov made music in a similar style at The Stray Dog. Arnold Schoenberg, visiting Petersburg, heard Evreinov's "Second Polka" and asked sarcastically, "*Und warum es notwendig ist, diese Sekunden?*" Schoenberg had reason to consider himself a connoisseur of cabaret music. For several years he had conducted the orchestra at the famous Überbrettl, Ernst von Wolzogen's Berlin cabaret.

Karatygin, one of the guiding spirits of the Evenings of Contemporary Music, performed at The Stray Dog as accompanist and also as author of musical jokes "with a strong dose of musical pepper in the form of sharp rhythms and brazen harmonies, strung onto curious and silly words."[86] Ilya Sats went even further in that direction, composing parody operas with names like "Revenge of Love, or The Ring of Guadelupe" and "Oriental Delights, or The Battle of the Russians and the Kabarda." Karatygin wrote about Sats's music, "I never saw such a musical mirror. By itself, it's nothing, zero. But light candles all around it and suddenly this music will shine and sparkle like fire. Isn't that enough?"[87]

Sats, rumpling his thick black hair and nervously chewing at his walrus mustache, wrote his biggest opus at The Stray Dog, the bal-

let *The Goat-legged,* first performed in Petersburg in 1912. Balanchine's future mentor, the choreographer Fyodor Lopukhov, was present at the premiere and as he confessed to me in a conversation in
1967, he "didn't understand a thing in Sats's music—all dissonance."
I asked him about Boris Romanov's choreography. "Very daring, bor-
derline pornography. It was a much more revealing spectacle than *The
Afternoon of a Faun* with Vaslav Nijinsky," Lopukhov replied
thoughtfully. "But Romanov was a very talented man. He experimented with free dance à la Isadora Duncan. And he found a beautiful dancer who wasn't even a professional. She was very, very sexy."[88]

Lopukhov meant Olga Glebova-Sudeikina, whose performance in
The Goat-legged created a sensation in Petersburg. The wife of the
artist Sudeikin, who had decorated The Stray Dog's interior, and closest friend of Akhmatova, Olga was one of the "fragile Europeans"
(Mandelstam's expression) who scintillated in the capital. Arthur
Lourié tried to describe her. "Glorious golden braids, like Melissande
or Debussy's *La Fille aux cheveux de laine,* enormous gray-green eyes,
sparkling like opals, porcelain shoulders and a 'Diana's bust,' nearly
revealed by her deeply décolleté dress, charming smile, lilting laughter, flying, light movements—who is she? a butterfly? Colombine?'[89]
    Discussing the Petersburg era with me in 1976, Vera Stravin-
sky, who married Sudeikin after taking him away from Olga, was
rather pejorative about her. "She was no actress, she couldn't sing or
dance, and basically was a rather empty-headed thing whose only interest was suitors."[90] Lourié, however, wrote that Olga Sudeikina
"was one of the most talented characters I had ever met."
    Lourié maintained that she was exceptionally musical, could
read poetry unforgettably, particularly Blok, and successfully translated Baudelaire into Russian. Lourié also recalled that Sudeikina
"knew the style of every epoch and her taste was impeccable. I remember how she liked to go to the Alexander Market, where she knew
all the shopkeepers. She would bring back all sorts of incredible things
dug out from the flotsam—old porcelain, snuff boxes, miniatures,
knickknacks."[91]
    For Lourié and the other bohemians of the capital, Olga
Sudeikina was the personification of the sophisticated Petersburg style
of the 1910s, its soul and its muse. She "expressed the refined era of
Petersburg of the beginning of the twentieth century just as Madame
Récamier expressed the early Empire."[92] Nadezhda Mandelstam said
wryly,

Akhmatova considered Olga the embodiment of all female qualities and was constantly giving me recipes for household work and for charming men according to Olga. . . . Dust rags must be gauze—you dust and rinse it out . . . cups must be thin and the tea strong. Among the beauty secrets the most important was that dark hair should be smooth and blond hair must be fluffed and curled. Kchessinska's secret for getting along with men was never to take your eyes off "them," hang on every word, "they" love it. . . . Those were the Petersburg recipes at the start of the century.[93]

Sudeikina and Akhmatova quoted Mathilda Kchessinska, the notorious star of the imperial ballet, for good reason. In prerevolutionary Petersburg, Kchessinska, the mistress first of Nicholas II when he was heir to the throne, then of two grand dukes, was the symbol and proof of the success to which an artist, a woman from the demimonde, could aspire.

The tabloids described Kchessinska's outfits, her diamond necklaces and pearls, the luxurious banquets in her honor at expensive restaurants, and her townhouse in the modern style. The director of the imperial theaters, Vladimir Telyakovsky, who hated her whims and intrigues, wrote in his diary that she was a "morally impudent, cynical, and brazen dancer, living simultaneously with two grand dukes and not only not hiding it but on the contrary, weaving this art as well into her stinking, cynical wreath of human offal and vice."[94]

But many people were in awe of Kchessinka's brilliance as a dancer. "Le tout Petersburg" came to her performances. A reporter for *Peterburgskaya gazeta* breathlessly described the audience at the Maryinsky Theater when Kchessinska was dancing on stage: "Innumerable ball gowns in every color and shade, diamonds sparkling on shoulders, endless frock coats and tails, small talk in English and French, the heady scent of fashionable perfume, in a word, the familiar scene of a social rout."[95]

The influential ballet critic Akim Volynsky should not have been interested in Kchessinska's social successes, but he too did not distinguish between her stage performance and her image.

Her demonic artistry sometimes gives off an icy chill. But at other times Kchessinska's rich technique seems like a miracle of a real, high art. At moments like that the audience bursts into wild applause and crazy cries of delight. And the black-eyed she-devil of ballet endlessly repeats, to the bravos of the entire hall, her incredible pas, her blindingly glorious diagonal dance across the stage.[96]

Praising Kchessinska's genius, "capricious and mighty, with a shade of sinful personal pride," the critic saw in her a symbolic and tragic figure. But for Telyakovsky, the director of the imperial theaters, Kchessinska's appearances on the stage were the triumph of "vulgarity, triteness, and banality."

The director was disgusted by the open, challenging, and indecorous sexuality of the ballerina, "her too short costume, fat, turned-out legs and open arms, expressing total self-satisfaction, an invitation to an embrace." The irony of the situation lay in the fact that the audience, loving the unheard-of energy of the spectacle, readily attributed the sexual explosion on stage to their presence. The cynical Telyakovsky knew better, when he wrote in his diary after another "trite and coarse" performance, "Kchessinska was in good form. The royal box was filled with young grand dukes, and Kchessinska made a real effort."[97]

Thus the connection between the huge stage of the Imperial Maryinsky Theater and the little halls of the Petersburg cabarets was made. Everywhere the intimate was becoming the purview of everyone, brought out for display and gossip. Private life no longer existed. The sexual relations (real or imagined) of the royal family or of two famous poets was the subject of public discussion and ballyhooed in the same way.

Kchessinska on the stage was almost within reach. One could undress her mentally and evaluate her physical charms (or flaws) with the same aplomb with which Akhmatova's tragic loves were gossiped about on the basis of her latest poems. Few were shocked that the niece of Alexander Benois, the twenty-eight-year-old artist Zinaida Serebryakova, entered the *Mir iskusstva* exhibits with nude self-portraits—under innocent titles like "Bather" or "In the Baths"—of incredible beauty, in which there was "a certain sensuality,"[98] as even her loving uncle admitted.

For Serebryakova and her friends this was a manifesto of moral and aesthetic emancipation. For the public it was yet another opportunity to feel drawn by a celebrity's sex appeal and to indulge their voyeuristic fantasies. In this charged atmosphere Kchessinska, Serebryakova, Akhmatova, and Sudeikina were all equal before the Petersburg public, which was ever hungry for sexy scandal and gossip.

A contemporary described Sats's *The Goat-legged* as "half-goats, half-humans lasciviously frolicking on stage."[99] But Sudeikina did not limit her appearances to the Theater of Miniatures on Liteiny Prospect, where Sats's ballet was appearing. In her memoirs, Akhmatova recalled that Sudeikina performed a Russian dance for Grand Duke Kirill at his father's palace. Akhmatova repeated the grand duke's reaction: *"La danse russe rêvée par Debussy."*

Grand Duke Kirill was often seen at performances of Kchessinska, who was the mistress of his younger brother, Andrei. An interesting connection appears—grand dukes, Kchessinska, Sudeikina, Akhmatova. To my knowledge, no one has noted that connection before, and yet it could partly explain the persistent and rather widespread rumor that Akhmatova had had an affair with Nicholas II or, at any rate, with someone from the royal family.

This myth, despite Akhmatova's sarcastic reaction to it, was typical of prerevolutionary Petersburg. The capital was all mixed up. Grigory Rasputin, a mystical Siberian peasant turned monk, had become the most influential person in the empire. (Akhmatova once saw Rasputin in a train and would later reminisce how his hypnotic eyes pierced her.)

Nikolai Klyuev, a peasant poet close to Rasputin, adored Akhmatova's work. She later maintained that Klyuev was intended to take Rasputin's place near the emperor and his wife. So no one would have been surprised if Akhmatova suddenly were to have become the "court poet." Rumors appeared and vanished daily in the capital's atmosphere of mysticism, sex, and poetry. Inevitably they touched the uncrowned empress of the Petersburg bohemians, who was reigning at The Stray Dog.

Akhmatova was ambivalent toward this bohemian world and her role in it. In late 1912 she wrote a poem called "In The Stray Dog," subtitled, "Dedicated to Friends." It begins,

> We are all revelers and tarts here,
> How unhappy we all are together!

And it ends with lines that could refer to Akhmatova or to her friend Sudeikina.

> And the one who is dancing now
> Will definitely end up in hell.

But having published the poem, Akhmatova continued to appear regularly at The Stray Dog, the living symbol of which she had become.

A kind of umbilical cord existed now between the place and the person. Without the majestic Akhmatova, without her stylized beauty, The Stray Dog was unimaginable. But Akhmatova apparently felt most comfortable in that cellar filled with smoke and the heavy scent of wine. As a poet later recalled, "We (Mandelstam and I and many others) began to imagine that the whole world was in fact concentrated at The Stray Dog, that there was no other life, no other interests than the Doggy ones."[100]

That cellar world, a part of and an attraction for elite Petersburg, shuddered along with the rest of the capital in the summer of 1914, for World War I had begun. "Everyone expected it and no one believed in it," Viktor Shklovsky later maintained. "We sometimes allowed that it might happen, but we were convinced that it would last three months at most."[101]

Events escalated swiftly and ominously. In response to the general mobilization ordered by Nicholas II, Germany declared war. The next day the tsar published a manifesto, greeted with great enthusiasm, on Russia's responding in kind. Thousands of people came out on Palace Square waving the flag, icons, and portraits of the tsar. When Nicholas and his wife appeared on the balcony of the Winter Palace, the crowd sank to its knees and sang the anthem, "God Save the Tsar."

The city was caught up in patriotic frenzy. German stores were attacked and the gigantic cast-iron horses on top of the German embassy were thrown down to the street. This wave of long-unknown patriotism and chauvinism is the only explanation for how the renaming of Saint Petersburg to Petrograd slipped through without serious debate in August 1914.

The reason for this fateful change was to discard the city's "Germanic" name in favor of a "Slavic" version. But in the frenzy of the war, two things were forgotten. The name originally given to the capital by Peter the Great was not German but Dutch. Second, turning the capital's name into Petrograd made it the city of Peter the man, Peter the emperor, whereas at the time of its founding the city had been named for Saint Peter, its patron. This was particularly ironic because Nicholas II, who personally ordered the name change, was highly ambivalent, to say the least, about his ancestor, the "miracle-working builder." He had said of Peter the Great, "This is the ancestor I like least of all for his enthusiasm for Western culture and violation of all purely Russian customs."

Obviously, it was not the time for pedantic discussions of the correctness of the capital's new name. Even Blok only noted laconically in his notebook, "Petersburg has been renamed *Petrograd,*" and moved on to more important matters, the bad news from the front. "We lost many troops. Very many."[102]

It was just five years later that Petersburg's bard Nikolai Antsiferov, with the advantage of hindsight, would analyze this fatal turn:

> The loss of its age-old name must have signified the start of a new era in Petersburg's development, an era of total consolidation with Russia that was once alien to it. "Petrograd" would become a truly Russian city. But in the name change many saw the tastelessness of contemporary imperialism and also its impotence. Petrograd betrays the Bronze Horseman. The Northern Palmyra cannot be resurrected. And fate is preparing another path for it. It would be not the city of triumphant imperialism but the city of all-destroying revolution. The resurrected Bronze Horseman would appear on his "loud-galloping steed" not at the head of victorious armies of his ill-starred descendant but ahead of the masses, destroying the past.[103]

Meanwhile, all observers agreed that the face of Petrograd, now in wartime, changed dramatically. The first breath of war, Livshits noted bitterly, blew the blush from the cheeks of The Stray Dog's regulars. Only now was the Russian capital, as Akhmatova repeated many times later, bidding farewell to the nineteenth century.

> And down the legendary embankment
>   Came not the calendar—
>   But the real Twentieth Century.

People in Petrograd, a contemporary recalled, immediately divided into two groups—those who left for the front and those who remained in the city. "The former, irrespective of whether they left as volunteers or were mobilized, considered themselves heroes. The latter readily agreed with that, trying every which way to expiate their vaguely felt guilt."[104]

Among those leaving with the army was Gumilyov, who received news of the war enthusiastically. Although exempted from military service because of his crossed eyes, he managed nevertheless to get permission to shoot from his left shoulder and headed for the front as a volunteer in the squad of the Life Guards of the Uhlan Regiment. By October, Gumilyov had seen battle and in late 1914 he received his first St. George's Cross.

"His patriotism was as unreserved as his religious faith was cloudless," wrote the critic André Levinson about his friend's state of mind in the early days of the war.[105] And this "enlightened and exalted" patriotism also found expression in Gumilyov's poetry.

> And truly radiant and holy
> Is the war's great goal,
> Seraphim, clear and winged,
> Are seen behind the soldiers' shoulders.

At the very start of the war, Gumilyov and Akhmatova lunched together with Blok. They spoke of the war, of course, and when Blok left, Gumilyov remarked sadly, "Will they really send him to the front too? It's like broiling nightingales."

Blok, German by heritage and pacifist by conviction, clearly did not share Gumilyov's enthusiasm for the war. Blok did not go to the front and he wrote about the war: "For a minute it seemed that it would clear the air. Actually it turned out to be a worthy crown to the lies, filth, and vileness in which our homeland was bathed."

Military action began favorably for Russia. In Petrograd they predicted that Russian troops would be in Berlin by Christmas of 1914, but then luck ran out. In the first eleven months of bloody battle, over a million and a half Russian men were wounded, killed, or taken prisoner. Rumors spread in the capital about a catastrophic shortage of weapons and ammunition, about the stupid, craven generals, about theft and bribery in the supply system. They spoke more and more openly about treason, about the German-born empress and her favorite, the all-powerful Rasputin, leading the country to ruin.

Petrograd came to be swollen with refugees from the western provinces. Under the curfew, people were allowed in the streets only until eight in the evening, but Viktor Shklovsky said that crowds of prostitutes roamed the Nevsky Prospect at night with impunity. It was somewhat ironic, since the number of men in the city had diminished steadily. Sometimes it seemed that Petrograd had become a woman's capital. Life for women became more difficult with food disappearing from the city. More and more wounded were on the streets. There were many benefit performances for the wounded, in which Akhmatova often took part.

The war sharply changed her way of life, and here Gumilyov's influence was without question. But Akhmatova's poetry also changed, and her muse responded to the war differently. They said that Gumilyov's experience of the war was easy and enjoyable. There wasn't a trace of joy in Akhmatova's poems about the war. Listening to them, the audience froze in painful presentiment. Her poem "The Prayer," published in the collection *War in Russian Poetry*, was particularly popular.

> *Give me bitter years of grave illness,*
> *Gasping, insomnia, fever,*
> *Take away my child and my friend,*
> *And my mysterious gift of song—*
> *That's how I pray at Your Liturgy*
> *After so many days of suffering,*
> *So that the storm cloud over dark Russia*
> *Will turn into a cloud in a glory of light.*

The self-oblivion of Akhmatova's "Prayer," which in 1915 may have seemed natural and timely, now first shocks, then horrifies. These are terrifying verses, almost blasphemous in their unprecedented, self-denying patriotism. They are particularly horrifying now because we know that none of the people who praised the poem during the war nor the author herself could even guess at how great the sacrifice Akhmatova offered would turn out to be.

Meanwhile, the war continued to chew up millions of human lives. A black cloud hung over Petrograd. To describe the prevailing conditions, Merezhkovsky coined the expression "brutifying," which was picked up by other Russian intellectuals. Blok, returning from a walk to the Bronze Horseman, wrote, "On Falconet's statue is a horde of boys, hooligans, holding onto the tail, sitting on the serpent, smoking under the horse's belly. Total decay. Petrograd is finis."

The gigantic state machine sputtered: it was falling apart. Nicholas II no longer held the reins of power. In a common view of the last Russian monarch, succinctly stated by one of his officials in his memoirs, "His wife ruled the state, and Rasputin ruled her. Rasputin inspired, the empress ordered, the tsar obeyed."[106]

Like any epigram, it was an oversimplification. Rasputin's murder by court conspirators in December 1916 did not stop the coming catastrophe. But the role of the personality (or rather its absence) in the fall of the Russian Empire is clear, if we mean Nicholas II himself. For in Russia, as an historian justly put it, "the ruler is not a symbol of the regime but *is* the regime."[107]

One often hears that the quiet, amiable, and educated tsar, a model family man and a loving, gentle father, would have been the ideal constitutional monarch in a country like England. But for the single-handed ruling of enormous Russia at a crucial time, Nicholas lacked the talent, the wisdom, and above all, the determination. Instead, the emperor displayed stubbornness and an absurdly unyielding conviction that the people and the army adored their Tsar Father, that only the intellectuals, encamped in their "rotten Petersburg," stirred up trouble.

This manner of ruling the country was unsurprisingly among the causes for Nicholas's dethroning. In July 1918, he and his family were executed by the Bolsheviks in the Urals, where the royal family had been kept under guard by the local Soviet.

But in early 1917 Nicholas II had not even imagined such a horrible possibility, even though his empire and its capital in particular were coming to a boil. Zinaida Hippius recalled,

> The war startled the Petersburg intelligentsia and heightened political interests. . . . Figures from the most varied spheres—scientists, lawyers, doctors, writers, poets—they all turned out to be involved in politics. For us, who had not yet lost human common sense, one thing was clear. War for Russia, in its present political condition, would not end without revolution.

By January 1917 even diehard monarchists like Gumilyov had lost faith in the efficacy of continuing the war. Gumilyov at that time, according to a friend, openly fumed about the "stupid orders" of the generals. This disillusionment with the system overtook the entire hierarchical ladder of the empire from Ensign Gumilyov to the highest officials. Telyakovsky, the director of the imperial theaters, kept amazingly frank diaries. "January 26, 1917. You have to be completely blind and stupid not to sense that the country cannot be ruled this way any more." "January 29. Life is bad in Russia and has been for a long time, but now it's becoming unbearable, because this is not merely bad ruling, this is a mockery of the subjects."[108] And so on, page after page.

Anarchy took over Petrograd, but it was just then that the Imperial Alexandrinsky Theater put on perhaps the most famous production of prerevolutionary Russia—Mikhail Lermontov's drama *Masquerade*, directed by Meyerhold and designed by Golovin. Everything about this production is legendary. Its endless rehearsals, ongoing for five years under Meyerhold, had turned into a theatrical ritual of sorts. Golovin had made four thousand drawings of costumes, makeup, furniture, and other props, setting a record for the Russian theater. *Masquerade* cost three hundred thousand gold rubles, an amazing sum even for the seemingly bottomless royal treasury.

Lermontov, who had been killed in a duel in 1841 at the age of twenty-six, never dreamed that his youthful drama, which he had never seen on the stage, would be presented with such sumptuousness. *Masquerade* was a typical romantic melodrama from the life of Petersburg high society, in which the hero, the jealous Arbenin, poisons his wife.

The impudent and independent Lermontov, an amateur artist, liked to depict Petersburg engulfed in a raging tide. "In those pictures," recalled Count Sollogub, "Lermontov gave free rein to his imagination, which craved sorrow." But even the fatalistic and pessimistic Lermontov could not have predicted that the production of *Masquerade*, which even the participating actors nicknamed "Sunset of the Empire," would be the last act of the old Russia, drowning in the waves of the revolutionary flood. Lermontov would have found such a coincidence the height of romantic irony.

Lermontov's unfinished novel, *Princess Ligovskaya* (1836), set in Petersburg, depicts the city's topography exceptionally accurately. In that sense as in many others, Lermontov was an innovator, presaging the detailed descriptions of the capital in Dostoyevsky's prose. As Levnid Dolgopolov noted, that topographical accuracy was due most probably to Lermontov and Dostoyevsky's shared military education.[109]

But Lermontov would not have recognized the long, straight prospects of Petersburg in those days of February 1917, filled as they were with unhappy crowds of people. The protest demonstrations were spreading. One of them even interrupted a rehearsal of *Masquerade*, when the actors rushed to the windows and watched fearfully as an avalanche of workers moved silently along Nevsky Prospect. Banners imprinted with demands for bread swayed over the demonstrators' heads. Yuri Yuriev, a popular actor playing Arbenin, recalled that "in that concentrated, silent mass was something threatening."[110]

Events around *Masquerade* developed in a grotesque and symbolic way. Despite the existence of a revolutionary situation in the city, the minister of the imperial court insisted that the premiere take place. Yet again in Russian history, ritual and appearance for the sake of appearance was of paramount importance.

Meyerhold, fully sensing the tragic irony of the situation, was nevertheless excited. This was not the first time his artistic intuition had led him to mount a production whose political naïveté bordered on the outrageous. In 1913 during the pomp and ceremony commemorating three hundred years of the Romanov dynasty, he staged Richard Strauss's opera *Electra,* with a scene of a royal beheading.

Meyerhold's challenge in *Masquerade* was to create a unique "director's score," according to which literally every word the actor spoke had an exact equivalent in his gestures or movements. At all those innumerable rehearsals Meyerhold sought to find an exact scheme for moving each of the hundreds of extras across the huge Alexandrinsky stage. A critic called the delicate orchestration of the actors in the play "an opera without music." Thus the basics were carefully laid down of Meyerhold's as yet unformed avant-garde theatrical teaching, "biomechanics," which would eventually become famous.

The premiere of *Masquerade* was set for February 25. The city was empty and eerie that night, but cars were parked in solid black rows in front of the Alexandrinsky Theater. Despite the high cost of tickets, the play sold out, and all the celebrities of the city were present. To his great astonishment, Yuriev saw grand dukes in the royal box.

Golovin had created a set that was a continuation of the audience. Intense black and red predominated. On stage, to Glinka's languid "Valse-Fantaisie," the imperial capital's high society made merry, intrigued, and ultimately rushed to its doom, all the while watched by the truly doomed high society of the capital. What romantic author could have come up with a more symbolic or melodramatic scene?

The action of *Masquerade* shifted from the gambling house to a masquerade where myriad masks swirled before the audience, then to a ball. The outstanding actors, especially Yuriev, the lavish sets, splendid costumes, and beautiful music blended into an overpowering tapestry. Even the most jaded regulars oohed at the mounting theatrical effects. Still, one critic did write, though after the revolution, that he had been shocked watching the play, "So close, in the same city, next to those starving for bread—this artistically perverted, brazenly corrupting, meaninglessly frenzied luxury for the sake of prurience. What was it—the Rome of the Caesars? What were we going to do afterward, go to Lucullus to eat nightingales' tongues, and let the hungry bastards howl, seeking bread and freedom?"[111]

The play ended with an eerie scene of a Russian Orthodox memorial service. The church choir Meyerhold had brought in seemed to be ringing the death knell for the regime, the country, and its capital. The curtain fell not only on Lermontov's *Masquerade* but on the extravagant, entrancing, and tragic masquerade of an era.

The applause seemed to have no end. Baskets of flowers and laurel wreaths piled up on the stage. When Yuriev came out for a bow, the audience stood. Then came a solemn announcement that a gift from Nicholas II had been bestowed upon Yuriev—a gold cigarette case ornamented with a diamond-studded eagle. Few could guess that this imperial gift would be the last in the history of the Russian stage. Ironically, theater connoisseurs exchanged glances.

Everyone knew that Yuriev was homosexual—he didn't hide his sexuality. Thus the gift from the prudish tsar was puzzling. The public still remembered the scandal of 1911, when Nijinsky was suddenly fired from the imperial theaters, the excuse being that his costume was too daring. But rumor had it that the dancer's love affair with Diaghilev had displeased the royal family.

Akhmatova, who saw Meyerhold's production of *Masquerade,* hadn't liked the show. "Too much furniture on stage. . . . And I never thought highly of Yuriev." What she remembered the most was the difficulty of getting home from the play. "There were shots on Nevsky Prospect and horsemen with bared swords attacked passersby. Machine guns were set up on roof tops and in attics."

Akhmatova did not have a car or private coach, and coachmen refused to take her from the theater to the Vyborg side, where she was living at the time. They explained in embarrassment that it was impossible to go that far, they might get killed. "Young lady, I have two children," one driver explained. Another agreed reluctantly. "He probably had no children," Akhmatova recalled with melancholy. And so her coach rolled past rebellious troops in the streets of Petrograd.

A few days later Nicholas II saw he was no longer capable of controlling events and reluctantly abdicated. The unthinkable had occurred: the monarchy in Russia had fallen. In Petrograd, power passed formally to the provisional government, which immediately declared an amnesty for political prisoners, and in fact into the hands of the Soviet of Workers' and Soldiers' Deputies, who controlled the army, railroads, post, and telegraph. Everyone agreed that the people's revolution had been a gigantic improvisation. According to Viktor Shklovsky, it "happened instead of being organized."[112] Shklovsky pictured this revolution as "a thing that was light, blinding, unreliable, and joyous."

Petrograd was shaken by innumerable rallies with fiery orators making speeches for hours to spellbound audiences. Still, the war with the Germans continued, even though the army and the nation were exhausted. Freedom from the tsarist regime had not brought bread, either, and the capital roiled with the anger of the hungry. Revolutionary developments zigzagged and soon it came to pass that Vladimir Lenin became one of the most famous politicians in Petrograd. Recently returned from exile, he was the leader of a small faction of the Russian Social Democratic Party called Bolsheviks.

Lenin and his party colleague, Leon Trotsky, were both known as hypnotic orators, each in his own style. Trotsky's temperament carried the audience away, while Lenin persuaded with seeming simplicity and logic. The provisional government could not explain to the soldiers why it was necessary to continue the war, to the workers why factories were shutting down, nor to the peasants why the land was not being redistributed to them. Speaking from the balcony of Kchessinska's town house (the dancer had fled during the revolution and the Bolsheviks turned her palace into their headquarters), Lenin told the crowds that the war must be ended and promised the people instant well-being as soon as the power of the bourgeoisie was destroyed. A politician of genius with a brilliant understanding of mass psychology, Lenin talked in language of immediate goals, persuading the tired and hungry masses that an instant solution was possible for all the complex problems at hand.

The Petrograd intelligentsia was in disarray. Their ears belonged to the moderate liberal party of the Constitutional Democrats (Cadets), which had set the tone for a while in the provisional government. However, seeing that the moderate elements were quickly losing ground, the more opportunistic members of the Petrograd elite tried to establish contacts with the Bolsheviks as well. One of the Bolshevik leaders in Petrograd was the columnist and playwright Anatoly Lunacharsky, considered an expert on culture among the party comrades. That is why Yuriev, the leading actor of the Alexandrinsky (formerly Imperial) Theater, unexpectedly invited Lunacharsky to his apartment in the fall of 1917 to discuss the fate of the capital's culture.

Arriving at Yuriev's, Lunacharsky found over forty famous actors in the cozy quarters with its velvet armchairs. To his surprise he recognized among them the imposing figure of one of the Cadets party leaders, Vladimir Nabokov, the father of the future writer. The diplomatic Yuriev explained that he understood, as did everyone else, that a political storm was gathering over the capital and it was not clear which party would be in power tomorrow. Therefore he was asking Lunacharsky and Nabokov, each of whom had a chance to become the next minister of culture, to state his views on the theater's future.

In response the wily Lunacharsky gave an eloquent ninety-minute speech, assuring the actors that in the case of a Bolshevik victory not a single "bourgeois" theater would be closed. Nabokov, in a manner typical of the Russian liberals, avoided a discussion with the Bolshevik parvenu and announced with an ironic smile that his party could not propose any utopian programs.

Nabokov must have imagined that he sounded quite respectable and realistic. But actually, he was losing ground to the Bolsheviks without firing a shot. In that decisive moment of Russian history a multitude of similar episodes were being played out in every sphere of life in Petrograd, with the same results. The Bolsheviks, unchallenged, were gaining everywhere.

Months passed in political maneuvering, in attempted coups from right and left, while the soldiers and workers of the capital continued rumbling, rallying, and making ever more radical demands. Finally, the Petrograd garrison voted to recognize the Soviet of Workers' and Soldiers' Deputies, which was dominated at the time by the Bolsheviks, as the only legal power in the capital. On the morning of October 25, 1917, posters were plastered all over the city proclaiming the overthrow of the provisional government and the transfer of all power to the Soviets.

That evening two ballets were presented at the Maryinsky Theater—*The Nutcracker* and Michel Fokine's *Eros*, set to Tchaikovsky's "Serenade for Strings." The audience excitedly exchanged the latest news, passing around the evening newspapers, which slowly floated along the rows like swans. Everyone expected the Bolsheviks to attack the Winter Palace, where the provisional government, virtually paralyzed by fear, was still sitting.

When the performance began, the audience jumped at the sound of shots. The cruiser *Aurora*, on the Neva River opposite the Winter Palace, fired a blank shot, which echoed deafeningly throughout the capital. The Bolsheviks burst into the Winter Palace and arrested the ministers of the provisional government. The head of the new government, called the Soviet of People's Commissars, was the short, barrel-chested Lenin, a forty-seven-year-old professional revolutionary with a maximalist program, confident in his messianic role.

But even Lenin, seizing power, could not have thought in those autumn days that he had led one of the most far-reaching upheavals of the twentieth century. It not only radically changed the historical course of one of the biggest countries on earth but also started a chain of major social changes and mortal conflicts throughout the world that was to last for most of the century. The effect of that fateful day was still being felt decades later in places far from the marvelous city on the Neva, among all kinds of peoples, some of whom didn't even know the city existed.

At the start of his rule, Lenin and his Bolshevik comrades in arms seriously doubted they would be able to hold onto the power that had fallen into their hands so unexpectedly. One young artist peeked into the empty Winter Palace the day after the coup and ran into the new minister of culture—People's Commissar of Education Anatoly Lunacharsky; the prediction of the actor Yuriev had turned out to be correct. Lunacharsky commented philosophically that the Bolsheviks apparently would not be able to stay here more than two weeks, "after which they would be hanged from those balconies."[113]

A joke widely circulated in the capital held that the provisional government held its sessions standing instead of sitting. The Bolsheviks, having founded in Petrograd the most radical communist regime in the world, also felt very uncertain. They were surrounded by a sea of hostility.

A few days after the coup the Petrograd theaters ceased working in protest against the "illegal government of Lenin and Lunacharsky." When Lunacharsky announced that he wanted to meet with intellectuals prepared to cooperate, only a few persons showed up, easily fitting onto one couch. Of course, among them were such extraordinarily talented individuals as Blok, Mayakovsky, Altman, and Meyerhold. (Meyerhold soon went even further and joined the Communist Party.)

This small but fairly representative group of intellectuals that was willing to collaborate with the Soviet authorities was soon joined by the leader of the *Mir iskusstva* group, Alexander Benois. In a secret report to Lenin, Lunacharsky wrote that Benois had "hailed the October revolution long before October."[114] This is what he meant.

In April 1917, when Lenin and the Bolsheviks kept attacking the provisional government's policy of "war to the victorious end," Benois reassuringly reasoned in an article,

> Calm down, friends, don't burn the ships of your idealism only because the dreadnought of Lenin and his leftist friends have entered the same port as you. You'll manage to coexist with them. Well, you'll have to make some concessions, some changes; well, it'll be less comfortable for you and, in any case, less familiar. But, first of all, life as a whole will not become worse, only better. And then is it so hard to part with a few things, if you are promised at the same time such great, maybe even absolute joy as the resurgence of purely human relations among people in general, if this kingdom of vileness, blood, and lies that is the war will end, if we will be able to think once more of the general well-being of the universe?

This eloquent but starry-eyed statement, which now seems so naive as to be almost touching, was actually a rather bold act in those days, because it went against common sense and public opinion, at least in the capital's intellectual circles. Not surprisingly, the Soviet authorities first accepted Benois with open arms. He and Blok took on thousands of big and small responsibilities—in particular, they participated in the discussion of the fairly major changes in Russian orthography undertaken by the Bolsheviks.

This was one of the innumerable reforms of the new regime. According to another, the first day after January 31, 1918, would be not the first, but the fourteenth of February, "In order to establish calculation of time in Russia that is the same as in all the civilized nations." Thus the country shifted from the Julian calendar, which had been used since 1699, to the Western (Gregorian) one.

This innovation was applauded even by monarchists. Count Dmitri Tolstoy, the director of the Hermitage Museum, wrote to his wife, "On the Bolsheviks' orders we have skipped fourteen days of life—this is the sole reasonable thing the Bolshevik rule will leave to Russia." The conservatives resisted orthographic changes and, for one, Igor Stravinsky (as did many other Russian émigrés) continued to write in the old orthography to the end of his days.

Life in Bolshevik Petrograd plunged into chaos as frenzied crowds looted everything from warehouses to wine cellars. In response the government started to destroy the wine supplies. Akhmatova recalled with a shudder how she was driving through Petrograd with Mandelstam and saw huge brown chunks of frozen cognac, which smelled powerfully.

Shots rang out constantly in the city. Despite Lenin's announced desire to sue for peace, the Germans pressed their advance and on February 20, 1918, they approached Petrograd. Blok wrote in his diary in his usual mystical style, "*Only*—flight and rush. Fly and tear yourself away, otherwise, there is destruction on every path." And further, "The Germans are still coming. . . . If you've done so many horrible things in your life, you must at least die honorably."[115]

On February 21 at the meeting of the Soviet of People's Commissars, Lenin promulgated an appeal. "The German generals want to establish their 'order' in Petrograd. . . . The socialist republic of Soviets is in the greatest danger." The Bolsheviks appealed to the "laboring populace": "All corrupt elements, hooligans, marauders, and cowards must be expelled ruthlessly from the ranks of the army, and if they attempt to resist—they must be wiped from the face of the earth. . . . In Petrograd, as in all other centers of revolution, order must be maintained with an iron hand."[116]

Rumors spread in Petrograd that the government headed by Lenin was prepared to flee to Moscow. The Bolsheviks announced officially that the rumors were lies; yet on the very day of this categorical denial, Lenin had approved the resolution to move the seat of government and reestablish Moscow as the country's capital.

At first this evacuation was euphemistically called an "unloading" of Petrograd. The intended flight from Petrograd of almost the entire Bolshevik leadership and the government apparatus was kept secret for fear of terrorist acts. Just recently, on January 1, 1918, Lenin's car had been attacked while he was returning from an army rally at the Mikhailovsky Manege.

When I emigrated to New York in 1976, I met the last living participant of that legendary assassination attempt, Nikolai Martyanov. The polite and gentle Martyanov told me that he considered Lenin a very lucky man. Among the terrorists were some of the best shots in the Russian Army, but Lenin escaped unscathed. "Amazing luck!"[117]

So in 1918, Martyanov, never giving up, began preparing a new attempt on Lenin's life, but somebody denounced Martyanov and his friends. They would have been executed by the Bolsheviks, but Lenin's orders came. "Stop the case. Free them. Send them to the front." As one of Lenin's comrades commented, "In this case, he showed great nobility."[118]

On March 10, 1918, Lenin and his entourage left Petrograd for Moscow on special train No. 4001. The journey was comparatively long, almost twenty-four hours, and in that time Lenin managed to write an article in which he proclaimed, "The history of mankind in our days is making one of the greatest and most difficult turns with—and it can be said without the slightest exaggeration—immense significance for world liberation." For Petrograd, at any rate, those days were truly historical.

On March 16, the All-Russian Congress of Soviets rubber-stamped Lenin's resolution, "In the conditions of the crisis the Russian revolution is undergoing at the given moment, the situation of Petrograd as the capital has changed sharply. In view of this, the Congress resolves that until these conditions change, the capital of the Russian Socialist Federated Soviet Republic will temporarily be moved from Petrograd to Moscow."[119]

That this declaration was intended only as a smoke screen is clear, in particular, from Lunacharsky's secret report to the Soviet of People's Commissars, written in early March 1918 but published only in 1971. "The government firmly and absolutely correctly decided to leave Petersburg and move the capital of Soviet Russia to Moscow even if we were to achieve a more or less stable peace." And further, continuing to call the capital Petersburg, as so many of its inhabitants did, Lunacharsky accurately and ruthlessly predicted the results of this fateful step. "Things will be hard for Petersburg. It will have to go through the agonizing process of reducing its economic and political significance. Of course, the government will try to ease this painful process, but still Petersburg cannot be saved from a terrible food crisis or further growth of unemployment."[120]

At that moment the majority of Petrograd's intellectuals did not view this dramatic change in the city's status pessimistically. The Bolshevik *Krasnaya gazeta* (*Red Gazette*) described their mood sarcastically in a lead article entitled "The Birdies Sang Too Soon." "In connection with the evacuation the bourgeoisie is overjoyed. They think that as hated Bolsheviks will leave Petrograd, the former government will somehow return to power, and bourgeois paradise will arrive at last."[121] Blok in his notebook for March 11 noted, " 'Flight' to Moscow, panic, rumors."

On March 16, the Bolsheviks signed a separate peace with the Germans and Petrograd was spared German occupation. The elite of the former capital experienced an ambivalent reaction. *Krasnaya gazeta* went on mocking,

There is a rumor in the city that Petersburg will be declared a free city. On the streets, in the trolleys and in cafés, you can hear a lot about the future "free" Petersburg. The so-called "clean public" is building its faith on that rumor so dear to their hearts of the evacuation of the capital and the government's move to Moscow. They say, "There's a reason they left, there's a secret paragraph in the peace treaty about making Petrograd an open city." The bourgeoisie is building the most fantastic hopes on ridiculous rumors, and everywhere that fat cats meet they talk about these hopes. And that's understandable. What else is left to the totally defeated bourgeoisie, but dreaming about what could have been?[122]

Who would find it surprising that in March 1918 the populace of Petrograd believed the most fantastic rumors more than the decrees and editorials in official newspapers? People refused to look truth in the eye, still not understanding that the circle of Russian history had closed. Pushkin once described Peter the Great's move of the capital of the Russian Empire from Moscow to Petersburg:

And before the younger capital
Old Moscow dimmed,
Like the porphyry-bearing widow
Before the new queen.

It was only in 1919 that Antsiferov admitted, "In the cosmic winds Russian imperialism found its tragic end. Petersburg stopped crowning Great Russia with its granite diadem. It became Red Piter. And Moscow, the porphyry-bearing widow, became the capital once again, the capital of the new Russia. And what of Petersburg?" And Antsiferov answered his rhetorical question, citing the prophetic lines from Andrei Bely's epic novel, *Petersburg,* written before World War I, "If Petersburg is not the capital, then there is no Petersburg. It only seems that it exists."[123]

The loss of status as capital was a horrible blow for Petrograd. Many of the site's inherent weaknesses, compensated for two hundred years by the massive influx of money and labor, suddenly pushed to the fore. All at once it was remembered that the former capital was quite removed from the rest of Russia, so food as well as raw materials for its industry had to be delivered from afar; that it was located too close to the border, open to foreign invasions; and that the climate was bad, and that the city was regularly flooded.

Clearly Lenin weighed these considerations before deciding to return the Russian capital from Petrograd to Moscow. As he described it, he felt like a military leader "taking the tatters of a defeated army or one shattered by panicky flight deep into the interior." But as was the case with Peter the Great's determination to establish his capital at St. Petersburg, there was an emotional, almost irrational aspect to Lenin's decision.

Lenin was the first to admit he didn't know Russia well. No fewer than fifteen years of his short life (he died in 1924, at age fifty-three) were spent abroad. For Lenin, Russia was embodied in Petersburg, with its all-powerful, tsarist institutions that constantly persecuted him, its police and prisons, in one of which Lenin spent fourteen months after his arrest in 1895.

Lenin felt great hostility to monarchical and bureaucratic Petersburg. But he also despised and hated the Petersburg intelligentsia, whom he considered spineless, drooling liberals and, most important, counterrevolutionary. Lenin's anti-intellectual position was confirmed in the recollections of many people, including those who admired him.

A typical, psychologically telling example is related by Lunacharsky. The writer Maxim Gorky, who had often defended the Petrograd intelligentsia before Lenin, came to him to complain about the arrest of people who had hidden many Bolsheviks, Lenin included, from the tsarist police before the revolution.

Lenin responded to Gorky's complaint with a laugh and said that all those idealist liberals ought to be arrested exactly because they are such "fine, kind people," who always aid the persecuted. First they hid Bolsheviks from the tsar, and now they protected counterrevolutionaries from the Bolsheviks. "And we," Lenin concluded sternly, "need to catch and destroy active counterrevolutionaries. The rest is clear."[124]

The move to Moscow was among other things an act of revenge, perhaps unconscious, on Lenin's part against the Petrograd intelligentsia, whom the Bolshevik leader called "embittered . . . understanding nothing, forgetting nothing, having learned nothing, *at best*—in the very rare best case—confused, despairing, whining, repeating old superstitions, frightened and frightening itself."[125]

Like Peter the Great breaking with Moscow to start Russian history afresh, Lenin left behind the former tsarist capital to assert his right to a radical experiment. In demoting Petrograd, Lenin demonstrated the seriousness of the new regime's rejection of the old Russia, its institutions, and its intelligentsia. After leaving Petrograd,

Lenin wrote to Gorky, who remained in the city: "The intellectual powers of the workers and peasants are growing in the struggle to overthrow the bourgeoisie and its helpers, the little intellectuals, the lackeys of capital, who consider themselves the brain of the nation. In fact they are not the brain, but the droppings."[126]

With the government's move to Moscow, Lunacharsky's dire predictions about Petrograd's fate immediately came to pass. Unemployment and economic dislocation increased not daily but hourly, and the population began to decline dramatically. In postrevolutionary Russia the population fell throughout the country, but overall decline and population losses were the greatest in Petrograd.

In 1915 Petrograd had 2,347,000 people. But on June 2, 1918, just two and a half months after the city lost capital status, there were only 1,468,000 people living there. This sharp downturn continued. The census of August 1920 reported only 799,000 people in Petrograd, that is, not quite 35 percent of the prerevolutionary level.[127]

The cold, hungry city was dying, and many recalled the curse of Tsarina Eudoxia, the wife Peter the Great exiled to a convent: "Sankt-Peterburg will stand empty!"

Pipes froze. People burned furniture, books, and the wood of their houses for firewood. The avant-garde artist Yuri Annenkov, who later emigrated to France, recalled,

> It was an era of endless hungry lines, queues in front of empty "produce distributors," an epic era of rotten, frozen offal, moldy bread crusts, and inedible substitutes. The French, who had lived through a four-year Nazi occupation, liked to talk of those years as years of hunger and severe shortages. I was in Paris then, too—an insignificant shortage of some products, a lowering of quality in others, artificial but still aromatic coffee, a slight reduction in electric energy and gas. No one died of hunger on icy sidewalks, no one tore apart fallen horses, no one ate dogs, or cats, or rats.[128]

Petrograders went through all that, but something kept them from total despair. Shklovsky maintained, "This city did not become provincial, it was not taken because it heated itself with its own fire, burned everyone who attacked it. Potatoes and carrots were bought like flowers; poems and tomorrow were sacred."

The factories stopped smoking, and the sky above Petrograd became cloudless and wrenchingly blue. Artists egocentrically found new beauty in the radically changed urban landscape.

You no longer saw luxurious carriages. The crowd of sated, strolling people vanished. The streets were deserted, and the city that could be seen only knee-high at last stood up at full height. Before that, when you drew it, you sometimes had to wait several minutes for a crowd of people to pass and let you see the pure line of a building's foundation, of the bottom of a column or statue, or the horizon over the river. Now everything was free.[129]

But even this incredible transformation did not seem adequate to many artists, especially in the avant-garde. They wanted to feel like the true masters of the former capital, if only for an hour, and play even more boldly with its still majestic and beautiful squares, prospects, palaces, and monuments.

Petrograd was called the Petrograd Labor Commune in those days. The editorial of the first issue in late 1918 of the semiofficial newspaper *Iskusstvo kommuny* (*Art of the Commune*), whose editor in chief was Akhmatova's future husband, Punin, was a poem by the futurist Vladimir Mayakovsky, "Orders on the Army of Art."

> *Wipe the old from your heart.*
> *The streets are our brushes.*
> *The squares our palettes.*

In another poem, which was soon placed in a Communist newspaper, Mayakovsky confidently proclaimed, "A new architect is coming. It is we, the illuminators of tomorrow's cities." The radical poet's declarations were not simply utopian manifestoes; rather, they summed up the fantastic artistic experiments already attempted by the avant-gardists on a citywide scale.

The first grand theatrical demonstration, imitating the legendary festivities of the French Revolution, rolled down the streets of Petrograd on May 1, 1918. Red banners, huge multicolored proclamations, garlands of greenery and flags covered the most important buildings, squares, bridges, and embankments. Giant posters showed soldiers and peasants, painted in bold orange and cinnabar. People's Commissar Lunacharsky rushed around the city in a car from one mass rally to another.

"It's easy to celebrate," he intoned, "when everything is going swimmingly and fortune pats us on the head. But the fact that we, hungry Petrograders, besieged, with enemies within, bearing such a burden of unemployment and suffering on our shoulders, still are celebrating proudly and solemnly—this is our real achievement."[130]

At the Winter Palace, renamed by the politically astute Lunacharsky the Palace of the Arts, Mozart's *Requiem* was performed for an audience of seven thousand. Many were listening to classical music for the first time, and as Lunacharsky recalled, a small boy in the front row thought that he was in church, sank to his knees, and stayed that way for the entire concert.

Aeroplanes soared overhead. The fleet on the Neva was festooned with thousands of flags. Fireworks blazed in the sky that night and the artillery sounded salutes from the Peter and Paul Fortress. And the memorable celebration ended with a parade of thousands of Petrograd's firemen in gleaming brass helmets carrying blazing torches—a scene worthy of a new Rembrandt.

By the time a lavish celebration for the first anniversary of the Bolshevik revolution was decided a few months later, there were already some attempts to push aside Petrograd's avant-garde artists. So for this occasion Lunacharsky handed out commissions to a group of some 170 artists, sculptors, and architects, among whom were many traditionalists. But the avant-garde painter Nathan Altman, for instance, still got permission to redesign Palace Square (renamed Uritsky Square, in memory of the recently assassinated prominent Bolshevik), and that symbol of the former monarchy, the Winter Palace, standing on it.

In 1966, Altman told me that he had passionately wanted to turn the square into a huge open-air auditorium, where the revolutionary crowd could at last feel at home. For that he had to "destroy the imperial grandeur of the square."[131] On the palace and other buildings around the square, Altman hung enormous propaganda posters, depicting the "new hegemonic forces"—gigantic workers and peasants. In the center of the square, near the Alexander Column, he placed a rostrum made up of bright red and orange surfaces, which in the evening light created the feeling of a wild cubist flame. This avant-garde rostrum seemed to be blowing up the the Alexander Column, which Altman associated with the old order.

In comparable fashion the avant-garde artists transformed the Hermitage, the Admiralty, the Academy of Sciences, and many other historic buildings of old Petersburg. When I asked Altman in 1966 where he got the material—the panels alone required tens of thousands of meters of canvas—the artist, smiling enigmatically, replied, "They didn't skimp back then."

This bold, lavish experiment in ruined Petrograd opened a new page in the history of urban design. But the hungry masses were

angered by the "Futurist showings off" of the leftist artists. A contemporary wrote, "Alien and uncomprehending columns of demonstrators walked past the red and black sails thrown onto the Police
Bridge by the artist Lebedev, past green canvases and orange curves
which covered the boulevard and the column on Palace Square at Altman's whim, past fantastically deformed figures with hammers and
rifles on Petrograd buildings."[132]

Even the workers, who supported the Bolsheviks, vaguely felt
that Petrograd was being subjected to some sort of ideological violence. For locals the modernist experiments with the city's squares and
palaces in November 1918 did not differ in the least from another
mockery carried out that same November of the historical values of
the former capital.

Several thousand participants had come to Petrograd for the
Congress of Committees of Peasants, and many of them were housed
at the Palace of the Arts. When they left after the debates, it was discovered that all the bathtubs of the palace—the official residence of
the imperial family before the revolution—and an enormous number
of Sevres, Saxon, and Oriental vases of museum quality had been filled
with excrement.

Outraged by the contempt of the country's new masters for its
cultural heritage, Maxim Gorky conveyed the shock of the Petrograd
intelligentsia: "This was done not out of need—the toilets in the palace
were fine and the plumbing worked. No, this hooliganism was an expression of the desire to break, destroy, mock, and spoil beauty."[133]

So Petrograd literature rushed to defend the city's cultural heritage as
if it had suddenly sensed the fatal threat to its roots. Music and art had
done it first, of course. Predicting the coming cataclysms, Tchaikovsky's
symphonies bewailed the great city in the nineteenth century. Benois
and his companions in *Mir iskusstva,* with the same prophetically nostalgic feeling, described and captured the essence of the capital at the
turn of the century. But contemporary literature, even the most modern, merely continued to damn Petersburg routinely. In that sense it remained hopelessly under the spell of Gogol and Dostoyevsky, the
undisputed idols of the Russian symbolists.

I should stress once more that many leading symbolists grew
up influenced heavily by Slavophile ideas. So while radically rethink-
ing some of Gogol and Dostoyevsky's heritage, the literary symbolists
remained much more under the influence of their Slavophile ideology
than the Russian artists of the turn of the century.

Even Benois and Diaghilev's comrades at *Mir iskusstva*—
Merezhkovsky and his wife, Hippius—did not go beyond what Gogol
had begun and Dostoyevsky had developed in their attitude toward
Petersburg. Hippius wrote skillful poetry and Merezhkovsky full-
blown entertaining historical novels that were very popular (among
them the eloquently named *Antichrist,* subtitled "Peter and Alexei,"
dealing specifically with Peter the Great), and whose contents, despite
all pseudo-philosophical trappings, could be easily reduced to the
forthright conclusion by Dostoyevsky that Petersburg was an alien
phenomenon in Russia and therefore doomed to destruction. "Sankt-
Peterburg will stand empty!" In the amusing middle-brow interpretation this old curse had turned into an ideological cliché.

A much more ambitious and significant attack on the imperial
capital was the novel *Petersburg,* written by the symbolist Andrei Bely,
who was born in Moscow in 1880 and died there in 1934. This monumental work, finished in its first version in 1913, is unquestionably
the peak of Russian symbolist prose. Nabokov held Bely's *Petersburg*
on a par with Proust's *A la Recherche du temps perdu,* Joyce's *Ulysses,*
and Kafka's *Metamorphosis,* an opinion shared by many specialists.

Bely's attitude toward Petersburg is profoundly negative, and
in that sense he is a faithful adherent to the Gogol-Nekrasov-
Dostoyevsky tradition. "Europe's culture was imagined by the Russians; the West has civilization; there is *no* Western *culture* in our sense
of the word; such culture in embryonic form exists only in Russia."
Such Slavophile passages are not unusual in the Muscovite Bely's writing. Therefore Bely's admission, made in a letter to his friend the Petersburger Blok, should not surprise us: "In Petersburg I am a tourist,
an observer, not an inhabitant."[134]

The fact that the most famous modernist text about Petersburg
belongs to a Muscovite is paradoxical only at first glance, for the
essence of Bely's *Petersburg,* no matter how one turns it or interprets
it, consists of artistically humiliating and philosophically destroying
the "illegal" capital. No wonder Bunin irritatedly rejected Bely's
novel. "What a vile idea the book has—'Petersburg will stand empty.'
What did Petersburg ever do to him?"[135] And Akhmatova in her later
years often said, "The novel *Petersburg* for us Petersburgers is so unlike the real Petersburg."

One of the impulses for writing the novel came to Bely with
the unveiling in Petersburg on May 23, 1909, of the equine statue of
Emperor Alexander III on Znamenskaya Square. Created by the sculptor Paolo Trubetskoy (1866–1938), who was born in Italy of an Amer-

ican mother and was the scion of one of the noblest Russian families, the monument caused a storm of controversy. It presented the heavy, gloomy emperor sitting on a stolid draft horse.

Many saw a political caricature in that statue, but Trubetskoy, who was famous for never reading books or newspapers and didn't know a word of Russian, replied to the question, "What is the idea of your monument?" with, "I don't care about politics. I simply depicted one animal on another."

To general amazement, the widow of Alexander III, Maria Fyodorovna, supported the project, since she believed the statue greatly resembled her late husband, and her son, Nicholas II, was forced to agree. As soon as the monument was erected, jokes began circulating around Petersburg. One ditty went as follows:

> On the square stands a commode,
> On the commode, a behemoth,
> On the behemoth, an idiot.

The ill-starred statue annoyed Nicholas so much that he wanted to move it to the Siberian city of Irkutsk but gave up the idea when he was told the latest bon mot going around town—the sovereign wanted to exile his father to Siberia. Ironically, the Soviets fulfilled the last Russian emperor's wish. In 1937 Trubetskoy's work was removed from its pedestal and exiled not to Siberia but to the backyard of the Russian (formerly, Alexander III) Museum.

Whenever I went through the museum, I always stopped at one of its big windows to look out at the monstrously heavy silhouette of the rider and horse, which was such a contrast to Falconet's Bronze Horseman. This contrast was felt even more acutely in 1909. In this respect Trubetskoy's monument was for many viewers, including Bely, just another proof of the dead end into which Peter the Great had led Russia. (In 1994 this equestrian statue at last found a home—erected not on its former site, but in front of one of the palaces of St. Petersburg.)

Of course, Bely brought Falconet's statue into his novel, as well as numerous themes from Pushkin's poem that was dedicated to it, but he removed Pushkin's dualism, which vacillated in its evaluation of the role of Petersburg's founder. For Bely the Bronze Horseman is a figure out of the apocalypse, still galloping through Petersburg in 1905, a horrible symbol of the vain attempts at Westernizing by the Russian Empire.

The detective plot of Bely's novel—the hunt for an important Petersburg official by revolutionary terrorists—is merely an excuse for fantastic situations, intense descriptions, and mystical theories (at that time Bely was a fanatical adherent of Rudolf Steiner and his anthroposophic teaching). The reader is virtually engulfed by a literary storm of enormous power. Bely uses irony, absurdity, pathos, and parody; in particular, he parodies Tchaikovsky's *Queen of Spades*. He is a virtuoso at using the entire arsenal of techniques first tried by his precursors Gogol and Dostoyevsky. He also creates brilliant new effects, incomparably mixing the horrible, the funny, and the tragic with the aid of masterful linguistic tricks. Yevgeny Zamyatin rightly observed that Bely's *Petersburg* has the same complicated relation to the Russian language that *Ulysses* has to English.

For Bely, heavily influenced by anthroposophy, Petersburg is on the border between the earthly and the cosmic on the one hand and between the West and Asia on the other. This is the novel's main intellectual innovation. Before Bely the imperial capital had always been viewed in the framework of West versus Russia. But Bely seems to soar into space and from there to see Petersburg caught between two realities—Western and Asiatic. This is a tragic situation for him. "The West stinks of decay, and the East does not stink only because it has decayed long ago."

Europe, Bely predicted, would inevitably die, swallowed up by Asia, and Petersburg, that loathsome example of the triumph of civilization over culture, would vanish. Russian writers before Bely, enjoying their fantasies about the destruction of their capital, expected three of the four elements to beset the city—Petersburg would perish in a flood, by burning, or by dissolving like a mirage. Bely introduces the fourth element, earth. In his novel Petersburg falls into a hole.

When inspired, Bely, opening wide his piercing blue eyes, read excerpts from his novel at Vyacheslav Ivanov's Tower, jumping up and practically taking off, so that his hair stood on end like a crown. The spellbound listeners, nodding in time to the hypnotically rhythmic prose, were prepared to consider the author a prophet.

But Blok—who had a love-hate relationship with Bely that was typical of the symbolists, further complicated by Bely's infatuation with Blok's wife—wrote after hearing the novel, "revulsion for the terrible things he sees; evil work; the approach of despair (if the world really is like that)."[136]

And Blok also noted in that "muddled novel with a stamp of genius" an amazing parallel with his own autobiographical verse epic, *Retribution*, which preoccupied Blok in those years and in which the image of Petersburg loomed large. Actually, for all their obvious differences in style, the similarity of the attitudes toward the imperial capital of the Muscovite Bely and the Petersburger Blok is astonishing.

The Slavophile symbolist doctrine, which rejected a Germanic Petersburg, was obviously stronger than direct experience even for such an independent personality as Blok. Blok's *Retribution* and his drafts of it are filled with Slavophile anti-Petersburg rhetoric. For instance, Peter the Great appears in Blok's work, as he does in Bely's novel, as an emanation of the devil.

> *Tsar! Are you rising from the grave again*
> *To chop us a new window?*
> *Frightening: in a white night—both—*
> *Corpse and city—are as one. . . .*

Similar symbolist clichés, the result of a mix of Slavophile and modernist-urbanist phraseology, fill Blok's correspondence, which bristles with italics: "again that horrible anger at Petersburg boils within me, *for I know* that it is a lousy, rotten nucleus, where our boldness wanes and weakens . . . we live *daily* in horror, stink, and despair, in factory smoke, in the rouge of lascivious smiles, in the roar of disgusting automobiles . . . Petersburg is a gigantic whorehouse, I feel it. You *can't rest, learn everything* there, a brief rest only where the masts creak, boats sway on the *outskirts,* on the islands, at the gulf, in twilight."[137]

Blok's paradoxical love for Petersburg's outskirts, like his hatred of the "pompous" center, was ideological in nature and originated in his Slavophile beliefs. But in this particular instance there were also some true and strong emotions involved, the happy result of which was a multitude of strange, moody poems in which Blok, not calling Petersburg by name, nevertheless lets us feel the longing, sadness, and charm of its outskirts.

The shades of "small" Petersburgers flicker in those poems—tramps, prostitutes, card sharks, drunken sailors. Blok's Petersburg is hostile to all those people. In the traditions of Gogol, Nekrasov, and Dostoyevsky, he depicts the metropolis as a monster. But we also feel an intensely personal note, comparable to Blok's observation of the city in his diaries, like this almost Dickensian one: "What dreariness—almost tears. Night—on the broad embankment of the Neva, near the university, barely visible among the rocks was a child, a boy. His mother (a peasant) picked him up and he wrapped his little arms around her neck—afraid. Horrible, miserable city, where a child gets lost. It chokes me with tears."[138]

It is only natural, therefore, that Blok, who at first greeted the Bolshevik coup enthusiastically, managed to create an astonishing picture of postrevolutionary Petrograd, its hackles raised, in his famous narrative epic *The Twelve*, written in January 1918. The twelve of the title are a Red Army patrol walking through the dark, ruined city, and at the same time they become in Blok's imagination the twelve apostles, led by Jesus Christ.

Petrograd in *The Twelve* appears in a series of impressionistic sketches—snow, ice, shoot-outs, and robberies on the streets, huge political posters flapping in a sharp wind. Despite the mystical image of Christ, the narrative presented some intentionally brutal and horrifying pictures. Therefore Blok's work pleased both the Bolsheviks and their foes. Still, controversy flared. Religious leaders were shocked that Blok had Christ leading the Red Army through Petrograd. In a letter to a friend, one writer was indignant: "But I and many millions of people are now observing something completely different from what Christ taught. Then why should he be leading that gang? When you see Blok, ask him about that."[139]

Blok's and Akhmatova's political positions diverged sharply then. At the start of the Bolshevik revolution Akhmatova published in liberal newspapers, which were soon shut down by the authorities. She also read her poetry at rallies with a marked anti-Bolshevik character.

At one of them organized to support political prisoners, victims of the Bolshevik terror, Akhmatova read her old poem "The Prayer," which took on an even more ominous tone in the new circumstances. She appeared with her closest friends; Olga Sudeikina danced and Arthur Lourié played the piano at the same concert. Blok, who did not attend, was told the audience shouted "Traitor!" at the mention of his name.

Tellingly, Akhmatova refused to participate in another literary evening when she learned that someone would be reading *The Twelve*. In his notebook a deeply wounded Blok called her decision "astonishing news."[140]

Much later, Akhmatova, recalling Petersburg after the Bolshevik revolution, remarked mournfully, "The city did not simply change, it determinedly turned into its opposite." Apparently, from similar observations of Petrograd in agony, Akhmatova and Blok drew different conclusions.

Such obvious disagreements between Akhmatova and Blok in interpreting the Petersburg mythos were dictated by several reasons. Age made a difference, as well as being from different social strata and feuding literary movements. The acmeists, Akhmatova included, were freer of the clichés employed by the Slavophile "professorial" culture. Therefore their attitude toward Petersburg was less prejudiced and more sympathetic.

In that sense the acmeists had much in common with Benois and his *Mir iskusstva*. They were also similar in their use of a flexible, confident line and well-drawn, lacelike detail. In the early poems of Akhmatova and Mandelstam, two leading acmeists, there is a definite resemblance to the drawings of the *Mir iskusstva* group. In their work, Petersburg at last ceases to threaten and takes on the intimate traits of a place that has been lived in. But there were also differences with *Mir iskusstva*, which became more apparent in time.

The acmeists considered their forefather to be the poet Innokenti Annensky (1855–1909), the author of the posthumously published "Petersburg," a most concentrated presentation of the symbolists' imagery of the city on the Neva.

> The sorcerer gave us only stones,
> And the Neva of brownish yellow,
> And the empty, mute squares
> Where people were executed before dawn.

Akhmatova had a special respect for Annensky that went beyond appreciation of his poetry. She recalled with great feeling Annensky's words when he learned of the wedding of his relative to Akhmatova's older sister: "I would have chosen the younger one." Akhmatova insisted, "I mark my 'beginning' from Annensky's poetry. His work, to my mind, is tragic, sincere, and whole-hearted."

For Annensky Petersburg was always tied to the "awareness of a damned mistake." For the acmeists, the existence of Petersburg was not an issue; the city was a given for them and belonging to it a source of pride. That's why they didn't borrow Annensky's Petersburg mythology but took to heart his dramatic precision in descriptions and his expressive landscape details, like the ones that open "Petersburg":

Yellow steam of the Petersburg winter,
Yellow snow, sticking to the stones. . . .

Viktor Zhirmunsky later announced that "Akhmatova's Petersburg landscape was her poetic discovery."[141] In fact, Akhmatova had borrowed extensively from Annensky in this respect, and also something from Blok and the other symbolists. But the landscape they saw as unpeopled, hostile, and historically illegitimate takes on roots in Akhmatova's work, is legitimized by her, and, most important, becomes "homey" and familiar. Akhmatova's "autobiographical" heroine moves around freely in the historical and temporal space of Petersburg.

For Akhmatova Petersburg is an enchanted place, as it is for Annensky. But in differing from him, she finds it even better. She does not feel herself a stranger—

Above the dark-watered Neva
Under the cold smile
Of Emperor Peter.

Peter's smile may be cold, but it is addressed to Akhmatova personally. In one poem of 1914 Akhmatova ties her entire existence to Petersburg. She calls it her "blessed cradle," "solemn bridal bed," and "prie-dieu of my prayers"—an amazing combination but typical of Akhmatova. This is the city in which her Muse lives, the city "loved with bitter love."

Not one of the *Mir iskusstva* participants would have ever spoken or even thought in such a way. At that period their attitude toward Petersburg was very loving but with a faint smile of condescension, as for an object that was quite lovely and dear but without question part of the distant past. Those artists delighted in Petersburg as antiquarians might.

The acmeists quickly overcame that approach. Akhmatova later insisted that Mandelstam "disdained" the *Mir iskusstva* love of Petersburg, but she herself had patiently studied the architecture of old Petersburg, and the reappraisal by Benois and Co. of that architecture had a significant influence on both her and Mandelstam. Mandelstam recalled,

When I was seven or eight, I regarded as something sacred and festive Petersburg's architectural ensemble, the granite and stone blocks, the tender heart of the city, with its unexpected squares, lacy gardens, and islands of monuments, the Caryatids of the Hermitage, the mysterious Millionnaya Street, where there were never any passersby and where among the marble buildings one tiny grocery store was hidden, and especially the arch of the General Staff Headquarters, the Senate Square, and "Dutch" Petersburg.

The acmeists' attitude—which was intimate and at the same time solemn and historically rooted—portended the horror with which Akhmatova responded to the sudden changes in the face of the city on the Neva after the Bolsheviks came to power:

> *When the Neva capital,*
> *Forgetting her majesty,*
> *Like a drunken harlot,*
> *Didn't know who was taking her . . .*

But Akhmatova's indignation quickly turned to pity in the escalating deterioration of her beloved city.

> All the old Petersburg signs were still in place, but behind them, there was nothing but dusk, gloom, and gaping emptiness. Typhus, hunger, executions, dark apartments, damp logs, people swollen beyond recognition. You could pick a bouquet of wild flowers at the Gostiny Dvor. The famous Petersburg wooden pavements were rotting. It still smelled of chocolate from the cellar windows of Kraft's. The cemeteries were torn up.

After the Bolshevik revolution Akhmatova did not leave for the West, as did numerous intellectual notables, many of them former ideological "foes" of Petersburg. Her refusal to emigrate was perceived as a conscious sacrifice, as were Mandelstam's and Gumilyov's. One of the many complex reasons for that fateful decision was Akhmatova's proclaimed desire to save at least some remains of Petersburg's grandeur, the "palaces, fire, and water" of the former capital.

The acmeists' identification of Petersburg's fate with the fate of Russia took on such a declarative character at the time that in Mandelstam's poetry, for instance, "the symbol of faithfulness to Russia in her misfortune became St. Isaac's Cathedral,"[142] according to Sergei Averintsev, even though the poet disliked that church from a purely architectural point of view.

Thus, the acmeists helped to usher in a new period in the history of the Petersburg mythos, in which the city began to be viewed as martyr. Anything that could be integrated into this mythos was once again—after a hiatus of one hundred years—regarded positively, even if a particular building or statue was not liked. After the *Mir iskusstva* group's rather sentimental look at the city, this was a significant new attitude, prompted by a totally different political and social reality.

To suffer together with Petersburg became a ritual. Partly because of this sacrificial rite, for the first time in the history of Russian culture Petersburg's inevitable downfall was interpreted as the first stage of its inexorable resurrection in some new form.

Thus Mandelstam, describing Petersburg's decay, simultaneously predicts the city's postapocalyptic existence:

> Grass on Petersburg streets—the first runners of a virgin forest, which will cover the place of modern cities. This bright, tender green, amazing in its freshness, belongs to the new animate nature. Truly Petersburg is the most avant-garde city in the world. The race of modernity is not measured by the existence of subway or skyscraper, but by merry grass breaking through the urban stones.

Akhmatova expressed her feelings for the dying Petersburg with even more mystical force:

> *Everything is stolen, betrayed, sold,*
> *The wing of black death flashed,*
> *Everything is gnawed by hungry depression,*
> *Why do we see light then?*

Akhmatova's irrational, almost ecstatic sensation that "The miraculous comes so close" to the collapsing dirty buildings of Petersburg is deciphered by Mandelstam: "Nothing is impossible. Like a dying man's room open to everything, the door of the old world is now wide open to the crowd. Suddenly everything became common property. Go and take. Everything is accessible: all the labyrinths, all the secret places, all the hidden passages."

In Mandelstam's poetry of that period, horror and despair at witnessing Petersburg's convulsions prevail. There is no one to complain to, and the poet must raise his voice to the heavens:

> *Translucent star, wandering fire,*
> *Your brother, Petropolis, is dying!*

But in Mandelstam's essay "Word and Culture," we can find autobiographical lines that cast a different light on current events. "At last we found inner freedom, real inner merriment. We drink water from clay pitchers as if it were wine, and the sun likes a monastery refectory more than a restaurant. Apples, bread, potatoes—they sate not only physical but spiritual hunger."

The artist Vladimir Milashevsky, a rather cynical observer, gave an ironic commentary to this sort of almost religious frenzy and obsession with cathartic ideas that were so prevalent in postrevolutionary Petrograd: "Meager nourishment and sluggish functions of the physical body affected the psyche. It gave rise to meager, strange, and distorted ideas. In monasteries the monks made a point of eating little, in order to believe more strongly, to have religious visions. 'I believe! I believe! I believe rapturously!' "[143]

By the 1920s Petrograd really did resemble a vision of some religious ascetic. We can judge that from a remarkable cycle of lithographs, "Petersburg in 1921," by Mstislav Dobuzhinsky (1875–1957). That series was Dobuzhinsky's farewell to the city he loved more than anything else on earth. Later, as an émigré in the West, the artist would recall, "The city was dying before my very eyes with a death of incredible beauty, and I tried to capture as best I could its terrible, deserted, and wounded look."[144]

A member of *Mir iskusstva,* all of whose participants were enraptured by Petersburg, Dobuzhinsky stood out even among them for his uncanny comprehension of the city's mood. He did not idealize old Petersburg. His attention from the first was captured by the newest parts of the city: "Those sleepy canals, endless fences, brick fireproof walls without windows, piles of black logs, empty lots, dark wells of courtyards—it all astonished me with its sharply drawn, even eerie features. Everything seemed extraordinarily original, imbued with bitter poetry and mystery."[145]

Dobuzhinsky's contemporaries had noticed early on that alongside the Petersburg of Pushkin, Gogol, and Dostoyevsky in literature appeared "Dobuzhinsky's Petersburg" in the visual arts. "When they looked at a foggy sunset in London, people said, like Oscar Wilde, that it was 'a Turner sunset,' and when they looked at the blind stone backs of Petersburg buildings, they saw 'Dobuzhinsky walls.' It was as if we were given different eyes for some objects, different glasses."[146]

Akhmatova once wrote that she observed her beloved city "with the curiosity of a foreigner." Dobuzhinsky's friend Milashevsky found something comparable in the artist's Petersburg works. "Dobuzhinsky has the feeling of a man seeing Petersburg for the first time. You have to be born elsewhere to see it in all its strangeness. Dobuzhinsky was not born in Petersburg like Somov, Benois, or Blok; he saw it for the first time as a young man and then as an adult artist. But Petersburg became the hometown of his soul."[147]

Dobuzhinsky readily admitted how enormously Dostoyevsky had influenced his artistic vision of Petersburg. It is through the prism of Dostoyevsky that Dobuzhinsky first saw the imperial capital, and so he started to capture its "nonimperial" aspects—the outskirts, dimly lit, empty, and sad. In Dobuzhinsky's work, Petersburg's walls, roofs, and chimneys formed fantastic landscapes filled with anxiety and anticipation.

Dobuzhinsky expressed his admiration for Dostoyevsky by illustrating his *White Nights,* which the writer had subtitled *A Sentimental Novel.* The seventeen stark, transparent drawings Dobuzhinsky did for *White Nights* in the early 1920s are his masterpiece. The exquisite drawings, with their sensitive contrasts of black and white, creating an atmosphere of quiet despair, can easily be called the best illustrations of Dostoyevsky. At the same time, they create probably the most inspired visual paean to Petersburg in all of Russian art. In that sense, Dobuzhinsky's series still has no rivals in Russian culture.

His album of lithographs, "Petersburg in 1921," is another incomparable document capturing the tragedy of the former capital. The artist fixes the city's farewell with Western civilization, which Akhmatova expressed in poetry in those same years:

> In the West the winter sun still shines
> And rooftops still glitter in its rays,
> While here death covers houses with crosses
> And calls the ravens, and the ravens come.

It is hard to imagine the shock Dobuzhinsky, usually slow to action and regally calm, so in love with Petersburg, must have experienced to give in to the hardships and humiliations of postrevolutionary life, pack his bags, and emigrate to the West while it was still possible, leaving behind forever the city and his friends, among them Akhmatova, and dying eventually, a heartbroken old man, in New York City.

In late 1920 and early 1921 decrees were issued in Petrograd eliminating fares on public transportation and admission to the steam baths and making apartments, water, and electricity free for residents. The problem was that the trolleys rarely ran then, the water froze, and washing at home, much less at the baths, was rare. Money didn't mean anything anyway, because there was nothing to buy. Food was distributed in ration parcels at work.

People who were not employed in factories or Soviet offices received a bread ration of half a pound a day, which was called "hunger rations." In order to survive, intellectuals started "ration hunting," finding parcels wherever they could.

The artist Yuri Annenkov, who drew the very successful cubist illustrations for the first edition of Blok's *The Twelve,* became the champion ration hunter. As a professor in the reorganized Academy of Arts, he received "scholar's rations," and as a founder of the cultural and educational studio for militiamen, he got their parcel, too. Annenkov found a job there for Dobuzhinsky, who lectured the militia on the Petersburg architectural monuments they were supposed to guard. Lecturing sailors guaranteed Annenkov the "special" rations parcel of the Baltic fleet. (The archives contain the topics of lectures sanctioned by the Bolsheviks for sailors in the winter of 1920: "The Origins of Man," "Italian Painting," "Mores and Life in Austria."[148]) But the most generous rations—for a breast-feeding mother—were given to Annenkov at the Maternity Center, now called the Rosa Luxemburg Drops of Milk, for lecturing the midwives on the history of sculpture.

Blok, who did not have to work for a living before the revolution, was hard up under the Bolsheviks, since he lacked the know-how to "ration hunt." The Communists treated him sympathetically at first. Annenkov recalled how he, Blok, Bely, Olga Sudeikina, and a few other friends had stayed late at someone's house in October 1919 and, because there was a curfew in Petrograd then, they decided to spend the night there.

They put Olga in the bed while Blok napped at a table. Toward dawn there was a commanding knock at the door: armed sailors led by the military commandant of Petrograd came to search the apartment in response to a report about "suspicious" guests from the vigilant neighbors of their "building committee of the poor." (The Bolsheviks created such committees in every Petrograd house.)

"Any strangers here?"

"Yes, as you can see: the poet Alexander Blok is sleeping at the table," replied the host. "He lives far away and would not have gotten back in time for the curfew."

"Detail!" The self-important Bolshevik was impressed. "Which Blok, the real one?"

"One hundred percent!"

After a peek at the sleeping poet, the commandant whispered, "To hell with you!" to the host and tiptoed out, leading away the sailors with their clanging weapons. Annenkov thought then that as a young man the Communist must have read Blok's *The Unknown Woman,* as so many of his contemporaries had. . . .

When Blok, Bely, and Annenkov left in the morning, a symbolic meeting of the new regime and the Petrograd intelligentsia took place on deserted Nevsky Prospect. They came across a bored militiaman with a rifle over his shoulder, legs apart, writing his name in the snow with his urine. Upon seeing that, Bely shouted, "I don't know how to write on snow! I need ink, just a little bottle of ink! And a scrap of paper!"

"Move along, citizens, move along," the militiaman muttered, buttoning his fly.[149]

Blok used to tell his friends who were making do with lecturing, "I envy you all: you know how to talk, so you lecture someone somewhere. I don't know how. I can only read from a text." But it was impossible to live on a writer's fees in those days. One writer calculated that to survive in Petrograd in 1920, Shakespeare would have had to write three plays a month, and Turgenev's fees for his novel *Fathers and Sons* could have kept him fed for three weeks.[150] So to survive, Blok took a job, as did many other Petrograd intellectuals, in the People's Commissariat of Education, that is, the Soviet Ministry of Culture, headed by Lunacharsky.

The poet worked in its theatrical department, sitting on all kinds of committees and on the editorial board of Vsemirnaya Literatura (World Literature) Publishing House. Here Blok and other intellectuals compiled an enormous list of masterpieces of all times and peoples that had to be retranslated into Russian and published for the proletarian audience. The first series alone was to include fifteen hundred titles of an academic nature with detailed commentary and another five thousand of a more popular kind.

It was Maxim Gorky's utopian idea, and in the impossible conditions of postrevolutionary Russia, it would have taken a hundred years to complete, but in the meantime, writers could get fed. One of them, André Levinson, later recalled bitterly in exile that their work was the "hopeless and paradoxical task of implanting the West's spiritual culture on the ruins of Russian life. . . . We lived in a naive illusion in those years, thinking that Byron and Flaubert reaching the masses even in the guise of the Bolshevik 'bluff' would enrich and astonish more than one soul."[151]

At meetings of the editorial board of Vsemirnaya Literatura Blok often met with Nikolai Gumilyov, who had returned to Petrograd in 1918 from Paris, where he had been serving in the office of the military attaché of the provisional government overthrown by the Bolsheviks. To the friends who tried to dissuade him from what they considered to be a foolish decision, Gumilyov said, "I fought the Germans for three years and I hunted lion in Africa. But I've never seen a Bolshevik. Why shouldn't I go to Petrograd? I doubt it's more dangerous than the jungles."[152]

Gumilyov behaved provocatively in Bolshevik Petrograd, announcing at every corner that he was a monarchist and crossing himself at every church he passed, which was considered almost a sign of madness in the conditions of official atheism and "red terror." Just as Gumilyov arrived in Petrograd a Russian writer was complaining to another by letter, "There are patrols in the evenings now—they search people for weapons. The decree says that if they find a gun and take it away and the person resists, he is to be shot on the spot. So where's the proclaimed abolition of capital punishment? In the past even regicides were first given a trial and only then hanged, but now they do it 'on the spot.' They've turned everybody into an executioner!"[153]

Still Lunacharsky and Gorky hired Gumilyov to work at Vsemirnaya Literatura; he also started to give lectures to Petrograd workers and sailors. Even for audiences like those Gumilyov declaimed his monarchist poems. He laughed. "The Bolsheviks despise conformists. I prefer to be respected."

Years later Akhmatova was asked why Gumilyov took part in various cultural enterprises under the aegis of the Bolsheviks: he translated, lectured, and led a seminar of young poets. She explained that he had been a born organizer—just think of the creation of acmeism. But at the time it would have been ridiculous to consider that he could go to the tsarist minister of education and announce, "I want to organize a studio to teach people how to write poetry." Under the Bolsheviks that became possible. Moreover, Gumilyov had to survive. Before the revolution he lived on his annuity, but under the Bolsheviks only by working in Lunacharsky's commissariat could he stave off starvation.

This was how Akhmatova justified Gumilyov's compromise with the regime. Still she herself did not go to work for the Bolsheviks despite her hunger. She admitted that once, when things got really bad, she went to Gorky to ask for some work. Gorky suggested she apply to the Communist International, the notorious Comintern, headed by the chief of the Petrograd Communists, Grigory Zinoviev. She would be given Communist proclamations to translate into Italian. Akhmatova refused the job. "Just think: I would do translations that would be sent to Italy, for which people would be arrested." Akhmatova's principles cost her dearly. A friend writing to his wife reported, "Akhmatova has turned into a horrible skeleton, dressed in rags."[154]

On Gumilyov's return to Bolshevik Petrograd, Akhmatova was quite laconic: "He loved his mother and was a good son." Their marriage had fallen apart even before the revolution. Gumilyov later confessed to a woman friend that soon after his marriage to Akhmatova, he began to cheat on her. "But she demanded absolute fidelity." According to the wayward husband, Akhmatova carried on a "love war" with him in the style of Knut Hamsun, that is, she was constantly having jealous rages with stormy scenes and stormy reconciliations. But Gumilyov hated "working out" their relationship.

In the sixties, Akhmatova stated that Gumilyov was a "complex man, refined but not soft. He could not be called responsive." In response to her demand, "Nikolai, we have to talk," he would typically answer, "Leave me alone, mother dear."

Even the birth of their son, Lev, in 1912 did not save the foundering marriage. "We argued over him, too," Gumilyov later complained. Akhmatova rarely saw the child, who was brought up by Gumilyov's relatives, and once when asked what he was doing, the child replied, "I'm trying to figure out the odds of my mother thinking about me."[155]

While holding Akhmatova's work in high esteem, Gumilyov could not forgive her for her poem of the war years, "The Prayer," calling it monstrous. He would quote,

Take away my child and my friend . . .

and comment indignantly, "She's asking God to kill Lev and me! After all, the friend here is meant to be me. . . . But thank God, that monstrous prayer, like most prayers, was not heard. Lev is—knock on wood—a sturdy lad!"[156] Gumilyov never learned that Akhmatova's prayer, embodied in a poem, was a prophecy of the true—and most tragic—course of events. When in June 1941 Akhmatova met Tsvetayeva for the first time, the latter asked her, "How could you write

'take away my child and my friend'. . . ? Don't you know that everything in poetry comes true?"

Right after Gumilyov's return to Petrograd Akhmatova told
him, "Give me a divorce." She recalled that he turned white and without any argument replied, "Gladly." Learning that Akhmatova was
marrying Vladimir Shileiko, Gumilyov refused to believe it, so outlandish was this young Assyriologist's reputation in Petrograd. Gumilyov immediately proposed to one of his women friends, the lovely
Anna Engelhardt.

In the sixties, Akhmatova would only shrug when asked for
the real reasons for the divorce. "In 1918, everyone was getting di-
vorced." She added, "I'm all for divorce." She always believed that
her request for a divorce had hurt Gumilyov badly and even hinted
that her former husband encouraged hostility toward her in his many
young poetry students.

This was one of the many paradoxes of the revolutionary era—that
cold, hungry Petrograd was positively seething with budding poets.
Their unquestioned idol was Blok at first. But after *The Twelve* many
recoiled from him and then Gumilyov was the pretender to the role
of leader. Politically, poetically, and psychologically, Gumilyov was
Blok's opposite. Akhmatova commented, "Blok did not like Gumilyov, and who knows why. There was personal hostility, but what was
in Blok's heart only Blok knew." Blok described Gumilyov's poems as
cold and "foreign." Akhmatova recalled, offended, how she was
changing from shoes to boots in a coatroom and Blok came up behind her and started to mumble, "You know, I don't like your husband's poetry."

Blok also found strange Gumilyov's idea that writing poetry
could be learned, that there were rules and laws of versification. Gumilyov, who admired Blok's poetry enormously, nevertheless attacked
The Twelve, maintaining that Blok had served the "cause of the Antichrist" in that work. "He crucified Christ a second time and executed our sovereign yet again."

It is remarkable, however, that in politics Blok and Gumilyov
were gradually moving closer to the same position. The latter apparently had come to the conclusion that the Bolsheviks had a fairly tight
grip on power. And even though Gumilyov did not accept the Communist platform, he started to be impressed by some aspects of their
policies. For instance, he announced that if the Bolsheviks moved to
conquer India, his sword would be with them. He also maintained

that "the Bolsheviks respect the bold, even as they execute them."[157] Romanticizing the Communists, Gumilyov elevated them to the rank of worthy opponents, or even potential allies.

Blok, on the contrary, was gradually becoming disillusioned by the romantic image he had created for the revolution. In an appearance before Petrograd actors, he complained, "The destruction has not ended, but it's on the wane. Construction has not yet begun. The old music is gone but the new music has not yet come. It's boring." Blok's diary is filled with grim notes such as "I'm so tired," "I feel I'm in a heavy sleep."

In February 1919, Blok was arrested by the Petrograd Extraordinary Commission (Cheka), the Bolshevik secret police. He was suspected of participation in an anti-Soviet conspiracy from the left. The next day, after two interrogations, he was released, with Lunacharsky's intercession. In 1920 Blok wrote in his diary, "under the yoke of violence human conscience grows silent; then man shuts himself up in the old; the more brazen the violence, the more firmly man shrinks into himself. That happened in Europe under the yoke of war and in Russia now."[158]

Blok had stopped writing poetry completely and answered questions about his silence this way: "All sounds have disappeared. Can't you hear that there are no sounds?" He complained to the artist Annenkov, "I'm suffocating, suffocating, suffocating! We're suffocating, we will all suffocate. The world revolution is turning into world angina pectoris!"[159]

Tellingly, the bass singer Fyodor Chaliapin, who lived in Petrograd in those years, would later describe that era in almost the same terms. Chaliapin acknowledged "that at the very basis of the Bolshevik movement there was a striving for a real restructuring of life on a more just footing, as it was perceived by Lenin and some of his comrades."[160] But Chaliapin, like Blok, was feeling oppressed by the growing bureaucratization of daily and artistic life, until the great singer felt that the "robot would choke me if I didn't get out of its inanimate embrace." Soon thereafter Chaliapin left Petrograd for the West.

Blok's eagerly awaited speech in February 1921 at an evening dedicated to Pushkin turned into a cry for help. Akhmatova was there and so was Gumilyov, who arrived in tails, a lady on his arm shivering from the cold in her deep-cut black dress. Blok stood on the stage in a black jacket over a white high-necked sweater, hands in his pockets. Quoting Pushkin's famous line, "There is no happiness in the world, but there is peace and freedom," Blok turned to a nervous Soviet bureaucrat sitting on the stage (one of those "who write nothing, but only sign," in Andrei Bely's sarcastic definition) and said, "They're taking away our peace and freedom, too. Not external peace, but creative peace. Not childish freedom, not the freedom to be a false liberal, but our creative freedom, our secret freedom. And the poet is dying because there is nothing for him to breathe; life has lost its meaning."[162]

After such a declaration, imbued with pathos and tragedy, made from a stage, the poet-prophet, as Blok was perceived (and perceived himself to be) could only die. And by the summer of 1921 Blok's health had deteriorated so much that Lunacharsky and Gorky asked Lenin to allow the poet to go for treatment in neighboring Finland. Four months earlier in response to a secret inquiry from Lenin, Lunacharsky had characterized Blok and his works this way: "In everything that he writes there is a unique approach to the revolution: a mixture of sympathy and horror of the typical intellectual. Anyway, he is much more talented than smart."[163]

Apparently, Lenin was intrigued by Blok. In the inventory of the Bolshevik leader's personal library at the Kremlin are at least a dozen books by or about Blok. Nevertheless, the Politburo of the Communist Party, in a meeting chaired by Lenin, refused permission for Blok to go abroad, fearing he would openly speak out in the West against the Soviet regime. That was also the opinion of the Cheka representative, which was often the deciding one in such questions. This circumstance irritated Lunacharsky, and he referred to the Cheka in a letter to Lenin as the "final court."

It was clear now that Blok was dying, and Lunacharsky and Gorky bombarded Lenin with appeals for immediate help. Lenin gave in, but it was too late. In an earlier conversation with Annenkov, Blok called death "abroad, where everyone goes without preliminary permission from the authorities." He went to that abroad on August 7, 1921. A brief notice ran on the front page of the Communist newspaper *Pravda*: "Last night the poet Alexander Blok passed away." That was all, without a word of commentary.

Blok died of endocarditis complicated by nervous exhaustion and severe malnutrition. But his contemporaries saw his death symbolically, as the poet had wanted; it was clear to them that Blok had suffocated from a lack of personal and creative freedom, from "spiritual asthma," as Bely called it.

In that sense Blok's death summed up an entire era. Akhmatova had predicted in the spring of 1917, "The same thing will happen that had happened in France during the Great Revolution, it might even be worse." But Blok had the most radiant hopes for the revolution, which were shared by some highly talented people.

Arthur Lourié, the composer of a modernist cantata set to Blok's poetry that was performed while the poet was still alive, recalled,

> Blok had an enormous influence on me; with him, and taught by him, I listened to the music of the revolution. Like my friends, the young avant-garde—artists and poets—I believed in the revolution and joined it immediately. Thanks to the support we got from the revolution, all of us, young innovative artists and eccentrics, were taken seriously. For the first time fantasy-spinning youngsters were told they could realize their dreams and that neither politics nor any other power would interfere with pure art. We were given complete freedom to do whatever we wanted in our realm; this was a first in history. Nowhere in the world had anything similar ever taken place.

Blok's death destroyed this faith in the "idealism" of the Soviet authorities and in the possibility of uncompromised coexistence with the Bolsheviks. Blok and his allies were not too troubled by the loss of material wealth that the revolution caused; the real tragedy for them was the loss of spiritual independence, the ability to express themselves freely. That is why, when Arthur Lourié wrote in an article dedicated to the poet's memory, "The Russian Revolution ended with the death of Alexander Blok," he expressed the general feeling of Petrograd's leftist intelligentsia.

Blok, in one of his last letters, found terrible, very Russian words for his self-predicted and anticipated death: "She did devour me, lousy, snuffling dear Mother Russia, like a sow devouring her piglet."[164] The last lines of his farewell letter to his mother were, "Thank you for the bread and eggs. The bread is real, Russian, almost without additives, I haven't eaten any like that in a long time."[165] Blok had not reached his forty-first birthday. . . .

The poet was buried on August 10; Kuzmin wrote in his diary, "Priests, wreaths, people. Everyone was there. It would be easier to list who wasn't."[166] Someone said that if a bomb had gone off then, not a single important member of the literary and artistic community would be left in Petrograd. They sang music by Tchaikovsky, that quintessential Petersburg composer. Annenkov, helping to lower the coffin into the grave, remembered Akhmatova weeping nearby. He did not know that on that day Akhmatova had learned about the arrest of her ex-husband, Gumilyov.

The circumstances of Gumilyov's arrest were wrapped in legend for almost seventy years. At the time, the Bolsheviks announced that Gumilyov had been part of the Petrograd Military Organization (PBO), a large underground association preparing an armed uprising against the Soviet regime. Akhmatova always insisted that there had been no such conspiracy and that Gumilyov did not take part in the anti-Soviet struggle. Once the materials of the "Gumilyov case" began to be published in the Russian press in the 1990s, the matter could be judged more objectively.

In the summer of 1921 the Petrograd Cheka made mass arrests, and only in the PBO case, according to Soviet sources, over two hundred people were detained. Grigory Zinoviev, Petrograd's party boss, thought it was time to put some fear into the intelligentsia. They did not like Zinoviev, who had introduced a dictatorial rule that was harsh even by Bolshevik standards. They called Zinoviev "baba au rhum," because he had taken the reins of power in Petrograd as skinny as a rail and had grown very fat over the lean revolutionary years. Also head of the Comintern, Zinoviev operated rather independent of Moscow.

It is clear now that there was no large anti-Soviet Petrograd Military Organization. That preposterous idea was fabricated by Yakov Agranov, a young Chekist and lover of belles lettres who later reminisced, "In 1921 seventy percent of the Petrograd intelligentsia had one foot in the enemy camp. We had to burn that foot!"[167]

Thus, the goal of the Zinoviev-Agranov campaign was preventive. The people arrested in the PBO case, including many leading representatives of Petrograd's scientific and artistic communities, had been scared and confused during the interrogations and were forced to denounce themselves and others.

Judging by the transcripts of the interrogations, Gumilyov was an easy mark for the Cheka investigator. He naively believed that first of all, there was a "gentleman's agreement" of sorts between him and the Soviet authorities, according to which he honestly cooperated with the Bolsheviks in the area of culture and they gave him the right to a certain freedom of thought and conscience.

Second, Gumilyov was sure that his enormous popularity in Petrograd would be a reliable shield against any provocations from the secret police. "They won't dare touch me," he often said. As the much more sober Vladislav Khodasevich observed, "He was extremely young at heart and maybe in mind. He always seemed a child to me." [168]

In the published records of the interrogation, Gumilyov seems to admit that he had talked with friends "on political topics, bitterly condemning the suppression of personal initiative in Soviet Russia"[169] and also that if there were a hypothetical anti-Bolshevik uprising in Petrograd, he "in all probability" would be able "to gather and lead a band of passers-by, using the general mood of opposition."[170] All that, even for those harsh times, was very minor stuff.

Gorky rushed to Moscow to ask Lenin for a pardon for Gumilyov. According to some very similar and probably reliable versions of the course of events, Lenin promised to talk with Felix Dzerzhinsky, the head of the All-Russian Cheka about releasing Gumilyov. If Gorky is to be believed, Lenin guaranteed that none of those arrested in the PBO case would be executed.

Gorky returned to Petrograd to learn that sixty of the prisoners, including Gumilyov, had already been shot, on the recommendation of the investigator, without any trial, even a Bolshevik one. With tears in his eyes, Gorky kept saying, "That Zinoviev held up Lenin's orders."[171]

An authoritative eyewitness account by the Russo-French revolutionary Victor Serge (Kibalchich), who was living in Petrograd then, says that the so-called independent decision of the Petrograd Cheka to shoot Gumilyov was actually approved in Moscow. "One comrade traveled to Moscow to ask Dzerzhinsky a question: 'Were we entitled to shoot one of Russia's two or three poets of the first order?' Dzerzhinsky answered, 'Are we entitled to make an exception of a poet and still shoot the others?' "[172]

There is reason to believe that Lenin's order of pardoning Gumilyov was part of a charade designed to keep Gorky at bay and that Zinoviev's holdup of the order had been agreed upon beforehand by Lenin.

The Bolsheviks achieved their goal. When news of the executions in the PBO case came, not only Petrograd but all of Russia shuddered in horror. Zinoviev strengthened his reputation for ruthlessness. The career of Yakov Agranov, the mastermind of the case, took off. After moving to Moscow, he became the director of the "literary subdepartment" of the secret police, a personal friend of Stalin, and a member of his secretariat. Agranov returned to the city once more in December 1934 to "investigate" Kirov's murder—in the preparation of which he himself had probably taken an active part.

I later learned more about Agranov in the early 1970s from Lilya Brik, the mistress of the late Mayakovsky. Agranov was Mayakovsky's personal patron and political control. When Mayakovsky committed suicide in 1930, Agranov was the first to read the poet's suicide note. He wanted to make sure there were no anti-Soviet statements in it. But faithful service to Stalin did not save Agranov: in 1938 he and his wife were shot on his boss's orders. Zinoviev had been shot in 1936. One Soviet source maintains that when he was led from his cell to his place of execution, he laughed hysterically.[173]

Gumilyov, according to the stories circulating in Petrograd in those days, died in the manner appropriate to his image of the fearless Russian officer: smiling, with a cigarette held in his lips. His death, at the age of thirty-five, became legendary instantly. It was because of Gumilyov that the PBO case was not forgotten in the long chain of mass executions by the Bolsheviks. Along with Blok's untimely demise, Gumilyov's execution marked a sharp break in the relations of the intellectuals with the Soviet regime. In Russia the poet had always been a symbolic figure. The attitude of the authorities toward poets signaled the regime's position on issues of culture, tradition, and human rights.

The policy of Lenin's government toward Blok and Gumilyov, for all the extraordinariness of the situation, was nevertheless characteristic. All the methods for dealing with the cultural elite later to be witnessed in the Soviet Union were already in place. The intellectuals were pushed firmly onto the path of serving the regime. They were given opportunities to educate the masses, but under the strict control of the Communist Party. Loyalty was generously rewarded, while deviation from the "correct" line was punished with greater and greater ruthlessness.

As long as the Bolsheviks did not feel totally in control, they pretended to acknowledge the cultural elite's right to ideological neutrality. But that relative tolerance quickly vanished, and then they demanded absolute fidelity from the intellectuals.

Gumilyov, by honestly responding to the Cheka investigator's questions, was re-creating—probably consciously although perhaps not—a famous moment of Russian cultural history. Pushkin, recalled from exile by Nicholas I in 1826 after the rebellion of the Decembrists had been quashed, told the emperor frankly that he would have joined the revolutionaries had he been in Petersburg on the day of the uprising.

As we know, Nicholas I pardoned Pushkin and favored him. The emperor appreciated the poet's honesty because he was comfortably certain of his own authority. A charitable gesture toward the famous poet would simply underscore the fact.

Gumilyov's mistake, which cost him his life, was in thinking the Bolsheviks were somehow descendants of the imperial Russian government, even though he himself was a monarchist and anti-Communist. The Bolsheviks, on the other hand, believed their rule to be scarcely legitimate; thus a show of charity would be taken for weakness. They could play cat and mouse with the poet, but any overt disobedience on his part had to be punished. Using Blok and Gumilyov as examples, the Bolsheviks showed that they regarded artists as their serfs.

It is telling that this first archetypal scenario of the relationship between the Soviet regime and intellectuals was played out in Petrograd. The city had been the stage of confrontation and cooperation between the authorities and the cultural elite for over two hundred years. In that time the autocracy weakened gradually and the intellectuals had grown in power and independence. The Bolsheviks set the destruction of that independence as their goal.

By punishing Gumilyov and Blok, the quintessential Petersburg poets, the Bolsheviks were consciously destroying the equilibrium in the capital between the state authority and the cultural elite that had been created during prerevolutionary times. In effect, they abrogated the old rules and replaced them with new ones. At the same time the city's reputation as the cultural capital of Russia was also under attack.

Petrograd was dealt an irreparable blow politically and economically when Lenin moved the government to Moscow. Now the Petrograd culture had to be cut down a peg. In that sense Moscow's wishes coincided with Zinoviev's desire to teach the disloyal Petrograd intelligentsia a lesson.

All this had a profound effect on the Petersburg mythos but in direct contradiction to the Bolsheviks' intent. Petrograd parted rather easily with political hegemony, but it refused to relinquish its cultural preeminence. Sprinkled with fresh blood, the Petersburg mythos took on a new life. From the very start, Akhmatova played an exceptional role in that complex and painful process.

In the eyes of the reading public, Akhmatova was inextricably tied to Blok and Gumilyov. And even though both were married and had left "legal" widows, so to speak (and Akhmatova herself was married to Shileiko), the public considered Akhmatova the "real" widow of both poets. Almost every account of the memorial services and interment for Blok mention Akhmatova's presence, her tragic figure in black mourning and heavy crepe veil.

In 1974 Balmont's daughter, Nini Bruni, told me with great feeling how Akhmatova grew faint at one of the many services for Blok.[174] Another witness recalled the service for Blok in the small cemetery chapel. "The choir sang. But everyone's eyes were directed not at the altar, or the coffin, but at where I was standing. I began looking around, to see why, and I saw right behind me, the tall, slender figure of Anna Akhmatova. Tears were streaming down her pale cheeks. She wasn't hiding them. Everyone wept and the choir sang."[175]

Akhmatova's "affair" with Blok, brought into the readers' consciousness by her poems beginning in 1911, had turned into a popular legend by 1914, one that Blok himself did not dispute. In 1916 one of Blok's correspondents wrote to him, "blessing" the union of the two poets: "I think Anna Akhmatova is the most marvelous and refined creature. Let her be happy. And you will be happy, too."[176]

One entry made in Chukovsky's diary in 1920 is very interesting; he was walking with Blok and they met Akhmatova. "It was the first time I saw both of them together. Amazing—Blok's face is inscrutable, but there was constant movement, trembling reactions, very subtle, around his mouth. And it was the same with Akhmatova. They met and they expressed nothing with their eyes or smiles, but *there* much was said."[177] Even the perceptive cynic and skeptic Chukovsky tended to read something romantic, almost fateful, into a casual meeting of Akhmatova and Blok.

Later, observing that permanent tie between Blok and Akhmatova in the readers' subconscious, Chukovsky wrote in his diary in 1922, "If you spend an hour in a bookstore, you will see two or three buyers who come in and ask, 'Do you have Blok?'

'No.'

'How about *The Twelve?*'

'Don't have *The Twelve.*'

A pause.

'Then give me Anna Akhmatova.' "[178]

One would think that the legend of the affair between Akhmatova and Blok would not have survived the publication in 1928 and 1930 of Blok's diaries and notebooks, which made it abundantly clear that there had been no affair at all. But Akhmatova's poetry once more proved to be stronger than the "scorned prose" of reality. And even in the 1960s one could hear an exultant but not very well-informed student exclaim, "Ah, you mean the Akhmatova that Blok shot himself over?"

Blok wrote an article months before his death that, harshly and in many ways unjustly, criticized the acmeists, especially Gumilyov; the only kind words he found were for Akhmatova, with "her weary, sickly, female, and self-absorbed" poetry manner. The political differences between them were greatly narrowed after Blok's anti-Bolshevik speech on Pushkin and were completely erased by his death. Akhmatova later claimed that Blok recalled her on his deathbed and muttered in his delirium, "It's good that she didn't leave" (emigrate, that is).

In the first days after Blok's funeral, Akhmatova's specially written memorial poem received the widest distribution, unofficial of course, throughout Petrograd. It started with the line "Today is the Smolensk Lady's birthday . . . ," an allusion to the fact that the poet had been buried at Smolensk cemetery on the feast day of the icon of Our Lady of Smolensk. The poem ended:

> *We brought to the Smolensk interceder*
> *We brought to the Holy Mother of God*
> *In our hands in a silver coffin*
> *Our sun, extinguished in suffering—*
> *Alexander, the pure swan.*

"To this day the best that has been said about my son was said by Anna Akhmatova in those five lines," wrote Blok's mother to a friend in September 1921.[179] In Moscow, Marina Tsvetayeva, believing as did everyone else that there was an Akhmatova-Gumilyov-Blok triangle, wrote a poem addressed to her in 1921 that referred to the two dead poets as Akhmatova's brothers:

> *Your brothers are high up!*
> *You can't call loud enough!*

The rumor that the deaths of Blok and Gumilyov had left the thirty-two-year-old Akhmatova inconsolable and bereft was so widespread that rumors about her actual suicide began in Petrograd, then in Moscow. Another version also made the rounds—that Akhmatova had literally caught her death of cold at Blok's funeral. Mayakovsky believed the false story and wandered around, in Tsvetayeva's words, "Like a gored bull." Tsvetayeva wrote to Akhmatova from Moscow, "All these days there have been grim rumors about you, growing more persistent and irrefutable with every hour. . . . In the last three days (*without you*) Petersburg no longer existed for me."[180]

It is very telling that for Tsvetayeva the image of Akhmatova is so tied to Petersburg that without Akhmatova the city disintegrates for her. This close identification of Akhmatova with the city was no doubt strengthened in the public imagination because the Akhmatova-Gumilyov-Blok triangle had become part of the Petersburg background. The trinity of poets glorified the Petersburg mythos, and the mythos, in turn, united the members of the trinity.

It was not important that Blok and Akhmatova were not tied by tragic love. It was not important either that Akhmatova and Gumilyov had actually parted several years before his death. The new Petrograd demanded new martyrs. Blok and Gumilyov became those martyrs. Although hardly saints in life, their death brought them canonization in the eyes of the Russian intelligentsia and contributed to the atonement for the sins of St. Petersburg. And even though Akhmatova did not die, this atonement was now personified by her tragic figure—both as poet and as woman.

The unity of those two aspects of Akhmatova's public image must be emphasized. In Russia the old romantic idea of the identification of the poet's life and work was traditionally realized to extreme limits. Petrograd's embattled cultural elite badly needed a symbolic figure serving as the "keeper of the sacred flame," and the role suited Akhmatova ideally.

At Blok's funeral, as became clear from memoirs, Akhmatova was perceived as his widow. And here is a description of the memorial service at the Kazan Cathedral for Gumilyov, held two weeks after Blok's funeral. Gumilyov's young widow is weeping, and, the eyewitness continues, "Akhmatova is standing by the wall. Alone. But it seems to me that the widow of Gumilyov is not that pretty, sobbing girl wrapped in widow's weeds, but she—Akhmatova."[181]

Akhmatova's relations with Gumilyov were probably even more a matter of public record than her imaginary "affair" with Blok. After all, Gumilyov had indeed been her husband, which she did not delay announcing in her first book, *Evening,* describing him there in rather realistic detail:

> He liked three things in life:
> Evensong, white peacocks,
> And worn maps of America.
> He did not like crying children,

He did not like tea with jam
Or women's hysterics.
. . . And I was his wife.

And if readers believed this description, written in 1910, a half year after their marriage began, then how could they not believe another poem, written a year later and also included in *Evening,* which was much more emotional and therefore more convincing. It began,

My husband whipped me with a patterned
Strap, folded in half.

Later Gumilyov complained, "Just think about it, those lines made me a sadist. They spread a rumor about me that I would put on tails (which I didn't even own in those days) and a top hat (which I did) and, with a patterned strap folded in half, would whip not only my wife, Akhmatova, but my young female fans, first stripping them naked."[182]

Readers continued to form a picture of Akhmatova's volatile relationship with Gumilyov through the poems she published, even though some of them were actually addressed to other men in her life. Then the war, the revolution, and finally, Gumilyov's execution provided Akhmatova with a new, patriotic and civic theme and gave her a new voice. Mandelstam was the first to write about it, noting that Akhmatova's poetry "had undergone a break toward hieratic importance, religious simplicity and solemnity."

Akhmatova herself said that tragic events of the postrevolutionary years radically changed her attitude toward blood and death: the word "blood" now reminded her "of the brown seeping blotches of blood on the snow and on the stones and its disgusting odor. Blood is good only when it is alive, the blood coursing in veins, but it is horrible and disgusting in all other situations."

In Akhmatova's untitled poem written after Gumilyov's arrest, this sensation was expressed as follows:

Russian soil
Loves, loves blood.

Later Akhmatova was to recall how that poem "came" to her in a crowded suburban train traveling to Petrograd. She "felt the approach of some lines" and realized that if she didn't have a cigarette immediately, nothing would be written. But she had no matches. "I went out onto the buffer platform. Some boys in the Red Army were out there, cursing wildly. They didn't have any matches, either, but fat red sparks flew from the locomotive and settled on the platform railing. I pressed my cigarette against them. On the third (approximately) spark the cigarette lit. The guys, greedily watching my cleverness, were delighted. 'She'll always get by,' one of them said about me."

In another poem of that period, which also mentions "Hot, fresh blood," Akhmatova expressed repentance:

> I brought on death to my dear ones
> And they died one after another.
> Oh, my grief! Those graves
> Were foretold by my word.

Of course, those lines were also interpreted by contemporaries as referring to Blok and Gumilyov. The more erudite among them recalled Akhmatova's "Prayer" and how it was coming to pass and that Mandelstam in one of his poems called Akhmatova Cassandra, the prophetic daughter of the king of Troy. Thus in the popular imagination Akhmatova was turning from eyewitness of Petersburg's doom and destruction to prophet of its imminent rebirth, a figure of immense symbolic power. (Mandelstam was more perceptive than most here, too, pointing out the symbolic undercurrent in Akhmatova's poems as early as 1916.)

When Akhmatova recommenced reading her poetry before audiences after a long absence, she was met "with tense, electrified silence." The recollections of that event describe not a real person but a potent symbol of popular aspirations.

> She was very pale and even her lips seemed bloodless. She looked into the distance, beyond the audience . . . tall, fragilely thin . . . hopelessly and tragically beautiful. And how she read! It wasn't a reading, it was magic. . . . She finished. She stood in the same spot and still looked out into the distance, as if she had forgotten that she was on stage. No one applauded, no one dared even to breathe.[183]

The stage was set for a confrontation. On one side, the triumphant, omnipresent, cruel, and manipulative regime determined to destroy and subjugate not only the remains of Petersburg in Petrograd but to recast the new Petrograd "in its own image and likeness" at any cost.

On the side of the regime was the full power of the government, the secret police, and the cultural apparatus with its carrots and sticks.

On the other side was just a woman with a handful of confederates, poor, unarmed, and deprived. Her only strength lay in being a great poet in a country where poets traditionally wielded enormous influence and commanded great respect. Therefore she could count on the attention and sympathy of at least part of the audience—the part that was not brainwashed by the ruling ideology, tricked by its slogans, frightened, or destroyed.

The struggle was for the soul of a city—what it would live on, think about, weep over, and delight in, and what it would be called. And since the city also played a special, decisive role in the fate of Russian culture, the struggle would be for the future of Russian culture as well.

If one simply judged from the apparent strengths of the two sides, the battle looked hopeless. And with every year it would seem ever more hopeless. Never in the history of Russia had the poet been up against such a powerful, clever, cynical, and merciless enemy. But on the other hand, never had a poet who was also a woman entered into such a desperate and uncompromising battle with the regime.

Akhmatova was prepared for humiliation and even death, but not for defeat. She believed in the city, in its inhabitants, in herself and her mission, in the power of the Russian word, and in the moral strength of Russian culture. In 1923, a book of her poems published in Berlin, *Anno Domini MCMXXI*, appeared in Petrograd. When readers opened the book, they virtually froze: the very first poem spoke of the fate of the city, their fate, their future. It was Akhmatova's manifesto, her call to arms. The poem was called "To My Fellow Citizens." It did not promise a speedy victory. On the contrary, it spoke of life "in a bloody circle." But the poem ended as might have been expected, prophetically:

> *Another time is drawing near:*
> *The wind of death chills the heart,*
> *But the holy city of Peter*
> *Will be our unwilling monument.*

CHAPTER

4

in which a young hero—renamed, like the marvelous city in which he was born and grew up— undergoes quite a few exciting adventures and mind-boggling experiences in that amazing city, so that when he quits his native shores hastily, he becomes at long last a celebrated choreographer and, along with his fellow émigrés Stravinsky and Nabokov, carries the glory of his birthplace to distant America. This is the Petrograd of George Balanchine.

O n December 6, 1916, according to the custom, all the churches in the capital of the Russian empire held a special service in honor of Nicholas II's saint's day. This time the feast of St. Nicholas was not marked with as much pomp as usual, because the bloody war with Germany had reached its third year. But for Georgy Balanchivadze (nicknamed "Georges"), a twelve-year-old charge of the Imperial Petrograd Theater School, and for his classmates, the occasion became quite special; he remembered and recounted it all his life.

Georges was learning to be a ballet dancer; he had been on a full scholarship for several years, paid out of the tsar's treasury, in an enormous building that stretched the entire length of Teatralnaya (Theater) Street. On the morning of December 6, Georges and the other pupils were led to a service at the school chapel and in the evening were taken in a six-seater coach to a performance at the Imperial Maryinsky Theater. They were there not as spectators but as proud participants. The ballet was Nicholas's beloved *Humpbacked Horse,* and Georges and his comrades were in the emperor's favorite number, the final march.

When the performance was over, the little dancers changed into their parade uniforms from the ballet school. Georges liked his uniform—a handsome, light blue military-looking suit with silver lyres on the collar and cap. After lining up the children in pairs, their supervisors led them to be presented to the emperor. It was a solemn moment and the children caught their breath with excitement, but they stayed in line with their habitual professionalism. Georges Balanchivadze marched along diligently, too.

> Everyone thinks that the royal box at the Maryinsky is the one in the middle. Actually, the tsar's box was on the side, on the right. It had a separate entrance, a special, large stairway, and a separate foyer. When you came in, it was like entering a colossal apartment: marvelous chandeliers and the walls covered with light blue cloth. The emperor was there with his entire family—the Empress Alexandra Fyodorovna, the heir, his daughters; we were lined up by size and presented—here they are, Efimov, Balanchivadze, Mikhailov. We stood at attention.
>
> The tsar wasn't tall. The tsarina was very tall, a beautiful woman. She was dressed luxuriously. The grand duchesses, Nicholas's daughters, were also beauties. The tsar had bulging light eyes and he rolled his Rs. He asks, "Well, how are you?" We had to click our heels and reply, "Extremely pleased, Your Imperial Majesty!"
>
> Then we received a royal gift: chocolate in silver boxes, marvelous ones! And mugs of exquisite beauty, porcelain, with light blue lyres and the imperial monogram.[1]

In 1981, in New York City, this is how the émigré George Balanchine, a celebrated seventy-seven-year-old choreographer, recounted this touching story to me, another Russian émigré who had come to America comparatively recently. It was one of many little legends that composed Balanchine's reminiscences of the city that he stubbornly continued to call Petersburg, despite official and widely accepted name changes.

Balanchine must have sensed the almost saccharine quality of the picture he was presenting. That may be why he invariably added an ironic touch: the other youngsters reverently preserved the chocolate from the tsar as relics until the candy grew moldy. But Georges ate his immediately. "At that time it wasn't in the least bit important to me."[2]

In Petrograd in 1916 perhaps it wasn't. But in New York in the second half of the century, it became very important indeed—to remember and tell others, with delight and nostalgia. Balanchine in America, along with the Russian émigrés Igor Stravinsky and Vladimir Nabokov, created a powerful mythos of Petersburg: the New Atlantis that sank beneath the sea in the stormy twentieth century. The mythos, which eventually flourished in the West, was basically musical and balletic at its roots. In Europe it was initially planted right after the Bolshevik revolution by Diaghilev and his colleagues, of the formerly influential art group *Mir iskusstva*.

The intertwining of the Petersburg mythos with music and ballet was, of course, no accident. Alexander Benois of *Mir iskusstva* had maintained that Petersburg's soul could be made manifest only through music. He added that the musicality of the Russian capital "seems to be encapsulated in the very humidity of the atmosphere." Petersburg's "theatricality" was considered just as organic. It could be seen as a magical consequence of the city's architecture.

It was noted long ago that the architectural ensembles of Petersburg resemble stage scenery in their majesty. In 1843 the splenetic Marquis de Custine informed the civilized world, "At each step I take I am amazed to observe the confusion that has been everywhere wrought in this city between two arts so very different as those of architecture and decoration. Peter the Great and his successors seem to have taken their capital for a theatre."[3]

The sharp-tongued marquis cut to the essence of the problem. Peter the Great had founded Petersburg with a dramatic gesture, and it is not surprising that his theatricality remained with the city forever.

From an architectural standpoint, one of the main reasons for Petersburg's beauty is that its buildings are stylistically unified throughout many parts of the city. In that respect the Russian capital differed radically from other great cities, which developed gradually over centuries. The comparative suddenness of the Russian imperial capital's appearance also added to the dramatic sensation.

The city's inhabitants were aware of that effect. In one of the first Russian historical novels, *Roslavlev, or the Russians in 1812*, written by Mikhail Zagoskin in 1831, the hero, arguing with a French diplomat in Petersburg, exclaims proudly, "Look around you! Tell me, did your ancestors build over the many centuries what we have erected in the course of one? Doesn't it remind you of a quick change of scenery in your Paris opera, this appearance of magnificent Petersburg among impassable swamps and deserted northern expanses?"[4]

At the start of the twentieth century, the theater metaphor was taken to an extreme by the members of *Mir iskusstva*. For Benois, the resemblance of Petersburg's architecture to scenery was so incontrovertible that he traced its existence to the effects of theater performances: "After the Russian people received such pleasure for the brief span of an evening theater spectacle, they felt it necessary to immortalize it in constructions of stone and bronze."[5]

Petersburg for the *Mir iskusstva* crowd, who in a typically Petersburgian mix were imperially oriented though politically liberal, was a gigantic stage, "the arena of mass, state, and communal movements."[6] "Street theater" (in the words of Benois) was constantly taking place there: stunning parades, solemn, pompous funeral processions, ritualistic public dishonoring of criminals. Even the changing seasons for Benois and company were "theatrically effective"; after the sudden, "violent" spring, which Stravinsky recalled at the end of his life as "the most wonderful event of every year of my childhood,"[7] came resplendent summer, then dramatic autumn led in terrifying winter.

Benois stressed yet another Petersburg tradition that had a theatrical aspect: "In the winter months, the Petersburg 'season' flourished—theaters played, balls were given, the main holidays were celebrated—Christmas, Epiphany, Mardi Gras. The winter in Petersburg was always harsh and severe, but in Petersburg people learned as nowhere else to turn it into something pleasant and splendid."[8]

The opera and ballet, both foreign flowers that had been transplanted in Russian soil in the first half of the eighteenth century and then quickly flourished, were the high points of the Petersburg season. In 1791 a Russian critic still had to justify ballet: "This art is not as vain as many imagine,"[9] but fewer than fifty years later Gogol in his article "The Petersburg Stage in 1835–36" was proclaiming, "The ballet and opera have completely conquered our stage. The public listens only to opera and watches only the ballet; the public talks only about opera and ballet. Thus it is extremely difficult to obtain tickets for the opera and ballet."

The soil for this flowering of opera and ballet was fertile because both theatrical institutions belonged to the emperor and were completely subsidized by the royal treasury. In Russia, the rulers traditionally did not skimp on support for the theater. When a reporter for the popular *Severnaya pchela* visited London in 1837, he had the opportunity to compare the staging of Rossini's opera *Semiramide* in the capitals of Britain and Russia. Here is what he reported: "In London the staging of operas is miserly. The scenery is average, the choruses are thin. How can one compare *Semiramide* in Petersburg with the London production? Ours is lush, full, animated; here [in London] it is poor, thin, weak. We do everything that is possible; here they do not even do half of what is necessary."[10] Another author observed, "Our productions surpass those of the Parisians in magnificence and luxury."[11]

In a typical Petersburg ballet of the period, the sets were changed half a dozen times, and during the same performance the audience might also see "various dances, games, marches, and battles," plus such effects as "mechanical rising and eclipse of the sun, earthquakes, mountains spewing flames, and the destruction of the Temple of the Sun."

Nicholas I enjoyed a laugh or two at a fashionable French vaudeville and could be deeply touched by stolid Russian patriotic dramas, but he truly relaxed only when watching the ballet. The emperor was not an ordinary balletomane but an ideological one. In the words of the poet Afanasy Fet, "Emperor Nicholas, convinced that beauty is a sign of strength, demanded and got from his astonishingly disciplined and trained troops total subordination and uniformity." These same qualities impressed the emperor in ballet, and it was no accident that the Russian corps de ballet became a model of discipline and training.

A witness of the Petersburg production of the ballet *La Révolte au serail* in 1836 gives a glowing account of how the corps was trained. The legendary romantic ballerina Marie Taglioni danced the part of a strong-headed beauty who led the army of concubines to rise against the sultan. Nicholas I sent his guard officers to train the "army" of dancers in military techniques.

At first this amused the girls, but then they got bored and grew lazy. Hearing of that, the tsar came to a rehearsal and sternly admonished the theater's amazons: "If they did not practice seriously, he would have them stand outside in the freezing cold for two hours with rifles, wearing their dancing shoes." You should have seen the zeal with which the frightened recruits in skirts went about their work.[12]

After the triumphant premiere of *La Révolte au serail*, Nicholas never missed a single performance, enjoying the sight of the ballet regiment, armed, in the words of a playful Petersburg reviewer, "with the white weapons of full shoulders and rounded little arms."[13]

The unprecedented uniformity and precision of movement made the performances of the Russian corps de ballet the artistic equivalent of the military parades and maneuvers so typical of Petersburg. Classical ballet and imperial army discipline found a common aesthetic ground. As Yuri Lotman put it, "The question: how will this end? becomes secondary in both ballet and parades" because "precision and beauty of movement are of more interest to the connoisseur than the plot."[14] It is tempting to speculate that this imperial-militaristic inattention to plot in dance was one of the many impulses for the subsequent development of Russian plotless ballet, with Marius Petipa as its founder, Michel Fokine's *Chopiniana* its first masterpiece, and George Balanchine its acknowledged master.

George Balanchine was born on January 9, 1904, the son of the Georgian composer Meliton Balanchivadze, who is still sometimes called "the Georgian Glinka." His Russian mother, Maria, was the daughter of a German, and thus, Balanchine had Georgian, Russian, and German blood. Born in Petersburg, he visited Georgia for the first time when he was fifty-eight.

The first Georgians appeared in Petersburg soon after the city was founded. Their number grew rapidly after 1801, when Alexander I annexed independent Georgia, a flourishing state in the Caucasus with an ancient Christian culture; this was done, as the imperial manifesto put it, "Not in order to add to our powers and expand our borders, but to end the sorrows of the Georgian people."[15]

At first the Georgian nobility lived in Petersburg, most of them forcibly moved there so they would not interfere with their country's absorption into the Russian empire. But when Georgia's loss of independence became a certainty, many young Georgians—like the youth of other nations that made up the Russian empire—started migrating to Petersburg by choice to obtain a European education.

The Georgians are a warrior people, so in Petersburg many of them entered the military academy. Another characteristic trait of Georgians is their love of music and dance. Therefore it is not sur-

ITEM CHARGED
Due Date: 09/03/2007 06:00 PM
Title: Soviet economic
             development from Lenin to
             Khrushchev / prepared for
             the Economic History
             Society by R.W. Davies.
Author: Davies, R. W. (Robert
             William), 1925-
Call Number: HC335 .D26 1998
Enumeration:
Chronology:
Copy: 1
Item Barcode:02558930

ITEM CHARGED
Due Date: 16/02/2007 06:00 PM
Title: Red empire
             [videorecording].
             Survivors / a Granite
             production for Yorkshire
             Television.
Author:
Call Number: DK246 .R43 1992 v.6
Enumeration:
Chronology:
Copy: 1
Item Barcode:02712271

ITEM CHARGED
Due Date: 09/03/2007 06:00 PM
Title: St. Petersburg : a
             cultural history / Solomon
             Volkov ; translated by
             Antonina W. Bouis.
Author: Volkov, Solomon.
Call Number: DK557 .V65 1995
Enumeration:
Chronology:
Copy: 1
Item Barcode:02343507

prising that among the first students of the Petersburg Conservatory, which opened in 1862, was the Georgian Kharlampy Savaneli, who became a friend of Tchaikovsky. Thirty-seven years later, the ambitious thirty-seven-year-old Meliton Balanchivadze left Georgia to enter the same conservatory.

By that time the elder Balanchivadze had already lived a stormy artistic life. The son of an archbishop, Meliton had studied at the seminary and at age seventeen became a singer with the opera theater in the Georgian capital, Tiflis—first in the chorus, then as a soloist in *Eugene Onegin* and *Faust*. His exuberance led him in various directions. While still in Georgia, Meliton composed the first native European-style art songs, which became quite popular, and established an ethnic choir. In Petersburg he first set about continuing his singing studies, but then, on the advice of the conservatory's director, Anton Rubinstein, he took lessons in composition with Nikolai Rimsky-Korsakov. In the Russian capital Meliton Balanchivadze started to write the first Georgian opera, *Tamar Tsbieri* (*Perfidious Tamara*), based on the epic poem of the national poet, Prince Akaky Tsereteli. According to the proud recollections of his son in New York City, he also "wrote choral works for all the big cathedrals" in the capital.

In Petersburg, the overactive Meliton continued to advocate Georgian folk music, which was little known there. He organized choirs, performed in special Georgian concerts, and published articles about the national style of singing. But he expanded in every possible (and often impossible) direction after winning an enormous sum in the state lottery; Balanchine spoke to me of one hundred thousand rubles.

Meliton gave the respected Petersburg musicologist Nikolai Findeizen the idea of collecting the letters of Mikhail Glinka, and paid for their publication, the first of its kind. Meliton threw his money around, making unrepaid loans to his numerous Georgian friends and financing Georgian restaurants all over the city, which went broke one after the other. Then he made a fateful mistake. According to Balanchine, his father wanted to get involved in a major financial operation—a crucible factory, which required importing special machinery from the West. He went bankrupt.[16]

In 1917, Meliton Balanchivadze returned from Petrograd to his homeland, where an independent Georgian republic with the first democratically elected socialist government in the world had been proclaimed. The republic lasted only a few years, however, before it was swallowed up by Communist Russia. Balanchivadze became a leader of musical life there, chairing numerous societies, councils, and committees, and died in 1937, a highly respected and decorated People's Artist.

At the time of his father's departure George (named for the saint) was in his fifth year at the Petrograd ballet school. His friends still called him "Georges," in the French manner. When in 1924 Georges became a member of Diaghilev's Ballets Russes in France, the famous impresario shortened his Georgian surname to the still exotic-sounding but easier-to-pronounce "Balanchine"; with his arrival in the United States in 1933, "Georges" would change to "George," the final transformation of his name.

Young Georges was nicknamed "Rat" because he was secretive, taciturn, and always wary and because he habitually sniffled, revealing his front teeth. In the enormous school where Georges and his classmates spent their days, he felt abandoned by his parents, despite the impressive appearance of the school building, designed by Carlo Rossi and located on one of the most beautiful streets of the city.

That was a typical Petersburg conflict—the pompous facade concealing a multitude of minor tragedies. And yet at the same time, again typically for Petersburg, the facade imperceptibly influenced the lives behind it, decisively forming (and deforming) the personalities of the building's inhabitants.

This Petersburg facade certainly had a powerful influence on Georges, who learned to mask his emotions. Born in Petersburg, he became the quintessential Petersburger. Restraint became the determining trait of his character. He later admitted that this restraint had been inculculated in him in Petersburg, and he spoke reverently of Theater Street.

Coming from a ballet family, Carlo Rossi, the street's architect, seemed fated to build the house for what would become the most famous ballet school in the world. The building is part of the architectural ensemble of magical harmony and severity. The secret of that magic was explained to me by the choreographer Fyodor Lopukhov. I once met him on Nevsky Prospect in the early 1960s. Resembling Gogol—if the writer had lived to a ripe old age—Lopukhov was hurrying back to his small apartment in the ballet school building. Before that, we had met in the Leningrad Conservatory, where Lopukhov headed the choreography department.

What luck to have had Lopukhov as guide, even for just twenty minutes! I still remember his exaltation when proclaiming that Rossi's edifice had no equal.

> Behold the Alexandrinsky Theater—there is nothing comparable in Europe! The Grand Opera in Paris, Covent Garden—they pale before Rossi's creation. I assure you! They say that Russians don't know how to work. It's not true! The entire Teatralnaya [Theater] Street was built in three and a half months, eighteen million bricks laid by hand!

Lopukhov made me realize that the entire street is basically two huge buildings. One had housed the Ministries of Education and Internal Affairs since 1834; the one across the street had been the site of the administration of the imperial theaters and the ballet school since 1835. "Do you know, when you walk down this street to the theater, the columns of the buildings literally start to dance? Believe me! You'll see, I'm right! I sometimes wonder—did Rossi do it consciously?"

Of course, I knew that the harmony of the street was the result of architectural calculation. It had been beaten into our heads since childhood that Theater Street is 220 meters long and the height of the buildings equals the width of the street—22 meters. In my Leningrad days the conventional wisdom was that walks along Theater Street (renamed by then to Rossi Street) cultivated the feeling for refinement and spiritual harmony. But I suspect the young Balanchine did not think much about it. It is hard to believe now, but initially he felt almost revulsion for his future profession. He was attracted by music, which he felt came from within and touched him, while dancing seemed forced on him from without.

The unexpected change came during a performance of Tchaikovsky's *Sleeping Beauty,* when little Georges appeared as a tiny cupid on the stage of the Maryinsky Theater. The curtain rose and Georges observed the Maryinsky Theater from the stage, with its breathtaking light blue and gold and a stylishly dressed audience. Contemporaries recall that for special occasions the lights were merely dimmed at the Maryinsky, and the audience and stage magically blended into one.

The music started, and Georges suddenly understood that he passionately wanted to be on that stage, as often as possible—he was prepared to spend the rest of his life there.[17] He was carried away by the spectacle made up of music, movement, scenery, light, and the response of the audience. But music in that inseparable union always remained the first among equals for Balanchine. And that feeling was probably what propelled him to become the greatest choreographer of the twentieth century.

The author of the ballet masterpiece that had inflamed Georges's imagination and changed his life was Marius Petipa, the Frenchman who came by boat to Petersburg at the age of twenty-nine in 1847. Balanchine came to America at the age of twenty-nine, also by boat, a significant coincidence for the superstitious Georgian. Living a long life, Petipa, whom many consider the greatest creator of classical ballet, served four Russian emperors "with faith and truth"—Nicholas I, Alexander II, Alexander III, and Nicholas II. He choreographed dozens of ballets for the imperial theater, including such world-famous masterpieces as *Sleeping Beauty, Don Quixote, La Bayadère,* and *Raymonda.* Together with Lev Ivanov, Petipa staged *Swan Lake;* much of the most popular version of *Giselle* today is his; and he also authored the scenario of *The Nutcracker.*

Balanchine never met Petipa, who died in 1910. But the teachers at the ballet school recalled the elegant old man with the neatly trimmed beard and gold pince-nez. The old-timers liked to repeat his comical Russian expressions (after sixty plus years in Petersburg, Petipa hadn't learned to speak Russian properly), remembered with awe his temper and demanding nature, and delighted in the wealth of his choreographic imagination. Petipa created his finest works at the close of his life. Ill and weak, he continued to rehearse; work was for him, as it would be for Balanchine, the best medicine. But Petipa's final years were clouded by conflict with Telyakovsky, the director of the imperial theaters, who considered the choreographer "old hat" and an obstacle to the progress of the Petersburg ballet.

On January 19, 1903, ten days after the birth of Georgy Balanchivadze, Petipa wrote in his diary: "They are rehearsing *Sleeping Beauty* at the theater. I am not going to the rehearsal. They do not inform me. . . . My marvelous artistic career is over. Fifty-seven years of service. Yet I have enough strength to work more. Presently, on March 11 I will turn eighty-six."[18] A day later, with barely disguised glee: "This evening is the 101st performance of *Sleeping Beauty.* My daughter is dancing. The emperor and dowager empress are present. Box office 2,866 rubles and 07 kopeks."[19] Petipa, it seems, never failed to note the exact amount of the ticket sales.

Balanchine read Petipa's diaries and memoirs attentively, describing them to me with his sympathetic half-smile as "sad." He was struck that Petipa had died an "unneeded and embittered old man." The older Balanchine saw Petipa as the ideal choreographer. Petipa was not only enormously talented; for Balanchine, he was the right man at the right time in the right place. Balanchine saw him firmly established in the social landscape of his time, yet still free enough to compose dances not under the whip but out of an inner drive. Petipa felt proud to be "in his majesty's service." The Frenchman was lucky; Russia at that time, in Balanchine's opinion, had a much greater life force than Petipa's homeland. One of the main proofs of that for Balanchine was the well-known fact that the tsar's treasury was the most generous in all of Europe for ballet.

Once Balanchine recounted to me an episode, recorded in Petipa's memoirs, that apparently took on a special significance for the Georgian. Petipa was at the theater rehearsing the "grand pas with rifle" from Jules Perrot's ballet *Caterina, or La fille du bandit* with the great dancer Fanny Elssler. Unexpectedly, Nicholas I arrived at the rehearsal. Seeing that Elssler was not holding the gun right, the emperor interrupted the rehearsal and said to her, "Come closer to me and do everything that I do." The emperor then demonstrated how to use the rifle. Elssler copied his movements with agility. Pleased with her efforts, the emperor asked her the date of the premiere and then said, "I will come and applaud you." Smiling mischievously, Balanchine added that when the courtiers learned of the incident the tickets to the premiere sold out immediately.

The director of the imperial theaters, Ivan Vsevolozhsky, once declared, "We must first of all please the royal family, then the public taste, and only third must we satisfy the purely artistic demands." Balanchine, of course, was uncompromising on important artistic issues, but he also never forgot the choreographer's duty to the public. And I suspect that in his American period Balanchine sometimes regretted the lack of august patrons.

That was the reason for Balanchine's desire to establish contact with Jacqueline Kennedy when her husband was president. In modern America, the Kennedys were the closest approximation of a royal family. Mrs. Kennedy seemed to Balanchine to be a new empress who could become, in his words, the "spiritual salvation" of America. Characteristically, Balanchine remarked approvingly of one American who donated a substantial sum for the production of a ballet, "In Russia he would have been a prince."

Another gift from Russia to Petipa, as far as Balanchine was concerned, was the "human material." Choreographers express themselves through dancers, and much depends on the particular gifts of each dancer. Elizaveta Gerdt, a Petersburg ballerina Balanchine adored, liked to recall how Petipa invented variations for a dancer as Gerdt looked on. The dancer's face showed that she was not happy. Petipa said, "Don't like, I change it." Then he started showing her another combination. Balanchine agreed that the choreographer could not be dogmatic and had to orient himself to a certain extent according to the individuality of each dancer.

According to Balanchine, Petipa was blessed in that regard: he had worked with Mathilda Kchessinska, Anna Pavlova, Olga Preobrazhenskaya, Pavel Gerdt (Elizaveta's father). Pavel, the quintessential danseur noble of Russian ballet, was one of Balanchine's teachers. The young Georges was impressed to learn that he had created the leading parts in *Sleeping Beauty, Nutcracker,* and *Swan Lake* in Petersburg.

Balanchine always considered the French refinement and humor of Petipa's choreography, the brilliance and wit of its inventiveness, and, most of all, its inexhaustible variety as the highest examples of what could be achieved in the art of ballet. But all these "French" traits were significantly complemented by specifically Russian softness and fluidity, which Petipa acquired while working with Petersburg artists. The great city influenced Petipa, too—the poetry of its white nights, the ever-present threatening breath of the stormy Baltic Sea, the harmony and grandeur of the classicist architecture, and the cult of high craftsmanship.

Some ballet critics have found in the famous shadow scene of Petipa's *La Bayadère* the choreographer's impressions of Petersburg's constant floods and made a convincing parallel between the exquisite "white" (in white tunics) compositions of Petipa and the beautiful white nights of Petersburg. Vadim Gayevsky even saw the dream sequence from Petipa's *Don Quixote* as a veiled portrait of the Russian capital: "Here is embodied the theme of Petersburgian idealism, one of the main themes in Petipa. Here is outlined the scheme of 'Petersburg dreams.' "[20]

This somewhat unexpected linkage with Gogol and Dostoyevsky is fair in the sense that the theme of lost purity can be found both in their works and in Petipa's. In *Swan Lake* Petipa created the fatal image of Odile, the Black Swan, the moral opposite of the White Swan, Odette, transfiguring in that way the Petersburg graphic contrast of black and white into a battle between good and evil on the ballet stage.

Gayevsky maintained, "Petipa is the first true urbanist in the history of European ballet. The ensemble—the planning principle of the great city—is at the foundation of his choreographic plans."[21] From here comes the grandiosity of many of Petipa's choreographic solutions. In the first version of the shadows scene in *La Bayadère*, he used sixty-four dancers. The sensation created by that cascade of white tunics on the stage of the imperial theater was overwhelming.

But the embryo of catastrophe always lay dormant in Petipa's vision of Petersburg's grandness. At the end of his career he decided to stun the capital's audience with a particularly opulent production. He began work on *The Magic Mirror*, in which the main scenic effect would be a huge mirror on the stage reflecting both the stage and the hall. The mirror was filled with mercury and apparently exploded at one of the final rehearsals. Mercury poured out of the cracks in silver streams: a horrible sight and a bad omen. The superstitious Petipa was shocked.

Not long before the disaster with the mirror Petipa wrote in his diary:

> My last wishes in regard to my funeral. Everything must be very modest. Two horses for the hearse. No invitations to the funeral, just an announcement in the newspapers. In this year of 1903 I am finishing my long artistic career—sixty-six years of work and fifty-seven years of service in Russia. I receive 9,000 rubles in annual pension, and will be listed in service until my death. That is marvelous. But I fear that I will not be able to use that marvelous pension.[22]

The sense of change characteristic of fin-de-siècle Petersburg and the hovering expectation of doom did not leave Petipa. This was undoubtedly one of the reasons for his love for Tchaikovsky, who worked, we could say, on the same psychological wavelength. Petipa could easily have remained with the music of Cesare Pugni, Ludwig Minkus, or Riccardo Drigo—after all, some of his biggest successes were collaborations with those minor composers: *La Fille du Pharaoh* and *The Humpbacked Horse* (Pugni), *La Bayadère* (Minkus), and *Les Millions d'Arlequin* (Drigo).

These composers were masters of pleasant ballet music, but their works could not be compared with Tchaikovsky's. However, an understanding of Tchaikovsky's enormous contribution came surprisingly late. Even Minkus was considered "too serious" by Petersburg balletomanes. The reviewers of the premiere of Tchaikovsky's first ballet, *Swan Lake,* ruled almost unanimously that the music was dry and monotonous. As one ballet fan summarized it, "Tchaikovsky put the audience and the dancers to sleep."[23] So the seventy-year-old Petipa's decision to take on the choreography of Tchaikovsky's *Sleeping Beauty* should be considered a daring step. While the composer called Petipa a "sweet old man," Petipa fully recognized the genius of his collaborator.

Tchaikovsky, who valued Petipa's classicism, had flirted successfully with classicism in such scores as *Serenade* for string orchestra and the *Mozartiana* suite, which Balanchine used later for his choreographic masterpieces. And Petipa was drawn to Tchaikovsky's music by its nostalgic character. Against the background of Tchaikovsky's music, Petipa's grand ball scenes and lush, mysterious rituals and ceremonies took on a new meaning. Ballet action soared beyond its conventional character, beginning to express complex contemporary emotions and moods.

Not long before that, the satirist Mikhail Saltykov-Shchedrin could wrathfully attack Petipa's ballets: "Does *The Pharaoh's Daughter* deal with convictions, honesty, love of homeland? Never!"[24] But by 1890 the premiere of *Sleeping Beauty* by Tchaikovsky and Petipa on the stage of the Maryinsky Theater enticed and inspired an entire group of aesthetically advanced young idealists, including Alexander Benois, Leon Bakst, and Sergei Diaghilev, the future organizers of *Mir iskusstva.*

Petipa had created a world where on the surface merriment and order reigned but that still lived precariously, as if threatened by an inevitable flood. The culmination of *Sleeping Beauty,* Petipa's greatest work, is an unexpected catastrophe, and not one of individual lives but of an entire civilization. Based on the fairy tale by Charles Perrault, *La Belle au Bois Dormant,* from *Mother Goose,* the parable by Tchaikovsky and Petipa about a kingdom plunged into a hundred-year sleep on the whim of an evil witch seemed to foretell the fate of Petersburg. The evil magic that was to freeze the kingdom in an age-long sleep: it was a prophecy that came to pass in Russia in the twentieth century. A pall of foreboding hung over the era that united Tchaikovsky, Petipa, and the *Mir iskusstva* crowd.

For all that, Benois and his friends, while giving Petipa his due, did not perceive him as a kindred soul, as they did Tchaikovsky. Their choreographic comrade-in-arms was Michel Fokine, who was born in Petersburg in 1880 and died in New York City in 1942.

□   □   □

Mir iskusstva's aesthetic program was always rather vague, determined largely by individual preferences and temperaments. But it is hard to imagine a more eccentric amalgam than the artistic tastes and strivings of Fokine. His was a mix of yearning for realism, impressionistic sketches, symbolist ideas and decadent excesses, a love affair with pictorial concepts, and a serious interest in music as the basis for ballet movement.

In thirty-seven years Fokine, toward whom Balanchine always remained ambivalent, choreographed over eighty ballets, of which only a few were preserved intact, and only two—*Chopiniana* (called *Les Sylphides* in the West) and *Petrouchka*—became repertory standards. But even those two masterpieces give some idea of Fokine's creative range. *Chopiniana* is often called the first completely plotless, abstract ballet. But one forgets that it appeared almost accidentally. After all, Fokine was not planning to make *Chopiniana* a manifesto of plotlessness in ballet. On the contrary, in its first version, staged in 1907 in Petersburg, *Chopiniana* was a series of romantic sketches "from the life of the composer," accompanied by Chopin's music in Glazunov's orchestration. Only when it was ridiculed by Petersburg critics did Fokine turn his ballet into an abstract work.

Balanchine told me what he valued most in Fokine: "In Petipa everything was drafted along straight lines: the soloists in front, the corps in back. But Fokine invented crooked lines in ballet. And for me he really invented the ensemble in ballet. Fokine took a small ensemble and designed interesting, strange things for it."[25]

Balanchine loved *Chopiniana* in his youth, and in the early 1970s he asked the ballerina Alexandra Danilova—one of his greatest "muses"—to revive Fokine's work for the New York City Ballet. The dancers in that production appeared on stage in practice clothes instead of the traditional long tulle dresses, and they were accompanied by a piano instead of an orchestra. The critics saw this as a manifestation of Balanchine's desire to clarify and stress the purely dance aspects of Fokine's ballet, but Danilova gave me a much simpler explanation for this austerity: "We did it out of poverty."[26]

Petrouchka was choreographed by Fokine for Diaghilev's Ballets Russes. The sensational premiere of this most Petersburgian of all Fokine's works took place in 1911 at the Châtelet Theater in Paris. This was an extraordinarily important moment in the export of the Petersburg mythos to the West.

In the twentieth century the figure of the Russian artist seeking creative freedom in the West is well known. When people speak of such exiles, the first that come to mind are refugees from the Soviet regime. But the first cultural émigrés from twentieth-century Russia appeared in the West before the Communist revolution of 1917. Diaghilev's Ballets Russes was in fact an émigré organization which began its Russian seasons in Paris back in 1907.

Diaghilev became an émigré not of his own volition; the logic of events led him to it. In the beginning, his greatest ambition was to take over the position of director of the Russian imperial theaters. He had all the necessary qualifications: refined taste, impressive erudition, an acute feeling for the new, and effective organizational skills. But handicapped by his lack of bureaucratic tenacity and ties to the court and his too-bold aesthetics, as well as his own open homosexuality, he couldn't achieve his goal either through frontal attacks or complicated backstage maneuvering. As a result, in 1901 he was fired as director of special assignments for the imperial theaters and banned from any state jobs.

From that moment, Diaghilev concentrated on proselytizing Russian culture abroad, far away from court and bureaucracy. In 1906 Diaghilev organized L'Exposition de l'Art Russe at the Salon d'Automne in Paris, and in 1907, at the same place, the Historical Russian Concerts with the participation of Rimsky-Korsakov, Glazunov, Rachmaninoff, and Chaliapin. In 1908 the Grand Opera ran *Boris Godunov* with Chaliapin in the title role. Then in 1909 Diaghilev inaugurated his Paris opera and ballet season. It was then that Parisians first saw Fokine's *Chopiniana,* which Diaghilev had renamed *Les Sylphides.*

At first, through some clever maneuvering, Diaghilev managed to obtain the tsar's support for his enterprise. He had to beg, intrigue, and explain the "state importance" of the export of Russian culture to Europe. In 1907 Diaghilev complained in desperation to Rimsky-Korsakov, "I must convince Grand Duke Vladimir that our enterprise is beneficial from a national point of view; the minister of finances that it is beneficial economically, and even the director of theaters that it could be useful for the imperial stage! And so much more!!!"[27]

A typical reaction of the Russian bureaucracy to Diaghilev's cultural initiatives was the highly irritated note in the diary of the director of the imperial theaters, Telyakovsky: "Basically this infamous spreading of Russian culture has brought the imperial theaters quite a bit of harm, for I still see little benefit from it."[28] By 1910 the Rus-

CHAPTER 4 263

sian embassies in Europe were forbidden by a special circular from Petersburg to give any aid to Diaghilev's enterprise. This meant not only a break in the ties between the court and Diaghilev but an open declaration of war. From then on, the Russian ambassadors in Paris, London, and other European capitals sabotaged Diaghilev's work as much as they could.[29]

The confrontation between the tsarist bureaucracy and Diaghilev prefigured a much fiercer war against exiles waged by the Soviet government. A Russian tradition is, in fact, at work here. With the probable exception of Catherine the Great, Russian rulers were not terribly interested in exporting the country's culture. For them, army bayonets were much more effective implements of Russian influence and prestige. Cultural exchange was one-sided—from the West to Russia, and even that was limited and strictly controlled from above. In essence, entertainment from the West was always suspected of being too decadent. Italian singers or French actors were fine for the cultivated elite, but the masses were to have the simpler, healthier native fare.

Mir iskusstva became the first Russian art group to desire close contacts with the West. The influence of the growing Russian bourgeoisie, which thirsted for mutually beneficial exchange with western Europe, was an important factor. Therefore, the appearance of someone like Diaghilev was to be expected. That he turned out to be more than a traveling salesman of Russian culture, in fact a genius with a unique creative vision, can be considered an unexpected premium. But for the ambitious careerist, his talent was sometimes more of an obstacle than an aid. It made it impossible for him to compromise with the all-powerful imperial bureaucracy, which did not need visionary but merely energetic servants, like Telyakovsky.

That is why Diaghilev's Ballets Russes turned into an émigré organization. It was basically *Mir iskusstva* transplanted from Petersburg to Paris, since Benois, like so many other members of *Mir iskusstva,* and Bakst before him became leading collaborators of Diaghilev's enterprise. They were joined by Stravinsky and Fokine. In 1910, this group created the work that many consider to be the peak of Diaghilev's Russian Seasons, *Petrouchka.*

The collaborative effort on *Petrouchka* was typical for *Mir iskusstva.* The main author was Stravinsky, who played an excerpt for Diaghilev while he was in Lausanne in 1910. The music came from a planned concert piece for piano and orchestra called *Cry of Petrouchka*. Diaghilev immediately wanted to develop this into a ballet, and he wrote to Benois in Petersburg, asking him to compose a libretto.

Benois was delighted. Petrouchka, the Russian Guignol, had been his favorite marionette character since childhood. Just recently Petrouchka had amused crowds in the capital at the fairs and shows set up on the Field of Mars during the pre-Lenten Mardi Gras, called *Maslenitsa* in Russian, or Butter Week. By the early twentieth century the tradition of popular festivities on the Field of Mars had died out, and Benois, a confirmed passé-ist, longed to immortalize that colorful Petersburg carnival.

Diaghilev returned to Petersburg, and the libretto for *Petrouchka* was born over the daily evening tea and bagels in his apartment. Then Stravinsky joined Diaghilev and Benois. Later Benois insisted that he had written almost the entire plot of *Petrouchka*, with the three dolls—Petrouchka, Ballerina, and the Moor—mysteriously coming to life and playing out their traditional drama of love and jealousy in the midst of the boisterous Russian carnival. But he admitted that sometimes the "program" was made to fit music that had already been written. As for Stravinsky, he was delighted by his collaborator: "This man is unusually subtle, clear-sighted, and sensitive not only to movement but to music."[30]

Benois later recalled that before the premiere, when they had to decide who would be presented as the author of the libretto, he suggested ceding the authorship to Stravinsky, and it was only after a *combat de générosité* that they decided both Stravinsky and Benois would be listed as authors. Stravinsky subsequently regretted the decision deeply, because it gave Benois the right to one sixth of the royalties not only from theatrical but also from concert performances of the ballet's music.

Stravinsky lived abroad after 1910, and *Petrouchka* was composed in Switzerland, France, and Italy, and first shown in 1911 in Paris. Nonetheless, it was a purely Petersburgian composition. Stravinsky admitted this even at the end of his life, when he usually tried to minimize the Russianness of *Petrouchka* by insisting that its characters and even the music had been inspired by E. T. A. Hoffmann. Stravinsky "forgot" to add that at the turn of the century Hoffmann had been expropriated by *Mir iskusstva;* there was even a going expression, "Petersburg Hoffmanniade," describing everything unusual, grotesque, or eccentric in the life of the capital. Benois constantly proclaimed that Hoffmann was his idol and artistic guide, and in that period Stravinsky used to acknowledge that he was fully in "Benois' sphere of influence."[31]

The audience for the Parisian premiere of *Petrouchka* saw a picture of the fair in Petersburg in the reign of Nicholas I, around the 1830s, with the spire of the Admiralty in perspective and striped lampposts in the corners. Benois and Fokine invented a multitude of colorful types in the fair crowds: merchants, coachmen, nursemaids, military men, policemen, gypsies with a bear. Against the background of this festival the tragedy of Petrouchka unfolded—a marionette caught up in the storm of human passions. This traditional theme in Russian literature, the suffering of the little man, was seen through the prism of Hoffmann. "You could find here Gogol, and Dostoyevsky, and Blok," stated a Russian critic after the show.[32]

And the influence of Blok's drama *The Fair Show Booth* on the concept of *Petrouchka* is evident. *The Fair Show Booth,* produced by Meyerhold in Petersburg in 1906, was the first to present the suffering marionette Pierrot (Petrouchka in Russia) on the Russian stage within the framework of a modernistic "little theater." In this production Meyerhold strikingly combined music, dance, and dramatic action.

In February 1910, when Fokine staged a small ballet to Schumann's *Carnival* for a benefit for the Petersburg magazine *Satirikon,* Meyerhold appeared as Pierrot. This was a reprise of his performance of Pierrot in Blok's *The Fair Show Booth,* where Meyerhold appeared in white overalls with long sleeves: a sad marionette with angular movements, emitting pathetic moans from time to time. Meyerhold's Pierrot was the direct predecessor of Nijinsky's Petrouchka, who captivated the Paris audience of the Ballets Russes.

Contemporary French critics also wrote about the influence of Dostoyevsky on *Petrouchka;* the initiated sought hints and parallels with the scandalous liaison between Nijinsky and Diaghilev, in which the impresario allegedly played the role of the magician manipulator, and the dancer that of the poor marionette; but no one mentioned Blok or Meyerhold.

Petersburg had first caught the imagination of the European literary audience through Dostoyevsky's *Crime and Punishment.* It was a mysterious metropolis, similar to Dickens's London and Balzac's Paris, but more severe and scarier because of its distance and strangeness. For the European reader of Dostoyevsky, the exoticism of Petersburg had sinister overtones. *Petrouchka* was a different matter altogether. The tragedy of its plot was deftly wrapped up in nostalgic ethnicity.

After his heady European success, Petersburg seemed to Stravinsky "sadly small and provincial."[33] But, in fact, *Petrouchka* was greeted by Western audiences as an exotic, nationalistic work that succeeded in presenting the theme of Petersburg from a new aspect. Following the London premiere, the *Times* wrote, "The whole thing is refreshingly new and refreshingly Russian, more Russian, in fact, than any ballet we have had."[34]

It was extremely significant for the fate of the Petersburg mythos in Europe that *Petrouchka* was perceived by Western critics as an innovative work. "It is supremely clever, supremely modern, and supremely baroque," marveled the London *Observer* in 1913, perceptively summarizing several of the striking features of the Petersburg avant-garde later echoed in the works of Vladimir Nabokov.[35]

The *Petrouchka* of Stravinsky-Benois-Fokine-Diaghilev was the first Russian work to give Western audiences an idealized and romanticized image of Petersburg. And how fitting that this nostalgic image was created primarily in western Europe, mostly by semi-émigrés under the aegis of a semi-émigré enterprise. This is probably the only way that truly nostalgic works are born.

The imperial ballet school where the young Georges Balanchivadze lived and studied functioned almost as a monastery. The life of the pupils moved in strict rhythm under iron control; diligence was rewarded and disobedience punished, often with the maximum public humiliation. Pupils rose early, washed with icy water from a huge tank with numerous faucets, went for a walk under the viligant eye of their supervisor, and at ten in the morning began their lessons in classical dance. Then they studied academic subjects: literature, arithmetic, geography, history. Toward evening they had another session of dance. In the evening they did their homework and played piano. At eleven they went to sleep in a huge dormitory.

They were fed four times a day at a long table covered with a white cloth; the food was hearty, varied, and tasty. They had to eat quickly and make no mess. Their spiritual needs were served by the school church: they had early prayers before breakfast, and, during Passion Week, the last week of Lent before Easter, they were expected to go to confession and communion.

Like his school friends Georges could be certain of his future.

After graduation, pupils were guaranteed a place at the Maryinsky Theater, the title of Artist of the Imperial Theaters, an excellent salary, and an early and generous pension. If they did their work diligently and flawlessly, they did not have to worry about anything else. It was often said in those days, "Those ballet people have all their brains in their feet."[36]

And that is probably why the only serious examinations in the ballet school were in the dance classes. Fokine complained that history, geography, and languages were taught and learned superficially: "At that time none of the artists traveled abroad, and French seemed like a totally useless torture to us."[37] Lopukhov claimed that Nijinsky, for instance, graduated without taking any exams in the academic subjects, because it was understood he would fail them anyway.

That was how the school was set up and it continued in that fashion for decades. The daily routine of the ballet monastery had its own appeal; it was in harmony with the state structure outside the school and yielded excellent professional results. As long as it was peaceful in Russia, it was peaceful inside the ballet school. But as the foundations of the imperial state started to tremble, unrest began among the dancers, too.

One of the first rebels was Fokine, soon followed by others. Lopukhov told me that at age fifteen he had decided he would not be "just some dumb little dancer." "Fokine taught us to ask questions," he recalled. "How had it been before? You came out on stage, did your work, and left. The important thing was for your pirouette to be good, but why you were doing it, whom you were portraying—most didn't even wonder about that. After Fokine, dancing meaninglessly became shameful."[38]

The enticing rumors coming from Paris about Diaghilev's enterprise had a profound effect on the school's pupils. Western Europe did not seem so distant or abstract anymore. The Russian ballet was popular there, but not the traditional, academic sort that they were taught at the school, but a much more experimental one. As Danilova, who joined the school in 1911, told me, "Suddenly everyone wanted to move forward, and not keep endlessly rehashing the old."[39]

At the ballet school, the conflict between the comfortable routine and the distracting outside world only increased. We do not know how it would have developed if the political situation in Russia had remained stable. But in 1917 two seismic revolutionary shocks hit the country. The first revolution swept away the monarchy, the second eliminated the bourgeoisie. And along with them, most of the institutions of the ancien régime were destroyed. But a particularly heavy blow befell the imperial theaters: they lost both their august patron and their most loyal audience.

In this catastrophic new situation, the ballet school was simply forgotten at first. Ballet and opera performances in revolutionary Petrograd continued as if in a somnambulist's dream, by momentum, while the former "monastery" was suddenly without supervision. Previously pupils had arrived at the Maryinsky Theater in special carriages under strict supervision. Now even the streetcars were not running, and the pupils had to get to the theater on foot.

In late autumn 1917, Balanchivadze and his classmate Mikhail Mikhailov performed in Glinka's *Ruslan and Lyudmila*. The incomparable Tamara Karsavina danced in the production, and one of the roles was sung by the legendary Chaliapin. Heatedly discussing the performance, Georges and his friend did not notice that the theater had emptied long ago. When they came out onto the street, it was already dark.

Petrograd at night was particularly eerie then. Shots rang out here and there and it was raining as well. Hunched over in their black topcoats, Georges and Mikhail jumped over big puddles to keep from getting their worn boots even wetter. No one had worried about the pupils' clothes in ages.

A well-dressed gentleman strode boldly through the puddles ahead of the young dancers. His insouciance was explained by his marvelous new galoshes, which shone even in the dark. Hopping after the striding man, the boys eyed those galoshes enviously. Suddenly several shots could be heard and the proud owner of the galoshes fell face down into a puddle.

Georges and Mikhail ran off in opposite directions. Mikhail hid in the nearest doorway, where the gentleman in galoshes was soon brought. He was wounded and groaned loudly, repeating that one of the shots had killed the boy in a black overcoat who had been next to him. "Georges!" thought the terrified Mikhail. He ran to the scene of the shooting but found no one. He wandered around the nearby streets for a long time, trying to find out from the few passersby where the dead boy had been taken.

In despair, Mikhail returned to the school. "You can imagine my joy when Georges ran out of our small, agitated anthill toward me," he later recalled. It turned out that Georges had also heard talk of a boy in a topcoat killed by the shots and decided that it had been Mikhail. He too had unsuccessfully looked for his friend and returned dejected to the dormitory, where he upset all his classmates with the terrifying story. Luckily, things had turned out all right that time.

Similar dramatic incidents were commonplace in the once-orderly life of the ballet school pupils. Previously insulated from the world outside, the school now reacted to every change happening around it. When Petrograd went hungry, so did the school. When the plumbing froze in the city, the children were without water, too. They were spared none of the horrors of a dying Petrograd. For Georges and his classmates, this sharp change in status must have been traumatic. Always resentful about his separation from his family, he was now deprived a second time of the comforts of a stable life and withdrew completely.

Still he made another attempt at "family life." In the spring of 1922, eighteen-year-old Georges married the lovely fifteen-year-old dancer Tamara Zheverzheyeva (whose surname Diaghilev would later shorten to Geva) and moved to the apartment of his father-in-law, Levky Zheverzheyev, in house No. 5 in Grafsky Alley.

Levky Zheverzheyev, who played an exceptional and still underappreciated role in young Balanchine's artistic development, was a Petersburg original. Of Oriental heritage, he inherited a lamé fabric plant from his parents as well as the capital's largest church supply store, on Nevsky Prospect. Balanchine told me, "Before the revolution the Zheverzheyev factory made vestments and miters for the patriarch and other high clergy. Do you know what a patriarch's vestment is like? The lamé cloth for it was thick and heavy, of pure gold. One inch of that cloth took a year to make!"

But Zheverzheyev's heart was not in business. An amateur artist, even as a teenager he began collecting unique materials on the Russian theater: first editions of plays, original posters and announcements over a hundred years old, various documents, sketches for scenery and costumes, portraits of famous actors of the past and the present. His library of rare books—close to twenty-five thousand volumes—was one of the richest and most extensive in Petersburg.

Paradoxically, besides collecting antiques, Zheverzheyev became interested in the avant-garde. Every Friday he invited a group of noisy modernist youths to his home. These meetings soon became a fixture of artistic Petersburg. A reflection of Zheverzheyev's reputation was the opinion of a leading innovator of that era, the director Meyerhold: "The city of Peter—St. Petersburg—Petrograd (as it is now called)—only it, only its air, its stones, its canals can create such men with such a desire to build as Zheverzheyev. To live and to die in St. Petersburg! What good fortune!"[40]

At "Zheverzheyev's Fridays" one could meet the futurist poets Vladimir Mayakovsky, Velimir Khlebnikov, and Alexei Kruchenykh, the artists Casimir Malevich, Vladimir Tatlin, and Pavel Filonov, the art critic Nikolai Punin, and the violinist, composer, and painter Mikhail Matiushin. One of the habitués of Zheverzheyev's salon recalled later, "The most modest and quietest person at the Fridays was the shy host, whom none of the guests noticed. He never took part in the heated discussions but sat in the corner and silently, attentively listened to the agitated, noisy speeches."[41]

The Russian avant-garde was going through its "heroic" period then. Despite the widespread misapprehension in the West, the leading Russian modernists were formed ideologically and artistically before the Communist revolution. Starting in the late nineteenth century, Russian culture had developed to an extremely swift tempo. The stunning changes in economic and social life were accompanied by radical shifts in aesthetic vision.

In 1895 Friedrich Engels wrote to a Russian fellow social democrat:

> In a country like yours, where major modern industry is grafted to primitive peasant communes and at the same time all the intermediate stages of civilization are represented, in a country which in the intellectual sense is surrounded by a more or less effective Wall of China, erected by despotism, there is nothing surprising about the appearance of the most incredible and bizarre combinations of ideas.[42]

These "combinations of ideas" became even more bizarre when the Wall of China that Engels wrote about gradually disappeared. During the latter part of the nineteenth century, Russian youth had the opportunity to assimilate unhindered the latest artistic experiments of the West. The results were fantastic. In the space of ten or fifteen years Russian art managed to absorb, digest, and boldly rework the product of Europe's lengthy process of development. The leading Russian avant-gardists rather quickly "left behind" impressionism, pointillism, Art Nouveau, symbolist aesthetics, and Cézannism. They tarried over cubism and for a while Picasso was their idol. But by 1912 Filonov announced that Picasso "had come to a dead end."

The Russian avant-gardists were maximalists. Maximalism is

characteristic of Russian culture in general, but in the feverish atmosphere after 1910, it grew more pronounced. Malevich and Tatlin and Filonov considered themselves not only artists but prophets of a new form of life. Artistic creation for them was a profoundly spiritual experience. Each of these artists was tied, in his own way, to the Russian religious tradition. In the paintings of each, one could find traces of the influence of ancient Russian icons. And in those artists' speeches, refrains from religious and mystical ideas often echoed.

This could not have escaped Zheverzheyev's attention, since he was a specialist in that area, owning a church supply store, after all. For him the ties between the Russian avant-garde and folk art were also obvious: they all adored the ancient designs, the primitive art of shop signs and serving trays, embroidery and ornaments. As a collector, Zheverzheyev knew those items well, too.

In the annals of the Russian avant-garde theater, there is an example of the influence on contemporary innovation of Zheverzheyev's collection and his interest in historical rarities. He commissioned a model of the famous "Scene in Hell," which was the finale of the once-popular old Russian show *The Secrets of Saint Petersburg Underground*. In the center of the model stood the figure of Satan, and from his open mouth demons in red tights jumped out, while hell fire and clouds of smoke surrounded all.

Mayakovsky came to the craftsman's studio while he was working on the project and peppered him with questions on the traditional techniques of folk fairy plays and mysteries. A while later Meyerhold produced Mayakovsky's new play, *Mystery-Bouffe*, which also had a scene in hell. The sets were by Malevich.

Every major Russian avant-garde artist wanted to be a leader and felt he had the right to be one. And among themselves, the artists fought fiercely. This worried Zheverzheyev, who wanted to make peace among these warring talents, believing it would be easier for them to confront the philistines among the public if they were united. So he took pains to help organize the Union of Youth, a society of avant-garde artists, in 1910.

The Union of Youth lasted almost four years, giving seven major exhibits, producing three issues of a daring magazine, publishing books, and holding debates that drew attention to the new art. None of this would have been possible without Zheverzheyev: the magazine, the exhibits, and all the rest were paid for out of his pocket.

And in general without his peacemaking and unifying presence, the Union of Youth could not have lasted as long as it did. As its chairman, Zheverzheyev insisted that Moscow avant-garde artists and futurist poets join this Petersburg society. Such a goal was not easy to achieve, but the results included two extraordinary theatrical presentations that left a deep impression on the history of the Russian avant-garde: the performances in Petersburg of the tragedy *Vladimir Mayakovsky* and the opera *Victory over the Sun.*

Russian avant-gardists believed the theater was the best instrument for expressing their ideas. This conception originated with the Russian symbolists, who had always maintained, "From art will come a new life and the salvation of humanity." For them, the theater was not simply inseparable from ethics and religion but became a means for transforming the spirit. Andrei Bely preached that "at the heart of the goals proposed by art there are religious aims: those aims are the transformation of humanity."[43]

These messianic ideas were vividly reflected in the late work of Alexander Scriabin, who conceived the great music and dance work *Mysterium.* Its performance, according to the composer, would lead to "the end of the world," when material force would perish and sheer spirit would triumph. All humanity would become participants in the *Mysterium,* the composer dreamed. Scriabin visualized an incredible theatrical happening in which there would be no distinction between actors and audience. This was the apotheosis of the symbolist concepts of the mystical role of the theater.

Scriabin's *Mysterium* remained, of course, a utopian conception, but that fact did not dampen the dreams of the Russian modernists. "The musicality of contemporary drama," wrote Bely, "its symbolism—does this not show the desire of drama to become a mystery? Drama came out of mysteries. And it will return there. And once drama returns to mystery, it will inevitably leave the boards of the stage and spread into life. Do we not have here a hint of the transformation of life into mystery?"[44]

Even though they attacked the "obsolete" symbolists, the Russian avant-gardists retained a mystical belief in the lofty mission of the theater. Their theater fixation was all-encompassing, as it was for the symbolists. Following the symbolists, the futurists were turning daily life into theater. The symbolists "theatricized" their relations with one another. The futurists brought this "home" theater into the streets. Malevich strolled down the streets with a large wooden spoon in his lapel. Mayakovsky showed off in a shirt of bright yellow, which had been designated the official color of futurism. The futurists painted their faces, drawing flowers on their cheeks and gilding their noses. They also earned pretty good money from shocking, theatricized debates, which attracted large, curious audiences.

Zheverzheyev organized one such debate in November 1912 at the Troitsky Theater of Miniatures, which he had founded and financed. This was one of the first theaters of its kind in Petersburg. Avant-garde art, rejected by established institutions, had access to the public on the stage of the Troitsky Theater (and similar small stages) and in the semiprivate cabarets like The Stray Dog. The manager of the Troitsky Theater was Alexander Fokine, the choreographer's brother, a colorful figure and former race car champion. An unknown but promising young poet and artist was recommended to Zheverzheyev as someone who could deliver a lecture on the latest in Russian poetry. He was brought to Zheverzheyev, the arts patron liked him, and thus the debut of nineteen-year-old Mayakovsky in Petersburg took place under the aegis of the Union of Youth.

Tall and handsome, Mayakovsky shocked the audience with a statement made in his velvety voice that "the word requires spermatization," and that in painting, as in other arts and literature, one needs to be a "shoemaker." As Mayakovsky's friend, the futurist poet Alexei Kruchenykh, who liked to wear a couch pillow tied around his neck with a string, explained, "so that it writes tight and reads tight, more uncomfortable than greased boots or a truck in the living room."[45]

And in the summer of 1913 in that "tight," rough language Mayakovsky wrote a tragedy that he intended to call either *The Rebellion of Objects* or *The Railroad*. But since the play was written in haste, the author sent it to the censors for approval with a title page that simply said, "Vladimir Mayakovsky. A Tragedy," that is, without any title. Once it was passed by the censors no changes could be made. Mayakovsky was pleased: "Well then let's call the tragedy 'Vladimir Mayakovsky.' "

That wording was particularly appropriate because the poet was in fact the main character of his play. A young Boris Pasternak was stunned when Mayakovsky read it to him:

I listened, forgetting about myself, with my whole entranced heart, with bated breath. I had never heard anything like it in my life. The title concealed a brilliantly simple revelation, that the poet is not the author but the object of lyric poetry, addressing the world in the first person. The title was not the name of the writer, but the name of the contents.[46]

Mayakovsky's tragedy was written under the obvious influence of the then-popular ideas on monodrama of the playwright and director Nikolai Evreinov, who was once sarcastically depicted thus by Viktor Shklovsky, an ally of the futurists:

> Hair combed back, trimmed, very handsome, an official sadist, who published *The History of Corporal Punishment in Russia*.
>   When you come to his house, he claps his hands, and the fat young maid comes in. Evreinov says, "Bring some pheasants."
>   "The pheasants are all eaten," the maid replies.
>   "Then bring tea."
>   This is called Theater for Oneself.[47]

Shklovsky, of course, was caricaturing the post-symbolist theater innovations of that great paradoxicalist, the "Russian Oscar Wilde," Evreinov. He maintained that life was a constant "theater for oneself," through which the personality defends itself from the chaos of the unknown world. He considered executions and torture as theater, too. Evreinov explained his concept of monodrama this way: "A dramatic performance, which, while trying to relate to the viewer the protagonist's spiritual state as completely as possible, presents on stage the world around him as it is perceived by the protagonist at a given moment of his stage life."[48]

Besides the Poet, the characters in the tragedy *Vladimir Mayakovsky* were Man Without Eye and Leg, Man Without Ear, and Man Without Head—all various versions of the author, as Evreinov had prescribed. The futurist Benedikt Livshits observed that in his play, "Mayakovsky fractured and multiplied in a demiurgic frenzy."[49]

In November 1913 posters were pasted all over Petersburg announcing that the Luna-Park Theater in early December would present "the world's first four productions by Futurists of the theater": *Vladimir Mayakovsky* and the opera *Victory Over the Sun* would each be given twice. Since the newspapers were writing a lot about the futurists then in the most sensational terms, the tickets sold out instantly, despite the high prices (as much as Chaliapin commanded). *Le tout Petersburg* attended.

The "Futurist Festival" opened with Mayakovsky's play. Meyerhold and Blok were present. The brazen spectacle was undoubtedly connected to their theatrical ideas—the dreams of the symbolists for a ritual theater in which poet, actors, and viewers blended into one.

The tragedy took place against backdrops by Pavel Filonov and Ilya Shkolnik, depicting the city. (The sets were lost in 1924 during major flooding in Leningrad.) One of the backdrops was particularly memorable: "an agitated, colorful city port with numerous, thoroughly painted boats on the shores and beyond them, hundreds of city buildings, each of which was detailed down to the very last window."[50] At least one viewer was stunned by the scenery: "Perhaps what I saw then on that cardboard was the truest depiction of a city that I had ever seen. . . . I felt a movement inside myself, I felt the movement of the city in eternity, its horror as part of chaos."[51]

Mayakovsky came out on the stage in his famous yellow shirt, supposedly playing himself. He was a marvelous actor, and many people in the audience were deeply moved when he melodramatically compared himself to an unneeded tear rolling down "the unshaven cheek of the squares."

That cry of desperation by the young poet against the background of Filonov's urban painting summed up the romantic and symbolist tradition of alienation in Petersburg. Pasternak, the Muscovite, recalling Pushkin, Dostoyevsky, and Andrei Bely's magnum opus, emphasized Mayakovsky's traditionality vis-à-vis Petersburg: "He saw beneath him the city that gradually rose up to him from the bottom of *The Bronze Horseman, Crime and Punishment,* and *Petersburg . . .* a city in the mist of eternal fortune-telling about the future, a needy Russian city of the nineteenth and twentieth centuries."[52]

All the performances were done under the aegis of the Union of Youth and paid for by Zheverzheyev. It was his finest hour. He recalled that the dress rehearsal of Mayakovsky's play was attended by

> the police chief himself (there were only four in the entire city) as well as the censor and the local policeman. In the breaks between acts and at the end of the rehearsal, the police chief pestered me with questions: "For God's sake, tell me honestly, is this truly only futurist showing-off and nonsense? To tell the truth, I don't understand a thing. There isn't anything in it that's . . . you know? . . . no? well, . . . seditious? There's nothing I can put my finger on, I admit . . . I admit . . . but I feel that something's wrong.[53]

That episode amply demonstrates the paradox and uniqueness of Zheverzheyev's position in Petersburg. For the authorities he was a wealthy and respected businessman, the owner of a famous store for church supplies; thus he was connected to the most traditional and stable institution in tsarist Russia. But Zheverzheyev gave all his sympathies to a small group of enthusiasts of a shocking new art. He was not pretending or being a hypocrite but lived naturally in two worlds that were far apart from each other. His quiet confidence helped him to persuade the police authorities of the "innocence" of Mayakovsky's play, which is now widely acknowledged as a pinnacle of the young futurist's early work.

Mayakovsky's avant-garde comrades complained that his tragedy was too accessible: "it never tears the word away from its meaning; it does not use the sound of the pure word as such."[54] This was the reaction of Mayakovsky's friend Mikhail Matiushin—violinist, composer, painter, and one of the founders with Zheverzheyev of the Union of Youth. Matiushin, who was over fifty, was the oldest of the futurists; Blok noted sarcastically in his diary that he was "futuristically trying to look young."

In the summer of 1913, Matiushin, Malevich, and Kruchenykh, meeting outside Petersburg, decided to write an opera. They proclaimed themselves the "First All-Russian Congress of Futurists" and issued a manifesto of their goal: "To swoop down on the bastion of artistic sickliness—the Russian theater—and to transform it decisively." Interestingly, this manifesto was immediately published by many Petersburg newspapers; the public curiosity in their domestic futurists was quite high.

Matiushin wrote music to Kruchenykh's libretto. They called the opera *Victory Over the Sun*, because in it two Strongmen-futurists knocked the sun, the embodiment of the traditional concept of "beauty," out of the sky. Matiushin recalled that the first rehearsals of the opera greatly inspired Zheverzheyev; and Alexander Fokine, the manager of the Troitsky Theater, shouted happily, "I like these fellows!'"

Only fragments of Matiushin's music survive. It resembled the neoprimitivist works of the French composer Erik Satie and the Russian composers of The Stray Dog circle. In some parts of the opera, Matiushin experimented with "ultrachromaticism," using quarter tone intervals. But the music did not make an impression on audiences. Its performers had not rehearsed sufficiently, the vocalists were third-rate, and to make matters worse, they sang to the accompaniment of an untuned upright piano.

The center of attention became the scenery and costumes by Casimir Malevich. He had been presented to Petersburg audiences more than two years earlier, also under the aegis of the Union of Youth. Afterward, Zheverzheyev organized a performance by Malevich at the Troitsky Theater of Miniatures. Shklovsky recalled that Malevich wanted to explain his painting: black-and-white women in the form of truncated cones against a red background. In the course of the explanation, he referred to the recently deceased artist Valentin Serov, who had been universally beloved and respected, as a "mediocre dauber." People were upset. Malevich calmly continued: "I'm not teasing, this is what I think." But he was not allowed to finish: a commotion ensued and an intermission had to be announced.

In his work on *Victory Over the Sun* Malevich, who had moved from postimpressionism to cubism in just a few years, came face to face with abstract art. Kruchenykh's libretto was constructed out of *zaum* ("non-sense" language). Malevich strove for the same effect in his costumes and scenery. The characters resembled animated cubist paintings. Matiushin recalled how Malevich dressed the Strongmen: "He gave them shoulders on the level of their mouths and made heads in the shape of a cardboard helmet—it created the impression of two gigantic human figures."

Malevich used lighting in a bold, new way: colored theater lights captured individual parts of brightly colored cardboard figures otherwise hidden in darkness—first hands, then heads, then legs. This underscored their geometric, abstract character. Part of the audience applauded, but the majority laughed and booed. Petersburg critics were outraged both by the play and the audience: "Shame on a society that reacts with laughter to mockery and that allows itself to be spat upon!"

The critics apparently had forgotten that in the theatrical city of Petersburg, the spectacle was all: it didn't matter how incongruous and outrageous a performance was, as long as it was unusual and amusing. Petersburg's cynicism and avowed curiosity for the new went hand-in-hand here. As a proud observer of his city, an artist, snob, and high-society denizen noted, "To admire an amusing bit of rubbish is not something given to everyone!"[55]

The Russian modernists fought desperately for success in the capital and power over the soul of skeptical Petersburg. With the opening of the Artistic Bureau of N. Dobychina in the fall of 1912, selling works of art became a real business in Russia. Nadezhda Dobychina (née Fishman) became the first professional dealer in the country; she not only organized exhibits for artists and sold their paintings but also directed their work. It was considered inappropriate for a woman, and a Jew-

ish one at that, to interfere so unceremoniously in the capital's artistic
life, and so Petersburg men spoke of Dobychina with grudging respect,
appreciating her power: "Yes, that woman was a hidden lever in the
life changes of many artists. . . . She was very ugly, and perhaps that
fueled her energy, life force, ambition, and desire to triumph."[56]

In December 1915, Dobychina gave the "Last Futurist Exhibition of Paintings 0,10 (Zero-Ten)" at her Artistic Bureau. Malevich
dominated the show, with close to forty works, next to which he hung
a sign Suprematism of Painting. These were geometric abstract works
of the greatest intensity and rigor. High in a corner, in a place Russians traditionally reserve for icons, reigned Malevich's painting *Black
Square*. Achieving notoriety, it became the icon of abstract art in Russia and, with it, Malevich proclaimed the leadership of the Russian
avant-garde in world art. This painting transmuted the deceptively el-
ementary form of the black square into a symbol of the new sensation of limitless space and universality of existence. *Black Square* was
fortified by Malevich's idea that abstract art would open the way for
the spiritual cleansing of the masses, hence the challenging unity of
form and color in his seminal work.

Malevich's letter to Matiushin explains the origin of the term
the artist used for the new direction in art he had created: "I think
that suprematism is the best because it means sovereignty."[57] The
painter's symbol of suprematism originated in a sketch he had done
for *Victory Over the Sun*, when the artist first drew the square on paper. Later Malevich wrote about that sketch, "This drawing will have
great significance in painting. That which had been done unconsciously is now yielding extraordinary fruits."[58]

Zheverzheyev understood the importance of Malevich's
sketches for *Victory Over the Sun*. At the same time as Dobychina's
exhibit, Zheverzheyev was showing "Monuments of Russian Theater" in Petrograd, consisting of precious materials from his legendary
collection. Right after the performances of *Victory Over the Sun*, he
bought nineteen sketches for the opera from the artist. Now they were
in the exhibit of Zheverzheyev's collection, next to posters from the
early eighteenth century.

Malevich pronounced, "Color is the creator of space. . . . The
keys of suprematism open what is still unconscious. My new art does
not belong to the Earth exclusively . . . in man, in his consciousness
lies the striving for space, the desire to break away from the planet
Earth."[59] Like every real missionary, Malevich tried to conquer avant-

garde Petrograd with his philosophy. And for that, he had first to conquer Nikolai Punin's circle.

At meetings of the club, the intense, brooding Malevich, according to Punin, spent hours "convincing you with astonishing pressure that was hypnotizing and forced you to listen, spoke as if piercing you with a rapier, putting things to you from the most unexpected angles; pushing hard, he would leap back from his interlocutor, shaking his hand and his short fingers, which trembled nervously."[60]

But Malevich had a mighty rival in his battle for Petersburg's heart. Someone brought a masterful cubist drawing by the Muscovite Vladimir Tatlin to Punin's circle. The members of the club were astonished, and chipping in ten to fifteen kopeks apiece, sent Tatlin a collective telegram: "Come! All Petrograd's young artists and critics await you as our teacher, laying a new path in Art. We're waiting!"

Tatlin immediately showed up in Petrograd. "He had a unique look," recalled a member of the Punin circle. "He was tall and ugly . . . his whitish hair lay in some kind of tresses on the back of his head. He resembled a pelican."[61] At that time, Tatlin, who had renounced painting, was obsessed with his innovative "counterreliefs." These were sculptural paintings that heralded constructivism—beautifully arranged strange and powerful combinations of various materials: metal, wood, and glass.

Tatlin's ideas were even more radical than Malevich's. His counterreliefs did not serve as symbols of some mystical yearnings, as did Malevich's paintings. They were not intended to give viewers spiritual impulses but simply stated the right of various materials and objects to sovereign existence as objects of art. The prosaic and utilitarian qualities masking the refined beauty of Tatlin's counterreliefs found resonance in restrained Petersburg, besides which Tatlin himself made an indelible impression on young artists there. As Punin recalled, "Then his every opinion, every thought he expressed about art was a breakthrough to a new culture, to the future."[62]

Under the powerful influence of Tatlin's ideas, the avant-gardists in Punin's circle began working enthusiastically

on constructing expansive models, on various kinds of selection of materials of different qualities, characteristics, and shapes. We sawed, planed, cut, rubbed, stretched, and bent; we almost completely forgot about painting; we talked only about contrasts, combinations, tensions, aces of intersections, textures. From the side, it might have looked rather strange, but actually, this was the creative tension of people who thought that through their efforts the world would at last shift away from the age-old canons and "enter into a new Renaissance."[63]

And so, *Space Composition* by the Petrograd wunderkind Lev Bruni utilized a large steel linchpin, stretched leather, glass, mica, and tin. Bruni's piece didn't make it through the years of the revolution; his widow, Nina, told me about it.[64] Pyotr Miturich's composition consisted of plywood, glass panes marked with wax, purple paper, and "silver" foil.

Punin spoke of the incessant rivalry between Tatlin and Malevich.

> For as long as I can remember them, they always divided up the world between them: the land, and the sky, and interplanetary space, establishing their spheres of influence everywhere. Tatlin usually claimed the earth for himself, trying to shove Malevich into the sky because of his abstractness. Malevich, not refusing the planets, did not yield earth, either, justly assuming that it too was a planet and therefore could be abstract as well.[65]

Malevich scorned Tatlin, accusing him of having a "narrow view" and maintaining that "iron blocks Tatlin's horizon." Tatlin responded in kind.

That war for spheres of influence was not limited to ideological clashes. Before the opening of a show at Dobychina's Artistic Bureau, the broad-shouldered Malevich and the agile giant Tatlin actually came to blows. Shows of the avant-gardists in Petrograd were becoming more like happenings at every occasion, but this soon-to-be-legendary fist fight contributed overwhelmingly to the overall theatrical nature of the event.

The ivory tower did not attract the Russian avant-gardists; they always thought of the potential audience and considered its possible reactions. That may be why attempts to reconstruct *Victory Over the Sun,* undertaken in the early 1980s in the United States and Europe, were not completely successful. Educated audiences reacted to the performance as to a landmark in the history of modern art. But respect was the last reaction the innovative authors wanted from the outrageous original production of 1913 in Petersburg.

The burning desire of the Russian avant-garde to conquer a

mass audience took on religious overtones. Their proselytizing left its mark even on their appearance: "Malevich looked like a hermit, Tatlin, a martyr, and Filonov, an apostle."[66] Their activity was a tightly woven combination of creative enlightenment and pragmatic calculation, mysticism and scholarly reckoning, utopian ideas and striving for immediate changes in daily life. They were all interested in the study of the "fourth dimension," a mystical "new reality," the quest for which became fashionable after the publication in Petersburg of two books by the Russian theosophist P. D. Ouspensky, *The Fourth Dimension* (1909) and *The Key to Mysteries* (*Tertium Organum*) (1912).

In May 1913 Malevich wrote to Matiushin that he could see a time "when big cities and the studios of contemporary artists would be held up on huge Zeppelins."[67] In 1917 he casually informed Matiushin, "back in the summer I proclaimed myself chairman of space."[68] Therefore, it is not surprising that many avant-gardists hailed the Communist revolution, thinking it would clear the way for the realization of their radical ideas.

For all that, most of the leaders of the new Russian art had little interest in the social and economic aspects of the Russian Revolution. They were primarily concerned with artistic and moral issues, and the liberating promise of the revolution. Punin later recalled with bitter irony, "We imagined art autonomous of the state, perhaps even a dictatorship of art over the government." The Bolsheviks, on the other hand, agreed to cooperate with the avant-garde only out of practical considerations. Most of the major art figures of a traditional orientation had emigrated or tried to sabotage the new regime. Someone had to run the enormous cultural empire that the Bolsheviks had inherited from old Russia. People's Commissar of Education Lunacharsky intoned, "The work of protecting the palaces and museums, definitively passed on to the people, must not be put off."[69]

Zheverzheyev was one of the first respected art figures of the capital to cooperate with the new regime. The Bolsheviks nationalized his enormous theater collection but named him its curator. Early in 1917 Zheverzheyev headed the Left Bloc of the Petrograd Union of the Arts. Its members included Mayakovsky, Punin, Meyerhold, and Nathan Altman. After the Bolshevik revolution they took top positions in the new apparatus for managing culture, and naturally did not forget Zheverzheyev.

Here is one of many examples. In 1918 Zheverzheyev applied to the state publishing house with a request to publish a manuscript

on African art by the artist and art historian Vladimir Markov (pseudonym of the Latvian Voldemar Matvejs), who had died young.
Markov was one of the most active members of the Union of Youth,
which formally ceased to exist some years before the revolution but
which, in Punin's words, still stood as a landmark over Petrograd.

At that time people in Petrograd were starving, and basic necessities were lacking. But Mayakovsky zealously supported Zheverzheyev's idea. At a meeting of the Petrograd Art Collegium, which
under the Bolsheviks managed the day-to-day business of the arts,
Mayakovsky said that the proposal to publish Markov's book came
"from comrade Zheverzheyev, whom we all know: during the dark-
est reactionary times, he held the banner of art high."[70] The history
of the culture of the twentieth century will note that in 1919 in Petrograd, where the plumbing had frozen, public transportation had
stopped, and a horse that had fallen on the street was stripped down
to the carcass by hungry citizens, one of the world's first serious studies of African art, Art of the Negroes, with a cover designed by Altman, was published through the joint efforts of Zheverzheyev,
Mayakovsky, and Punin.

A unique and curious child born of the bizarre combination of
events in revolutionary Petrograd was propaganda porcelain: dinner
services and commemorative plates depicting the slogans and symbols
of the new regime, as well as portraits of its leaders. In a period of extreme shortages of many necessities, including paper on occasion, Petrograd's porcelain factory miraculously discovered large supplies of
unpainted plates left over from imperial days.

Russian porcelain production was one of the oldest in Europe.
By the beginning of the twentieth century it had lost its artistic attractiveness. New ideas in this field, as in others, were presented by
members of the Mir iskusstva group, primarily Sergei Chekhonin, an
accomplished artist of mousy appearance whom friends called a
"lurking mosquito."

Chekhonin's imagination blazed after the revolution, when,
working in his factory studio, he painted virtuoso renditions of revolutionary appeals on porcelain plates and cups intertwined in intricate designs. This paradox could not exist anywhere but the Petrograd
of those years, a hungry city in which exquisite dishes worthy of the
most luxurious table were decorated with blunt Communist slogans,
rendered with the greatest imagination.

Chekhonin collected a group of innovative artists around him,
and the Bolsheviks wisely decided to use that creative potential for

their propaganda goals as well as profit. The dinnerware and figurines produced in Petrograd were sold in the West for much-needed hard currency. As a result, Western collections today display the exquisite porcelain plates painted by Chekhonin, Dobuzhinsky, Altman, Kustodiev, and even such avant-garde artists as Malevich and Nikolai Suetin.

Another paradox of that terrible and fantastic era was the proliferation of theaters. Zheverzheyev, who had a wealth of experience as a producer, became the head of a new theater, the Hermitage. He and Meyerhold had come up with the idea of it together. The Hermitage Theater was registered as the forty-fifth in the city; at that time in dark, hungry Petrograd, over forty different productions were available almost every evening.

Zheverzheyev had worked with Meyerhold before, when the latter had produced Mayakovsky's *Mystery-Bouffe* in Petrograd for the first anniversary of the Communist revolution. Malevich did the scenery. His sketches for *Mystery-Bouffe* did not survive and they are rarely mentioned now.

Meyerhold had begun experimenting in his studio on Borodinskaya Street in Petrograd, even before the revolution, in the area of "people's theater," that is, a theater with mobile troupes that could, theoretically at least, perform on public squares, in the streets, and at fairs. Meyerhold worked with his actors on improvisation and acrobatics and took them to the circus, suggesting that they study with the jugglers. He devoted a lot of attention to pantomime with musical accompaniment, and he always made his students move "on the music," and not "to the music"—subsequently one of the most important elements of Balanchine's aesthetics. Among the numerous guests of the studio, the young Sergei Radlov, the dandy and future avant-garde director, stood out. Leaning casually against the door jamb, Radlov closely observed Meyerhold's experiments.

After the revolution Meyerhold spoke with unfeigned enthusiasm of art for the broad masses. But his proposal to present plays for the mass audience at the Hermitage Theater apparently had not been wholly serious; the charming hall, built in the late eighteenth century and then reconstructed by Carlo Rossi, had only two hundred seats. Plays for the imperial family were staged there, and sometimes its members took part.

And now Zheverzheyev was proposing turning the Hermitage Theater into "the bearer of new forms of theater art." Just how avant-garde the new enterprise was to be is clear from Zheverzheyev's list of designers, including Altman, Chagall, and Tatlin. The whole concept was going to be under the aegis of the People's Commissariat of Education, where modernists like Mayakovsky, Punin, and Arthur Lourié set the tone in the arts section.

Zheverzheyev, however, met many obstacles right off the bat. Meyerhold, who could not stand the hungry life, fled south from Petrograd. The city authorities did not allow performances at the Hermitage Theater, citing the danger of fire. (Curiously, the same excuse was given to me when, half a century later, I tried to obtain permission to use the Hermitage Theater for the struggling Experimental Studio of Chamber Opera).

But in the end, the avant-garde artist Yuri Annenkov managed to produce under Zheverzheyev's auspices an influential production of Leo Tolstoy's play *The First Distiller* at the Heraldry Hall of the Winter Palace. Annenkov had audaciously transformed Tolstoy's didactic parable about the dangers of drinking into a circus show with acrobats, dancers, clowns, accompanied by accordion and balalaika players. The second act of Tolstoy's morality play took place in hell, and Annenkov later recalled that it gave him the opportunity to go all out:

> The scenery was made up of multicolored crisscrossing ropes, slightly camouflaged trapezes, various swaying platforms suspended in space and other circus equipment, against a background of abstract blobs of color, primarily in a fiery spectrum. The devils flew and tumbled in the air. The ropes, trapezes, and platforms were in constant movement. The action developed simultaneously on the stage and in the audience.[71]

This "people's" production was banned after four performances because the Bolsheviks were offended on Tolstoy's behalf and found this "bourgeois modernization of the classics" unacceptable. However, Annenkov's radical experiments were immediately picked up and continued by Sergei Radlov, who opened his theater, the "People's Comedy," in the Iron Hall of the Petrograd People's House in 1920.

The observant Shklovsky noted, "Radlov, coming in a direct line from Yuri Annenkov, proceeds tangentially from Meyerhold's pantomime."[72] In Radlov's productions the actors also improvised, did complicated acrobatic turns, and juggled fire. Only a few of them came from traditional theater (one of them was Lyubov Mendeleyeva, Blok's wife), for Radlov had recruited most from the circus or variety stage. The action could take place in Russia, Paris, or New York, with transformations, fights, and almost cinematic chase scenes.

During Meyerhold's absence from Petrograd, the energetic Radlov became the recognized head of the avant-garde theater. But Meyerhold soon returned and made directly for Radlov's theater, where he created a loud scene, accusing his follower of plagiarism. The horrified actors watched the infuriated Meyerhold, dressed in the Bolshevik "uniform": leather jacket, rough boots, and cap with a badge depicting Lenin, also in a cap. Meyerhold ran from the Iron Hall shouting curses. As of that moment, he and Radlov were mortal enemies. But Zheverzheyev continued to maintain friendly relations with both.

A little taller than average, well built, and always calm, Zheverzheyev was self-confident in the stormy seas of Petrograd's artistic avant-garde. His temperament made him the ideal arbiter for settling the innumerable disputes and conflicts of superinflated egos. Before the revolution, the authorities had respected him for being rich. After the revolution the new authorities continued to respect Zheverzheyev because he had given up his wealth easily and gracefully. The avant-gardists respected him before and after the revolution for his steady support for their experiments and for his organizational skills. In the early 1920s Zheverzheyev was still in the middle of Petrograd's cultural life.

For the young Balanchine, Zheverzheyev's apartment was a haven, and its owner must have become a father figure. George even began imitating Zheverzheyev, who wore his hair long and parted on one side. Balanchine got the same hairdo. Zheverzheyev had beautiful hands (his daughter Tamara described them as "Botticelli-like"), and George started paying attention to how his hands looked.[73]

It was in 1922, when Balanchine moved in with the Zheverzheyevs, that the young dancer was in particular need of advice and support. Petrograd's ballet people were bewildered, discouraged, and frightened. That year the Kremlin seriously discussed shutting down the Maryinsky Theater for economic and ideological reasons. The government was catastrophically short of money. Expenditures for opera and ballet in those circumstances seemed particularly extravagant. Those arts were proclaimed not only useless but even reactionary and harmful to the masses. The leader for "proletarian culture," the Bolshevik Platon Kerzhentsev, wrote, "Opera and ballet in their essence are more appropriate to an authoritarian regime and to bourgeois hegemony."[74]

But the most important reason was the opinion of Bolshevik Number One: Vladimir Lenin, who considered opera and ballet "a piece of purely big landowning culture."[75] Trying to save the Maryinsky Theater from the "present attempt to stifle it," Lunacharsky appealed to Lenin with a desperate letter ("Urgent and for him personally!"), in which, with some exaggeration, he pressed the case for opera and ballet as a necessary and useful entertainment for the proletarian masses: "Literally the entire laboring population of Petrograd treasures the Maryinsky Theater so much, since it has become an almost exclusively working-class theater, that its closing will be perceived by the workers as a heavy blow."[76]

The pragmatic Lenin was more impressed by Lunacharsky's argument that guarding the empty Maryinsky Theater would cost almost as much as maintaining the acting troupe. As a result, the state subsidy for the Maryinsky Theater, which had been cut to a minimum, was retained.

But the ideological storms surrounding the ballet did not quiet down. Ballet was rejected by many of Zheverzheyev's avant-garde friends. Tatlin proclaimed that the modern factory was the highest form of ballet. Mayakovsky sarcastically spoke of dancing "Elfs, Zwelfs, and syphilides." Yet Mayakovsky remained one of the young Balanchine's idols, and he became "a walking encyclopedia on Mayakovsky, quoting his pronouncements, and once met the author and was terribly proud of this acquaintance."[77]

Balanchine told me that he had seen the Petrograd production of *Mystery-Bouffe* in 1918. The play and particularly the scenery by Malevich had made a great impression on him, but he had not known then that one of the producers was Zheverzheyev. Balanchine recalled that Tamara Zheverzheyeva had introduced him to Mayakovsky. Balanchine explained to me in 1981 in New York,

> In those years I liked to recite Mayakovsky, because I was young and did not have much taste in poetry. Mayakovsky's poetry is made up of striking aphorisms. I thought that I could find the answers to all my questions in it. It was the poetry of adolescence. For instance, when I courted girls, I recited Mayakovsky's
>
> *If you want—*
> *I'll be irreproachably tender,*
> *not a man, but a cloud in trousers!*
>
> and that sometimes made the needed impression.[78]

Balanchine had no trouble when he was near eighty quoting Mayakovsky's narrative poem *A Cloud in Trousers*. His memory for poetry set him apart in his youth. At the ballet school, he was often recruited for performances in the Imperial Alexandrinsky Theater when a boy was needed in a small dramatic role. The actor Yuri Yuriev, in the classical comedy in verse *Woe from Wit,* by Alexander Griboedov—the story of a failed rebellion by a young Russian intellectual named Chatsky against the hypocrisy of his conservative milieu—made an indelible impression on Balanchine. To the end of his life Balanchine would declaim Chatsky's final monologue, which in Yuriev's presentation had elicited tears from young Georges, as he himself admitted in later years:

> *I flee, without looking back, I will seek*
> *A place in the world for injured feeling!*
> *My carriage, my carriage!*

Those romantic lines practically foretold Balanchine's future. His emotional reaction to their open melodrama lifts a window into the choreographer's soul that subsequently was shut forever.

Balanchine knew a lot of Pushkin by heart, particularly from *The Bronze Horseman.* For a true Petersburger, this was obligatory and served as a kind of password. In avant-garde circles, the equivalent was reciting Mayakovsky by heart. The artist Milashevsky recalled that he made the acquaintance of young Viktor Shklovsky in the summer of 1913, when he began reciting Mayakovsky aloud in the street and Shklovsky joined him.

Shklovsky was among the first to respond to *A Cloud in Trousers* when it was published in 1915: "In Mayakovsky's new mastery, the street, which had been deprived of art, has found its words, its form."[79] Even earlier, as a twenty-year-old student, Shklovsky, who looked like "a rosy-apple-cheeked boy who had leaped into Futurism straight from the nursery,"[80] read an aesthetically and politically radical lecture entitled "The Resurrection of the Word" at The Stray Dog. Shklovsky announced there that the avant-garde was saving culture, returning it to its face and soul: "We are removing filth from precious stones, we are awakening Sleeping Beauty." Shklovsky warned that Mayakovsky and other futurists, whom their contemporary audience considered at best harmless madmen, were actually "clairvoyants, who sense with their raw nerves the coming catastrophe."[81]

That was December 1913, getting onto three in the morning, and the Petersburg nouveaux riches who had come to The Stray Dog to view the fashionable avant-gardists did not quite understand which catastrophe he meant. But Shklovsky's persuasive powers were such that he forced "the large audience, half made up of 'tuxedos' or low-cut ladies to listen without a murmur."[82]

Shklovsky quickly became one of the leading figures of avant-garde Petersburg, taking part in the work of the Union of Youth and befriending Mayakovsky, Matiushin, Tatlin, and Zheverzheyev. A group of young linguists who had gathered around Shklovsky created in 1914 the Society for the Study of the Theory of Poetic Language, or Opayaz, the acronym of the Russian name. Shklovsky recalled, "And then we had the idea that poetic language differs from prose in general, that it was a special sphere in which even lip movements are important; as is the world of dance: when muscle movements give pleasure; as is painting: when vision gives pleasure."[83]

According to the young Shklovsky and his friends, art was the sum total of the devices (*priemy*) used in it. The "content" of art dissolved without a trace in its form. Therefore, the "content" of an author's work had no interest or significance for him. The "content" was merely an excuse for using whatever formal devices the author desired.

These views, first formulated by Shklovsky in a bombastic and categorical manner, unusual for a scholar, created some shock waves. The members of Opoyaz, among whom were the linguists Yevgeny Polivanov, Lev Yakubinsky, Yuri Tynyanov, and Boris Eikhenbaum, were dubbed "formalists." This militant group made some extraordinary theoretical discoveries. For instance, the formalists introduced the important distinction in the theory of narrative between *fabula* (story) and *suzhet* (plot). They used *fabula* for the chain of events described in the work; *suzhet* referred to the actual presentation of those events by the author. *Fabula* is "what actually happened," and *suzhet* is "how the reader learned about it."

Shklovsky wrote "How *Don Quixote* Is Made," and his close friend Eikhenbaum wrote "How *The Overcoat* Is Made" (punning on Gogol's famous Petersburg story). One of the characters in the tragedy *Vladimir Mayakovsky* is named Old Man with Dry Black Cats, who is several thousand years old. If you pet the cats, Mayakovsky used to say in his public lectures, you get electric sparks. Shklovsky later explained,

> The point of the cat was this: you can get electricity from a cat. That's what the Egyptians did. But it's more convenient to get electricity using a power station, rather than messing with cats. Traditional art,

we thought in those days, obtained artistic effects the way the Egyptians obtained electricity, while we wanted to get pure electricity, pure art.[84]

Shklovsky created his theoretical works in a completely unacademic setting. Born in Petersburg to a Jewish family he didn't even finish university because he volunteered for the army during World War I and was awarded the coveted St. George Cross for valor in battle. He took part in the overthrow of the tsar but did not support the Bolshevik revolution and even participated in an anti-Communist conspiracy. He was heavily wounded; while taking a shell apart to retrieve the precious explosive, the shell burst in his hands, peppering him with shrapnel. He recalled, "They couldn't remove the pieces, there were too many. They came out by themselves. You'd be walking along and your underwear would creak: that was a piece of shrapnel that came out. You could remove it with your finger."

Shklovsky was constantly generating ideas, which, in fact, came out of him like the pieces of shrapnel. It was he who invented the cultural term "*ostranenie*" (defamiliarization), which became fashionable worldwide. Our actions and perceptions, Shklovsky maintained, gradually become automatic: "Automation devours things, clothes, furniture, your wife, and the fear of war."[85] Art struggles against automatic perception, placing a usual thing in an unusual context, describing it from a different angle or as if the object or phenomenon had never been seen before. This concept was popularized by Bertolt Brecht and became famous as the "alienation effect."

Shklovsky described other devices the author uses: parallelism, contrast, retardation. The critic Prince Dmitri Sviatopolk-Mirsky (D. S. Mirsky) called Shklovsky "the father of almost all ideas by which contemporary aesthetics lives."[86] The ideas Shklovsky generously imparted and that first seemed too radical and lacking in scholarly respectability were quickly picked up and assimilated by the mainstream academic audience. By 1922 Mandelstam wrote that Shklovsky was "the most daring and talented literary critic of new Petersburg, coming to replace Chukovsky, a real literary battleship, all stormy flame, sharp philological wit, and literary temperament for a dozen."[87] Fewer than ten years later, Shklovsky would be forced to renounce formalism in print, to repent his literary "sins," and to denounce his "mistaken" ideas. But they would flourish in the West.

The similarity between Opoyaz and the Anglo-American New Criticism is striking. But the methodology of Russian formalism was widely used in later years not only in the theory of literature but in linguistics, history, semiotics, and anthropology. Eventually Shklovsky's categories of automation and alienation found application in the theory of computers.

Shklovsky died in December 1984, two months short of his ninety-second birthday. I visited him in his Moscow apartment in the winter of 1975–1976. He sat in his armchair, his shiny bald head, popularized by caricaturists, resembling a mushroom cap. Explaining why he had married a second time, Shklovsky joked, "My first wife told me I was a genius, my second that I was curly-haired." He let flow a cascade of brilliant monologues onto his captive listener on every imaginable topic, his favorite, apparently, the life and films of Sergei Eisenstein. Shklovsky spoke the way he wrote, in brief, choppy phrases connected by association—the speech of an incorrigible formalist.

He told me,

> Music is not my forte. But I like Shostakovich. I wrote about him. I even wrote about the ballet. There was a time when I went to the ballet, in Petrograd, in the early twenties. Everybody started going then, because it was no fun sitting around in cold, dark apartments, and it was light at the Maryinsky. I saw Mandelstam, and Akhmatova and Kuzmin there. Even Zoshchenko went to the ballet. Probably to meet ballerinas. The audience at the ballet in those years was rather fantastic. My neighbor, some soldier or sailor, would often ask, "And when are they going to start singing or declaiming?"

Shklovsky's article on ballet, printed in the journal *Petersburg* in 1922, is typical of his no-nonsense, aphoristic style.

> The Russian classical ballet is an abstract matter.
>   Its dances are not depicting a mood or illustrating something. Classical dance is not emotional.
>   This explains the pathetic and silly nature of the old ballet librettos.
>   They were barely needed. Classical *pas* and their combinations existed according to the inner laws of art.
>   Classical ballet is as abstract as music, the dancer's body does not determine the construction of a step so much as serve as one of the loveliest of abstractions in itself.[88]

Shklovsky transferred his idea of art as a sum of its own devices to ballet. The modern, sophisticated viewer brought up on Balanchine's choreography is unlikely to argue with Shklovsky's opinions. But at the time, his article was revolutionary, especially in Russia. Classical ballet was a formalized art to the highest degree. But it flourished—and this was the paradox—in Russia, where art traditionally was given an active social role. It was demanded that art be useful. And the dubious social usefulness of ballet was constantly being debated by many liberal critics. It was fashionable to attack ballet from the right and the left, and its very existence was questioned. The defenders of classical dance preferred to overlook its abstract tendencies and stressed ballet's "emotional content."

That is why Shklovsky's blunt article created such a stir in the Petrograd ballet world of 1922. It was perceived not without reason as a ballet "manifesto" of the formalists and the radical dancers and choreographers allied with them. Sixty years later in New York, Balanchine still recalled that article with great satisfaction. "I met with Shklovsky, talked to him, and had attended several of his lectures," Balanchine told me in 1982.

It was difficult listening to Shklovsky, because he kept getting side-tracked. But his article on ballet was another matter. It was written like a poem. And it seemed very important right away. I was young then and I wanted to be progressive. And who was I then? "Ballet boy," "dancer-prancer"—we were always called names. People didn't take us seriously. That's why I am so grateful to Zheverzheyev. He introduced me to all these modern things through the back door, so to speak. The front door was closed to people like me.

"Take Mayakovsky," Balanchine went on.

I adored him, but he didn't pay any attention to me. He didn't understand a thing about ballet. Zheverzheyev had exhibits in his living room on Saturdays, mostly from his own collection. I saw the works of many left artists, including Malevich. I liked the pictures, even though I didn't understand them completely. The artists came to Zheverzheyev's, had tea, talked. They mocked ballet: "it's funny," "no one needs it." You see, whenever I read that in the newspaper or a magazine, I got very upset. I was ashamed: why was I bothering with something so useless? But then I saw those people at Zheverzheyev's. And I thought, well, they may be geniuses, but they're not gods. They are still men. And they don't understand ballet. That's why I was so happy when I read Shklovsky's article in a magazine. Shklovsky was also a very progressive, very left person. But he wrote of the ballet with respect, not trying to kill it off. He explained why

ballet didn't need complicated plots. And why you could dance without "emotions." And it was written clearly and simply—not like the
muddled and verbose articles on ballet by Volynsky."[89]

Akim Volynsky (his real name was Chaim Flekser) was, with André
Levinson, the first truly professional ballet critic in Russia, and in the
opinion of some dance historians, in the world. Small and thin with
a yellow, wrinkled face and always wearing an old-fashioned black
suit coat, he was a Petrograd landmark. Volynsky could talk about
ballet for hours in grandiloquent passages. He wrote the same way
"in language combining an educational tract with a lover's muttering,
a laboratory analysis with a religious service," in the words of a sympathetic contemporary.[90]

In the spirit of the symbolists, Volynsky maintained that ballet must return to its source—religious ritual. Lopukhov reminisced
about him, not without irony:

> Starting with raptures in honor of Duncan and praise of the glory of
> Hellenism, he then moved over to the salon of Mathilda Kchessin-
> ska and began singing the praises of the most rigid classical ballet,
> discovering in it the same Hellenism. Now his adulation went to
> Kchessinska and his damnation to Fokine.

Balanchine, discussing Volynsky with me in New York in the early
1980s, was even more sarcastic (and unfair): "He loved ballet girls
and built a whole ballet theory around them: that the most important
element in ballet was eroticism and so on. He used to describe the big
thighs of his favorites."

Volynsky saw Fokine as the destroyer of classical ballet and
the assassin of ballet stars like Pavlova, Karsavina, Nijinsky. Volynsky never tired of repeating that Fokine's choreography was merely
an illustration of the music. That was the criticism from the right. But
in Petrograd of the twenties, Fokine was also attacked from the left,
because some young avant-gardists became enthralled with ballet, despite its "archaic" principles.

Balanchine told me that he met Shklovsky at the home of his
friend Yuri ("Tuka") Slonimsky. The apartment of Slonimsky, who
was two years older than Balanchine and a student at Petrograd University, was next to the ballet school, on the corner of Fontanka
River and Chernyshev Alley. In 1918 Balanchine started giving
Slonimsky private ballet lessons and soon became a virtual member

of the household, sometimes improvising at the piano for hours on end.

Slonimsky recalled that Balanchine "had the amazing ability to make you like him instantly."[91] He was, according to Slonimsky, one of the "desperadoes"—the term Yevgeny Mravinsky, then an extra at the Maryinsky Theater and later the conductor of the Leningrad Philharmonic Orchestra, used for his friends—wild Petrograd youths obsessed with art.

In 1919 two other desperadoes joined Slonimsky and Balanchine's crowd—Boris Erbstein and Vladimir Dmitriev, who were students of the respected modernist painter Kuzma Petrov-Vodkin at the Academy of Arts and had studied with Meyerhold. Dmitriev, the oldest in the group, soon became its leader. "That young man was not what you call handsome, but he was pleasant in a feminine way. A maiden's face with gentle contours. It was that Slavic type that was so highly valued at the slave markets of Baghdad—of course, in the era of Scheherazade and Sinbad the Sailor," was how the artist Milashevsky described Dmitriev, with some extravagance.[92] But Dmitriev's eyes were steely gray. He spoke little, in a low voice and curt phrases— and one sensed the weight and experience behind every word. It was Dmitriev who brought Stendhal's *De l'Amour* to his friends, recommending it as "the higher mathematics of love." According to Slonimsky, they made Stendahl's book their bedside reading, having discussed it from cover to cover and constantly checking it against "practice."

The friends also devoured Stefan Zweig's melodramatic novellas about love; their favorites were *Amok* and *Twenty-Four Hours in a Woman's Life*. Alas, the wild, romantic escapades were mostly imaginary; real-life circumstances were much more prosaic. When Balanchine and Slonimsky dared to take two young women from the graduating class of the ballet school to the theater to see the popular American play *Romance,* by Edward Sheldon, there was a scandal. The next day the school inspectress, known as "hateful Varvara," ruthlessly interrogated the young women in front of the rest of the school, accusing them of "depravity." Balanchine and Slonimsky were declared "seducers of young souls."[93]

Dmitriev, Slonimsky, Erbstein, and Balanchine spent almost all their free time together attending the theater, exhibitions, lectures, and all kinds of cultural disputations. Dmitriev commented on everything. He could address Meyerhold as an equal as well as Kuzmin, and the artist Golovin, who was a mentor. Dmitriev spoke proudly of a meeting with Blok, to whom Meyerhold himself had introduced him. Blok, of course, was an idol of Dmitriev's. Slonimsky recalled how the friends had gone to one of Blok's final appearances in Petrograd, and on the day of his funeral had been present when the body was brought out of the church. They also walked part of the way to the cemetery.

Dmitriev was an inveterate Petersburger. He could lead his friends around the city for hours, reciting from Gogol's *Petersburg Tales* or Dostoyevsky's novels. Dmitriev frequently recalled *The Queen of Spades*—both Pushkin's and Tchaikovsky's. Later, the scenic design for the opera was perhaps Dmitriev's best work. I remember virtually shuddering when the curtain rose in the Bolshoi Theater, where *The Queen of Spades* was performed with Dmitriev's design until the early 1970s, and saw the gloomy grandeur of a deserted Palace Embankment on a snowy Petersburg night. It was a visual symphony of black, dark blue, white, and gold—an unforgettable landscape by a great master, creating a Dostoyevskian atmosphere subtly enhancing the tragic music.

The year 1922 was the hundredth anniversary of E. T. A. Hoffmann's death. In Dmitriev's circle the phrase "Petersburg Hoffmanniade" became popular once again, signifying the phantasmagorical aspects of the city's mythos, which was so fascinating for these young people. The friends found that eccentric Hoffmann touch in Tchaikovsky's *Nutcracker* and in Meyerhold's staging of *Masquerade*. Dmitriev used to bring up Bely's novel, *Petersburg*. And then, as if to counter the complicated symbolism of that work, he would recite the precise, severe poems of Akhmatova about Petersburg.

But the main topic of conversation by members of Dmitriev's group was, of course, ballet in all its aspects. They discussed the stars of the Maryinsky Theater; they spoke most of the ballerina Olga Spessivtseva, with whom Dmitriev was madly in love. She died near New York City in 1991 at the age of ninety-six, and was hailed as perhaps the greatest Giselle in the world. Spessivtseva was a legendary figure in Petersburg in the 1920s. "I saw O. A. Spessivtseva in the box and I was stunned. Do you know who she reminded me of? A heroine out of Maupassant," wrote young Shostakovich to his friend the composer and future critic Valerian Bogdanov-Berezovsky.

In 1970 in Leningrad, Bogdanov-Berezovsky, who had become my mentor, recalled,

> Shostakovich, naturally, was in love with Spessivtseva. So was I, and how! Sometimes I thought that all Petrograd was in love with her.

How can I describe her? An astonishingly lovely face, dark hair, big sad eyes. It was the Akhmatova type. Who knows, that may be why Spessivtseva was so incredibly mysterious and attractive. Akhmatova herself was crazy about her. Spessivtseva danced tragic roles, making them even more so, extremely tragic. Even recalling that is torment. She was taciturn, and wore an all-concealing black dress, like a nun. All of that also reminded you of a heroine of Akhmatova's poetry.[94]

Slonimsky maintained that Spessivtseva, who was not very impressed by innovation in ballet, made an exception only for Balanchine. Alexandra Danilova, in a conversation with me, recalled Balanchine's relations with Spessivtseva with slight jealousy:

George adored her. Spessivtseva was a goddess: a marvelous figure, marvelous legs. But she was eccentric. George did *La Chatte* for her at Diaghilev's. The music by Henri Sauguet was rather simple—not like Stravinsky. But Spessivtseva was very unmusical, so even that simple music, you had to count out for her backstage, and then push her on stage and pray that she hit the beat. I remember Balanchine went to Paris to do a ballet for Spessivtseva. That was in 1929. He got sick and Lifar finished the ballet. And ten years later Spessivtseva left the stage and spent twenty years in a mental hospital. That was a tragic fate, almost like Giselle's.[95]

The Dmitriev group hotly debated Fokine's ballets. Dmitriev himself defended them fiercely; Balanchine and Slonimsky were more critical. They were thrilled by the plotless *Chopiniana* but were rather skeptical of *Petrouchka*. Slonimsky even insisted that Fokine's *Petrouchka* was not ballet at all but a brilliant pantomime. The friends also rejected *Eros*, Fokine's ballet to Tchaikovsky's *Serenade for Strings*. One of the impulses that led Balanchine to create his signature ballet *Serenade* in 1934 to the same music was his desire "to cleanse" Tchaikovsky's work from Fokine's interpretation.[96]

Isadora Duncan's tours of Petrograd added fuel to the debate on the direction ballet should take. A passionate supporter of the Bolsheviks in those days, Duncan settled in Soviet Russia and often performed to the music of revolutionary songs and the "Internationale," wearing a red tunic and waving a red banner. In a dance to the music of the *Slavonic March*, according to a rave Soviet review, she depicted the "thorny path of the Russian working class, oppressed by the tsarist boot, and eventually tearing off its chains."[97] Balanchine was furious.

Danilova told me that he had said scornfully of Duncan, "She dances like a pig."[98]

Shklovsky, egged on by Dmitriev and his friends, wrote haughtily, "We hail Duncan from the high shore of classical ballet." That poisonous phrase became popular in ballet circles in Petrograd and was repeated almost like a password. When in 1927 Duncan died in a car accident, Shostakovich's closest friend and a pal of Balanchine's Petrograd days, the critic Ivan Sollertinsky, summarized the attitude toward the dancer this way: "Duncan danced only herself. Her dancing was a curious combination of morality and gymnastics. She did not have a free mastery of her 'liberated' body. Her movements were monotonous and schematic: leap, bent-knee position, run with arms held high."[99]

The experiments in free dance by the Muscovite Kasyan Goleizovsky, who brought his Chamber Ballet to tour Petrograd in the fall of 1922, made a much more serious impression on Balanchine. He presented vivid, highly erotic miniatures, performed by almost naked dancers, and some critics, accusing Goleizovsky of attempting to shock the public, wrote in irritation about "constant embraces with legs." Goleizovsky used sophisticated music for his numbers—Prokofiev, Scriabin, Nikolai Medtner. Balanchine's friends recalled that at first he was practically delirious about Goleizovsky and went to the hotel where the Moscow guests were staying to express his praise. Goleizovsky liked Balanchine. At one time Goleizovsky planned to move his Chamber Ballet permanently to Petrograd, away from the Moscow authorities, and have Balanchine teach a special class in "choreographic improvisation."

But from Balanchine's friend Slonimsky we know that the Dmitriev group gradually grew disenchanted with Goleizovsky. Another comparatively brief surge of interest came for the dance experiments of two other Muscovites—Lev Lukin (who, like Goleizovsky, choreographed erotic numbers to avant-garde music like Prokofiev's "Sarcasms") and Nikolai Foregger. Resembling the film actor Harold Lloyd in his horn-rimmed glasses, the tranquil and elegant Foregger gained fame as a creator of "mechanical dances," or "dances of machines," in which the performers imitated the work of complex, fantastic mechanisms. The lasting impressions from Foregger's productions undoubtedly were reflected later in Balanchine's *Prodigal Son*, with music by Prokofiev, which was premiered by the Diaghilev company in Paris in 1929.

(Top) A group portrait of *Mir iskusstva* (World of Art) by one of its members, Boris Kustodiev. This dynamic collective changed the course of Petersburg arts and crafts, but many of its members ended in exile after the Bolsheviks came to power in 1917.

(Above left) Alexander Benois, guiding spirit of *Mir iskusstva*, became one of the most influential makers of the Petersburg mythos at the turn of the century. Portrait by Leon Bakst, 1898.

(Above right) The organizational genius and impeccable taste of Sergei Diaghilev brought Petersburg art, music, and ballet into the world arena. Portrait by Valentin Serov, 1908.

(Top left) Michel Fokine, who choreographed the first plotless ballet, *Les Sylphides*, died in exile in New York in 1942.

(Top right) Igor Stravinsky, for whom St. Petersburg was dearer "than any other city in the world," helped create, along with Vladimir Nabokov and George Balanchine, a powerful new vision of Petersburg in the West. Portrait, 1933, by Vassily Shukhaev, an émigré who returned to Leningrad and spent ten years in Stalin's labor camps.

(Top left) Nikolai Rimsky-Korsakov, founding father of the highly influential school of composition to which Stravinsky, Prokofiev, and Shostakovich—three of the most popular composers of the twentieth century—belonged.

(Top right) Sergei Prokofiev's music ranged from neoclassicist to futuristic, reflecting the vitality of the artistic scene in prerevolutionary Petrograd. Portrait by Alexander Benois.

(Right) During Alexander Glazunov's tenure as director of the St. Petersburg Conservatory, that institute produced some of the greatest performers of the century. Photo of Glazunov with youthful violinist Nathan Milstein, 1923.

(Opposite bottom) Petrouchka, a collaborative effort by Stravinsky, Benois, and Fokine, was the first work to offer the Western audience an idealized image of Petersburg. This is Benois' sketch for the 1911 Paris premiere.

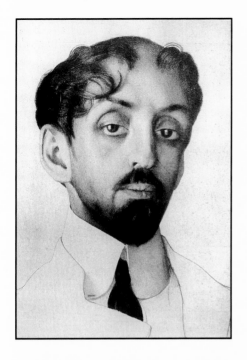

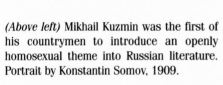

(Above left) Mikhail Kuzmin was the first of his countrymen to introduce an openly homosexual theme into Russian literature. Portrait by Konstantin Somov, 1909.

(Above right) Matilda Kchessinska, notorious star of the Imperial Ballet and mistress of Nicholas II when he was heir to the throne, was proof of the success to which a woman artist from the demi-monde could aspire in St. Petersburg.

(Right) Alexander Blok, the most famous Petersburg poet of his time: "In those days there wasn't a single 'thinking' young woman in Russia who wasn't in love with Blok."

(Opposite top) In her poetry and her person Anna Akhmatova came to symbolize the endurance of the city on the Neva, and she was its courageous voice. Portrait by Nathan Altman, 1914.

(Opposite bottom) Akhmatova with her first husband, poet Nikolai Gumilyov, and their son, Lev: all three were destined to be swept up in the city's tragic fate. Photo,1916.

(Top) Seeing off futurist Benedikt Livshits to war in 1914 after the city was renamed Petrograd. From left: poet Osip Mandelstam, critic Kornei Chukovsky, Livshits, artist Yuri Annenkov. Only Chukovsky lived to an old age in Russia; Annenkov fled to Paris, and Mandelstam and Livshits perished in the years of Stalin's Great Terror.

(Bottom) At the futurist exhibition in Petrograd of 1915, *Black Square* by Casimir Malevich is seen hung high up at the corner of the gallery, the position traditionally reserved for sacred icons. It did, in fact, become the icon of abstract art.

(Above) Revolution in Petrograd, 1917: the rubble consists of burned police files.

(Left) Vladimir Lenin moved the capital of the country from Petrograd back to Moscow in 1918. He disliked the city intensely, but, ironically, after his death in 1924 it was renamed Leningrad in his honor. Portrait drawn from life by Nathan Altman, 1920.

(Top) Propaganda porcelain: exquisite dishes in a hungry city. Tray, 1921, by Sergei Chekhonin, who died in exile in 1936.

(Bottom) Propaganda poster, 1920, by Vladimir Lebedev: Petrograd's revolutionary artists attempted to reinvent the role of art in the city's life.

But Balanchine soon had a new idol—the Petrograd choreographer Fyodor Lopukhov. Slonimsky wrote,

> The revolution brought Lopukhov out of anonymity. If not for the revolution, Lopukhov would have perished in the stifling atmosphere and stagnation of the imperial theater of the early twentieth century.[100]

In 1922, when it became clear that Fokine, who had emigrated to the West, would not return to the Maryinsky Theater, Lopukhov became the artistic director of the ballet troupe. An enthusiast and dreamer always in pursuit of one idea or another, Lopukhov tried to involve the whole company in his bold experiments:

> In the evenings, at the theater, he got into fierce arguments with young people in the artists' box or sat backstage on a stepladder like a huddled, skinny bird, and reacted violently to what was happening: approving some, encouraging others, ruthlessly criticizing those who made even trifling mistakes.[101]

Lopukhov, whose sister, Lydia, was a star in the Diaghilev ballet and married the famous economist Lord Keynes, was a quintessential Petersburg avant-gardist, that is, the desire "to change everything" coexisted within him with a profound respect for the old masters, especially Petipa, whom Lopukhov adored. Lopukhov began his career as head of the Maryinsky ballet with a revival of the Petipa-Tchaikovsky *Sleeping Beauty*, and the following year he revived *The Nutcracker*. He introduced some changes in both productions, and the debates about the suitability of those changes polarized Petrograd's ballet world.

Balanchine naturally sided with Lopukhov. Besides, even the head of *Mir iskusstva*, Benois, wrote an article called "Piety or Sacrilege," reflecting the heat of the debate, in which he announced that the old ballets must not be treated like "embalmed remains." Benois, a passionate fan of *Sleeping Beauty*, had been rather pleased: Lopukhov's pastiches were so close to the original that to this day some of them (for instance, the Lilac Fairy's variations) are performed throughout the world as the work of Petipa himself.

Volynsky, who plotted in vain to have Lopukhov dismissed from his position in order to take his place, responded to Lopukhov's revisions of Petipa's ballets with a vitriolic article entitled "Lousy House Painter," referring to Pushkin's famous lines:

> It's not funny, when a lousy house painter
> Ruins Raphael's Madonna for me.

Volynsky spewed forth even greater invective over Lopukhov's *Grandeur of the Universe*, to the music of Beethoven's Fourth Symphony—a unique attempt at a new ballet genre, which the choreographer called *tantssimfonia* (dance symphony). Lopukhov's idea, which he had started to work on in 1916, was that the leading elements of ballet should be the classic dance in its most intricate and complex form, based on great symphonic music without resorting to what Lopukhov considered distracting literary plots, elaborate scenery, and sumptuous costumes. Balanchine later introduced similar asceticism in his New York productions.

Lopukhov began rehearsing his *tantssimfonia* in the summer of 1922 with a group of young enthusiasts that included Balanchine, Danilova, and Pyotr Gusev. His production brought out, to the music of Beethoven's opening adagio, eight young men bathed in blue light, who slowly walked past the viewers, one hand covering their eyes, the other extended forward. A chain of eight young women followed the men. Lopukhov explained that this symbolized "The Birth of Light." Then came "The Birth of the Sun." Later in *tantssimfonia* Lopukhov commented on the idea of evolution with rather abstract dance patterns of the "Pithecanthropuses," "Butterflies," and "Birds." *The Grandeur of the Universe* ended with "Perpetuum Mobile," in which all the participants, now in red light, formed a spiral symbolizing the universe.

Lopukhov did not try to use dance to illustrate literary concepts. He was inspired primarily by Beethoven's music and followed the unfolding of the large symphonic canvas, creating parallels and counterpoint to it through bold, abstract movements. Balanchine used some of Lopukhov's innovative ideas in his first American ballet, *Serenade*, which eventually won immense popularity.

Tantssimfonia had a different fate. It was shown only twice—first in September 1922 in the rehearsal hall of the Maryinsky Theater for specially invited colleagues and friends and then on March 7, 1923, at a benefit for the corps de ballet, after *Swan Lake*. Besieged by doubts, Lopukhov wrote in the margins of his libretto, "Won't there be even one person who understands me?"

He could have found the answer to this bitter question at rehearsal, where Balanchine, enthralled by the avant-garde concepts of his mentor, enthusiastically explained to the worried dancers how best to realize the choreographer's innovations. One of the participants in *tantssimfonia* recalled, "All the rehearsal work, all the finishing and detailing was done by the performers. Lopukhov would come and just sit there happily, observing the embodiment of his dream ... he burned, glowed, and was as pleased by every successful trifle as a child."[102]

Dmitriev's group came to the closed viewing of *The Grandeur of the Universe*, in which Balanchine had taken such an active part, in full complement and supported Lopukhov vociferously. At the ensuing discussion, Petrograd's leading avant-garde critics, Asafyev and Sollertinsky, both recognized the immense importance of *tantssimfonia*. But at the performance for the regular audience of the Maryinsky Theater, the reaction was just the opposite: "Instead of the usual roar of applause, there was deathly silence. The audience did not applaud, or laugh, or boo—it was silent."[103] Lopukhov's political enemies took advantage of this failure, and *The Grandeur of the Universe* vanished from the repertoire.

Sollertinsky tried to excuse the lack of success of *Universe* with the mass audience as follows: "The form seemed too abstract and scholarly; the added-on murky metaphysics with cosmic circles and world hierarchy completely mixed up the viewers."[104] Sollertinsky insisted that compared with the experimentation of Fokine, Lopukhov's work had made an important step forward:

> As opposed to the intuitive Fokine, Lopukhov is a rationalist to his bone marrow. Starting off with a music score, Fokine was inspired by its pathos and emotional flight. Lopukhov, on the contrary, takes it apart to the smallest units, and carefully invents appropriate primary choreographic movements for them.[105]

This could just as well be an analysis of Balanchine's future productions in New York.

To explain the lasting influence of *The Grandeur of the Universe* on Balanchine's work, it is important to understand that Lopukhov, as opposed to Goleizovsky, continued to use classical dance. In the work of Lopukhov, even when he was introducing heretofore unheard-of acrobatic tricks into ballet, the general silhouette of the dance remained Petersburgian: severe, finished, elegant.

That is why some Russian dance historians consider Lopukhov's *Grandeur of the Universe* the first neoclassical production in ballet theater.

In review of the post-premiere discussion of the *tantssimfonia*, the author's speech was summarized: "Lopukhov believes that this idea will not die."[106] That faith was not unwarranted; Yuri Slonimsky, the Dmitriev's group leading theoretician, later recalled, "The *tantssimfonia* became the main stimulus in the life of the younger generation, and personally in Balanchivadze's. Other Lopukhov productions too. The revival of the complete *Sleeping Beauty*, too."[107] But it was a long way to that belated admission, and when it came, Lopukhov was merely a shadow of his idealistic, energetic, and prophetic young self.

The persecution began right after the premiere of the *tantssimfonia*. The attack was headed, alas, by Volynsky, who began his devastating review of *The Grandeur of the Universe* this way: "Once a promising staff scribbler dreamed of the grandeur of the universe," and so on in that mocking tone. Furious, Balanchine retaliated with a review of the graduating concert of a private ballet school headed by Volynsky. In the fashion of the times, Balanchine used a literary allusion in his title, filled with heavy irony: "The junior officer's widow, or How A. L. Volynsky whips himself" (a reference to a character in Gogol's comedy *The Inspector General*). Balanchine was no less sarcastic than his foe Volynsky; he described the students of the school as "provincially saccharine shop clerks with pretensions to solo roles."

Balanchine did not spare Volynsky's school: "It lacks the basic rules of classicism. . . . It all creates a depressing impression." And as a final observation of the school's effort, "It is left with nothing but a broken trough," another literary reference, this time to Pushkin's popular fairy tale.[108]

Teatr, the magazine in which Balanchine's lampoon appeared, featured the attack and printed the artist's photograph on the cover: Balanchine, in heavy makeup like some decadent Pierrot, stared piercingly as if playing the role of a libertine, cynic, and skeptic.

The same magazine later published a playful satire on Volynsky entitled "The Demise of Theaters. Horrible Events in Ballet." It described the fantastic "nightmarish tragedy" of the Maryinsky Theater, when Volynsky was allegedly confirmed as its director (the ballet world in Petrograd knew that this was his dream). Volynsky the director decided on a ballet performance and then asked Volynsky the writer to lecture the audience before the start of the show and invited Volynsky the critic to read his review at the end of the performance right from the stage. This led to a tragic end, according to the satire: listening to Volynsky's endless presentation, "one of the audience died . . . and dying, whispered, 'Too much water!' " (In Russian, "water" in a speech or lecture is like water in a ham—unnecessary filler.) Soon afterward, the rest of the audience followed suit and died, the magazine reported in mock horror.[109]

The satire on Volynsky was not signed, but ballet connoisseurs knew that it was written by Grigory Kozintsev and Leonid Trauberg, the already notorious leaders of the Factory of the Eccentric Actor (FEKS). It was an avant-garde theater studio, but the word "studio" seemed hopelessly old-fashioned to its creators, who replaced it with "factory." In the anthology *Ekstsentrizm* (*Eccentricity*), published as the cover announced in the city of "Eccentropolis (formerly Petrograd)," Kozintsev proclaimed the "Americanization of the theater":

> *Life demands art that is hyperbolically crude*
> *overwhelming, grating on the nerves,*
> *openly utilitarian, mechanically precise,*
> *instantaneous, fast,*
> *otherwise they will not hear, see, or stop.*

Further, Kozintsev defiantly listed the "parents" of FEKS:

> In a word—the chansonette, Pinkerton, an auctioneer's cry, street brawls.
>> In painting—the circus poster, the cover of a trashy novel.
>> In music—the jazz band (a Negro makeshift orchestra), the circus march.
>> In ballet—American dance music.
>> In theater—the music hall, the movies, circus, dance café, and boxing.

On September 25, 1922, FEKS performed *The Marriage* ("Not after Gogol") to a stunned Petrograd audience; the poster had promised operetta, melodrama, farce, film, circus, variety, and grand guignol all in one. The whole thing was called "A Trick in Three Acts," and Kozintsev and Trauberg were its "engineers," rejecting the antediluvian term "director." The characters in this amazing *Marriage* were Albert Einstein, Charlie Chaplin, and three suitors who came on stage on roller skates: robots running on steam, electricity, and radioactivity. The latter explained, "Marriage today is ridiculous. The husband goes away, the wife suffers. Radium, a new force, works at a distance. A radioactive marriage is truly modern."

The outraged public, suspecting it was being mocked, went wild. Kozintsev came out on stage and thanked the shouting patrons "for a scandalous reception of our scandalous work." The action of *The Marriage* was a cascade of acrobatic tricks, satirical couplets, tap dancing, fox trot music, and sound-and-light effects. The performers had to be specially trained, because no one in Russia knew how to do all these things. The Factory of the Eccentric Actor prepared them in a marvelous old town house whose owner had fled to the West. Here seventeen-year-old Kozintsev and twenty-year-old Trauberg and their acolytes lived according to the motto borrowed from Mark Twain, "It's better to be a young pup than an old bird of paradise." Leading Petrograd avant-gardists were announced as teachers: Punin, Annenkov, Evreinov, and Lourié. But in fact they did not take part in the studio's work.

One of the reasons could have been the excessive cockiness of the inventors of eccentricity. This is a description by Sergei Yutkevich, a leader of the early FEKS, of a visit to Annenkov, who was already a famous avant-garde artist and director, in a letter to Eisenstein from Petrograd:

> Yuri Annenkov, a fine fellow, joined eccentricity, and our respect for him grew when he came to see us in striped pajamas (black and orange), in which he previously appeared in the circus, riding on the back of a donkey. Besides which, he can do handstands, tap dance, and draw smutty pictures. But that doesn't matter! He wanted to get in on an exhibit of eccentric posters and we said: well, well, where were you before?[110]

But Kozintsev and Trauberg did invite Balanchine to teach dancing and acrobatics. Later one of the participants in FEKS, the talented actress Elena Kuzmina, recalled him as one of her favorite teachers. Other classes at FEKS included boxing, fencing, horseback riding, and "cinema gestures." FEKS's experimentation resembled (in some cases outstripped) the attempts by Meyerhold and the early Eisenstein. In a huge hall with marble figures in niches along the walls reflecting in a multitude of mirrors, students dressed in "feksosuits"—white shirts and black overalls with big breast pockets and wide shoulder straps—

boxed, tumbled, and danced the foxtrot to piano accompaniment. Balanchine felt right at home.

Kozintsev declared in the FEKS manifesto: "The double soles of an American dancer are dearer to us than five hundred instruments of the Maryinsky Theater." But for all that, Kozintsev and Trauberg were habitués of the Maryinsky. They were great fans of Lopukhov's productions, including his revivals of the Tchaikovsky ballets, and they pressed Balanchine for the subtleties of classical dance. Balanchine, in his turn, shared the FEKS love of American movies.

It was then that Balanchine developed his taste for Westerns and American comedies with madcap chases. Even earlier, in the winter of 1920–1921, he was stunned by Griffiths's film *Intolerance*, to which their progressive director, Andrei Oblakov, took the students of the ballet school. Long after the show, the young people continued to reenact scenes from the film. Balanchine would pretend to be King Balthasar and his partner, Lydia Ivanova, was "the girl from the mountains."

At FEKS Balanchine learned as he trained the young artists; he became more casual, daring, and eccentric. There, he was assured that the love of supposedly "low" entertainment—music hall, circus, movies, and jazz—was not a sign of poor taste or aesthetic "backwardness." On the contrary—that was the real avant-garde of the most audacious and potentially the most fruitful kind. The "Americanization" of Balanchine started at full speed at FEKS, long before he arrived in New York City.

Balanchine's life, like that of Petrograd and all of Russia, changed sharply in the spring of 1921. After several years of total state control, Lenin—sobered by the explosion of anger and dissatisfaction in the country—decided to loosen the reins somewhat. He had been particularly shocked that when in March 1921 the sailors at Fort Kronstadt, not far from Petrograd, rose against the Bolsheviks, many people in the city supported them.

Petrograd was threatening to become the center of a new, anti-Bolshevik revolution. Lenin worried that a rebellion in that unpredictable city could once again change the fate of all Russia, so he decided to act first. On his orders, the Kronstadt uprising was cruelly suppressed, and then, using the carrot after the stick, he announced significant economic liberalization, which he called the New Economic Policy (NEP).

Retreating from his rigorous Communist ideals, Lenin once

again allowed the existence of small private businesses. The effect of that decision was astonishing. Most food and fuel shortages evaporated. Many stores appeared, cafés and restaurants opened where, for the first time in almost four years, one could order a bottle of wine and have some pastry.

Numerous new private theaters, cabarets, and variety shows flung open their doors. Multicolored advertising reappeared on gray building walls. Currency speculators on Nevsky Prospect were selling dollars, pounds, and marks. There was something febrile in life under the NEP. Everyone sensed that this breathing spell could not last long, so people tried to get as much as possible out of it.

With their wives wrapped in expensive furs, the newly rich filled the casinos, restaurants, dance halls, and movie theaters springing up in the new environment. To amuse their clientele, the owners of these establishments needed floor shows—preferably with dancing, definitely made up of short numbers, and most certainly with an erotic motif.

One of the popular producers of this sort of entertainment in Petrograd under the NEP was Balanchine, who began choreographing short numbers for his friends while still in ballet school. As a dancer Balanchine was considered good but no one raved about him; some of his peers were much more popular with audiences. But as a choreographer, he gained a reputation very quickly.

Balanchine felt that his first successful attempt was a piece to the art song "Night," by Anton Rubinstein. This work already showed traits that would be present in Balanchine's later productions: no plot, quasi-classical steps, and eroticism.

As Danilova recalled, "At the end of the piece the young man lifted the girl in an arabesque and carried her offstage. Today that is the usual thing, but then it was shocking. The impression was that the girl had given herself to her partner without a word." The inspectress, "hateful Varvara," cried in shock, "It is amoral!"[111] But the students of the Petrograd ballet school, at whose graduation concert in 1920 "Night" first saw the light of day, were delighted. The number quickly became popular.

Another production by Balanchine that appeared on many Petrograd stages was "Valse triste" to the music of Sibelius, which Balanchine did for Lydia Ivanova. She appeared before the audience as if fleeing some evil pursuer, perhaps Death itself. Like a blind woman or a somnambulist she moved toward the edge of the stage, and just as the spellbound public expected her to fall into the orchestra pit, she turned abruptly and froze with her back to the audience.

In the finale of "Valse triste," Balanchine boldly used an expressionist device reminiscent of the works of Edvard Munch but undoubtedly reflecting the influence of silent movies: emoting horror, Ivanova opened her mouth in imitation of a cry for help, without uttering a sound. The effect was extraordinary. The number was repeatedly staged in Russia after Balanchine left for the West, but without his name; it became public property. He later revisited and developed the motif of somnambulism in his ballet *La Somnambula*.

The young Balanchine's reputation was also based on the respect his musicianship elicited. They knew at the Maryinsky Theater that even Marius Petipa had never learned to read a musical score. As Lopukhov recalled, the ballet school usually graduated "poorly educated people, even though they knew how to wear a ballet costume and conscientiously perform their dance parts."[112]

Of course, Michel Fokine played the mandolin well, and Lopukhov was known as an excellent guitarist. But Balanchine, with his broad musical education, had moved far beyond that. Even in the ballet school he had amazed his peers with his piano improvisations. He had also organized an amateur orchestra for which he arranged music using some very eccentric "instruments": pots and pans, jars, tubs, and combs. As a friend of those years, Pyotr Gusev, recalled, in the finale of the overture to *Carmen* (orchestrated for combs), when the fate theme sounded, some of the performers fell as if dead at the first chord and the others followed suit on the second. It was a clever idea, and the public always reacted with enthusiasm to this amusing trick.

In 1919, while still a student at the ballet school, Balanchine decided to enter the Petrograd Conservatory. With the encouragement of the director, the composer and author of the ballet *Raymonda*, Alexander Glazunov, he was accepted in the piano class of Sofia Zurmüllen, who had been brought to the conservatory by Rubinstein.

The sixty-three-year-old Zurmüllen had reason to be pleased with her student: Balanchine quickly learned quite difficult works, soon playing Beethoven sonatas and Chopin études. In those years Balanchine enjoyed improvising at the piano and also composed a lot, primarily piano pieces in the style of Rachmaninoff and Scriabin, as well as art songs.

Balanchine wrote an art song to the poetry of Yevgeny Mravinsky, later a celebrated conductor and the first interpreter of many of Shostakovich's symphonies but at the time an extra at the Maryinsky Theater and a pianist at the ballet school. In 1982 Balanchine recalled wryly, "I wasn't very knowledgeable about poetry then, and I thought, well, he seems sensible, a poet. So why shouldn't I write music to his poem? And so I did."[113] Balanchine set great store by Mravinsky's interpretation (with his orchestra, the Leningrad Philharmonic) of Tchaikovsky's symphonies. Mravinsky's recordings of the symphonies were kept in a conspicuous place in Balanchine's office at the New York City Ballet.

Balanchine even showed his compositions to Leonid Niko-layev, a respected composer in Petrograd who was famous as a professor of piano at the Petrograd Conservatory. His students included three rising stars—Vladimir Sofronitsky, Maria Yudina, and Dmitri Shostakovich. Later in life Balanchine felt little love for Shostakovich, finding his work esthetically alien. But Shostakovich admired Balanchine in his Petrograd years both as a choreographer and as a dancer.

There is curious documentary proof of the latter. Young Shostakovich and his best friend of those years, Bogdanov-Berezovsky, carried on a lively correspondence in the early 1920s, even though both lived in Petrograd. When Bogdanov-Berezovsky died in 1971, over one hundred of Shostakovich's letters from his collection were returned to the composer. The letters, as Bogdanov-Berezovsky himself once told me, were priceless: the sixteen-year-old Shostakovich unabashedly shared his impressions of books he had read, plays he had seen, and concerts he had attended. After he got the letters back, Shostakovich destroyed them. When I later asked him why, he looked away and, drumming on the table with the fingers of his right hand, replied laconically, "Too many four-letter words, you see. Youth!"

But in his lifetime, Bogdanov-Berezovsky managed to have published a few fragments from those letters. One was even reproduced in facsimile in one of Bogdanov-Berezovsky's books. In this miraculously preserved fragment (extraordinary in its open, joyful pleasure that vanished almost completely in the later Shostakovich), the composer lists the stars of the Petrograd ballet he liked: "My dear, why is so much in this world so good? Long live our Ballet!!! Long live M. A. Kozhukhova, Gerdt, Danilova, Ivanova, G. Bolshakova, Dudko, Balanchivadze, Ponomarev, Chekrygin, Leontiev, Khristapson, and many other glories, hurra-a-ay!!!"[114]

Dmitriev's group was fascinated by ballet; they argued about it and dreamed of new paths ballet might take. But the only ballet professional in the circle was Balanchine. Moreover, he was the only professional musician. This explains why Dmitriev asked Balanchine to head a small group of young dancers for ballet experimentation.

About fifteen people showed up for the first meeting of the future ensemble. One participant later recalled, "We united to try to use our common efforts (as we so proudly put it) to push our art from its dead spot. Of course, the only justification for our daring was our youth."[115] And so they called the new dance group the "Young Ballet." It is unlikely it would be remembered today if its chief choreographer had not been Balanchine, all of nineteen years old.

Dmitriev had made the right choice, becoming the first "impresario" to trust Balanchine. Others followed, including Diaghilev and Lincoln Kirstein. Balanchine was always "selected" to lead companies. He never forced himself, not knowing how nor caring to insist on his superiority. Either that superiority was recognized or the choreographer walked away.

In choosing Balanchine to lead the Young Ballet, Dmitriev had several considerations in mind. Being part of the world of theater and art, Dmitriev proudly recalled, "Meyerhold considered me an adopted son . . . and was jealous of everyone."[116] The twenty-three-year-old artist, a snob at heart, was impressed that Balanchine's father-in-law was the famous patron of the arts and influential collector Zheverzheyev, who was respected by Meyerhold, Mayakovsky, and Dmitriev's teacher at the Academy of Arts, Kuzma Petrov-Vodkin. Dmitriev believed that being related to Zheverzheyev gave Balanchine an entrée to the artistic elite of Petrograd.

Moreover, Dmitriev adored eccentricity. He styled himself a "Petersburg eccentric." His best friend, the theater designer Boris Erbstein, had walked on all fours along the Nevsky Prospect on a dare, to shock the "NEPman shits." Dmitriev considered Zheverzheyev to be a Petersburg eccentric, too. Balanchine basked in the reflection of his father-in-law's eccentricity. The fact that Balanchine was a clothes horse was important, too. His white summer trousers were the envy of all his friends. In short, he was a "personality": Dmitriev's highest category.

Balanchine was the ideal leader for the Young Ballet not only because of his choreographic gifts; he also knew how to use his talent to help his troupe. Before the NEP theaters did not have to worry about the box office because they were fully subsidized by the state and tickets were handed out free of charge in factories, offices, and military units. Thus Petrograd theaters usually played to full houses.

The reactions of the new public were often unexpected. Sailors and soldiers laughed loudly when Othello killed Desdemona. Ballet audiences stamped their feet and whistled when they got bored. "Today's audience is much more expansive than the old one," was the cautious assessment of the leader of the Maryinsky Theater's ballet company in 1918 to a newspaper reporter.

This changed abruptly with the start of the NEP. The state cut back subsidies even to such established theaters as the Maryinsky. Theaters were forced to raise prices and the audiences diminished. The situation was even worse for many private enterprises. They fought for their lives to draw audiences. The experimental "People's Comedy" run by Sergei Radlov, addressed to a proletarian audience, was forced to shut down under the new conditions. For Balanchine, who had often attended Radlov's plays at the Iron Hall of the People's House, this catastrophe was a harsh lesson.

Balanchine explained to me in New York,

> The Iron Hall was called that because its two levels were made of iron constructions. The lacework railings of the balconies were also iron. Radlov's audiences were the simplest people, among them many street urchins. They also had opera at the People's House, the audience was a bit better there. But the opera itself was rather bad. They had no money. I remember they had to do the Polovtsian dances in *Prince Igor*. They could afford only two dancers, and they invited me and my friend to dance. I accepted, I accepted everything then. The two of us quite successfully presented the Polovtsian masses.[117]

His unpretentiousness and flexibility as both dancer and choreographer made Balanchine the ideal leader for a small ballet ensemble during the NEP. He knew how to survive. Danilova maintained that in hard times Balanchine stole food to keep from starving.[118] His character as well as the existence he led completely turned Balanchine away from snobbery. He was no longer affected by Volynsky's attacks, who in an attempt to publicly humiliate Balanchine sneered in a newspaper article that "he is treading the Petrograd stages in a specific type of piquant, unbridled dance."[119]

Shostakovich in his later years liked to quote Chekhov: "I write everything except denunciations." Balanchine could have signed that *profession de foi*, a statement typical of a Petersburg professional of high caliber who combines pride in his or her craft, respect for the so-called "low" art genres, and a quiet, ethical purity.

Although the revolution deprived Balanchine of imperial patronage, it taught him to work for the audience. The NEP in Petrograd completed Balanchine's education. Now he would make a face whenever anyone said he "created" ballets. "Only God creates," he would counter with a shrug. "I am only a chef cooking up another dish for the audience, that's all." That idea, repeated throughout his life with slight variations, would be the linchpin of Balanchine's aesthetics.

On June 1, 1923, a few months after the group of enthusiasts met and elected Balanchine director of the Young Ballet, the new ensemble gave its first concert in a theater appropriately called the Experimental. It was in the building of the former City Duma, located on October 25th Prospect (formerly Nevsky, renamed to commemorate the Bolshevik revolution). "The star turn of the program was Chopin's 'Marche funèbre' choreographed by Georges Balanchivadze," recalled one of the participants.

> It was performed by almost all the females in our little troupe and several men. We moved on the stage in self-oblivion, wearing the fantastic black costumes that barely covered our bodies, designed by Boris Erbstein. We diligently performed the movements invented by the choreographer, shifting groups and poses that were imbued with deepest depression and grief.[120]

The public liked the Young Ballet. As for the critical reaction, it was predictably divided along aesthetic lines. Volynsky attacked Balanchine; a young critic, Yuri Brodersen, who was under his influence, called the performance "a whole evening of stage triteness." The progressive critics, among them the authoritative Alexei Gvozdev, an admirer of Meyerhold's, were approving.

Balanchine got the hall of the Experimental Theater for the debut of the Young Ballet from the director of the theater, Vsevolod Vsevolodsky-Gerngross, who also headed the Institute of the Living Word. Vsevolodsky was one of the first to reconstruct and perform authentic ancient Russian rituals: weddings, wakes, and circle dances. He was fascinated by the folkloric, preprofessional roots of the theater. "We are also for a 'left theater,' but a Russian theater," he announced. "We are not interested in Americanism, or constructivism, circuses, fox trots, or the cinema—no! We want to develop a line of spirituality in the new Russian theater!"[121]

Vsevolodsky wanted to assert what he called "the theater of

Logos." In practice, this meant the domination of declamation, in which Vsevolodsky's Experimental Theater became incredibly virtuosic. One of his most sensational productions was a performance, jointly with Balanchine's Young Ballet, of Blok's narrative poem *The Twelve*. Balanchine's group danced to the accompaniment of a chorus of Vsevolodsky's students declaiming Blok's verse.

As a participant later recalled, Balanchine did not produce an illustrative pantomime but a complex dance in Russian folk traditions. Blok's verse, which Vsevolodsky's ensemble performed using sharp contrasts of tempo and dynamics, juxtaposing chorus and soloists and male and female voices of the most varied timbres, provided a sophisticated rhythmic base. It was a striking and entertaining show.

Before the revolution the music of Blok's poetry lulled the audience. *The Twelve*, that portrait of revolutionary Petrograd that Shklovsky compared to Pushkin's *Bronze Horseman*, had a completely different effect. As the perceptive Shklovsky commented, "*The Twelve* is an ironic work. It is written not even in ditties but in the 'criminal argot' style. The style of the street couplet à la Savoyarov."[122]

Shklovsky meant Mikhail Savoyarov, a chansonnier popular in Petrograd then, who worked in the "ragged genre": he appeared on stage in the costume and makeup of a clochard. Balanchine never forgot Savoyarov singing the famous satirical ditty "Alyosha, sha, take it a half-tone lower." He often recalled other variety stars of Petrograd—Vassily Gushchinsky, Leonid Utesov, and Alexei Matov, and he could sing large chunks of the street argot songs. Balanchine particularly liked "Bubliki" ("Bagels": "And on this lousy night,/take pity on miserable me,/a private vendor") and "The Apple" ("Hey, apple,/where are you rolling?/If you end up at the Cheka,/you'll never come back!").[123]

Balanchine absorbed this repertoire and the music of innumerable fox trots, shimmies, and two-steps, dancing with his wife, Tamara, in numbers he created for such golden spots of NEP-time Petrograd as the Casino gambling club, the rooftop restaurant at the Evropeiskaya Hotel, or the small stage at Maxim's. His need for such performances kept increasing, since his miserly salary at the Maryinsky could not keep up with the inflationary spiral of the NEP. (Lunacharsky later admitted, "In the early years of the revolution the real earnings of our artists equalled 18 percent of what we gave them officially, and what we gave them was approximately 1/4 of what they got before the war," meaning, of course, World War I.)[124] The infrequent concerts of the Young Ballet were not especially profitable, either. Still, the concerts gained popularity for Balanchine in avant-garde circles, and the young choreographer began getting work from the city's established theaters.

He was asked to stage oriental, exotic dances for Rimsky-Korsakov's opera *The Golden Cockerel* and George Bernard Shaw's *Caesar and Cleopatra*. Radlov, a family friend of the Zheverzheyevs, was hired by the former Imperial Alexandrinsky Theater to carry out a rejuvenating operation there, so he brought in Balanchine for his debut on that venerable stage, remembering him from the Iron Hall at the People's House.

Radlov had a subtle sense of the ballet. Later, in the early 1930s, he became the artistic director of the former Maryinsky Theater, and in 1935, with his old friend Sergei Prokofiev, wrote the scenario for Prokofiev's ballet *Romeo and Juliet*. Radlov also was stage director of its famous production of 1940, with Galina Ulanova as Juliet.

Radlov's career was interrupted during the war years, when he was arrested and exiled. It was only in 1953, after Stalin's death, that Radlov was allowed to return to directing—in Daugavpils, a provincial Latvian town. The theater came to Riga to perform when I was living there. Still a child, I saw Radlov at one of the performances in the mid-fifties, when he came to take a bow after the show. It had been a flashy review in the style, as I later learned, of Radlov's early Petrograd productions, and the gray-haired director, despite his trials and tribulations, took pleasure in the delighted ovations of the Riga audience. Radlov died soon afterward.

Radlov adored Dmitriev. In 1923, together with Balanchine, this trio produced on the stage of the Alexandrinsky Theater the new expressionist play by the German revolutionary Ernst Toller, *Miserable Eugen (Hinkenmann)*. The play became the sensation of the season, and the connoisseurs particularly noted the sophisticated cubist scenery by Dmitriev and the vivid dances that Balanchine presented as silhouettes in the brightly lit windows of the "restaurants" onstage. The production re-created the exciting atmosphere of postwar Berlin, the capital of the Weimar Republic. And while the Petrograd critics rattled on about how Radlov and his friends "have exposed the sociopolitical contradictions of contemporary Germany" and were "reflecting the sunset of Europe," the audiences rushed to the show to get a glimpse if not of Western life for real, then at least its theatrical version: chic hair styles and fashionable costumes, and the latest dances to the music of Kuzmin, with their contemporary Western rhythms.

It could be presumed that Balanchine was already dreaming of being there as he worked on this nostalgic show about Berlin. In 1981, I asked him why he had emigrated to the West, and he replied,

> It was impossible to live in Russia, it was terrible—there was nothing to eat, people here can't understand what that means. We were hungry all the time. We dreamed of moving anywhere at all, just to get away. To go or not to go—I never had the slightest doubts about it. None! I never doubted, I always knew: if there were ever an opportunity—I'd leave![125]

The opportunity arrived when an aspiring manager got permission from the authorities for a small group of performers to tour the West for "cultural propaganda." The group included Balanchine and his wife, as well as three other stars of the Young Ballet: Danilova, Lydia Ivanova, and Nikolai Efimov. The same pretext was used the following year by two other émigrés—the pianist Vladimir Horowitz and his friend the violinist Nathan Milstein.

The unexpected and sudden departure, which was kept secret from the other members of the Young Ballet, was darkened by tragedy: during a boat ride on the Gulf of Finland Lydia ("Lida") Ivanova drowned. A rumor spread through Petrograd that this was no accident; in the obituaries Ivanova was openly compared to Adrienne Lecouvreur, the celebrated French actress of the eighteenth century who was the victim of court intrigues. Ballet circles were convinced the secret police had had a hand in Lida's death. Balanchine insisted to me: "I think it was a put-up job. I had heard that Lida knew some big secret and they did not want her to go to the West."[126]

Akhmatova was a great admirer of Ivanova, whom she watched at the Maryinsky Theater in the twenties. Akhmatova kept Ivanova's picture for many years and referred to her as "the biggest wonder of the Petrograd ballet." This opinion was shared by many. Kuzmin wrote that Ivanova's name was dear to all who were interested in the future of Russian art and described her gifts as "childlike purity, occasional humor, attentiveness, piercing seriousness, restrained emotion and strongly expressed feelings."[127]

This characterizes the Petersburg type of performance. Ivanova loved Tchaikovsky, and not long before her death she wrote in her diary a touching comment that many later talked about in Petrograd:

"I would like to be one of the tones created by Tchaikovsky, so that I could sound gently and sorrowfully and then dissolve in the evening mists."[128]

With her death, the Petrograd balletomanes recalled one of her most popular numbers, which now seemed prophetic, "Valse triste" to Balanchine's choreography, in which the dancer was pursued and finally caught by Death. This story had a strange and unsettling parallel in 1956, when Balanchine's new wife, his fourth, Tanaquil LeClerq, was stricken with polio. Many people recalled that a decade earlier the choreographer had composed a short ballet in which he danced the symbolic figure of Polio and touched LeClerq, who fell paralyzed.

Undoubtedly, the flight of Balanchine to the West caused him psychological trauma whose effect grew with the years rather than diminishing. Moving to the West from Soviet Russia had taken on threatening political overtones. The revolution had caused mass emigration. Exact figures are still lacking, but some one and a half to two million people must have fled. They were primarily well-educated, ideologically motivated foes of bolshevism, many of whom had taken up arms against Soviet power. A great number of them considered their emigration temporary, particularly in Germany, France, the Baltics, and the Balkan countries.

For the Soviet regime this "white" emigration, as it was then called, presented a definite threat. The Communists attacked the emigration politically, mocked it, infiltrated it, and tried to divide, tame, and disarm it. Relations with the émigrés were an important aspect of Soviet foreign and domestic policy; each departure for the West was perceived as a hostile act and, later, as unpardonable treachery.

The problem of emigration was particularly acute for ballet dancers. Their regular trips abroad had begun before the revolution, with Diaghilev's company, the first alternative to the state (then still imperial) Russian ballet. After the revolution, the cultural emigration increased. In 1922 the press revealed that thirty-four ballet artists from Petrograd had left for the West. It was "almost all the top dancers of the former Maryinsky Theater," Lopukhov admitted. Some of the new émigrés wrote to Petrograd from the West, and their letters were widely read and discussed in ballet circles.

The attitude of the artistic world toward the émigrés was complex; they were both envied and despised. A later statement by Lopukhov is typical. He declared that the ballet émigrés, "afraid of deprivation, thought about nothing but a sated existence and 'security.' They thought that they had no obligations to their own theater, to their people, that they were free to dispose of their talent as they saw fit and sell it to whomever they wanted."[129]

These bitter, unjust words seem to be addressed to Balanchine. We know that the members of the Young Ballet who remained in Petrograd viewed his unexpected departure as a betrayal. Balanchine's flight was an irreparable blow to the Young Ballet, which fell apart soon afterward, the members going their own ways. Dmitriev's career was the most brilliant. Disavowing the avant-garde enthusiasms of his youth, he moved to Moscow, where he became Stalin's favorite theater designer and received four Stalin Prizes—more than any other Soviet stage designer—while the best friend of his youth, Boris Erbstein, was arrested, then exiled, and faded out of the picture.

Dmitriev died wealthy and famous in 1948 at the age of forty-seven, having designed no fewer than five hundred productions. Even in his lifetime, the official press flattered him with the term "classic," for his realistic scenery for Chekhov's plays and Tchaikovsky's operas remain unparalleled in their own way. Until the end of his life, Dmitriev—despite all his successes a privately embittered and frightened man—was obsessed with Petersburg landscapes and returned to them over and over in his theater work and easel paintings.

Leaving behind Dmitriev, Erbstein, Slonimsky (who later became a leading historian and theoretician of Soviet ballet as well as a successful ballet librettist), and the other Young Ballet members must have been hard for Balanchine. But here his characteristic fatalism—which grew in later years and was undoubtedly rooted in religion—played a part. Everything had been decided for Balanchine: the idea of leaving, its plan, even the composition of the touring troupe. He merely had to join in.

Balanchine was superstitious, as were Diaghilev and Stravinsky. He considered it providential that the manager and organizer of the troupe had the same name as Balanchine's best friend, Vladimir Dmitriev, even though this man was not related to the young artist. The two Dmitrievs were not even acquainted. (However, they are still being confused in the Western literature on Balanchine.)

When Balanchine and his small group left Petrograd on July 4, 1924, on a ship bound for Germany, the young dancer and choreographer's material belongings were minimal, but his spiritual and artistic baggage was huge. He had attended the world's best ballet school and worked in the troupe of the Maryinsky Theater, at the time the center of world ballet, with a classical repertoire of over two dozen works that had been preserved for the most part in their original form. No other ballet company could match that. Moreover, Balanchine's musical education had been at the country's finest conservatory, where his schoolmate had been Shostakovich.

Balanchine appeared on the Maryinsky stage in Petipa's classic masterpieces and in Lopukhov's neoclassical experiment. He had appreciated both the charm of Fokin's plotless *Chopiniana* and the exoticism of Goleizovsky's erotic miniatures and Foregger's Americanized "dances of machines." Balanchine was among the first participants in the Factory of the Eccentric Actor and the bold post-Meyerhold attempts to "circusize" the theater, undertaken by Sergei Radlov. He had recited by heart Blok's *The Twelve* and Mayakovsky's *A Cloud in Trousers*, read Akhmatova and Shklovsky, fought with Volynsky, admired and discussed Malevich's designs and Tatlin's constructions, and taken in the music of Scriabin, Prokofiev, and Stravinsky. At the apartments of Zheverzheyev and Slonimsky he had plunged into the whirlpool of the latest theories of modern art. And he had headed his own experimental ballet ensemble, working with some of the most talented young artists of his generation.

That is why the meeting of Balanchine and Diaghilev in Paris in November 1924 was only to be expected. Diaghilev's troupe had been in the West for fifteen years, going through dizzying ups and downs. World War I and then the revolution greatly complicated Diaghilev's ties with Russian culture in general and with the Maryinsky Ballet in particular; he desperately needed fresh, new talent. Otherwise his innovative company was in danger of going stale, which meant certain death. That is why Diaghilev did not delay in inviting Balanchine's group to audition.

The first thing Diaghilev asked Balanchine after his dancers had shown the veteran impresario a few of the numbers they had brought from Russia was this: could the young choreographer quickly stage dances for opera? Balanchine replied without hesitation in the affirmative. And so Diaghilev established easy working relations with Balanchine based not on favoritism but mutual trust. The source of the trust was the Petersburg culture both men shared, which overcame differences in age, status, and sexual orientation.

Boris Kochno, in those years one of Diaghilev's closest aides, recalled his impression that Balanchine had appeared before the skeptical impresario pretty much formed as an artist, with his own understanding of music and its choreographic potential. Diaghilev's early misapprehension disappeared quickly. A particularly pleasant surprise for him was Balanchine's firm grasp of Stravinsky's music. Balanchine's choreographic debut in the Diaghilev seasons was the ballet *Nightingale's Song*, to music by Stravinsky, which he knew well; in Petrograd Balanchine had participated in Meyerhold's rehearsals for Stravinsky's opera *The Nightingale*, from which the music for the ballet came.

Balanchine's early understanding of Stravinsky's music was the result of many influences. Balanchine was familiar with Stravinsky's ballets *Firebird* and *Petrouchka* from the Maryinsky. But the composer's symphonic and chamber works were often played in Petrograd in the early twenties; Stravinsky's émigré status at that time was not yet enough to remove his works from the repertoire.

Stravinsky's ardent admirers were Balanchine's friends. Watching Vsevolodsky's experiments in Russian folklore prepared Balanchine for an innovative, "defamiliarized" interpretation of that same folklore by Stravinsky in his *Les Noces* and *Renard*. Finally, in the early twenties Balanchine had choreographed a number to Stravinsky's *Ragtime*, and just before leaving Petrograd he had started working on his *Pulcinella*. Thus, his involvement in Stravinsky's music of various periods and genres was a professional one, from the inside.

Balanchine's background, aesthetic inclinations, and temperament prepared him well for becoming Stravinsky's ideal collaborator. Their first important joint effort was the ballet *Apollon Musagète* for Diaghilev in Paris in 1928. This ballet, with its mythological story of three muses, Calliope, Polyhymnia, and Terpsichore, competing for the attention of their leader, the young god Apollo, was used as a pretext for the music and choreography that corresponded to it ideally— outwardly restrained but dramatic in its peculiarly linear way; with hindsight it seems like an ideal manifesto of the neoclassical movement between the two world wars. Neoclassicism flourished then in Germany, Italy, France, and the United States, but the émigrés from Petrograd played a special role in its development.

Paul Valéry and T. S. Eliot had expressed important ideas for classicism, and by 1915 Picasso was drawing in the style of Ingres. For Picasso, however, this was only temporary, as were many of his enthusiasms. Stravinsky's neoclassical period lasted no fewer than thirty years, from the early twenties to the early fifties. And the most loyal ally of Stravinsky for that entire period was Balanchine, whom the composer esteemed highly as a refined musician and unique interpreter of his compositions.

Many historians link the appearance of neoclassicism with the aftershocks of World War I, when people tried to find a haven from the dislocation in an art that was clear, balanced, and majestic. Russian refugees from the Bolsheviks in Europe reacted acutely to the perceived triumph of barbarism and the collapse of the world order.

Petrograd culture tended toward neoclassicism even before the revolution; for example, there was a strong classicist tendency inside *Mir iskusstva*. The manifestoes of the acmeists in the years before World War I called for simplicity, clarity, precision, and economy in the selection of words; many of the poems of Kuzmin, Gumilyov, and Mandelstam were quintessentially classical. Before the revolution this orientation was presumed to be primarily aesthetic, with reference to Petersburg traditions. After the Bolshevik seizure of power the political underpinnings of neoclassicism suddenly became much clearer.

Some of the major Petersburg neoclassicists emigrated and lived in Paris in the early twenties. The leader of *Mir iskusstva* and the main theoretician of Russian artistic neoclassicism, Alexander Benois, settled in Paris with his niece, Zinaida Serebryakova, who while in Petrograd had painted neoclassical portraits of the dancers Lydia Ivanova and Alexandra Danilova. Dobuzhinsky and Somov, members of the older generation of the *Mir iskusstva* crowd, also lived in Paris. The neoclassicists Alexander Yakovlev and Vassily Shukhaev, graduates of the Petersburg Academy of Arts, worked there, too; Shukhaev produced a splendid portrait of Stravinsky in 1933.

The émigré ballet critic and translator André Levinson, who in Petersburg had won a reputation as a fierce defender of the heritage of Marius Petipa, became in Paris an influential interpreter of the aesthetics of classicism in dance. The former Petersburger D. S. Mirsky, a critic of postsymbolist poetry, leading specialist in modern Russian literature, and author of still the best history of Russian literature (first published in English in 1926–1927), often visited Paris from England, where he had settled. Stravinsky later made special notice of his friendship with Mirsky, who returned to Soviet Russia from emigration only to be arrested and die in the camps.

Bolshevik Russia watched the successes of émigrés with poorly disguised hostility. Mayakovsky's articles published in Moscow in 1923 on the subject of his visit to western Europe were filled with scorn for "Parisian" Russians. Mayakovsky was angered even by the fact that a portrait by Yakovlev, exhibited at the Autumn Salon in Paris, depicted a woman holding a book of Akhmatova's poetry. The predictable but even then dubious conclusion Mayakovsky reached was: "We, workers in the arts of Soviet Russia, are the leaders of world art, the bearers of avant-garde ideas."[130]

Prokofiev, who while living in Paris continued nevertheless to flirt with the Bolsheviks, described in a letter to Moscow in 1928 the production of Stravinsky's *Apollon Musagète*, without even deigning to mention the choreographer:

> I saw and heard that thing in Diaghilev's production and am com-
> pletely disappointed in it. The material is absolutely pathetic and
> stolen out of the most shameful sources: Gounod, and Delibes, and
> Wagner, and even Minkus. It's all served up with extreme cleverness
> and mastery, which would be all right if it were not for the fact that
> Stravinsky missed the most important thing: it's terribly boring.[131]

(Prokofiev, of course, knew Mayakovsky's reaction to Stravinsky's music, after Stravinsky had shown his works to the poet in 1922: "It makes no impression on me. He is considered an innovator and a re-viver of the baroque at the same time! Prokofiev is more what I like.")

The Russian pro-Bolshevik "left" readily equated neoclassi-cism with counterrevolution. For them the "restoration" of classical forms evidenced the desire to restore old Russia, so the neoclassicists were perceived as enemies. Gumilyov was shot on charges of coun-terrevolutionary conspiracy. Akhmatova and Mandelstam were un-der suspicion as being "internal émigrés." The Bolsheviks and their fellow travelers tried to persuade themselves and others that the neo-classicists were aesthetic and political corpses.

Now it is hard to determine the actual political views (or lack thereof) of young Balanchine in Russia. There is evidence that allows us to assume he was very devout, even though his enthusiasm for Mayakovsky's often sacrilegious poetry seems paradoxical in that light. The politics of Diaghilev and Stravinsky before the revolution could be described as rather liberal. But the hostile attitude of the Bol-sheviks toward émigrés in general and their political attacks on neo-classicism in particular inevitably pushed Diaghilev, Stravinsky, and Balanchine into the conservative camp.

The three shared a cult of Pushkin, Glinka, Tchaikovsky, clas-sical ballet, and its genius, Petipa. Diaghilev began propagandizing Tchaikovsky in Europe in 1921, presenting his *Sleeping Beauty* (par-tially reorchestrated by Stravinsky) in London. In connection with the premiere, Stravinsky published an open letter to Diaghilev in the Lon-don *Times* in which he glorified Tchaikovsky, whose talent Stravinsky considered "the greatest of any Russian musician": "The fact is that he was a creator of melody, which is an extremely rare and precious gift."[132]

In his production Diaghilev restored Petipa's choreography, which Stravinsky remembered from his childhood. The first performance little Igor ever saw at the Maryinsky Theater was *Sleeping Beauty*. The ballet delighted the boy, and his devotion to classical dance, in which the mature Stravinsky saw "the triumph of studied conception over vagueness, of the rule over the arbitrary, of order over the haphazard," never left him.[133] (It was this production that also converted Benois, Levinson and Balanchine to the "ballet faith.") Neoclassical Stravinsky openly proclaimed his "profound admiration for classical ballet, which in its very essence, by the beauty of its *ordonnance* and the aristocratic austerity of its forms, so closely corresponds with my conception of art."[134]

Inspired in part by his work on *Sleeping Beauty*, Stravinsky wrote his own "Petersburg" one-act opéra bouffe, *Mavra*, in 1921, based on Pushkin's comic narrative poem "The Little House in Kolomna" and dedicated to "the memory of Pushkin, Glinka, and Tchaikovsky." It was a demonstrative act in relation to the West and the East. In Europe none of the three dedicatees were in especially high esteem. In Communist Russia their names were in fact surrounded by a negative aura just then. Pushkin and Glinka were considered monarchists, and Tchaikovsky was dubbed a pessimist and mystic, hostile to proletarian audiences.

Stravinsky, who a few years later would be called by Moscow a "mystic who moved to bestial fascism," knew all that, of course. But Pushkin, Glinka, and Tchaikovsky symbolized Petersburg culture to him, and as he strongly felt aesthetic and ethical ties to that culture, he intended to promote it in western Europe. However, his attempts were not overly successful with the Western intellectual elite. The classically oriented art of his Petersburg idols was considered by many in the European capitals as being too traditional. The efforts of Diaghilev did not help, either. His production of *Sleeping Beauty* in London and its next version, shown in Paris, were both commercial failures.

Purely aesthetic reasons aside, an important role was played by the general political and intellectual climate of the times. The Bolsheviks had won the civil war decisively, and the pragmatic Western politicians began to see Communist Russia as an inevitable and formidable reality. As a result Russian émigrés in Europe began to seem a nuisance. And the avant-garde elite of London and Paris, disillusioned by capitalism, were attracted by Communist ideas. In these conditions all attempts to inculcate Petersburg aesthetics and values on European soil seemed doomed to failure, since they appeared hopelessly obsolete.

Vladimir Nabokov, born in Petersburg in 1899 when it was still the capital of the Russian Empire, exemplifies the cultural hardships of surviving emigration. His father, a prominent Cadet political figure, was expected by some to become minister of culture, after the tsar was deposed. Instead, Nabokov Senior died in Berlin in 1922, shielding the provisional government's former minister of foreign affairs, his political mentor, from the bullets of right-wing assassins. Young Vladimir made his debut as a poet in Petrograd, but his real literary career developed after he emigrated, in 1919.

Nabokov's poetic attempts, although not without their admirers, were not up to the level of Tsvetayeva or Khodasevich, who also emigrated, or even of such minor masters as Georgy Adamovich and Georgy Ivanov, who had belonged to the acmeists in Petersburg and went on to create the so-called "Paris note" school. But Nabokov's Russian prose immediately put him in the front ranks, right next to the acknowledged master of émigré literature, Bunin.

In the first twenty-odd years of his European émigré life, Nabokov published some important works, and his experimental novels—*Luzhin's Defense* (1930), *Despair* (1936), *Invitation to a Beheading* (1938), and *The Gift* (1938), in which one finds similarities to Proust, Joyce, and Kafka—marked the appearance on the international scene of a Petersburg brand of literary modernism.

Bely's *Petersburg* is mentioned most frequently as a precursor to Nabokov, but his work also owes much to the prose of Pushkin and Gogol and the poetry of Blok and the acmeists. The world of exaggerated Petersburg theatricality triumphs in Nabokov's novels; their refined style, playful inventiveness, and existential significance were evidence of the birth of a great talent. Still, the establishment of London and Paris were in no hurry to recognize Nabokov. Often they refused to translate and publish him simply because he was a refugee from the Bolsheviks, and therefore—in the eyes of the leftist Western intelligentsia—a reactionary.

When Nabokov's novels did break through to European readers, the critics were sometimes outright hostile. Sartre's review of *Despair* may be taken as an example. Anticipating the arguments of

Stalinist critics of the late forties, Sartre accused Nabokov of lacking national roots and compared him unfavorably with Soviet writers, who, in Sartre's opinion, were useful members of socialist society.

The position in prewar European culture of another émigré, Igor Stravinsky, was somewhat different. Nabokov was still a little-known writer, while Stravinsky was a recognized master of the European musical avant-garde. But even Stravinsky had difficulties in those years in France. After 1925 most of the commissions for new works, including two ballets (*Apollon Musagète* and *Jeu des Cartes*) and the Symphony of Psalms, came from America. When Stravinsky was a candidate for the French Academy in 1935, he lost the vote: four in favor, twenty-eight against. That humiliating rejection was gleefully bandied about in the French press, which reflected the attitude of French audiences in general, who were mostly unsympathetic to Stravinsky.

That is why the composer gratefully accepted an invitation from Harvard University and moved to the United States. Nabokov, who could not get permission to work in France, arrived in America in 1940. The war in Europe also influenced his decision. And Balanchine had moved to the United States even earlier, in 1933, at the invitation of a recent Harvard graduate, the young American aesthete and ballet connoisseur Lincoln Kirstein.

Neoclassical ideas had a powerful influence on Kirstein. In the twenties T. S. Eliot's "Tradition and the Individual Talent" became "code and guide" for him. In the late twenties and early thirties Kirstein also read the works of André Levinson, a Russian ballet reviewer in Paris, and later called him "the most erudite, perhaps the only contemporary critic of dancing."[135] Kirstein and his friends were thus prepared intellectually and aesthetically to transplant classical ballet to America in its most severe traditional form. Balanchine had no more illusions about his career in Europe; according to Kirstein, who met Balanchine in London, he was "intense, convinced, not desperate but without hope."[136] America held out that glimmer of hope.

In hindsight, we could suppose that the emigration from Russia of Stravinsky, Nabokov, and Balanchine, for all the differences in their backgrounds and ambitions, was no accident. Stravinsky left his homeland before the revolution, and it seems likely Nabokov and Balanchine would have chosen that same path even if the Bolsheviks had not come to power.

All three had been born in Petersburg and developed, independently of one another, a cosmopolitan aesthetics based on classical principles, but they gave those principles a modern twist. All three felt constrained within traditional Russian culture, which proclaimed the supremacy of content over form and demanded that art be actively involved in the social and civic ferment of the times.

To realize at least some of their creative concepts in an international setting was for all three a natural desire. The Russian Revolution had created new realities that made the emigration of Stravinsky, Nabokov, and Balanchine irreversible. As a result these three artists, along with others less prominent, created what I call the Petersburg branch of modernism abroad. These three were stifled in the nationalistic atmosphere of Europe between the wars. They imagined the United States as a safe refuge, free of European political labels and prejudices.

Stravinsky spent over thirty years and Balanchine almost fifty in America, and died in New York City; Nabokov's "American period" lasted close to twenty. In those years Balanchine created a tradition of classical ballet that has become an American national possession; and Stravinsky and Nabokov powerfully influenced their American colleagues with their distinctive skills; the adjectives "Stravinskian" and "Nabokovian" became commonplace. All three became loyal American citizens, and, in fact, American artists. Nabokov even made the ultimate conversion: he stopped writing in Russian. Thus, their presence in America turned this branch of Petersburg modernism abroad into a specifically American version.

At the same time, the three planted a version of the Petersburg mythos in America in works oriented for American audiences that then traveled the world and, against all odds, returned to their native city, where their creators could not venture.

Teaching Russian literature in American universities, Nabokov tirelessly promoted Gogol, stressing the formal perfection and existential vision of his Petersburg works and pointing out the glaring deficiencies of the existing English translations. In the forties, Nabokov wrote a brilliant book about Gogol that remains the single best introduction to the genius of Petersburg for foreign readers.

Nabokov's accurate translation and meticulous commentary on Pushkin's *Eugene Onegin* remains unsurpassed; after Shakespeare, Nabokov considered Pushkin the greatest poet and once said that steady reading of Pushkin would increase the readers' lung size. Published in four volumes in 1964, this controversial work kindled a new wave of interest in Pushkin in the English-speaking world. It demonstrated, among other things, Pushkin's close connections with European culture, an important point for the cosmopolitan Nabokov, and his compatriot Stravinsky.

But Nabokov's greatest contribution to the creation of the American image of St. Petersburg is his *Speak, Memory*, which many consider among the best autobiographies ever written. Serialized in *The New Yorker* and other American magazines in the last years of the forties and published as a book in 1951 (with the title *Conclusive Evidence*, which was later changed; in 1954 the Russian version appeared as *Drugie Berega*), Nabokov's autobiography was enthusiastically received by critics both then and in 1967, when the author revised and expanded what was probably his most personal book.

Petersburg was a leading theme in Nabokov's poetry. The émigré existence added nostalgic overtones: Nabokov tirelessly returned in his poems to his native city, lovingly going over the fading images of "my light, my airy Petrograd." (I had a unique opportunity to examine the notebook in which the young Nabokov wrote his poetry; its title page had a drawing of a Petersburg landscape.) In his verse Nabokov responded to the death of his beloved Blok and the execution of Gumilyov. One of Nabokov's best poems of his Berlin period ("Memory, sharp ray, transform my exile . . .") paints a fantastic picture of Petersburg in the style of Dobuzhinsky and is dedicated to the artist, a fellow émigré who in Petersburg gave the teenaged Nabokov drawing lessons, which the writer applied gratefully, as he put it, "to certain camera-lucida needs of literary composition."

In *Speak, Memory*, Nabokov's tour de force, the writer emphasizes the role of the artists of *Mir iskusstva*, Dobuzhinsky and Benois, in the creation of that stylized image of "modernist" Petersburg, which Nabokov in turn wanted to engrave in the consciousness of the American reader. The main themes of that autobiography are memory, fate, freedom, and the possibility/impossibility of choice; the main mystery is the nature and essence of time. At almost every turn in the narrative Nabokov somehow touches on Petersburg, which becomes the leitmotif of the book.

The portrait of the city, first purely descriptive, then social and political, forms kaleidoscopically as if from a multitude of pieces of colored glass, a favorite method of Nabokov's. The writer teases the reader, distracting his attention and then, like the experienced professor he was, suddenly gives a brief but stern lecture. The sharp homilies attempted to dispel the prejudices and doubts of American intellectuals about the existence of a liberal and cosmopolitan culture in prerevolutionary Petersburg, of which Nabokov proudly considered himself a rightful member and heir.

It was not an easy task. In 1949, *The New Yorker* refused to print the chapter of *Speak, Memory* in which Nabokov insisted that there was more freedom in tsarist Russia than under Lenin—a thesis at odds with the grim picture of tsarist Petersburg created by Dostoyevsky in *Crime and Punishment* and still current in the popular imagination. Nabokov's firm political convictions, supported by his literary mastery, did, however, have their effect. Gradually, as his literary reputation grew, he worked his vision of Petersburg into the intellectual center of the American elite. By the time Nabokov's autobiography appeared in print, it was greeted as a masterpiece. And his Petersburg took its place next to that of Dostoyevsky—a pioneering achievement of historical and cultural importance, opening the door for other practitioners of the American branch of Petersburg modernism.

As modernists with Petersburg roots, Nabokov and Stravinsky had much in common. They were related by the theatricality of their works, the paradoxicality of their creative thought, the love of playing with art "models" (literary ones for Nabokov, musical for Stravinsky), as well as an incorrigible tendency toward irony and the grotesque.

Nabokov's novels are full of literary mystifications and allusions; often the "literary scenery" and point of view shift suddenly to reveal the presence of the omnipotent author. Alfred Schnittke, in his essay concerning paradoxicality as a trait of Stravinsky's musical logic, analyzed the similar methods in the work of the composer (in particular *Apollon Musagète*):

> This is not simply "in the old style," but "in the old style through the eyes of Tchaikovsky" (the seventeenth century via the *Serenade for Strings*), that is, mystification with a triple bottom: the first impression is that of Lully's ballet theater with a classical plot and typical orchestral score ("Les Vingt-quatre Violins du roi"), a closer look reveals the swanny Maryinsky ballet with its elegant pastoral air, and finally we see above the stage the shadow of the Magician controlling everyone; and here we notice that the ballet is for puppets and is really staged today.[137]

In contrast to Nabokov, Stravinsky did not need "to conquer" America; his reputation had preceded him. Even before moving permanently to the United States, Stravinsky was the subject of a special New York festival in 1937, and as part of it the Metropolitan Opera staged two of his most Petersburgian works—the ballets *Apollon Musagète* and *Le Baiser de la fée*. Both ballets (and also *Jeu de cartes*) were choreographed by Balanchine; this was his first work with Stravinsky's music in America.

Le Baiser de la fée, composed in 1928, after Alexander Benois's idea, was Stravinsky's "Tchaikovskiana." The composer included in it numerous themes from Tchaikovsky's piano pieces and songs. The plot, from a fairy tale by Hans Christian Andersen, was an allegory: the Muse, "choosing" a newborn with a kiss, subsequently takes him away at his wedding. This theme Stravinsky and Balanchine shared, the primacy of art over life, an echo of the old argument between the Russian "realists" and "idealists." Stravinsky and Balanchine considered Tchaikovsky an ally in that argument, and the ballet was dedicated to him.

Moving to America, Stravinsky periodically included Tchaikovsky's Second and Third Symphonies and his *Serenade for Strings* in programs when he conducted, but *Le Baiser de la fée* became his final homage to Tchaikovsky. Nabokov, Stravinsky, and Balanchine all tried to enter the mainstream of American life and to become as Americanized as possible. Still, Petersburg never let go completely.

With *Speak, Memory*, Nabokov was the first to present the theme of Petersburg in the new American context. Stravinsky followed with his autobiographical dialogue books with Robert Craft. The impetus for those books was the numerous requests for interviews in connection with the composer's seventy-fifth birthday. Stravinsky always wanted to control his interviews, another trait he shared with Nabokov, who responded only in writing to questions presented in advance and always demanded that resulting texts be reproduced without any cuts. Like Nabokov, Stravinsky discovered that the interview genre could also be profitable.

An important similarity of Nabokov's and Stravinsky's memoirs is that they attempt to impose an artistic order on the vision of their Petersburg childhood. They both guarded their past, and for both, this childhood was an inexhaustible reservoir of creative impulses.

During 1959–1968, six books of dialogues between Stravinsky and Craft were published in the United States. The tone of the first is comparatively impersonal, especially when it comes to memories of Stravinsky's youth. The watershed comes in the third book, *Expositions and Developments*. Here the approach becomes positively

Nabokovian. Many episodes resemble *Speak, Memory*; and if it is accidental, it is all the more impressive, underscoring the common cultural and emotional basis of the creative development of both men.

In *Expositions and Developments*, Stravinsky first found the
strength to confess that "St. Petersburg is so much a part of my life
that I am almost afraid to look further into myself, lest I discover how
much of me is still joined to it. . . . it is dearer to my heart than any
other city in the world."[138] The composer begins a journey to the realm
of his childhood, evoking—in Nabokov's style—the memory of the
light of a street lamp that came through the parted curtains into the
room of little Igor in the Stravinsky's Petersburg apartment. That light
led him to a world "of safety and enclosure," with reminiscences of
the nurse, cook, butler, the priest at the gymnasium, which Stravinsky begins with a typically Nabokovian passage that "memories themselves are 'safeties,' of course, far safer than the 'originals,' and
growing more so all the time."[139]

Stravinsky takes pleasure in bringing to life the sounds, smells,
and colors of Petersburg of the late nineteenth century, insisting on
their connection with his later musical work (*Petrouchka, Nightingale, Le Baiser de la fée*). With special tenderness, "consumed with
Petersburger pride," Stravinsky recollects his visit to the Maryinsky
Theater: "To enter the blue-and-gold interior of that heavily perfumed
hall was, for me, like entering the most sacred of temples."[140]

The books of Stravinsky's conversations with Craft became
perhaps the most influential of their kind in the intellectual life of
America in the sixties. They were avidly read in Europe, too, by the
cultural elite. At the same time, Nabokov's *Speak, Memory* was made
part of the curriculum of modern American literature at universities
throughout the country. It was then that Nabokov was proclaimed (in
a book review in the *New York Times*) to be the world's greatest living writer. Stravinsky's reputation as arguably the greatest modern
composer was established by then. It could be said that the American
branch of Petersburg modernism had flowered gloriously. That is why
the image of prerevolutionary Petersburg created by Nabokov and
Stravinsky had such an impact.

The American cultural climate of the 1960s was especially receptive
to that flowering. The fiftieth anniversary of the Russian Revolution,
observed in 1967, drew much interest in Russian history and focused
the attention of large audiences on "the remote, almost legendary, almost Sumerian mirages of St. Petersburg," in the words of Nabokov.

The mystery of the city, its historical fate, its rulers and inhabitants were analyzed and described on various levels and from different points of view in such disparate works as *The Icon and the Axe* by James H. Billington (1966) and *Nicholas and Alexandra* by Robert K. Massie (1967). The movie industry, after a long hiatus, returned to the theme of Rasputin (*Rasputin the Mad Monk* with Christopher Lee in 1966, and *I Killed Rasputin* with Gert Frobe in 1968); somewhat later *Nicholas and Alexandra* was brought to the screen.

Against the background of this heightened interest in Petersburg in the "high" and "low" spheres of American culture, Balanchine's role and influence became very prominent. He succeeded in combining disparate aspects of the Petersburg mythos into a single enduring iconic image that had an enormous impact on the perception of Petersburg traditions by the American, and ultimately, the world audience.

When Kirstein invited Balanchine in 1933 to come to the United States to head a ballet company, the choreographer set one important condition: "But first a school." Kirstein's agreement determined in great part the future of American ballet, because for Balanchine schooling was never merely a question of technique. Kirstein recalled how the mother of one of the first potential students asked Balanchine, "Will my daughter dance?" Balanchine's answer, in French, was neither simple prognosis nor polite avoidance: "La Danse, Madame, c'est une question morale."[141] Treating dance as a moral consideration was something Balanchine had inherited from the Petersburg masters, especially Petipa.

The school, according to Balanchine, had to lay the foundation both of the craft and of morality; they were not mutually exclusive. The attitude toward ballet as an entertainment did not hinder a serious opinion of its possibilities within the framework of high culture. Petipa saw himself simultaneously as court confectioner and enlightener. This Petersburg dualism unmistakably colored Balanchine's activity in America.

And it was in New York City that Balanchine felt he was continuing Petipa's work. It was only there that he could see himself as a sophisticated European, who had arrived—as Petipa had come from France to Petersburg—in a country of unlimited opportunity with a mission of converting the natives to the classical ballet. And like his illustrious forebear, Balanchine almost completely integrated himself into the culture of the country that had taken him in, in the process, as Petipa had done in Russia, molding from a traditional, highly stylized and constricted endeavor a vital, contemporary, and unquestionably national form of artistic expression.

In the United States, Balanchine's neoclassicism, whose roots went back to the aesthetics of Petipa, took on unheard-of modern traits to become the "American style." In Petersburg Petipa used the extraordinary Russian human material in building up the grandeur and lyricism of his ballets; in New York Balanchine was able to choose from that great American pool "bee-like little girls"—big thighs, nipped-in waists, pin-heads—who seem to be bred to the eminent choreographer's specifications."[142]

This observant comment of Stravinsky's is inaccurate on only one point: "Balanchine's ballerinas," as they were soon to be called, were not little but as a rule tall women. They moved with incredible speed, accuracy, and musicality. They had that specifically American combination of athleticism, unbounded physiological joy in doing their turns and leaps, and a natural feel for complex, syncopated rhythms.

This made American dancers the ideal performers for Balanchine's ballets set to Stravinsky's music. Two émigrés from Petersburg formed a unique duo in the United States. In his lifetime, Balanchine choreographed almost thirty works by Stravinsky, from *Ragtime* in Petrograd in 1922 to *Perséphone* in New York in 1982. The great majority of these productions occurred in the American period. Balanchine felt much more the missionary about Stravinsky's music than Petipa did about Tchaikovsky's. Many people considered Stravinsky a father figure to Balanchine.

It was Balanchine's achievement that Stravinsky's late serial compositions—such as *Movements for Piano and Orchestra*—which initially met with resistance in the concert halls, were received rapturously when danced at the New York City Ballet. The 1957 production of *Agon*, the composer's third ballet "on Greek themes" after *Apollo* and *Orpheus*, was a turning point. *Agon*'s tense and "alienated" eroticism and its modernist sparseness stunned American intellectuals.

The dance critic Arlene Croce recalled that "After one of the first performances of *Agon* a well-known New York writer said joyfully, 'If they knew what was going on here, the police would close it down.' "[143] Tickets were impossible to get for the "twelve-tone nights," performances at Balanchine's theater composed exclusively of ballets set to avant-garde music. Balanchine sensed the parallel between the discipline of classical dance and the discipline of twelve-tone composition, a comparison that was gradually absorbed also by the intellectual audience of his modernist ballets. First drawn to Balanchine's theater by the innovation of his repertoire, they began to accept classical dance in his interpretation as a truly modern phenomenon, worthy of the most serious attention. This was a cultural event of the greatest importance. As Nathan Milstein, a witness to this aesthetic revolution, commented to me later, "Balanchine saved ballet as an art form for the twenty-first century."[144]

In the early decades of the twentieth century the international appeal of ballet was the result of the proselytizing of Diaghilev, who considered himself the child of Petersburg aesthetics. With Diaghilev's death in 1929, the Petersburg connection with classical dance weakened and perhaps would have come to naught if not for the efforts of Balanchine. Balanchine also revived the Petersburg aura of Tchaikovsky's music, which had waned significantly by the middle of the century.

Balanchine's love of Tchaikovsky did not fluctuate with fashion. Among the first ballets he choreographed in America were *Mozartiana* and *Serenade*, to Tchaikovsky's music. Each ballet evolved in its own way into signature pieces of Balanchine's theater. The melancholy *Serenade*, with its flowing lines and an allegorical subtext, became one of Balanchine's most popular works. *Mozartiana*, after several revisions, turned into an enigmatic homage to Tchaikovsky.

Returning regularly to Tchaikovsky's music and to the works of Glinka and Glazunov, Balanchine set these compositions and his choreographic interpretation of them in a Petersburg context. This tradition began with *Ballet Imperial* (later renamed as *Tchaikovsky Piano Concerto No. 2*), produced in 1941 with scenery by *Mir iskusstva* member Dobuzhinsky as a specific "tribute to St. Petersburg, Petipa, and Tchaikovsky." Subsequently, the imperial and court associations were persistently used in Balanchine's Petersburg works.

This is particularly interesting because there was nothing "imperial" or "courtier-like" in Balanchine's character, habits, and tastes. Of course, he was a courteous Petersburg gentleman, but it would be hard to call his behavior overtly aristocratic. As Milstein noted, Balanchine "was a monarchist and a democrat, one does not preclude the other at all."[145] His monarchism was nostalgic and aesthetic. Though Balanchine loved hamburgers and cowboy movies, in the rehearsal hall he became an autocrat. In that sense his theater could be called a tiny monarchy, with the choreographer at its head.

Paradoxically, the monarchist idea refracted through Balanchine's ballets gained sympathy among the American liberal elite. Audiences left the traditional American egalitarian values at the doorstep of Balanchine's theater, where elegance, brilliance, and pomp and-circumstance reigned. Imperial Petersburg was rehabilitated there, and along with it, Tchaikovsky's music. Its romantic impulses were no longer held in suspicion by ballet connoisseurs, for Tchaikovsky was being interpreted by the same company that had proven its-modernist allegiance with its productions of Stravinsky's most avant-garde works. So it might be said Stravinsky finally "rehabilitated" Tchaikovsky partly through the New York City Ballet by the coexistence of his works with those of Tchaikovsky on the stage of Balanchine's theater.

Balanchine's 1954 production of *The Nutcracker* was the decisive breakthrough in that direction. That ballet, which has turned into a Christmas season ritual of sorts, made Tchaikovsky practically a national American composer. *The Nutcracker*, imbued with Petersburg associations, made the fantastic city of Tchaikovsky-Balanchine seem homey and familiar to Americans. Majestic and mysterious Petersburg took on cozy and intimate traits that were first introduced to Western audiences by Nabokov and then elucidated by Stravinsky in his dialogues with Craft. Balanchine functioned here as a great synthesizer.

Zinaida Hippius is credited with a well-known phrase (which may also have originated with Nina Berberova) that the Russian émigré cultural elite in the twentieth century were in the West "not as exiles, but as emissaries." This was a reference to the cultural and political "mission" of the group, which had a two-part goal: to preserve the Russian heritage that had come under attack by the new Communist masters of Russia, for world civilization; and to warn about the tragic consequences of the Communist experiment if it were to be attempted in the West.

The influence of Russian émigrés on the policies of Western governments was, of course, negligible. Their cultural message was much more effective, and it too divided into two parts: it was addressed to the modern Western public but also to a certain future "post-Communist" audience in Russia. The power of the signal to the future depended significantly on the success of the idea in the present, that is, on the talent, dynamism, and conviction of the Russian cultural figures in exile. Also exceptionally important was the environment, its receptiveness, lack of prejudice, and enthusiasm.

In that sense the Petersburg modernists and America were a

happy match. Neither Stravinsky nor Balanchine nor Nabokov had planned to become American artists or citizens. But western Europe proved inhospitable to the Petersburger's strain of refined, aristocratic modernism. It was only in the United States that the Petersburg modernists could formulate, then plant in the Western mind a legendary, mystical image of their native city in that tragic period, when the Petersburg mythos was being systematically uprooted in their homeland.

CHAPTER
5

in which our long-suffering city is renamed af-
ter a tyrant, undergoes dreadful ordeals in the
Great Terror and the most horrible siege in re-
cent history, and turns from a "crazy ship" into
a "ship of the dead," to be mourned in elegies
and sung in requiems. This is the Leningrad of
Dmitri Shostakovich.

T here are black days in people's lives. They are like eclipses of the sun."[1] This is how Galina Serebryakova, the writer and one-time lover of Dmitri Shostakovich, looked back in the 1960s at January 21, 1924, the day the glorified leader of Soviet and world Communists died, the ruler of Russia for over six fateful years, a clever polemicist, brilliant tactician, and ruthless politician, a man who spoke with a thick burr and had a skull shaped like that of Socrates or Verlaine—Vladimir Lenin.

The coffin with Lenin's body was laid out in the Hall of Columns of the House of Unions in Moscow. The poet Vera Inber described the endless line of people come to say their farewells to the legendary Bolshevik. "A cloud composed of the breath of hundreds of thousands blanketed those waiting in line. The frigid air was motionless. In the sky, a triple halo that occurs only in extreme frosts veiled the moon."[2] Inside the Hall of Columns "the light of the chandeliers, wrapped in crepe, as if through a dark haze of fog, illuminated the coffin, banked with blood-red tulips."[3]

It is difficult now to establish the actual emotions of the crowd that passed before Lenin's bier. One thing is clear: everyone, even the enemies of Lenin and communism, recognized the significance of the moment. The history of an enormous country, which had always depended on the personal characteristics of its ruler, was once again at a crossroads. It was time to exclaim as Pushkin had in *The Bronze Horseman*, "Where are you galloping, proud steed,/And where will you plant your hoofs?" It is only by appreciating the apocalyptic mood of the Russian people in the first days after Lenin's death that we can understand how Mikhail Bulgakov, who had fought in the recent civil war against the Communists and who had no sympathy for the Bolsheviks, could have written in January 1924, "This coffin will be visited for four days through the cold of Moscow and then throughout the centuries across the faraway caravan routes of the yellow deserts of the globe, there where once, at the birth of humanity, an eternal star rose above its cradle."[4]

Next to Bulgakov's passage, the reaction of seventeen-year-old Dmitri ("Mitya") Shostakovich, a student at the Petrograd Conservatory and a beginning composer (expressed in a letter to Tatyana Glivenko, with whom he was in love), seems almost like an understatement: "I'm sad, Tanechka, very sad. I'm sad that V.I. Lenin has died and that I will not be able to say farewell to him because he is being buried in Moscow. The Petrograd Soviet applied to have his body moved to Petrograd, but this application must have been refused."

On January 26, the Second All-Union Congress of Soviets was convened, and at its first session, dedicated to Lenin, the general secretary of the ruling party spoke. Joseph Stalin was a Georgian of medium height with a neatly trimmed mustache and a pockmarked face. (Today the two most famous Georgians in the West are Stalin and George Balanchine.) In his low, resonant voice heavy with a Georgian accent, Stalin declared "As he left us, Comrade Lenin willed us to preserve and strengthen the dictatorship of the proletariat. We vow to you, Comrade Lenin, that we will not spare any effort to obey honorably this commandment of yours as well!" To immortalize the memory of their leader, the congress decided to establish a special day of mourning, to build a mausoleum for Lenin on Red Square in Moscow, and to publish his complete collected works.

The Congress, "fulfilling the unanimous request of the workers of Petrograd," also renamed the city Leningrad, explaining in a special resolution, "In Petrograd the great proletarian revolution had its first, decisive victory. . . . Like an unscalable cliff, Red Petrograd stood high all these years, and remains today the first citadel of Soviet power. . . . The first workers' and peasants' government in the world was created in this city. . . . Let this major center of the proletarian revolution from this day forward be connected with the name of the greatest leader of the proletariat, Vladimir Ilyich Ulyanov-Lenin."[5]

The city's renaming, the second in fewer than ten years, was, like the first, hasty, momentous, and ill-fated. When St. Petersburg was renamed Petrograd in August 1914 by Nicholas II, it was intended to "Slavicize" the capital of the empire at war with Germany. At the time many considered the tsar's action not so much in bad taste as filled with evil portents. Alexander Benois, who had always maintained that of all the mistakes made by the tsarist regime the most unforgivable was this "betrayal of Petersburg," insisted, "I am even disposed to believe that all our misfortunes were a punishment for that betrayal, for the fact that puny ancestors dared to denigrate Peter's 'testament,' and that with no comprehension they decided that there was something humiliating and unworthy for the Russian capital in the name that Peter had given it."[6]

Benois, the leader of a movement for the restoration of old Petersburg's glory and grandeur, pointed to several reasons why the city's renaming seemed a tragic mistake. In naming the city Sankt-Peterburg, Peter the Great placed it "under the special protection of the saint who had already once blessed the idea of spiritual dominion of the world."[7] By making St. Peter the patron of the city, the tsar was announcing his own cosmopolitan ambitions. "Slavicism" was alien to the first Russian emperor. Changing the capital's name to a more Slavic-sounding version, his descendants conspicuously rejected universal, cosmopolitan aspirations. This renaming inadvertently narrowed the city's spiritual sphere of influence.

In addition, Nicholas II had made yet another mistake. He thought that by publicly venting his hostility to Petersburg, he was expressing the feelings of "simple" Russian people. Benois felt that this was a fatal error. In violating the will of Peter the Great, the last Russian emperor undermined the idea of sovereignty so important to the first. Nor did he garner the people's support. Though Nicholas was the first, he was not the only ruler to tinker with the Petrograd mystique. The Bolsheviks followed him, at least in this, but in a much more decisive if even less rational manner.

The initiative to rename Petrograd Leningrad formally belonged to the Petrograd Soviet of Worker, Peasant, and Red Army Deputies. Actually it was the idea of the Soviet's chairman, the ambitious Grigory Zinoviev, who as one of the rulers of the Communist Party had obvious reasons for this. When Lenin moved the capital to Moscow in 1918, it radically diminished the importance of Petrograd. In the new situation, when Lenin was rapidly being transformed into a Communist saint, endowing the city with his name would give Zinoviev, the city boss, a political advantage. In 1919, Zinoviev was also the chairman of the Executive Committee of the Comintern (Communist International), which made Petrograd the natural center of the world Communist movement. With all its "regalia," especially the name Leningrad, the city could aspire to become the official "Party" capital of the country and of the entire "proletarian" world. The Communists hoped to perform a radical re-creation of the city's mythos in the service of Communist ideology. Petersburg, the lighthouse of Russian artistry, would become Leningrad, the torch of the Communist movement.

Zinoviev had grounds for imagining himself leader of the Party. He had always been one of Lenin's closest friends. The reputation of another major Party leader, Leon Trotsky, was waning. Stalin was still considered little more than an effective but unimaginative Party bureaucrat. In the coming intraparty power struggle, Zinoviev's move to rename the city was clever.

This move was also, paradoxically, an application for reviving the city's international status, but with a Communist aura. After all, Lenin and his comrades had always assumed that after the revolution in Russia, the Communists would seize power throughout Europe. Thus, Leningrad would be the natural capital of the future commonwealth of European Communist states. In his imagination Zinoviev could already see himself mounted on a bronze horse (or at least in a bronze car).

Zinoviev's dreams did not come to pass. But in 1924, the rest of the party leaders supported Zinoviev, each for his own reasons. Renaming cities after revolutionary leaders had become a kind of reward. A Petrograd suburb had been renamed Trotsk even earlier, and also in 1924 the cities of Elizavetgrad and Yuzovka were renamed Zinovievsk and Stalino, respectively.

Decisions made by the Party elite were not subject to wide discussion, debate, or appeal. It was only abroad, in Russian émigré circles, that the renaming of the former imperial capital was met with a squall of protests and mockery. In particular, it was pointed out correctly that Lenin had spent relatively little time in Petrograd during his life, apparently had not liked the city, and moved the Soviet government to Moscow at the first opportunity. For the Russian émigrés and for many others as well, it was clear that the process of "plebeianization" of the city, which began with renaming Petersburg Petrograd, had taken another giant step. A popular joke circulated in the city that if the Bolsheviks had the nerve to give Lenin's name to the creation of Peter the Great, then the famous "proletarian poet" Demyan Bedny could just as easily demand that "the works of Pushkin" be changed to "the works of Bedny."

Young Shostakovich was one of the people who was not afraid to express outrage over the renaming of the city. Ignoring the danger of possible inspection, he wrote to Tatyana Glivenko, "Lenin was always against ceremony.... If I become as great a man as Lenin, when I die will the city be renamed Shostakovichgrad?" And later Shostakovich liked to joke about the cult of Lenin that reigned in the Soviet Union. "I love the music of Ilyich," he would proclaim. Using only the patronymic was the affected way in Russia to refer to Vladimir Ilyich Lenin, who, as we know, did not compose music. After savoring the confusion of his interlocutor, Shostakovich would explain gravely, "Naturally, I mean the music of Peter Ilyich Tchaikovsky."

From the ideological point of view, such jokes were not harmless. The Lenin mystique was being broadly inculcated; even superficial deviations from the official cult were perceived as heresy. So it was only among close, trusted friends that Shostakovich would sometimes sing, after having a few drinks, the song of the Baltic sailors: "Burn bright, candle in Ilyich's ruddy backside."

The terrible flooding of Leningrad in September 1924 was seen by many as a punishment for the name change. Olga Freidenberg, the poet Boris Pasternak's cousin, recalled, "The city was turning into a vessel. The water rose from the bottom up to the sky. We stood by the window and watched floors of buildings disappear. Even though our apartment was on the fourth floor, the terror we felt is impossible to describe."[8] Veniamin Kaverin described the foreboding of Leningraders when suddenly "the water imposed chaos and a silence unknown in the city from the days of its founding. When the lights went out in all the houses. And the signal cannon boomed every three minutes. When the schismatics, trapped at the common graves on the Field of Mars prayed loudly, rejoicing that at last the time had come for the destruction of the city, built by the Antichrist on the swamps."[9]

Shostakovich hastily informed his Moscow friend, the pianist and composer Lev Oborin, that "the city, especially the Petrograd Side and Vasilyevsky Island, are badly damaged. Huge boats lie on their sides on the embankments. It'll take colossal amounts of money to clean it all up. Lots of valuable sets and scenery were soaked and washed away from the Maryinsky Theater. Lots of animals perished in the zoo and the botanical gardens are totally destroyed. It's a disaster."[10]

Pasternak immediately pointed out the historical and poetic parallels: "A strange coincidence. It's exactly the hundredth anniversary of the flood that was the basis of *The Bronze Horseman*."[11] The famous flood of November 7, 1824, had given rise to numerous symbolic and mystical interpretations. The fact that Alexander I died almost exactly a year after it was a favorite point. In 1924 rumors connected the flood with Lenin's death and the subsequent renaming of the city. Pushkin's *Bronze Horseman* was more popular than ever.

Just a half century before that, the attitude toward *The Bronze Horseman* was much more ambivalent. Pushkin's status as the national poet was in doubt, under direct attack from the nihilists. They criticized *The Bronze Horseman*, which according to the radical guru Chernyshevsky, had "no characters, only pictures."

That makes it all the more noteworthy that in 1863 the nineteen-year-old coast guardsman Nikolai Rimsky-Korsakov used *The Bronze Horseman* as an example in the arts in a letter to his mother, sent to Petersburg from aboard the clipper *Almaz* while cruising the Baltic Sea. He had started his first symphony and commented,

> As for whether the public will like my symphony, I can tell you that it will not. It's tricky for a decent work to please the audience. There are exceptions, but they are due to effective orchestration and a more or less dance rhythm, like, for instance, Glinka's *Jota aragonesa*. It combines both prerequisites, but I doubt that the audience appreciates its true beauty. That is also the situation with my symphony.[12]

These lines show many characteristics of the young Rimsky-Korsakov, scion of a noble family, whose father was a highly placed official under Nicholas I and whose grandfather and great-grandfather were admirals in the Russian Navy. They evince his confidence in his talent, his direct nature, common sense, rational approach to art, tendency toward a technical analysis of music, and even his love of Glinka. Most interesting, two of the most popular works by Rimsky-Korsakov in the West, the symphonic show pieces *Capriccio espagnol* (1887) and *Scheherazade* (1888), are in fact orchestrated most effectively and propelled by a strong rhythm, particularly *Capriccio*. The orchestral innovations of these works were used by the French: Debussy, Ravel, and Paul Dukas.

In Russia, Rimsky-Korsakov is particularly revered for his fifteen operas (as many as Glinka, Mussorgsky, and Tchaikovsky wrote together); the most popular are the touching fairy tale *The Snow Maiden* (1880–1881); the vivid and melodic *Sadko* (1894–1896), based on an old Russian epic; and the entertaining and dramatic *Tsar's Bride* (1898). His lofty *The Legend of the Invisible City of Kitezh and the Maiden Fevronia* (1903–1904) is considered a masterpiece of Russian spiritual music; its mystical revelations are all the more astonishing because the composer was an agnostic. Now, as before the revolution, Rimsky-Korsakov's symphonic overture *Svetly prazdnik* (*Easter Overture*) is played during the Easter holidays, a musical interpretation, the author explained, of the transition "from the dark and mysterious night of Holy Saturday to the unfettered paganreligious merriment of the morning of Easter Sunday."[13]

One of Rimsky-Korsakov's main achievements was the creation of a highly influential school of composition, of which three of the most popular composers of the twentieth century are members: Igor Stravinsky, Sergei Prokofiev, and Dmitri Shostakovich. The music of each composer is so individual, their aesthetic and political views developed in such different directions, that one easily forgets all three have common roots.

Stravinsky and Prokofiev were the master's students, and his favorite student and son-in-law, Maximilian Steinberg, taught composition to Shostakovich. Thus, Stravinsky and Prokofiev can be considered Rimsky-Korsakov's composing children and Shostakovich his grandson. However, this common lineage is mentioned at best only in individual biographies of the respective composer; they are never examined as the products of one system of teaching, with a shared background of beginning rules.

The very concept of a Petersburg school of composition, unlike that of the Second Viennese School, did not become part of the aesthetic lexicon of the twentieth century, even though the music of the former is performed much more frequently than that of the latter (Arnold Schoenberg, Alban Berg, and Anton von Webern). And it is unlikely that this trend in popularity is going to flag in the near future.

The Petersburg school of composition has been neglected for both aesthetic and political reasons that, as so often happens, are tightly intertwined. The aesthetics and music of the Second (or New) Viennese School (named after the "First" Viennese School of Haydn, Mozart, and Beethoven) filled the European cultural vacuum after World War II. Hitler had persecuted modernism, and therefore its triumph in the fifties was perceived not only as an aesthetic victory but as a matter of political justice. Schoenberg, Berg, and Webern not only personified the break with Nazi ideology with their highly individualistic, innovative works, but at the same time they reestablished the authority and leadership of German-Austrian music. Those composers were deservedly promoted in postwar Germany and Austria, then practically elevated to the canon. In Europe and America this canonization was accepted with sympathy and understanding and by some with hearty approval. Innumerable books, studies, theoretical conferences, and seminars were the process by which members of the Second Viennese School were fixed in positions of influence among music professionals.

In contrast, no one was interested in glorifying the achievements of the Petersburg school. The very word "Petersburg" has been missing from the map for over three quarters of the twentieth century. In the Soviet Union, one preferred not to recall the former glory of the city. In addition, Stravinsky, Prokofiev, and Shostakovich at various times were considered ideological enemies by the Soviet government, with many of their works banned from performance. The first Soviet biography of Stravinsky appeared only in 1964; as recently as 1960 he was still called "a political and ideological renegade" who had lost "all ties with the spiritual culture of his people." Clearly, in such conditions, there could be no talk of propagandizing the Petersburg school of composition, even though it included the leading names of Russian music.

At the source of this school was Mikhail Glinka. By the middle of the nineteenth century Glinka had moved Russian national music forward with a mighty shove, as Pushkin had done several decades earlier with literature. The good fortune of the new Russian culture was that its founders turned out to be such harmonious and protean creators. Both managed in their works to be simultaneously profound and light, complex and simple, tragic and playful, refined and folk-like. Never again in Russian culture would an artist achieve a comparable balance.

Both Glinka and Pushkin were, like Janus, simultaneously Westernizers and nationalists. That is why their work could be claimed as models by representatives of opposite camps. People in Russia inevitably returned to Glinka and Pushkin again and again. No matter how strong the clashes, the basic tradition that the two titans represented remained a common inheritance. Thus, Glinka remained a model both for Tchaikovsky and for the Mighty Five, even though aesthetically they held hostile positions. Tchaikovsky was impressed by the Western tendencies in Glinka's music. The members of the Mighty Five, Mussorgsky in particular, elevated Glinka's nationalism.

The question was which interpretation of Glinka's heritage would become the more influential, and consequently, which path would the Petersburg school follow. It would seem that Tchaikovsky, the star of the first graduating class of the Petersburg Conservatory and an audience favorite, held all the cards. The talent and aggressiveness of the Mighty Five were no substitute for a systematic professional education so necessary for the building of any musical academy—besides which, Tchaikovsky had the sympathy of the court and of the Russian musical bureaucracy.

But in fact Tchaikovsky was edged out of Petersburg, where the musical tradition began forming to a significant degree outside his influence. This took place largely because of the efforts of Rimsky-Korsakov, who possessed all the qualities needed for the methodical construction of the edifice for the Petersburg musical academy, which eventually became the "school of Rimsky-Korsakov."

Rimsky-Korsakov spent thirty-seven of his sixty-four years as professor of the Petersburg Conservatory, bringing up several generations of composers. A list here will give some idea of his "offspring": Alexander Glazunov, Anatoly Liadov, Anton Arensky, Mikhail Ippolitov-Ivanov, Alexander Grechaninov, Mikhail Gnessin, Nikolai Tcherepnin, and Nikolai Myaskovsky, as well as musicians who became leaders of their national cultures: the Latvians Jāzeps Vītols, Emīls Dārziņš and Emilis Melngailis; the Estonians Artur Kapp and Mart Saar; the Ukrainian Nikolai Lysenko; the Armenian Alexander Spendiarov; the Georgian Meliton Balanchivadze.

Two outstanding figures of Petersburg modernism, Kuzmin and Evreinov, also studied with Rimsky-Korsakov. And for five months in 1901 Ottorino Respighi, a musician from Bologna, studied composition with Rimsky-Korsakov. His brilliant orchestrations reveal the influence of the Petersburg master.

In 1921 the Opoyaz group published "Dostoyevsky and Gogol (Toward a Theory of Parody)," a brochure that explains much about artistic inheritance written by one of its members, Yuri Tynyanov, when he was twenty four years old. Tynyanov proposed that tradition in culture is not passed in a straight line, from the elder representatives of a school to the younger ones: "Succession is first of all a struggle, the destruction of the old whole and a new construction from the old elements."[14] In the course of this struggle, people do not clash as fiercely with representatives of another school or another tradition, he noted. "You simply go around them, rejecting or revering, you struggle against them by the very fact of your existence."[15] In other words, talented students often rise up against their own teachers and older friends, while they simply ignore their enemies.

Tynyanov's analysis is an excellent illustration of the situation inside the Petersburg musical academy. One of the students described it more colorfully:

> Rimsky-Korsakov's severe rectitude as a teacher and his extraordinarily warm concern at the same time for the achievements or failures of his students, their loyalty toward their teacher and also their struggle against him, leaving him and returning with repentance— these complex relations filled with ideals and emotions between the great teacher and his students, sometimes very talented ones, were somewhat reminiscent of Leonardo da Vinci and his school.[16]

The tall, gray-bearded Rimsky-Korsakov, with his thin, wrinkled face, round glasses, and deep voice, seemed unfriendly and aloof to many people. But Igor Stravinsky, like his other close students, saw a surrogate father figure in the master. Stravinsky first showed his compositions to Rimsky-Korsakov in the summer of 1902, when the younger man was twenty years old. By the time he began regular studies with Rimsky-Korsakov in early 1903, the young composer had recently lost his father and became extremely close to his teacher.

Stravinsky was accepted in the Rimsky-Korsakov home and was good friends with his son, Andrei. The master apparently realized that his student had an unusual gift; that is probably why he did not recommend that Stravinsky enter the Petersburg Conservatory but nevertheless taught him the fundamental technical knowledge in composition. Stravinsky's technique is undoubtedly rooted in his private studies with Rimsky-Korsakov.

At first, the master tried to turn Stravinsky into a true professional in the Petersburg sense of the word. That meant in particular a rational approach to the process of composition, rigorous self-discipline, accuracy, and neatness, elevated to aesthetic principle. Rimsky-Korsakov urged Stravinsky to compose his first symphony, believing his student would develop these qualities more quickly working in a large form. Stravinsky dedicated that symphony, opus 1, to his teacher.

Rimsky-Korsakov left a brief formulation for a course of composition for gifted musicians like Stravinsky:

> In fact, a talented student needs so little; it is so simple to show him everything needed in harmony and counterpoint to set him on his feet in that work, it is so simple to direct him in understanding the forms of composition, if one goes about it the right way. Just one or two years of systematic study in the development of technique, a few exercises in free composition and orchestration, assuming a good knowledge of the piano—and the studies are over.[17]

At the conservatory there were many students in the famous professor's class, and this irritated the fifteen-year-old Sergei Prokofiev, who wanted Rimsky-Korsakov's undivided attention. The maestro sat at the piano and looked through all the exercises in counterpoint his students brought him. He played endless fugues, preludes, canons, and arrangements, but refused to look through a student's work if written in pencil, declaring, "I do not wish to go blind because of you." (Later Shostakovich would also insist that his composition students write their scores in ink.)

Rimsky-Korsakov would begin his first class at the conservatory this way, according to one of his students, Nikolai Malko: "'I will speak, and you will listen. Then I will speak less, and you will start to work. And finally I will not speak at all, and you will work.' And that's the way it was," Malko concluded. "Rimsky-Korsakov explained everything so clearly and simply that all we had to do was to do our work well."[18]

Prokofiev had trouble breaking through the crowd that surrounded the maestro.

> The ones who knew how much they could learn from Rimsky-
> Korsakov got the benefit despite the crowding. I approached
> the lessons half-heartedly, and the Schubert marches for four
> hands that Rimsky-Korsakov made us orchestrate I found clumsy
> and uninteresting. My instrumentation did not satisfy Rimsky-
> Korsakov. "Instead of thinking, you simply choose on your fingers
> whether it should be oboe or clarinet," he used to say. Shutting his
> eyes, he would twirl his index fingers and then try unsuccessfully
> to make them meet. I would look triumphantly at my comrades,
> to gloat at the old man being angry, but their faces would be
> serious.[19]

Despite the fact that Prokofiev was offended by the maestro's attitude
toward him, the ambitious teenager was thrilled by Rimsky-
Korsakov's opera *The Legend of the Invisible City of Kitezh*, which
premiered in February 1907. Prokofiev was captivated by the grand
mystical fresco that told in epic tones of the miraculous salvation of
the ancient Russian city from the Tatar invasion.

The legend of Kitezh became popular in the elite circles of Petersburg. Kitezh, which was inundated by God's will and made invisible, was discussed in the fashionable religio-philosophical societies
of those years as a symbol of the desired purity that was unattainable
in modern times. Zinaida Hippius even juxtaposed the legendary
Kitezh and the real Petersburg, mired in sin.

Rimsky-Korsakov's opera was almost immediately compared
to Wagner's *Parsifal*. Interestingly, Akhmatova thought more highly
of *Kitezh* than of *Parsifal*; for all the similarity in approach of the two
composers to a mystical theme, Akhmatova sensed a false piety in *Parsifal* and an intuitive, pure religious feeling, typical of the Russian people, in Rimsky-Korsakov's work.[20]

Akhmatova also noted the exceptional literary quality of the
libretto of *Kitezh*, written by Vladimir Belsky. The libretto's influence
is apparent in Akhmatova's lengthy mystical poem of 1940, *The Way
of All Earth*, in which she considers herself a denizen of the vanished
Kitezh. At that moment, she associated the legendary Kitezh with the
beloved city on the Neva that had lived through such horrible trials.
By 1940, Petersburg's image was transformed from the antithesis of
Kitezh to its twin.

Prokofiev was awed by the fantastical orchestration in *Kitezh*, its rhythmic diversity, the psychological complexity of the characters, especially the "Dostoyevskian" part of the traitor Grishka Kuterma, performed by Ivan Ershov, Petersburg's best Wagnerian tenor, "with extraordinary brilliance and drama," as Prokofiev recalled. "But most of all I liked *The Battle of Kerzhenets*, which at the time I thought was the best thing Rimsky-Korsakov had written."[21]

The astounding symphonic picture depicting the decisive battle of the Russian troops against the fierce Tatar horde was the high point of *Kitezh*. The fact that the confrontation was depicted by the orchestra and not on stage merely emphasized the opera's epic character. If one can call Mussorgsky's vocal ballad "Forgotten" a brilliant battle engraving, then *The Battle of Kerzhenets* was the greatest Russian musical fresco about war until Shostakovich. This work seemed to foretell the further metamorphosis of the Petersburg mythos by not praising the victors but the vanquished—their valor in the face of inexorable evil power. As Prokofiev wrote, "It was all new and astonished the imagination."[22]

When Rimsky-Korsakov died in 1908, even Prokofiev, a man not given to sentimentality, admitted that he was "profoundly saddened: something hurt my heart. I loved Rimsky-Korsakov's music, especially *Kitezh, Sadko, The Snow Maiden*, the piano concerto, *Capriccio espagnol, Scheherazade, Fairy Tale*." And the vain but honest Prokofiev added, "I never had the opportunity to become close to him personally: there were many students in his class and he did not distinguish me from the rest."[23]

If Rimsky-Korsakov had managed to live another four years to hear the premiere of Prokofiev's daring First Piano Concerto, it is unlikely he would have clasped the twenty-one-year-old composer to his breast. Even though his last operas, especially the fairy tale-based *Kashchei the Immortal* and *The Golden Cockerel*, toyed with modernism, introducing unusual harmonies and "prickly" melodies, Rimsky-Korsakov was increasingly intolerant of the musical avant-garde of his day; for example, he was very critical of Claude Debussy and Richard Strauss.

After hearing Strauss's *Salome* for the first time in Paris, Rimsky-Korsakov's wife wrote in horror to her son in Petersburg, "It is so disgusting, there is nothing worse in the world. Even Papa hissed for the first time in his life."[24] Strauss repaid the debt by describing a concert (under the aegis of Diaghilev) of Glinka, Borodin, and

Rimsky-Korsakov thus: "Even though it was all very nice, we, unfortunately, are no longer children."[25]

Rimsky-Korsakov undoubtedly would have also rejected Stravinsky's *Petrouchka* if he had lived to hear it. The maestro of the Petersburg school's "ideal" student was Alexander Glazunov, his junior by twenty-one years. The teacher adored Glazunov, never ceasing to be impressed by his protégé's talent, taste, sense of measure, and mastery of counterpoint and orchestration. The premiere of sixteen-year-old Glazunov's First Symphony in 1882 at the Assembly of the Nobility was a sensation, according to Rimsky-Korsakov: "It was a truly great day for all of us, the Petersburg representatives of the young Russian school. Young in inspiration, but already mature in technique and form, the symphony was a great success. Stasov bubbled and hummed at full blast. The audience was stunned to see that the composer who came out for bows was still in the uniform of a gymnasium student."[26]

Among the admirers surrounding the young man at the premiere, besides the colorful figure of the boisterous Stasov, was a handsome man of middle age with an expressive face framed by a mane of hair. Mitrofan Belyaev, the Petersburg timber millionaire, saw in Glazunov a new genius and a "pillar of Russian music," who had to be supported in every way possible.

An amateur musician, Belyaev's taste was formed under the influence of another outstanding student of Rimsky-Korsakov, the composer, conductor, and teacher Anatoly Liadov, ten years older than Glazunov. Famous as the "sixth," junior member of the Mighty Five, Liadov was a master of refined piano and orchestral miniatures, of which the most famous were written in the last decade of his life (1905–1914): "Baba Yaga," "Kikimora," and "The Magic Lake." But Liadov composed his little masterpieces (whose orchestral innovations most probably influenced Stravinsky) extremely slowly, "a teaspoon per hour," as the Russian expression puts it.

When Diaghilev needed a Russian fairy tale ballet for his Paris company, he first approached Liadov with the idea for *The Firebird*. Only when he saw that Liadov would never write the ballet did he approach Stravinsky. It was also assumed that the first Russian ballet on the Scythian theme would be written by Liadov; but as we know, Prokofiev realized that idea. There is something symbolic in this: "the fathers" were incapable of keeping up with the times and, kicking all the way, gave up the limelight to their rambunctious "children."

Liadov's phlegmatic nature was legendary. Yet many considered him an inspiring teacher. Malko, who studied harmony with him at the conservatory, maintained, "Liadov's critical comments were always precise, clear, understandable, constructive, and brief. . . . And it was done indolently, without haste, sometimes seemingly disdainfully. He could suddenly stop in midword, take out a small scissors from his pocket and start doing something with his fingernail, while we all waited."[27]

Liadov was the first to point out Glazunov's gifts to Belyaev. Pleased first with Glazunov's work, the millionaire then decided to take an entire group of national composers under his patronage. He created a large, noncommercial music publishing house unprecedented in Russia and in the world and an organization he called Russian Symphonic Concerts, all to promote the new works of those Russian musicians dear to his heart. Both the publishing house and the concerts were set up on a large scale; Belyaev spent tens of thousands of rubles on them annually.

He also held "Fridays" for musicians in his spacious Petersburg apartment. They performed quartets (Belyaev played the viola) and then repaired to a luxurious dinner with copious amounts of alcohol. These Fridays eventually grew, as a continuation of the Petersburg musical tradition, into the Belyaev Circle.

The Belyaev Circle succeeded the Mighty Five as the dominant musical force in Petersburg. Rimsky-Korsakov became head of the Belyaev Circle, and he defined their difference from the Mighty Five as follows:

> The Balakirev circle corresponded to the period of Sturm und Drang in the development of Russian music, the Belyaev circle to the period of calm forward movement; the Balakirev was revolutionary, the Belyaev progressive. The Balakirev circle was exclusive and intolerant, the Belyaev was more indulgent and eclectic.[28]

But in fact it requires a stretch of the imagination to call the Belyaev Circle "progressive"; it was more accurate to call it "moderately academic." Several significant musicians (Liadov and Glazunov, for instance) belonged to it, but the majority were merely erudite composers whose works were derivative. They turned technical accomplishment into an end in itself. The desire for technical perfection had always characterized the Petersburg academy, and the productions of the Belyaev Circle composers demonstrated the dead end to which this road could lead. The Belyaev group regarded with suspicion everything that violated the canons it established.

"Rimsky-Korsakov followed his age, and each new work was yet another concession of genius to his times and to modernity,"[29] Asafyev wrote in his *Book About Stravinsky*. It could be said that Rimsky-Korsakov was urged forward by his great talent. One of his favorite expressions was, "Well, if we're going, we're going, said the parrot when the cat pulled it out of the cage." After Rimsky-Korsakov's death the movement of the Belyaev Circle came to a halt. Petersburg academism triumphed and there could be no talk now of tolerance for the ever-more impatient Russian musical avant-garde.

Prokofiev, who had shown Liadov his school works, recalled that even the most innocent innovations drove the latter crazy. "Shoving his hands in his pockets and rocking in his soft woolen shoes without heels, he would say, 'I don't understand why you are studying with me. Go to Richard Strauss, go to Debussy.' This was said in a tone that meant 'Go to the devil!' "[30] Yet Liadov told his acquaintances about Prokofiev. "I am obliged to teach him. He must form his technique, his style—first in piano music."[31]

In 1916 Glazunov left the concert hall during the premiere of Prokofiev's *Scythian Suite* and, as the newspapers reported with relish, "did not spare words" in evaluating the new work. Ten years later, Glazunov wrote to a pianist friend, "I never considered Stravinsky a good musician. I have proof that his ear was never developed, as his teacher Rimsky-Korsakov had told me."[32] Glazunov was so hostile toward Stravinsky that he did not even return his greeting when he bumped into him in Paris in 1935, the year before Glazunov's death. At the time, both composers were émigrés and their political positions (which was very important in those days) basically coincided. But the aesthetic gap turned out to be too great for Glazunov to bridge. Stravinsky repaid Glazunov by belittling his music at every opportunity, turning him into the personification of the Petersburg academism he so hated.

In 1905 Glazunov, with Rimsky-Korsakov's active support, was appointed director of the Petersburg Conservatory. He remained at that post for over twenty years, becoming a legend. Heavyset, lost in thought, Glazunov moved quietly along the conservatory halls, cigar in hand, leaving a scent in the air. Students would sniff and say, "The director was just here."

As a composer, Glazunov was highly respected in that era. Even the irreverent Prokofiev was impressed for a while by his eight symphonies and at first enjoyed playing them in a four-handed version with his conservatory friend Myaskovsky. Pianists eagerly performed Glazunov's two piano concertos, and his melodic Violin Concerto (1904), which enjoyed great popularity among violinists. And everyone hailed Glazunov's romantic ballet, *Raymonda*, which was choreographed by Petipa in 1898, performed with unfailing success at the Maryinsky Theater, and became a repertory staple throughout the world. From time to time Glazunov conducted this brilliantly orchestrated ballet himself, because he was drawn to conducting like a child to a favorite toy, even though he had no talent for it. Nevertheless, he liked to joke, "You can criticize my compositions, but you can't deny that I am a good conductor and a remarkable conservatory director."

Everyone knew that Glazunov gave his all to the conservatory. As Prokofiev recalled, "he would either be off to see Procurator Korsak to intercede on behalf of a student who was going to be exiled for revolutionary activity, or appealing for a residence permit for a talented Jew or giving away his director's salary for scholarships for the students."[33] And Glazunov remained just as dogged a defender of the conservatory after the Bolsheviks came to power. Undoubtedly, the main reason why he did not emigrate immediately after the revolution was the desire to defend his beloved conservatory from the destruction that threatened it. Together with his students, Glazunov went through difficult times; he lost weight and grew haggard, his worn suit hanging from his once corpulent body as if from a hanger. But the director continued the ritual inspections of the institution entrusted to him, albeit without the cigar, a commodity impossible to obtain in those years.

The Bolsheviks were impressed by the composer's European fame, and Glazunov managed even in the hardest of times to obtain special food parcels for particularly gifted students. Viktor Shklovsky wrote down the following story, which was recounted to him by Maxim Gorky, whom the conservatory director visited in the hungry year of 1921.

"Yes," Glazunov says, "I need a food parcel, even though our candidate is very young—he was born in 1906."

"A violinist? They start young. Or a pianist?"

"A composer."

"How old is he?"

"He'll be fifteen. The son of a music teacher. He brought me his work."

"You like it?"

"Its awful! It's the first music I can't hear just by reading the score."

"Then why have you come?"

"I don't like it, but that's not the point. The future belongs to this boy, not to me. Well, I don't like it. Too bad. This will be our music, and we have to get an academy food parcel for him."

"I'm putting him on the list. Name?"

"Shostakovich."[34]

Unlike Stravinsky and Prokofiev, Shostakovich did not study with Rimsky-Korsakov. In 1919, when the thirteen-year-old Mitya Shostakovich entered the Petrograd Conservatory, Rimsky-Korsakov had been dead for eleven years. In that period the Petersburg school of composition was often called the "school of Rimsky-Korsakov-Glazunov." As the caretaker of Rimsky-Korsakov's legacy, Glazunov's influence on Petrograd's musical life was all-encompassing.

It was Glazunov who appreciated Prokofiev's childhood works and insisted that he enter the Petersburg Conservatory; it was then that he gave the remarkable thirteen-year-old a copy of Glinka's score for his *Valse-Fantaisie*, inscribed "To dear co-brother Seryozha Prokofiev from Glazunov." But the "dear co-brother" turned out to be too insubordinate for Glazunov's taste. In conversations with me in the 1970s Shostakovich often emphasized that he, not Prokofiev, had been a very "obedient" student.

Glazunov was moved by Shostakovich's talent and gave the young musician the highest grades on composition examinations (a five in the Russian five-point system), with remarks such as: "Exceptionally vivid and early-maturing gift. Worthy of awe and delight. Marvelous technical ability, interesting, original content (5+)," or "Vivid outstanding creative gift. In music much imagination and inventiveness. In a period of finding himself (5+)."[35]

Yet in purely creative terms the young Stravinsky and Prokofiev could be placed in Rimsky-Korsakov's orbit much more than Shostakovich. Stravinsky's early symphony, when first publicly performed in Petersburg in 1908, was perceived as a composition, according to Asafyev, "displaying the complete mastery of the methods of his favorite teachers, including Glazunov."[36] Rimsky-Korsakov even felt that in this symphony Stravinsky was "imitating too much" both Glazunov and himself. It is not difficult to determine that Stravinsky's first ballet, *The Firebird* (1910), was written by a student of Rimsky-Korsakov. The exotic harmonies of Rimsky-Korsakov's operas *Kashchei the Immortal* and *The Golden Cockerel* surely are reflected in Stravinsky's opera *The Nightingale*, first produced by Diaghilev in 1914. The early Stravinsky's orchestral palette was also heavily indebted to the Petersburg maestro.

Rimsky-Korsakov's influence on Prokofiev is probably even more profound. Prokofiev's symphonies are built more as paintings in the style of Rimsky-Korsakov's symphonic poems than as developing psychological dramas in the manner of Rimsky-Korsakov's rival, Tchaikovsky. It was Shostakovich who picked up Tchaikovsky's symphonic technique.

But Shostakovich also adopted Rimsky-Korsakov's attitude toward orchestration as a quality of musical thought and not something external that is added to the composition like a dress on a hanger. Rimsky-Korsakov said this about his *Capriccio Espagnol*: "The opinion of the critics and audience that the Capriccio is a brilliantly orchestrated piece is incorrect. The Capriccio is a brilliant composition for the orchestra."[37] In other words, the orchestration is born with the music being composed; it is a characteristic of it, not a later "addition."

For Shostakovich this idea became a leading artistic principle, and it explains why he was dubious about Prokofiev's later practice of allowing other musicians to orchestrate his works. Shostakovich was not satisfied by the explanation that Prokofiev made rather detailed preliminary sketches for them. Shostakovich usually imagined a new composition in the form of a full score that he had to write down himself, even though in his last years, when he had difficulties in using his right hand, doing so was quite a problem for him.

As he did with Prokofiev, Glazunov persuaded Shostakovich's parents to let the youth study composition at the conservatory. Glazunov was the guest of honor at Shostakovich's fifteenth birthday party in 1921, when the young composer's father, a noted chemist at the Main Chamber of Weights and Measures, was still alive. Mitya was made uncomfortable by the close relations between the conservatory director and his parents. He told me the reasons much later.

Glazunov was subject to bouts of heavy drinking. Early in their regime, the Bolsheviks had banned the official sale of wine and vodka. Yet Shostakovich's father had access to strictly rationed spirit alcohol through his work. Learning this, Glazunov sometimes asked him to get him some of the precious liquid. These requests were transmitted through Mitya, who was bothered by this for two reasons. First, he feared Glazunov's requests were endangering his father. The times were hard and it was impossible to guess whom the Bolsheviks would suddenly decide to shoot as a lesson to others. The recent execution of Gumilyov was on everybody's mind. Second, Mitya did not want his success at the conservatory to be attributed to bribery.

Maximilian Steinberg, Shostakovich's teacher, was head of the composition department of the conservatory then. He adored his student, according to Bogdanov-Berezovsky.[38] Steinberg was a typical representative of the Belyaev Circle, but his conservative orientation did not keep him from considering Shostakovich the most talented young composer in Leningrad and the hope of Russian music.

Then and later, Shostakovich could be rather skeptical about Steinberg, but it was nothing compared with the violent emotions Stravinsky seemed to have about the teacher. Stravinsky told the conductor Malko in 1934 (and only partly tongue in cheek, it seems), "So many people died in the revolution, why did Steinberg survive? I'm not bloodthirsty but . . . they shot engineers, why did these people keep on living? I left because I couldn't bear the life that those obscurantists created for me. And now Steinberg's at the conservatory." A bit taken aback, Malko reminded Stravinsky that he must have liked Steinberg at one time; he had dedicated the orchestral fantasy *Fireworks* to Steinberg on the occasion of the latter's wedding to Rimsky-Korsakov's daughter. Stravinsky replied with a sigh, "Yes, and so now I'm tied to Steinberg for the rest of my life. But now I don't want to know him. He's a mediocrity."[39]

In the same conversation with the conductor, Stravinsky noted that he heard Malko conducting Shostakovich on the radio: "I liked him—you can see tradition in him. I like being able to see where a person has come from."[40] He was undoubtedly speaking of Shostakovich's First Symphony, which was first played under Malko's baton on May 12, 1926, in Leningrad. Shostakovich began composing the symphony in 1923, when he was sixteen. Malko, who was then the chief conductor of the orchestra of the Leningrad Philharmonic, decided to perform it even though some conservative musicians felt Shostakovich could wait another year.

Before the concert Shostakovich was consumed with anxiety, nervously enumerating the possible complications in a letter to a friend in Moscow:

What if it doesn't sound right? That would be a humiliating scandal. I mean, if they boo the symphony, that would hurt. So, there are lots of worries, I can't list them all. Besides worries like this, there are even more unpleasant ones. What if they cancel the concert? What if Malko gets sick or misses the train and doesn't get back in time? It's all very unpleasant. And very tiring and enervating.[41]

The premiere in the acoustically marvelous hall of the Leningrad Philharmonic (the former Assembly of the Nobility) was a triumph. The nineteen-year-old composer, thin, wearing glasses, still a boy, with a forelock that would become famous, awkwardly took his bows. The audience kept looking over at Glazunov, who sat in his usual sixth-row-aisle seat. He had no intention of quitting the hall (as he had with Prokofiev); on the contrary, he smiled and applauded, even though the young composer had not followed his persistent recommendation to change a bad-sounding (to the maestro) part in the introduction.

This was a significant moment in the history of the Petersburg school of composition. Forty-four years earlier in the same hall, Glazunov's First Symphony had been performed, and ever since he had been the leading composer of his generation, the "Russian Brahms." Shostakovich's symphony had an even more brilliant future; just a year later it was conducted in Berlin by Bruno Walter, and soon after it was included in the repertory of Leopold Stokowski and Arturo Toscanini. Shostakovich had no intention of remaining a model student of the Petersburg school. But at that moment very few people guessed that.

In Shostakovich's symphony, the first audiences heard the influence of the later Rimsky-Korsakov and his students, Stravinsky and Prokofiev. The more attentive could have pointed out traces of Scriabin, Richard Strauss, and some Mahler. The accent in the symphony was on continuing tradition rather than breaking with it. In that city musicians did not merely value tradition—they worshipped it. It seemed particularly important to preserve it in an era of unprecedented social upheaval. The fact that talented young people respected tradition was a comfort.

As it was, the Petersburg school of composition had just entered a period of convulsions. Its time as a school exclusively of the Rimsky-Korsakov–Glazunov line had ended. Once Rimsky-Korsakov had managed to supersede Tchaikovsky in Petersburg. Now Tchaikovsky's music was coming back with a vengeance.

Beginning composers were also becoming more and more influenced by the musical world of Mussorgsky. In his day Rimsky-Korsakov had done more than anyone to preserve the heritage of his late comrade from the Mighty Five. He completed and orchestrated his opera *Khovanshchina*, and edited and reorchestrated *Boris Godunov*. With the help of Rimsky-Korsakov, these works won world fame.

Rimsky-Korsakov had not foreseen that Mussorgsky's acclaim and influence would exceed his own. Nor would he have imagined that Mussorgsky, whom he considered a technically helpless dilettante who tossed snatches of confused ideas onto paper, would become a model for several generations of Russian composers. For Stravinsky, Prokofiev, and Shostakovich, the works of Tchaikovsky and especially Mussorgsky occupied an incomparably higher place in the pantheon of Russian music than Rimsky-Korsakov and Glazunov. Shostakovich even repeated Rimsky-Korsakov's enormous labor and redid the orchestration of *Boris Godunov* in 1940 and of *Khovanshchina* in 1959. (In 1913 Stravinsky worked with Ravel at Diaghilev's request to reorchestrate the original numbers from *Khovanshchina* omitted by Rimsky-Korsakov.)

Shostakovich's editions did not win out over the Rimsky-Korsakov versions. In the twentieth century, the idea took hold that Mussorgsky should be performed whenever possible in the composer's own versions. What Rimsky-Korsakov saw as "carelessness," "clumsiness," and "composer's deafness" was now perceived as visionary breakthroughs. The movement for Mussorgsky's rehabilitation began in Petersburg in the 1910s and received its strongest impulse in Leningrad in 1928, when *Boris Godunov* had its first performance in the author's version. And so Mussorgsky gradually became a part of the Petersburg canon.

This helped guarantee the viability of the Petersburg musical tradition. The Petersburg school of composition retained its characteristic striving for form, brilliant orchestration, and exotic harmony but also acquired a taste for the emotional, "wavelike" development of musical material à la Tchaikovsky and the dramatic "Dostoyevskian" contrasts à la Mussorgsky.

Placed by history among particularly harsh conditions, sometimes struggling for its very existence, the Petersburg school of composition nevertheless continued to develop. It absorbed the creative heritage of its famous pupils, in particular the structural and rhythmic innovations of Stravinsky and Prokofiev's methods of melodic development. Later, the school came to be associated with the tradition of the so-called philosophical symphonies in the style of Shostakovich, the composer of fifteen symphonies, a man recognized by many as one of the world's giants in this genre in the twentieth century.

Shostakovich, pleased by the success of his First Symphony on the night of its premiere, probably did not think about Mussorgsky, Tchaikovsky, Rimsky-Korsakov, and the fate of the Petersburg school just then. After the concert Steinberg, Malko, and Mitya's young friends went to the Shostakovich home to celebrate.[42] Steinberg gave Shostakovich a score of Beethoven's Ninth Symphony. Malko, more agitated than usual, returned late at night and could not sleep. He wrote a letter to a friend that night: "I have the feeling that I have turned a new page in the history of symphonic music and discovered a major new composer."

Shostakovich had the gift of charm and easily won over new acquaintances. He was particularly comfortable and animated with adults, despite his apparent awkwardness and a certain shyness. He was even perceived by some of his older friends as being "electrically charged."[43]

When Shostakovich was only seventeen, the Petersburg journal *Teatr* called him a genius. Early fame naturally attracted attention. But the young Shostakovich also projected the impression of an intense inner life. The first famous portrait of Mitya, done in charcoal and bloodred in September 1919 by the Petrograd artist Boris Kustodiev, depicts him deep in thought.

Kustodiev, who was forty-one, inscribed the portrait, "To my little friend Mitya Shostakovich from the artist." Shostakovich had been introduced to the artist by a classmate, Kustodiev's daughter, but it was the father who became his friend. For Kustodiev Shostakovich played Grieg, Chopin, Schumann, and his own first compositions. Kustodiev called him Florestan, after one of the characters in Schumann's *Carnival*, impetuous and poetic: apparently Mitya was not too embarrassed to reveal himself to the artist, with the piano an intermediary in their communication.

For Shostakovich, Kustodiev personified a link with the Russian past. He was a member of *Mir iskusstva*, in which he had played an important role. Benois, the leader of *Mir iskusstva*, and the majority of his comrades were committed Westernizers. What interested them the most in Russian history was the classicist eighteenth century, where they found ties and parallels with western Europe. Kustodiev, who was enormously popular, felt out of place among the refined members of *Mir iskusstva*. The themes of his paintings were mostly folk Russian: fairs, holidays, dressed-up crowds, merchants, clerks, peasants, white churches with golden domes, troikas—all painted colorfully, with overflowing feeling, not at all in the style of *Mir iskusstva*. As Petrov-Vodkin recalled, the leaders of *Mir iskusstva* were silent before Kustodiev's paintings. Some critics considered his works a revival of the traditions of the Wanderers, the final fireworks of that movement.

The women painted by the *Mir iskusstva* group were usually refined Petersburg ladies, whereas the women Kustodiev painted were of the merchant class—big-boned, calm, epitomizing spiritual and physical health. Russians use the expression "Kustodiev woman" the way "Rubenesque" is used in the West. But only at first glance do Kustodiev's works appear to be the apotheosis of triumphant flesh. As a Russian critic noted, "In the voluptuousness of the full-bodied beauties you sense the artist's irony, anxiety, and longing—the spirit of the Russian intellectual on the cusp of two centuries."[44]

Kustodiev's ambivalence toward his constant merchant wife heroine was forcefully expressed in his illustrations for Nikolai Leskov's short story "Lady Macbeth of the Mtsensk District," done in 1922–1923, when Shostakovich was a frequent guest at the artist's home. The tale of the provincial merchant's wife, Katerina Izmailova, who became a murderer out of passionate love, was interpreted by Kustodiev in Dostoyevskian, sometimes grotesque manner. (It is not surprising that Dostoyevsky was the first to publish Leskov's story in 1865 in his journal *Epokha*.) Kustodiev's drawings first appeared in a book in 1930; and it was that edition that started the renewed popularity of Leskov's "Lady Macbeth of the Mtsensk District," which had been almost forgotten by then. Shostakovich read the book and, inspired by Leskov's tale and Kustodiev's work, decided to write an opera based on Leskov; it was to become one of the most famous operas of the twentieth century.

Kustodiev did not live to see either the notable edition or Shostakovich's opera. He died in 1927 at the age of forty-nine, spending the last ten years of his life in a wheelchair as the result of a sarcoma of the spine. The artist, whose canvases were filled with healthy, strong people, could barely move and sometimes suffered intolerable pain. Surgery did not help. Doctors suggested that he seek better treatment in the West. He sought permission for a long time but got his passport too late.

The writer Yevgeny Zamyatin, whose play *The Flea* (also based on Leskov) was produced with sets by Kustodiev that thrilled Leningraders, compared the artist to the Old Russian saints, "with the only difference that his exploit was not in the name of saving his soul but in the name of art."[45] Usually skeptical and rational, Zamyatin was amazed and touched: "What creative willpower must one have to sit like that in a wheelchair, jaws clenched with pain, and paint all those pictures."[46] And Kustodiev, when appearing before his guests, including Shostakovich, was almost always animated, amiable, and elegantly dressed, wearing a tie and white collar. His blond hair was neatly brushed, his mustache and small beard carefully trimmed. He shaved off the beard when it began to show gray, explaining to his wife, "A lot of young people visit us; sometimes there are pretty girls, and the beard ages me."

Kustodiev complained only rarely. "Legs—well, they're a luxury! But when my arm starts to ache, that's a shame."[47] And it was this invalid who painted a six-foot canvas of Fyodor Chaliapin, which was not only the best depiction of the bass but a symbol of the Russian artist. In it, Chaliapin in beaver hat and "boyar" fur coat stands on a hill with a Russian landscape receding into the distance. Kustodiev enlivened the landscape with a country fair. Chaliapin was perhaps the most national of Russian performing musicians: a giant of a man who could be equally supercharged on stage as tsar or peasant. He was a man of the people and understood them. And he was also their mouthpiece, the expression of their emotions, the embodiment of their potential. Kustodiev captured this relationship of the Russian musician with his country, explaining the Chaliapin mystique in these words: "Here you have the immeasurable power of a natural gift and a peasant's clever mind, and a refined mastered culture. A totally unique phenomenon!"[48]

Kustodiev's portrait vibrates and breathes. That symphony of colors made a lasting impression on Shostakovich, not least because he had watched the artist create it. A block and tackle attached to the ceiling of Kustodiev's studio allowed the artist to move the canvas away and toward his wheelchair without assistance. So he worked as if he were painting a church ceiling while in constant pain. For Shostakovich, it was a lesson in professional courage that he recalled some forty years later, when he began losing strength in his right hand and began training the left so he could continue composing. Kustodiev's portrait of Shostakovich hung in the composer's apartment in a place of honor. Bogdanov-Berezovsky liked to say that whenever he thought of that picture, he recalled the lines a young poet, a mutual friend, dedicated to the composer:

> *I love the spring sky,*
> *Right after a storm.*
> *That is your eyes.*[49]

By the beginning of the twentieth century, the Petersburg Conservatory was recognized as one of the world's leading musical academies, preparing first-class performers. It was fitting that its founder was Anton Rubinstein, one of the two greatest pianists of the nineteenth century (the other was Franz Liszt). Rubinstein had brought such European luminaries as the pianist Theodor Leschetitzky and the violinist Henryk Wieniawsky to teach at the conservatory. They both left their mark on Petersburg, spending many years there.

Leschetitzky's influence was particularly strong. One of his most talented students, Annette Esipova, became his second wife. Esipova toured the world many times; New York critics were thrilled by her, and even the sardonic George Bernard Shaw was impressed by her flawless technique. In the late nineteenth century Esipova settled in Petersburg, where she became a professor at the conservatory, making her appearances like a queen surrounded by a retinue of assistants and students. Being accepted in her class was considered a great achievement. One such fortunate student was Prokofiev.

At first he, like everyone else, was in awe of his professor's fame, and considered himself as part of the "conservatory guards." But soon the composer grew disillusioned with Esipova. His rebellious, impatient nature was exasperated by the severe discipline of Esipova's teaching system. In addition, she demanded a clear, "pearl-like" technique, her trademark, from her students, while Prokofiev had trouble dropping his habit of playing rather carelessly.

Nevertheless, he performed powerfully on his final exam in the spring of 1914 and won the Rubinstein Prize, a grand piano given to the best graduating pianist. (There were 108 graduates that year and over twenty-five hundred students at the Petersburg Conservatory in 1914.) Later Prokofiev became a renowned interpreter of his own works, and gave concerts in Europe and the United States.

One of the main musical attractions of Petersburg in the early twentieth century was the much discussed piano trio of Esipova, the violinist Leopold Auer, and the cellist Alexander Verzhbilovich. Auer had appeared in Petersburg in 1868, and after Wieniawsky left he became the leading violin teacher at the conservatory. The list of Auer's students reads like a who's who of twentieth-century violin playing: Yascha Heifetz, Mischa Elman, Efrem Zimbalist, Nathan Milstein. No other pedagogue of the nineteenth or twentieth centuries could boast of such a roster. Auer's class was legendary, and students from all over the world flocked to him.

In his last years Auer did not accept "rough draft" work: he demanded that the student come to class with the music already learned; only then would Auer concentrate on the artistic problems. Milstein recalled Auer's advice: "Practice with your head, not your fingers."[50] That meant the priority of analysis and imagination over mechanical practice. According to Milstein, the impatient professor would not only yell at slow students, he would throw their music at them; even the incomparable Heifetz was not safe from Auer's flashes of anger.

Yet Auer took an individual approach to each of his phenomenal students. He would help a violinist of lyric bent to discover highly dramatic colors, expanding his artistic palette that way. He would lead a student with a fiery temperament toward a more controlled interpretation. All pupils were expected to play with a beautiful, noble sound and in a lofty style.

Auer was a marvelous performer (Tchaikovsky wrote his Violin Concerto for him). The composer Yuri Shaporin recalled the following incident. Shaporin was studying at the Petersburg Conservatory when the word of Professor Auer's extraordinary new student, Yascha Heifetz, circulated through the school. Only Auer's students were permitted to attend his classes. In order to hear the prodigy play, Shaporin sneaked into the small space between the two doors leading to the classroom and scraped away some of the paint covering the glass of the inner door. With his eye glued to the "peephole," Shaporin saw a curly-haired youth in a sailor suit, admirably playing the Glazunov concerto, which Auer himself had premiered in 1905.

When he had finished, Heifetz turned to the professor and asked, "Like that?"

"I don't know."

"Then how?"

Then Auer, who was in his late sixties, got out of his deep armchair, took the boy's little violin, and played the Glazunov concerto from beginning to end with such brilliance and inspiration that Shaporin stood entranced behind the door.

When he had finished, Auer said to Yascha, "Like that!"[51]

Undoubtedly, the aesthetics of both Auer and Esipova developed to a great degree in parallel to the artistic strivings of the Belyaev Circle. No wonder Glazunov dedicated his Violin Concerto to Auer. The similarities in their musical principles are noteworthy: a striving for grandeur and dignity. Both the composer and the teacher valued clarity of thought, neatness of detail, and technical perfection. With the years both Auer and Esipova demanded from their students an ever more serious, restrained, and "objective" approach to their playing.[52]

This Petersburg style of playing might be called academic were it not for the overpowering temperament and acuity manifested in the playing of its most talented representatives. It was rather too full of color and life to be academic. Rather, the style—like the best works of some members of the Belyaev Circle—retained traits of Petersburg pseudoclassicism, which at that very period had become the leading architectural style in the capital of the Russian Empire.

A great distance separates pseudoclassicism from neoclassicism. The former is incomparably more conservative. This is particularly visible in composition; it is enough to compare Liadov's pseudoclassical "Musical Snuff Box" with any piece in Stravinsky's neoclassical *Pulcinella*. But in musical performance the situation is not as clear-cut. Here the transition can be much smoother, since performance is a reproductive art. Consequently, a violinist's or pianist's aesthetic evolution can be so much less painful than that of a composer. Still, the leap from pseudoclassicism to neoclassicism that was made by some of Auer's students is astounding. Particularly Heifetz and Milstein are the exemplars of neoclassicism in the art of violin playing.

Both violinists came to Petersburg as outsiders. For Russian Jews from the Pale of Settlement, one of the few ways to a great career, fame, and wealth was mastery of the piano or, especially, the violin. Entering the Petersburg Conservatory made it possible. Glazunov gave his patronage in every possible way to talented Jews. A Russian, he was even called "King of the Jews." Shostakovich told me about Glazunov's famous response to the inquiry from the Russian prime minister, Pyotr Stolypin, about the number of Jewish students at the Petersburg Conservatory: "We don't keep count."

But Glazunov inspired the respect of young musicians not only because he was a caring director. For Heifetz and Milstein he was the

"Russian Brahms," a renowned composer and for many years the symbol of musical Petersburg. In falling in love with Glazunov, Heifetz and Milstein, like hundreds of other young musicians from the provinces, fell in love with Petersburg. Milstein recalled the time spent in the Russian capital as the happiest period of his life.[53] Petersburg was the inspiration for the majestic, restrained playing of the young violinists, a style that corresponded well to the city's architectural style. The role of the Petersburg school of composition in this development is clear.

Their move to the West rapidly accelerated the changes in their playing. As the neoclassical tendencies of Heifetz and Milstein matured, their playing became even more refined, but also more expressive and modern. They can be considered a rightful part of the Russian neoclassical group in the West. The aesthetic closeness of Heifetz and Milstein to Stravinsky and Balanchine is obvious. In the United States, Milstein became one of Balanchine's closest friends. With a nudge from Milstein, Balanchine created some of his best neoclassical ballets, for instance, *Concerto Baroque*, to the music of Bach's Double Violin Concerto in D minor.[54]

If Heifetz, Elman, and Milstein had not emigrated to the West but remained in the USSR, the development of the Soviet school of violin playing probably would have proceeded in a very different direction. But the cosmopolitan nature of their talent "pushed" them beyond the borders of Russia, as it had Stravinsky, Nabokov, and Balanchine. Once they moved to the United States, these violinists, together with Arturo Toscanini and Sergei Rachmaninoff, exerted an enormous influence on the American style of music making. Through recordings this style spread to the rest of the world, becoming in the end one of the most distinctive performing styles in the twentieth century. Professor Auer and the Petersburg Conservatory had every reason to be proud of their graduates.

In 1927 the magazine *Muzyka i revoliutsiia* (*Music and Revolution*) published a review of a concert by piano students of Leonid Nikolayev, a professor at the Leningrad Conservatory. The review stated, in part,

> Almost all the performers control the instrument like first-class masters, they all have a large, multifaceted, amazingly free and light technique; they all have an unforced, very beautiful and gentle tone; an enormous sound range; exceptionally delicate pedaling; a high mu-

sical culture and a truly artistic approach. In terms of their devices, they are extremely restrained and economical, but their movements are absolutely relaxed and free; they have a subtle feeling for the keyboard.[55]

Among the performers in that concert was twenty-year-old Dmitri Shostakovich, who was singled out by the reviewer. Shostakovich was one of Nikolayev's favorite students; the professor had taken on Esipova's mantle as the most outstanding teacher of piano in the city on the Neva. Nikolayev, a well-known homosexual in Leningrad, was of medium height, taciturn but charming, with a neat part in his hair and clear gray eyes. He was a respected composer of the academic style (Horowitz and Milstein performed his Violin Sonata with great success),[56] but he was sympathetic to the avant-garde. In particular, Prokofiev worked out his graduation program with Nikolayev, because Esipova was gravely ill by then. Nikolayev voted, against Glazunov's objections, for awarding the prize to the young rebel. And Nikolayev was one of the first to proclaim far and wide that Shostakovich was a genius.

Shostakovich made great strides in Nikolayev's class. My piano teacher in Leningrad, Iosif Shvarts, who had been Nikolayev's student and lover of many years, told me how Shostakovich, then fifteen, played Beethoven's demanding *Hammerklavier* Sonata: with profound thought, steely rhythm, restraint but true lyricism, and polished to the smallest detail. (Nikolayev could not stand sloppy but confident playing, calling it, as Shvarts recalled, "negligé with valor."[57])

Shostakovich had two strong rivals in Nikolayev's class: Maria Yudina and Vladimir Sofronitsky. He spoke of them even a half-century later with agitation and some obvious jealousy. Sometimes Shostakovich's enormous ambitions as a pianist are forgotten. Yet he was selected by Nikolayev to represent his class at the Chopin Competition in Warsaw in 1927, the first international competition for pianists in interwar Europe. Shostakovich prepared for the event with great intensity, locking himself in his room and even taking a break from composing. That made it all the more painful when he received only honorable mention in Warsaw. According to many observers, the jury's decision was unfair, but the support of the audience and the press was of little consolation to Shostakovich.[58] After his defeat at the competition he gave up the idea of a concert career and concentrated on performing his own works.

Yudina and Sofronitsky had a different life. Known in the West only to connoisseurs, they were enormously popular in Russia, becoming cult figures. Their significance went far beyond that of musical performance. In a closed, hierarchical society, in which every member had to know his or her place as determined by the authorities and perform all duties in accordance with prescriptions handed down from above, Sofronitsky and Yudina became—in different ways—symbols of inner freedom and cultural protest.

Tall, thin, pale, and mysterious, Sofronitsky was considered one of the most handsome men in Leningrad. Women were said to have left their families and attempted suicide over this romantic musician. Sofronitsky was compared to Byron, and it was often said that he was "the ideal Hamlet."[59] He played Chopin and Scriabin incomparably and was married to the latter's daughter for a while. The general opinion was that after Scriabin's death, Sofronitsky was the best interpreter of his works. Before the revolution Scriabin's oeuvre was considered in Russia as the highest expression of creative genius; under the Bolsheviks, his music fell into disgrace. First he was called a mystic, then a decadent, and finally a formalist. Sofronitsky stubbornly continued to play Scriabin, even giving concerts consisting only of his works, which instantly made him more than just a pianist, even a great one.

In 1942 Sofronitsky was brought out of Leningrad, which at the time was besieged by the Germans, and taken to Moscow. In 1943 he received the Stalin Prize, and in 1945 Stalin took Sofronitsky with him to the Potsdam Conference to show him off to President Truman, an amateur pianist. (Besides a trip in 1928–1929 to Warsaw and Paris, this was Sofronitsky's second and last appearance in the West.) Despite this official attention, the pianist's alienation from the Soviet cultural apparatus continued to grow. Sofronitsky's son recalled how in 1948, when Shostakovich and other composers were being denounced by the authorities, Sofronitsky was playing at home and suddenly slammed down the lid of his piano, exclaiming, "I can't play! I keep thinking that a policeman will come and say, 'You're not playing the right way!' "[60]

Trying to defend his inner freedom, Sofronitsky became an alcoholic and dope addict. His audiences knew it. People held their breath when Sofronitsky brought his famous white handkerchief to his nose, right on stage. This meant that the pianist felt the need for an additional snort of cocaine.[61] This behavior was a challenge to the strict norms of Soviet life. For the pianist and his admirers, it was a desperate declaration of the right to spontaneity and rebellion.

The next step was Sofronitsky's refusal to tour Russia and then to give practically any public performances at all. He could be heard only at the small auditorium of the Scriabin Museum in Moscow, playing before specially invited guests. He was also reluctant to make recordings, reiterating, "Recordings are my corpses." Nevertheless, his fame continued to grow. Legends spread about his rare semiprivate performances, each of which was turned into a mystical rite. Amateur tapes made without the pianist's permission were passed around, precursors of the Soviet *magnitizdat* (to parallel *samizdat*, banned literature that was typed and passed clandestinely to readers), illegal tapes of nonconformist content.

Sofronitsky's favorite authors were Dostoyevsky and Blok. Bogdanov-Berezovsky, who had known the pianist well, once told me that Sofronitsky was a character out of Dostoyevsky who resembled Blok. Sofronitsky liked to say, "Think how many people went mad or committed suicide over Blok's poems. What power they have!" He was perfectly aware of the magic impact of his playing, too.

When Sofronitsky died at the age of sixty in 1961, his health ruined by alcohol and drugs, Russian intellectuals perceived him as the lonely, persecuted Hamlet described by Pasternak in the poetry of his novel, *Dr. Zhivago*, a martyr musician who had disdained the cultural dogmas forced on him by the authorities and who had burned his candle at both ends but who had not given in to ideological dictate.

Maria Yudina graduated from the conservatory in Nikolayev's class the same year as Sofronitsky. They performed together at the graduation concert, which Shostakovich considered one of the strongest musical impressions of his youth. Yudina looked just as striking as Sofronitsky: with large gray eyes on a maidenly face, she was sometimes compared to the Mona Lisa.[62] She always wore a black pyramid-shaped dress with long, flowing sleeves and a large pectoral cross on a chain. Yudina, who was Jewish by birth, converted and became a fanatical Orthodox Christian, devoting considerable effort to church affairs. Her behavior naturally put her on a collision course with the atheistic Soviet state. Yudina was expelled from Leningrad Conservatory, where she was a teacher, and unlike Sofronitsky she never received any awards and was never allowed to perform outside the Soviet Union.

On and off the stage, Yudina was a proselytizer. Her interpretations, which drew overflow crowds, were always passionate sermons, delivered with imperiousness and conviction. Yudina destroyed forever the stereotype of "female" piano playing as something gentle and tender. Her performances were majestic, with sharp contrasts. Her programs were full of contrasts, too. She would play Bach and Beethoven and then, skipping Chopin, Liszt, Tchaikovsky, and Rachmaninoff—that is, the most popular part of the repertoire—turn to contemporary works.

Before the war Yudina promoted the music of Stravinsky, Hindemith, and Shostakovich, and then of Bartok and Webern, and in the final years of her life, she was taken with the works of Boulez, Stockhausen, and Luigi Nono. She was a powerhouse of ideas and information about the avant-garde. Her influence was revolutionary and liberating in that area, but it was not confined to just that. With equal passion, Yudina studied the lives of the saints, church architecture, and the poetry of Leningrad dadaists, many of whom had been friends of her youth. An admirer and connoisseur of Malevich, Tatlin, and Filonov, she was capable of suddenly interrupting her concert to start reciting the poetry of the futurist Khlebnikov or the banned Pasternak. Every such performance was regarded by the regime as a political act, of course. Although Yudina was often banned from performing, she was never arrested.

A possible explanation for the authorities' toleration is a story I first heard from Shostakovich that was later corroborated by others. Stalin, allegedly hearing Yudina playing a Mozart piano concerto on the radio, demanded a recording of the performance. No one dared tell him that it had been a live broadcast. Yudina was hastily called to the studio to produce a special record overnight—one copy for Stalin.

When Stalin received the record, he sent Yudina a large sum of money. She thanked him in a letter, explaining that she was donating the funds to her local church and would pray for God to forgive Stalin his grievous sins before the people. This seemed like a suicidal act, but contrary to expectations, nothing happened to her. It is rumored that Yudina's Mozart recording was on the record player near Stalin's bed when he was found dead.

Like Sofronitsky, Yudina was a passionate partisan of Petersburg. In her old age, she was flattered by comparisons to Peter the Great. In fact, her aquiline profile, especially when she was playing, did resemble that of the emperor. On stage, she sometimes placed a picture of the Bronze Horseman on the piano. After a concert in which her playing had been particularly compelling, she explained, "I was in the thrall of the Bronze Horseman today, and I wanted to convey the hoofbeats, the chase, the fear."

Yudina could be called the emissary of the American branch

of Petersburg modernism in the Soviet Union. When the New York City Ballet brought Balanchine's works there for the first time, she compared them with the Pergamon Altar, Bach's Passions, and Wagner's *Parsifal*.[63] Yudina adored Stravinsky and played almost all his piano works. When Stravinsky came to Russia in 1962, the elderly composer was very embarrassed that Yudina, at age sixty-three, tried to kneel and kiss his hand at every meeting.

Yudina was a personality given to exaltations. Many people, including Shostakovich, who had the greatest respect for her musical talents, found her behavior affected and pretentious. But I always believed Yudina's extravagant gestures manifested the same fierce temperament that surged in her performances. She violated one convention after another. She never married, wore sneakers even in winter, and could spend weeks sleeping in the bathtub. When we met, she tried to convert me to Russian Orthodoxy with her first words, refusing to discuss musical topics. But since our conversation lasted over five hours, I managed to turn it to questions of culture. The result was the only published conversation with Yudina that I know of, covering aesthetic themes and her musical credo. Alas, it first appeared in Leningrad only in 1972, almost a year and a half after her death at age seventy-one.

Yudina could have used Akhmatova's poem of 1961 to speak for herself:

> No! Not beneath foreign skies
> Or the protection of alien wings—
> I was with my people then,
> Where, to their misfortune, they were then.

Heifetz and Milstein, who belonged to the same school as Yudina but left for the West for "the protection of alien wings," conquered the world with their art and significantly expanded the cultural horizons of multitudes of music lovers. They began interpreting music in a new way, creating a revolution of sorts in their sphere. Remaining in Russia, Yudina and Sofronitsky also achieved unique musical heights. In fact, their musical evolution paralleled in many ways the development of Heifetz and Milstein in the direction of severe neoclassicism. In addition, Yudina and Sofronitsky also became models of behavior and examples of inner independence for artists in the Stalinist and post-Stalinist Soviet state. Their ethical role was enormous, even though it has been little described until now. Thus, the influence of Yudina and Sofronitsky was both narrowed (since they could be heard only in the USSR) and expanded (moving beyond the purely musical into the ethical and political spheres).

An analogous situation developed with the great alumni of the Petersburg school of composition. Stravinsky chose life "beneath foreign skies" and became arguably the leading composer of the twentieth century. Modern music is impossible to imagine without his achievements. Shostakovich remained "with his people," and his music, which has sometimes been accused of aesthetic provincialism, became a diary of the Soviet era. Prokofiev emigrated but then returned to the Soviet Union. Interestingly, the fate of his music reflects his ambivalence: it did not acquire universal traits, as did Stravinsky's work, but it is not tied so closely to recent Russian history as is Shostakovich's music. Diaghilev realized this, saying in 1929 about Prokofiev, "He needs to strengthen the ethical base of his creativity. That is why I insisted on his doing *The Prodigal Son*."[64]

The question does not arise here of which path was preferable and more in keeping with the spirit of Petersburg. Even far from his home town, Stravinsky, like Balanchine and Nabokov, remained true to it. On the other hand, some of the compromises Shostakovich was forced to make caused him to be criticized for violating Petersburg's stringent ethical norms. It is important to emphasize that having gone through the Petersburg school, a talent could develop and realize itself both in Russia and beyond its borders. Besides the sense of belonging to a glorious tradition, this school imparted a solid grounding of craftsmanship, professional curiosity, restrained irony, and nostalgia without sentimentality.

The city in which Shostakovich grew up was wide open to the temptations of modern culture. In art, literature, and theater, avant-garde influences from the West cross-pollinated with bold native attempts. In 1923 the first research center in the world for the avant-garde was founded in Petrograd, the State Institute of Arts Culture (GINKHUK). Its director was Casimir Malevich, who had moved to Petrograd from Moscow and continued to develop his visionary suprematist ideas; the institute's departments were headed by Matyushin, Punin, and Malevich's eternal rival, Vladimir Tatlin.

In 1923 at GINKHUK Tatlin produced a play based on *Zangezi*, a *"zaumny"* ("non-sensical") dramatic poem by the futurist poet Khlebnikov. In Petrograd, Tatlin also created the much discussed Monument to the Third International: he planned for a gigantic metal spiral (he intended it to be four hundred meters tall) to straddle the Neva River in the middle of the city, like the mast of a huge sailing ship or utopian spaceship. This bold symbol for the new Petrograd was supposed to have replaced the Bronze Horseman, but it was never built and remained but a model that teased the imagination, delighting Punin and his friends. They already viewed Petrograd as the capital of the international avant-garde movement.

In the twenties Petrograd-Leningrad was visited by many leading modern composers of the West. The most important was Alban Berg, who came to see his opera *Wozzeck* in 1927. Béla Bartók, Paul Hindemith, Darius Milhaud, Alfredo Casella, and the émigré Prokofiev came to perform. Igor Stravinsky did not show up then, but his works were regularly performed in Leningrad at that time. We know that Shostakovich heard many of Stravinsky's works, including *Renard, Song of the Nightingale, Histoire du soldat,* and the opera *Mavra,* and that he had taken part in the Leningrad premiere of *Les Noces* in 1926, as the second piano player (Yudina played first piano). Shostakovich also played Stravinsky's Serenade in A and his piano concerto, which, he said, he sometimes imagined that he himself had composed.

One of Shostakovich's most influential advisers after he graduated from the conservatory was the inveterate modernist music critic, Boris Asafyev. Asafyev spoke in a soft, hypnotic voice, but his erudite articles, published under the pen name Igor Glebov, silenced his opponents. He was a dedicated proselytizer of avant-garde music in Leningrad. Glazunov considered Asafyev not without justification as the main reason that modernist works were constantly being performed at the city's two opera houses and the philharmonic. A musician from the hostile camp fumed,

> Just look at Asafyev's subtle tactics: first as the critic Igor Glebov he publishes a detailed article in the newspaper praising and advertising a new decadent work, unknown to anyone; then as artistic consultant to both theaters and to the philharmonic, Asafyev makes sure it is performed. And finally, once again as critic Igor Glebov, he hails that performance in print, handing out medals and honors to absolutely everyone involved. Now, how could the conductors resist?

Asafyev headed the music department at the Institute of the History of the Arts, a research institute founded before the revolution by Count Valentin Zubov, called "the red count" because he cooperated with the Bolsheviks and voluntarily gave them his luxurious town house on St. Isaac's Square. The institute attracted some of the most brilliant minds of the Opoyaz association for its literature department: Tynyanov, Eikhenbaum, and Tomashevsky. Work was in full swing in the Zubov House; people from all over the city came to hear the eloquent lecturers who proposed new ideas on the cutting edge of modern cultural theory. The theater department, where the idol was Meyerhold, created radical new conceptions of the interaction between actors and audience. Under the institute's aegis, there were concerts and exhibitions, evenings devoted to playing and discussing the music of Stravinsky, Hindemith, Schoenberg, Milhaud, and Satie. Sofronitsky played Scriabin; Yudina and Steinberg gave a recital in memory of Dante. Shostakovich attended these concerts regularly.

In that heady atmosphere of modernism, Shostakovich took a decisive step in the direction of the avant-garde. He burned a pile of his early, traditional works, including an opera based on Pushkin's *Gypsies*. The musical language of Shostakovich's new compositions grew more radical, using constructivist principles in developing the melody and harmony, dissonances, sound clusters, and even a factory whistle as an orchestral instrument. These works also bore revolutionary titles and texts: a piano sonata (1926) was called "The October," in honor of the Bolshevik revolution, and in the Second Symphony, "Dedication to October" (1927), the chorus sang in the finale:

> *We have understood, Lenin, that our fate*
> *Is to bear the name: struggle.*

Shostakovich's Third Symphony (1929) was called "First of May," after the day of international solidarity of the proletariat, an official holiday in the Soviet Union. It too had a choral finale, with a text that included these words:

> *March, roar in our ears,*
> *Raising the sun of the banners.*
> *Every first of May*
> *Is a step toward socialism.*

Any translation would only improve the quality of this "poem," which in Russian sounds like poorly rhymed slogans. Shostakovich understood that, of course, and he wrote to a friend as he began to compose the "Dedication to October" symphony, "I received Bezymensky's poetry, which upset me very much. Very bad poetry."

Why then did Shostakovich feel the need to use this "very bad poetry" in his avant-garde symphony? The answer is simple: the symphony was written on commission from the Propaganda Department of the music sector of the State Publishing House (that is, the Soviet government) especially for the tenth anniversary of the Bolshevik revolution. The commission was an honor and a well-paying one, and Shostakovich, who needed the money, tried to complete it on time and without friction with his employer. There could be no question of rejecting the text for the finale, which had been proposed from above. The "Dedication to October" was immediately performed in Leningrad and Moscow.

Reading the art articles and creative manifestos of the twenties, one is struck by the constant reappearance of just a few cultural terms. The most common are "proletarian culture," "fellow travelers of the revolution," and "social commission." At different times, different people endowed these terms with different meanings. At first the creation of proletarian culture was the official goal of the Communist Party, which proclaimed that in the new state of workers and peasants, the corrupt bourgeois civilization would wither away, making way for proletarian art for the proletariat.

Many theoreticians of socialism sincerely believed that the creative powers of "liberated" people would instantly produce thousands of proletarian Shakespeares and Beethovens and that very little would be left of the old culture. Entry into the Communist paradise was closed to Tchaikovsky's Petersburg works, for example. "Tchaikovsky's music is melancholy, imbued with a specifically intellectual psychology, and expresses the yearnings of a frustrated life; we do not need it."[65]

However, it soon became obvious that a mass manifestation of proletarian geniuses was not to be expected in the near future. In practice, the term "proletarian culture" came to mean merely politically correct—from the point of view of the authorities—works done by people who managed to prove their proletarian origins. Naturally, it was but a small part of the general flow of contemporary Russian culture. But it was these works, though mostly of very poor quality, that were used as a model by the leaders of the Russian Association of Proletarian writers (RAPP) and its sister organization in the music field, the Russian Association of Proletarian Musicians (RAPM), founded in the 1920s. All other culture in Soviet Russia loyal to the new regime was created by "fellow travelers of the revolution," in the Bolshevik definition. When the term was introduced by Leon Trotsky, one of the new leaders, it had positive overtones. But the never-ending attacks by "proletarian" cultural figures on the "fellow travelers" made their status unstable and ambiguous.

The cultural administration in Soviet Russia manipulated the term "fellow traveler" quite arbitrarily. In fact, most of the intelligentsia that remained in the country were "fellow travelers" to some degree. The only ones who protested loudly against the Bolsheviks were Russian émigrés in the West, who did not risk their lives by doing so. Inside Russia, the opportunity for open political protest was rapidly being reduced to nought. But the range of ideological and cultural cooperation with the state was still broad: from utter servility to a false service that barely disguised the author's subversive intentions.

For the authorities, the main criterion separating good cultural fellow travelers from bad ones was the acceptance or rejection of the social commission, that is, the readiness to fulfill "in high-quality artistic form" the current needs of the ideological apparatus. Silence or work "for the desk drawer," in the Russian expression, were regarded in these circumstances as hostile acts—and were punished accordingly. For many talented and honest intellectuals, the question was, how does one reconcile the conditions of the state's "social commission" with the demands of creative conscience?

Making his way in the artistic ferment of Leningrad in the twenties, the sensitive and impressionable Shostakovich could observe the innumerable variations of that deadly game of cat-and-mouse with the authorities. His genius was threatened from two sides: it could be stifled while still in its infancy by the state, but it could also be corroded and gradually dissipate as the result of a multitude of small compromises, or one big one, with the authorities. There were more than enough models for both kinds of behavior. Shostakovich chose the course of survival, but not at any cost.

He was in luck: RAPM greeted "Dedication to October" with enthusiasm and embraced the composer. (The modernists were also delighted by Shostakovich's Second Symphony.) Asafyev tried to persuade Shostakovich to write an opera, because Berg's *Wozzeck*, which had come to Leningrad thanks to Asafyev's efforts, had made an indelible impression on the young composer. After an intensive search for a subject, Shostakovich settled on Gogol's *The Nose*, from his cycle of Petersburg tales.

Written in two and a half months, *The Nose* became the early Shostakovich's most "Petersburg" composition. Created at a critical moment in the development of the Petersburg mythos, *The Nose* seemed to sum up the contemporary efforts to destroy that mythos and simultaneously feel around for a path to its continued development. When *The Nose* was performed in Leningrad in 1930, one critic called it "an anarchist's hand grenade." The opera did go off at the height of official efforts to obliterate the mythos. An army of cultural workers was needed for that campaign, but the anarchist Shostakovich slipped from their ranks.

In 1921 the Petrograd journal *Dom Iskusstv* (*House of the Arts*) printed an article by Yevgeny Zamyatin, entitled "I am Afraid," which caused a great stir. He openly declared that the Soviet regime was stifling Russian literature, encouraging accommodating hacks and forcing honest writers to be silent. "Real literature can exist only where it is done not by obedient and dependable clerks, but by madmen, hermits, heretics, dreamers, rebels, and skeptics."

Zamyatin's passionate protest made an even greater impact because it came from an author loyal to the revolution (he had at one time been a member of the Bolshevik Party) and who was respected for his independence. His incorruptibility was well known in Petrograd. "Fastidious and restrained, he never made a single gesture that resembled kowtowing. . . . So many writers could, by comparing their behavior with that of Zamyatin, determine unerringly the degree of their deviation from the true and straight path."[66]

It was said that Zamyatin carved his works as if out of ivory, weighing and polishing every word, neatly creating a composition that in its mosaic and geometric shape resembled, as D. S. Mirsky pointed out, a cubist canvas. That is the way Zamyatin wrote the symbolic story "The Cave," in which reviewers saw a requiem for the intellectual dwellers of old Petersburg, doomed to destruction in the grim conditions of the early postrevolutionary years.

> The general background of the story is the dying, frozen Petrograd, returned to the Ice Age (by whom? by what?—let the reader decide), and against it, the barely moving shadows of half-dead cultural figures. . . . The impression is chilling and oppressive. Yes. This is how the intellectual, chilled to the bone by the severe weather of the times, died out in the struggle with the elements.[67]

Zamyatin's most famous work is his novel *We*, completed in 1921 in Petrograd, an ambitious anti-utopia and precursor of Huxley's *Brave New World*, as well as an influence on Orwell's *1984*. It was published in New York City in English in 1924 but was immediately banned by the censors in Zamyatin's homeland and not published there until the late 1980s. Nevertheless, *We*, which was almost unknown to Soviet readers, was subjected to a constant barrage of hostile criticism in the press, as were most other works by Zamyatin. He complained about this in a letter to the Soviet authorities in 1929: "Since 1921 I have been the main target of Soviet criticism. Since that year, the reviews of my work have been nothing but a dictionary of foul language, beginning with 'class enemy,' 'kulak,' 'bourgeois,' 'double-dyed reactionary,' and 'bison' all the way to 'spy.' "

In 1922 the authorities arrested Zamyatin and put him in solitary confinement. An ironic twist of fate had him in the same prison (even the same cell block) as the one in which he had spent time before the revolution for being a Bolshevik. After his release, they first planned to expel him to the West but then changed their minds. Zamyatin went abroad only in 1931, after appealing to Stalin with a desperate letter stating that he preferred exile to "literary death." Zamyatin died in Paris in 1937. In his own country he was recalled only a half-century later, even though some of the most noted Soviet writers were his pupils.

Called the "grand master of literature" in Petrograd, Zamyatin believed that the craft of writing could be learned. He was an outstanding mentor for Petrograd prose, as Gumilyov had been for Petrograd poetry. In the former palace of the merchants Eliseyev (renamed the House of the Arts), Zamyatin founded a literary studio. In a small room that smelled like a tobacco shop, and furnished with a metal bed and a rickety chair, Zamyatin, dressed elegantly in the British manner, offered students a course of lectures on the mastery of fiction, with titles like "Plot and Story," "Rhythm in Prose," "Style," "Spacing Words," and "The Psychology of Creativity." This was like a monastery for budding authors, with a strict, demanding, but just abbot.

The most talented of Zamyatin's students organized a literary group in 1921 called the Serapion Brothers, after the novel by E. T. A. Hoffmann. ("They were going to call themselves Nevsky Prospect originally," recalled Viktor Shklovsky.[68]) They were young men but rich in life experience; according to one of the Serapion Brothers,

> Eight people embodied among themselves an orderly, a typesetter, an officer, a cobbler, a physician, a fakir, a clerk, a soldier, an actor, a teacher, a cavalryman, and a singer; they had to hold down dozens

of the most menial jobs, they had fought in a world war, participated in a civil war, and could not be impressed by hunger, or disease, for they had looked death in the face too long and too often.[69]

The Serapions insisted on their apolitical stance. When asked whether they were for or against the Communists, they would reply, "We are with the hermit Serapion." This sounded quite daring under a Communist dictatorship. Lev Lunts, the group's theoretician, insisted: "We do not want utilitarianism. We do not write for propaganda."

Besides Zamyatin, another strong influence on the Serapion Brothers came from Shklovsky, who was so attached to his disciples that he considered himself part of their group. Encouraged by Zamyatin and Shklovsky, the Serapion Brothers blissfully experimented, especially in the area of plot, which they tried to make entertaining and fast-paced in the Western manner. In general, the Serapion Brothers' Western orientation made them a typical Petersburg group. Gorky wrote of the Serapions, "They understand that Russia can live normally only in constant communication with the spirit and genius of the West." Zamyatin even compared these young writers with the acmeists. Both groups shared a desire to avoid abstract symbolism, a heightened awareness of the objects of everyday life, a striving to make each word meaningful, and a love for vivid psychological detail, often with an exotic flavor.

But of course next to the Serapion Brothers, the acmeists seemed like relics from another era. After all, they did not write about the dens of thieves as did Veniamin Kaverin, or partisans who kill an infant, like Vsevolod Ivanov, or about soldiers who, crazed by blood, performed a lynching, like Mikhail Slonimsky. Those were shocking subjects. But the most daring and also the most famous of the Serapion Brothers was the satirist Mikhail Zoshchenko. He rejected many traditions of Russian classical literature. Though all around, demands were aired for a "red Leo Tolstoy" to hail the revolution in epic novels, Zoshchenko started writing short humorous stories from the life of urban dwellers instead, explaining, "Until now we still have the tradition of the former intelligentsia's literature, in which the main object of art is the psychological life of the intellectual. We must break down this tradition, because we can't go on writing as if nothing had happened in the country." And what had happened was that after the dislocations of war and revolution, many peasants poured into the cities, creating a huge new stratum. These new urban dwellers were now often setting the tone in social and public life. Traditionally oriented Soviet literature continued cautiously to avoid this type; but Zoshchenko changed that almost single-handedly.

Not only did he make this triumphant "new man," uneducated and unsightly, the sole hero of his works, but he began writing in the persona of that obnoxious Philistine. He created the literary mask of a dull, angry, greedy, and aggressive human amoeba, insisting that this amoeba was the true author of his works. Not only the dialogue but the entire fabric of Zoshchenko's early prose consists of the phantasmagoric Soviet "newspeak": the grotesque, ridiculous attempts of his narrator hero to express himself with authority by means of wild neologisms and meaningless but pompous-sounding word combinations (which make Zoshchenko's best works practically untranslatable). This real revolution in Russian literature was all the more effective because Zoshchenko's stories were stylized with virtuoso panache and polished with lapidary precision.

Zoshchenko's attitude toward his hero was complex: he hated him, feared him, and pitied him. The average reader, fooled by the superficial comedy and simplicity, did not sense this ambivalence in Zoshchenko's stories. Zoshchenko said sarcastically, "I write very compactly. My sentences are short. Accessible to the poor. Perhaps that is why I have so many readers." Hundreds of thousands of these new "poor"—financially, morally, emotionally—readers made Zoshchenko one of the richest writers in the Soviet Union. His books came out in dozens of editions, in huge printings, and sold out immediately. He received thousands of letters. He had only to step into the street to be surrounded by a crowd, like Chaliapin. Yet unlike Chaliapin, Zoshchenko was not an impressive sight. Shklovsky described him as "a man of medium height. He has a yellowish face. Ukrainian eyes. And a careful tread. He has a very soft voice. The manner of a man who wants to end a big scandal very politely."[70]

This desire of Zoshchenko's "not to stick out" was noted by Chukovsky, too. "Zoshchenko is very careful—I would say, fearful."[71] Yet Zoshchenko had been a courageous officer in World War I and was decorated many times. The "table of contents" of his life, which Zoshchenko compiled in 1922, is telling:

arrested—6 *times*
sentenced to death—*1 time*
wounded—*3 times*
attempted suicide—*2 times.*

Zoshchenko had lofty and even slightly old-fashioned ideas of honor and dignity, but he wanted to be published and censorship was pervasive. All the Serapion Brothers had problems with the censors. Chukovsky recorded a conversation in 1928 with Mikhail Slonimsky, who complained, "I'm writing one thing now that certainly will not pass censorship—it's for myself, and it will spend all its time in my desk drawer; and I'm writing another one for publication, a terrible one." Chukovsky agreed with him: "We are in the clutches of a censorship worse than any that had ever been in Russia, that is true. Every publishing house, every journal has its own censor, and their ideal is propagandistic cliché elevated to ritual."[72]

In that situation, one had to make accommodations—both psychologically and as a purely practical matter. Daily life was difficult and often disgusting. But blaming the government for that became riskier every day. In that sense Chukovsky's notation made in 1927 after a walk with Zoshchenko is characteristic. "He cursed contemporary times, but then we both came to the conclusion that nothing can be done with the Russians, and that we can't come up with anything better, and that the fault is not that of communists but of those little Russian people whom they are trying to remake."[73]

Comparisons were made early on between Zoshchenko and Gogol. Zoshchenko had studied not only the works but also the biography of Gogol, in which he found much in common with his own life as a writer: the same lack of understanding from critics and readers who wanted only "a good laugh"; the same difficulties with the censors; the same desire to "improve the morals" of society through satire. Both writers ended their lives in madness. But there was little in common between them in their daily lives, because conditions had changed so much. Zoshchenko could not, like Gogol, escape to Italy from the Russia which had become unbearable to him. Left face to face with his hero, the modern "little man," who unexpectedly for the intellectuals had taken charge, Zoshchenko regarded him all the more closely, and that gradually led to a tragic closing of the gap between the writer and his prose characters. As Kaverin stated about Zoshchenko, "He was particularly interested in insignificant, unnoticeable people, with a broken spirit. . . . And in life he tended to socialize with people who were mediocre, dullish, and ordinary."[74]

It is interesting to follow this process in Zoshchenko's letters, which with time came to resemble fragments from his stylized works. And the same thing happened to him in his contact with others:

Zoshchenko began speaking in the abbreviated, clumsy language of his protagonists. The author himself confirmed that he had consciously stylized not only his literary manner but his behavior as well. "I was born into a family of the intelligentsia. I was not essentially a new man or a new writer. And my innovation in literature was totally my invention. . . . the language that I took and that, at first, seemed funny and intentionally distorted to the critics was, in fact, extremely simple and natural."

This acceptance of the moronic language of the masses as "simple and natural" was an important step for Zoshchenko, and not only for him. Many Petersburg intellectuals, young Shostakovich among them, began to stylize their everyday speech to match that misapplied bureaucratese that came to be known as "Zoshchenkoese." Psychologically it eased the burdens of daily life in an often hostile environment that was, unfortunately, dominant. At the same time pretending to buy into the new ideology sent an almost subversive message in a superficially acceptable political packaging.

This duality becomes particularly clear in the attitude of Zoshchenko and his followers to the Petersburg mythos. On the one hand, their work and behavior could be regarded as a last ditch attack on that mythos, as it had developed in the prerevolutionary era, that should have satisfied the new regime. On the other hand, the attack was launched in such an open and absurd manner that it cast doubt on the sincerity of the "new nihilists" and discredited the revolutionary idea behind them. In fact, the mythos mocked in such an eccentric way became only stronger.

The literary and life mask created by Zoshchenko was the result of virtuoso craftsmanship and careful stylistic polish. Shostakovich appreciated that. Throughout his life he considered Zoshchenko a great writer, could recite pages of his work by heart, and sought opportunities to work with him. After Zoshchenko's death, he made a pilgrimage to his grave near Leningrad. Zoshchenko used to say that Shostakovich's understanding of his writing was "very correct, even faultlessly so. His opinion was always dearer to me than the opinion of a professional critic."

Zoshchenko's characterization of Shostakovich is very perceptive. "Hard, caustic, extremely smart, probably strong, despotic, and not quite kind. . . . He is made up of enormous contradictions. One cancels out the other in him. This is conflict in the highest degree. It is almost a catastrophe."[75]

In adopting Zoshchenko's style as a tool for everyday communication, Shostakovich (and some of his friends) were making a gesture of accommodation but not capitulation to the regime. Zoshchenko could announce, "I am temporarily representing the proletarian writer." But the very awkwardness and naïveté of that statement was, of course, parodic. There was a game on, in which the border between political engagement and mocking that engagement became blurred. Life under the Communists was accompanied by constant, ironic self-commentary. This simultaneously made life easier and also made it unbearable. Very few people could take that tension, and Zoshchenko broke completely toward the end. Shostakovich had greater endurance.

Yuri Tynyanov gave a sympathetic review to the anthology of the Serapion Brothers, published in 1922, noting "the decline of the poetic wave." "Prose must soon take the place that just recently had belonged exclusively to poetry." In fact, a boom in prose came quickly, and it resulted in a phenomenon I call the "new Petersburg prose," a term I am introducing to distinguish the "new" from the "old," which was created in the nineteenth century.

At the turn of the century poetry was decisively ahead of prose, and the leading literary figures were all poets. Prose came into its own in the first half of the 1920s, pulling both poets and theoreticians of literature into its orbit. I call it "Petersburg" not only out of geographic considerations but also because one of its main themes was the city of Petersburg-Leningrad, old and new. It measured itself against the old Petersburg masters, their motifs and symbols, and distorted and parodied them.

It was a powerful movement that yielded more than one masterpiece. Yet it was never gathered under a single literary umbrella. But almost all the creators of the new Petersburg prose knew one another and read and learned from one another. Many even shared the same roof, since they lived at or regularly visited the House of the Arts, founded by Maxim Gorky to bolster the Petrograd intelligentsia, who were dying out from hunger and cold. Before the revolution the enormous dark red building at the intersection of Nevsky Prospect and the Moika River had housed a major bank, the luxurious quarters of the Petersburg millionaire Eliseyev, and also the English Shop, visits to which are described in *Speak, Memory* by Nabokov, who is tied by many threads to the new Petersburg prose.

It was at the House of the Arts that the Serapion Brothers group was born. There lived the poets Khodasevich and Mandelstam, the ballet critic Volynsky, the literary theoretician Shklovsky, and the writer Olga Forsh, who described the house as a "crazy ship." This was the title of her experimental roman à clef (even the modern Shklovsky found it "unbalanced"), which compared life in the city to a stormy sea, where the Petrograd Noah's Ark was buffeted by the powerful waves: "It seemed that the house was not a house at all, but a ship that appeared out of nowhere and was speeding somewhere." Forsh's vigorously written book was not made up of traditional chapters but instead was divided into "The First Wave," "The Second Wave," and so on up to the ninth, which "washed away" the last refuge of the writers and poets, banned by Petrograd boss Zinoviev.

The ship metaphor, which for a time seemed to have replaced the bronze horseman, was popular in the new Petersburg prose. One of its founders and masters, Zamyatin, began his short story "Mamai," which was published in 1921 in the *House of the Arts* magazine, as follows:

> In the evenings and at night, there were no more buildings in Petersburg: there were six-story stone ships. A ship speeds along the stone waves, a solitary six-story world, amid other solitary six-story ships; the ship sparkles with the lights of its innumerable cabins onto the stormy stone ocean of streets. And in the cabins there are no residents, there are only passengers.

The whole city seemed to be a huge ship that had broken away from its anchor and with its desperate passengers was being pulled by an overpowering current to its doom. Mandelstam wrote these apocalyptic lines in that period:

> *Monstrous ship at a terrifying height*
> *Speeds, spreading its wings. . . .*
> *Green star—in lovely poverty*
> *Your brother, Petropolis, is dying.*

This poem, like many others in those years comparing the former capital to a ship, is undoubtedly tied to the ancient image of the "ship of the dead," which is how its inhabitants perceived their city. That ship wandered between sunrise and sunset, birth and death. Another traditional image was combined with it—the flood. An ark floating between life and death gave hope for a future rebirth—an important theme of Mandelstam's poetry and prose about Petersburg.

Mandelstam was one of the strangest and most colorful passengers of the Crazy Ship; according to Shklovsky, "he grazed like a

lamb around the building, seeking shelter in the rooms like Homer."
Because he was short and his literary style so imposing, the residents
of the House of the Arts called Mandelstam "the marble fly." In turn,
he called Shklovsky the "merry cobbler" because he liked to sing while
he worked (and more stingingly, "the professor from the high road,"
apparently because of Shklovsky's strident polemics). Mandelstam
saw Zoshchenko almost daily in that period because the latter almost
never left the House of the Arts, the cradle of the new Petersburg prose.
The atmosphere on the Crazy Ship was aptly described by Annenkov:

> Lectures, conferences, debates, readings, laughter, curses, more
> laughter, arguments, sometimes wild arguments—about Cervantes,
> chicken pox, Dostoyevsky, cholera, roast chicken . . . oh, yes: about
> roast chicken. I remember that Zoshchenko once said that roast
> chickens must have learned to fly very well, since you can't seem to
> catch any at all nowadays.[76]

As Shklovsky recalled, "We sailed, talking, we were still young." Being on the Crazy Ship, it was impossible to avoid mutual influence:
everyone lived openly in close quarters, the "passengers" reading their
latest works to one another; everyone knew who was working on what
and how everyone was evolving. It was a marathon literary workshop
of numerous talented individuals in close professional interaction.
Typically, Mandelstam knew many of Zoshchenko's short stories by
heart, as if they were poems.

This attitude toward Zoshchenko's prose as if it were "high
Biblical lyricism" (Chukovsky's expression) seems paradoxical in
view of Zoshchenko's style and protagonists. But the Petersburg connoisseurs had an acute awareness of Zoshchenko's ties to the works
of Gogol and the early Dostoyevsky. In Zoshchenko's novella *The
Nanny Goat*, the petty clerk Zabezhkin goes out onto Nevsky
Prospect "out of curiosity: after all, there was a variety of people, and
the stores had god only knows what, and it was funny to read what
people were eating in which restaurant." In his imagination,
Zabezhkin, in an allusion to Gogol's *Nevsky Prospect*, saves a lady in
a black dress and veil from some hooligans; she turns out to be the
daughter of

> some trust's director. Or even simpler: A little old intellectual is walk-
> ing along. And suddenly falls. As from dizziness. Zabezhkin says to
> him . . . "Oh, oh, where do you live?" . . . "A coach!" . . . "Hold him
> up!" . . . And the little old man, may a mosquito fly up his nose, is

an American citizen. . . . "Here," he'll say, "here's a trillion rubles for you, Zabezhkin."

This evokes the classic passage from Gogol: "But even stranger are the things that happen on Nevsky Prospect. O, don't trust that Nevsky Prospect! I always wrap my cape more tightly around me when I walk on it and I try not to look at all at the objects I come across. It's all deceit, all dreams, it's all not what it seems!"

Zoshchenko's affection for the Nevsky Prospect sung by Gogol is broken by the prism of parody. This is the alienation described by Shklovsky. The alienation effect is achieved by an intentionally infantile tone of the narrative. And Mandelstam, who according to Akhmatova regarded Zoshchenko very highly, used the same method in his prose work about Petersburg in the 1920s, called *The Noise of Time*. Mandelstam described "the grandeur of a military capital as seen through the glowing eyes of a five-year-old" (as Akhmatova put it).

With the years Zoshchenko's prose became more and more "transparent," moving in that sense from Gogol to Pushkin. The basic elements of Pushkin's prose Zoshchenko once defined as "entertainment, brevity and clarity of narration, extreme grace of form, and irony." Undoubtedly, this is also Zoshchenko's secret self-description, as well as that of the new Petersburg prose as a whole.

A writer who surpassed Zoshchenko in a desire for simplicity and laconic writing was Leonid Dobychin, a remote and lonely man who managed to produce three small books before vanishing in 1936 after a vicious critical campaign against him for his "formalism" (he is believed to have committed suicide). Dobychin's works, which were greatly esteemed among Leningrad writers, were met with hostility by the critics as collections of "man-in-the-street gossip, foul anecdotes, and operetta episodes." A critic reviewing Dobychin's book fumed, "The streets of Leningrad are filled with various people, most of whom are healthy, life-loving and energetic builders of socialism, but the author writes: 'Gnats bustled.' "[77]

Dobychin's stories were formed of short, "naked" sentences: "They were breaking into stores. It reeked of oil. Rooks with twigs in their beaks flew up." The narrative constantly breaks off; the halting rhythm emphasizes the horror and dislocation in which Dobychin's characters find themselves—petty clerks terrified by the Soviet regime and desperately trying to adjust to it. Memories of the old life flash through their distorted imaginations like ugly visions:

"In Petersburg I saw someone once," said the round-cheeked Suslova, dreamily staring at the cups (one had the Winter Palace, the other the Admiralty Spire). "I don't know, maybe it was the empress herself: I was walking past the palace and suddenly a carriage pulls up, a lady leaps out and flutters into the entryway."

"Maybe it was the housekeeper with the shopping," replied Kozlova.

Dobychin's work was an extreme expression of the attempts by some masters of the new Petersburg prose to achieve simplicity and a laconic tone. At the opposite pole was the loquacious surrealist story, "The Ratcatcher," by Alexander Grin, perhaps the best "mythologized" depiction of Petrograd's dangerous life in the early 1920s.

Grin, described by his neighbor Shklovsky as being "gloomy and quiet, like a convict in the middle of his term," also lived in the House of the Arts. Grin rarely left his small, cold room and the denizens of the house quipped that he must have been training his cockroaches. Grin worked furiously on his manuscripts at a kitchen table, jumping up occasionally to pace in order to warm up. Back in February 1914 he had published a visionary story about the destruction of Petersburg by earthquake. There was still half a year before World War I, but Grin's vivid prose was already painting prophetic pictures of chaos and destruction. Their prophecy was recalled in the horrible days of the German blockade of the city in 1941–1944:

> Frozen in place, I saw an abyss opening into the bowels of the earth; people, crumbling walls of buildings, corpses and horses, fell and vanished in the gaping emptiness with the speed of a waterfall. The sundered earth shook. . . . Blasts like cannon fire roared from every direction; it was the sound of houses falling, flattened to the ground. Following that overwhelming roar came another, growing like an avalanche—the screams of dying Petersburg.

Grin had close ties to the Serapion Brothers in his passion for entertaining and avant-garde fantastic subjects, which he made seem quite plausible through the use of numerous convincing details, both descriptive and psychological. For his "Ratcatcher," which ostensibly described an incredible event that took place in Petrograd in the spring of 1920, Grin used a real but eerie-looking scene he had observed in the building where he lived. As Mandelstam recalled, "The rooms were underheated, but the building had virgin reserves of fuel: an abandoned bank, around forty empty rooms knee-deep in thick bank cardboard boxes. Anyone could go pick them up, but we didn't dare, however Shklovsky would sometimes go into those woods and return with his quarry. The fireplace would crackle with mounds of office papers." Grin regularly accompanied Shklovsky on these expeditions for lifesaving paper for the fire, and he placed the hero of "The Rat-catcher" in the endless corridors and passages filled with paper snow-drifts and made him meet the evil and powerful rats, who could take on human form at will, and who were planning to conquer Petrograd. It was a powerful allegory for the struggle for survival in that quickly emptying and dying city.

The House of the Arts was also the theme of Khodasevich's memoir, published in the late 1930s in Paris. In describing the Petrograd of the early 1920s he expressed an idea that was very important for understanding the genesis of the new Petersburg prose: "There are people who grow better-looking in the coffin; I think that was the case with Pushkin. Undoubtedly, that was the case with Petersburg. That beauty is temporary, ephemeral. It is followed by the terrible ugliness of decomposition. But in contemplating it there is an inexpressible, thrilling pleasure." Khodasevich also compared the House of the Arts with "a ship, sailing through darkness, blizzard, and rain."

Writers had an acute sense of the moment's historical significance and tried to capture Petersburg's image in unprecedented transition before it was too late. No other comparably brief period of time—just a few years—in the city's history had elicited such an upsurge of memoir and quasi memoir that was stylistically and ideologically intertwined.

Shklovsky reminisced about life on the Crazy Ship in his best book of memoirs, *Sentimental Journey:*

> Imagine a strange city.
> They don't distribute firewood. That is, they do somewhere, but a line a thousand people long is waiting and can't wait long enough. They create red tape to make a person give up and go away. There's not enough anyway.
> And all they give is one bundle.
> Tables, chairs, cornices, and butterfly boxes have all been burned.
> A friend burned his library. But that is terribly hard. You have to tear the books up and burn the pages in wads.

Shklovsky's evocative, crisp style is typical of the new Petersburg prose. Borrowing his title from his favorite writer, Lawrence

Sterne, Shklovsky uses a quotidian voice to speak of the most terrible things. Khodasevich noted that in the face of impending separation with the past, you develop a desire to preserve memories of it as thoroughly as possible. That emotion urged Shklovsky to write stylized, ironic memoirs. Shklovsky's colleague in Opoyaz, Tynyanov, also a leading theoretician of the formalist school, expressed that feeling of farewell to an era in intense fiction disguised as history, even though it was in fact filled with contemporary allusions.

> People of the twenties had a hard death, because the age died before them.
> In the thirties they had a certain sense of when a person was to die. Like dogs, they chose a comfortable corner for dying. And they no longer expected either love or friendship before death.
> What was friendship? What was love?
> They had lost friendship back in the previous decade, and all that was left was the habit of writing letters and appeals for guilty friends—at that time there were many guilty ones.

This excerpt from Tynyanov's historical novel, *The Death of Vazir-Mukhtar*, written in 1927, ostensibly describes the harsh ending of an era after the Decembrist rebellion was crushed in 1825. In fact, of course, he is also talking about the tragic situation one hundred years later, when Tynyanov and his comrades were feeling the iron pressure of Soviet ideology, which constantly sought more "guilty ones" with the inexorability of the Inquisition.

The era of the Crazy Ship was receding into the past. The ship had already sunk by then, and its passengers had scattered—some slipped away to the West, some vanished, destroyed by the Soviet regime, some were in hiding, and some went on working, trying to make sense of the dizzying changes and to preserve their ties with the past. The real fate of the city no longer depended on them, at least that is how the situation must have seemed to them in those trying years, but they were still able to mold its image.

The new Petersburg prose took an active part in the transformation of the Petersburg mythos. The contributions of Mandelstam, Shklovsky, and Tynyanov were the most significant. Mandelstam, according to Akhmatova, "saw Petersburg as semi-Venice, semi-theater." Akhmatova explained that Mandelstam "managed to be the last writer about Petersburg's mores—precise, vivid, dispassionate, and unique. In his writings the half-forgotten and many times vilified streets reappear in all their freshness." Undoubtedly, Mandelstam's *Noise of Time* influenced the later prose memoirs of Akhmatova and also Nabokov's *Speak, Memory*. The Russian émigré press printed many reactions to Mandelstam's work when it appeared, and O. S. Mirsky noted in 1927 in *The London Mercury* that Mandelstam's Petersburg "is crystallized into images of gem-like colour and hardness. It is a book apart, and one of our generation's greatest contributions to the nation's literature."[78]

In the same article Mirsky called Shklovsky's *Sentimental Journey* the most representative book of the new Russian literature, drawing readers' attention to the unbearable but inspired life of intellectuals in dying Petrograd. Shklovsky's book, first published in Berlin in 1923, also elicited enormous interest among Russian émigrés and became one of the most influential works in the creation of Petersburg's new image as victim city. And even though *Sentimental Journey* was later banned in the Soviet Union and not reprinted for over sixty years, the sections on Petrograd were frequently retold and repeated by Shklovsky in his other books, thereby constantly setting the conceptual tone for descriptions of the city in the revolutionary era.

Tynyanov's role may have been even more substantial. After the revolution, the tsars and tsarinas were sharply criticized, and almost all their actions were pronounced useless or harmful. Petersburg as the creation of the tsars was also undone. One of the innumerable examples of that occurred in the speech of a well-known theoretician of proletarian literature, Vladimir Yermilov: "You know that there was a lot of construction done under the empress Catherine II. But, comrades: compare the scope of construction of Catherine and Peter with the unprecedented scope of the resolution of the Central Committee and the government on socialist Leningrad—and the work of the nobility will seem pathetic, impoverished, and skimpy to us."[79]

The reigning formula then was "history is politics turned on the past," and consequently the sole task of historical prose was to be the direct proof of the legitimacy of the Bolshevik revolution. Before it conditions in the country were so bad that the only way out was the overthrow of the ancien régime, with the consequent destruction of all its roots. Dozens of Soviet historical works can be reduced to this simpleminded thesis.

Tynyanov ostensibly accepted this paradigm but used it in his work in an unexpected way. He was one of the first Soviet writers to use historical prose effectively to create anti-Bolshevik allusions. His story "Lieutenant Kije," based on a true incident from the days of Emperor Paul I about a nonexistent officer created by a clerical error who successfully rose up the army ladder while a live man accidently listed as dead lost the right to exist, turns this anecdote into an allegory of life in Stalinist Russia, where the bureaucratic document became more important than the individual. In *The Waxen Effigy*, published by Tynyanov in 1932, the parallel was clear between his description of the wax figure of Peter the Great being installed in the Petersburg Kunstkamera in 1732 and the placing of Lenin's mummified body in a special mausoleum by the Bolsheviks. In Tynyanov's novella, Peter's comrades betray his ideas immediately after the emperor's death, the harsh lifestyle dehumanizes the people, and denunciations and torture reign across the land. For the careful reader, these hints were very clear.

A Leningrader wrote, "Tynyanov's books, which appeared every few years, were read by the intelligentsia eagerly and anxiously."[80] Nikolai Chukovsky, the son of Kornei Chukovsky, felt as did many others that Tynyanov's main theme was the clash of Russian statehood with the individual trying to protect his dignity and rights, that is, the theme of Pushkin's *Bronze Horseman*. He recalled that Tynyanov's "stories about the past agitated contemporaries more than stories by others about the present, because the Bronze Horseman was still galloping after the fleeing Yevgeny and with every year the ringing hoofbeats sounded louder along the stunned cobblestones."[81]

Tynyanov's heroes were not one-dimensional political caricatures. Tynyanov, who died in 1943 at the age of 49 after a twelve-year struggle with what must have been Alzheimer's disease, was a writer with a virtuoso literary technique who drew on his knowledge of historical material. As demanding a critic as Dobychin considered Tynyanov a great master.

In Leningrad's cultural circles the cult of mastery and craftsmanship still reigned. That cult was characteristic of the new Petersburg prose as well. Surprisingly, the regime accepted this for a time. The censors passed Tynyanov's barely veiled historical allegories. Proletarian writers pretended that Zoshchenko's stories (which Russian émigrés reprinted with delight as satirical depictions of the collapse of morality under the Bolsheviks) were close in spirit to proletarian literature. This created a special cultural climate in Leningrad that allowed some exotic plants to flourish. Among them was Shostakovich's opera *The Nose*, which began with this rather unusual dialogue for the opera stage but natural enough within the corpus of Gogol's work:

"Ivan Yakovlevich, your hands always stink."
"Why would they stink?"
"I don't know, brother, but they do."

Many people at the Leningrad premiere of *The Nose* in 1930
were stunned. Gogol's absurdist story from his cycle of Petersburg
tales, published by Pushkin in his *Sovremennik* magazine in 1836, had
not lost its ability to shock; even in 1930 one critic called it "a clumsy,
delirious joke." It was even more shocking as an opera. Shostakovich,
who did not follow the current fashion of totally rewriting the classics, re-created Gogol's plot rather faithfully: Petersburg Major Kovalyov suddenly loses his nose, which then brazenly walks around
town in a uniform trimmed in gold and in a plumed hat. Kovalyov
confronts his nose at the Kazan Cathedral, where the nose is praying
"with an expression of great piety," but he is unable to persuade his
nose to return to him. Kovalyov is in despair, but the city police capture the nose, which was "already getting into a carriage and planning to go to Riga." Once his nose returns, Kovalyov cannot figure
out how to stick it back on his face. But then the nose miraculously
rejoins the face of the boundlessly happy Kovalyov. In conclusion,
Gogol mockingly noted that such stories as his bring "no benefit whatever to the homeland." With a total lack of humor, the Soviet critics
almost a century later posed a question after the premiere of
Shostakovich's opera: Could this work "attract the attention of the
progressive laborer?" They answered with a resounding, "Of course
not."

And this was despite the fact that Shostakovich, like Tynyanov,
whose fiction and theoretical works the composer read avidly, used
the ruse of calling his opera "a satire on the era of Nicholas I." The
critics sensed something was wrong. Of course, they were irritated by
the frankly avant-garde character of Shostakovich's opera. (Analogous criticisms were often aimed at Tynyanov.) And in fact, along with
Mussorgsky's *Marriage*, also based on Gogol, *The Nose* is probably
the most experimental work in Russian operatic literature, with uncompromising vocal demands, a complex polyphonic orchestration
in which the percussion instruments play a great part (one of the
entr'actes is written only for percussion), and a breathless tempo, with
one surrealistic episode quickly following another.

The production added to the impression of the work's boldness. The movie director Kozintsev recalled, "To dashing gallops and
lively polkas Vladimir Dmitriev's settings whirled and spun: Gogol's

phantasmagoria became sound and color. The youthful Russian art, boldly experimental and tied to urban folklore—hanging signs of shops and taverns, tacky art, cheap dance bands—has burst into the kingdom of *Aida* and *Trovatore*. Gogol's grotesque imagery throbbed: what was farce here, what was prophecy?"[82] Dmitriev, who had just recently been the guiding spirit of Balanchine's avant-garde group Young Ballet, had become the leading designer for Leningrad's musical productions and Shostakovich's favorite theater artist. He would soon design the premiere for Shostakovich's opera *Lady Macbeth of the Mtsensk District*.

But critics were made wary not only by the opera's stunning avant-garde aesthetics. The satire of Shostakovich's *Nose*, like Tynyanov's satire, was uncomfortably directed not so much against the era of Nicholas I as against contemporary life, in which the police, secret and otherwise, were taking bribes and enjoying unlimited power to decide whether someone was a clerk "in a state position and a rather significant one" or was simply a runaway "nose," a phantom subject to removal from the system. Shostakovich also depicted the terrible force of mass psychosis, the mechanism of rumors and fears that arise in the atmosphere of the near total censorship.

The Leningrad critics must have also been challenged by Shostakovich's announcement that one of the coauthors of *The Nose*'s libretto was Zamyatin. He had just been derided in the Soviet press as "an open enemy of the working class" for the publication abroad of his novel *We*, which was officially characterized as a "lampoon of communism and slander of the Soviet system." Though Zamyatin's actual participation in the writing of the libretto was rather insignificant, including him in the list of coauthors was a gesture that cost Shostakovich dearly. After sixteen performances, *The Nose* was removed from the repertoire, not to reappear on the Soviet stage for more than forty years.

Soon after the premiere of *The Nose*, Shostakovich, discouraged by the hostile reviews, wrote to the director of the production: "The articles will do their work and no one who's read them will go to see *The Nose*. I'll get over that in about a week, another two months for the gloating of 'friends and acquaintances' that *The Nose* was a failure, and then I'll calm down and start working again, but I don't know on what. I'd really like to do *The Carp*."[83]

The libretto for the projected opera was to be written by a leading Leningrad dadaist, the poet Nikolai Oleinikov, a handsome man with rosy cheeks and blond curly hair, who possessed, according to some, a demonic charm.[84] Oleinikov, like Leningrad's other avant-gardists of the time, approved of Shostakovich's music, while Shostakovich was smitten by Oleinikov's absurdist poem "The Carp," which, although unpublished, was nevertheless popular in Leningrad's elitist circles.[85] It was a parody of a passionate Gypsy love song that recounted the tragic story of the unrequited love of a carp for the "marvelous madame," a smelt. The rejected carp throws himself into a net and ends up in a frying pan. The poem concludes with a requiem for the passionate lover:

> Roil on, murky
> Waters of the Neva.
> The little carp
> Won't be swimming anymore.

The plots of "The Carp" and *The Nose*, for all their superficial dissimilarity, are united by the way a tragic theme is rendered as a parody. In Oleinikov's poems, Shostakovich saw parallels with Zoshchenko's prose.[86] Both authors wrote in brief, intentionally primitive phrases, using and mocking the clumsy language of urban masses. Both hid behind the mask of a frightened and almost retarded observer.

Lydia Ginzburg, who knew Oleinikov well, wrote that he

> was formed in the twenties, when there existed (along with others) the type of the *shy man*, who feared lofty phraseology, both official and vestigial-intelligentsia versions. Oleinikov was the expression of that consciousness. These people felt the inadequacy of 'high' values and 'big' words. They used jokes and irony as a defensive cover for their thoughts and feelings.[87]

Oleinikov, Zoshchenko, and Shostakovich appropriated this specifically Petersburgian mask of the "shy man," who was simultaneously infantile and ironic. For Zoshchenko and Shostakovich it became a second face. Oleinikov used it in a more theatrical manner. He was helped by the tragically carnivalesque atmosphere of Leningrad in the mid-twenties, when the acute and tragic awareness of the disappearance of the old city and its values was transformed into a marked theatricality in the intellectual elite's daily life.

And at this dramatic moment in the life of Petersburg-Leningrad came the Oberiu group, to which Oleinikov belonged. The acronym Oberiu referred to the Association for Real Art. The name reflected in part the unwillingness of the group's members to associate themselves openly with "avant-garde" or "left" art and their desire to avoid labels of any "-ism," like acmeism or futurism. In their manifesto, published in 1928, they insisted, "We are the creators not only of a new poetic language, but creators of a new sensation of life and its objects. Our will to create is universal: it overflows all forms of art and tears into life."

The central figure of Oberiu was twenty-two-year-old Daniil Yuvachev, who took the pseudonym Kharms (according to one version, forming it from the English words "charm" and "harm"). A poet, prose writer, and playwright, Kharms stylized himself as the classic Petersburg eccentric. Tall and long-haired, looking, as one of his friends said, like both "a puppy of good pedigree and the young Turgenev," Kharms strolled around Leningrad in an unusual getup for a Soviet city: a British-style gray jacket, vest, and plus fours tucked into checked socks. The image of "mysterious foreigner" was completed by a starched collar, narrow black velvet ribbon on his forehead, thick walking stick, pocket watch the size of a saucer on a chain, and crooked pipe.

Kharms insisted that he was a wizard and frightened friends with stories of his strange magic powers.[88] His apartment was filled with books on black magic, satanism, chiromancy, and phrenology, as well as a book for interpreting dreams, for Kharms was very superstitious. He would return home if he met a hunchback on the street, and drank milk only if all the windows and doors were shut tight and the smallest cracks were stuffed with cotton. In Kharms's bedroom, which was full of wires and springs stretching in all directions, on which bounced occult symbols and all sorts of demons and imps made of paper, stood an ancient harmonium on which the wizard host liked to play works by his beloved composers Bach and Mozart. (Kharms used to show off an old medallion depicting a severe-looking man in a powdered wig, telling people that this was a unique portrait of "Ivan Sevastyanovich himself," that is, Johann Sebastian Bach.)

Kharms's domestic imps were undoubtedly descended from the private furnishings, known all over town, of another legendary Petersburg eccentric, the writer Alexei Remizov, who by 1921 had already emigrated to the West. A subtle stylist who tried to purify and vivify the Russian language the way it had been "before Peter the Great," Remizov was an important influence on Zamyatin and on the Serapion Brothers, including Zoshchenko. He also gave the young people of Petrograd a lesson that they remembered for many years, living as if in a subtle literary game. One of the Serapions, Konstantin Fedin, called Remizov one of the most terrible and most miserable harlequins of Russian literature, "who were hindered from tasting earthly delights by the mask they wore. O, of course, it was all stylization! Their whole life was stylization, and their writing, too—almost a joke, a trifle, but what a fatal trifle and what a heart-breaking joke!"[89]

Remizov invented a literary order called The Simian Great and Free Chamber, whose members, with appropriate titles—bishops, princes, cavaliers—were his writer friends: Blok, Zamyatin, and the Serapion Brothers. Shklovsky's rank was "short-tailed monkey." Remizov had a marvelous calligraphic hand. Stoop-shouldered, hook-nosed, and half-blind, he would sit in his tiny Petrograd cell, inscribing filigreed "simian certificates" and turning scraps of paper and wool into little imps that he hung up with string all around his room. So Kharms's love for hand-illustrating his own texts, inventing cryptograms and hieroglyphs, and organizing various societies, into which he included (and excluded) his friends, echoed Remizov's eccentricities.

At the literary evenings of the "oberiuts," as the members of Oberiu were called, the heavily powdered Kharms would be wheeled out on the stage on top of a huge black lacquered wardrobe, from which he would begin reciting in a singsong his intentionally infantile verses:

> Once granny waved
> and the steam engine instantly
> served the children and said:
> eat your mush and trunk.

Other members of the group declaimed their works while bicycling around the stage. The culmination of the oberiuts' theatrical ambitions was their 1928 production of Kharms's absurdist play, *Elizaveta Bam*. The composer of the music for this performance was Pavel Vulfius, later my mentor at the Leningrad Conservatory. Smiling somewhat mysteriously, he would tell me about what he called a dadaist opera: "*Elizaveta Bam* was layered with music and the actors often switched from rhythmic declamation to song, and the beginning of the play was a half-parody, half-homage to Glinka's *Life for the Tsar*." (Glinka was one of Kharms's favorite composers; he loved to sing his song, "Calm down, emotions of passion," sometimes in a duet with another Oberiu member, the poet Nikolai Zabolotsky.)

The day after the play the Leningrad *Krasnaya gazeta* (*Red Gazette*) printed a review that described *Elizaveta Bam* as "cynically

frank muddle, in which virtually no one could tell what the hell was going on." This was a blatant overstatement because the cream of
Leningrad's avant-garde was at the performance, and they certainly
would have understood the connection between Kharms's play and
Blok's *Fair Show Booth,* as well as the futurist masterpieces, the tragedy
Vladimir Mayakovsky, and the opera *Victory Over the Sun.* Kharms
sent out invitations to the performance to the creators of *Victory Over
the Sun,* Matyushin and Malevich, to members of FEKS, and to other
leading cultural experimenters in Leningrad. The oberiuts consciously
strove to unite various directions in Leningrad modernism—artists,
musicians, theater people, poets, and writers—in what came to be
called "happenings" in the 1960s. The traditional collectivist spirit of
Petersburg innovators was strong in them.

When the oberiuts turned to Malevich for support, he replied,
"I'm an old hooligan, you're young ones—let's see what happens." In
those years there was already a feeling in the air that the "left front" in
the arts was in its final battle with the winning Philistines. The oberiuts
demonstrated this sense of being part of a common cause, lofty but
doomed, by appearing, as one later recalled, "in full complement" at the
premiere of Shostakovich's *Nose.* "It seemed that everyone in the audience knew one another (and in fact that was very much the case!) and,
as if they had planned it, they had all come to enjoy a last triumph."[90]

The performance of *Elizaveta Bam* by Kharms was another such
demonstration of solidarity. It took place in the Leningrad House of the
Press, which was located in the former aristocratic town house on the
Fontanka River embankment not far from Nevsky Prospect. The director of the House of the Press, who sympathized with left art, invited
Filonov and his students to paint on the walls of the lobby and the theater. The audience for the oberiuts play saw an unforgettable sight:

> On canvases, depicted in soft, transparent colors, were purple and
> pink cows and people, who seemed to have had their skin removed
> by some marvelous surgery. The veins and arteries and internal or-
> gans were clearly visible. Through the figures grew pale green run-
> ners from trees and grasses. Elongated proportions and a strictly
> measured composition made one think of the frescoes of the ancient
> masters, spiritual and devoid of physical solidity.[91]

Filonov, who with Zheverzheyev was one of the founders in
Petersburg of the art association Union of Youth in 1910, was one of
the masters beloved of the futurists and oberiuts. Khlebnikov described his "cherry eyes and pale cheekbones." The Russian avant-

gardists were fanatical figures, but even among them Filonov was distinguished by his unprecedented single-mindedness, the stubbornness with which he set his goals, and his frenzied proselytizing. Leningrad had a surfeit of art schools—those of Malevich, Matyushin, Petrov-Vodkin. Filonov's school had the most students, up to seventy followers, the most faithful of whom formed a collective in the late twenties that they called Masters of Analytical Art.

Filonov had started with expressionistic canvases and then came to the "principle of doneness," which became the guiding light of his method. He taught, "Draw every atom stubbornly and accurately." He painted large works with small brushes, often starting in a corner and gradually spreading across the canvas, because he was convinced that the painting "must grow and develop just as organically, atom by atom, as growth occurs in nature." The result of such work was that even his small canvases and watercolors were so thickly "inhabited" by intertwining forms, figures, and faces that in reproduction they seem to be monumental frescoes. Filonov's works are at once abstract and figurative, because the artist synthesized the myriad component details into complex symbolic images, which he often called "formulas," for instance, *Formula of Spring, Formula of Revolution*, and *Formula of the Petrograd Proletariat*.

Filonov's art is nationalist and original because its roots go back to primitive Russian folk art and Orthodox icons. A student of Filonov's recalled that he "rejected the existence of the soul and the spirit and, of course, of God." But Filonov's works are spiritual in the highest degree, as happened with certain other Russian artists whose private lives were not marked by devoutness, for instance Mussorgsky and Rimsky-Korsakov. That is why even though Filonov's themes are often tragic, his paintings do not have a depressing effect. The current in Filonov's art is sympathy for the underdog. Many of his paintings are populated by workers and other humble citizens. Filonov poeticized their life, and the working-class neighborhoods of Petrograd were transformed in his works into a carnival of multicolored forms, figures, and faces.

Filonov worked like a man possessed, without commissions, often half-starving. He wrote in his diary, "sometimes I stretch a pound of bread for two days." On August 30, 1935, he wrote, "I made the last pancake with my last pinch of flour this morning, preparing to follow the example of many, many times—to live, not knowing for how long, without eating."[92] And he refused to sell his paintings, because he wanted to hang all of them in his imagined grand museum of analytical art. But the Soviet state was getting more hostile toward Filonov and other modernists.

In 1932 Filonov wrote about a conversation with Malevich. "He started complaining about his lot and told me that he spent three months in prison and was interrogated. The investigator asked him, 'What's the Cezannism you're talking about? What's this cubism you are propounding?' "[93] The secret police were questioning Filonov's students about the artistic and political views of their teacher. Then his two stepsons were arrested. Filonov was effectively excluded from the artistic and social life of Leningrad. In 1941, in the first winter of the Nazi siege of Leningrad, he died of starvation, forgotten by all but his most faithful pupils.

After the war Filonov's name was no longer mentioned, as if he had never existed. His works, over three hundred of them, were preserved by his sister, the singer Yevdokia Glebova. With an introduction, one could come to her apartment to view the paintings. In the early sixties I was among the lucky few. I went there with two friends. In a heavily curtained room in a Leningrad communal flat a gravely imperious woman first read us excerpts from Filonov's theoretical works and then showed us several dozen paintings. The effect was as if a new world had opened before us, because Filonov had created his own universe, in which animals, people, buildings, and plants existed as a sparkling colorful mass, simultaneously solid and weightless, soaring upward. We lived under a profound impression of those amazing works for a long time. Unfortunately Filonov's paintings were not available to large audiences until 1988, when an exhibition of his works was organized in Leningrad and the Soviet press happily announced "the discovery of yet another artist almost unknown until now."

Despite his tragic end, one could say Filonov had been lucky in Stalinist Russia. He himself had not been arrested, had not been beaten during interrogations by the GPU or the NKVD (acronyms for the secret police), had not rotted away in a Siberian prison camp. The fate of many other Leningrad avant-gardists was much worse than the poor artist's.

"Stunned by a blow from the back, I fell, started to rise, but there was another blow—in the face. I lost consciousness. I awoke, sputtering in the water someone was pouring over me. I was lifted up and I thought they were tearing off my clothes. I passed out again. No sooner had I come to than some strangers dragged me down the stone corridors of the prison, beating me and mocking my defenseless-ness."[94] This was a description of one of his interrogations by the poet Nikolai Zabolotsky, an Oberiu member arrested in 1938.

The Leningrad dadaists were persecuted with particular cru-elty. Oleinikov died in prison. A friend recalled that Oleinikov had come to visit a few days before his arrest and said nothing, even though the friend could see he wanted to talk. "What about? That he was cer-tain of his doom and, like everyone else, could not move, was just waiting? What to do? His family? How to conduct himself—*there*? We'll never know."[95] The same fate befell the poet and member of Oberiu Alexander Vvedensky, who disappeared without a trace. Kharms was arrested in August 1941, soon after Germany attacked the USSR. He was declared mentally ill and sent to a prison psychi-atric hospital, where he died two months later—it is not known whether of hunger or forced "treatment."

Zabolotsky survived prison and the camps, his health ruined by heavy forced labor. Then he lived in exile in Kazakhstan and was released in 1946 through the efforts of friends, but he was not reha-bilitated until five years after his death, in 1963.

Zabolotsky went through his incredible trials attempting to maintain a sense of his own dignity and the restraint that had been typical of him since youth. Those who knew him commented that there was very little of the poetic about him: a smooth pink face and, behind round bookkeeper glasses, almost expressionless eyes with short lashes. But he soon became the most famous poet of Oberiu, with a special interest in contemporary Petrograd.

A born Petersburger, Kharms was worried by the disappear-ance of his city. Peter the Great and Nicholas II appear in his *Com-edy of the City of Petersburg*. Nicholas poses the rhetorical question: "O Peter, where is your Russia? Where is your city, where is pale Pe-tersburg?" The echoes in Kharms's work of Pushkin's *Bronze Horse-man* are not even the typical dada parody but more of an homage. These parallels with the classics were important for Kharms, which is why he made a point of bowing to every ancient lamppost when he strolled through the city: for him those lampposts were animate crea-tures that had seen, perhaps, Pushkin himself.

Zabolotsky, who viewed the transformation of the Petersburg mythos as a personal trauma, also loved *The Bronze Horseman* and considered Kharms's *Comedy* to be the author's best work. But Zabolotsky saw the city with the eyes of a provincial visitor, bowled over by the ugly contrasts of life in the metropolis, with the "drunken

paradise" of its noisy bars, the hypocrisy of Nevsky Prospect "in glitter and dreariness" (almost a Gogolian image), and simple-minded
but crowd-pleasing entertainments at the People's House (where a few
years earlier Balanchine and a friend had presented the "Polovtsian
masses" in *Prince Igor* for the unsophisticated audience). Zabolotsky
describes the city circus, which "shines like a shield"; wandering musicians, singing in narrow Petersburg courtyards, "amid tall dug-out
pits"; and a wedding where "the pound-heavy wine glasses roared."

Zabolotsky created one of the most poignant images to convey the mystical effect of the white nights, using the new surrealistic
imagery:

> *Thus a fetus or an angel,*
> *opening its milky eyes,*
> *sways in a formaldehyde jar*
> *and begs to be returned to the skies.*

But he brings along the fantastic picture of a flea market on the Ob-
vodny Canal, with its brazen speculators, crippled beggars, and the
coach drivers who resembled sultans. This is the world of
Zoshchenko, whose heroes Zabolotsky regarded with markedly naïve
astonishment. It is not surprising that it was Zoshchenko who noted
in an early review of Zabolotsky's poetry, "But this is seeming child-
ishness. Beyond the naive verbal picture there is almost always visible a bold and clear stroke. And that naïveté works as a justifiable
device."

This defense of Zabolotsky by Zoshchenko is characteristic of
the cultural state of affairs in Leningrad during the late twenties and
early thirties, when experimental authors demonstrated solidarity in
the face of the ever-growing hostility from the authorities. They all
knew one another, meeting constantly at literary, artistic, philosophical, and religious salons and circles, entering loose creative associations that formed, then fell apart. Zabolotsky admired Shostakovich,
and Filonov was one of his favorite artists. In turn, Filonov and his
students were brought into the production of Gogol's comedy *The Inspector General* by the poet and director Igor Terentyev, one of the
brightest figures in avant-garde Leningrad.

This play was shown at the same House of the Press, in which
Filonov's Masters of Analytical Art had done paintings on the walls
of the theater and lobby. Now Filonov's "analytical" method triumphed on the stage: the costume of the postmaster was made up of
envelopes sealed with red wax and huge postal cancellations; the po-

liceman's uniform featured leg irons, chains, locks, and keys; the tavern waiter had a wine bottle and hams on his head and a large sausage dangling from a strategic place. They were called "speaking costumes" and elicited a stormy reaction. The sophisticated audience was as delighted as the critics were outraged by Terentyev's handling of the text of Gogol's comedy, which was known to everyone in the country. The characters suddenly switched to French, Polish, or German or burst into Gypsy song and even arias from Rimsky-Korsakov operas in the middle of their monologues.

The play based on *The Inspector General* was filled with music and staged for the most part as parody; for instance, the hero proceeded solemnly to the toilet to the sounds of Beethoven's Moonlight Sonata. In general, the toilet played an important part in Terentyev's production: the actors were constantly heading off for it and interpolating grunts and moans into Gogol's original text. This was highly unusual for Soviet audiences, as was the blatantly erotic interpretation, which embarrassed even the avant-garde critics.

The premiere of the Gogol-Terentyev *Inspector General*, which received a hostile reception from the Leningrad establishment, took place in the spring of 1927 and had an undoubted influence on Shostakovich's *Nose*, which he began soon afterward. Another striking theatrical phenomenon in Leningrad that entranced Shostakovich was the Theater of Worker Youth (TRAM), which arose in 1922 as an amateur studio at the House of Communist Upbringing. Shostakovich lived nearby and saw many performances by that ensemble, which was headed by one of the most popular theater figures of the city, Mikhail Sokolovsky, the idol of "proletarian" youth. TRAM quickly won a wide audience and realized the secret dreams of the most radical "left" theoreticians of the theater. Sokolovsky, whose energy and enthusiasm could overwhelm any doubters, rejected the most important elements of the old theater. Instead of presenting plays traditionally, the basis of their performance became the "dramatization," which Adrian Piotrovsky, a TRAM theoretician, later described thus: "The dramatization of a remembered event or asserted slogan was the linchpin onto which were threaded actions, movements, dialogues, and songs."[96] According to Piotrovsky, for the avant-garde an important distinction between a "dramatization" and the old psychological drama was the fact that this new theater form "strove not 'to show,' but 'to prove,' 'to persuade,' to change lives."

In that sense TRAM was the embodiment of all the utopian manifestos of Russian theater symbolism and the later futurism. What had seemed an unrealizable ideal before the revolution suddenly became possible in Communist Petrograd. In the early years after the revolution the authorities allowed and encouraged all sorts of dramatic performances in which thousands of people took part. The avant-gardists were granted an artistic license that had not existed before; they could use "word, song, athletic march, military parade, smoke screen, cannon fire from a fortress, fireworks, projectors from battleships."[97] For Soviet avant-gardists these were exercises in preparation for the total theater of the future, which according to their plans would have to blend into life and which they visualized as a never-ending carnival.

But gradually those mass theatrical productions dwindled to nothing. The "obsolete" traditional theater withstood the attacks of the innovators and clearly had no intention of vanishing. Now all the hopes of the left theater people were tied to TRAM, where the indefatigable Sokolovsky banished professional actors as well as the traditional play and replaced them with young laborers. This allowed TRAM to claim to be the bastion of "proletarian" art. More or less protected by his orthodox label, Sokolovsky could undertake any experiment he wished.

Sokolovsky was primarily interested in theater's unmediated effect on audiences. His actors lived and worked like a creative commune, which Sokolovsky dubbed the Monastery.[98] TRAM's performances, which usually consisted of a chain of brief episodes with a generous use of lights, music, and songs, were dedicated to such themes as alcoholism, anti-Semitism, juvenile delinquency, and the questions of free love versus traditional marriage.

Sokolovsky encouraged direct interaction with the audience, and the actors had the right to change the text while onstage, depending on audience reaction. Often as they started a performance, the actors did not know how they would end it—for instance, whether the heroine would die or whether they would decide to let her live. (This was called "total freemenry" in TRAM jargon.)[99] As a result, each TRAM performance was a passionate improvised dispute that included the audience and often dragged on until dawn.

Shostakovich was attracted by the theatrical form of Sokolovsky's productions and the bubbling atmosphere around them. For three years he was the musical director of the Leningrad TRAM and wrote the incidental music for several of its productions. For Shostakovich, brought up in the severe "intelligentsia" tradition, the intoxicating carnival life of TRAM was liberating, a source of im-

portant new creative impulses. Participating in Sokolovsky's efferves-
cent productions gave the composer the illusion of continuing his voy-
age on the Crazy Ship.

The word "carnival," according to some lexicographers, is tied ety-
mologically to the image of a ship on wheels, the ancient ritual char-
iot (*carrus-navalis* in Latin). In the mid-twenties in Leningrad a
philosophical-religious circle met at the home of the pianist Maria Yudina and at a few other apartments. Its leader was Mikhail Bakhtin, an
original and influential humanist thinker. As Yudina told me, even then
one of Bakhtin's favorite themes was the influence of the carnival on
world culture. Bakhtin later developed this idea in his classic work on
Rabelais. But the concept of the liberating function of the carnival was
polished in the private discussions in a city for which one of the basic
metaphors in those days was a flying ship. "The carnival is a spectacle
without footlights and without separating into performers and viewers. In a carnival everyone is an active participant," Bakhtin later
wrote. In those words we can hear the echo of theatrical performances
in Petrograd in the early postrevolutionary years. Sokolovsky, the creator of the carnival-like TRAM, would have signed that statement.

Bakhtin noted once that the carnival life "is life taken out of
its usual ruts." It would be difficult to imagine a city more torn out
of its usual trajectory than Petersburg after the Russian Revolution.
In that sense it was the quintessential carnival city. All the hierarchical barriers that had formed over centuries were broken down there,
traditional values were tossed out the window, religion was subjected
to "carnival" profanation, and numerous eccentrics of various types
floated to the surface. These were all important signs of a carnival
culture, according to Bakhtin. They were reflected in Shostakovich's
music, Zoshchenko's prose, Zabolotsky's poetry, and Kharms's eccentricity. Filonov's paintings are also filled with the carnival spirit.
This is urban art, just as Bakhtin's philosophy was urban.

Bakhtin's discussion group was a phenomenon of underground
culture, typical of Leningrad in those years. A network existed in the
city of unofficial literary, philosophical, and religious societies, often
consisting of just a few people each.[100] Feeling a threat to their ideological monopoly, the authorities ruthlessly persecuted these underground groups, even though they were not anti-Soviet organizations
by any stretch of the imagination. Bakhtin's circle discussed Kant,
Henri Bergson, Freud, Christian theology, and Eastern philosophy.[101]
Although disabled by osteomyelitis, Bakhtin was a charismatic figure.

A major thinker whose ideas influenced literary and social history, linguistics, the philosophy of culture and language, psychology and anthropology, Bakhtin was also an inspiring lecturer. Few people knew about Bakhtin outside his narrow circle of friends, but among them were the leading lights of Leningrad's intellectual elite.

In 1929 the Leningrad publishing house Priboi released Bakhtin's book *Problems of Dostoyevsky's Creative Works*, with Nathan Altman's engraving of Dostoyevsky on the cover. In this groundbreaking monograph Bakhtin offered a new interpretation of Dostoyevsky's novels. In Bakhtin's opinion, Dostoyevsky had created a type of novel that Bakhtin called "polyphonic." In a polyphonic novel the author does not predominate; the narrative develops as a result of the constant dialogue of many voices that exist independently of the author.

The concept of dialogue is central to Bakhtin's cultural philosophy. His ideas on dialogue are exemplified by a megalopolis where people talk to each other without listening and pass each other without seeing. Thus Bakhtin describes the existence of the hero of *Crime and Punishment* as follows:

> Everything that he sees and observes—the Petersburg slums and the monumental Petersburg, all his random encounters and petty incidents—all this is brought into dialogue, responds to his questions, poses new ones before him, provokes him, argues with him or confirms his thoughts.

For Bakhtin Dostoyevsky is not only a great novelist but also the creator of a new type of artistic expression and, more broadly, of a new artistic model of the world. Using Dostoyevsky's works as an example, Bakhtin tries to solve the general problems of human intercourse: "Only with an inner receptivity to dialogue does my word find itself in the closest connection with another's word, but at the same time it does not blend into it, does not engulf it, and does not dissolve its significance, that is, it preserves fully its independence as a word."

Bakhtin's call for dialogue, understanding, and attention to "another's word" could be construed as a political statement, but it appeared at a time when any meaningful discourse was becoming more and more problematic. Bakhtin's book on Dostoyevsky was published in May 1929, a few months after the author had been arrested during a secret police dragnet to liquidate underground philosophical and religious circles in Leningrad. The fact that the book came out anyway speaks of the comparative lack of teeth in Soviet cultural policy in that period. Lunacharsky, living out his final days at his post as the cultural czar, even published a lengthy and on the whole positive review of Bakhtin's work. A surviving copy of the book, which had belonged to Lunacharsky, has a marginal note that reads, "But the problems are posed in an interesting way, and work on them could lead far."

It is quite probable that Lunacharsky's intercession saved Bakhtin from death in a labor camp; he was "merely" exiled to Kazakhstan—his work did "lead far," but not in the sense Lunacharsky meant—where seventy-five years earlier, during the reign of Nicholas I, the subject of Bakhtin's research, Dostoyevsky, had spent his exile. Unlike Dostoyevsky, however, Bakhtin never returned to the city on the Neva. The last few years of his life (he died in 1975) were spent in Moscow in an apartment obtained for him by the members of the "new" Bakhtin circle. He had lived long enough to see the beginnings of his international fame and recognition.

Bakhtin's best work stylistically, *Problems of Dostoyevsky's Creative Works*, can be read as a graceful literary work in its own right, which then leads to parallels with another great Russian thinker; the first book of the religious philosopher Vassily Rozanov (1856–1919) was also a work on Dostoyevsky that brought its author fame, at least in Russia. Published in 1894, this book was the first to assert Dostoyevsky's religio-philosophical significance. Rozanov wrote that Dostoyevsky was a "flexible, dialectical genius whose almost every thesis is transformed into an anti-thesis."

Rozanov's writing style is quite similar to Bakhtin's manner of expression. In both cases, the reader seems to hear the author's voice intoning his text with extreme conviction, sometimes sharpening his thought to the point of paradox for better effect. But for Bakhtin refinement and paradox were not an end in themselves. With Rozanov, this did happen. However Rozanov, an unattractive individual who lisped, drooled, twitched his knees and shook his red beard in conversation, went decidedly beyond any other Russian philosopher in the attempt to capture on paper barely perceptible emotional states and feelings, the "cobwebs of life," as he put it.

Rozanov developed (not without Nietzsche's influence) an aphoristic style that had an enormous impact on the new Petersburg prose. In his later books he created, in fact, a new literary genre. According to Shklovsky, who studied Rozanov closely, it was a sort of novel of the parodic type: " 'Yes' and 'no' exist simultaneously on one page—a biographical fact elevated to the rank of stylistic fact."

The Petersburg modernists esteemed Rozanov highly, despite his political cynicism and anti-Semitism. Mandelstam wrote almost lovingly of him,

> An anarchic attitude toward everything, total confusion, nothing counts, there's only one thing I can't do without—that's living without words, I cannot survive separation from the word! That is an approximation of Rozanov's spiritual organization. That anarchic and nihilistic spirit recognized but one authority—the magic of language, the power of the word.

Right after the revolution Rozanov began to speak of an iron curtain:

> With creaks, screeches, and clanks an iron curtain descends over Russian History.
> "The show is over."
> The audience rises.
> "Time to put on your fur coats and go back home."
> They look around.
> But their fur coats and homes are gone.

Rozanov's innovative prose is "polyphonic," to use Bakhtin's term. Its pages are filled with arguing voices that are seemingly independent of the author. This disturbing prose, which lures readers into its magic circle to make them take part in a philosophical dispute, seems to have been created for Bakhtin's analysis.

As befits the author of the carnival theory, Bakhtin liked to surround himself with carnival personalities—exceptionally gifted eccentrics. The radical break in traditional culture gave rise to highly unusual situations and eccentric personalities. One observer noted, "In eccentricities, strangeness, and incongruities the intelligentsia expressed its need to deal with its past. . . . Just the way, after an explosion, the dust remains for a long time, settling slowly, and individual dust specks, totally unconnected and unattached, perform the most inventive pirouettes."[102]

In Bakhtin's Leningrad circle one of the most remarkable figures of the carnival type was the young poet and prose writer Konstantin Vaginov. The son of a fabulously wealthy colonel in the tsarist gendarmes, who was taught western European languages by his private tutors, Vaginov was a cocaine addict and bibliophile. He likened the victory of the Russian Revolution, which ruined his family, to the triumph of the barbaric tribes over the Roman Empire. For Vaginov, Petersburg had been a magical stage for that cultural tragedy, and he sang the praises of the spectral city in dadaist poems (which also showed the influence of Mandelstam), in which "pale blue sails of dead ships" appeared tellingly. Mandelstam, in turn, rated Vaginov highly, including him as a poet "not for today but forever" in a list with Akhmatova, Pasternak, Gumilyov, and Khodasevich.

Vaginov was part of the left wing of Oberiu. Like the group's leader, Kharms, he also wrote experimental prose, which he read aloud to his friends. They were particularly interested in Vaginov's novel *The Goat Song*. According to one witness, the listeners followed the thin, stoop-shouldered author from apartment to apartment to hear excerpts from the novel again and again in his masterly reading. This avid curiosity existed primarily because *The Goat Song* was a roman à clef: its characters were easily recognizable as some of the Bakhtin group members and other notable figures of literary Leningrad.

With the frightening speed of change in historical eras, people and events were instantly "bronzed," becoming natural fodder for fiction that grew directly out of memoirs or for fictionalized memoirs, like Georgy Ivanov's entertaining *Petersburg Winters*, published in Paris in 1928, which could also be considered new Petersburg prose.

Ivanov's memoirs and Vaginov's novel were written at approximately the same time, and it is not difficult to find much in common between them, especially the acute sense of and mourning for the end of the Petersburg era, the destruction of the Venice of the North. Both Ivanov and Vaginov agreed that the rose of Petersburg culture was about to fade anyway and that the unexpected revolutionary frost had merely hastened its demise. But in his memoirs, Ivanov, a subtle poet of the acmeist circle, an aesthete and snob, provides a nostalgic description of the decadent charms of prerevolutionary Petersburg. The book's origins in newspaper columns is evident in the amusing albeit not always reliable anecdotes and vivid, prejudiced sketches of Blok, Gumilyov, Akhmatova, Mandelstam, and the carnival world of Vyacheslav Ivanov's Tower and The Stray Dog cabaret.

Vaginov's novel, on the other hand, while written in equally translucent prose and imbued with a melodic quality characteristic of a "poet's prose," is a philosophical work, filled with learned allusions to obscure ancient and medieval authors. Even the title *The Goat Song* is a literal translation of the Greek word "tragedy." For Vaginov, Petersburg was "Athens on the Neva," the center of a refined Hellenism. The protagonists of *The Goat Song* carry on profound eschatological discussions à la Rozanov or Bakhtin, vainly trying to escape from the ugliness of Soviet reality in a "tall tower of humanism." Vaginov describes these people with love, irony, and pity. He understands their utter doom but hopes for a renaissance of the old values in a new quality. When this will happen Vaginov does not know. He states sadly, in a sarcastic refutation of the clichéd official designation of Leningrad as the "Cradle of the Revolution," "Now there is no Petersburg. There is Leningrad; but Leningrad has nothing to do with us. The author is a coffin maker by profession, not a master of cradle works."

Vaginov, who died of tuberculosis in 1934 at the age of thirty-five, depicted himself in *The Goat Song*, with ironic allusions to Blok and Akhmatova, as the last inhabitant of Hellenic Petersburg:

> On a snowy hill, on Nevsky, now hidden by the blizzard, now reappearing, stands an unknown poet: beyond him there is emptiness. Everyone had left long ago. But he does not have the right, he cannot leave the city. Let everyone flee, let death come, but he will remain here and protect Apollo's high temple.

Kharms did not share the messianic cultural illusions of his friend Vaginov. The hero of his absurdist prose exists not in the mythical Hellenic Petersburg but in the real nauseating Leningrad.

> The house on the corner of Nevsky is being painted a revolting yellow. Have to turn off onto the street. I am pushed by people coming toward me. They all recently moved here from villages and haven't learned to walk on the streets yet. Their clothes and faces are filthy. They come trampling from all sides, growling and shoving.

Most of the characters in Kharms and Zoshchenko are related, they "growl and shove" in the same world: one that is dark, cruel, and threatening, a world that has nothing to do with the "temple of Apollo" that came to Vaginov in a dream. Khodasevich had taken ninety-nine short stories by Zoshchenko and found at least ninety-nine characters who break the law in some way: they kill, cheat, counterfeit, and brawl—drunk and sober. They do it for absurd reasons, suffering neither doubts nor pangs of conscience "à la Dostoyevsky," vaguely feeling that they are both "masters" of the new life, as they are told by the posters all around them, but also its victims.

In Kharms's prose, the darkness gets ever thicker. One of his characters replies this way to a charge that includes rape: "First of all, she wasn't a virgin anymore, and secondly, I was dealing with a corpse, and she's not going to complain now. What of the fact that she was supposed to give birth any minute? I pulled out the baby, didn't I?" But in Kharms's cruel and surrealistic short parables, which he called "incidents" and which have parallels with Kafka and Céline, there appear also alienated intellectuals, closer to the frightened and despairing heroes of Vaginov.

"A man with a thin neck climbed into a trunk, shut the lid, and started to suffocate." Thus begins one such metaphorical narrative by Kharms, in which the typical representative of the Leningrad intelligentsia of those years sets up a humiliating experiment on himself to test the ability to survive in a hostile environment. In another "incident" called "The Dream," a certain Kalugin was reduced to such nervous exhaustion by a recurring nightmare involving a dreaded policeman that when a medical-sanitation inspection team going through the apartments "found him antisanitary and useless," it had him tossed into the garbage: "Kalugin was folded in half and thrown out like trash." Akhmatova, commenting on similar surrealistic moments in Kharms's prose, said, "He managed to do what almost no one else could, write the so-called prose of the twentieth century. When they describe, for instance, how the hero went out into the street and suddenly flew up into the air, no one else can do that convincingly, only Kharms."

In the epilogue to his *Goat Song*, Vaginov described the forced dissolution of Bakhtin's circle and, echoing Rozanov's lamentations, concluded sadly, "But it is time to lower the curtain. The performance is over. It is confusing and quiet on the stage. Where is the promised love, the promised heroism? Where is the promised art?" Vaginov, like many others, thought that everything was over. But this perception was not universal among the Leningrad elite; even among Vaginov's loyal followers there were a few extraordinary personalities, who—at least at first—managed to find an application for their outstanding gifts within the limits of officially recognized culture, without making total compromises. The example of the musicologist and critic Ivan Sollertinsky is edifying in that sense, although not typical.

The son of a high-ranking tsarist bureaucrat, Sollertinsky quickly became a local landmark, the "city genius." He walked around

Leningrad in a shabby coat and when asked why he, such a famous lecturer, could appear in trousers worn to a sheen, replied, "It is the sparkle of Soviet musicology!" His genius pose was also a mask for dealing with life, but of a different sort than Zoshchenko's. Sollertinsky enjoyed playing the absentminded professor, even though he never missed an opportunity to jab an opponent with a sarcastic remark. In a public discussion of a derivative symphony by a Leningrad composer, he said, "It's the water in which Rachmaninoff's chamber pot was rinsed!"[103]

The eccentric genius mask helped Sollertinsky survive. Celebrities arriving from the West always asked for a meeting with that "phenomenal scholar who knows fifty languages."[104] Sollertinsky in fact was fluent in at least two dozen languages (thirty-two, counting dialects), from Latin to Sanskrit; in the latter he usually made his most private diary notations. His vast and extremely varied knowledge coupled with the temperament of an activist quickly made Sollertinsky one of the leading proselytizers of the new art in Leningrad. He was an intimate of Bakhtin's but also met frequently with Kharms and the other oberiuts and was highly esteemed by the choreographer Fyodor Lopukhov. Balanchine spoke respectfully of Sollertinsky to the end of his days.[105] Sollertinsky had a photographic memory: after a quick glance at the most complex text, he could repeat it by heart. Shostakovich liked to remind us that Sollertinsky had memorized "all of Shakespeare, Pushkin, Gogol, Aristotle, and Plato." When they met in 1927 Sollertinsky pronounced Shostakovich a genius, and the composer immediately fell under the spell of the scholar who was four years his senior and became his best friend.

Sollertinsky defended Shostakovich's Nose from hostile critics, stating that "The Nose is not a product for instant use and disposal. It is a laboratory factory, where new music and theater language are being created." Sollertinsky compared Shostakovich's opera to the works of Swift and Voltaire. "The Nose has no positive characters: only masks." Bakhtin would have called this work one of "carnival" but not of "dialogue." Shostakovich made the leap from Gogol's carnival world to Dostoyevsky's dialogue world in the opera Lady Macbeth of the Mtsensk District, based on the story of Nikolai Leskov, a Petersburg writer of the late nineteenth century whose careful treatment of every word and mastery of the phrase earned the respect of Zamyatin and the Serapion Brothers, who considered Leskov among their teachers.

A literary maverick, Leskov liked fanciful plots to which baf-fled critics did not know how to react. His "sketch" about the mer-chant wife Katerina Izmailova, whose fatal love leads her to commit multiple murders, had remained in obscurity for over a half century; Shostakovich's opera brought it world fame. The paradox lies in the fact that Shostakovich had radically rewritten Leskov's story; as Sollertinsky put it, "The evaluation of the roles has been changed: the victims become executioners, the killer—the victim." In Shostakovich's version, Katerina kills in self-defense and the composer vindicates her. Leskov's misogynist work is transformed into a feminist apotheosis.

Sollertinsky believed that "in the history of Russian musical the-ater nothing of the scope and depth of *The Queen of Spades* appeared until *Lady Macbeth*." In his operas Tchaikovsky sympathetically treated his women characters. Shostakovich continued that tradition. His Katerina is a "polyphonic" heroine, strong passions and deep emo-tions battle within her; she can be tender, passionate, caring, and cruel. Sollertinsky was among the first to note that killer Katerina's part "is completely lyrical, with deeply felt melodies," and that the opera as a whole has "a tragic—Shakespearean rather than Leskovian—sweep."

Lady Macbeth has sharply contrasting parts: expressionist de-pictions of the brutish merchant life, satirical carnival vignettes of the police apparatus, and dramatic scenes from the life of hard labor, à la Dostoyevsky. Another striking similarity between Shostakovich's opera and Dostoyevsky's polyphonic novels is the criminal plot, which keeps the audience in constant suspense and develops in a sweeping way that leads to important social and philosophical conclusions.

Bakhtin discussed with his circle the idea of a special "poly-phonic creative thought" that went beyond the limits of the novel. In his second opera Shostakovich showed himself to be the master of that type of thought. He does not judge Katerina Izmailova but gives her the opportunity to express herself through contradictory actions and emotions. This work was influenced by the Bakhtin circle's aesthetics. A prominent participant in the circle, Sollertinsky was Shostakovich's closest adviser in the years he was writing the opera. He was present at all the rehearsals, commenting freely, encouraging, inciting, and provoking the conductor, the soloists, and the composer.

The 1934 premiere in Leningrad was a great success; in its first five months the opera was performed thirty-six times to sold-out houses. The happy Shostakovich could allow himself to write to a friend, "The audience listens very attentively and makes a run for their

galoshes only after the curtain falls."[106] *Lady Macbeth* was staged triumphantly in Moscow, too, but with catastrophic consequences. In
January 1936 Stalin attended a performance. The opera infuriated
him and he left before the end.

The best barometer of Stalin's reaction was the editorial that
appeared in the Party newspaper, *Pravda*, two days later, called "Muddle Instead of Music," almost certainly dictated by Stalin:

> The listener is stunned almost from the first minute by the opera's in-
> tentionally dissonant and muddled avalanche of sounds. Snatches of
> melody, embryos of musical phrases drown, escape, and vanish once
> more in clangs, creaks, and squeals. Following this "music" is diffi-
> cult, remembering it is impossible. . . . The music quacks, grunts,
> pants, and gasps, the more naturally to depict the love scenes. . . .
> The predatory merchant woman, who seized wealth and power by
> murder, is presented as some kind of "victim" of bourgeois soci-
> ety. . . . This glorification of merchant lust has been called satire by
> some critics. But there isn't even a breath of satire here. By all avail-
> able means of musical and dramatic expression the author is trying
> to elicit the audience's sympathy for the crude and vulgar desires and
> actions of the unscrupulous Katerina Izmailova.

It is not hard to believe that Stalin was personally offended by
the music's expressionistic excesses, its unprecedentedly frank, erotic
character, and the opera's strongly feminist statement. But Stalin
had more in mind than public expression of personal dissatisfaction.
That became clear when *Pravda*'s editorials followed, fiercely attacking all kinds of "formalists" and "pseudo innovators" in Soviet
art. The headlines—crude, peremptory, sounding like harsh sentences—are characteristic: "Balletic Falsity," "Cacophony in Architecture," "About Dauber Artists," "External Shine and False Content."

The campaign that followed these publications was unparalleled in its ferocity and scope. Articles from *Pravda* were reprinted by
every newspaper in the country. "Discussions" of the articles were
mandatory, and terrified writers, composers, and artists accused one
another of formalism, alienation from the people, and other mortal
sins, and exercised knee-jerk self-criticism. Virtually no major figure
in Soviet art was spared public humiliation in some degree. Accounts
of hundreds of such meetings were also obligatorily printed in national and regional newspapers and broadcast on the radio.

The *Pravda* editorial that started the avalanche clearly presented the official harsh formula not only for the arts but for cultural

expression in the broadest sense: "Leftist freakishness in opera grows from the same source as leftist freakishness in painting, poetry, pedagogy, and science. Petit bourgeois 'innovation' leads to a break with real art, science, and real literature." One phrase in particular sounded a very Stalin-like threat: "This is playing with nonsensical things, which could end very badly."

The articles in *Pravda* were correctly perceived as direct instructions. *Lady Macbeth of the Mtsensk District* was immediately taken out of the repertory in both Leningrad and Moscow. Criticized books were removed from libraries and destroyed, plays were banned, art exhibits shut down. One cultural bureaucrat later recalled being sent "to set things straight" at the Leningrad Russian Museum, which had a valuable collection of Russian avant-garde art. At the museum, he found piles of garbage in the halls, works by Malevich and Filonov sticking out. His orders were to destroy the paintings. Risking his neck, he hid them in deep vaults, saving them for future generations.[107]

The cultural convulsions of 1936 were the culmination of a lengthy process in the course of which Stalin, the supreme manipulator of public opinion, shaped Soviet art and literature according to his far-reaching propaganda goals. By 1932 he had dissolved all literary and artistic associations, including the omnipotent Russian Association of Proletarian Writers (RAPP), which had been a pillar of support for him until then. The terms "proletarian culture" and "fellow travelers of the revolution," which RAPP juggled so deftly, were replaced by new ones—"Soviet culture" and "Soviet writers." The sole organization allowed was the new Union of Soviet Writers, created as a model for the bureaucratic coordination of all "creative" professions, including composers, artists, and architects.

At the same time it was officially announced that the road to the development of Soviet culture was to be realism, and not ordinary but "socialist" realism. The intention was for Soviet cultural forces to glorify socialism in traditionally realistic forms. An atmosphere was created in which, with growing rigor, any attempt at experimentation in art was declared "formalism," and "formalist" became the worst label one could hang on a writer, artist, or composer.

The frightened, broken leaders of the Soviet avant-garde capitulated one after the other; in the thirties this was called *"perestroika,"* or "restructuring." For example, Malevich tried to restructure himself. He stopped working in his suprematist manner and began painting realistic portraits. They are interesting and significant works, but in his heart Malevich must have continued to consider himself primarily the creator of nonfigurative suprematism. When he died in 1935, Lydia Ginzburg described the funeral: Malevich was "buried with music and in a Suprematist coffin. People lined Nevsky, and people said: Must be a foreigner! . . . The Suprematist coffin was made from a design by the deceased. For the cover he had planned a square, a circle, and a cross, but the cross was rejected, even though it was called an intersection of two planes."[108]

The observation that the mass audience perceived the avant-gardists as foreigners was a shrewd one. In Russia, experimental art had never taken root. At all times civic-oriented culture was highly valued, and the demand for "realism," understood primarily as a naturalistic similarity to life and first presented by populists in the 1860s, acquired legitimacy in intellectual circles. As Akhmatova commented bitterly in the 1960s, "The good things that the *narodniki* (populists) called for, no one accepted. But their 'realism' was accepted right away. And for a long time."[109]

In the early years of the twentieth century the symbolists and especially the members of *Mir iskusstva* succeeded in reeducating a significant number of the Russian intellectual elite, particularly in Petersburg. New perceptions about the possibilities and goals of culture started to take root; this Silver Age prepared the soil for the wild flowering of the Russian avant-garde. But the broad circles of intelligentsia, not to mention the general public, remained outside of this process. When the avant-garde captured a few commanding positions for a brief period after the revolution and tried to expand their influence, the cultural counterrevolution was not long in coming.

Petersburg, as the most Western-oriented Russian cultural center, accepted the ideas of the modern sooner than other locales and remained a platform for avant-garde experimentation longer than any other city. In the postrevolutionary years, the cultural "left front" in Petrograd-Leningrad produced dazzling things: the canvases of Malevich and Filonov, the constructions of Tatlin, the theatrical productions of Sokolovsky and Terentyev, the Factory of the Eccentric Actor, the choreography of Lopukhov and Balanchine, the new Petersburg prose, Oberiu, and the symphonies and operas of Shostakovich. But this highly original work, the impulse for which came from the innovations of the Silver Age and which the poet Lev Loseff suggested calling the Bronze Age, took place in an unconducive atmosphere, under constant and increasing pressure both from above and below.

The pressure from above came from the bureaucratic state apparatus that grew stronger with every passing month. From below, the peasant masses that poured into the city brought pressure. An aggressively conservative Philistine taste in culture was common at the top and the bottom. In those circumstances, the Bronze Age was doomed in Leningrad and in the rest of the country.

Inside the country the "left front" did not fulfill even a small part of its goals. But it did become immensely popular in intellectual circles of the West. In that sense a comparison with *Mir iskusstva* is revealing, whose leaders except for Diaghilev did not become cultural icons in the West; the same could be said about the Russian symbolists. Yet inside Russia the cultural goals of *Mir iskusstva* and the symbolists were realized in large part. Of course, the "socialist realists" managed to crowd out many recognized figures from *Mir iskusstva*. But this happened later, in the forties and early fifties, and affected Leningrad least of all, where *Mir iskusstva*'s authority remained unshakable, even in the most difficult years of Stalin's cultural clampdown and in defiance of the prevailing attitude.

The left front in culture was for Stalin not only an aesthetic but a political threat. He considered it part of the left opposition to his political line. Very adept at using art for political gain, Stalin always regarded it in a broader social context. Even though his moves in the political and cultural spheres were not necessarily always simultaneous, the general direction of his strategy in both almost always coincided. And often clamping down in cultural life was a harbinger of pressure in the political sphere. Thus, the bureaucratic centralization of cultural activity and the imposition of socialist realism preceded one of the turning points in prewar Soviet history: the assassination on December 1, 1934, in Leningrad of the Communist Party leader Sergei Kirov, which some historians dubbed "the murder of the century."

This killing, which stunned the Soviet Union, had tragic consequences for Leningrad. A high Party official and friend of Stalin, Kirov had been his satrap in Leningrad since 1926, replacing Zinoviev, Lenin's comrade-in-arms, who did not suit Stalin and was a leader of the internal Communist Party "opposition." The subsequent development of events turned Kirov into a national hero, while Zinoviev was presented for years afterward only in a negative light. In this respect the case of Kirov resembles the situation with Lenin: reminiscences by people who knew him blend contemporary feelings with an overlay of emotions added later.

Energetic, attractive, and a good orator, Kirov was a comparatively well-read man who followed contemporary literature and devoted a lot of attention to Leningrad culture.[110] He was a patron of

Lopukhov, encouraging the choreographer's experiments in using modern plots in ballet.[111] Kirov also frequently attended the opera. He did not care for *The Nose*, but that did not lead to the immediate removal of the production from the repertory.[112] Kirov no doubt tried to cultivate the image of a "democratic" leader, as opposed to Stalin. That made him popular but also probably annoyed Stalin, who had eliminated Zinoviev and with him the threat of a powerful center of opposition in Leningrad. Then less than a decade later, Stalin perceived that Leningrad was trying to slip from his control again.

That Kirov might have been killed on Stalin's orders was discussed openly in the Soviet Union after the mid-fifties. But the rumor spread in Leningrad almost immediately. Kirov was shot in a corridor of the former Smolny Institute, which became the Communist Party's headquarters in Soviet times. A popular jingle of the period went:

> Oh, horrid things got even horrider,
> Stalin got Kirov in the corridor.

The official reaction to Kirov's death was naturally quite different. It was immediately announced that the enemies of the Soviet state were behind the murder. Many people were truly shocked and frightened. Zabolotsky dedicated a poem to Kirov that appeared in the newspaper *Izvestiya* three days after his murder. It began

> Farewell! A mournful word!
> A wordless dark body.
> From the heights of Leningrad
> The cold sky looked down austerely.

Kirov's bier lay in state in the Tauride Palace, with Stalin, who had arrived by special train from Moscow, as one of the honor guards. "Huge crowds of Leningraders moved along Shpalernaya Street to bid him farewell. I also walked in that sorrowing and anxious crowd, also felt in that event something of a watershed, a transition to a new era that promised we knew not what," recalled Nikolai Chukovsky.

The most terrible foreboding of the city's inhabitants came to pass. Mass arrests and executions began instantly. "The words 'execution' and 'shoot' became so ordinary in our daily lives that they lost meaning. Only the shell remained, an empty combination of sounds. The real meaning of the word did not reach our brains. It was worn off, like a counterfeit coin," wrote Lyubov Shaporina, the author of one of the rare surviving honest diaries of the period.[113]

The "investigation" of the circumstances of Kirov's death—ac-

tually nothing less than the organization of mass terror in Leningrad—
was entrusted by Stalin to the infamous Yakov Agranov, who in 1921
had fabricated the "case" against Gumilyov on Zinoviev's orders. But
now Agranov was obeying Stalin, and one of his first victims was Zinoviev. Stalin accused Zinoviev of being the mastermind behind
Kirov's murder. This gave him the opportunity to put an end for good
to opposition within the Party. But the consequences of the Kirov case
reached much farther. It was Stalin's pretext for unleashing the Great
Terror of 1936–1938, in which millions of people perished.

That terror was like the black plague attacking the Soviet Union,
infecting more and more strata of society, who came to be branded "enemies of the people." The country was caught up in a madness of
denunciations, mutual accusations, and self-incriminations extracted
under torture. Leningrad was singled out for specially ruthless treatment: Stalin hoped to destroy the city's oppositional spirit once and
for all.

The Great Terror in Leningrad was described by an impassioned witness, Yevgeny Shvarts:

> A storm broke, swirling everything around it, and it was impossible
> to guess who would be killed by the next bolt of lightning. And no
> one ran and no one hid. A man who knows he is guilty knows how
> to behave: a criminal gets a false passport and flees to another city.
> But the future enemies of the people stood without moving, awaiting
> the blow of the terrible Antichrist brand. They sensed blood, like bulls
> in a slaughterhouse, they sensed it, but the 'enemy of the people' brand
> kills without selection, anyone at all—and they all stood there, obe-
> diently, like bulls waiting for the blow. How can you run if you know
> you're not guilty? How do you behave during interrogations? And
> people died, in a nightmare, confessing to unheard of crimes: espi-
> onage, terror, sabotage. And they vanished without a trace, and after
> them were sent their wives and children, entire families.[114]

It was hard to find a family in Leningrad that was not affected
in some way by the terror. Its horrible shadow reached Akhmatova:
in 1935, at the height of the repressions following the Kirov case, they
arrested her son by Gumilyov, Lev, and her husband at the time, Nikolai Punin. Both had been arrested before and were already "marked":
Gumilyov, as the son of an "enemy of the people" executed in 1921,
and Punin as an influential theoretician of the avant-garde in art and
one of the leading figures in Leningrad's cultural life. On the advice
of friends, Akhmatova wrote a short letter to Stalin himself, pleading

for the release of her son and husband. It ended with the entreaty, "Help, Iosif Vissarionovich!" A few days later Lev and Punin were home.

In 1938 Lev Gumilyov was arrested again. Among the other absurd charges was the following. Akhmatova was allegedly inciting her son to avenge his father's death by killing Andrei Zhdanov, the new Party boss of Leningrad installed by Stalin to replace Kirov. New interrogations and beatings followed, but Lev did not sign any of the confessions they tried to force out of him, even though many people who could not withstand the torture "assembly line," as it was called, incriminated not only themselves but their friends and relatives.

Zabolotsky, arrested also in 1938, later described the behavior of his cellmates in a Leningrad prison: "Here you could observe all forms of despair, all manifestations of cold hopelessness, convulsive hysterical merriment, and cynical disregard of everything in the world, including one's own fate." The atmosphere changed dramatically at night, when the multistoried prison was illuminated by lights and the army of investigators set about its ruthless "work" in its innumerable offices: "The enormous stone courtyard of the building, onto which opened the windows of the offices, would gradually be filled with the groans and heart-rending screams of people being beaten. The whole cell shuddered, as if an electric current had run through it, and mute horror appeared once again in the eyes of the prisoners."

Lev Gumilyov was condemned to be shot. It is not known whether a new appeal, sent by Akhmatova to Stalin, had any effect or whether other circumstances were involved, but his sentence was commuted to exile in Siberia, where he was fated to spend fourteen years in prison and labor camps.

During the more than seventeen months that Gumilyov was imprisoned in Leningrad, Akhmatova spent hundreds of hours in prison lines. The women of Leningrad, who formed most of the long queues by the prison wall, were trying to learn at least something about the fate of their arrested relatives and to deliver food parcels to them. The exhausted Akhmatova, almost fifty years old then, her face ashen, was noticed by many people in the lines, even though in her worn old coat and crumpled hat she must have been hard to recognize.

One of the tensest moments when Akhmatova was turning over a parcel for her son was later described by her neighbor in that horrible line: "It was her turn, she came up to the crevice of a window—inside were insignia and an unapproachable dummy; softly, almost without opening her mouth, she said the required: 'Akhmatova for Gumilyov.' "[115] Akhmatova recalled that a woman who stood behind her burst into tears at hearing her name.

They were tears of shock. For many Leningraders Akhmatova must have seemed like a ghost from the past. In 1925, when an unofficial Party directive was issued about her ("Do not arrest, but do not publish"), her new poems ceased to appear. Akhmatova could have been considered deceased long ago, and in fact many thought she was. A favorite theme of the official critics, when her work was submitted for publication, was its blatant incompatibility with the new progressive "socialist way of life." In her late years, Akhmatova often ironically quoted one such article. "The new people remain, and will remain, cold and unmoved by the whining of a woman who either was born too late or did not die in time."

Hardest of all for Akhmatova was that this official hostility coincided with a certain cooling toward her poetry among the Leningrad poetry connoisseurs, who preferred to listen to Oberiu avant-garde poets like Zabolotsky or Vaginov. Akhmatova was losing contact with her audience and that may have been one of the reasons for the decline in her productivity. There were years when she wrote only one or two poems or none at all. For a lyric poet such muteness is worse than death, and Akhmatova suffered greatly.

The Great Terror brought to Akhmatova, as it did to millions of her fellow citizens, fear, sorrow, and inexpressible suffering, but it also gave her a new poetic voice and a renewed sense of sharing the nation's fate. Between 1935 and 1940 Akhmatova wrote the main body of the verse cycle *Requiem*, which is arguably the greatest contemporary artistic testimony to the Stalin terror. *Requiem* also played an important role in the later evolution of the Petersburg mythos.

The tsars had created Petersburg as an artificial capital, summoned to exert control over the Russian Empire, and many Russian creative geniuses keenly felt that the city's influence was that of the devil. Yet over two centuries, Petersburg grew deep roots in the native soil. And now the Communists' abrupt return of the capital to Moscow was regarded by the locals as violence against history and tradition. Stalin's vendetta against "oppositionist" Leningrad merely strengthened that impression.

The Petersburg elite of the nineteenth century, in opposition to the regime, felt alienated from their own capital. At the turn of the century, only isolated individuals began to feel a certain sympathy for Petersburg. But by the time Petrograd had lost its political significance under the Soviet regime, wide circles of the intelligentsia had come to love and revere their city.

The city's imperial traditions made it the ideal focus for remembrance; this was understood well by its enemies, too. When in the early 1920s Nikolai Antsiferov's book, *The Soul of Petersburg*, appeared—the first attempt to provide a comprehensive outline of the Petersburg mythos in its literary and architectural manifestations—the proletarian writer Alexander Serafimovich wrote an irritated partisan review:

> The book draws the city's "face," the face and soul of Petersburg. But it draws it exclusively from the point of view of the representative of the former ruling class. It presents (rather vividly) the image of the central part of the city—its palaces, gardens, churches, and monuments—but does not present at all, does not even mention, the large area where there were factories, poverty, and slavery, as if there existed only the center, full of interest, life, movement, and uniqueness, while the rest was just deserted, dead, mute, and unneeded. This creates an incorrect, anti-proletarian perspective.[116]

The Great Terror in Leningrad destroyed the juxtaposition of the "imperial" and "proletarian" parts of the city. Right after Kirov's murder in 1934, Lyubov Shaporina, describing the start of the deportation of the Leningrad elite, wrote in her diary, "Who is being exiled? For what reasons? What do all those people have in common? They are the intelligentsia. And the majority are native Petersburgers." The subsequent terror of the late 1930s spread a much wider net. It was not that just a part of Leningrad was destroyed; the whole city was a victim now. These tragic events paved the way for a decisive change in the Petersburg mythos, while the city became a martyr city. The work that cemented that radical change of the city's image was Akhmatova's *Requiem*.

Stalin had declared a genocidal war against his own people, and Leningrad was one of his most visible victims. And yet the terror wanted to remain anonymous, unnamed. "Enemies of the people" were harangued daily on the radio, in newspapers, at countless meetings, but it was forbidden to speak of where they were being sent as they disappeared. The words "terror," "prison," "camp," and "arrest" were not spoken aloud and seemed not to exist in the everyday vocabulary. The infamous black vans that carried off the arrested had fake signs of their sides: "Meat" or "Milk."[117] People called them Black Ravens or Black Marias. Lydia Chukovskaya (daughter of Kornei Chukovsky) recalled that in the "prison lines women stood in silence or, whispering, used very impersonal forms of speech: '*they* came,' 'he *was taken.*' " The official slogan for the country, by which everyone allegedly lived at that time, was Stalin's constantly quoted "Life has become better, life has become merrier." In that atmosphere it took enormous inner strength for Akhmatova to violate that taboo and write about her officially "merry" times:

> It was when only the dead
> Smiled, glad of the peace.
> And like an unnecessary bangle
> Leningrad dangled around its prisons.

A mythos without names is impossible; every mythos demands that people, things, and events be named. Naming is an ineluctable part of mythos creation. The ritual importance of naming is confirmed by the principle *Nomina sunt odiosa* ("names are odious," that is, they may not be spoken), prevalent in many ancient cultures. In *Requiem*, Akhmatova fearlessly named things:

> The stars of death stood above us,
> And innocent Russia writhed
> Beneath the bloody boots
> And the Black Marias' tires.

The fifteen verse fragments of *Requiem* form a terrible mosaic of daily life in terror-stricken Leningrad: arrest, desperate pleas for mercy, endless lines by the prison wall, sentencing. The emotional culmination of *Requiem* are two stanzas called "Crucifixion," in which Akhmatova compares the fate of her arrested son to the trials of the crucified Christ and she accents the suffering of Mary. Those two fragments are Akhmatova's tour de force and the key to *Requiem*, which would be better called *Stabat mater dolorosa*.

Akhmatova had an old Russian musical model, the *kondak*, a liturgical song of Byzantine origin that relates in dramatic form episodes from the life of Jesus Christ and his mother, Mary. The epigraph to "Crucifixion" is taken from a *kondak* and indicates this connection. In her work Akhmatova even loosely followed the *kondak* structure: introduction—relating the drama—and a final edifying conclusion. Like the *kondak*, Akhmatova's *Requiem* is a kind of mystery play, retelling the Passion of Christ for a modern audience.

Akhmatova's use of traditional religious imagery echoed a similar experience of Stravinsky's, who in 1930 composed his Symphony of Psalms, one of Akhmatova's favorite musical works. But she was facing a task of extraordinary difficulty: she was the first to find the words and the art form to respond to a genocide unmatched in world history. Later attempts to describe and interpret the Holocaust showed how difficult it is to treat such a horrible theme artistically. Words, pictures, and music seem inadequate to depict simple, horrible facts. In addition, Akhmatova was working in total isolation against Stalin's enormous propaganda machine, selecting grain by grain the needed words of grief, despair, and protest.

Alexander Solzhenitsyn, meeting Akhmatova in the early 1960s when he was collecting material for his monumental work on the Stalinist labor camps, *The Gulag Archipelago*, said of *Requiem*, "It's too bad that in your poetry you are talking about only one person." Solzhenitsyn thought that the accent on the suffering of mother and son narrowed the scale of the national catastrophe. As if in response to him, Joseph Brodsky noted, "In fact Akhmatova was not trying to create a national tragedy. *Requiem* is still the poet's autobiography, because everything it describes happened to the poet."[118]

Requiem's power lies in the way its mirroring of the fate of its author and her son reflects the tragedy of a city and a nation. Akhmatova's talking about her personal experiences personalizes a tragedy that in its bare facts is beyond human comprehension. That is the key to the poem. Akhmatova says in *Requiem* that she is writing it

> *Listening to my delirium*
> *That seems by now to be another's.*

As to the mechanism of *Requiem*'s creation and its emotional effect, Brodsky commented,

> But really, such situations—arrest, death (in *Requiem* it always smells of death, people are always on the edge of death)—well, such extreme situations rule out the possibility of an adequate reaction. When a person weeps, it is the weeper's private concern. When a writer weeps, when he suffers, he actually benefits somehow from suffering. A writer can really suffer, really grieve. But describing that grief, those are not real tears, not real gray hair. It is merely an approximation of a real reaction. And the realization of that alienation creates a truly mad situation. *Requiem* is a work that is constantly balancing on the edge of madness which is the result not of the catastrophe itself, not the loss of a son, but of that moral schizophrenia, that schism, not of reason but of conscience. The schism between sufferer and writer. That is what makes this work so great.[119]

During World War I, Akhmatova announced in her frightening poem "The Prayer" her readiness to sacrifice on the altar of Russia her child, her friend, and her mysterious gift of song. Twenty years later her offer was accepted, but only in part, and with truly Faustian conditions: both her friend and her child were taken away (which did not lessen Russia's suffering, however, as she had requested in "The Prayer"); but it was these tragic events in her own life, so terrible for Akhmatova the woman, that gave a powerful impetus to the inspiration of Akhmatova the poet. Her son sensed this acutely. After returning to Leningrad from his many years in exile after Stalin's death, he once reproached his mother in the heat of an argument, "It would have been even better for you [as a poet] if I had died in the camps."[120]

The Communists' execution in 1921 of Akhmatova's first husband Gumilyov and the death of Alexander Blok left the poet with the halo of "poetic widow." She was on her way to becoming a national symbol, but further developments left her in relative isolation. The tragic turns in her son's life and then in the life of her third husband somehow returned the moral authority of the seer Cassandra to Akhmatova, making her the priestess of the national destiny. It was then that she fully felt herself the guardian defender and even—to some extent—the creator of the nation's historical memory.

> *I was with my people then,*
> *Where, to their misfortune, they were then.*

Politically, artistically, and emotionally Leningrad no longer juxtaposed itself to Russia as a whole. Languishing under the weight of the Great Terror, the city suffered like the rest of the country—only more so. In that sense it continued to be the symbol of all Russia, but a hidden, esoteric symbol: officially there was no terror.

The new mythos of the martyr city was being created, as befits a mythos, in deep secrecy, underground. At first only her closest friends knew about the existence of Akhmatova's *Requiem*. For many years she did not commit it to paper but secreted it in the memories of several trusted friends. They were to be the bearers of that still hidden mythos until such time as the secret could be revealed. Lydia Chukovskaya, one of those living depositories, recalled meeting with Akhmatova in her bugged apartment:

> Suddenly, in the middle of a conversation, she would stop, and looking up at the ceiling and walls, she would pick up paper and pen;

later she would say something quite social very loudly, "Would you like some tea?" or "You've gotten quite a tan," and write on the scrap of paper in a quick hand and give it to me. I would read the verse, memorize it, and silently return it to her. "We're having such an early fall this year," Akhmatova would say loudly, strike a match, and burn the paper over the ashtray. It was a ritual: hands, match, ashtray—a beautiful and bitter ritual." [121]

In every mythos, there are esoteric and exoteric elements. For many years, *Requiem*, known only to initiates, formed the esoteric part of the new Petersburg mythos. In 1941 a work appeared that announced to the whole world the exoteric message of that mythos: Shostakovich's Seventh Symphony, which came to be called "Leningrad." It appeared in circumstances that were no less dramatic than those of *Requiem*, and it followed another important symphonic work by Shostakovich, also directly tied to the Great Terror and its horrible psychological trauma.

The Great Terror bypassed Shostakovich personally; however, because his compositions were subject to official attacks for their "formalism," he had to expect the worst and confided to his closest friends more than once, "Who knows what will happen to me, they'll probably shoot me." Like millions of his fellow citizens, he did not sleep well at night, awaiting the arrival of the secret police to arrest him. (As Yevgeny Shvarts recalled, "For some reason it seemed particularly shameful to stand in your underwear before the messengers of fate and pull on your trousers before their eyes." [122]) But arrests did take people close to the composer—his older sister's husband, his wife's family. Under these circumstances, he was compelled to recall his Mahlerian Fourth Symphony, but despite that the creative impulse flourished, as it did with Akhmatova. Shostakovich vowed to a friend, "If they chop off both my hands, I'll still write music with a pen between my teeth." [123] Prokofiev reacted in a similar way to the enormous pressure of the Great Terror, confiding to Ilya Ehrenburg, "Now I must work. Only work! That is salvation."

Shostakovich wrote his Fifth Symphony very quickly, between April 18 and July 20, 1937; the central part of the symphony, the long Largo, was composed in just three days. *Le tout* Leningrad came to the symphony's premiere on November 21, 1937, conducted by the rising star, thirty-four-year-old Yevgeny Mravinsky. This was a brilliant crowd, dancing on the volcano, the intellectual elite of the city, leading a precarious existence in those terrible days. Theirs was a sur-realistic world, the nights spent listening for the Black Maria, guess-ing on which floor the elevator bearing unwelcome callers would stop, the days pretending that everything was fine. Shvarts, a member of the elite feasting during the plague, described its emotions: "We lived outwardly as we had before. There were evenings at the House of the Writer. We ate and drank. And laughed. In our servile condition we laughed at the general misfortune—but what else could we do?"[124]

The first audience of the Fifth Symphony entered the hall dressed to the nines, exchanging pleasantries, flirting, gossiping, and wondering what the "disgraced" Shostakovich would offer up for their judgment. But from the very first sounds, reflexive, jagged, filled with nervous tension, the music captured them and did not release them until it ended. The Fifth Symphony developed like a grand mono-logue without words, in which the protagonist led the audience through the thicket of his doubts and worries, through his private hell, which was painfully familiar to every Leningrader. Shostakovich's mu-sic expressed the feelings of the intellectual who tried in vain to hide from the menacing outside world, which nevertheless found him everywhere—in the great outdoors, on the street, at home—ruthlessly pushing its hapless victim against the wall.

The Fifth Symphony moved the audience; when the music ended, many were weeping.[125] The audience rose as one for a thirty-minute ovation. Mravinsky waved the score over his head. The or-chestra had long left the stage, but the public would not leave the hall. They understood that this music was about them, about their lives, their hopes and fears. The Fifth Symphony from the very beginning was interpreted by Leningraders as a work about the Great Terror. Of course, it was impossible to say that. As Isaac Babel commented with bitter irony, "Now a man talks frankly only with his wife, at night, with the blanket over his head."

Therefore the premiere of the symphony was wrapped by the author and his friends in "protective" words to blunt its impact. Shostakovich gave an interview in which he tried to avoid arousing the ire of the authorities against his work. "At the center of the concept of my work I placed man with all his feelings," he explained vaguely. The reporter published this interview under a headline typical of the times, "My Creative Reply" (Shostakovich's reply, that is, to the allegedly "just" rebukes for formalism and other mortal sins of the period).

For Shostakovich, as for other Soviet artists, this was a routine feint, a half-hearted attempt to cover his tracks. Shklovsky compared such behavior with the weary circling of a cat with a can tied to its tail. "The cat races around, and the tin can rattles across its tracks." But Western critics, not understanding or not willing to understand the reality in which Shostakovich lived, accepted the legend that his Fifth Symphony was conceived and written as "an artist's creative reply to justified criticism." As a result, this tragic and highly personal symphony, which has won popularity worldwide as perhaps the most frequently performed of Shostakovich's works, for many years was interpreted in the West as an act of creative capitulation before the Stalinist regime.

Nevertheless, the first Soviet reviewers described the Fifth Symphony rather accurately, discovering "traits of physiological horror" and the "coloring of mortality and despair." "The thrust of suffering in a number of places is taken to a naturalistic scream and howl. In some episodes the music is capable of eliciting an almost physical sense of pain," stated a critic. Another critic maintained that in Shostakovich's symphony "the emotion of dazed mourning is elevated to the heights of tragedy."

The paradox is that these critics were not trying to help Shostakovich. At the height of the Great Terror their perceptive judgments were in fact intended as political denunciations of the composer who dared to create a tragic work in the paranoic atmosphere of enforced optimism. Shostakovich's symphony truthfully reflected the emotions of the populace, exhausted by mass arrests and executions, yet the press rebuked the work for its "concentratedly gloomy musical colors" and its "horror of numbness." But precisely because the Fifth Symphony continued to be performed and to be discussed in the press, it became the subject of public debates, unlike Akhmatova's *Requiem*. And so Shostakovich's work played a certain role in the crystallization of the mythos of Leningrad as a martyr city.

Shostakovich's Fifth Symphony could be called the Bronze Horseman Symphony because, like Pushkin's *Bronze Horseman*, it deals with the eternal question for Russia about the conflict between the individual and the state. Like Yuri Tynyanov in his prose, Shostakovich reinterpreted the problem under Soviet conditions. In his symphony the basic conflict occurs in the finale, which caused the greatest arguments. The critics, especially those in the West, saw an unconditional apotheosis in the finale, an anthem to the status quo. Yet the first Soviet listeners perceived the music quite differently. One of them noted that the start of the last movement is "the iron tread of

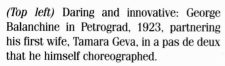

(Top left) Daring and innovative: George Balanchine in Petrograd, 1923, partnering his first wife, Tamara Geva, in a pas de deux that he himself choreographed.

(Top right) Levky Zheverzheyev, Tamara's father and prominent patron of modern art; his role in developing Balanchine's taste and artistic outlook cannot be overestimated.

(Right) Vladimir Dmitriev, cofounder with Balanchine of the experimental Young Ballet. He received the Stalin Prize for his stage designs four times, but after the arrest of his wife by the secret police he lived in fear and died of a heart attack at the age of 47.

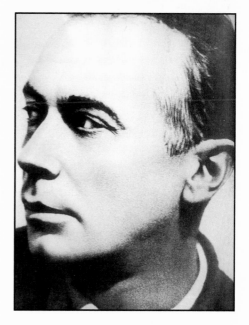

(Above left) The cover of the booklet containing drawings for Fyodor Lopukhov's neoclassical ballet *The Grandeur of the Universe*; Balanchine fully absorbed Lopukhov's bold ideas.

(Above right) "Speaking" costume design for the avant-garde production of Gogol's *The Inspector General* in Petrograd, 1927. The policeman's uniform depicts chains, lock and keys, and prisoners behind bars.

(Right) Vladimir Lebedev's illustration for a children's book about a circus; the book was attacked as "formalist" by the authorities. In 1931 a number of Leningrad writers and artists for children were arrested on charges of "counterrevolutionary convictions."

(Opposite top) Film directors Grigory Kozintsev (at left) and Leonid Trauberg (second from right), founders of the Factory of the Eccentric Actor, with their colleagues. Shostakovich wrote music for their films.

(bove left) Dmitri Shostakovich was the darling of the Leningrad artistic élite until *avda*'s 1936 editorial denounced his opera *Lady Macbeth of the Mtsensk District* as ıuddle," not music. Portrait by Nikolai Akimov, a prominent stage director, 1933.

bove right) The satirical writer Mikhail Zoshchenko in a 1923 photograph, at the ight of his enormous popularity. After party boss Andrei Zhdanov called him a coundrel of literature," Zoshchenko was no longer published. He died in 1958, bro-ı in spirit and half mad.

(Above left) "Stunned by a blow from the back, I fell, then started to rise; but there was another blow—in the face. I lost consciousness." Thus Leningrad poet Nikolai Zabolotsky described one of his interrogations by the secret police in 1938.

(Above middle) A few months before his influential book on Dostoyevsky appeared in 1929, Mikhail Bakhtin was arrested by secret police, and, in the course of an operation to liquidate Leningrad's underground philosophical and religious circles, he was sent into internal exile.

(Above right) A leading Leningrad dadaist, Daniil Kharms was arrested in 1941, declared mentally ill and placed in a prison hospital, where he soon died.

(Opposite top) Joseph Stalin, with Zhdanov, at the bier of Leningrad Party leader Sergei Kirov, who was killed in 1934 on—it is now believed—Stalin's orders. Stalin was hostile to Leningrad, regarding it as a hotbed of political and cultural opposition, and he used Kirov's murder as a pretext for mass repressions.

(Right top) Threatening the city with obliteration, the 900-day siege of Leningrad by the Germans in World War II claimed innumerable lives and cemented the new image of the city as martyr. Poster by Nikolai Tyrsa, 1941.

(Right bottom) After the war, a new generation of Leningrad artists challenged the official dogma: a drawing by Richard Vasmi mockingly depicts one of the city's many monuments to Lenin.

(Top left) As did Stravinsky's reappearance after decades of exile, Balanchine's triumphant visit to Leningrad in 1962 reconnected émigré and native halves of the modern Petersburg culture. The reconnection took hold slowly; Nabokov's works were accepted in Russia only in the late 1980s. *Photo of Balanchine by Marianna Volkov.*

(Top right) The poetry of Joseph Brodsky, exiled to the West in 1972 and awarded the Nobel Prize in 1987, opened a new chapter in the life of Petersburg's cultural tradition. He, too, is now published widely in Russia. *Photo by Marianna Volkov.*

(Above) For the younger generations, Akhmatova's late work fused past and present threads in the city's self-image. Solomon Volkov (at left) is seen with his group after playing Shostakovich's Ninth String Quartet for Akhmatova at her summer dacha. *Photo courtesy of Slava Osipov, 1965.*

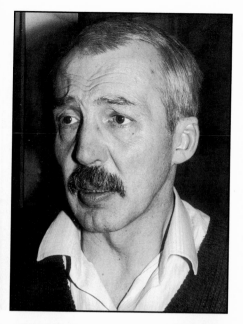 

(Top left) The prose of Andrei Bitov presented an unmistakably Petersburg type—restrained, observant, hiding a profound ambivalence behind a mask of irony. *Photo by Marianna Volkov.*

(Top right) Conductor Valery Gergiev revitalized the Maryinsky Theater, making it once again a premier Russian opera house. *Photo by Marianna Volkov.*

(Above left) In his rebellious songs rock star Boris Grebenshikov expressed the yearnings of multitudes of the city's alienated youth. *Photo by Marianna Volkov.*

(Above right) Alexander Kushner, describing the city's twilight beauty in his poems, makes a ritual journey "from Leningrad to Petersburg." *Photo by Marianna Volkov.*

This monument to Peter the Great by Mihail Chemiakin was unveiled in 1991, just before the city won the right to return to its historical name, St. Petersburg. *Photo courtesy of Mihail Chemiakin.*

a monstrous power trampling man." Upon first hearing the symphony, Alexander Fadeyev wrote in his diary, "The end does not sound like an outcome (and ever less like a triumph or victory), but like a punishment or revenge of someone."

The finale of the Fifth Symphony is tied in its imagery with Pushkin's *Bronze Horseman*, in which poor Yevgeny entered in vain battle with the awesome statue of Peter the Great, the embodiment of the idea of the Russian state. Yevgeny lost his mind and died, and the state triumphed. But Pushkin, as we recall, refused to make a final judgment, as if "suspending" the conclusion of his poem. This allowed various and often contradictory interpretations of his work, depending on the critic's ideological persuasion. Symphonic music tends to ambiguity more than literature does, allowing even more room for various interpretations. This gave Shostakovich the chance to "speak out" in an atmosphere that otherwise made open public discussion impossible for Soviet intellectuals.

The ambiguity of Shostakovich's Fifth Symphony helped it to surface, while Akhmatova's *Requiem* continued to exist in the underground. All critical attacks on the music's "horror," its "mortality and despair" were of a general character. Its detractors were not able to provoke a political scandal, and the discussion of the Fifth Symphony was largely confined to an aesthetic realm. The name of Leningrad, for understandable reasons, was not mentioned in connection with the symphony. The new Petersburg mythos of the city as martyr remained hidden. The decisive push toward its public acceptance—both in the USSR and in the West—came from the war with Nazi Germany.

On June 22, 1941, Shostakovich was chairman of the final examinations for pianists at Leningrad Conservatory, where he had been a professor since 1937. The exam was interrupted by terrible words resounding in the hall: "War with Germany!"

Many Soviet people had feared that Hitler would one day invade their country. A Leningrader recalled the mood of those years, "Somewhere in Europe the war is on, for several years now—so what? Our country is outside the war; we were told that it was good that the capitalists were fighting among themselves, we could only profit from that." This same person continued, "It was not considered appropriate to worry about international events, to exhibit, as they used to call it, 'unhealthy moods.' We were lulled by a popular song that went: "Our favorite city can sleep peacefully, and dream, and grow green in spring.' "[126]

The shock was great. The Germans had striking success in the early days of the war, causing unprecedented damage to the Soviet Army and occupying huge chunks of Soviet territory. By July 14 German troops were at the gates of Leningrad. On September 8 they completed their encirclement of the city. On September 22, 1941, German Naval headquarters issued a secret directive called "On the Future of the City of Petersburg," which stated,

> The Führer has decided to wipe the city of Petersburg from the face of the earth. . . . After the defeat of Soviet Russia there is no interest in the further existence of this large inhabited area. . . .We propose blockading the city tightly and to level it through artillery shelling of all calibers and constant bombing from the air.[127]

Secret Nazi Party instructions, detailing the need for great caution in conversations with Russians, pointed out that most dangerous were discussions with residents of the former Petersburg: "The latter are good dialecticians by nature and have the ability to persuade one of the most incredible things."[128] The Nazi leadership considered Moscow a semi-Asiatic village whose residents could be worked over and possibly still forced to serve the interests of the German Reich. But the Nazis were of a different mind when it came to residents of the former capital. The logical conclusion was that Leningrad, the heir of Petersburg, had to be destroyed by German military might.

Stalin's own prewar policies were clearly aimed at bleeding Leningrad dry. But the German invasion instantly changed the situation. Now Leningrad became a prominent part of Stalin's defense against Germany.

On August 21, 1941, Andrei Zhdanov, Leningrad's party leader, appealed to the people of the city with a declaration:

> The enemy is trying to break into Leningrad. He wants to destroy our homes, capture the factories and plants, steal the people's wealth, flood the streets and squares with the blood of innocent victims, rape the peaceful populace, and enslave the free sons of our Homeland.[129]

Zhdanov's appeal was posted on the walls of many Leningrad buildings. And on September 14, Leningraders heard the writer Vsevolod Vishnevsky on the radio: "The Fascists want to turn our people into numbered cattle, deprive them of honor, rights, and dignity. 'Hey, you, from Leningrad, Sankt-Peterburg! This is the city that first made revolution. So go to the wall, or go to hard labor.' "

Among the evils listed by Zhdanov and Vishnevsky were none that had not already been perpetrated in Leningrad by Stalin and his henchmen. But Stalin's rape of Leningrad took place in secret. After the German invasion, Leningrad's salvation suddenly became a legitimate theme. It became possible to speak and write openly about the city's struggle for survival.

In these dramatically changed circumstances Shostakovich started writing down his new work dedicated to the fate of Leningrad, a work that became famous as the Seventh ("Leningrad") Symphony. I emphasize the term write down, not compose: Shostakovich typically worked fast, because in many cases he was writing down a work that had been completed in his mind, with just a few preliminary sketches. Therefore Shostakovich wrote the orchestration of his symphonies in ink. "But, even in light of Shostakovich's typically accurate preliminary conception of sound, this was a special case, a notation of unusual clarity, fullness, and speed," his Soviet biographer averred.[130]

Shostakovich could not stand talking about his "creative plans," preferring to announce his completed works. Nevertheless, his Seventh Symphony was included in the program for the Leningrad Philharmonic's 1941–1942 season, that is, before the German invasion. That could have been done only with the composer's consent and indicates that Shostakovich had a clear idea of his Seventh Symphony and was sure he would complete it by the fall season.

Undoubtedly, the shock of the war created a new psychological background for the composer's work and influenced the final result. We know that at that time Shostakovich was seriously considering using words from the Psalms of David, for a soloist to sing. Sollertinsky, who was knowledgeable about the Bible, helped him select the texts. Excerpts from the Ninth Psalm were chosen:

> When He maketh inquisition for blood, He remembereth them: He forgetteth not the cry of the humble.

> Have mercy upon them O Lord; consider my trouble which I suffer on account of them that hate me; thou hast lifted me up from the gate of death.

For Shostakovich the words about "inquisition for blood" were of particular importance, corresponding with the composer's outrage over Stalin's oppression. Though before war broke out he could not even think about a public performance of a work to that text, after the invasion, the opportunity arose, at least in theory. The reference to "blood" could now be applied to Hitler. Moreover, Stalin, stunned by the country's setbacks, was trying to appeal to the patriotic and religious feelings of the Russian people. Orthodox themes and images were no longer suppressed by the authorities. Ehrenburg recalled the cultural situation in that period: "Usually war brings with it the censor's scissors; but in Russia during the first eighteen months of the war writers felt much freer than before."[131]

Shostakovich had another, professional reason for turning to the Psalms. Igor Stravinsky had used them in his 1930 Symphony of Psalms. Shostakovich did not hide the fact that Stravinsky was always at the center of his attention. "Stravinsky's work had a big influence on me. Every work made a strong impression and elicited enormous interest," Shostakovich confessed.

As soon as the score of the *Symphony of Psalms* (which Stravinsky began writing to a Russian text and only later switched to Latin) reached Leningrad, Shostakovich transcribed it for piano for four hands and often performed the work with students in his composition class at Leningrad Conservatory. When he began composing the Seventh Symphony, he clearly intended to compete with his idol.

Eventually, Shostakovich gave up the idea and the Seventh Symphony turned out to be a work "without words" and with a vaguely programmatic theme. But the spirit of the Psalms of David hovered over it, especially in the first movement, with its elevated intonations and in the grand orchestral chorale of the third movement. Thus, the theme of "inquisition for blood" remained in the symphony. But echoes of the German siege of Leningrad burst into the symphony, as well.

Leningrad authorities declared a state of siege. The Germans bombed the city ruthlessly from the air and bombarded it with heavy artillery from the surrounding territory. To save the Bronze Horseman from destruction, the equestrian statue of Peter the Great was placed in a special "sarcophagus" of sand and wooden boards but remained standing in the middle of the city. Inhabitants recalled the legend that the city would be impregnable as long as the Bronze Horseman retained his original spot. Along with other Leningraders, the teachers and students of the conservatory, including Shostakovich, dug anti-tank trenches around the city. Then Shostakovich, along with the pianist Sofronitsky, was drafted into the fire brigade that kept watch from the conservatory roof. He also wrote songs and musical arrangements to entertain soldiers at the front.

But of course, his primary occupation was the feverish work on the symphony, with the first three movements—an hour or so of music—ready by late September. In early October Shostakovich, along with other cultural figures considered to be of importance by the regime, including Akhmatova and Zoshchenko, was taken out of blockaded Leningrad by special plane on government orders. Among the few things Shostakovich took with him were his transcription of the *Symphony of Psalms* and the manuscript of his Seventh Symphony.

Before being evacuated Shostakovich had time to show what he had written to a few friends. As Bogdanov-Berezovsky recalled, the guests at Shostakovich's apartment were stunned by what they heard.

> Everyone unanimously asked him to play it again. But sirens rang out, another air raid alert. Shostakovich suggested that we not end the musicale but take a short break. He had to bring his wife and the children, Galina and Maxim, to the shelter. Left to ourselves, we sat in silence. Any words we could use seemed inappropriate after what we had heard.

A section of the first movement, later called by critics the "invasion episode," made a particularly strong impression on its first listeners: an evil "marionette" march theme is played in eleven variations by different instruments, rising in volume like Ravel's *Bolero* and reaching a powerful, screaming climax with a level of sound that is unbearable physically and mentally. It has become commonplace to explain this episode in a naturalistic way: Shostakovich wanted to depict the march of the Germans across the burning Soviet land.

However, many of the symphony's first listeners, especially those who were part of the composer's circle, spoke much more ambiguously about this music, preferring to discuss the images of universal evil and violence that it embodied. For instance, the conductor Mravinsky, who usually chose his words with extreme care when describing Shostakovich's music, insisted that when he first heard the Seventh Symphony on the radio in March 1942, he had thought that the "invasion episode" was the composer's depiction of unrestrained, shameless stupidity and crudeness.

The composer in the last years of his life often said in private conversations that his Seventh Symphony contained a protest against two tyrants—Hitler and Stalin. But how did Shostakovich explain this clearly programmatic music right after it was written, during the war years? The answer became known only a half-century later, when the Russian press began publishing the testimony of witnesses who had been forced to keep silent before the era of Mikhail Gorbachev's *glas-*

nost. The music critic Lev Lebedinsky, who had been Shostakovich's friend for many years, confirmed that the Seventh Symphony had been conceived by the author before the war and explained,

> The famous theme in the first movement Shostakovich had first as the Stalin theme (which close friends of the composer knew). Right after the war started, the composer called it the anti-Hitler theme. Later Shostakovich referred to that "German" theme as the "theme of evil," which was absolutely true, since the theme was just as much anti-Hitler as it was anti-Stalin, even though the world music community fixed on only the first of the two definitions.[132]

Another important testimony comes from the daughter-in-law of Maxim Litvinov, the Soviet foreign minister before the war who was then dismissed by Stalin. She recounted attending Shostakovich's piano performance of the Seventh Symphony in a private house during the war years. Later the guests discussed the music:

> And then Shostakovich said meditatively: of course, it's about fascism, but music, real music is never literally tied to a theme. Fascism is not simply National Socialism, and this is music about terror, slavery, and oppression of the spirit. Later, when Shostakovich got used to me and came to trust me, he said openly that the Seventh (and the Fifth as well) was not only about fascism but about our country and generally about all tyranny and totalitarianism.[133]

Shostakovich could speak this freely, of course, only in a very narrow circle of friends. But even in his statements for the Soviet press, he attempted to hint as much as possible about the hidden agenda of his Seventh Symphony, insisting, for instance, that the "central place" in the first movement was not the "invasion episode," which was the first thing journalists asked about, but the tragic music that followed the episode, which the composer described, characteristically, as "a funeral march or, rather, a requiem." And Shostakovich continued his commentary, trying to imbue every carefully chosen word with hidden meaning for future listeners. "After the requiem comes an even more tragic episode. I do not know how to characterize that music. Perhaps it is a mother's tears or even the feeling that the sorrow is so great that there are no more tears left."[134]

Shostakovich's words echo in a remarkable way not only the general mood of Akhmatova's *Requiem* but especially one of her "memorial" poems that belong to the same period—a poem written in 1938 in response to news of the demise of a close friend, Boris Pilnyak, in the cruel machine of the Stalinist terror:

> O, if I awaken the dead with this,
> Forgive me, I cannot do otherwise:
> I miss you like my own
> And envy all who weep,
> Who can weep in this terrible hour
> For those who lie at the bottom of the ditch.
> But my tears have boiled dry without reaching my eyes,
> There have been no tears to refresh my eyes.

Shostakovich's Seventh Symphony and Akhmatova's *Requiem* are brought together not only by the same horrible initiating impulse (the Stalinist terror in Leningrad), not only by a common artistic model (Stravinsky's Symphony of Psalms) and the requiem character dominant in both works, but also by the similarity of creative method, which permitted Shostakovich and Akhmatova to tackle such a daunting theme. The effect of the *Requiem* was achieved in large part by the almost schizophrenic splitting of the central figure of the narrator into the images of mother and poet. Shostakovich also brings in the composer as a protagonist of his symphony.

In Shostakovich's later works the autobiographical element is announced unambiguously by including the composer's musical signature, the motif DSCH (D, E-flat, C, B). In the Seventh Symphony Shostakovich signals his presence more subtly. For instance, in the second movement he introduces a wild theme that could be called the "theme of the condemned." The programmatic meaning of this musical theme can be deciphered without doubt because of the way Shostakovich used it subsequently with words in two later instances—in "Six Songs" to the words of English poets (1942) and in the Thirteenth Symphony ("Babi Yar," 1962). Both times Shostakovich uses that particular theme to illustrate the same image—a defiant dance of the condemned man before execution:

> Sae rantingly, sae wantonly,
>   Sae dauntingly gaed he,
> He play'd a spring, and danc'd it round
>   Below the gallows-tree.

Undoubtedly, in choosing this poem by Robert Burns, "MacPherson's Farewell," for his vocal cycle, Shostakovich was identifying himself with its hero, who exclaimed,

I've liv'd a life of sturt and strife;
  I die by treacherie:
It burns my heart I must depart,
  And not avengéd be.

Another side of the author's personality in the Seventh Symphony appears in the third movement, where the hero seeks shelter from mortal concerns in high art. Shostakovich characterized this movement as an "adagio with pathos, the work's dramatic center." The composer tied the genesis of this music to his strolls through the city during the white nights, when the majestic architecture of old Petersburg was particularly impressive against the pale background of the shimmering gray Neva and the pearly skies.

Shostakovich could have added that in a musical sense this movement is the most indebted to Stravinsky, this time for his *Musagète* ballet of the late 1920s, *Apollon Musagète*, with its imperious themes carried by the strings. For Shostakovich the connection of Stravinsky's ballet with Petersburg's architecture was indisputable. In the Seventh Symphony he pays homage to both with the help of musical borrowings from *Apollon Musagète*, adding in the process his own lonely figure to the idealized Petersburg landscape. In that sense the third movement can be interpreted as the composer's attempt to flee the harsh real world, the realm of unbridled terror, into an imaginary ideal world of art, ruled by Apollo and his muses.

This attempt to escape was doomed to failure, both in art and in life. Even though the Seventh Symphony was conceived as an esoteric work, a radically different fate awaited it.

As early as September 17, 1941, just two months after Shostakovich started writing down the symphony, he was summoned to Leningrad radio to tell the whole country about his new work. As one of the producers of the broadcast later recalled, a special car was sent for Shostakovich and as they drove to the Leningrad Radio Committee, the composer was given the editorial "The Enemy Is at the Gate," in the latest issue of *Leningradskaya pravda*: "Leningrad has become a front. The enemy is counting on the workers of Leningrad to lose heart and become confused, not to think clearly and thereby disorganize the defense of our great city. The enemy has miscalculated!"[135]

It was explained in no uncertain terms to Shostakovich that his radio talk had to be a variation on this theme. And he read a prepared text that announced he was writing his Seventh Symphony "so that the Leningraders who are listening to me now will know that life in our city is going on normally."

The life of Leningrad, like that of any besieged city, had very little normalcy about it, but for the major propaganda machine that was gearing up, this fact was insignificant. After the radio announcement, Shostakovich's new patriotic work made the newspapers—first the local ones, then Moscow's *Pravda*, which set the tone for subsequent coverage in newspapers throughout the USSR. The fact that Shostakovich was composing a symphony in besieged Leningrad was turned into a national symbol of the determination of the city and the country to resist the Nazis to the very end. The talented writer Alexei Tolstoy, a leading propagandist of the Stalin era, captured that well in his lengthy article in *Pravda*, "At a Rehearsal of Shostakovich's Seventh Symphony," written in the dramatic style of the day.

> The Seventh Symphony is the creation of the conscience of the Russian people, who have undertaken mortal combat with black forces without hesitation. . . . Hitler didn't scare Shostakovich. Shostakovich is a Russian man, and that means an angry man, and if you get him good and angry, he's capable of fantastic exploits.

The performance of the symphony was organized with great urgency, considering the war. Shostakovich completed the orchestration on December 29, 1941, in Kuibyshev (Samara), where leading ministries and theaters had been evacuated from Moscow, including the Bolshoi. And on March 5, 1942, the Bolshoi Theater orchestra, one of the best in the Soviet Union, performed it under the confident baton of Samuil Samosud, who had earlier performed the premieres of Shostakovich's operas *The Nose* and *Lady Macbeth*. The concert was broadcast all over the country, and it was announced that the performance was in Moscow, not Kuiybyshev, where it was really taking place; this was part of the propaganda plan.

On the title page, Shostakovich had inscribed "Dedicated to the city of Leningrad." In that way, the "secret" dedication, as the composer had planned it before the war, became an open one. But he continued to worry, often repeating before the premiere, according to his friends, "They won't like the symphony, they won't like it," in his nervous manner. He was afraid that the audience would not get its hidden message.

Shostakovich's anxieties were unfounded: the premiere and subsequent performances drew tears from listeners. But even this fact was used by the Soviet propaganda machine. The Seventh Symphony was a real find for them: it was a work of world-class stature, expressing tragedy and pathos. It truly moved audiences but, like any symphony, it was subject to the most general interpretations. A spate of ecstatic reviews followed the premiere, and on April 11, *Pravda* published the decree bestowing the country's highest cultural award, the Stalin Prize first class, on Shostakovich.

Stalin put great store by propaganda aimed at Britain and America, his allies in the anti-Hitler coalition. The Seventh Symphony fit his plans beautifully. Shostakovich's name had been known in the West before the war, but news of the Seventh, which spread quickly in the British and American press, made him particularly popular. Curious details surrounded the work, written up by Western correspondents languishing in Kuibyshev, who were permitted neither in Moscow nor at the front lines.

For instance, a photo taken earlier in besieged Leningrad appeared in publications around the world, depicting Shostakovich, in full fire-fighting uniform and helmet, "putting out a fire" on the Conservatory roof. Later a Shostakovich friend admitted,

> Of course, it was a stage show of sorts. The brass fireman's helmet was becoming to Shostakovich's antique features. And he looked amazingly effective in the photograph in his uniform and holding a nozzle. Later we ran into each other, and I reminded Shostakovich of that photo. He merely lowered his eyes in response.[136]

But in Britain and America, where people were eager to learn more about their unexpected mysterious Soviet allies, the clever propaganda photo was met with delight. The image of Shostakovich in the golden fire helmet against a background of burning buildings appeared on the cover of *Time* magazine, captioned "Fireman Shostakovich" and subtitled "Amid bombs bursting in Leningrad he heard the chords of victory." The magazine wrote about the coming U.S. premiere of the Seventh Symphony: "Not since the first Manhattan performances of *Parsifal* (in 1903) had there been such a buzz of American anticipation over a piece of music."[137]

In addition to the dramatic story of the symphony's creation, *Time* rehashed the excitement of getting the microfilmed score to the United States—by plane from Kuibyshev to Teheran, by car from Teheran to Cairo, by plane from Cairo to New York—and the sensational battle of the most famous conductors for the right to premiere the symphony for American audiences. Millions of Americans heard the broadcast from New York's Radio City played by the NBC Orchestra, under Arturo Toscanini. After that the concert premiere of the work was done by Serge Koussevitzky, the director of the Boston Symphony Orchestra, who announced,

> It is my deepest feeling that there never has been a composer since Beethoven with such tremendous appeal to the masses. No one since Beethoven has had the esthetic sense, the approach to musical material that Shostakovich has. He is the greatest master of musical wealth; he is the master of what he desires to do; he has melody without end; his language is as rich as the world; his emotion is absolutely universal.[138]

During the 1942–1943 season the symphony was played more than sixty times in the United States—unprecedented success for a modern work of classical music lasting over an hour. Often those performances were turned into demonstrations of support for the Soviet war effort and of sympathy for besieged Leningrad. Shostakovich's contemporaries in the music world were nonplussed. Virgil Thomson, expressing the opinion of many American musicians, wrote condescendingly that if Shostakovich were to continue composing in the same manner, it "may eventually disqualify him for consideration as a serious composer."

The usually restrained Béla Bartók, who was living in New York City at that time, was so incensed that he vented his anger by including a parody of the "invasion" theme from the Seventh Symphony in his Concerto for Orchestra. Bartok bitterly told a friend about his disappointment in the huge success of a work that he felt did not deserve it in the least.[139] Stravinsky privately expressed similar feelings while enthusiastically supporting the Russian War Relief and hailing any news of the successes of the Red Army that he had earlier hated.[140]

The political situation, however, made a dispassionate aesthetic discussion of the symphony's merits unfeasible, which had a negative effect on its postwar reputation. For many years it disappeared from the repertory of Western orchestras, a victim of both artistic ostracism and cold war mentality. But the symphony's startling and, for many, unjustified move beyond the notice of connoisseurs to the large Western audience during the Allied coalition became an important support for the international fame of Leningrad as a martyred city. The Seventh Symphony became an acceptable universal symbol of Leningrad's suffering. Its success in America and Britain boomeranged back to the Soviet Union and forced *Pravda*, which had attacked Shostakovich's music in 1936, to write this about him: "His unique talent developed in a great city, beloved by all Soviet people, dear to all progressive humanity."

This "love for Leningrad," decreed from on high, was the result of the city's special status as a strategic besieged fortress, symbolizing the heroic efforts of the Soviet people to repulse the German invaders. The German blockade lasted from September 1941 until January of 1944. Those twenty-nine months were the most tragic in the city's existence and entered history as the 900 Days, during which between one and two million of the almost three million inhabitants of the city were lost to bombings, shellings, disease, and, most of all, to starvation. The exact figure for the victims of the blockade will probably never be determined, like that for the victims of the city's original construction. Soviet statistics are notoriously unreliable and, in the case of the siege of Leningrad, the authorities tried to hide and distort the actual situation for political reasons, so that the hopelessly muddled existing data will always be open to different interpretations. In those months the 240-year-old curse of Eudoxia seemed about to come true: "Sankt-Peterburg will stand empty!"

Historians continue to debate whether the defense of the city was needed or justified from a military point of view. Should Stalin have ceded the city and thereby spared the civilian population its suffering? It is almost certain that Leningrad's capitulation would not have saved it. Hitler thirsted for its destruction more than Stalin had before the war. The two evil spirits hovered over the city, nearly annihilating it by their joint efforts. Many other cities might have succumbed under such pressure. But Leningrad's stubborn, proud spirit prevailed.

The worst scourge was hunger. Workers were given 200 grams of bread per day and members of their families, 175 grams (two thin slices). White-collar workers received the same rations. Shostakovich, who had been evacuated to Kuibyshev, wrote to a friend in 1942, "I get occasional letters from Leningrad that are incredibly painful to read. For instance, my dog has been eaten, several cats have been eaten." An eyewitness recalled the conversation of some students in a bread line: "They found that cat meat was quite good—like rabbit. The unpleasant part was killing the cat. It defends itself desperately. If you go about it wrong, you can get seriously scratched."[141]

In the first months of the blockade, pet birds were eaten, canaries and parrots; then came the turn of street birds, pigeons and crows. Then the hungry turned to the mice and rats. With amazing inventiveness, people tried to extract the edible components of everything around them: they scraped flour paste from wallpaper and book bindings, boiled leather belts, used up all kinds of medicines and drugs, petroleum jelly, and glycerine. They ate dirt—the peat around Leningrad was considered nutritious and one could trade a piece of bread for two mugs of peat.

There were periods when up to thirty thousand people a day died of hunger. Yevgeny Shvarts recalled, "The first to die of hunger in our building was a young actor named Kramskoy, who was rumored to be the artist's grandson. He died instantly—fell down in the hallway."[142] Olga Freidenberg wrote of the same thing:

> People walked and fell, stood and toppled. The streets were littered with corpses. In pharmacies, doorways, entries, landings, and thresholds there were bodies. They lay there because people threw them there, like foundlings. The janitors swept them out in the morning like rubbish. Funerals, graves, and coffins had been forgotten long ago. It was a flood of death that no one could handle. The hospitals were crammed with mountains of thousands of corpses, blue, emaciated, horrible. People pulled bodies silently down the street on sleds. They sewed them up in rags or simply covered them, and they were all long, dried out somehow like skeletons. . . . Whole families vanished, whole apartments with several families. Houses, streets, and blocks vanished.[143]

The heartbreaking diary of twelve-year-old Tanya Savicheva, who died of malnutrition in 1944, survives; in a childlike hand, she recorded the terrible fate of her family on seven sheets of paper:

> Zhenya died Dec. 28 at 12:30 A.M. 1941. Grandmother died Jan. 25 at 3 P.M. 1942. Lyoka died March 17 at 5 A.M. 1942. Uncle Vasya died Apr. 13 at 2 A.M. 1942. Uncle Lyosha May 10 at 4 P.M. 1942. Mama May 13 at 7:30 A.M. 1942. The Savichevs are dead. Everyone is dead. Only Tanya remains.

The real Petersburgers—noble, restrained, scrupulous—died first as a rule: it was harder for them to adjust to the inhuman conditions of existence, to the struggle for survival. The artist Pavel Filonov died in his studio on December 3, 1941—he had been on hunger rations even before the blockade; his exhausted body did not last long.

Children suffered in particular from hunger, turning into wizened little beings very quickly. Like the adults, they thought and talked about food constantly. One Leningrad woman recalled her son, five-year-old Tolya:

> He was so skinny that he rarely got out of bed, and he kept saying, "Mama! I could eat a whole bucket of porridge and a whole sack of potatoes." I tried to distract him. I tried telling him stories, but he kept interrupting, "You know, Mama, I'd eat a loaf of bread this big"—and pointed at the washtub. I said, "No, you wouldn't. It wouldn't fit in your tummy." And he argued, "I would, Mama, I would. I'd stay up and eat and eat and eat." He looked like a baby bird, just a mouth and big brown eyes, such sad eyes.[144]

Little Tolya suggested to his mother several times that he be killed, maybe by gas. "At first it would make my head ache, but then I would fall asleep." Many children spoke in those terms during the blockade. One girl consoled her mother, "If I start dying, I'll do it very quietly, so as not to frighten you."[145]

Rumors of cannibalism circulated in Leningrad, which were never reflected in Soviet publications. But some survivors of the siege did touch on this taboo topic with me. One woman told me, "I once traded a chunk of bread for a piece of jellied meat. I brought it home, we started to eat, when my father spat it out. 'It's made of human flesh.' And who was to know whether it was human flesh or not. But we didn't eat it, we couldn't. How could we have looked each other in the eye afterward?"

The dying experienced a strange sense of liberation. The academician Dmitri Likhachev, who survived the blockade, wrote, "Only someone dying of hunger leads a real life, can perform the vilest deed or the greatest sacrifice, without fear of death." Similar emotions were expressed by Olga Berggolts, the bard of the blockade, whose line "No one is forgotten and nothing is forgotten" is carved on the stela of the monument commemorating the victims of the siege. Her poem reads,

> *In mud, in darkness, hunger, and sorrow,*
> *where death, like a shadow, trod on our heels,*
> *we were so happy at times,*
> *breathed such turbulent freedom,*
> *that our grandchildren would envy us.*

More than one survivor of the blockade described this sense of inner liberation, an emotional flight, to me. It involves the physiology of hunger, when the body seems weightless and visionary impulses are sharpened, heightening the potential for sacrifice and mysticism. And many Leningraders justifiably felt superpatriotic once again: the city's inhabitants often recalled that never had an enemy set foot on Petersburg soil, and it was not to be this time, either.

These intense and noble emotions and the heroic behavior of Leningrad under siege were skillfully exploited by Stalin's propaganda machine, which cleverly mixed truth with lies. On the one hand, articles, poems, and songs appeared about the exploits of the Leningraders; on the other hand, the terrible facts of the siege were classified. Olga Freidenberg, who spent the entire blockade in Leningrad, recalled,

> The hunger and the killing of people in Leningrad were a deep secret for Moscow and the provinces. The censors had a legal (military) right to check all our letters. You could not tell, nor complain, nor appeal. The newspapers and radio screamed about the courage and valor of the besieged; the deaths were vaguely termed "sacrifices on the altar of the Fatherland." There was something bizarre about having these besieged people, these starving ghosts, left without water and fuel, be proclaimed officially as the luckiest people in the country. . . . Our hardships were not only hidden from the world, but the official version spread the rumor that things were better in Leningrad than in the rest of the country, including Moscow. But the people stubbornly insisted that "Stalin does not like our city, if Lenin were alive, things wouldn't be like this."[146]

As far as Freidenberg was concerned, the siege of Leningrad was a "double act of barbarity, Hitler's and Stalin's." Typically, Hitler's propaganda acted in unison with Stalin's when it came to the city on the Neva. The Germans had a good picture of the horrible conditions inside the city but preferred not to publicize it. When they needed to make a propaganda point about hunger on Soviet territory, German newspapers published photographs of emaciated children in the city of Kuibyshev. There wasn't a word about Leningrad. The German tactic was explained this way: "The population of Leningrad not only had to be wiped from the face of the earth, it had to be forgotten."[147]

Soviet photographers in besieged Leningrad did their best to falsify the tragic situation. In the seventies, the Soviet writer Daniil Granin went to the official archives in search of photographs of the blockade years. He was particularly interested in pictures taken at Leningrad plants and factories. Granin recalled "factories destroyed by bombs, exhausted people who tied themselves to the lathes and machines to keep from falling." He found nothing like it in the archives. "We went through thousands of photographs taken by reporters in those years. We saw people at work, laborers—men, women, stern or smiling, but invariably hearty. And very few signs of hunger or suffering."[148]

One of the main acts of Stalin's propaganda was the performance on August 9, 1942, of Shostakovich's Seventh Symphony in the besieged city. This performance had been prepared and carried out like a military operation. It was run by Alexei Kuznetsov, Zhdanov's right-hand man. Additional musicians were deployed from the front to the Leningrad Philharmonic over the objections of the generals, who asked, "Make music, not war?"[149] But the Party bosses explained to the generals the political significance of performing the symphony. Its score was delivered by special military plane from Kuybyshev to Leningrad.

Because important Party and military leaders of the city were expected at the concert, Soviet forces had to protect the Leningrad Philharmonic from German fire. This was the task of Lt. Gen. Leonid Govorov (later marshal of the Soviet Union), commander of the Leningrad front. A few weeks before the performance, military intelligence actively searched out German artillery batteries and observation posts. Three thousand large-caliber weapons were provided for the operation—code name Squall. As a result, the Soviet artillery was able to open heavy fire on the enemy on the day of the concert. The stunned German artillery was put out of commission during the time of the performance.

The Leningrad premiere was broadcast on the radio. Before it started, the announcer stated solemnly,

> Dmitri Shostakovich has written a symphony that calls for struggle and affirms faith in victory. The very performance of the Seventh Symphony in besieged Leningrad is evidence of the inextinguishable patriotic spirit of the Leningraders, their stalwartness, faith in victory, readiness to fight to the last drop of blood, and to win victory over the enemy. Listen, comrades.

As Bogdanov-Berezovsky later recalled, Philharmonic Hall (formerly the Assembly of the Nobility) was overflowing, and he had the impression that the whole city had turned out for the concert. In the boxes sat Kuznetsov, Govorov, and other party and military leaders. The weary and hungry Bogdanov-Berezovsky thought that the brightly illuminated Great Hall of the Philharmonic, with its beautiful combination of blinding white, gilt, and gentle raspberry velvet tones, and its flawless architectural proportions, looked even more festive than it had during the most solemn prewar concerts. Compared to the facades of the buildings on the streets, full of wounds, it seemed like an apparition from a wonderful fairy-tale world.

The program said that the Seventh Symphony was dedicated to Leningrad. It is hard to imagine a more grateful audience. Everyone realized that this was a historic occasion. "No one will ever forget this concert on August 9. The motley orchestra, dressed in sweaters and vests, jackets and collarless shirts, played with inspiration and agitation. . . . When they played the finale, everyone in the audience stood up. It was impossible to listen to it sitting down. Impossible."[150]

Many in the audience wept, as had happened during the premiere of Shostakovich's Fifth Symphony. In both cases such a reaction was the result of shock created by the unexpected emotional attack, when the music spoke of common tragedy. To the sounds of the Seventh, Leningraders wept for their fate and that of their city, slowly dying in the grip of the most ruthless blockade of the twentieth century.

Shostakovich's music accompanied the crystallization of the new legend of Leningrad the victim city, martyr city, city of suffering. A hundred years earlier, Gogol and then Dostoyevsky had created the image of Petersburg as the cold, inhuman colossus, the center for oppression and humiliation of simple folk. Years passed; bearing blow after blow, the city lost the prerogatives of power and grandeur: first it ceased to be the capital, then it was devastated by the Great Terror. The German siege was supposed to destroy Leningrad completely. But a miracle happened: even though it was physically broken, the city's spirit soared, buoyed by the sea of compassion from the nation and world.

Once upon a time the anti-Petersburg legend grew in the national consciousness, deep underground, and only later burst to the surface in the prose and poetry of leading Russian writers. In the twentieth century the mythos of the martyr city was also born in the underground, this time not in folk legends but in such brilliant and sophisticated works as Vaginov's novels and Akhmatova's *Requiem*. Shostakovich's Seventh Symphony was conceived in the same vein, a hidden message about Leningrad's tragic fate. A dramatic zigzag in history turned that symphony from an esoteric into an exoteric work.

Talk of Leningrad's horrible fate grew louder. The joint efforts of
Hitler's and Stalin's censors failed; rumors of the starvation and destruction of Leningrad spread widely and it was impossible to sup-
press them. The underground legend surfaced and, breaking through
official barriers, became a national one.

Akhmatova was one of the first to sense it. It was much too
soon to think about publishing the anti-Stalinist *Requiem*, but she did
manage to publish a cycle of poetry dedicated to the Leningrad of the
war years, when there was a brief window of opportunity, in which
she discreetly incorporated some of the main themes from *Requiem*.
For the rapidly changing Petersburg mythos, this was a historic moment: the whole country heard Akhmatova's great tragic poem, perceived by all as a requiem for the victims of the Great Terror and the
martyrs of the 900 Days.

> *And you, my friends of the last draft!*
> *My life was spared to mourn you.*
> *Not to stand like a weeping willow over your memory,*
> *But to shout your names out for the world to hear!*
> *But then, names or no names, you're always at our side!*
> *Everyone, on your knees!—the crimson light pours in,*
> *And Leningraders pass again through gloom,*
> *The living with the dead: glory has no dead.*

CHAPTER

6

in which the city becomes the hero of the Poem Without a Hero *and, surviving against all odds and nurturing its own mythos in the underground, wins the right to get its original name back. The Bronze Horseman continues its eternal gallop into history—but where to? This is the Petersburg of Joseph Brodsky and his friends in creativity—the independent and tenacious poets, writers, artists, and musicians on whom the spiritual fate of this astonishing city depends.*

On January 26, 1945, on Stalin's command, the highest award of the land, the Order of Lenin, was bestowed upon Leningrad "for outstanding achievements by the workers of Leningrad for the Motherland, for the courage and heroism, discipline and steadfastness displayed in the fight with the fascist invaders under the difficult conditions of an enemy blockade." Stalin did not wish the city well, but he had a genius for propaganda, and at that moment the promotion of Leningrad suited his political tactics. His main goal was a complete victory over Hitler, and Leningrad had made a signal contribution to that end. For this, Stalin officially designated Leningrad a "hero city," an accolade that even Moscow had not yet been awarded.

For a brief time Stalin's acolytes chorused songs of glory and praise to Leningrad. Typical was Vsevolod Vishnevsky's radio address to the nation in 1946:

> The city cannot—whatever losses it sustained in the nine hundred days of the blockade—weaken its historical push, its drive, its will.

It is used to being in the front ranks—always, unfailingly. This city
on the Neva has been entrusted by the people to bear Lenin's name,
to protect his name—and the city has responded worthily. . . . O father city, accept my filial greetings, offered with trembling heart! The
whole country honors you, your medals and wounds, your victories
and your labor, which serve as examples for all. And everyone knows
that you will speak bravely to the country once again.[1]

Vishnevsky, a crafty propagandist, offered an artful mix of truth and
lies. It was true that Leningrad's moral status after the war against
Hitler was higher than ever. There was briefly no impediment for
the nation's heartfelt respect for Leningrad's suffering to surface
unchecked. This allowed the mythos of Leningrad the martyr city
to take root in the national consciousness. Additionally, the mythos
took on international resonance—an extremely important circumstance for Russia, which even under Stalin jealously followed its image abroad.

The result was a radical change in the city's image from that
of the previous hundred years or so. A symbol of oppression turned
into a symbol of suffering. Morally and culturally, this was an incredible triumph. Now Leningrad wore a double halo: an architectural marvel celebrated in story and song and a city of majestic exploits
and unmatched suffering.

But did Leningrad, exhausted by the Great Terror and the siege,
have the strength for the "historical drive" so grandiloquently described by Vishnevsky?

The truth was that the stifling of the city, which began after the
capital was moved to Moscow from Petrograd in 1918, had continued unabated for many decades. It was a process initiated by Lenin
and continued after his death by Stalin. Culture was the great victim
because in a centralized state it was supported exclusively by subsidies from above. The artist Milashevsky observed, "The great city
dried up like a great river. Water was leaving the soil. There was no
cash or it was cut. Moscow was taking all the money and all the people's energy and initiative."[2]

Back in 1919 a clever poet had suggested joining Petrograd and
Moscow and calling the new city Petroscow. (This project was resus-
citated a half century later; then the megalopolis was to be called
Moscowleningrad.) Nothing came of this plan, but it reflected the
spirit of the times and the desire of some Leningraders to at least retain a link with capital status.

In practice, the stifling process involved a shift of talent out of Leningrad into Moscow. In the early thirties several leading Leningrad ballet dancers, including Marina Semyonova and Alexei Ermolayev, moved to Moscow. Leningrader Viktor Semyonov became the new artistic director of the Bolshoi Theater's ballet school. Fyodor Lopukhov even became (albeit briefly) the chief choreographer of the Bolshoi.

The Petersburg poet Mandelstam ended up in Moscow, trying to explain it thus:

> In the thirty-first year of the century's life
> I returned, no—make that forcibly
> Was returned to Buddhist Moscow.

It was then too that Mandelstam wrote, "Living in Petersburg is like sleeping in a coffin." The writer Valentin Kataev called the Leningrad of that era a "strange, half-dead kingdom."

Stalin's Great Terror and the almost nine-hundred-day German siege of Leningrad had together ruined the city almost irreversibly. In 1944 there were fewer than six hundred thousand people left. The city's water, sewage, and central heating systems were destroyed, its trolleys and buses not functioning. When the writer Ilya Ehrenburg came to the city in 1945, he was stunned: every house was scarred. But the passersby on Nevsky Prospect depressed Ehrenburg even more. There were so few native Leningraders! Kataev imagined that the soul of Leningrad had "flown away like a bee swarm that abandoned its lovely hive."

Anna Akhmatova returned from evacuation in June 1944 and later recalled how she had been struck by the "terrible ghost that pretended to be my city." Akhmatova told a friend then, "The impression of the city is horrible, monstrous. These houses, these two million shadows that hover above us, the shadows of those who starved to death. It should not have been allowed to happen. It was a monstrous mistake by the authorities."

But Leningrad, revived, albeit slowly. The moral basis of that rebirth was the growing awareness of the city's heroic survival. The poet Olga Berggolts put it thus:

> My sister, comrade, friend, and brother,
> It is we who were baptized by the blockade!

Together we are called Leningrad,
And the world is proud of Leningrad.

Trying to capitalize on the idea that the country owed Leningrad an enormous debt, the city's Party leaders, especially the young Alexei Kuznetsov, proposed a highly ambitious plan for the city's restoration and expansion. Leningrad claimed once again the role it had played before the revolution: window into Europe.[3] The Party leaders even spoke incautiously of the possibility of returning the capital to Leningrad from Moscow.

This idea was picked up by some of the foreign correspondents in the Soviet Union. One was the young American Harrison Salisbury, who later published a best-selling book on the Leningrad blockade, *The 900 Days.* In 1944, after a visit to Leningrad, he wrote an article for the *New York Times* that was, in his words, "an open plea that Leningrad again be Russia's capital." But the article was not passed by the Soviet censors.[4]

Such vague dreams were part of a general mood in Soviet society at the end of the war. Though it took tens of millions of lives, World War II had ended victoriously for the Soviet Union. Its authority in the world was at its peak, and the Soviet government seemed to many to be one of "national unity." Millions of Russian soldiers had marched through Europe, where they had been hailed as liberators from the Nazi yoke; they had seen how much better people lived in the West. Now they wanted more consumer goods and an end to mass repression. The not very bold hopes of the artistic intelligentsia included communication with Western colleagues and correspondents, a greater access to travel abroad, and even—the ultimate dream!—the latest films from America.

"The people have gotten much smarter, that's for sure," Marshal Govorov, the commander of the Leningrad front during the war, said to Ehrenburg. The writer later described Govorov as a quintessential Petersburger—educated, a lover of poetry, able to hide deep passion behind a mask of restraint; a man of precise calculation, of clear and sober thought. It had been the troops of Govorov, one of the youngest Soviet marshals, that had repelled the Germans from Leningrad in 1944.

In 1946 Govorov, discussing the future of Leningrad and the country with Ehrenburg, suddenly began declaiming Pushkin's *Bronze Horseman,* the part where the poet in meditation and anxiety turns to the equestrian statue of Peter the Great that had come to symbolize the Russian state:

> *Where are you galloping, proud steed,*
> *And where will you plant your hoofs?*

Govorov was typical of a large group of new Soviet military leaders, men who had marched victoriously through Europe, who were decisive and full of initiative, reminiscent somehow of the young Russian generals who had routed Napoleon in 1812–1813. Many of those officers had joined the Decembrist uprising in Petersburg in 1825. Knowing Russian history, Stalin must have seen this dangerous parallel. He decided to strike a warning blow. As he had with the Great Terror, he chose Leningrad as his first target.

Akhmatova often said that she considered August her unluckiest month. Her first husband, the poet Nikolai Gumilyov, had been shot by the Bolsheviks in August 1921; another husband, Nikolai Punin, had been arrested for the last time in August 1949 (he died in 1953 in a concentration camp in Siberia, presumably also in August). Finally, in August 1946, a quarter century after Gumilyov's execution, the infamous resolution of the Central Committee of the Communist Party was passed, aimed primarily against Akhmatova, Leningrad's leading poet, and Zoshchenko, Leningrad's leading prose writer. To this day the resolution is attributed to Zhdanov, since at that period Andrei Zhdanov, the former Party boss of Leningrad, was the national Party ideologue and "specialist" on arts questions.

In fact, the initiative for this and subsequent cultural threats during the period called Zhdanovshchina came from Stalin himself. He had summoned to the Kremlin a group of party and literary administrators from Leningrad and then had unleashed on them a series of crude, often profane attacks centering on Akhmatova and Zoshchenko. These attacks set the tone for the dramatic events that followed.

On Stalin's orders, Zhdanov gave two speeches in Leningrad to Party and literary elites, who were forced to attend. He repeated Stalin's directives but added touches of his own. The result was both insulting and illiterate. About Akhmatova: "The range of her poetry is pathetically limited—the poetry of a crazed lady, chasing back and forth between boudoir and chapel. . . . Neither nun nor whore, or rather, both whore and nun, whose lust is mixed with prayer." Zoshchenko was characterized as "an unprincipled and conscience-less literary hooligan" and a "scoundrel of literature," who "is used to mocking Soviet life, Soviet mores, and Soviet people, covering that mockery with a mask of silly entertainment and inappropriate humor . . . depicting people and himself as vile, lustful animals."

A writer present at Zhdanov's speech recalled, "The audience grew silent, frozen, petrified, until it had turned in the course of three hours into a solid white lump." One young woman writer grew faint. She tried to leave the hall, but two armed guards blocked her path: it was forbidden to leave before Zhdanov. And he was still shouting: "On what basis do you permit Zoshchenko to stroll around the gardens and parks of Leningrad literature? Why does the Party of Leningrad and its writers' organization allow these shameful facts?!"

For the Leningrad intelligentsia gathered in the room, this outburst was totally unexpected. After enduring war and blockade, they had hoped for a thaw. They thought that Leningraders' sufferings gave them the right to expect lenient treatment from Stalin. But they were once again threatened with repression.

It was obvious that Stalin would not rest until he had destroyed the Petersburg remnant within Leningrad. That was the only explanation for Zhdanov's statement:

> Leningrad should not be a haven for all kinds of slimy literary rogues who want to exploit Leningrad for their own goals. Zoshchenko, Akhmatova, and their like do not hold Soviet Leningrad dear. They want to see it as the personification of another sociopolitical order and of another ideology. Old Petersburg, the Bronze Horseman, as an image of that old Petersburg—that is what is before their eyes. But we love Soviet Leningrad, Leningrad as the progressive center of Soviet culture.[5]

The meeting ended after midnight. Several hundred people left silently. No one even whispered. A huge question mark hung over each of them and over the city.

As it turned out, Stalin put off a new strike against the Party and bureaucratic elite of Leningrad for several years, until Zhdanov left the scene. A loyal satrap, the short and plump Zhdanov, whose puffy face sported a dandified mustache, had headed the Leningrad Party organization for ten years after Kirov's death in 1934. Transferred in 1944 to Moscow, he continued to supervise Leningrad. For organizing its defense during the war, Zhdanov received high honors from Stalin and the rank of major general, but his national and world fame (including an appearance on the cover of *Time*) came as "overseer of ideology" (as Stalin mockingly called it), in which capacity came his harsh attacks on Akhmatova, Zoshchenko, Shostakovich, and Prokofiev, among others.

Stalin observed Zhdanov's growing celebrity with increasing irritation; Zhdanov's sudden death in August 1948 was thus suspicious. (Stalin later attributed Zhdanov's death to the "sabotage" of his doctors.) By mid-1948, though, Stalin had already begun preparing to liquidate Zhdanov's former Leningrad aides and protégés, about two hundred people in all. They were all arrested in 1949, charged with various state crimes, tortured, and executed.

Yet again, Leningrad and its leadership had become national pariahs. Numerous arrests and firings followed, and former Leningraders were hunted down nationwide. In essence, they were accused of creating a criminal "Leningrad sect," which plotted to restore Leningrad's cultural and economic preeminence, including returning to the city its status as capital of the nation. This mass action of repression and persecution came to be known as the Leningrad affair.

But while alive, Zhdanov was Stalin's point man in the campaign to completely subdue Soviet culture. After Akhmatova and Zoshchenko were denounced, a series of aggressive Party resolutions attacked theater critics, filmmakers, and "composers hewing a formalistic, antipeople line," the last of whom included Shostakovich, Prokofiev, and Aram Khachaturian. Though each resolution seemed to be passed for a specific reason, the press and radio immediately absolutized and generalized them as new Communist commandments.

Millions of people living in the devastated, hungry country repeated and memorized the formulas of these Party resolutions, as if they were magic spells, with frightening numbness at thousands of meetings. A contemporary recalled, "Life went from meeting to meeting, from campaign to campaign, and each was more total, all-encompassing, more ruthless and ridiculous, than the last. The atmosphere of guilt was heightened, a general and individual guilt that could never be expiated."[6]

Stalin relied more and more on nationalism and isolationism. In 1947 he invited to the Kremlin the film director Sergei Eisenstein and his favorite actor, Leningrader Nikolai Cherkasov, celebrated for his roles as Alexander Nevsky and Ivan the Terrible in Eisenstein's eponymous films. The conversation turned to Russian history, and Stalin expressed the opinion that Peter the Great had opened the gates of Russia too wide and that too many Germans and other foreigners had come in. "The wisdom of Ivan the Terrible consisted in standing on a national point of view and not letting foreigners into his country." Two and a half months later Stalin repeated these thoughts to a group of writers, saying that Peter began the "obsolete tradition of kowtowing before shitty foreigners."[7] Stalin announced that this attitude toward Western culture had infected all of the contemporary Soviet intelligentsia. "They lack a proper sense of Soviet patriotism."

The obscurantist ideas of the aging, paranoid leader were perceived as directives to immediate and energetic action. In all areas of Soviet life, the struggle against "cosmopolitanism" began. Leningrad was singled out yet again: Stalin considered the city, the direct descendant of Peter the Great's Petersburg, the source of the contagion. All ties with the West, real or imaginary, were to be axed.

Ridiculous things happened. Edison Street disappeared; the Nord Café was renamed the Sever (North); Camembert became "snack cheese," and French bread Moscow bread. But much more important were the human aspects of this Stalinist ideological campaign. Thousands of people were fired, and many were arrested. With a creak and a clang, an iron curtain fell between the Soviet Union and the West.

Nikolai Punin, art historian and critic, was arrested and sent to Siberia where he died. The arrest was preceded by a series of attacks in official speeches and newspaper articles that accused Punin of "openly propagandizing decadence, the perverted art of the West and such representatives of it as Cézanne, Van Gogh, and others. These extreme formalists are called geniuses, great artists by the cosmopolitanizing gourmand Punin." Once the newspapers added Punin to the list of "sworn enemies of Soviet culture," his fate was sealed. Friends begged him to leave Leningrad quickly. "I'm no rabbit to be running around Russia," he replied. When Akhmatova learned of Punin's death in the camps in 1953, she wrote a poem to his memory:

> And your heart will no longer respond
> To my voice, joyful and sad.
> It's over. . . . And my song rushes
> Into the empty night, where there is no more you.

In 1949 Grigory Gukovsky, a forty-nine-year-old specialist in Pushkin and Gogol and a leading Leningrad literary historian, was arrested; he died in prison soon after. Other Leningrad scholars—Boris Tomashevsky, Viktor Zhirmunsky, and Boris Eikhenbaum—were not allowed to teach or publish. At meetings they were denounced for "bourgeois cosmopolitanism" and "kowtowing to the West." After one such meeting Eikhenbaum noted in his diary, "You need incredible health and iron nerves." Another eyewitness, recently back from the war, confessed to a friend, "I led my squad to attack. It was scary. But this is worse."[8]

Eikhenbaum was then one of the most notable intellectual figures of Leningrad. He had great authority even in prerevolutionary Petersburg, and Nikolai Gumilyov had tempted him to head acmeism as theoretician of the movement. Instead Eikhenbaum became a leader with Shklovsky and Tynyanov of the Opoyaz, an innovative group studying literature as the sum of "formal devices." He also devoted a lot of time to Lermontov and Leo Tolstoy, and in 1923 he wrote the first major study of Akhmatova's poetry. Ever ready with an ironic comment, the small and elegant Eikhenbaum (whom Shklovsky called the marquis), flawlessly dressed in blinding white collar, was a fixture at the Leningrad Philharmonic.

Valerian Bogdanov-Berezovsky told me of a conversation with the sixty-two-year-old Eikhenbaum in 1948, after the music of Prokofiev and Shostakovich had been denounced for formalism. Strolling outside of town, Eikhenbaum drew Bogdanov-Berezovsky's attention to a complicated cobweb. "Here is the symbol of a composer's work! What fantastic mastery, what subtle calculation! What painstaking, exhausting work! But all it takes is a hostile storm, and there won't be a trace left. That is the composer's lot."

Eikhenbaum's pessimism was understandable: many of the works by Prokofiev and Shostakovich had been banned, and it seemed that the ban would endure. With far-reaching limitations on many areas of cultural and spiritual life, the atmosphere seemed unbearable, and the old Petersburgers were certain that they would not live to see better days.

When Eikhenbaum was fired from his post as dean at Leningrad University, he wrote in his diary, "I'm through, thank God, with the department. I should finish up with life, too, really. Enough, I'm weary. Only curiosity is left: what else will history come up with and how will it laugh at me?"[9] Lydia Ginzburg confirmed that the general feeling among the Leningrad elite in that period of total repression (1946–1953) was one of doom: "It came from the repetition (no one expected a repetition), from the horror of recognition of a model that had therefore not changed. As someone put it then, 'It used to be a lottery, now it's a queue.' "[10]

The head of that queue was eventually reached by the pride of Leningrad's culture, the world-famous Lenfilm studios. In the early 1950s Lenfilm was practically shut down on Stalin's orders. For the studio's workers this was doubly shocking and unfair, since it had seemed that if there was anything at all that Stalin did like in Leningrad's culture, it was Lenfilm.

"Of all the arts the most important for us is film." This was said by Lenin, but it was Stalin who made Soviet film a powerful and effective political weapon. In the cultural sphere—according to writer Konstantin Simonov, who knew the leader's tastes well—Stalin "did not program anything as consistently and thoroughly as future films, and this program was tied to contemporary political goals." Stalin often met with leading Soviet filmmakers, proposing ideas for films (which, naturally, were instantly made), attentively read and edited screenplays, actively participated in the discussion of completed works, and generously rewarded their authors if he felt they deserved it. In this sense Stalin was like a Hollywood mogul, but with the fundamental difference that a mogul could only cut off an actor's salary, while Stalin could take off his head as well.

The all-powerful Kremlin producer watched the work of Lenfilm with avid interest. Before the revolution 90 percent of the Russian industry had been concentrated in Moscow. Filmmaking in Petrograd was created—almost from scratch—by the efforts of immensely gifted outsiders: the Jews Grigory Kozintsev, Leonid Trauberg, and Fridrikh Ermler and the Karaite Sergei Yutkevich. Through them, Lenfilm developed a style that was eccentric and daring despite a tendency to stylistic excess; but the studio also had an opportunistic bent and willingly acceded, though admittedly under increasing pressure, to every whim of the Party and of Stalin.

Lenfilm's first headquarters were in the former Aquarium, a popular *café chantant* of tsarist Petersburg, and the directors were given office space in the old "private rooms," where prostitutes accommodated the highest officials of the empire, including the legendary Grigory Rasputin. The young Lenfilm directors noted ironically that, after all, their position in Stalinist Russia often resembled that of highly paid prostitutes.[11]

For all that, the atmosphere at Lenfilm, especially in the early years, was rather heady. The studio worked as a single group, a "collective of committed individualists," as it was sometimes called. Their first important models were American serials and German expressionist films. The complex system of training silent-film actors developed at the Factory of the Eccentric Actor (FEKS), founded by Kozintsev and Trauberg, was put to use by them in the film *The Adventures of Oktyabrina,* in which a young female revolutionary in military helmet and miniskirt rode a motorcycle among the majestic colonnades of Petersburg, creating a grotesque contrast.

As Trauberg recalled, "We didn't know how to do anything, we didn't know anything, but we dealt cruelly and joyfully with the city of Blok."[12] The authors insisted that *The Adventures of Oktyabrina* had all the necessary ingredients for the authorities: satire of the bourgeoisie and the West, antireligious propaganda, and "agitation for a new lifestyle." But the reviewer for a Soviet newspaper didn't buy it: "A worker will not understand a thing in this picture, he'll simply shrug."[13]

Kozintsev and Trauberg continued their experiments in the deconstruction of imperial Petersburg in *The Overcoat,* with a screenplay by Yuri Tynyanov. This was a fantasy based on Gogol's short story, in which Petersburg—in accordance with contemporary ideological considerations—was depicted as an enormous prison. The beauty of the imperial city was rejected derisively by the young directors. The critics tied their film to the 1918 manifesto "How 'The Overcoat' Is Made," by Eikhenbaum (like Tynyanov, a leading figure in Opoyaz). At first coyly denying the article's direct influence, Trauberg later did admit, "There were three Leningrad writers and scholars—Eikhenbaum, Tynyanov, and Shklovsky—for whom we always had not only understandable respect but unlimited tenderness."[14]

As theoreticians of culture, the members of Opoyaz treated film rather disdainfully at first. "Cinematography is in its very essence outside art," Shklovsky proclaimed. Eikhenbaum wrote something similar. But Tynyanov saw in cinema's "poverty," its flatness and monochrome, the aesthetic base of a new type of art.

In 1927 an anthology called *The Poetics of Cinema,* edited by Eikhenbaum, was published in Leningrad. Besides his own article, "Problems of Film Stylistics," there were works by Shklovsky and Tynyanov. This anthology exerted great influence on the European theory of montage in film, but on a practical level personal contacts with the Opoyaz group—lectures, friendly chats, and the participation of Eikhenbaum and especially Tynyanov (who became head of the screenwriting department at Lenfilm in 1926) in the studio's daily work—had an even greater significance for Leningrad filmmakers.

Movies became an important source of income for Eikhenbaum and Tynyanov. Perhaps that is why they seemed unperturbed by the radical changes made in their screenplays. *The Overcoat* was filmed and edited in under two months, and, according to Trauberg, the scenario was "cut and sewn anew." This did not keep Tynyanov from defending the completed film when the Leningrad press called for sweeping the filmmakers from the studio. One Leningrad critic's reasoning went something like this: Gogol was a national treasure, and the authors of the screen version of *The Overcoat* distorted and ruined it; therefore, they should be prosecuted.

An even more hostile reception was accorded *New Babylon* (1929), a film about the Paris Commune by Kozintsev and Trauberg. The Young Communist League (Komsomol) attacked it as an ideologically harmful work. In addition, *New Babylon* failed at the box office. Even the help of sympathetic theater managers was not enough. One manager proudly announced, according to Trauberg, that after an advertising campaign and special educational lectures, the audience at his theater had doubled for *New Babylon:* instead of twenty people, he had forty. It was a silent film, and the customers were particularly outraged by the music. The composer was the young Dmitri Shostakovich, who had been hired by Kozintsev and Trauberg when they learned that he had written an avant-garde opera based on Gogol's story "The Nose," which was close in spirit to their *Overcoat.*

Shostakovich arrived at the studio dressed in a soft gray hat and a white silk scarf. Kozintsev was presumably appreciative; he himself typically sported a colorful scarf and a thin cherry walkingstick. He also spoke in falsetto. The short, plump, and slow Trauberg must have seemed like Sancho Panza to Kozintsev's Don Quixote.

The directors, whose combined age was under fifty, had never worked with someone even younger. They wanted a completely new approach from Shostakovich. As Kozintsev later explained, "in those years film music strengthened the film's emotional content or, as they used to say, illustrated the shots. We immediately decided with the composer that the music would be tied to the inner meaning and not the external action and that it would develop contrary to the events, in opposition to the scene's mood."[15] For instance, the tragic episode of the attack of the German cavalry on Paris was accompanied by a melody reworked from an Offenbach operetta, effectively caricaturing the scene. The average filmgoer in the late 1920s found Shostakovich's music, in the words of a contemporary review that presaged Stalin's later condemnation of the composer, "a muddle that gets in the way of understanding." The acclaim for this forgotten score only came forty years later, when the restored *New Babylon* made a triumphant tour of European capitals.

Despite failure with the public, Shostakovich's talent was appreciated and recognized immediately at the Leningrad film studio. He was hired for all the major productions. One such project, commissioned by the state to commemorate the fifteenth anniversary of the Bolshevik takeover, was *Counterplan,* which hailed the efforts of a Leningrad plant to build a powerful turbine before the deadline. The production was personally supervised by Kirov, who compared making *Counterplan* with "crucial economic and political work."[16] Stalin himself impatiently awaited completion of the film, which had an enormous budget (including construction of a set to represent a huge turbine-building plant). *Counterplan* was intended to praise the achievements of the Soviet five-year plans for developing industry. It was also the first Soviet film to depict the saboteur engineer as a full-blown villain; this was the start of a theme soon to dominate Soviet culture—"the hidden enemies."

Unlike *The Overcoat* and *New Babylon,* with their themes of defeat and impotent protest, their ghostly characters, and their over-complicated style and technique, all of which made them unacceptable to the authorities, *Counterplan* was out-and-out agitprop, albeit masterfully done; it therefore received unqualified approval from the Soviet state. The film was shown everywhere, and the song Shostakovich wrote for it quickly became a hit; it even became fashionable in leftist intellectual circles in the West. After World War II it was designated as the anthem of the United Nations. (Most people were unaware that the author of the lyrics, the Leningrad poet Boris Kornilov, had died in one of Stalin's purges.)

Counterplan made celebrities of its two young directors, Sergei Yutkevich, a founding member of FEKS, and Fridrikh Ermler, who came to the film studio straight from the Soviet secret police. Yutkevich, an aesthete, and Ermler, an autodidact, were united by opportunism: both were ready to tailor the form and ideology of *Counterplan* to the Party's wishes. Once they moved to the front ranks, these directors began to set the tone at Lenfilm, which was beginning to change from a refuge for eccentrics to a state factory of ideologically correct dreams.

□ □ □

The leaders of FEKS, Kozintsev and Trauberg, sensed the changes in the rules of the game. FEKS ceased to exist as a part of the Leningrad film studio after completion of *New Babylon* in the late twenties. It became clear that its avant-garde aesthetics did not suit the state's purposes. The directors' attempts to find a new path led in the mid-thirties to their film *Maxim's Youth,* a fictional story of a simple fellow from a working-class suburb of Petrograd who is transformed into a professional Bolshevik revolutionary.

Kozintsev and Trauberg, having lost their ideological virginity by then, wanted to create a work accessible to a mass audience. *Maxim's Youth,* Kozintsev explained, was an attempt at a Soviet biographical novel in film. "The audience had to fall in love with Maxim not for his incredible looks or for his general 'good qualities,' but because Maxim had to represent the best qualities of his class. The strength of his class. The humor of his class."[17] In other words, the film had to be ideologically instructive as well as entertaining.

Kozintsev and Trauberg made *Maxim's Youth* entertaining; it had good actors (but, tellingly, not former FEKS members), and the musical score was again by Shostakovich. Against a backdrop of mediocre Soviet films and an almost total absence of movies from the West, *Maxim's Youth* caught on with Russian viewers. But more important for the former FEKS leaders was Stalin's approval.[18] The Soviet leader was preparing his major political purges, in which almost all the leading Bolsheviks who had seized power in 1917 with Lenin were to disappear from the stage and people's memories. Therefore, Stalin hailed the creation of new heroes to replace old ones: the mythical Maxim would supplant the real Trotsky, Zinoviev, and others doomed to destruction and oblivion.

Stalin likewise gave broad support for *Chapayev,* the 1934 film produced in Leningrad about a minor commander in the Red Army who drowned in action in the civil war. The film's directors, Georgy and Sergei Vasilyev (not related, even though people referred to them as the Vasilyev brothers) single-handedly made Chapayev a national hero. This suited Stalin, who planned to (and soon did) liquidate the real revolutionary military leaders.

Chapayev was the most popular Soviet film of the prewar period. Legend has it that many teenagers saw *Chapayev* dozens of times, hoping against hope that this time their beloved hero, played by Boris Babochkin, would be saved. Other Lenfilm productions were extremely popular with audiences, too.

Many in the West were impressed by the Moscow filmmakers Sergei Eisenstein, Vsevolod Pudovkin, and Dziga Vertov, but their works, which lacked traditional plots and likable heroes and which used metaphorical, so-called poetic montage, did not find a mass audience at home. But the well-crafted, accessible productions of Lenfilm touched the Soviet public. Their conscious emphasis on "prosaic" cinema was both acceptable to the authorities and eagerly consumed by the masses. Indeed, the Leningrad films were the only truly popular Soviet art of the period.

Lenfilm and its directors thus became the cultural darlings of the Stalinist era. In 1935 Stalin, using the fifteenth anniversary of Soviet cinematography as an excuse, awarded the Order of Lenin to Lenfilm, making it the first Soviet "creative collective" to receive the country's highest honor. The order was also bestowed upon Kozintsev, Trauberg, Ermler, and the Vasilyevs (Eisenstein did not get one). That same year at the International Film Festival in Moscow, the first prize went to Lenfilm for a program that included *Chapayev, Maxim's Youth,* and Ermler's *Peasants,* a film about class struggle in the countryside. This official recognition as the country's best film studio was the peak of success for Lenfilm.

That success was achieved at the cost not only of the directors' youthful avant-garde ambitions but also of even the illusion of independence of the Party line, no matter how much it zigzagged. The directors themselves later admitted the cost. Trauberg bitterly recalled how his old friends rebuked him after *Maxim's Youth,* which led to two acclaimed sequels. "Why did you move away from *The Overcoat* and *New Babylon*? A violinist should not switch to drums."[19]

Ermler underwent an even more radical evolution, going from a film based on "The Cave," a story by the 1920s Leningrad nonconformist Yevgeny Zamyatin, to *The Great Citizen,* the most notorious film of the 1930s. *The Great Citizen* presented, thinly disguised, the story of Kirov's life and death in an interpretation that came from Stalin: the hero fights opposition leaders, spies, and saboteurs and dies at their hands. Stalin's written reaction to the screenplay is known to us. "It is composed with indisputable political literacy. Its literary qualities are also indisputable."[20] The film's writers announced breathlessly, "If our work receives critical appreciation from Soviet viewers, if it is of benefit in mobilizing vigilance, in exposing and destroying the enemies of the people, we will be happy knowing that our creative duty has been done."[21]

Ermler's *The Great Citizen* was both a justification of and an inspired hymn to the Great Terror. According to contemporaries, viewers left the movie theaters prepared to tear apart any opposition villains who tried to move the country from Stalin's course. Trauberg's reaction was understated. He called it "a splendid film with highly interesting characters." Its effect was enhanced by Shostakovich's music. *The Great Citizen* received, for its political and popular acceptability, the Stalin Prize first class.

Ermler was proud of *The Great Citizen* to the end of his days (1967), stubbornly insisting, "I am a soldier of the Party!" Shostakovich avoided talking about his early films in general and *The Great Citizen* in particular, merely saying that "one had to make a living." However, it is clear that working on such projects was more than a source of income for him. Participation in film work sanctioned and supported by Stalin was a safe-conduct pass for Shostakovich. The composer did his work well and received an appropriate fee, but the real goal was to survive in a totalitarian state where his music was often branded "anti-people." Many times he told his students, "Take up film scores only in case of extreme need, extreme need."

Paradoxically, in his film work Shostakovich took unexpected creative leaps. For films with revolutionary themes, particularly the *Maxim* trilogy, Shostakovich often used Russian protest melodies from the turn of the century. These quotations made a powerful impression on the audiences, inspiring as they did memories of happier days past.

In the years of Soviet rule, the old revolutionary songs and revolutionary traditions in general underwent significant cultural revision. Stalin shunted them aside in favor of paeans to the exploits of the contemporary Communist Party and its great leader. The new "pseudo-revolutionary" songs were pompous and cold. The old ones—sincere and spontaneous—still had the spirit of protest. Gradually they became part of the new cultural "Aesopian language" characteristic of the Soviet era.

In that coded language, references to the revolutionary past—in a novel, play, or film about the Decembrists or nihilists, for instance—took on a special meaning. Words like "liberty," "tyrant," and "prison," while formally referring to the past, were signals of the present situation as well. This technique became particularly popular after Stalin's death, in the fifties and sixties. In that period even some of the revolutionary films of the twenties and thirties provoked an emotional impact of another sort. The romantic image of "revolutionary Petersburg" was juxtaposed with the contemporary drab and faceless Leningrad, where the slightest sign of nonconformity was eradicated and punished severely. Struggles against tsarist gendarmes, distribution of underground leaflets, and antigovernment demonstrations were elements of that contrast, formed in part by the film trilogy of Kozintsev and Trauberg about the ever-hopeful "fellow from the suburb," Maxim.

It is against this cultural background that we must examine the appearance in 1957 of Shostakovich's Eleventh Symphony, which came to be known as *1905* Symphony. The revolutionary events of Bloody Sunday, January 9, 1905, when tsarist troops shot at a demonstration by unarmed workers, had taken on the status of martyrdom.

Mandelstam had written about Bloody Sunday as a tragedy that

> could have unfolded only in Petersburg—its plan, the disposition of its streets, the spirit of its architecture left an ineradicable mark on the nature of the historical event. The ninth of January would not have happened in Moscow. The centrifugal force of that day, the proper movement along radii, from the outside to the center, that is to say, the entire dynamic of January ninth was determined by the architectural and historic meaning of Petersburg.

Even in 1922 when he wrote these words, Mandelstam realized the significance of Bloody Sunday for the creation of a new legend of Petersburg, when "the liberated new soul of Petersburg, like a tender orphaned Psyche, wandered along the snows." Thirty-five years later the memory of Bloody Sunday fit organically into the underground mythos of Petersburg the martyr city.

Shostakovich's Eleventh Symphony was a grand portrait of that city. A master of symphonic development, Shostakovich here, somewhat unexpectedly, extended his hand to the Mighty Five, basing the symphony on revolutionary folk songs. By using these familiar melodies, the words of which were known to most people, Shostakovich introduced the multifaceted imagery of revolutionary romanticism into his symphony. The sound of the songs inevitably elicited freedom-loving associations, or, as Soviet cultural bureaucrats used to put it, "incorrect allusions."

Hearing the refrain of a well-known Russian prison song in the first movement, the audience could recall its words.

Like treachery, like a tyrant's conscience,
The autumn night is dark.
Blacker than the night
Is the grim vision of the prison in the fog.

The same effect ensued in the finale with the revolutionary melody "Rage on, Tyrants."

Rage on, tyrants, mock us,
Threaten us with prison and chains;
We are stronger in spirit, even if our bodies are broken—
Shame, shame, shame on you, tyrants!

Intimations of code words like "prison" and "tyrants" created a charged environment for Soviet audiences of those years, attuned as they were to the slightest dissident hint. Even Akhmatova, a strict critic and no idealizer of revolution, was strongly moved by Shostakovich's use of the revolutionary songs. According to Lydia Chukovskaya, Akhmatova responded with delight to the Eleventh Symphony: "The songs fly across the horrible black sky like angels, like birds, like white clouds!"[22]

For more aware listeners, the music elicited a contemporary parallel, one intended by the composer: the cruel suppression by Soviet tanks of the 1956 Hungarian anti-Communist uprising. In the second movement Shostakovich ostensibly depicts the shooting on the Petersburg demonstrators on Bloody Sunday. But at the Leningrad premiere of the symphony, one woman was heard to say, "Those aren't rifle shots, that is the roar of tanks crushing people."[23]

This stratum of Leningrad society also took to heart the musical depiction of Petersburg as an oppressed city. The introduction to the first movement evoked the mood of some scenes in *The Queen of Spades*. The music may in general be characterized as a "symphony of catastrophe." This depiction of Petersburg as a backdrop for tragedy unites Tchaikovsky, Shostakovich, Mandelstam, and especially Akhmatova, who maintained that "Leningrad is at bottom extraordinarily well suited for catastrophe. . . . That cold river with heavy storm clouds always over it, those menacing sunsets, that operatic, frightening moon. . . . Black water with yellow reflections of light. . . . It's all frightening. I cannot imagine how catastrophes and trouble look in Moscow: they don't have all that there."[24]

□ □ □

Alas, by the time the Eleventh Symphony was written, Shostakovich had a good idea of what catastrophe looked like in Moscow. He had moved there permanently in the spring of 1943, a move sanctioned as part of Stalin's general policy for the cultural deprivation of Leningrad. He was there when the infamous Party resolution of 1948 condemned composers of a "formalist, anti-people tendency," including Shostakovich, Prokofiev, Myaskovsky, and Khachaturian. This resolution, issued by Zhdanov on Stalin's orders, cut Shostakovich out of the mainstream of Soviet music. Even so, Shostakovich was allowed to work in film—also on Stalin's orders—and his music accompanied many of the hit films of the final years of the Stalin era.

Practically all these films were made in Moscow. The significance of Lenfilm dwindled in those years. The successful duo of Kozintsev and Trauberg had broken up, but Shostakovich continued working with Kozintsev. They were brought together by their Shakespeare project. Back in 1941 Kozintsev staged a production of *King Lear* with music by Shostakovich. The sets and costumes were designed by Nathan Altman, with whom Kozintsev had studied art.

This prewar *King Lear* was a Leningrad sensation. Shakespeare had always been one of the most admired writers in the country, both before and since the revolution. Interest in him rose at crisis moments, when productions of his plays became political statements in disguise.[25] Kozintsev's production of *Lear* was a closet commentary on the madness of Stalin's purges in Leningrad. Altman's scenery prominently featured scaffolds with dangling nooses, a menacing and easily understood visual hint. The Leningrad critic Naum Berkovsky wrote in Aesopian terms about Kozintsev's production, talking about a city exhausted by terror. "For Shakespeare there is tragedy in a regime that does not emanate from human personality, which does not seek justification for itself there . . . society has abandoned public morality, it has turned to random cohabitation, it fosters low, base, crude behavior in people and leaves noble deeds to languish unnoticed or punishes them."[26]

In 1954 Kozintsev produced *Hamlet* at the former Alexandrinsky Theater. Once again Shostakovich and Altman were part of his team. This outstanding production, mounted soon after Stalin's death, opened a new era in Soviet interpretation of Shakespeare and prepared the way for two films by Kozintsev—*Hamlet* (1964) and *King Lear* (1971)—which were to be his swan song. They rank among the Lenfilm's greatest achievements.

Yevgeny Shvarts called Kozintsev "a mix of mimosa and nettle," a description that could apply equally to Shostakovich.[27] The two men were drawn together by a certain shared emotional restraint that Petersburgers like to think of as characteristic of their upbringing. Shvarts noted that habit as well, saying about Kozintsev, "In his snobbish, aristocratic nature, formed in the twenties, he is ridiculously reticent. Like Shostakovich. Their strict bandbox neatness trains them for tidiness and meticulousness of the spirit."

Kozintsev, himself a master of Aesopian language, noted approvingly the subtlety of Shostakovich's music. After hearing the Eleventh Symphony, he wrote in his diary, "The beginning was frightening: ice cold on the square and damned tsarism beating a small drum. And then—cruelty, desperation, an evil force destroying all life, pain, heartrending grief; and the question—what was all this for?"

These musings became the leitmotif of Kozintsev's Shakespeare films, in which the texts, in unorthodox translations by Boris Pasternak, sounded like commentaries on the news. In *Hamlet,* done in severe black and white, the visual metaphor of Elsinore as prison permeates the film. The cult of personality of the pathetic usurper is juxtaposed with the proud independence of Hamlet, played nobly and impetuously by the popular Innokenty Smoktunovsky. Shostakovich himself was often compared to the prince, and Hamlet-like traits had been noted in his works since the Fifth Symphony. Shostakovich wrote a harsh, elliptical score for Kozintsev's film, some critics consider it the most successful musical interpretation of *Hamlet,* and many see it as one of Shostakovich's best works. Kozintsev, who understood the enormous role played by Shostakovich's music in shaping the hidden message of his *Hamlet,* had considered calling the film a "cinema symphony."

Kozintsev, who died in 1973, summed up his life's work, as well as that period of Lenfilm history, in *King Lear.* The film was shot in black and white, like *Hamlet,* but was even more severe, with several shocking naturalistic scenes. Kozintsev personified the avant-garde roots of Lenfilm, the studio's youth and early maturity when Stalin was its main patron. Kozintsev—like few other directors—though a favorite of Stalin's, still appealed to mass audiences and elicited respect from critics both in the Soviet Union and in the West even in the post-Stalinist period. His *Hamlet* and *King Lear* are rightfully considered treasures of world film as treatments of Shakespeare. Kozintsev, an ambitious and proud man, knew full well the impact of Shostakovich's music. "Without it, and without Pasternak's translations, I could not have made the Shakespeare films."[28]

Kozintsev tried to formulate why Shostakovich's music was so important to him, a Leningrader of the new era.

> What seems most important in it? The sense of tragedy? Philosophy, universal thoughts about the world? . . . But still, another quality is most important. A quality that is hard to write about. Goodness. Kindness. Charity. But a special kind of kindness. We have an excellent word in our language: fierce. There is no goodness in Russian art without a fierce hatred of what destroys man. In Shostakovich's music I hear fierce hatred of cruelty, the cult of power, the oppression of truth. This is a special kindness: fearless kindness."[29]

In the late forties and early fifties Akhmatova and Zoshchenko lived in Leningrad like shadows. They were expelled from the Writers' Union, they were not published, and they maintained an impoverished existence, shunned as lepers. Former friends crossed the street when they saw them coming. They expected to be arrested at any moment.

One contemporary theory was that Stalin allowed Akhmatova and Zoshchenko to remain free in order to continue the ideological campaign ad infinitum.[30] The Party resolution of 1946 directed against them was "studied" at innumerable meetings all over the country and then made part of the school curriculum so that class after class of Soviet youngsters learned it by heart. To millions of Soviet people, Zoshchenko was a "literary hooligan" and Akhmatova "either a nun or a whore" whose poetry was corrupt and decadent.

Leningrad in those years lived by inertia. Everything it had been proud of was taken away; many cultural figures were in disfavor, others moved to Moscow. Stalin's fabricated Leningrad Affair clouded the city. Even the glory of the 900-day siege was now being belittled. The popular Museum of the Defense of Leningrad, founded in 1946, was shut down in 1949, its administration arrested, and many precious exhibits destroyed.

The main sentiment of that difficult time was hopelessness. These were probably the gloomiest years in the history of Leningrad culture. People felt that the stifling monotony, brightened only rarely by an anniversary or some still-tolerated icon of national culture, would reign forever.[31] The self-awareness and self-esteem of the city on the Neva seemed past all hope of renaissance.

Yet even then there existed (at least in outline) a work that foretold the fate of the Petersburg legend in the second half of the twentieth century. I am referring to Akhmatova's *Poem Without a Hero,* begun at the end of 1940 and completed in first draft in 1942. The fate of *Poem Without a Hero* is unusual: Akhmatova continued working on it for some twenty years, adding lines, prefaces, dedications, and commentaries. As a result, the final version is almost twice as long as the first. And the text has the additions of *Prose About the Poem* and sketches for a ballet libretto intertwining various themes from *Poem Without a Hero*.

Akhmatova was aware of the historic and cultural significance of her magnum opus. That is why she gave the first part of the poem, "1913," the subtitle "A Petersburg Tale," thereby creating a direct parallel with another famous "Petersburg Tale," Pushkin's *Bronze Horseman*. In fact, the role of Akhmatova's poem in forming the latter-day Petersburg mythos is comparable to the impulse given to the birth of that mythos by Pushkin's poem. In the opinion of Lev Loseff, *Poem Without a Hero* is a " 'historiosophical' poem, not so much about the events of history as the mechanism of history, which Akhmatova sees in the cyclical nature of the ages, in the endless repetition, which is what brings it close to Pushkin's historical vision."[32]

Poem Without a Hero lacks a developed narrative. The embryo of a plot can be reduced to the traditional love triangle, Pierrot-Columbine-Harlequin, beyond which can be seen the real drama that agitated the artistic circles of the capital in 1913. A young poet and officer, Vsevolod Knyazev, committed suicide by shooting himself in the chest. Rumor tied this suicide, typical of Petersburg's "prewar, lascivious and threatening" atmosphere, in Akhmatova's words, to Knyazev's unrequited love for Akhmatova's friend, the dancer Olga Glebova-Sudeikina. Knyazev's lucky rival was said to be the poet Alexander Blok. At her son's funeral, Knyazev's mother lashed out at Olga. "God will punish those who made him suffer."

Knyazev, his poetry, and the tragic story of his love were buried by World War I and the revolution; they seemed destined to oblivion. (The death in 1945 of Olga Glebova-Sudeikina from consumption in Paris also went unnoticed.) But Blok remained popular after the revolution, and his untimely death in August 1921 only added to his mystique and made him one of the most revered poets in the history of Russian literature.

Blok played an exceptionally important part in Akhmatova's life, both as a poet and as a symbol of his era. In the 1910s Akhmatova started a risky literary game with Blok, hinting in her published poems of her love for an unnamed poet with features—like his famous gray eyes—that made him easily recognizable.

The legend that Akhmatova and Blok had had an affair survived the poet's death and even the publication of his diaries and notebooks. The average reader did not notice what Akhmatova's eye caught instantly: "As is clear from Blok's notebooks, I had no place in his life."

Angry protestations and ironic puzzlement became part and parcel of Akhmatova's conversations with acquaintances old and new, including me. In 1965 I would not have dared suggest to her that the obvious source for the legend was Akhmatova's early—and quite popular—love poems. Be that as it may, the Blok elements in *Poem Without a Hero* form a crucial layer of the work, a knot of themes, images, allusions, and direct citations all leading to Blok.[33]

Blok appears as an androgynous hero, a demon with a woman's smile and a dual image. He is not only Harlequin but also Don Juan "with dead heart and dead gaze." Akhmatova took the epigraph to the first chapter from Mozart's opera *Don Giovanni:*

> *Di rider finirai pria dell'aurora.*
> *(You will stop laughing before dawn.)*

As usual for Akhmatova, the reference hides a deeper parallel—with the classic Russian interpretation of the Don Juan legend, Pushkin's *Stone Guest* (on which Alexander Dargomyzhsky, the spiritual father of the Mighty Five, based his imaginative opera of the same name).

Shortly after World War II Akhmatova wrote a work on *The Stone Guest;* she later revised and expanded it several times. In this essay she maintained that Pushkin projected his own emotions onto his Don Juan: fear of happiness and eternal fidelity. For her, Pushkin's Don Juan "truly was transformed during his assignation with Donna Anna and the whole tragedy lies in the fact that at that instant he loved and was happy, and instead of salvation, from which he was just a step away, there came disaster."

It has practically become a truism that Akhmatova often hints at a correlation between Pushkin's life and work and her own. She compares Pushkin's Don Juan with a Petersburg rake and calls his friends "golden youths." The well-versed reader of turn-of-the-century Russian poetry (Akhmatova's intended reader) will readily recall "the Petersburg Don Juan" Alexander Blok and his famous 1912 poem "The Commendatore's Footsteps," in which the autobiographical hero, called Don Juan, meets the Commendatore, who has come for him, and exclaims,

Maid of Light! Where are you, Donna Anna?
Anna! Anna!—Silence.

These lines are themselves an imitation of the last line of Pushkin's tragedy ("I perish—it's over. O Donna Anna!").

This brings us back to the love triangle, Pierrot-Columbine-Harlequin, at the nucleus of *Poem Without a Hero*. Beyond the triangle are two poets, Knyazev and Blok, and Akhmatova's friend Olga Glebova-Sudeikina. Akhmatova admitted that she used secret writing ("invisible ink" and "mirror writing") and that this box, in her own words, had two "false bottoms." She directly addresses Olga this way: "You are one of my doubles"; she thereby gives enough cause for the reader to substitute Akhmatova for Olga in the poem and to see Blok as Don Juan, who in "The Commendatore's Footsteps" called his beloved by the name that is also Akhmatova's:

Anna, Anna, is sleep sweet in the grave?
Is it sweet to see unearthly dreams?

Knyazev's place in this new imaginary triangle will be taken by another poet and officer, Akhmatova's first husband, Nikolai Gumilyov. "The Commendatore's Footsteps" then becomes a secret confession of love for Anna (Akhmatova), and Blok becomes the repentant Don Juan, who—like the hero of Pushkin's tragedy—finds true love only on the brink of death. (Akhmatova claimed that Blok thought of her in his deathbed delirium.) Thus, Akhmatova, asserting the poet's right to transform reality, presented in a coded way (but open to the careful reader) a continuation of her imaginary affair with Blok in *Poem Without a Hero*.

Reorganizing her own biography thus, Akhmatova entered into a complex relation with history. In accordance with Russian tradition and her own philosophical system, the poet was not only the bearer of the nation's historical memory but the catalyst of important contemporary events. Invisible but sturdy threads stretch from the poet to pivotal personalities and dramas of the twentieth century.

In particular, Akhmatova had an acute sense of a personal tie with Stalin even though she never met him. As he had done with the cinema, Stalin took Russian literature under his personal control. He followed the latest books year after year, he met with writers (sometimes in informal settings) and phoned them. Some of these telephone conversations (with Bulgakov and Pasternak, for instance) were much talked about in literary circles.

Akhmatova first appealed to Stalin in 1935, asking for the release of her current husband, Nikolai Punin, and her son Lev. They were freed almost as soon as her letter was given to Stalin; word of that miracle spread far among the Soviet intelligentsia. When her son was again arrested, though, a second letter did not secure his release. But in 1939 Stalin asked at a meeting with writers how Akhmatova was doing and why her poems were not appearing in print. After that, the leaders of the Writers' Union showed "heightened attention" to Akhmatova, and soon after, a collection of her poems appeared, the first in many years. From that time on, Akhmatova felt—probably with reason—the leader's attentive gaze. She reasonably connected Stalin with the unexpected remission of her son's death sentence to a term in the camps and with her own timely evacuation from besieged Leningrad during the war.

Akhmatova assumed that Stalin had spared her because he had formed an image of her as a secluded, ascetic woman, talented but modest, completely devoted to her literary work. (Pasternak had described Akhmatova that way in his letter to Stalin.) According to Akhmatova, Stalin periodically inquired, "Well, how's our nun doing?" But a fateful event in 1945 shattered that image forever.

Isaiah Berlin, then a young and intellectually curious staffer of the British Embassy in Moscow, came to Leningrad and, knowing Russian well, decided to visit Akhmatova, whose poetry he had long loved. This was late November 1945. Probably Berlin did not fully realize that Stalin perceived all Western diplomats as real or potential spies and therefore kept them under constant surveillance.

Akhmatova was also being watched, and the meeting between Berlin and Akhmatova was immediately reported to Stalin. She always felt that Stalin's anger was caused by the fact that the thirty-six-year-old Berlin stayed until morning. As Akhmatova told it, when Stalin learned of the nighttime rendezvous, he cursed and shouted, "So our nun receives foreign spies!" The invisible thread that, Akhmatova believed, connected her to Stalin was broken.

She felt that this chain of events led to the infamous Party decree of 1946, directed against her and Zoshchenko. The decree, in turn, led—in her opinion—closer to the Cold War. She wrote about her meeting with Isaiah Berlin in *Poem Without a Hero*:

He will not become a dear husband,
But he and I will pay in a way
That will confound the Twentieth Century.

This pronouncement may seem far-fetched, and the significance of her almost random meeting with Berlin blown out of pro-
portion. But that is so only at first glance. Close examination suggests
that her interpretation is logical and psychologically sound. Though
the Cold War would have begun anyway, the vicious campaign against
Akhmatova and Zoshchenko noticeably chilled the postwar eupho-
ria, especially among the leftist Western intelligentsia, and hastened
the descent to hostility.

When I arrived in the West in 1976, I saw how painfully fresh
the Akhmatova-Zoshchenko affair was in the minds of local Rus-
sophiles. As one who had borne the brunt of Stalin's wrath, Akhmatova rightfully could feel that she had played a central role in world
events, especially if we accept the view that some outbursts of the aging Stalin were linked to random or irrational causes.[34]

In these skeptical times the novels of Alexandre Dumas *père*
are read, if at all, only by children, and we tend to forget the roles that
chance and individuals play in history. In *Poem Without a Hero*,
Akhmatova tried to challenge historical determinism; in that sense her
work is a polemic with and a parallel to Pushkin's *Bronze Horseman*.
But, just as it is in Pushkin's poem, fate is stronger than the characters in *Poem Without a Hero*, including the author. All of them, in
Akhmatova's mythology, are inhabitants of a legendary, doomed Atlantis pulled to the bottom of the sea both by the undertow of world
history and by a shared sense of guilt.

The theme of general guilt—and even more important, personal
guilt—is central to *Poem Without a Hero* and traditional in Russian
literature. Nor was it original to project such guilt onto Petersburg,
the new Rome, generally decadent and richly deserving destruction
at the hands of twentieth-century barbarians. But the transformation of the theme of sin and guilt into the theme of expiation through
suffering, wherein the city and Akhmatova follow the way of the cross
of humiliation, torment, and transfiguration—that is both new and
essential.

Akhmatova begins by unfolding a rich tapestry of the carnival
life of Petersburg in 1913 (here the influence of Mikhail Bakhtin's
ideas on the central place of carnival in culture is evident). During a

New Year's carnival the author is visited by legendary characters of prerevolutionary Petersburg (recognizable among them are Blok, Mayakovsky, and Mikhail Kuzmin), dressed as Don Juan, Faust, Casanova, "Prince of Darkness." But the action immediately opens out onto the expanses of Petersburg, and Akhmatova deftly weaves the city's cultural symbols into the panorama. Thus, in the text of the poem, the "inaccessible swan," the ballerina Anna Pavlova, appears, as does the voice of the great bass Fyodor Chaliapin, which "fills hearts with trembling." When Akhmatova writes

> *The denouement is ridiculously close:*
> *Petrouchka's mask behind the curtains,*
> *Coachmen dancing around bonfires . . .*

she evokes in the reader's mind scenes from another work that had become a symbol of prerevolutionary Petersburg—the Stravinsky-Fokine-Benois ballet *Petrouchka,* the first major work built around the theme of nostalgic longing for the capital of the old Russian Empire, a theme developed around the same love triangle that is the basis of *Poem Without a Hero* (in Stravinsky's ballet Pierrot-Columbine-Harlequin become Petrouchka-Ballerina-Moor).

Yet another character in Akhmatova's carnival is the leading avant-garde theater director of that era, Vsevolod Meyerhold. In 1906 Meyerhold had staged Blok's symbolist fantasy *The Fair Show Booth,* which also embodied the ubiquitous Pierrot-Columbine-Harlequin triangle. That production became a manifesto of Petersburg modernism. A few years later Meyerhold staged Arthur Schnitzler's pantomime *Columbine's Scarf,* where the same characters whirled in carnival ecstasy. Meyerhold created a touching figure, a blackamoor who was remembered by many in the audience, including Akhmatova. She includes "Meyerhold's blackamoors" in the action of *Poem Without a Hero.* As usual, this detail has many meanings. It recalls another Meyerhold production with blackamoors—a *Don Juan,* based on Molière's, which Meyerhold directed at the Alexandrinsky Theater in 1910. Akhmatova uses every chance to remind the reader of the core theme of *Poem Without a Hero* (which is also the leitmotif of the Don Juan legend): sin and its punishment.

Akhmatova herself considered Meyerhold's work a mainspring for the creation of *Poem Without a Hero.* She tied its genesis to her impressions of his 1917 production of Lermontov's drama *Masquerade.* The play sounded then like a requiem for imperial Petersburg; it was that memorial note that Akhmatova captured in *Poem Without a Hero.*

Another Meyerhold production that may have played as great a role in the genesis of *Poem Without a Hero* was his innovative 1935 production in Leningrad of *The Queen of Spades.* Akhmatova had a complex relationship with this work. She was captivated by Tchaikovsky's music, and besides, *The Queen of Spades* was a favorite of Blok and Arthur Lourié, who both considered it central to the Petersburg mythos.[35]

In a published letter Blok identified Pushkin's *Bronze Horseman,* Lermontov's *Masquerade,* and Tchaikovsky's *Queen of Spades* as variations on the same Petersburg theme. For him magical Petersburg was a city of masquerades (carnivals) where " 'Apollonic' Pushkin fell into the abyss, pushed there by Tchaikovsky—*magus and musician.*" Akhmatova, who studied Blok's letters closely, could not have missed this observation. But she was shocked by the liberties taken in Tchaikovsky's opera, radically transforming its literary source, the Pushkin story.[36] Part of what made Meyerhold's production of the opera so memorable was that the director tried to "re-Pushkinize" the plot, even commissioning a completely new libretto that revealed more sharply the linchpin of Tchaikovsky's music—guilt and its redemption (this theme was clear in Lermontov's *Masquerade* as well).

Meyerhold's production split the intellectual elite of Leningrad into two camps: one fiercely attacked it taking liberties with Tchaikovsky's opera, the other—including Shostakovich—considered it a work of genius.[37] Meyerhold himself announced that he wanted to convey the "mood of *The Bronze Horseman.*" He structured the production around the contrast between the twilit urban landscape and Petersburg's decadent entertainments. Akhmatova later built this contrast into her *Poem Without a Hero,* endowing it also with veiled reminiscences of and parallels with *The Queen of Spades.*

Tchaikovsky sensed the possibility of the death of Petersburg, so dear to his heart, and he was horrified and worried by that possibility. His music—particularly *Sleeping Beauty, The Queen of Spades,* and the *Pathétique* Symphony—embodies his requiem for the imperial capital. (In conversation with Akhmatova we discussed using the *Pathétique* for a ballet of *Poem Without a Hero.*) For Akhmatova, Tchaikovsky's music represents a core element in the classic Petersburg mythos. *Poem Without a Hero* is in effect an encyclopedia of that mythos. Its citations—obvious, hidden, and encoded—from works of Petersburg authors make it the quintessential postmodernist text.

It sometimes seems that the poem, unlike anything else in Russian literature, is, as Mandelstam said of the *Inferno,* "a real quotation orgy." Akhmatova admits her habitual use of this technique in the first lines of the verse dedication:

> . . . *and since I ran out of paper,*
> *I am writing on your draft.*
> *And so another's word appears,*
> *And like that snowflake on my hand,*
> *Melts trustingly and without rebuke.*

The key term is "another's word," arising out of Bakhtin's literary concept of "reported speech." Bakhtin was particularly interested in the use of "reported speech"—that is, citation—in medieval literature, where "the borders between another's and one's own speech were fragile, ambivalent, and frequently intentionally convoluted and confused." When Bakhtin spoke of citations that were "clearly and reverently emphasized, half-hidden, hidden, half-conscious, unconscious, correct, intentionally distorted, unintentionally distorted, deliberately reinterpreted, and so on" in medieval literature, he could have been describing *Poem Without a Hero.*

According to Bakhtin, reported speech inevitably becomes not only a constituent part of the work in which it is included but its theme. Something like this occurs in *Poem Without a Hero,* where the quotations and images from Pushkin, Gogol, Dostoyevsky, Blok, and Mandelstam turn into mirrors in which Akhmatova regards herself, using the past to tell the future—her own and the city's.

A contemporary of Akhmatova's, the Leningrad critic Efim Dobin, compared *Poem Without a Hero* to Velázquez's famous painting *Las Meninas,* in which the artist depicted himself painting his subjects:

> The artist is in two worlds at once. Outside the painting. And inside it, next to his creations. In the world that exists in reality. And in the poetic world he has created. The whole painting is a mirror, everything that is depicted in it. Like Velázquez, Akhmatova wrote herself into an ancient drama. She stood next to the heroes in order to have uninterrupted dialogue with them.[38]

Akhmatova's tragic experience is woven into the horrible history of twentieth-century Petersburg, the culmination of which was the 900-day siege. Though she was evacuated, the blockade confirmed her theories about the unity of the poet's and the city's destinies:

> *You did not become my grave,*
> *Seditious, disgraced, dear,*
> *You've grown pale, emptied, still.*
> *Our separation is illusory:*
> *I am indivisible from you,*
> *My shadow is on your walls.*

The suffering of the city is personified in Akhmatova, and the city's way of the cross includes her torments. When Akhmatova began *Poem Without a Hero,* she announced, "From 1940, as if from a tower, I look at everything." It might have seemed to her that the Petersburg of 1913, like Sodom and Gomorrah, deserved to be destroyed. Yet the more scandalously Akhmatova painted prerevolutionary Petersburg, the more terribly stood out the later history of the city:

> *And the decades pass:*
> *Torture, exiles, and deaths.*
> *I cannot sing in this horror.*

But the weakened city and the weakened poet continued to live. To this half-dead city Akhmatova brought her *Poem Without a Hero,* in which all the elements of the new Petersburg mythos were synthesized. She even brought in Shostakovich's Seventh ("Leningrad") Symphony; a verse about it at one time ended the poem. (In fact, an early subtitle for the poem was "A Tragic Symphony.")

Poem Without a Hero has in fact two heroes: the author and her city. They maintain a constant dialogue above the heads of listeners and readers. Often Akhmatova intentionally encodes that dialogue, ironically justifying it thus:

> I noticed that the more I explain it, the more mysterious and incomprehensible it becomes, that everyone sees that I can not and will not (dare not) explain it completely, and that all my explanations, for all their ornament and inventiveness, merely confuse things—it came from nowhere and went off into nowhere, explaining nothing.[39]

Akhmatova considered Pushkin's *Bronze Horseman* a terrifying, hopeless, gloomy work. Thus, how ambivalent is the epigraph she chose for the final part of *Poem Without a Hero*, a line from *The Bronze Horseman*: "I love you, Peter's creation!" There is no doubt in Akhmatova's love for Petersburg, but for the reader, Pushkin's solemn pronouncement is colored by the grim shadow of twentieth-century events described in Akhmatova's work.

In the Russian cultural sphere *The Bronze Horseman* and *Poem Without a Hero* form the two bases of a majestic arch, an imaginary space under which lies the Petersburg mythos. In *The Bronze Horseman*, the heartbreaking story of Yevgeny and his bride, sacrificed to the fanatical idea of the building tsar, is reminiscent of ancient sacrificial legends: "no significant city can stand if in the erection of its fortifications a live man, or at least, his shadow, is not placed in the wall."[40] In Akhmatova's work, Petersburg, erected on the bones of numberless, nameless workmen, becomes a victim of the mighty forces of history and thereby expiates its guilt. Having walked to Calvary, Petersburg earned the right to resurrection.

This idea is realized in *Poem Without a Hero* to magical effect. For all its complexity, confusion, and allusiveness, *Poem Without a Hero* goes down in a single cathartic, almost joyful gulp.

I felt this clearly when I first read *Poem Without a Hero* in the spring of 1965. Akhmatova inquired if I had come across a typescript copy circulating in Leningrad and Moscow. I replied that I had read only excerpts in poetry almanacs and journals.

"Well, that means you don't know the poem," she noted sadly. "I treated it badly, I see that now, not like a caring mother. I shouldn't have published it in pieces." Then she read me a section intended for the final part:

> *And behind the barbed wire,*
> *Deep in the heart of the taiga,*
> *I don't know for how many years*
> *Now a handful of camp dust,*
> *Now a tale from a scary story,*
> *My double goes to be interrogated.*

Declaimed by Akhmatova in her hierarchical, solemn manner, slowly and carefully, each word stunned me. The publication of such a text in those years was of course unthinkable.

For me the essence of Akhmatova's philosophy of history and her ideas on the evolution of the Petersburg mythos are most succinctly expressed in the lines, "Just as the future ripens in the past,/So the past smolders in the future." This formula came to Akhmatova from her own experiences and therefore has a convincing ring. The role of "history's lightning rod" almost always falls on the poet. Though historical epochs mirror one another, the terrible predictability is visible only to the poet, whose role is to create all-encompassing historical myths.

Poem *Without a Hero* brought the creation of a new Petersburg mythos to its culmination, one to which all Russian culture of the preceding 250 years had contributed. Akhmatova's crucial achievement was the melting down of important elements of previous incarnations of that mythos into a new, indivisible whole. She takes her reader through Petersburg's entire history: from imperial capital to the city where the poet can only

> *weep freely*
> *Over the silence of fraternal graves.*

Her model in the complex relations between poet and history was Pushkin. She once said, of his verse novel *Eugene Onegin,* that its "aerial enormity, like a cloud, stood over me." In the middle of the twentieth century, Akhmatova became the ethical compass for a new generation of Leningraders. *Poem Without a Hero* embodied for them the new Petersburg mythos, that "aerial enormity" in whose shadow a new generation of Leningrad intellectuals grew. They were to be the ones to carry the legend of the city and the poet, Petersburg and Akhmatova, around the world.

On February 18, 1964, in Leningrad, in the Dzerzhinsky district court—a grubby room with a spit-covered floor—there began the hearing of Joseph Brodsky, who was already well-known in the city. The twenty-three-year-old Brodsky was charged with "malicious parasitism"—that is, being out of a job—which was a violation of Soviet law. Tall and thin, with red hair and bright cheeks, Brodsky (with a guard next to him) spoke calmly, trying to explain to an ignorant and hostile judge that his work was writing poetry. She and Brodsky had the following exchange, which was written down clandestinely by the sympathetic journalist Frida Vigdorova.

JUDGE: And who recognized that you are a poet? Who listed you among poets?

BRODSKY: No one. (*Dispassionately.*) Who listed me a member of the human race?

JUDGE: Did you study this?

BRODSKY: What?

JUDGE: To be a poet? Did you try to graduate from a school where they prepare . . . where they teach . . .

BRODSKY: I don't think that it comes from education.

JUDGE: What then?

BRODSKY: I think that it's . . . (*bewildered*) . . . from God.[41]

This was like something out of Kafka or an absurdist play. The judge sent Brodsky under police escort to a psychiatric hospital to determine his sanity. Things were very tough there: he was forcibly given sulfur injections, which caused the slightest movement to be unbearably painful.

A favorite amusement of the male nurses was to wrap Brodsky in a sheet, dip him in an icy bath, and then toss him, still wrapped in the sheet, alongside a radiator. They called this the "cold-damp envelope." As it dried, the sheet tore off Brodsky's skin.[42] His roommate committed suicide by slitting his veins with a razor at night, and Brodsky was afraid that he would never leave the hospital alive. His sufferings during that terrible period are reflected in the long philosophical poem "Gorbunov and Gorchakov."

Forensic psychiatrists found Brodsky sane, and he went back to court. The same judge who committed him asked him, "What good have you done for your homeland?"

Brodsky replied with quiet persistence, "I wrote poetry. That is my work. I am convinced . . . I believe that what I write will be of service to people, and not only now but for future generations."[43]

All Brodsky's attempts to explain fell on deaf ears. The predetermined sentence read, in part, "Brodsky systematically does not fulfill the duties of a Soviet man in the production of material goods. . . . He wrote and recited his decadent poems. From the report of the Commission on Work with Young Writers, it is clear that Brodsky is not a poet. . . . Brodsky is to be sent to remote areas for a term of five years at forced labor."[44]

This cruel sentence of a young man who already had heart trouble infuriated many Leningrad intellectuals. A secret KGB report informed the Party which writers had called Brodsky's trial illegal, that Kornei Chukovsky and Dmitri Shostakovich were among those who rose to Brodsky's defense, and that in artistic circles the Brodsky case was considered a "turn back to 1937."[45]

The worries of Soviet intellectuals, based on years of bitter experience with the authorities, were not unfounded. After Stalin's death on March 5, 1953, the new leader of the Communist Party, the sly Nikita Khrushchev, renounced many of the excesses of his ruthless predecessor and at first steered a course toward liberalization of political and cultural life. This policy became known as the Thaw. Mass arrests on the Stalinist scale were ended. Many victims of the Great Terror were rehabilitated; those who had survived were released from the camps. After a long hiatus Russia was beginning, albeit feebly, to reestablish cultural contacts with the West, and a certain—a very limited—deviation was permitted from the total conformity enforced by Stalin.

But the liberal experiments of the down-to-earth Khrushchev were erratic at best and turned out to be short-lived. He soon began to tighten the screws impatiently, wanting the intellectuals to toe the Party line. In late 1963 Khrushchev attacked a group of famous Soviet writers and artists in crude and abusive language. Brodsky's trial was symptomatic of the tightening. And many feared that it was only a prelude to a harsher repression.

There is evidence that Khrushchev, who had a deep distrust of intellectuals, was planning just that, but in October 1964 he was unexpectedly removed from power by his Party colleagues, who had tired of his endless reshuffling of the political apparat, his unpredictable policy zigzags, and his uncontrollable outbursts. The new Party leader was the imposing Leonid Brezhnev, whose chief goal was to rock the ship of state as little as possible. The "stagnation period" had begun.

Under Khrushchev and then Brezhnev, Leningrad became even more a second-rate city. Of course, it remained an important industrial and scientific center with a stress on military production. Its population increased from slightly over a half million people in 1944 to four and a half million in the 1970s. But where culture was concerned, the various Party bosses were interested only in maintaining the status quo. It was no accident that the first major post-Stalinist trial of a writer (Brodsky's trial) took place in Leningrad. The city had a particularly reactionary local climate, one conducive to conflict between the authorities and the resident intellectual elite.

In Moscow it was easier for poets with liberal leanings to gain official publication or to find a large audience. These young poets thus had something to lose and hence were more easily manipulated by the authorities. So a public game of cat-and-mouse ensued: a writer would release a nonconformist work, then was censured by the government for so doing; in order to smooth relations, he would write several more acceptable works; he could then regain popularity with another liberal work.

The Leningrad authorities were less willing to play this game; local artists thus had fewer temptations than their Moscow contemporaries.[46] Also, they had the towering moral model of Anna Akhmatova, the only living representative of the Silver Age.

The poet Yevgeny Rein brought his friend Brodsky to visit Akhmatova at her dacha in Komarovo, near Leningrad, in the summer of 1961.[47] At first Akhmatova did not make any special impression on the cocky Brodsky. "It was only one fine day as I was returning from Akhmatova's house in a crowded commuter train that I realized—you know, it's as if the scales fell away—with whom, or actually with what, I was dealing," Brodsky later confessed. "I recalled something she said or the turn of her head—and suddenly everything fell into place. After that it wasn't that I became a frequent visitor, but I did see Akhmatova fairly regularly. And I even rented a dacha in Komarovo one winter. Then we saw each other literally every day. It wasn't a question of literature at all, but a purely personal and—dare I say it?—mutual attraction."[48]

By the time he met Akhmatova, Brodsky, who was born in Leningrad in 1940, had led a colorful life, especially for an urban Jewish young man. Like other residents of Leningrad, he and his mother had nearly starved during the blockade (his father, who served in the navy, took part in breaking it). One of Brodsky's most vivid childhood memories was of his first white bread roll. "I am standing on a chair and eating it, and my adult relatives are watching me."[49]

When "the great leader and teacher" Stalin died, the thirteen-year-old Brodsky was already independent enough to refrain from the hysterical mourning that was widespread in those anxious days. "We school children were called into the auditorium and our class mentor (Zhdanov himself had pinned the Order of Lenin on her—we all knew about that and it was a real big deal) came out on stage," Brodsky recalled. "She began a funeral oration and suddenly cried out in a wild voice: 'On your knees! On your knees!' Pandemonium broke out. Everyone was howling and weeping and it was somehow expected of me to cry too, but—to my shame then; now, I think, to my honor—I couldn't. When I got home, my mother was also crying. I looked at her with some astonishment, until my father suddenly gave me a wink. Then I realized for sure that there was no particular reason for me to get upset over Stalin's death."[50]

At the age of fifteen Brodsky dropped out of school and went to work as a milling machine operator at the Arsenal defense plant in Leningrad. He had at least thirteen jobs between 1956 and 1962 and traveled around Russia with geological groups. One of his more unusual jobs in that period was assistant in the dissecting room of the morgue of a district hospital, where he cut up corpses, sliced off the tops of their skulls, removed their internal organs, and then sewed them back up.

Brodsky left that job after a very unpleasant scene. That summer many small children in the Leningrad region were dying of toxic dyspepsia. Among them were a pair of Gypsy twins. When their father came to the morgue for the bodies and saw that they had been autopsied, he began, knife in hand, chasing Brodsky around the morgue, trying to kill him.

"I ran from him among the tables with sheet-covered corpses," Brodsky told me. "Now that's surrealism that makes Jean Cocteau seem like nothing! Finally, he caught me, grabbed me by my shirt, and I knew that something awful was about to happen. I managed to get hold of a surgical hammer that lay nearby and hit him on the hand. His hands unclenched, he stopped, and started to weep. And I felt very eerie."[51]

When Brodsky started writing poetry, his early experiences contributed to the appearance of the themes of loneliness and alienation, their primary source being the tragic and romantic character of Brodsky's gift. But a highly important role, according to Brodsky himself, was played by the fact that his native city was Leningrad, which Brodsky always chose to call "Piter," in defiance of its official name, like many of his contemporaries.

Brodsky explained that Petersburg was built on the edge of the state, almost outside it, and thus a writer living there willy-nilly becomes an outsider. As a witness to Brodsky's first poetry readings in Leningrad put it, "Alienation was the only accessible road to freedom for young Brodsky. That is why separation—from life, from a woman, city, or country—is so often rehearsed in his poems."[52]

Brodsky as a rule picked the outskirts of "Piter" to describe in his poetry. A poem from 1962, which Brodsky titled "From the Outskirts to the Center," describes the "peninsula of plants, a paradise of workshops, and Arcadia of factories." Brodsky commented, "At that time no one wrote about that part of the city, about that world. But I was always impressed by the industrial landscape. The vision of newly started construction projects, the sense of open space filled with protruding structures, was close to me. It all gave rise to thoughts of loneliness and dislocation."[53]

In the same poem, where Brodsky's emotions include "sadness from a brick chimney and a dog's bark," the poet makes a startling prediction, echoing Akhmatova's "Prayer" in its tragedy. "Thank God that I am left on this earth without a homeland." As Akhmatova had predicted the horrible sacrifices to come in her life, Brodsky here either guessed his future or determined it.

According to Brodsky, the centrifugal idea of the poem "From the Outskirts to the Center" can be explained this way: "The outskirts represent not only the end of the familiar world, but the start of the unfamiliar world, which is much larger, huger. The idea of the poem is that in moving to the outskirts, you remove yourself from everything in the world and thereby go out into the big world."[54]

This new view of Leningrad contrasts with a more traditional approach expressed in "Stanzas to a City," also written in 1962, in which the poet thus addressed the city:

> . . . During the white night
> Let your immovable earthly glory
> Dawn on me, a fugitive.

Even here there is the persistent theme of escape, which conflicts with Akhmatova's constant insistence on her inseparability from the city's fate. Akhmatova nevertheless included Brodsky in the circle of young poets that formed around her and that she dubbed the "magic choir."

That choir included, besides Brodsky and Rein, the poets Anatoly Nayman and Dmitri Bobyshev, who took closer to heart some of the acmeist principles of Akhmatova's work, such as her demand that the poet be brief. Brodsky constantly violated this principle. Some of his poems stretched to two hundred lines and more; after a while even Akhmatova began to like them. She said of Brodsky's poetry that she had not read anything like it since Mandelstam, and she used one of Brodsky's lines as an epigraph to her poem "The Last Rose."

What Akhmatova liked in Brodsky was his furious poetic temperament. She jokingly called him "a cat and a half": she had given that nickname to a neighbor's cat, a huge, noisy, orange beast. When Brodsky was arrested and tried, Akhmatova actively took up his defense and grieved at his punishment. At the same time, she noted acerbically that the authorities who persecuted Brodsky so maliciously were helping him. "What a biography they're creating for our redhead! You'd think he hired them."

The repressive Leningrad apparatus was not misguided in selecting Brodsky as the focus for punishment, even though his poems were not overly political. They did give off, as did Brodsky himself, a specific Petersburgian air of liberty and independence that the authorities perceived as threatening. Brodsky wrote about this later, recalling his Leningrad friend, the writer Sergei Dovlatov, "The idea of individualism, a man on his own, all by himself, was our proud property. But the possibility of realizing it was minuscule, if it existed at all."

Once at a debate, Viktor Shklovsky, a leader of the Petrograd Opoyaz circle of formalists, sarcastically asked his Marxist critics, "You have the army and navy on your side, and we're just four people—why are you so worried?" In fact, the answer was clear to both Shklovsky and his opponents: with its position consolidated, the Soviet regime wanted absolute obedience, and to get it, the state generously wielded the stick and the carrot. In the 1920s and 1930s, the authorities not only broke up Opoyaz but to varying degrees forced some of its members to compromise. This they did not manage to do with Brodsky.

Of course, the pressure was not as focused in the 1960s as it had been in the Great Terror. But Brodsky's "existential nonconformism" and his unwillingness to collaborate turned out to be unusually steadfast. In 1964 Brodsky went north to exile unintimidated and unrepentant.

The city that Brodsky left behind lived a contradictory cultural life. Creative processes of considerable vitality survived, but for the most part they were hidden from the national and international communities.

Though local authorities did everything they could to prevent the unpredictable in Leningrad, the performing arts flourished. It was in this area that the characteristics of Petersburg culture could thrive: high professionalism, refinement, and a reliance on long-standing European tradition.

The Leningrad Philharmonic prided itself justly on being the only world-class orchestra in the country. It was headed for a record fifty years, until his death in 1988, by the greatest Russian conductor of the twentieth century, the Petersburger Yevgeny Mravinsky. Scion of an old noble family, the tall, thin, haughty, and taciturn Mravinsky was an imposing figure. The musicians were in awe of their leader, whose endless rehearsals and attention to detail were legendary. Mravinsky's interpretations were frequently illuminating and structurally revealing.[55]

Mravinsky's repertoire was a bit small by Western standards. His favorite composers were Tchaikovsky (whose portrait the conductor carried like a talisman) and Shostakovich; Mravinsky's performances of their music were incomparable. His recordings of Tchaikovsky's symphonies, particularly the *Pathétique,* were renowned. George Balanchine recalled his friendship with Mravinsky in Petrograd in the 1920s. In those days Mravinsky made money as an extra at the Maryinsky Theater, and the future choreographer set a poem by the future conductor to music.[56]

Mravinsky and Shostakovich had a close-knit relationship. In 1937 the composer trusted Mravinsky with the premiere of his Fifth Symphony. It was a triumph. The conductor subsequently premiered another five Shostakovich symphonies, including the monumental Eighth, which was dedicated to him. In Mravinsky's performances, Shostakovich's symphonies seemed more like Greek tragedy than modern drama.

The approach had pluses and minuses, creating as it did a certain distance between the horrible events of daily life and their musical reflection in Shostakovich's music. This Petersburg classicism worked until the late 1950s, when editorial tendencies began to predominate in the composer's work (he was by then living in Moscow). A mutual dissatisfaction developed between composer and conductor; though suppressed at first, it surfaced after Mravinsky's refusal to conduct the premiere of Shostakovich's Thirteenth ("Babi Yar") Symphony.

Mravinsky was accused of cowardice: the Thirteenth Symphony, which set the topical poetry of Yevgeny Yevtushenko, dealt with politically touchy themes, including anti-Semitism. But the conductor had not been fainthearted in even grimmer times. Mravinsky, a firm anti-Soviet, considered Shostakovich's music important. "Shostakovich's greatness is defined for me first of all by the significance of the public and moral idea that runs through his entire work. It is the thought that things should not be bad for people, that they not suffer because of wars and social catastrophes, injustice, and oppression."

In 1948, when Shostakovich's music was denounced and banned, Mravinsky put the disgraced composer's Fifth Symphony on the program of the Leningrad Philharmonic. The performance was a great success; the curtain calls would not stop. In response to the applause, Mravinsky held the score high over his head. The audience stood, realizing that this was a challenge, a desperately brave act. Mravinsky was risking a lot, perhaps even his life. His defiant gesture became part of the history of Petersburg culture.

The differences between Mravinsky and Shostakovich in the mid-1960s were thus less political than aesthetic. When, late in life, Shostakovich composed the introspective and textless Fifteenth Symphony, Mravinsky immediately added it to his repertoire.

Mravinsky was a religious man and did not hide the fact, which in the officially atheist state strongly complicated his relations with the authorities, who were forced to disregard this "eccentric" behavior because of the conductor's international fame. He took to his heart Beethoven's Missa Solemnis and Bruckner's symphonies, music through which he could express his spiritual ideas. Mravinsky also became a zealous exponent of Stravinsky's works. He gave the first Soviet performance of Agon, a serial work, and included the neoclassical Apollo and Baiser de la fée in his programs.

Mravinsky stressed the Petersburg roots of these Stravinsky works. Was the conductor thus shielding himself from reality, losing himself in the realm of the Petersburg mythos? His search for the ideal was tortuous. Mravinsky was often mired in despair (a fact few people knew); he would go off to his dacha and drink heavily.

One such time, his wife played a recording of Apollo for him. He listened intently and then exclaimed, "Oh, my God! I am so miserable! They play so well, the form is so perfect. I wouldn't be able to do that with my musicians!"

"That's you," Mravinsky's wife told him. "That's your orchestra."

Mravinsky broke down and sobbed like a baby.

When Mravinsky died, the score of Shostakovich's Fifth Symphony lay on his desk. He had first performed it in 1937; fifty years later the conductor was still working on it. This attitude was typical for Mravinsky, who expanded his core repertoire with caution.

He rarely performed works by the Leningrad composers of the

generation that followed Shostakovich. Among the few exceptions were the works of Galina Ustvolskaya, Shostakovich's favorite student at the Leningrad Conservatory. From the very beginning Ustvolskaya stood out for her uncompromising nature and indifference toward success. She worked for years over her compositions, keeping them hidden and destroying many of them. Her music did not imitate Shostakovich's, but spoke in its own voice: ascetic, unornamented, built on strong contrasts.

Ustvolskaya's chamber works are as monumental as a symphony, and her symphonies are as translucent as chamber music. Though partial to titles like *The True, Eternal Goodness* (Second Symphony, 1979) and *Jesu Messiah, Save Us!* (Third Symphony, 1983), she insisted that her music was "spiritual but not religious." Her brand of expressionism delighted Shostakovich, who told Ustvolskaya, "You are a phenomenon, while I am just a talent."

Shostakovich spent a lot of time with Ustvolskaya, who was short and girlish looking. He wrote to her frequently, sometimes twice a day. He confessed to his son, Maxim, that he had never loved anyone as he did her.[57] When his wife died suddenly in 1954, Shostakovich proposed to Ustvolskaya but was refused outright, which caused him great grief. Traces of his passion may be found in a melody by Ustvolskaya that Shostakovich used in two major works: the Fifth String Quartet (1952) and the Suite to Poems by Michelangelo (1974), one of his last pieces.

Ustvolskaya did little to promote her music, which therefore was known to only a narrow circle in Leningrad, where it developed cult status. When Ustvolskaya began teaching, the defiantly ascetic character of her life and her works created a great impression on her students. One of them was Boris Tishchenko, who subsequently did graduate work with Shostakovich. In the years when modern Western culture was in effect banned, Ustvolskaya introduced her students to the works of Mahler and Stravinsky, to which Shostakovich had introduced her. Thus was preserved in Leningrad music the sense of an uninterrupted cultural tradition.

Ustvolskaya's creative energy, devoutness, and personal eccentricity reminded people of the pianist Maria Yudina. Like Yudina, Ustvolskaya spent a lot of time with her students in discussion and listening to music; such "Socratic" sessions had gone on in Leningrad since the days of the Bakhtin circle.

This underground method of passing on culture was typical of Leningrad of that era. Thus, a group of young artists gathered around

Vladimir Sterligov—a student of Malevich's who had returned to Leningrad from the camps, where he had been sent during the Stalin terror after Kirov's murder—and Sterligov's wife, Tatyana Glebova, a student of Filonov's. Sterligov and his group discussed Malevich's suprematist ideas and Filonov's "principle of doneness" and declaimed the dadaist poems of the Oberiuts. Here, too, special emphasis was placed on the spirituality of art.

The "principle of doneness" of Pavel Filonov, who died of starvation during the Leningrad siege, held that the artist built a painting out of the tiniest strokes, working with a small brush and creating a complex composition that incorporated seemingly incompatible elements. When the Leningrad artist Mihail Chemiakin first saw Filonov's works in the late 1950s, the technique stunned him. Chemiakin proceeded to form an art association with his nonconformist friends; they called it Sankt-Peterburg.

The total informational vacuum of the Stalin era gradually broke down but it was a slow and arduous process. It was particularly hard for artists, because the work of the Russian avant-garde was hidden deep in the cellars of museums; the little that came from the West—an occasional album—was worth its weight in gold. Chemiakin collected reproductions of modern art however he could.

I once brought him a German recording of Arnold Schoenberg's music with a portrait of the composer by Oskar Kokoschka on the album cover. Chemiakin's room held an ancient harmonium, a press for etchings, a horse's skull, and a Limoges crucifix. He was wearing black leather pants and a vest with buttons depicting the Russian imperial eagles; the other guests were dressed no less eccentrically. Played with the Leningrad white night outside the window and lit candles inside, Schoenberg's *Verklärte Nacht* evoked a near trance. Stunned, Chemiakin talked me into leaving the record, priceless in those days, for further study. I never saw it again; the reproduction of Kokoschka's painting probably became an addition to Chemiakin's collection.

The cult of old Petersburg reigned in Chemiakin's circle. When a film version was being made in Leningrad of Dostoyevsky's *Crime and Punishment* in the mid-1960s, the production unit re-created a corner of the city of that era near Haymarket Square. Chemiakin and his friends would go there at night, dressed in period costumes, and wander around the sets until dawn, getting a feel for vanished Petersburg.

This passion for the Petersburg mythos, which was out of official favor in those years, found reflection in Chemiakin's celebrated exhibit at the Leningrad Conservatory in 1966. (Chemiakin's reputation among musicians was very high, even though the Artists' Union rejected him totally; he was even asked to create the masks for an experimental conservatory production of Shostakovich's opera *The Nose*.) Chemiakin's stylized Petersburg landscapes revitalized the almost lost tradition of tragic depiction of the city by the artists of *Mir iskusstva*, Benois and Dobuzhinsky. These calligraphic works are very sophisticated. To many viewers their ironic carnival spirit came as a revelation. His exhibit was a huge success. The authorities quickly sounded the alarm: the conservatory was pressured, and a week after its opening, the exhibit was shut down. Chemiakin was back in total isolation, surrounded by official hostility.

The situation of Leningrad music was significantly more liberal, thanks to the efforts of Andrei Petrov, a stammering but quick-witted composer of popular songs, who became head of the local Composers' Union in 1964. Petrov tried to create a beneficial atmosphere for moderately modernistic works by Leningrad composers in a period when even the concept of a distinctive Petersburg school of composition was rejected by Moscow. In this Petrov stood out from two other pop-song writers who had earlier headed the city's composers—Isaak Dunayevsky and Vassily Soloviev-Sedoi. While talented in their genre, they were very conservative.

Petrov aided Boris Tishchenko in particular. Petrov expedited the publication and performance of Tishchenko's sprawling symphonies in the manner of Shostakovich and arranged lucrative commissions for theater and film scores. The income made Tishchenko's daily life comfortable—he eventually moved into a well-appointed apartment in a prestigious neighborhood—but left him in an awkward position in 1966 when he completed his *Requiem* for soprano, tenor, and orchestra, based on Akhmatova's poem.

Tishchenko wrote the music in secret since Akhmatova's anti-Stalinist text, despite the Khrushchev thaw, was still strictly taboo. I first heard Tishchenko's *Requiem* at a private performance in a piano reduction played by the composer, and the work made a strong impression on me and all the others present. Though a local performance was out of the question in those years, Tishchenko always refused any proposal to premiere the piece in the West.

The reason was undoubtedly Tishchenko's fear of open confrontation with the authorities, which would lead to a loss of the privileges he enjoyed, a loss that even Petrov could not prevent. So the first publicly performed musical setting of Akhmatova's *Requiem* became that of the British composer John Tavener, which premiered at the Edinburgh Festival in 1981. Accenting the religious aura of Akhmatova's poetry, Tavener's *Requiem* drew the attention of musicians in the West to the Petersburg mythos in the dark years of the Brezhnev stagnation.

Moscow looked askance at the Leningrad composers' attempts at rebelliousness. When a concert of Leningrad music was held in 1965, an official in the Composers' Union sneered, "Petersburg chopped a window into Europe and now some Leningrad artists have fallen out that window!" This was a reference to the experimental works of Sergei Slonimsky, who called himself a "white crow" for sticking to the traditions of Prokofiev in a city where Shostakovich's followers were the majority.

In the 1960s Slonimsky toyed with and then abandoned the idea of basing an opera on a short story by Solzhenitsyn; but even his opera on Mikhail Bulgakov's novel *The Master and Margarita* was rejected by the authorities. Slonimsky noted bitterly that if Mussorgsky's *Boris Godunov* had been written in the years of the Soviet regime, it would never have made it into print or onto the stage.

The son of one of the active members of the Serapion brothers, the influential literary association of the 1920s, Slonimsky had an ear for poetry and was one of the first in the post-Stalin era to set the works of Akhmatova, Mandelstam, and Kharms. In the mid-sixties, around when Tishchenko first set the poems of Brodsky, Slonimsky used the poetry of Brodsky's friend Rein for a song cycle. When Slonimsky presented this difficult music (in the presence of the agitated poet) at an informal recital at the conservatory where he taught composition, the large classroom was overflowing. Students watched the ruffled composer introduce his new opus, which used devices unknown to most of those present: he strummed, plucked, and banged on the strings of the piano, eliciting unusual and attractive sounds.

Slonimsky could not have hoped for a better audience. Leningrad musical youth of the sixties were hungry for the new and unknown. We filled Maly Hall of the Leningrad Philharmonic for the premieres of Shostakovich's quartets, the intimate works of a wounded soul that was dear to us. But we also wanted to hear other music, outspoken and avant-garde.

The work of the émigré Stravinsky had been banned comparatively recently; he was invariably called a "rootless cosmopolite" or a "political and ideological renegade." But after 1962, when the eighty-year-old composer visited Moscow and Leningrad after a half century's absence and was received by Khrushchev himself, the situation changed somewhat for the better. Stravinsky's later works were still performed rarely and reviewed dismissively, but his "Russian" works—*Firebird, Petrouchka, Le Sacre du printemps*—gradually entered the repertoire.

This breakthrough coincided with the start of the partial rehabilitation of other Russian émigrés; in particular, some of the *Mir iskusstva* group. I remember the instant sellout of the first postcard reproductions of watercolors by Alexander Benois. In 1962 the memoirs of choreographer Michel Fokine were published in an edition of thirty thousand copies, and Diaghilev's Ballets Russes could be mentioned favorably. Some books illustrated by Dobuzhinsky were reprinted.

They were returning our past to us: cautiously, reluctantly, drop by drop. But we were persistent and resourceful. The poets of the Silver Age could be taken from the libraries only with special permission, so we would show up armed with official-looking letters testifying to our need to familiarize ourselves with the poetry of Kuzmin and Mandelstam for "ideological debates." A bouquet of flowers for the librarian could open up the way to getting the piano score for the still-banned *Lady Macbeth of the Mtsensk District*. I remember a friend bringing a roll of film he had taken of a book by Oberiut Zabolotsky published in 1929, and we spent the night in a stuffy darkroom, printing the book, page by page on photo paper; we wanted to share our discovery with other students.

At the former Maryinsky Theater—which, though renamed for the murdered Kirov, retained the luxury of tsarist times—we listened with delight to the operas of Glinka, Mussorgsky, Borodin, Tchaikovsky, and Rimsky-Korsakov, under the batons of Sergei Yeltsin and Konstantin Simeonov, as well as the occasional Prokofiev opera, but our hearts longed for the new. Benjamin Britten jolted our imagination, presenting several of his operas in Leningrad in 1964, including *The Turn of the Screw*, based on the Henry James story, which astonished us with its psychological subtlety. My friends and I, all students at the Leningrad Conservatory, decided to create our own experimental studio for chamber opera, and overcoming a multitude of bureaucratic obstacles, we produced several works.

We were the first to stage Veniamin Fleishman's opera *Rothschild's Violin*, based on the Chekhov story. This young Jewish student of Shostakovich died in 1941 defending Leningrad from the

Germans in the ranks of the home guard. With two other composition students, Fleishman fired on enemy tanks from a pillbox that was finally surrounded and blown up. The home guard consisted of hastily selected, ill-trained, and poorly armed workers, students, and intellectuals of Leningrad. Zhdanov used them during the siege as cannon fodder; almost none survived.

Among the dead was the former director of the avant-garde Theater of Worker Youth (TRAM), Shostakovich's friend Mikhail Sokolovsky. Shostakovich suffered the loss of his friends badly. Torn by guilt, he completed and orchestrated Fleishman's unfinished opera. The premiere was successful, and Shostakovich was happy that the memory of his talented student was thereby preserved.

The Fleishman-Shostakovich opera was lyrical and tragic. But we wanted to laugh, too, and so I wrote an absurdist libretto, based on the old parody play *Lyubov and Silin,* for a friend, the composer Gennady Banshchikov. Banshchikov worked on the opera at night, and in order to wake up mornings, he constructed a device that blasted out Stravinsky's *Le Sacre* when the alarm went off (he was a skilled mechanic, too); the wild sounds roused his neighbors as well. Banshchikov's opera was bold and barbed; it attacked cultural censorship, xenophobia, and the illiteracy of the bureaucratic elite.

We asked another young iconoclast, Alexander Knaifel, to set to music Lenin's letter (of which we were all sick and tired, forced to memorize it at school) in which he called for the start of revolution in Petrograd. The innocent-looking Knaifel brought us a score in which the words, familiar to every Soviet citizen from childhood, were sung menacingly by a unison chorus of basses. The effect was hilarious, absolutely surrealistic. Rumors of Knaifel's musical satire quickly reached Leningrad Party headquarters, from which came an edict banning its performance. They shut down our enterprise for good, despite the fact that the popular bass Yevgeny Nesterenko, soon to become famous with the premieres of Shostakovich's late vocal works, was part of our group. This time, the last laugh belonged to the authorities.

One of the first people to whom we showed the just-completed *Lyubov and Silin* was Nikolai Akimov, director of the Leningrad Comedy Theater. His opinion was important to us, and we all heaved a sigh of relief when he responded positively. Akimov was small and scrawny, but he had a large head, a long nose, and a sharp gaze. Though his enemies mocked his erudition, intellectualism, and seemingly endless capacity for work, he was one of the country's leading theater directors. Akimov first became famous in 1932 for an irreverent production of *Hamlet* as a farce.

Young Shostakovich wrote appropriately impertinent music for Akimov's production. A scandal ensued that almost destroyed the director's career. However, things were smoothed over, and despite the "formalist" label that followed Akimov throughout his life, his Comedy Theater, situated in the center of Nevsky Prospect, remained one of the city's most popular theaters. Audiences laughed at his productions of French farces and American comedies, while catching the hints about the absurdity of Soviet reality in his productions of Leningrad playwrights.

Akimov's brilliance as a theater designer played an enormous part in the success of his productions. Sometimes Akimov the artist outshone Akimov the director, from the first costume sketches to the lobby posters advertising the next premiere. In the 1950s and 1960s Akimov may have been the most famous and beloved artist in the city: his colorful posters, depicting in an intriguing way the essence of the play and the production, stood out in the quotidian atmosphere of those days, eliciting delighted attention from thousands of Leningraders.

Akimov had to wage exhausting battles with the censors over each poster. As he later recalled, "No one banned posters in general, but almost each poster specifically was banned. The excuses were quite subtle: 'Does not express the play's idea,' 'insufficiently optimistic,' 'the text is not visible from a distance,' 'the title is too aggressively presented,' and the favorite, which fit any occasion, 'isn't there some formalism here?' " For one play Akimov drew Moscow at night; the authorities perceived it as an attempt by a Leningrader to undermine Moscow's international reputation as a sunny city and consequently termed it a "crude political error."

As a painter (he adored doing grotesque portraits of his friends and left a huge series depicting Leningrad's intellectual elite), Akimov was a major representative of the prerevolutionary Petersburg neoclassicism that grew strong under the aegis of the Petersburg Academy of Arts. The academy, founded in 1757 by Empress Elizabeth, was given the title "imperial" by Catherine the Great a few years later, reflecting the traditional Russian idea that art must serve the monarch and the state.

Even in Petersburg, which readily assimilated all things foreign, the Academy of Arts remained an exotic flower, embodying a taste for the nude in a city where religion, climate, and mores were obstacles to unclothed bodies. Perhaps that is why the academy, having trained several artists like Karl Briullov, capitulated so quickly in the mid-nineteenth century to the attacks of Ivan Kramskoy and his fellow Wanderers. It reestablished its authority only in the early twentieth century, when the pedagogue Dmitri Kardovsky turned it into a bastion of Russian neoclassicism, "setting the eye and the hand," as the professionals put it, of such outstanding masters as Boris Grigoryev, Alexander Yakovlev, Vassily Shukhaev, and Boris Anisfeld.

The clear-thinking Kardovsky stressed drawing, and his best students bore comparison to the greatest artists of the past. Soon after the revolution Anisfeld emigrated to the United States and Grigoryev, Yakovlev, and Shukhaev went to France. They all were successful in the West, cleverly responding to the demand for the neoclassical with a touch of the exotic just as everyone's attention was caught by the corresponding works of Igor Stravinsky.

Yakovlev's and Grigoryev's Western careers were cut short by untimely death (1938 and 1939, respectively). Shukhaev returned to Leningrad from Paris at the invitation of the authorities to take over the ailing Kardovsky's class. Shukhaev taught at what was then the Soviet Academy of Arts for two years before he was arrested and sent to Siberia, from which he returned ten years later, morally and physically broken.

Akimov, who had studied with Yakovlev, revered his demonic-looking mentor (he had been wildly popular with women and had had a long, turbulent affair with Anna Pavlova in the West). Akimov's apartment faced the Neva and was filled with his many portraits of famous men and beautiful women (his friends called it the wizard's cave); in it the place of honor was given to a drawing by Yakovlev, which had miraculously survived all the trials of Leningrad life, even the siege. It was a museum-quality drawing of large reddish hands and a huge foot.

Every self-respecting director dreams of discovering a great playwright. In the early 1930s Akimov believed he had made his discovery when he met a modest young man, the Leningrad playwright Yevgeny Shvarts. At the time Shvarts was at a crossroad. He was a successful children's writer, but he had a quarrel with the influential poet and editor Samuil Marshak, whose word in children's literature, then and later, was law.

Marshak and Kornei Chukovsky could be called the fathers of

twentieth-century Russian children's literature. Chukovsky had begun writing his brightly rhymed poems in 1916, and to this day children all over Russia memorize them. Before the revolution Chukovsky had tried to free children's literature from treacly verse and goody-goody stories and afterward relentlessly fought the attempts of the Soviet authorities to turn children's literature into an instrument for ideological brainwashing.

In those days any fairy tales that caused "harmful fantasies" in children were banned by the censors. Even traditional dolls were taken out of circulation for inspiring "hypertrophy of maternal feelings." Instead girls were given propaganda dummies depicting fat, repulsive priests in order to elicit antireligious emotions. But the little girls, responding to their hypertrophic maternal feelings, stubbornly gave the dolls baths in toy tubs, fed them, and put them to bed.

This obvious failure did not stop the authorities from urging further ridiculous innovations. Chukovsky eventually wearied of his struggle (he bitterly described the "shameful history of my children's books—they were stifled, persecuted, sedated, and banned by the censors") and yielded the leadership in children's literature to Marshak, who had not only an uncommon poetic gift but fantastic organizational skills.

The bespectacled, chain-smoking Marshak reigned on the fifth floor of the House of Books, located in the former headquarters of the Singer Company on Nevsky Prospect, over a team of writers, poets, and artists. Marshak cleared the way for the dadaist Oberiuts—Kharms, Oleinikov, and Vvedensky—into print. They produced several children's magazines, full of vivid poems, counting games, and stories, on which several generations of young readers were to grow up.

Marshak created a new genre in Russian children's literature: stories of experienced people—sailors, pilots, divers, geologists, polar explorers. One man he brought in was Boris Zhitkov, a navigator and engineer who had circled the world several times in a sailing ship. Marshak sat up nights with Zhitkov, prodding him to develop a new Leningrad style of prose for children.

The fifth floor of the Singer building was crowded with people bearing manuscripts and drawings and ideas for new books. The floor shook with laughter, and some visitors were so overcome with the general hilarity that they left the building staggering, holding onto walls like drunkards. Shvarts, Oleinikov, and Kharms were particularly good at comic improvisations. An absurd sense of humor was the most esteemed. For instance, Kharms talked of a trained flea that bit its master and then rubbed the bite with its tiny legs. When he was asked his telephone number, Kharms replied, "It's very easy to remember: thirty-two, fifteen. Thirty-two teeth, fifteen fingers."

Only one man seemed to remain totally serious and unperturbed: Marshak's favorite artist, Vladimir Lebedev. He was one of the golden boys of Soviet culture, like Shostakovich or Kozintsev. Lebedev graduated from the Petersburg Academy of Arts and, on the first anniversary of the Bolshevik seizure of power, joined others in a provocative display of semiabstract compositions. As a painter and graphic artist, Lebedev quickly moved from cubism to nonfigurative experiments, creating a series of works by the early 1920s that are still considered among the cream of the Russian avant-garde.

Lebedev's art was always political, and he is properly considered one of the creators and masters of the Soviet political poster. But by the early 1920s he had also become a social critic, doing several series of satiric sketches of contemporary life, depicting nouveaux riches, their vulgar girlfriends, and colorful urban toughs. Lebedev's works revealed a different world; it seemed that after the long hegemony of *Mir iskusstva*, a new leader had appeared in artistic Petrograd. No wonder that Punin, who had supported and propagandized Tatlin in his time, published a monograph on Lebedev in 1928, based on the materials of the artist's solo show at the Russian Museum. Now Punin made Lebedev the benchmark.

But Lebedev was not cut out for leadership. He called himself a lone wolf, and his favorite poet was Kipling. Shvarts, who knew the artist well, said of Lebedev, "He was impressed not by fame, but power. Like Shklovsky and Mayakovsky, he believed that the times were always right."[58] Lebedev did not wish to fight the times. Having already renounced nonfigurativism, he preferred now to abjure social satire. He moved to children's books, where his collaboration with Marshak caused a sensation.

In the 1920s Marshak and Lebedev produced a series of illustrated children's books that became classics of the genre. These books had a seemingly utilitarian goal: to introduce the small child into the adult world, to explain how things worked—a repair shop, the plumbing, the circus, a typewriter, or an electric light bulb. But these editions were also works of art in which the combination of Marshak's polished verse and Lebedev's vivid drawings created an original whole.

Each subsequent Marshak-Lebedev book was a treat for young and old, reprinted over and over. A "Marshak school" and a "Lebedev school" sprang up in Leningrad: talented writers and artists working in the style of the masters.

Lebedev's loyal cohorts could be seen daily at the Leningrad printing house Pechatny Dvor, which published the best children's books. The Lebedevites were there round the clock, creating dummies, selecting fonts, setting type, and running off copies, as well as doing the actual drawing. Some artists, like Yevgeny Charushin or Alexander Samokhvalov, also wrote texts for their illustrations.

Many members of the Lebedev group had no competition in their field: Valentin Kurdov was celebrated for his depictions of horses, and Yuri Vasnetsov for his variations on the imagery from old Russian folk pictures. Mikhail Tsekhanovsky, who produced the book *The Post Office* with Marshak, became an experimenter in cartoons. He even began a satirical cartoon opera with Shostakovich. This was in 1933, seven years before Walt Disney's *Fantasia*. But the authorities did not allow Tsekhanovsky and Shostakovich to complete the work, and only fragments survived.

A bit apart from Lebedev's young artists were the old Petersburgers Dmitri Mitrokhin and Nikolai Tyrsa, whose illustrations added elegance to Leningrad book production. In sum, Leningrad literature for children was done by highly qualified professionals for whom quality and artistic worth were more important than ideological imperatives.

This led to an immediate attack by the Moscow press on the "harmful literary practice of the Leningrad group," which allegedly juxtaposed "aristocratic form" and "crude content." The attack against the "Marshak-Lebedev group" was not limited to words: in 1931 a number of Leningrad writers and artists for children were arrested on false charges of "organizing on the basis of their counter-revolutionary convictions" an underground anti-Soviet cell. Among the arrested was the artist Vera Ermolaeva, one of Malevich's closest colleagues, who was working with Marshak and the Oberiuts.

Ermolaeva always said, "Leningrad is the last citadel of new art in Russia." Always on crutches (her legs were paralyzed after a childhood fall from a horse), Ermolaeva was surrounded by loyal students. Her achievements in children's literature rivaled those of Lebedev.

Released after her first arrest, Ermolaeva was detained once again and sent to a camp in Kazakhstan in 1934, when a new wave of arrests and and sanctions rolled over Leningrad in the wake of the murder of Sergei Kirov. Sterligov, who was taken to the camps in the same group as Ermolaeva, recalled how the convoy soldiers mocked the handicapped artist, ordering her around at the daily roll call: "Stand up!" "Lie down!" "Stand up!"

After several years in the camps, where Ermolaeva's legs were amputated, she was given an automatic second term. Finally, she and other inmates were loaded onto a barge and sent onto the Aral Sea (Sterligov witnessed the event). All the prisoners were left on a desert island. No one ever heard from Ermolaeva again. All that was left of her in Leningrad were a few works and some photographs and letters.

For Lebedev, Ermolaeva's fate was a terrible blow and a warning. Events moved quickly: by the end of 1937, the new Leningrad's children's literature was destroyed. Arrests of writers and artists continued unabated, but Marshak and Lebedev were not arrested, despite the fact that the press invariably referred to their group as "a counterrevolutionary, sabotaging gang of enemies."

Lebedev was terrified. He, like Shostakovich, was personally attacked by *Pravda*; in those days that was a reliable signal of coming extermination. Lebedev's wife, Irina Kichanova, recalled,

> The fear did not leave Lebedev from that moment. And he tried to escape the fear in the city. The walls of the house stifled him, did not save him from fear, while he knew the city like no one else and loved it like no one else. And with the obsessiveness of an explorer he began showing it to me. We went off on long excursions on the Petrograd side, along Vasilyevsky Island, down the canals, to the Summer Gardens, the Neva, the Palace Embankment, I saw the house of the Queen of Spades, the English Embankment. . . . It was a strange feeling, sometimes very hard. That was not how you love art or architecture. That was how you love someone's soul, living and elusive.[59]

Such fear-induced attacks of claustrophobia were typical in those years among the Leningrad elite. The theatrical designer Vladimir Dmitriev (George Balanchine's best friend in the early 1920s) had his wife taken away in the middle of the night by the secret police; they pulled her from the cradles holding their sleeping seven-month-old twins. Dmitriev told Maria Konisskaya how he "spent the ten best years of his life in constant icy fear. Sometimes he would drop his work, jump on any train and go wherever it went, then change to another one in another direction, looping around, choking on fear." Commenting on this confession of Dmitriev, who received the Stalin

Prize four times for his designs, Konisskaya concluded sadly, "I'm not surprised that he died of a heart attack at forty-seven."[60]

It was almost impossible to avoid the omnipresent fear. The bravest people felt it. Someone said to Akhmatova in 1938, "You are fearless. You are afraid of nothing." She replied, "Not at all! That's all I do, is feel fear." Akhmatova always added when she told this story, "Really, how could you not be afraid? They would take you and before killing you force you to betray others."

Lydia Ginzburg described the surrealistic fear in Leningrad's cultural circles. "The horrible background never left your mind. The people who went to the ballet and to visit friends, played poker and rested at their dachas were the ones who got news in the morning of the loss of relatives, who themselves froze every time the doorbell rang at night, waiting for their uninvited guests.[61] Shvarts recalled this, too. "Love was still love, life was life, but every moment was imbued with horror. And the threat of shame."[62]

Everyone dealt with this daily, exhausting horror differently. Lebedev never missed a sports event—he went to soccer games and wrestling and boxing matches. Shostakovich went with him everywhere. Lebedev's wife said they were "united by fear and by love of sports."[63] Shostakovich's devotion to soccer is now often mentioned, usually in terms of a genius's amusing hobby. But in those difficult times it was one of the few available forms of spontaneous emotional release and, for Leningrad intellectuals like Lebedev and Shostakovich, also perhaps an unconscious attempt at social mimicry.

In those conditions it was natural to bend or break, psychologically and artistically. The greatest test was in creative work. Lebedev, like Dmitriev and Kozintsev, belonged to a generation whose creative potential gave them the ability to work at the highest level of modern culture, while the exigencies of life pushed them toward politically dictated, albeit professional, hackwork. Only a strong character could survive this unequal battle with a ruthless age.

In Shvart's severe judgment, "Lebedev believed in today, loved what was powerful that day, and scorned weakness and failure as something unacceptable in polite society."[64]

Such an attitude was a betrayal of the age-old traditions of Russian culture, which had always risen to the defense of the "insulted and injured." For that betrayal Lebedev, who continued to illustrate children's books to the end of his life (he died in Leningrad in 1967, at the age of seventy-six), paid with the emptiness of his late style. It is his early works that are now reprinted.

□ □ □

The children's texts of Yevgeny Shvarts were also very popular in their day; indeed, they were praised by the notoriously hard-to-please Mandelstam. But Shvarts earned his place in the history of Russian literature with his plays, which were commissioned by Akimov. They include *The Naked King, The Shadow,* and especially *The Dragon.*

In form the plays are fairy tales (*The Naked King* and *The Shadow* are based on stories of Hans Christian Andersen), but they were intended primarily, though not exclusively, for an adult audience. Shvarts used a broad spectrum of expressive devices, blending fantasy, irony, parody, lyricism, and lampoon. His plays can be read as parables, but they are most effective on stage, amusing and touching.

Like the historical political allegories in Tynyanov's prose, Shvarts's plays were filled with political hints and allusions, which Soviet audiences easily understood. Like Tynyanov, Shvarts transcended the political situation of his time, thanks to which his plays remain topical. But unlike Tynyanov, Shvarts had to suffer much at the hands of the Soviet censors. The authorities subjected plays and films to much greater scrutiny than books, and all of Shvart's best works underwent lengthy periods of being banned.

The censors were right to be upset by the characters Shvarts created: the Cannibal, who worked for the police; the Shadow, who ran affairs of state; the Vampire Bureaucrat. The greatest indignities were visited on *The Dragon,* written in 1943, one of the best Russian plays of the twentieth century. Shvarts tells of a magical city ruled by a terrible Dragon, which any Soviet citizen would recognize as Stalin. The Dragon frightened and corrupted his subjects. "Armless souls, legless souls, deaf-mute souls," he says with contempt.

As Kaverin, who read *The Dragon* in manuscript, recalled, the first readers were stunned by Shvarts's brutal analysis of Soviet conformity. "The impossibility of struggling against violence, the attempt to justify what is unjustifiable—that is ours, lived through." A traveling knight kills the Dragon, but true liberty still does not come to the people: power in the city is seized by the monster's loyal aide, the obnoxious Mayor. The Dragon may be gone, but tyranny "with a human face" continues.

In 1944 Shvarts and Akimov tried to bring *The Dragon* to the Soviet stage in the guise of an "anti-fascist satire." But even in the war years, when ideological censorship was comparatively temperate, the play was instantly banned. It was produced in Leningrad only in 1962, four years after the author's death.

Everyone rushed to see *The Dragon* at the Comedy Theater (Akimov both directed and designed the sets and costumes). They wanted to see the play before it was closed down. This possibility was real, since people saw in the social-climbing Mayor who replaced the Dragon-Stalin none other than the brutish Khrushchev. Shvarts's *Dragon,* like his other plays, had been prophetic.

Along with Shvarts's *Shadow,* which had been permitted on stage after a twenty-year hiatus (alas, after the author's death), *The Dragon* was Akimov's signature piece. A similar relationship linked another Leningrad director, Georgy Tovstonogov, to two plays by Alexander Volodin, like Shvarts a Leningrader. Twenty years younger than Shvarts and badly wounded in World War II, Volodin tried to express the feeble hopes of Leningraders in the period of Khrushchev's brief thaw.

If Shvarts resembled Andersen, then Volodin resembled Chekhov. The heroines of his plays (Volodin almost always had a woman at the center of his works)—saleswomen, telephone operators, secretaries—tried to find meaning and a little happiness in the grim life around them. It never occurred to them to confront the regime, but neither were they Soviet literature's traditional obedient cogs in the state machine.

Volodin's characters were not given to lofty declarations; they spoke and behaved like real people. This recycling of Chekhovian technique irritated official critics. As Volodin, painfully shy—not unlike his characters—later recalled, "Even before I completed the play *Five Evenings,* they came up with the formula that this was malicious barking from around the corner. However, there was no barking at all, no criticism of reality—it is beyond that, either beneath or above it, as you like. Then they changed the formula: 'These are just little maladjusted people, pessimism, petty themes.' And they all repeated it every time: whatever I did, it was a petty theme and pessimism."

Conservative reviewers fought doggedly to get Volodin's plays off the stage since their very existence undermined socialist realism. Thus, becoming Volodin's champion—which is what the sober and cautious Tovstonogov did—demanded quite a bit of courage.

At the Bolshoi Dramatic Theater Tovstonogov staged Volodin's *Five Evenings* in 1959 and *The Older Sister* in 1961. Audiences followed the uncomplicated twists of Volodin's plays, which appeared to be carelessly constructed but actually were crafted with great subtlety. These were plays about themselves, "ordinary Soviet people," as they were patronizingly described in the media, about *their* feelings. Volodin's works, an amalgam of sadness and tenderness, were touchingly played by Tovstonogov's accomplished actors— Tatyana Doronina, Zinaida Sharko, Efim Kopelyan, Yevgeny Lebedev, and Kirill Lavrov.

Both Akimov and Tovstonogov dominated their theaters, heading them, respectively, for twenty-seven and thirty-three years. (During the campaign for eradicating "formalism and kowtowing before the West" in Leningrad, Akimov was removed from the Comedy Theater; he was given his troupe back only seven years later.) These two directors were intellectually characteristic of Leningrad dramatic art. In Akimov's theater, the director's first visual impulse determined the concept and form of the play, and the actors sometimes seemed no more than strikingly dressed chess figures, moving in foreordained patterns. Tovstonogov's theater was first of all a showcase for his incomparable actors.

Tovstonogov needed first-class performers to embody his creative ideas, and he knew where to find them. He discovered Sergei Yursky, who later delighted audiences with his interpretation of Chatsky (in Alexander Griboedov's comedy *Woe from Wit*) as the prototype of a modern dissident. Tovstonogov likewise launched the career of Innokenty Smoktunovsky (known in the West as the Hamlet in Kozintsev's film), offering the thirty-two-year-old actor the difficult role of Prince Myshkin in a stage version of Dostoyevsky's *The Idiot.*

That 1957 play took on a legendary aura comparable to that of Meyerhold's production of Lermontov's *Masquerade* in the first half of the century. Meyerhold's production had reflected the emotions of Russian society on the eve of revolutionary cataclysm. A similar sense, that life could now be arranged in completely different ways, imbued Tovstonogov's production.

Prince Myshkin appeared meekly on stage, returning from a long absence in Petersburg—just as those victims of the Great Terror who had managed to survive Stalin's camps were returning to contemporary Leningrad. "His figure is narrow, with elongated arms and legs, not so much a human body as an outline of a body, a poor diagram for life in the flesh,"[65] wrote Naum Berkovsky, an influential Leningrad critic of those years. Smoktunovsky represented the Russian school of spiritualized acting at its peak.

The production was also a manifestation of the return to Leningrad of the tradition of Dostoyevsky, who had been banned by Soviet ideologists as a "reactionary" and "mystic." In that period Dostoyevsky's works began to reappear, and with them surfaced the religious dimension of the Petersburg mythos. In the play *The Idiot*, Smoktunovsky created on stage every evening a visionary space; the audience saw in him a new Russian saint. This theatrical experience became something to tell one's children and grandchildren about.

Another temple of high art in the fifties and sixties was the Kirov (formerly the Maryinsky) Theater—home to one of the world's great classical ballet companies. Existing symbiotically with its famous ballet school, the company cultivated and preserved the technique of classical dance. Surviving the revolutionary hurricanes, the Great Terror, and the war years, these institutions remained true to the principles of Petersburg professionalism.

Here the legendary names of Anna Pavlova and Vaslav Nijinsky were remembered and revered. Their rise in Petersburg and subsequent fairy-tale careers in the West are well-known parts of ballet history. Pavlova created an audience for ballet in the West, particularly in the United States. Nijinsky, who with Tamara Karsavina became the focus of choreographic innovation in Diaghilev's company, speeded audience acceptance of classical dance as a central part of twentieth-century culture. The exotic sets and costumes of Benois and Bakst and the gripping music of Stravinsky and Prokofiev furthered a ballet revolution born in Petersburg.

But mid-century Leningraders had only heard of this revolution. Local ballet battles had had more impact. One concerned the patronage of "choreodramas," the Soviet version of *ballets d'action*, which gained the dominant aesthetic position over the experiments of Fyodor Lopukhov, Balanchine's mentor, and Leonid Yakobson.

Since the early 1930s most successful new productions at the Kirov had been choreodramas. Compared with traditional classic dance, of which people had tired, the form seemed to promise interesting things. *Flames of Paris* (1932; choreographer Vassily Vainonen), *The Fountain of Bakhchisarai* (1934; Rostislav Zakharov), *Laurencia* (1939; Vakhtang Chabukiani), and *Romeo and Juliet* (1940; Mikhail Lavrovsky) all devoted more attention to plot development, psychological motivation, and dramatic expressiveness in corps scenes than to the invention of complicated dance steps. Most of them, including *Romeo and Juliet*, involved the outstanding theater director Sergei Radlov, a follower of Meyerhold, who was artistic director of the Kirov Theater in the second half of the 1930s.

Ivan Sollertinsky, a defender of the genre and a close friend of Shostakovich, wrote, "Orthodox balletomanes are not delighted by *The Fountain of Bakhchisarai*: not enough dancing! There are no dizzying variations with thirty-two fouettés, no pearls of the Italian school technique, no lush parade of symmetrically dancing corps-de-ballet masses in white tunics."[66] In response to these disgruntled "conservatives," Sollertinsky claimed that "*Bakhchisarai* was a happy step forward"; it at least had dramatic action and living characters. He concluded, "No wonder the production was performed by the company with a true creative enthusiasm."[67]

The truth was that the Kirov dancers enjoyed performing in the later much-maligned choreodramas because it gave them an opportunity to expand their repertoire and broaden their audience appeal. Marina Semyonova and Galina Ulanova were masters of classic dance, but many think some of their most vivid achievements were in choreodrama. Ulanova's Juliet became her signature part in Russia and abroad. The two premiere danseurs of the Kirov in that period, Chabukiani and Alexei Ermolayev, made their mark in the new repertoire. Their leaps, poses, and dramatic insight delighted Leningrad audiences and prepared the way for Rudolf Nureyev and Mikhail Baryshnikov.

Stalin closely watched the triumphs of the Kirov troupe; many of its brightest figures, including leading choreographers, were transferred to the Bolshoi. The vitality of choreodrama evaporated, and the genre took on parodic elements in "boy meets tractor" productions. The last effective choreodrama was *The Bronze Horseman*, produced by Zakharov in 1949 in Leningrad, with Konstantin Sergeyev and his real-life wife, Natalya Dudinskaya, in the roles of Yevgeny and his beloved Parasha.

Zakharov, following the party line, interpreted the conflict in *The Bronze Horseman* from the point of view of "historical inevitability." Yevgeny, who lost his beloved in a terrible Petersburg flood, is wrong to blame Peter the Great, who founded Petersburg in a swampy place; state interests supersede ordinary men's desires. To express that idea, the composer Reinhold Glière closed the ballet with an "Anthem to the Great City," which became a kind of unofficial anthem of Leningrad.

But Sergeyev and Dudinskaya turned the choreographers' ideas upside down, eliciting pity and compassion for their characters.

Sergeyev sometimes brought tears to the eyes of the audience. "The downtrodden Yevgeny, transformed by love, seems to rise above all around him. Yevgeny in the world of dreams. And then, a man overwhelmed by disaster. . . . An enormous all-engulfing grief. . . . The mad scene is the highest note of human tragedy, the way Sergeyev did it," recalled a viewer.[68]

Despite success and official recognition, the genre had implacable foes, among whom was the irascible Agrippina Vaganova, a former soloist at the Maryinsky and then a leading teacher of classical dance, who had trained a generation of principal dancers for the Leningrad ballet, including Marina Semyonova, Galina Ulanova, Natalya Dudinskaya, Alla Shelest, Irina Kolpakova, and Alla Osipenko. Vaganova created her own teaching method in the 1920s, which was published as *Fundamentals of the Classic Dance* in 1934 and reprinted many times at home and abroad. (She was helped in writing the book by Lyubov Blok, the widow of the great Petersburg poet, who had become a knowledgeable ballet historian.)

In her book Vaganova laid out the distinctive technical goals of the Petersburg ballet: clarity, precision of movement, and a clean line. Vaganova's pedagogical forte was her ability to assess the artistic potential of her little pupils. As Fyodor Lopukhov recalled, "She took into account the individuality of each girl, the most subtle characteristics, which didn't strike you right away but which the real pedagogue has the sensitivity to sense."

Vaganova did not waste words. Other teachers might give general orders: "Jump! Higher! More grace!" Vaganova's comments were always concrete: "Lift your right side," "take hold of your right hip and bring it back harder," and so on. Vaganova selected specific exercises for each student to strengthen the leg muscles, effecting thereby a painless transition to the most difficult dance combinations. But she never let her students forget that every virtuoso step had to make emotional sense.

Vaganova's counterpart in male dancing was Alexander I. Pushkin, whose method of teaching, like Vaganova's, developed his pupil's best qualities through carefully chosen individual exercises. The unruly and temperamental Rudolf Nureyev was on the brink of being expelled when Pushkin took him into his class; in three years (instead of the customary nine) Pushkin shaped the young rebel into a dancer who stunned the graduation concert audience in 1958 with his animal energy and grace.

Nureyev, who much of the time lived at Pushkin's house, de-

scribed him as a second father.[69] Pushkin steadfastly supported
Nureyev's attempts to expand the expressive boundaries of men's
dancing and nursed his young charge after Nureyev tore a ligament
in his right leg and feared he would never dance again.

Pushkin defended Nureyev in his conflicts with the ballet authorities. These conflicts grew ever more serious. The Kirov ballet,
though detached from the routine of Leningrad life, was still a mi-
crocosm of the Soviet state. The spirit of hierarchical obedience was
deepened by traditional Russian bureaucratism and Soviet ideology.
Indoctrination was pervasive, discipline and conformity were valued
above all else, and manifestations of independence were regarded with
suspicion.

The explosive Nureyev, who resembled the heroes of his
beloved Dostoyevsky (he would later dance the role of Prince Myshkin
in the Valery Panov ballet *The Idiot*), was shrilly lectured on how he,
despite his phenomenal success, was "poisoning the atmosphere" and
"corrupting the collective."[70] Nureyev felt that he could no longer
breathe.

The chance to escape the Soviet system came to Nureyev in
1961 in Paris, while the Kirov Ballet was performing there. He made
his leap to freedom at Le Bourget Airport, fighting off his two husky
"bodyguards." This was a story in the Cold War period, and reper-
cussions of that event were felt in Leningrad. As the flight of a major
artist from the Soviet Union, Nureyev's departure was discussed endlessly not only in ballet circles but among Leningrad intellectuals, despite the extraordinary measures taken by the authorities to hush up
the incident and to force Nureyev's fans to forget their idol.

Soon a new jolt struck the city's cultural elite. In the fall of
1962, on the heels of Stravinsky's triumphant visit to Leningrad, came
fifty-eight-year-old George Balanchine with his New York City Ballet. Balanchine, though he had left thirty-eight years earlier, was in
no hurry to go back. For him, a staunch anti-Communist, the name
Leningrad was deeply offensive. Besides which, he feared being in-
terned by the Soviet authorities.[71]

Under pressure from the Department of State, Balanchine
did go to Russia, where the tour seemed tiring and rather depressing. He thought that he was being followed and that his hotel rooms
were bugged; he was annoyed by the meaningless "aesthetic" discussions with officials from the Ministry of Culture; and he was
deeply saddened by the fact that the authorities had turned Kazan
Cathedral on Nevsky Prospect into the Museum of the History

of Religion and Atheism.[72] (It was restored as a place of worship in 1991.)

But for Leningrad's artistic youth, the visits of Balanchine and Stravinsky were determining events. One memorable moment was a performance of Balanchine's ballet to Stravinsky's *Agon* at the Kirov Theater. Many older dance lovers mockingly called it "Agony," complaining that the Americans did not so much dance as "solve algebra equations with their feet." The dancing and the music seemed abstract and cold; conversations buzzed with the ubiquitous charge of formalism.

But for Leningrad's young musicians and dancers, *Agon* was a breath of fresh air. Even the stage looked different, as if a gigantic sponge had washed off the dusty scenery. *Agon*'s frank physicality (irritating to the old) seemed natural to us, suggesting a society with fewer restrictions than our own. On top of that, we heard jazz rhythms in *Agon;* this too was sexy, like the jazz broadcasts over Voice of America or the glossy pin-up covers of *America,* the propaganda magazine of the U.S. government.

Discovering *Agon* in Leningrad, we appreciated for the first time the unrealized possibilities of the stifled Petersburgian avantgarde. Some said wistfully, "Balanchine brought us the future that was not allowed to flourish in Russia." Balanchine and Stravinsky personified Petersburg culture at its apex, a cosmopolitan art that had achieved world success and recognition.

It turned out that the Petersburg mythos was being realized in the international arena and was not the property of our domestic underground alone. The figure of Akhmatova was suddenly plugged into a global cultural context for us, and this unexpected shift gave a new vitality to the Petersburg mythos. It was also becoming contemporary for us.

The effect of the personal "materialization" in Russia of the titans of the world avant-garde cannot be overestimated. Tales of what they saw and said became for many years the barometer of local good taste in intellectual circles. Even their eccentricities became the object of intense gossip. Brodsky recalled how he came to Akhmatova's house and announced that he had just seen Stravinsky on the street. He began to describe him—small, hunched, with a fashionable hat. "And basically, all that's left of Stravinsky is his nose." "Yes," added Akhmatova. "And his genius."[73]

For a long time the Western branch of Petersburg modernism could not even be mentioned in Russia, at least not with praise. When its two leading representatives—Stravinsky and Balanchine—were allowed to return in triumph, even if only for a short time, to their hometown, the result was a rush of optimism in Leningrad's creative circles and an impulse to accelerate their own artistic experiments.

For thirty-five-year-old Yuri Grigorovich, then a staff choreographer with the Kirov company, Balanchine's work was confirmation of his own conviction that choreodramas were destructive of Russian ballet. In his recent success, *Legend of Love,* Grigorovich had tried complex ballet forms, bringing onto the Kirov stage dance combinations in the style of Fokine. Grigorovich insisted that Fokine and Lopukhov were masters of dance and that Russian ballet had to learn from them and drop all the nonsense about formalism.[74]

Another Kirov choreographer who used the American visit to serve his own creative battles was Leonid Yakobson, Balanchine's contemporary. The resident modernist of the Kirov (he was called the Chagall of ballet, sarcastically by his enemies and delightedly by his fans), Yakobson was having trouble fighting off the attacks of conservative critics of his recent ballet based on Mayakovsky's futurist comedy *Bedbug.* In it Yakobson had mixed elements of pantomime, free dance à la Isadora Duncan, Fokine-style impressionism, and near surrealism.

Yakobson was considered the enfant terrible of the Leningrad ballet. His escapades were overlooked, and his "madness" was a given. I witnessed Yakobson calling cultural bureaucrats idiots to their faces. They merely shrugged it off: the "crazy" Yakobson could get away with things that would cost others their heads.

The more adventurous dancers of the Kirov company were crazy *about* Yakobson; many got the opportunity of their lives through him. For the twenty-one-year-old Natalya Makarova, Yakobson created a lyric role in his satiric *Bedbug:* Zoya, a frail, naive worker who hangs herself over unrequited love. This was a character taken from life, an unhappy woman similar to characters in the contemporaneous Leningrad plays of Alexander Volodin. This role was a turning point for Makarova, exposing her to modern influences.

Yakobson gave a similar impulse seven years later to the career of the twenty-one-year-old Mikhail Baryshnikov with a cameo ballet, *Vestris,* for the international ballet competition in Moscow. Portraying Auguste Vestris, the French eighteenth-century dancer, Baryshnikov's vivid performance of an amalgam of neoclassical steps and pantomime movements astonished the jury, which included Maya Plisetskaya, Ulanova, Grigorovich, and Chabukiani. Plisetskaya, herself a devotee of Yakobson's talent, proclaimed *Vestris* the "ballet theater of my dreams" and gave Baryshnikov thirteen out of a possible twelve. He won the gold medal.

Like Nureyev, Baryshnikov had a classical training under Alexander I. Pushkin. Nureyev's flight left Pushkin with an emotional vacuum, which Baryshnikov, ten years younger than Nureyev, with his curiosity, humor, and charm, managed to fill. Pushkin was the only one to believe that the short-statured Baryshnikov would ever be more than a character dancer.

Pushkin pushed his student to spend long hours over exhausting exercises. At his graduation performance in 1967, Baryshnikov, who had developed balance, musicality, and confidence of execution, proved no less a sensation than Nureyev had been in his day, and he soon took a leading position in the Kirov company.

Baryshnikov had not seen the New York City Ballet perform in 1962, but their second tour in 1972 made him dream of someday working under Balanchine. Curious about the new, Baryshnikov tried to expand his horizons, using new contacts in the Leningrad underground art milieu. Baryshnikov recalled,

> You get no information in the Soviet Union. Not even magazines. And so you read every page of *Vogue,* or other fashion magazines that somebody smuggles in, from beginning to end. You even read who is editor and you remember the names. And there is a black market for art books, just like for underground literature and poetry. Somebody arrives from abroad and the first few nights they don't sleep, because their friends just move in and read and read the forbidden books.

Baryshnikov's reputation in Leningrad as a free spirit was so widely known that when Natalya Makarova defected in 1970, some members of the Kirov commented, "Why, we expected Baryshnikov to do it." Four years later Baryshnikov became the third star of the Kirov Ballet to flee to the West.

These defections cumulatively played an important cultural role. They engendered an extraordinary amount of attention from the Western media and as a result helped to make classic ballet accessible to a wider audience than ever before. They also helped change the attitude of some in the West to Soviet émigrés. Intellectuals here had traditionally been uneasy about them, wary of their "reactionary" attitudes. The appearance in the West of Nureyev, Makarova, and Baryshnikov allowed the debate to focus on the question of artistic freedom and get away from politics. The liberal Western cultural elite felt more comfortable on those grounds, and this shift had an immediate effect on the tone and volume of media coverage of the new émigrés.

The Western version of the Petersburg mythos consequently took on added meaning. Like Fabergé eggs, the ballet was a part of the tsarist heritage that elicited universal enthusiasm. In the wordless, mostly plotless, and therefore apolitical sphere, even Balanchine's "monarchism" seemed somehow acceptable, like a form of artistic nostalgia. The idea of Petersburg as a twentieth-century Atlantis took hold primarily thanks to the efforts of the old Petersburg modernists— Nabokov, Stravinsky, and Balanchine. The new refugees introduced the theme of preservation of classical tradition in contemporary Leningrad into the discourse.

This was quite a shift. All that was needed for the mythos of Leningrad as the cultural heir of imperial Petersburg to take root in the West was a strong intellectual leader. That part was taken by Joseph Brodsky, who had been expelled to the West in 1972.

Brodsky's arrival in the United States had been preceded by dramatic events. In March 1964 the Soviet authorities had sent him north into internal exile, where Brodsky was supposed to spend five years at manual labor to cleanse himself of "harmful" ideas. But Brodsky's trial had turned into a cause célèbre in the Soviet Union and in the West. The transcript, made surreptitiously by an enterprising female journalist, was circulated widely in *samizdat,* the underground method of distributing banned works in the Soviet Union, wherein people "self-published" books by retyping or photographing texts and handing out copies to trusted friends for reading and further copying.

Samizdat handled anything banned by the censors: political tracts, prose, and poetry, including Akhmatova's *Requiem,* which achieved great popularity thereby. The poet Natalya Gorbanevskaya later described how copies of *Requiem* grew. "At least a hundred copies came from me alone during the winter and spring of 1963 (even though I didn't have my own typewriter). I typed at least five versions with four carbons and gave them out on the principle, 'You return my copy and another one,' which I sent out further. Many others did the same thing."

In post-Stalinist Russia, *samizdat* was a revolutionary phenomenon that underlined the weakening of the authorities' control over cultural processes. For the first time, a writer had the opportunity to create a reputation outside official channels. This is what happened with many of Brodsky's poems. Another development was the establishment of regular contacts between Soviet intellectuals and the Western media. Many works from *samizdat* were clandestinely sent to the West, published there in translation (and sometimes in Russian), then returned to the USSR, but in print form—magazines, anthologies, or books.

Brodsky's poems began being published in the West in 1964. The transcript of his trial—the first such document to reach the West—was also widely known. This awareness explains the appearance of a document that played, as we can see today, a substantial role in further developments: a private letter from Jean-Paul Sartre, dated August 17, 1965, to Chairman of the Presidium of the Supreme Soviet of the USSR Anastas Mikoyan.

> Dear Mr. President,
>
> I allow myself to appeal to you with this letter only because I am a friend of your great country. I often visit your country, meet many writers, and know that what the Western foes of peaceful coexistence are already calling the Brodsky Affair is nothing more than an inexplicable and regrettable exception. But I would like to inform you that the anti-Soviet press will use it to start a wide campaign and present this exception as a typical example of Soviet justice; it has gone as far as reproaching the authorities for hostility toward the intelligentsia and anti-Semitism. Until the early months of 1965, we proponents of a broad juxtaposition of various cultures had a simple reply to this scurrilous propaganda: our Soviet friends had assured us that the attention of the higher courts is turned to the Brodsky case and the decisions of the court will be reviewed. Unfortunately, time passed, and we learned that nothing had been done. The attacks of the enemies of the USSR, who are also our enemies, are becoming more and more harsh. For instance, I want to note that I have frequently been asked to express my opinion publicly. Until the present time I have been refusing to do so, but remaining silent is becoming as difficult as responding.
>
> I want to let you know, Mr. President, about the anxiety we are undergoing. We are not unaware of how difficult it is within any social system to review decisions that have been made. But knowing your profound humanity and your interest in strengthening cultural ties between East and West within the framework of ideological struggle, I am daring to send you this highly personal letter, to ask

you in the name of my sincere friendship for socialist countries, on which we pin all our hopes, to come to the defense of a very young man, who already is or, perhaps, will become a good poet.[75]

Obviously, Sartre, who in his time had attacked Nabokov for doing nothing—unlike Soviet writers—to build a socialist society, would send such a request (found in the Party archives by the Moscow newspaper *Literaturnaya gazeta* in 1993) only as the result of extraordinary social pressure. The Kremlin must have understood this. In November 1965 Brodsky was given early release from his northern exile and returned to Leningrad.

A few months later he (and many others of us) suffered a cruel blow: on March 5, 1966, thirteen years to the day after Stalin's death, Akhmatova died of a heart attack at the age of seventy-six. She had not lived to see the official publication of *Requiem* or the full text of her masterpiece, *Poem Without a Hero*. But she knew that these works would not vanish without trace, since they had been bred into the bone of the Russian intellectual elite by then.

Akhmatova also knew that she was leaving behind a poetic movement she had created; the "magic choir," as she had dubbed them, consisting of Brodsky, Bobyshev, Nayman, and Rein, were now part of the Petersburg literary mythos. (After Akhmatova's death, the group got another name coined by Bobyshev—Akhmatova's orphans.)

Brodsky recalled that when someone began a eulogy at her funeral with the words, "With Akhmatova's departure has ended . . . ," everything inside him rejected those words. "Nothing had ended, nothing could or would end as long as we existed. Choir magical or not. Not because we remember her poetry or whether we write or not, but because she had become part of us, part of our souls, if you will."[76]

According to Akhmatova's wishes, the funeral service was at the Nikolsky Cathedral, where a large crowd (perhaps as many as fifteen hundred people) gathered on the cold morning of March 10. They were mostly Leningrad's young people; an old beggar woman at the church gate said, "They keep coming, more and more, and they're all her students!" A memorial tribute was held for her at the Writers' Union. Akhmatova's son, Lev Gumilyov, a former inmate of the Stalin camps and at this time a famous historian, asked me to play something at the ceremony, adding hastily, "But I'd like it to be a Russian

Orthodox composer." We agreed on Prokofiev. But that evening, at a private wake where Gumilyov was not present, we played Bach, whose works Akhmatova loved.

Music played an important part in Akhmatova's life. With me she talked about, among others, Schumann, Mussorgsky, and Tchaikovsky, especially his *Pathetique* Symphony. Akhmatova also talked about Shostakovich and Stravinsky, whose books of conversations with Robert Craft she had read attentively, paying particular attention to the inaccuracies in the description of their mutual friends in old Petersburg.

Conversations with Akhmatova tended to take place on two planes, the everyday and the transcendent. Brodsky formulated it accurately: "Of course we talked about literature, of course we gossiped, drank vodka, listened to Mozart, and laughed at the government."[77] And yet because of the power of Akhmatova's mind and her special place as witness to history and preserver of the Petersburg mythos, according to Brodsky, "there was always a field around her that permitted no access to scoundrels. And belonging to that field, to that circle, determined the character, behavior, and attitude toward life for many—almost all—of its inhabitants."[78]

After Akhmatova's death the moral atmosphere of Leningrad changed substantially: the figure that had connected eras was gone, the person against whom people checked their behavior and whose judgments they awaited and feared. This depressed the already grim city even further. The Leningrad Party hacks of the period were more reactionary and vengeful than their Moscow counterparts. This condition manifested constantly, in important decisions and in trifles.

When the local authorities banned a Western film that was allowed in Moscow and someone spoke up about it, he might get the smug response, "Leningrad, comrades, does not need to repeat Moscow's mistakes!" The director of the Leningrad Philharmonic was fired because the performance by a Western ensemble of one of Bach's church cantatas accidentally fell on Russian Orthodox Easter, a holiday that the Party was trying to eradicate from the popular consciousness.

The Leningrad artist Gavriil Glikman recalled that once, during the regime of Vassily Tolstikov, one of the most unpredictable and stupid Leningrad bosses, Shostakovich said to him sadly, "I think that you should hide your works carefully. Dig a hole, line it with concrete, and put your canvases in there. Who knows, today Tolstikov is in a good mood, but tomorrow they might all be destroyed." (It is said that when Tolstikov received a delegation of American congressmen and one asked about the city's mortality figures, Tolstikov replied confidently, "There is no mortality in Leningrad.")

Upon Brodsky's return from exile, Party officials tried to influence him with the usual carrot and stick. They gave him the opportunity to publish a few poems. At the same time that people were being arrested for keeping typewritten copies of the trial transcript, they offered to publish a collection of his works. However, the authorities made it a condition for publication that Brodsky agree to collaborate with the secret police as an informer. In a confrontational meeting with the KGB officials, Brodsky said, echoing an old remark of Shklovsky's, "This conversation is absurd, because we're not talking as equals. Behind you is an enormous system, and behind me is half a room, my typewriter, and nothing else."[79] The planned collection of Brodsky's poems was canceled.

This game continued until May 1972, when Brodsky was called in to the visa department of the local police and told to leave for the West immediately. When Brodsky asked, "And if I refuse?" the police colonel replied with an unambiguous threat, "Then, Brodsky, in the very near future you will have a very hot time."[80]

Trying to forestall the inevitable, Brodsky appealed directly to Leonid Brezhnev in a letter asking for repeal of his deportation. "It is bitter for me to leave Russia. I was born, grew up, and lived here, and I owe everything I am to it. Everything bad that was my lot is more than compensated by the good, and I never felt injured by the Homeland. I do not feel that way now. For though I cease being a citizen of the USSR, I do not cease being a Russian poet. I know that I will return; poets always return: in the flesh or on paper. I want to believe that it will be both."[81]

Brodsky did not receive a response. If Brezhnev read the poet's letter, its tone must have seemed strange and unusual. "We are all condemned to the same thing: death. I, who am writing these lines, will die, and you, who are reading them, will die, too. Our work will be left, but even that will not last forever. That is why no one should interfere with another in doing his work."[82] Free of philosophical ruminations, Sartre's letter in defense of Brodsky demonstrates a greater understanding of how a Soviet apparatchik's brain functions. Brodsky was in Austria by June; he later came to the United States and eventually settled in New York City.

His elderly parents were left behind in Leningrad, and Brodsky never saw them again. The Soviet authorities would not allow them to visit their son in America. When they died, the authorities vengefully kept Brodsky from attending their funeral in Leningrad. He also left behind his four-year-old son, Andrei, whose mother was the artist Marianna Basmanova, to whom Brodsky had dedicated his 1983 collection *New Stanzas to Augusta*—eighty love poems written over the course of twenty years.

Brodsky's expulsion deprived him of communication with his devoted readers in Leningrad, whose attention, understanding, and support had made his readings so memorable. He would gradually raise his guttural voice to something like singing and, shamanlike, bring his audience under his spell.

Soviet authorities counted on such separations to have a traumatic effect. Exile had ended the creative life of more than one Russian writer. For Brodsky the event was an unhealing wound. But his tormentors had underestimated his strength of character and cosmopolitan turn of mind. The acmeist ideology, "longing for world culture," which Brodsky had learned through Akhmatova, also eased his transplantation. In addition, Brodsky was not long without Russian companionship in the West.

As the result of the Soviet policy to push potential troublemakers out of the country, a significant number of new émigrés from Leningrad had gathered in America (primarily in New York); many had been acquaintances or friends of Brodsky's from his youth. Among them were the poets Lev Loseff, Dmitri Bobyshev, and Konstantin Kuzminsky, the writer Sergei Dovlatov, the cultural critics Boris Paramonov and Gennady Smakov, and the artists Mihail Chemiakin and Igor Tulipanov.

The Party's ideological strategists were sure that all these creative personalities would—after some initial interest in them—soon sink to the bottom, never to return. They based this strategy on the fact that the old Russian émigrés had never managed to develop a successful political dialogue and even less so a union with liberal Western intellectuals. To make sure that it would not happen this time either, Soviet propagandists denounced the new émigrés, many of whom were Jewish, for fascistic leanings.

To the horde of unfinished-off fascist lackeys and criminals come petty little people reaching for their toady's hunk of meat, "at long last" having reached the West, people who just recently had declared their loyalty to the ideals of pure art and creative freedom, who had bombastically bleated about their love for their Homeland. . . . And now works like "Pushkin and Brodsky" are being scribbled about these "newest" arrivals, works that elicit nothing but revulsion. Those who are capable of treachery become traitors. They made their choice and took the path of betrayal. They have been turned, not to put it too harshly, into ideological jesters.[83]

The effect of this propaganda barrage was negligible, however. Soviet Communism had lost its attractiveness, and Western intellectuals no longer had anything against contacts with Soviet nonconformists. The authorities had to resort to crude pressure, which sometimes (more frequently in Europe than in the United Stated) had the desired effect. For instance, the Spoleto Festival withdrew its invitation to Brodsky (whom Soviet propaganda now called "sponger off Western secret services") after the Soviet ambassador to Italy threatened to rescind the promised performances of the Perm Ballet.[84]

Despite these minor setbacks, Brodsky's intellect and erudition quickly made him a member of the American creative elite, so that he had every reason as early as 1976 to write in a poem addressed to his fellow Leningrad émigré and new friend, Mikhail Baryshnikov,

And as for where in space and time one's toe end touches,
well, earth is hard all over; try the States.

A noted American liberal intellectual once confessed to Brodsky that he had made Soviet nonconformity acceptable to her and to people like her. This acceptability extended to the latest incarnation of the Petersburg mythos, which Brodsky had brought with him from Leningrad.

Culturally, Brodsky became an heir to the three great representatives of the old Petersburg modernism in America—Stravinsky, Nabokov, and Balanchine. Brodsky was once called a "skeptical classicist," and in that sense his aesthetics are close to that of this great troika. Like them, Brodsky constantly used classical models and mythogeny, transforming and breaking them, subjecting them to ironic reworking and philosophical commentary. Brodsky's aesthetic, like theirs, was formed in great part by the Petersburg landscape, "so classicist that it becomes tantamount to a person's mental state. It's a kind of rhythm, completely conscious."[85]

While attesting ironically, "I am infected with normal classicism," Brodsky subjected it to every possible test of modernism and existential Russian philosophy (his favorite thinkers are Nikolai Berdyaev and Lev Shestov). In this he was also following Stravinsky, Nabokov, and Balanchine. Brodsky is a constant experimenter, complicating the shape of his lines, extending or shortening their length, often using complicated or archaic linguistic constructions, introducing exotic rhymes and refined puns. Brodsky deploys these devices with the ease of his Russian predecessors.

On the ideological level, at least one parallel exists between Brodsky's Petersburg mythos and Balanchine's work. The imperial theme is important for both. In Balanchine the line is clearly drawn in several of his major ballets, primarily those to music of Tchaikovsky. Identifying Petersburg with the empire was typical of Russian poets as early as the eighteenth century. Two of them—Antioch Kantemir and Gavriil Derzhavin—were particularly dear to Brodsky, for whom the concept of empire became central. In that sense Brodsky, like Mandelstam, can be called a "state-thinking" Russian poet.

The metaphor of empire is attractive to Brodsky because, paradoxically, in the closed imperial hierarchy he imagines, the poet holds a central position along with the emperor. The poet is in opposition to the tyrant, but in the organized space of the empire, they inevitably clash only to be reunited by the imperial course of events.

In *Anno Domini,* written in 1968 and dedicated to Marianna Basmanova, Brodsky re-created a mythological Roman Empire and with two or three strokes makes the governor general, fallen into disfavor, somehow reminiscent of the Leningrad Party boss Tolstikov, who was teetering on the brink of removal over differences with the Kremlin. He immediately introduces an autobiographical theme that links the fates of the poet and the tyrant: ". . . him the Emperor does not want to see, nor me—my son and Cynthia." According to Brodsky, "the idea of an artistic bohemia can be really achieved only in a centralized state, since it appears as a mirror reflection of that centralization."[86]

Peter the Great, according to Brodsky, played the role of the first Russian cosmopolite against the background of the "wild sets" of his new capital. One of Peter's main achievements was his decision to found the capital by the sea—not for a military or economic purpose but for the metaphysical concept of freedom, which comes from the sea when "movement is not limited by the earth." The literature created in Petersburg is marked by "the awareness that it is all being written from the edge of the earth. And if we can speak of some general concept, or tonality, or tuning fork of Petersburg culture, it would be alienation."[87]

These ideas and others about the Petersburg mythos were imparted to Western audiences in Brodsky's lectures, poetry readings (he gave over sixty in his first eighteen months in America), and especially the series of essays dedicated to his native city ("Less Than One: A Guide to a Renamed City"; "In a Room and a Half") and its writers: Dostoyevsky ("The Power of the Elements"), Mandelstam ("The Child of Civilization"), and Akhmatova ("The Keening Muse"). The essays were collected in *Less Than One* (1986), which won the National Book Critics Award for criticism.

Very soon quotations from Brodsky's Petersburg essays began appearing in Western meditations on Leningrad next to quotations from Nabokov's *Speak, Memory*. The intellectual elite had apparently absorbed the latest vision of the Petersburg mythos as presented by Brodsky and the image of contemporary Leningrad tied to that vision. Typical is Hortense Calisher's casual comparison of Leningrad to a "decoratively bleeding heart."[88] The Russian and foreign branches of Petersburg modernism finally came together in the minds of Western intellectuals; this was due to Brodsky, who became the link between Mandelstam and Akhmatova on one side and Stravinsky, Nabokov, and Balanchine on the other. In the person of Brodsky, the West recognized the contemporary vitality of the Petersburg tradition.

A significant sign of this recognition was the not-unexpected Nobel Prize for Literature in 1987 for his poetry and essays. In his Nobel lecture Brodsky emphasized the successional nature of his work, its ties with the past; he spoke of that in many interviews. But Brodsky told me that the strongest emotional experience connected with professional recognition was the news, arriving while he was still in Leningrad, that the British publisher was preparing a collection of his poems with a preface by W. H. Auden. Everything else, he said, was in a sense an "anticlimax." He added, "Of course, it's a pity that my mother and father did not live to see the Nobel Prize."[89]

Despite the fact that Mikhail Gorbachev had been head of the Soviet Union for two years by then and *perestroika* and *glasnost* had become state slogans, Soviet officialdom greeted the award of the Nobel Prize to Brodsky with suspicion and hostility. A special secret memorandum prepared by the KGB for the Soviet leadership stated that the prize "is a provocative political act by reactionary circles in the West, intended to halt the growing sympathy of public opinion in the world for our country's peace-loving foreign policy."[90]

Damage control went into effect. Nowadays, of course, Soviet ideologists could not act as crudely as they had done during the anti-Brodsky campaign of 1964, when the editor-in-chief of *Literaturnaya gazeta* announced in New York, "Brodsky is what we call scum, simply ordinary scum." In 1987 a foreign ministry spokesman was more diplomatic, muttering that "the tastes of the Nobel Prize committee are somewhat strange sometimes." For internal consumption, however, Moscow decided that the most effective policy would be silence.

The Leningrad intelligentsia received the news of Brodsky's Nobel Prize with rejoicing. It was recognition and vindication of the "parasite" and "scum" Brodsky and of all of the Petersburg literature that had been stifled from Blok and Gumilyov to Mandelstam and Akhmatova. In Brodsky the international community was honoring the other Petersburg geniuses who had never been so honored.

The prize was a reason for spiritual self-rehabilitation. The intelligentsia had not been able to protect Brodsky from persecution by the authorities either in 1964 or in 1972, and ever since his expulsion to the West, it had felt like a group without a leader and under constant siege. Any excuse to persecute Leningrad intellectuals was seized upon, such as the continuing underground dissemination of Brodsky's poems. In 1974 Vladimir Maramzin, a satiric writer like Zoshchenko, was arrested for compiling a samizdat collection of Brodsky's works. Mikhail Kheifetz, who wrote the introduction to the collection, was sentenced to four years in the camps and two years in exile; the sentence read, "Kheifetz's intentions to undermine and weaken Soviet power is proven by all his actions."

Brodsky's trial, with its symbolic overtones, had been enough to put the poet into the mythological ranks of the martyrs of the Petersburg pantheon: Blok-Gumilyov-Mandelstam-Akhmatova. His expulsion to the West completed the process, for in those years the émigrés vanished completely, both physically and spiritually. From those who remained, there could be no talk of return; even public mention of the exile's name was forbidden.

For Leningrad poetry lovers Brodsky was dead, and the news that sometimes reached them from America was like news from "the other side." His poetry was perceived as a contemporary classic. The situation was similar to the growth of Gumilyov's fame after his execution by firing squad in 1921. A contemporary Petrograder commented then, "Whenever the state clashes with a poet, I feel so sorry for the poor state. What's the worst the state can do to a poet? Kill him! But you can't kill poetry, it is immortal, and the poor state suffers defeat every time."[91]

The youth of Leningrad, seeking new paths, came into contact with the Petersburg mythos through Brodsky's poetry, whose thought, style, vocabulary, diction, and technique spoke to them. Brodsky is a philosophical poet; his work is founded on Kierkegaard, the existentialists, and early-twentieth-century Russian religious philosophers. This foundation, as well as Brodsky's complex dialogue with the Judaeo-Christian ethic, attracted the sympathy and interest of new readers of underground literature in Leningrad and throughout the USSR. Many sought in his poems the key to the "secret garden" of the old Petersburg culture, vanished, some thought, forever.

For the elite, one unexpected impression created by the new poems and essays that reached them from the West through clandestine channels was their "westernization." Even when he lived in Russia, Brodsky had exhibited a lively interest in the English metaphysical poets John Donne and George Herbert and in Robert Frost and W. H. Auden. He also translated Tom Stoppard's play *Rosencrantz and Guildenstern Are Dead*. In the West Brodsky immersed himself further in modern English-language poetry.

Every new Western-influenced work by Brodsky that reached Leningrad was consumed and debated. Readers were fascinated to learn that Brodsky wrote poetry in Russian with a pen and essays in English on a typewriter. The cosmopolitan streak had grown quite weak by then, the result of decades of enforced isolation from any suspicious outside influences. The former "window into Europe" was slammed shut so firmly that Leningraders began calling the once-sparkling capital "a great city with a regional fate." Brodsky's work helped the Leningrad intelligentsia pry open a crack in the window.

"The barbarians have taken over a country with a high civilization—that was the message of the life around us," said a Leningrad writer, thus characterizing the era's bleak outlook. He added a description of the "Brodsky effect" in Leningrad. "World culture, that was the name of the distant captured land to which our membership was returned to us by Brodsky's poems. They came as news that not the whole country had been occupied and defiled, that a free island survived somewhere. And that gave birth to a happy guess: perhaps we were not barbarians either."[92]

One of the leading cultural figures of Leningrad in these years was the poet Alexander Kushner, specifically Petersburgian in many aspects of his talent. First published in his early twenties, Kushner—unlike Brodsky, four years his junior—released collection after collection of his works through Soviet publishing houses apparently without any obstacles. This surprised many people, since Kushner—Jewish, like Brodsky—did not make ideological compromises with the authorities and did not write odious official verse: his classically oriented works, focused on the fading beauty of his native city, celebrated the twilight world of the Leningrad intellectual.

A bespectacled, almost shy reader, Kushner was loved in Leningrad for the tenderness of his creations, their refinement, and the dignity with which he defended the right to an independent inner life where pompous state propaganda could not intrude.

Kushner recalled how Brodsky maintained that the poet must upset the reader, "grab him by the throat." Such an attack on the reader would be inconceivable for Kushner, for he and Brodsky are poets of diametrically opposed temperaments. Brodsky noted with understanding that Kushner's works were marked by "a restrained tone, an absence of hysteria, loud pronouncements, and overwrought gesticulations." Others described the obvious incompatibility of the two poets as Sergei Dovlatov did. "The difference between Kushner and Brodsky is the difference between sadness and anguish, fear and horror. Sadness and fear are reactions to the times; anguish and horror, reactions to eternity."

Kushner and Brodsky share the theme of inner freedom and its attendant imperial strain, as well as the "longing for world culture" about which their idol Mandelstam spoke. But fate kept Kushner within the limits of Leningrad, and it increasingly became the main subject of his works.

Kushner was making a ritual journey in his poems "from Leningrad to Petersburg," taking with him a contingent of fellow travelers. For him this imaginary transport was becoming a narcotic. For Leningrad readers, too, Kushner's poetry was an escape because in it they could meet the shades of Pushkin, Nekrasov, Dostoyevsky, Blok, Mandelstam, and Akhmatova. Kushner, in a typically Petersburg manner, sowed his works with literary images, parallels, and allusions.

In some poems, those in the know found a hidden portrait of exiled Brodsky.

While Kushner's works may have been a kind of literary drug, real narcotics and alcohol were flooding intellectual Leningrad. This too was a long-standing Petersburg tradition. The city's founder, Peter the Great, had been a tireless drinker. Alexander Menshikov, Petersburg's first governor, was also a drunkard. The sprees and binges of the aristocracy became a cliché in Petersburg's artistic circles as a sign of independence and challenge to the government.

A high official of Nicholas I's regime recalled that "in close familiarity with all the innkeepers, whores, and wenches, Pushkin represented the filthiest debauchery."[93] For Pushkin and his contemporaries, immoderate imbibing among friends was tantamount to a symbolic sacrifice on the altar of liberty. The first major Petersburg artist to die of alcohol abuse was Mussorgsky. A contemporary bitterly recalled that "drunkenness was almost inevitable for a talented man of the period."[94]

The Russian reforms of the 1860s—the emancipation of the serfs and its attendant circumscribed liberalization—brought confusion and ferment to the minds of the Petersburg intelligentsia described by one observer thus:

> The more sensitive, more responsive writers in society saw that the freedom they had imagined was not at all what they got in reality, that individuality was still enslaved, that arbitrary rule still reigned in Mother Russia along with the most shameless, most vile brute force. And these wise men, the salt of the Russian earth, all of them young and life-loving, were driven to drink from the goblet of green wine.[95]

Almost one hundred years later in Soviet Leningrad, vodka (as well as some narcotics, like morphine, which could be gotten at hospitals) was still a potent symbol of confrontation with the authorities. The poet Lev Loseff admitted that "we drank fantastic amounts," explaining, "I owe everything good in my life to vodka. Vodka was the catalyst of spiritual emancipation, opening doors into interesting cellars of the subconscious and at the same time teaching me not to be afraid—of people, or the authorities."

Sergei Dovlatov commented on the Dostoyevskian world of the Leningrad cultural underground. "The years of miserable existence affected the psyche. The large amount of mental illness is evidence of that. And of course, the constant companion of the Russian writer reigned here—alcohol. We drank a lot, indiscriminately until we passed out and hallucinated." Dovlatov, who had periodic bouts of wild drinking himself, described how the esoteric Leningrad poet Mikhail Eryomin stepped out of a window when drunk and became crippled for life after landing on the concrete courtyard below. The tempestuous Gleb Gorbovsky, who called himself a "never-drying jester" and admitted to drinking any liquid with alcohol in it (including varnish, cologne, and dandruff lotion), later lamented the destructive role of vodka in the lives of Leningrad nonconformists: "So many brilliant talents died, broken halfway on the road to self-discovery!"

Gorbovsky recalled the fate in the early 1960s of Rid Grachev, the avant-garde prose writer and student of French existentialism, "The last time I saw the man was in a nuthouse, where I was with the D.T.'s. I remember it clearly: down the corridor of the former women's prison comes Rid Grachev toward me and, despite everything, smiling. Not at me—at the whole world."

Andrei Bitov, the major writer in the Petersburg tradition of recent decades, considered Grachev a leader and one of his teachers in prose. Bitov started out as a poet in the late fifties in one of the many literary associations in Leningrad—at the Mining Institute where Bitov was a student. Bitov and his friends were joined by Kushner and Gorbovsky, who later maintained that this collective of young poets put "the accent of its creative efforts on fighting official literary policy, on participation in the spiritual renewal of society in the fog of the moral thaw of those times."

Leningrad's Party authorities watched those young poets closely, and when censors found poetry with "hidden anti-Soviet subtext" in their first collection, of which 300 copies had been printed, the books were publicly burned in the courtyard of the Mining Institute.

Despite such measures, the popularity of the budding poets grew, and in the best Petersburg traditions, they joined aesthetic battle among themselves but mostly in the underground. The Mining Institute poets were jealous of the "magic choir" around Akhmatova (Rein, Nayman, Bobyshev, and Brodsky), considering it too refined. Some of the Akhmatova circle, in turn, were not very kind to the young

Leningrad "avant-gardists," who were yet another grouping, which consisted of Vladimir Ufliand, Loseff, Eryomin, and Viktor Krivulin.

When in 1957 the Mining poets invited the leading older female poet to meet them, it was not Akhmatova they asked, but the bard of the siege of Leningrad, Olga Berggolts. To invite Akhmatova "was just as unimaginable as inviting Princess Trubetskaya from the Decembrist era to a communal flat."[96] But the young poets felt Berggolts was one of them: approachable, unaristocratic, someone who brought them "the truth about the desperate unsettledness of the hungry and disorganized world."[97]

They particularly loved Berggolts's unpublished poems (which were widely known in samizdat) about her horrible years in the Great Terror, when the then-pregnant poet was arrested by the Leningrad secret police shortly after her former husband, Boris Kornilov (lyricist of Shostakovich's song for the film Counterplan). Kornilov was shot, but they released Berggolts after cruelly kicking her in the belly over and over. She miscarried and lost the ability to bear children. After this suffering and the siege, Berggolts took to the bottle and was almost never again seen sober.

I came to Berggolts's apartment in the 1960s to interview her. She opened the door herself; she was still in her fifties then. I had an idea of her condition, but I was still rather frightened to see a woman in a robe tossed over her naked body, her hair limp and sticky, her gaze unfocused. She could barely stand and hoarsely invited me into her room.

The conversation, which wandered at first, inevitably came to Kornilov's death. She lit a cigarette and spoke about his suffering and her own with interruptions from a hacking cough. This Dostoyevskian image was far from Akhmatova's majesty. But it was as the drunken madonna of Leningrad that Berggolts attracted the compassion of the Mining poets, including Bitov.

Bitov recalled the "strange friendships" with older Leningrad writers, who during the Khrushchev thaw

> suddenly gained the childlike ability to talk about what interested them, and in us they found a grateful audience. Since they were richer, they could put a bottle of vodka and some food on the table and invite the young people. Kushner used to visit Lydia Ginzburg, the last surviving student of Tynyanov. Then he brought me to see Ginzburg. We did not know then that she wrote excellent prose. We were also invited by one of the Serapion brothers, Mikhail Slonimsky. We

visited Professor Berkovsky, erudite and charming. They all enlightened us.[98]

Leaving poetry for prose, Bitov was one of the first to present
and analyze the character of the new "superfluous man" in Russian
literature, the young Leningrad intellectual, disillusioned by official
ideals and clumsily feeling his way, tripping at every step, toward a
still inchoate system of moral values. (Bitov was particularly attentive
to the description of tiny moral vacillations.)
    Bitov's hero, usually a first-person narrator, aimlessly wan-
dered the streets of the city and, in the classical tradition, tried to stifle the depression gnawing at him in skid row dens frequented by local
bums. "Here they smoke and here they drink vodka, here they live
their ended lives. Here is hubbub and familiar faces. And apparently
even the liquor authorities understand that it is useless to try to combat this. The red vending machine spits out my beloved Volzhskoe
wine and will spit it out as often as I want it. I want it more times than
I can remember."
    Even though Bitov's work had, from the very beginning (he
was first published in 1960, when he was in his early twenties), a
marked autobiographical character, a distance was maintained between the narrator and the author, a distance that Bitov probably
wanted to dissolve in the flow of lyric prose. He did it by developing
his own form of the Russian travelogue genre, covering the entire Soviet Union in search of creative stimuli and impressions—in particular, joining geological expeditions in the Kola Peninsula, beyond Lake
Baikal, in Central Asia, and in Karelia.
    This was a fashion of the times, probably started by Brodsky.
For Brodsky (unlike the professional mining engineer Bitov) such an
expedition was a way of "breaking out" of the system and simultaneously achieving poetic self-assertion. Thanks to Brodsky, who
boasted that he "filled geological expeditions with schizophrenics, alcoholics, and poets," this not easy but romantic way of making money
was taken up by many Leningrad writers, including Gorbovsky and
Kuzminsky. It was an escape.
    But for Bitov distant travels were an opportunity to describe
sensibilities and problems in a more multifaceted way. In that sense,
Bitov's travel sketches (particularly popular were his descriptions of
voyages to Armenia and Georgia), often marked by the more or less
direct influences of Proust, Joyce, and Nabokov, and ruminating on
the common cultural and political dreams of the peoples who inhab-

ited the country, were a direct continuation of the imperial theme of Russian literature, which went back to Pushkin. Even on the outer limits of the empire, Bitov remained an unmistakably Petersburgian type: restrained, observant, ironic, and uncertain about matters great and small.

Petersburg—both the imperial city of Pushkin and its Leningrad mutation—became one of the main characters of the experimental novel *Pushkin House,* planned by Bitov as a requiem for the Petersburg intelligentsia. He sat down to write it in 1964, at the very end of the Khrushchev period, sensing, as he called it, the despair of a dying era. (He later admitted that the despair could have also been the shock of Brodsky's trial, which Bitov attended as a frightened spectator.)[99]

The novel's hero, the young philologist Lev Odoevtsev, worked at Pushkin House, the Institute of Russian Literature of the Academy of Sciences in Leningrad, the oldest research institution of its kind in the country. It had been praised by Blok in a 1921 poem, a line from which is used as the novel's epigraph. But the title *Pushkin House* (Bitov had considered *A la Recherche du destin perdu* and *Hooligan's Wake*) carried symbolic significance: this was all of Petersburg, all of Russia, and most important, all of Russian literature.

The introduction of the classics of the Petersburg canon into the novel's fabric is a constant factor: epigraphs, citations (open and hidden), borrowings, and allusions to Pushkin (particularly *The Bronze Horseman*), Lermontov, Dostoyevsky, and Zoshchenko collide, re-creating the inner world of a hereditary Leningrad intellectual of the late twentieth century.

It was important for Bitov that his hero be an aristocrat, a prince, but perhaps more important, that both his hero's father and grandfather be professional philologists. This provided an opportunity to draw parallels between the history of the Odoevtsev family and the history of twentieth-century Russian literature as well as to decorate his otherwise static plot with a garland of essays about great Russian writers.

The lot of *Pushkin House* was a hard one, simultaneously typical and not; what Bitov called "a strange life."[100] The novel grew in fits and starts and was completed in the fall of 1970. Bitov recalled how after a sleepless night spent finishing the last few pages, he went out to bring the manuscript to a publishing house and on Nevsky Prospect ran into Brodsky ("who was no Nobel laureate then, but just a hoodlum like the rest of us," Bitov added). Brodsky asked, "Where are you going?"

"I've just finished my novel; it's called *Pushkin House;* I'm taking it to the publisher."

"I got a postcard today from Nabokov about my *Gorbunov and Gorchakov*," said Brodsky.

"And what did Nabokov have to say?"

"That in Russian poetry one encounters such meter extremely rarely."

Having boasted to each other in this way, Brodsky and Bitov parted. Bitov's hopes, however, were not justified: the publishing house refused to print his novel.[101] Thus began *Pushkin House*'s existence as a *samizdat* text.

Bitov persisted in getting at least parts of the novel past the censors. And by hook and by crook, after agreeing to major changes, he did manage to publish a series of excerpts under various titles, making up only a third of *Pushkin House*. It was a humiliating experience. The novel's key moments—including the culminating scene of the hero's Homeric drinking bout that precedes a duel with ancient (Pushkin) pistols—never reached the average reader, and the symbolic aspect of *Pushkin House* as a wake for the Russian intellectual remained hidden.

After waiting a few more years and concluding that further compromises were unacceptable, Bitov took a daring step: he allowed *Pushkin House* to be published (in Russian) in 1978 by Ardis, the American publishing house whose authors included Nabokov and Brodsky. Bitov later recalled his emotions when he finally held a copy of this version of his long-suffering novel: "astonishment, then fear, then hope—'maybe I'll get away with it.' "[102]

Though not openly subjected to repressions, *Pushkin House* remained on the "proscribed list" of the Soviet censors until 1987, when, seventeen years after its completion, it was printed by the Moscow journal *Novy mir* and became a sensation of the *glasnost* era.

Over the years *Pushkin House* became larded with author's comments, notations, and essays that belonged to the pen of either Bitov or his philologist hero. In this postmodernist structural openness Bitov's work somewhat resembled Akhmatova's *Poem Without a Hero,* which curiously Bitov had not originally appreciated. After Akhmatova had given Bitov a typewritten variant of *Poem Without a Hero* to read, he returned it with a sheepish remark about "not being a master of compliments." Akhmatova quickly sized up the situation: "Well, why aren't you a master?" and slammed the door in his face. The dialogue had failed.[103]

The structural manipulations of *Pushkin House,* which transformed the novel into an essentially open text, as well as the author's descriptive experiments and use of interior monologue and stream of consciousness, place Bitov's work among the landmark modernist prose works about Petersburg, including Bely's *Petersburg,* Vaginov's novels, Kharms's *Incidents,* Zoshchenko's stories, and Nabokov's *Speak, Memory.*

Gorbovsky once compared the rhythm of Bitov's prose with "the movement of a solitary swimmer among the waves of a commonplace emptiness when the swimmer seems about to drown, but again and again his head is seen above the surface; the loneliness of such swimmers is no tragedy, nothing sad about it, but almost a worldview or even a religion." Bitov's experience of "outsideness" had as one source Petersburg's outside location and position vis-à-vis the rest of the country.

Bitov's earliest memories involved the siege of Leningrad ("bombs, corpses all around—that wasn't scary, what was scary was being hungry"). Like many others, he felt that he had been raised by the city itself. "We read Leningrad like a book."[104] A contemporary of Bitov's, Viktor Sosnora, the author of tragic, surrealist poems and historical prose about Petersburg, confirmed that sense. "Petersburg's scenery and sets create a special psychological climate that basically forms you as a writer."[105]

In *Pushkin House* Bitov described—and mourned—the defeat and destruction of the Leningrad intellectual by a hostile cultural machine. In some ways he thus summed up the fate of his generation. The dark convolutions of Leningrad life became the main theme for Bitov's contemporaries and friends in the "radiant underground" (as Bitov dubbed their precarious existence), including the absurdist writer Viktor Golyavkin and the lyrical stylist Valery Popov, whose works combine naturalism and bizarrerie. As Alexander Volodin, whose melancholy autobiography *Notes of an Unsober Man* was begun in those years, commented, "Life, its most secret vices and illnesses cannot remain unreflected in art. Like twin stars, life and art are joined by an invisible thread. If an attempt is made to stretch that thread, sooner or later it will break, and art will strike a belated and thus particularly cruel blow."

Leningrad's older generation of writers—Yevgeny Shvarts, Nikolai Chukovsky, Mikhail Slonimsky, and Lydia Ginzburg—were also at that time working at their memoirs ("interstitial literature" was Ginzburg's term) and circulating them in intellectual circles (through private readings, *samizdat,* and the rare publication). According to Bitov, "These were common efforts to create a Petersburg prose for new times: based on fact, but at the same time artistic, psychological, and strange. The city was giving birth to this. And what is important, all this was not bought up the authorities, as it often happened in Moscow."[106]

Despite the iron curtain, the desire for cultural communication with the West (which Mandelstam dubbed "longing for world culture"), a long-standing component of Petersburg, continued to glimmer. Bitov told me that in the early 1960s, when he heard that Faulkner was going to be printed in Russian for the first time, he and his friends went every day to all the city bookstores in anticipation.[107] Twentieth-century American literature was highly esteemed in Leningrad, but any interesting foreign book that reached the intelligentsia became the subject of discussion and debates. The same happened with American and European films and also with the rare—and wildly expensive—Western art books, which could generally be bought only at a special Leningrad black market for books.

Brodsky recalled this pro-Western orientation in Leningrad. "When you long for world culture, you let your imagination off the leash. And it gallops ahead. And sometimes it catches up and passes what's going on in Western culture. Like on the firing range—sometimes it doesn't reach, sometimes it's an exact hit. And often, as in the case of Mandelstam himself, it can go past the target. And as opposed to real shooting, in culture this is most valuable."[108]

But among Leningrad bohemians there was another movement—Slavophilia, which developed primarily from the aesthetics of Russian futurism, especially the early Mayakovsky, Khlebnikov, and Alexei Kruchenykh (author of the libretto for the avant-garde opera *Victory over the Sun,* which premiered in Petersburg in 1913). The followers of this movement in contemporary Leningrad started Slavophile happenings: dressed in traditional Russian shirts and blacked boots, they sat in public, gulping down kvass sprinkled with bread and diced onions out of a common bowl with wooden spoons, and declaiming Khlebnikov's pan-Slavic poems.

Despite the seemingly innocent character of these demonstrations, to the Leningrad authorities orthodox patriotism could only be

"Soviet," and the Slavophile tendencies were persecuted. The Party's misgivings were confirmed when during an official holiday parade in Leningrad, a few young Slavophiles were observed crying out "Down with Khrushchev's clique!" instead of the approved slogans. The proletarian crowd, not listening closely, mechanically responded with "Hurrah!" Serious measures were taken against the young bohemians.

Khrushchev's false thaw was quickly replaced with cruel frosts, which were then followed by the long hibernation of Leonid Brezhnev, famous for his inarticulate speech, bushy eyebrows, and fantastic corruption. In the stagnant atmosphere of those years, many Leningrad rebels—poets, artists, and philosophers—renewed the Russian tradition of "going to the people." Rejecting intellectual professions, they went to work as loaders on the Leningrad docks, sailors on small freighters, janitors, and night watchmen. Some took jobs as stokers in the city boiler rooms (Dmitri Bobyshev called them "the copper youth"). Most were heavy drinkers; drugs were also popular. Clashes with the police and frequent arrests were commonplace. The poet Sosnora, who spent six years as a metalworker in a factory, wrote, "I'm off—so long!—on a beeline through the bars!"

Bravado and daring were present here but also a tragic sense of marginality. The poet Kuzminsky commented, "This is how we felt: if you're making us into outcasts, then we'll be even bigger hooligans. We became professional lumpen proletariat."[109] The colorful Kuzminsky, with his yellow leather pants and walking stick, could be seen loudly declaiming his futurist-influenced poems at the favorite bohemian gathering place—a café informally called Saigon. Kuzminsky (later, in American exile, he put together a large anthology of Russian nonconformist culture) thus explained the café's name: "The café was yet another 'hot spot' on the planet. It was the home for all of Leningrad's drug addicts, black marketeers, lumpens, poets, and prostitutes."[110]

This was already the second generation of postwar Leningrad bohemians; its pioneers had been a group of neorealist artists (and their bard, Roald Mandelstam—no relation to Osip Mandelstam—a *samizdat* poet who died young) headed by Alexander Arefyev, a charming man fond of wearing a striped sailor's shirt, who had served two terms in the camps and was under constant police surveillance. Arefyev, whose energy awed those about him, had by the early 1950s led his fellow thinkers—Vladimir Shagin, Rikhard Vasmi, Valentin Gromov, and Sholom Shvarts (all of whom were under twenty-five)—onto the streets of Leningrad, which became their main subject.

They depicted the city's underbelly: its Dostoyevskian court-yards and stairs, its brutal dance halls, seedy steam baths, and de-pressing factory suburbs. Shagin, for instance, did a sketch in the Stalinist years of a policeman dragging an arrested man. Nothing like that could ever appear at an official exhibit in those years. Moreover, even to sketch such a scene was dangerous, and the artists in Arefyev's group were held by the police more than once.

The Leningrad neorealists were early Russian beatniks and led an ascetic life (their rooms held only books and records) with a ten-dency to psychedelic experimentation. Arefyev and Shagin slept in cemetery crypts and lived on the deposits of bottles and cans that they collected. They did not even try to reach an audience and exhibited publicly for the first time at the December 1974 exhibit of Leningrad's unofficial art at the culture club of the Kirov Plant.

The authorities reluctantly agreed to this exhibit under pres-sure from the growing international publicity around Russian non-conformist artists and in the hope of compromising the underground once and for all. Announcing that they would not allow paintings that were "anti-Soviet, pornographic, or religious," the overseers ended up permitting the exhibition of close to two hundred works by fifty-two painters, but only for four days.

Given the total absence of advertising, no one expected that, under the vigilant eyes of police units, long lines would form before dawn, lines of people eager to learn about nonconformist art in Leningrad. They were hustled into the building in groups and given only fifteen minutes to see the entire exhibit. And yet they had time to see the canvas of Igor Sinyavin, where they were invited to sign their name with a marker; the conceptual presentation—an iron nail in a board—by Yevgeny Rukhin, who died in a suspicious fire a few years later; and the canvas by Vadim Rokhlin, in the middle of which was a mirror framed by four aggressive male figures. (Another non-figurative painter of the period, Yevgeny Mikhnov-Voitenko, refused to exhibit his works out of sheer contrariness.)[111]

Those four days in December were important in Leningrad's modern cultural history because they were the first time that the

Leningrad underground surfaced, even briefly, and attracted a sympathetic audience. The authorities were furious. One prominent cultural bureaucrat attacked Arefyev and Shagin at the exhibit, shouting, "We don't need artists like this!"

The stamina and self-dramatizing behavior of the Leningrad bohemia looked back to the futurists and Bakhtin's "carnival" and forward to the early 1980s appearance of a group called Mitki. The name was the nickname of one of its founders, the artist Dmitri Shagin (son of the neorealist Vladimir Shagin and therefore a second-generation bohemian). Mitki embodied a stylized, local variant of Western hippie culture with a strong Russian accent. The younger Shagin was joined by the artists Vladimir Shinkarev and Alexander Florensky and his wife, Olga, who revived the craft of "lubok," folk pictures with clever captions.

The main artistic achievement of the group was its ritualized lifestyle, described by its "ideologist" Shinkarev in a witty manual called *Mitki,* which was widely circulated in *samizdat.* According to Shinkarev, Mitki dressed like outcasts: striped sailor shirts (the Soviet bohemian uniform inherited from the Leningrad neorealists), old quilted jackets, Russian felt boots, and mangy fur hats with earflaps. Mitki drank from morning till night, but only the cheapest vodka and rotgut wine, and snacked on pasteurized cheese. When the members drank with outsiders, they used three main strategies for dividing up the alcohol: "share equally" meant each got the same amount; "share like brothers" meant Mitki got the bigger portion; and "share like Christians" meant Mitki got it all.

But even when drunk, Mitki remained friendly and gentle because aggressiveness was organically alien to them, as was the desire to have a career. Mitki communicated primarily through quotations from popular television shows. Still, Shinkarev's manual quoted Henry David Thoreau and contained references to Brueghel the Elder and to Mozart, whom the author actually considered predecessors of Mitki, adding that "Mozart was Russian."

Mitki found a like-minded person in the poet and artist Oleg Grigoryev, who composed short, grim poems in the style of the early Leningrad dadaist Oberiuts:

> "Well, and how is it on the branch?"
> Asked the bird in the cage.
> "The branch is like the cage.
> But the bars are farther apart."

Grigoryev's absurdist and irreverent humor was unacceptable for official publications, and so his poems were circulated primarily in *samizdat*. But some things were published (just like the Oberiuts in the 1920s and early 1930s) in children's books, attracting attention thereby and recalling the heyday of children's literature. Living in slum rooms, which he decorated with masks of his own making, Grigoryev led the typically desperate life of a Leningrad bohemian. Constant confrontations with the authorities, arrests, time in the camps, and heavy bouts of drinking eventually led to the poet's early death in 1992.

"The seventies. . . . Dead, inert times. Fatal for art's breathing." The poet Gorbovsky thus described the Leningrad situation in the Brezhnev era. There was little left to breathe in Leningrad—even literally, thanks to unchecked industrial pollution in the city. Freshly fallen snow turned black overnight. The chemical-laden Neva was covered with toxic green sludge.

The stifling atmosphere hastened the disintegration of talent and led to an increase in suicide and early death among the young, including the promising poet Leonid Aronson. Some potential intellectual leaders emigrated to the West, and many of the remaining were forced to make humiliating compromises with officials. Censorship seemed all-powerful.

A terrible blow fell on the budding Soviet feminist movement, which for a while had been centered in Leningrad. Women had long been cultural leaders in the city: Akhmatova, Yudina, Ermolaeva, Berggolts, Ustvolskaya, Ginzburg, and the translator Tatyana Gnedich. In the 1960s a group of original women poets appeared— Elena Kumpan, Nina Koroleva, Lydia Gladkaya, and a bit later, Elena Shvarts. Maya Danini and Inga Petkevich wrote interesting prose. So the late-1970s appearance in Leningrad of the first Russian samizdat feminist magazines, *Woman and Russia* and *Maria,* was natural.

"Our magazine caused such a sensation, such a furor, which even I had not expected," recalled one of the editors of *Woman and Russia,* Tatyana Mamonova. "People passed around our little volume, it was retyped over and over." The secret police reacted with searches, interrogations, and harassment. Mamonova was expelled to the West, as were other Leningrad feminists—Tatyana Goricheva, Natalya Malakhovskaya, and Yulia Voznesenskaya.

The writer Alexander Zhitinsky compared the Leningrad authorities with a boa constrictor. "We froze, like rabbits, in the stare of the state's unsleeping eye."[112] Cultural Leningrad was demoralized. At that moment there appeared a new and unprecedented force—Russian rock and roll; as Zhitinsky recalled, "Rock and roll burst into our country at the most terrible time, when freedom seemed unnecessary, and we invented the stagnation period for ourselves, so we could sit quietly."[113]

The rock movement in Leningrad, which started in the mid-sixties, owed its birth to the influence of the Beatles, who created a revolution in the consciousness of young Russian nonconformists. The popular Leningrad rocker Mikhail ("Mike") Naumenko sang about this later in his hit, "Right to Rock":

> I remember that every Beatles record
> Gave us more than a year in school.

Records by the Beatles, which quickly reached Leningrad through tourists and seamen, excited musically receptive young people. The Beatles craze engulfed even Brodsky, who translated "Yellow Submarine" into Russian in the 1960s.

The pioneering Leningrad rockers, who had more or less mastered their homemade instruments (the necks of their guitars were sometimes sawed out of the headboards of their parents' beds) and slavishly imitated Western bands, performed primarily in schools, dormitories, and cafés. They did not become a strong social presence until the early 1970s, when they began composing original music on topical Russian texts. The trailblazer was the band Sankt-Peterburg, led by Vladimir Rekshan, the self-styled "first real star of rock music in Russia." Official propagandists were offended by the group's name and immediately charged the band with monarchist leanings.

Rekshan described the expansion of the Leningrad rock scene: "Rock groups multiplied like rabbits, and every Saturday there were concerts in dozens of places. Daring fans exhibited the ingenuity of urban guerrillas in getting into concerts. The most successful got in through women's toilets. Others climbed up rainspouts. Sometimes they took apart the roof and came in through the attic."[114]

Emboldened by their young audiences, Leningrad rock bands became more defiant in their songs, reflecting "the taste of those years—astringent, with a touch of rebellion, through which the new generation in the big cities, lost in the thickets, tried to find themselves."[115] The rockers sang about the alienation of young people from Soviet society, which they saw as hypocritical and hostile, about their distrust of the official system of values, and their vague search for alternative paths.

For Leningrad's apparatchiks all this was totally unacceptable. The authorities, trying to isolate the rockers from their audience, organized a hostile campaign, both backstage and in the media, whose main theme was sarcastically summarized in a song by Konstantin Kinchev, a devotee of the poetry of Gumilyov and Brodsky.

> *You are all fags,*
> *Addicts, Nazis, thugs!*
> *All socially dangerous,*
> *All ready for jail.*

Despite the official attacks (or thanks to them) the influence of rock on Leningrad's youth spread like wildfire. This phenomenon, which eluded state control almost completely, was largely due to *magnitizdat,* homemade tapes circulated like manuscripts in *samizdat.* Leningrad became the center of Russian magnitizdat, perhaps because of the city's desire to register its achievements promptly and reflect upon them intensely.

The roar of local rock bands deafened almost every courtyard in Leningrad, scaring away the ghosts of Dostoyevsky's Petersburg novels. What the rocker Yuri Shevchuk had promised had come to pass: "The star of Russian rock will rise over our Northern Palmyra!"

One of the brightest stars was Boris Grebenshikov. When the tall, slim Grebenshikov, who resembled David Bowie, ran out on stage in his white suit, the audience would roar with delight.

When he was eleven, Grebenshikov first heard the Beatles and "understood the point of living." He organized his rock band Aquarium in the early 1970s, becoming its guitarist, lead vocal, poet, composer, and driving force. Grebenshikov's lyrics show the influence of the acmeist poets of the start of the century (Innokenty Annensky, Gumilyov). The official cultural ideologists noted the influence quickly, and their reaction to Aquarium's early performances was, "This is some sort of symbolism! Akhmatovism!"

This odd connection between the rocker Grebenshikov and the classical Petersburg tradition was further expressed in his preference for sophisticated melodies arranged in the style of folk rock; he also made his performances seem like absurdist rituals. In his Bob Dylan–like tenor Grebenshikov would sing,

I have nothing left
That I would want to save.
We are in full flight on this strange path
And there are no doors along the way.

They used to say in Leningrad that Aquarium wasn't simply a rock band but a way of life. Members of the group and fans close to them lived as a family, sharing Grebenshikov's literary, philosophical and religious interests, including American sci-fi, the writings of Lao Tzu, and Zen Buddhism. A meeting with Mitki, important for both groups, increased the nationalist tendencies in Aquarium's music and led to a democratization of the band's image.

In the late 1980s Grebenshikov's popularity in Leningrad had reached enormous proportions and became the subject of a dadaesque prose by Shinkarev, one of the Mitki, who were also gaining a large following in the city.

> Oh, yes, dear brothers, there's nobody poorer than Boris Grebenshikov.
> He's even afraid to go outside—can you imagine!
> The family says: go get some milk and take out the garbage. Just try to get past the fans with the garbage pail! Nobody's going to offer, "Boris, I love your music, so let me take out your garbage." No way! "Here," they say, "here's a glass, have a drink with me, and I'll tell everybody that I got high with Grebenshikov."
> But Grebenshikov's face is red enough to light a butt with already from all that expensive cognac he's had, his hands shake so hard he can't hold a guitar. He can't stand the sight of those glasses, it makes him puke.
> So he comes to the door with the garbage and listens: it's quiet. He peeks out: nobody there.
> Grebenshikov quick slips out the door, but as soon as he steps on the landing, someone grabs him from behind and forces his head back. The garbage pail spills, he falls, his feet in the slops, and before he can call for help, they force his teeth open with a knife and pour in a glass of moonshine.
> Boris lies there gasping, half-blind, battered—while his fans grin and go down the stairs satisfied: they had a drink with Grebenshikov!

Mocking the idol-worshiping young and the cult of the "mysterious Slavic soul," this narrative reflected, nevertheless, the dark side of Leningrad rock, with its major presence of alcohol and drugs. Rekshan posed a rhetorical question, "And who can explain why it's easier to get drugs in Leningrad than toilet paper?"[116] He recalled how one of his musician friends, high on drugs, decided to commit suicide: he fastened two scalpels point up on a table and then dropped his face onto them, trying to get them into his eyes. He lost one eye and went completely mad. Life on the edge led to early death for some stars of Leningrad's rock movement: "Mike" Naumenko, Viktor Tsoy, and Alexander Bashlachev.

Grebenshikov liked to say, "Rock is subversive by definition. If it's not subversive, it's not rock." The energy and ferocity of Leningrad rock shook up the stagnant city that Grebenshikov described in song:

> *The courtyards are like wells here, but there's nothing to drink.*
> *If you want to live here, rein yourself in,*
> *Learn to run and then to slow down,*
> *While tripping your neighbor.*

The appeal of rock as an unsanctioned cultural movement was a remarkable sign of coming ideological and political changes in the Soviet Union. The totalitarian system created by Lenin and Stalin, which had seemed eternal to many, was beginning to crack under the pressure of external and internal factors. Mikhail Gorbachev—the new Party leader who came to power in 1985, younger and more pragmatic and energetic than his ossified Politburo colleagues—tried to cope with the crisis, which had suddenly become apparent to all, through a series of political and economic measures. He introduced words that soon became current even in the West—*perestroika* (which referred to structural changes in the centralized administration of the country) and *glasnost* (which referred to substantial liberalization, at least in Soviet terms, in culture and mass media).

One of the last Leningrad Party bosses of the Brezhnev "stagnation period" (1964–1982) was the dogmatic Grigory Romanov, who spent thirteen years in his post. His surname led to many sarcastic parallels with the Romanov dynasty, which had ruled Russia for over three hundred years (it was founded in 1613 by Mikhail Romanov, Peter the Great's grandfather, and ended only with the revolution of 1917). One joke was quite popular in Leningrad. A workman enters a grocery store with absolutely empty shelves, loses his patience, and starts cursing Romanov. He is immediately arrested and asked why he was attacking comrade Romanov. "Because," the workman answered, "the Romanovs were in charge of Russia for three hundred years and they couldn't store up enough food to last for even seventy."

This joke was taken quite seriously by Anatoly Sobchak in his sweeping reinterpretation of the history of Soviet rule. (Sobchak, an economic law professor and prominent politician in the *perestroika* and *glasnost* years, was elected Leningrad city council chairman in 1990 and later mayor.)

> For seven decades we lived by exploiting what had been amassed by the people and nature herself, and we wanted to enter the Communist future through the momentum of former development. We consistently depleted the country's human, social, natural, and moral resources. Without exception the "successes" of the Communist doctrine—from the victory over Hitler to space flights, from ballet to literature—were all taken out of the pocket of Russian history.[117]

This tirade reflected the spirit that swept through Soviet society when the Communists, unable to control reforms that had taken on a momentum of their own, began to lose their many monopolies, not least the monopoly on information. Political, economic, and cultural information broke through the dam, washing away old dogmas that had so recently seemed immutable.

This ideological liberation brought decisive changes in the way of life of the new Petersburg mythos. In the years of Khrushchev and Brezhnev, it had existed as something semiforbidden. The intellectual elite nurtured it but quietly, among themselves. The mythos could not be publicly formulated or debated, and its greatest works were either unpublished, like Akhmatova's *Requiem,* or appeared only with major cuts by the censors, like her *Poem Without a Hero* (whose hero was Petersburg, of course).

In order to bring the poems of Akhmatova or Mandelstam to a wider audience, some courageous television journalists in Leningrad tried various subterfuges; for instance, they used banned verses in voice-overs to nature footage without naming the authors. The ruse worked because ignorant Party censors never expected to hear banned poets on television. Émigré literature remained out of bounds in Leningrad; the works of old émigrés, like Zinaida Hippius, Merezhkovsky, Zamyatin, and Nabokov, and of new ones, like Brodsky, still circulated only in the underground.

□ □ □

All this started to change under Gorbachev. "The process was under way," as Gorbachev liked to say, beginning with the rehabilitation of the poet Gumilyov. His works had not been printed in the Soviet Union in over sixty years; even in the early 1950s charges of having a picture of the "counterrevolutionary" author could lead to ten years' exile in Siberia. But Gumilyov's underground fame and reputation remained high all those years thanks to manuscript copies of his poems that circulated from hand to hand.

Gumilyov's hundredth birthday fell in 1986, and though Soviet journals and newspapers published his poetry (thanks, it is said, to the support of Raisa Gorbachev, a fan) and articles about him that gave him his due as a poet, they mentioned his execution very gingerly. It was only in 1990 that the materials on the "Gumilyov affair" (from the archives of the secret police) were published. It became clear that Akhmatova had been right in insisting that the charges against Gumilyov of "active counterrevolutionary activity" were largely fabricated.

Gumilyov had remained, throughout the decades of Soviet rule, a hero and martyr of the underground Petersburg mythos; therefore, his rehabilitation by the state signaled changes in the status of the mythos. At the same time, the authorities began reviewing the cases of a large number of victims of the Stalinist political terror, whose reputations had remained in a social limbo ever since the Khrushchev thaw. This meant the recognition of the innocence of such political groups as the "Leningrad opposition," led by Grigory Zinoviev; of those arrested and exiled after Kirov's murder; and of the victims of the postwar "Leningrad affair."

It became possible to speak openly of Mandelstam's death in the Stalinist camps, of the extermination of the Leningrad dadaists from the Oberiu group, and Zoshchenko's death in 1958, hounded and half mad, writing in his last letter to Chukovsky, "A writer with a frightened soul has lost his qualifications."

Published in the spring of 1987, almost half a century after its creation, Akhmatova's *Requiem,* that poetic memorial for all the dead of the Great Terror, and one of the most important documents for the new Petersburg mythos and its image of the city as martyr, was at last freely available to the ordinary reader.

Every such step met fierce opposition from Party hard-liners. A battle ensued over the reputation of Andrei Zhdanov, Stalin's ideologue. As recently as 1986 Soviet newspapers had referred to him in glowing terms. "In the city of Lenin, the cradle of socialist revolution, he unfolded his marvelous abilities and special gifts as a political figure. His name is treasured in the national memory." But by 1988 it was possible to write, "There are many thousands of streets, plants, factories, ships, universities, kolkhozes, schools, even kindergartens and pioneer palaces (in Leningrad as well) named for Zhdanov. Stalin's name is almost gone, but Zhdanov's name is all over the place. This is a record of sorts. But a record of what? A record of the cynicism of those who consciously do not wish to stop glorifying that name?"[118]

When the Party orthodox saw that further defense of Zhdanov's heritage was unfeasible, they reluctantly gave it up. The infamous Zhdanov resolution of the Central Committee, directed against Akhmatova and Zoshchenko, was rescinded in 1988, forty-two years after it was passed. Zhdanovism in culture, with its demagogic labels and accusations of formalism, cosmopolitanism, and kowtowing to the West, was officially proclaimed a mistake; and Zhdanov Leningrad State University (founded in the Pushkin era) became simply Leningrad State University.

Zhdanov's role as leader of the defense of Leningrad was also re-evaluated. Sobchak made public the information that, as multitudes starved, peaches were flown in to Zhdanov in the winter, while anyone who "spread rumors" about Leningrad's hunger was in danger of the camps and almost certain death.[119] The truth about the blockade, with all its attendant horror and suffering, began to emerge. This new understanding hastened the legitimization of the image of Leningrad as martyr city.

Attention was again focused on the Silver Age, that cultural flowering at the beginning of the twentieth century, which Zhdanov in his report of 1946 had called, misquoting Gorky, "the most shameful and most mediocre decade in the history of the Russian intelligentsia." Zhdanov's label was for years the mandatory one. It was memorized and quoted in school examinations and chewed over in innumerable articles and books. A welcome contrast was the mass reprinting in the mid-eighties of the works of the Russian symbolists, acmeists, and futurists to the great delight of the reading public. A typical reaction was, "The Silver Age is turning out to be, speaking in the language of analogy, the key to the treasure box of the twentieth century."[120]

The hundredth birthdays of Akhmatova and Mandelstam, celebrated with great solemnity in 1989 and 1991, respectively, aided the consolidation of their reputations as national classics. In 1990 a foreign tourist at a Leningrad police station on business was astonished to see on a young policewoman's office wall not the obligatory pictures of Lenin and Gorbachev but a large poster with Nathan Altman's 1914 portrait of Akhmatova. *Poem Without a Hero* was recognized as a monument to the Silver Age and as the philosophical encapsulation of the fate of the Petersburg legend in the twentieth century. A special room in the Akhmatova Museum, opened in Leningrad in 1989, was devoted to *Poem Without a Hero;* another held the materials relating to *Requiem.*

In the perception of the general public, the Petersburg text expanded swiftly. The movies of Lenfilm's leading directors—Ilya Averbakh, Alexei German, and Alexander Sokurov—which had been banned or shelved during the era of stagnation, received wide distribution and high praise. The works of the Oberiu group—Kharms, Oleinikov, and Alexander Vvedensky—previously available only in samizdat, were now properly published. The surrealistic novels of Vaginov and the early satiric stories of Zoshchenko were reprinted. And Nabokov, who had been strictly forbidden even recently (his name could not be mentioned in print)—"Nabokov descended on us like an avalanche," a Soviet critic announced. "Nabokov's gigantic heritage, the whole baker's dozen of his novels, and everything around it—has fallen on us all at once. This means that everything that we could have handled naturally over fifty years of regular and timely reading is now coming at us like a flow, a flood."[121]

The effect of this belated and dramatic meeting with Nabokov on the Petersburg mythos was profound. Of the three émigré giants the first to reappear was Stravinsky; soon after him came Balanchine. But their impact, while extraordinary, was short-lived. Stravinsky was played and praised cautiously. Balanchine's ballets appeared in the Kirov's repertoire only in 1989, thanks to its chief choreographer, Oleg Vinogradov.

But intellectual Russia has always been and remains logocentric. It was therefore only the "discovery" of Nabokov that led to broad discussion of the role of the émigré culture in shaping the new Petersburg mythos and its enormous significance in the making of Petersburg modernism.

The assimilation by the Petersburg mythos of the achievements of modernism was particularly problematic for the general reader. The eccentric dadaist texts were accepted with much less resistance (but perhaps more superficially). A lively polemic developed around

Nabokov's work: much in it seemed self-consciously "aesthetic" and condescending. Responding to accusations against Nabokov, Andrei Bitov noted, "It is not clear what there is more of—pride and snobbery or shyness and modesty." Bitov, whose Nabokovian novel *Pushkin House* had reached a wide audience by then, continued, "I do not believe that Nabokov taught English to the Russian language, but to some degree he managed to teach Russian to the English language, and that is no small feat. Perhaps this will be said someday of Brodsky, too, who for now continues teaching English to the Russian language."[122]

The name of Brodsky, as the heir to the American line of Petersburg modernism, is often mentioned nowadays alongside Nabokov's. The first Soviet edition of Brodsky's poetry appeared in 1990 and quickly sold out its printing of two hundred thousand copies. It was followed by many other printings. But Brodsky's work elicited hostile reviews as well: the popular newspaper *Komsomolskaya pravda* maintained that one poem was "imbued with the most inappropriate irony, which extends literally to everything" and another was just "a flood of rhymed banalities, tackiness, and cynicism."[123]

Some sympathetic readers were surprised at the absence of overt homesickness, which even sophisticated Russians expect from émigré literature. This unfamiliar discretion was characteristic of other former Leningrad writers who had moved to the West. Sergei Dovlatov, who died in New York in 1990, ten days before his forty-ninth birthday, wrote graceful, ironic stories, which emphasized detail, narrative rhythm, and the significance of each word. He never used two words starting with the same letter in a sentence. The reader, as a rule, does not notice this limitation: Dovlatov's prose flows easily and naturally as it limns the tragicomic adventures of Leningraders at home and abroad.

The mythos underwent a deconstruction in the refined, postmodernistic poetry of the New Hampshire hermit Lev Loseff. Though Brodsky was speaking of Dovlatov when he said that he was "remarkable, first of all, in his rejection of the tragic tradition (which is just a grandiose name for inertia) of Russian literature," his words are just as true of the skeptical, philosophical poems of Loseff. The polar opposite, stylistically and emotionally, of the émigré literature about Petersburg is the religious poetry of Dmitri Bobyshev, dedicated to the blessed Xenia of Petersburg. Canonized by the Russian Synodal Church in the United States, Xenia was an eighteenth-century holy fool whom the devout Bobyshev hailed as a heavenly protector of the city.

The introduction of émigré literature into Leningrad's cultural realm was not a painless process. Both sides felt a certain ambivalence, which was expressed on the émigré side by former Leningrader Vladimir Maramzin, who lived in Paris, in an angry and sarcastic open letter to Soviet publishers. "I am disgusted by memories of your state, which dragged me through humiliations and knocked any desire to write out of me for a long time. I don't want to play prodigal son, happily returned to the wide open arms of the all-forgiving executioner. I do not want to be published in your country. I do not want to visit you."[124]

But other Leningrad émigrés accepted with delight the opportunity to be published, to perform, or to exhibit in the homeland. Natalya Makarova and Rudolf Nureyev, whose names had been dropped from the Soviet ballet encyclopedia, returned to dance at the Kirov Theater (whose name was soon to revert to Maryinsky). A major civic event was the June 7, 1991, unveiling—at the Fortress of Peter and Paul, opposite the cathedral where the Romanov tsars were buried—of a monument to Peter the Great by the artist and sculptor Mihail Chemiakin, who lives in the United States.

A huge crowd had gathered, despite the rain, for the solemn ceremony. Musicians in bright red uniforms and white wigs played military marches of Peter's time. Exactly at noon the white covering slid slowly from the statue, and the audience saw the life-size figure of the emperor seated in an armchair.

Chemiakin's model was the famous wax figure of Peter kept in the Hermitage Museum, which was made right after the emperor's death by the Italian Carlo Rastrelli, father of the great Petersburg architect. The postmodern, collage-like aspect of Chemiakin's sculpture is underlined by the fact that the head is a cast of a life mask of Peter made by Rastrelli in 1719.

We know that the mask, also in the Hermitage collection, was studied closely by Falconet when he created the Bronze Horseman. But the head of the Bronze Horseman, made by Falconet's student Callot, was idealized in keeping with the requirements of the times, framed by beautiful curls and the traditional laurel wreath. In 1815 the poet Alexei Merzlyakov described the general impression of the monument to Peter the Great, unveiled in 1782:

On a fiery steed, like a god, he flies:
His eyes see all, and his hand commands.

In contrast, Chemiakin's Peter, with his wigless skull, puffy face, and huge hands, was emphatically unglamorous and static. But there was a mystery about him that brought to mind the sphinxes unearthed in 1820 at the site of Thebes, the ancient capital of Egypt, and brought to Petersburg twelve years later, where they stand in front of the Academy of Arts.

The solemnity of Chemiakin's work also suggested parallels with the Bronze Horseman and prompted discussion among the observers, some of whom saw the new sculpture as a polemic, conscious or not, with Falconet's equestrian monument. Some were outraged at the naturalism or found Chemiakin's interpretation insulting. Debate did not stop even after the sun went down, when the figure of the city's founder took on an eerie presence. One curiosity of the continuing dispute was the daily appearance of fresh flowers at the pedestal of the new statue. The greatest and most mysterious of Russian tsars remained at the center of the fate of his city.

The controversy surrounding Chemiakin's work was part of a much larger reevaluation. Seemingly permanent evaluations and conclusions—from development of the Petersburg avant-garde to the number of victims of the siege—were questioned and revised. Blacklisted names were reestablished as great classics. What could only be whispered became, overnight, the rage of the next day. Overblown reputations, formerly supported by the propaganda of the state, burst suddenly.

Countless textbooks, encyclopedias, and reference books became useless. New information came in an avalanche. The Petersburg mythos, finally vindicated after many decades of persecution, surfaced like the city in Pushkin's description:

> And Petropolis surfaced like Triton
> Submerged in water to his waist.

The ground beneath the feet of the hard-liners was shaking. The Bronze Horseman of the Petersburg mythos was threatening to knock them down and trample them.

The culmination of these changes was the return of the city's original name: on October 1, 1991, Leningrad was officially renamed Sankt-Peterburg. But this change had been preceded by tense and unsettling events.

There had been talk of returning to the traditional name since the early years of *glasnost*. The idea, which had first seemed utopian, was gathering popularity. It was being discussed—with growing boldness—at work, in lines, and even at meetings. Then, in 1991, through the efforts of reform-minded deputies in the Leningrad city council, it was brought to a citywide referendum, and the campaign turned into a political and cultural war.

The poet Alexander Kushner wrote expectantly, "I had the fortune to be born in Leningrad and I will die, God willing, in Petersburg." His opponents were much more resolute. A member of the hastily organized Committee for the Defense of Leningrad announced, "The idea of renaming Leningrad is political speculation serving evil goals and promoting an increase in societal confrontation. Many people recall that the German name 'St. Petersburg' was on the maps of Hitler's commanders and that they intended to rename Leningrad right after they took it. What the fascists did not manage to do, the deputies of the Leningrad city council want to achieve."[125]

Reformers were accused not only of fascism and disrespect for the memory of the victims of the siege but also of monarchism. Typical was a letter published in the pro-Communist Leningrad newspaper *Sovest'* (Conscience), "Why rename our city? So that dead tsarism can breathe on us?" The Communist Party in a special appeal called on people "not to allow mockery of the name of glorious Leningrad, a hero city, a warrior city, and a laborer." A leading Communist, Yegor Ligachev, said that the Party considered a return to the traditional name "unwise." "Leningrad earned its name with its blood."[126] Gorbachev's official position was the same.

But the opponents of the Communists were growing stronger. A conservative newspaper complained, "Strange things are happening here in Leningrad. Almost the entire press of the city has become 'democratic.' It's become good manners to predict civil war, to propagandize a total renaming of all the streets, and to publish caricatures of Lenin."[127] A popular Leningrad television program regularly featured a picture of Lenin with the word "Enough!" written in bold letters across it. Liberals organized a noisy demonstration in front of the Maryinsky Theater, shouting, "Lenin's name is a shame for a great city!"

These efforts were supported by the Russian Orthodox Church. The writer Alexander Solzhenitsyn, who also considered a change necessary, nevertheless spoke out against using St. Petersburg, which was foreign, and suggested a Russified rendering: Svyato-Petrograd. This was the first time a change in a city's name had become the subject of such an all-encompassing discussion. The passions aroused showed that people saw an apparently symbolic act as one that was profoundly important. "They are invoking the most mysterious part of Russian history," an observer noted.[128]

It seemed that many residents of the city had instinctively grasped the significance of this act. Names play a central part in every mythos. But in the Petersburg mythos the part was particularly obvious. The first time it changed its name, the city was subjected to horrible trials. A second change produced the same result.

The power in the name "Petersburg" was evidenced by the fact that, despite everything, everyone stubbornly called the city Piter. As Brodsky put it, "The reason for our loyalty to the word 'Petersburg' was not our anti-Sovietism but the nonsemantic content of the name. Even from the point of view of pure euphonics, the word, especially in its final 'g,' has a certain solidity, like a rock, for the Russian ear."[129] Faith in the power of a name, of a word per se, is typical of Russian intellectuals. In returning an old name to a great place, they passionately hoped to see a rebirth of its old grandeur.

The result of all this wrangling and soul-searching was a narrow victory at the referendum, held in June 1991, for the proponents of the name change. Mayor Sobchak reacted reasonably: "I think that the city's residents made the right choice, and my position was the same. A city, like a person, must bear the name given it at birth, like it or not. By the way, Peter the Great had named our city in the Dutch manner, not the German."

A delighted Brodsky gave his unconditional support. "After all, we are talking about a continuity in culture. Returning the city's previous name is a means of at least hinting at continuity, if not establishing it. I am extremely pleased by this event. Because I am thinking not so much about ourselves as of those who will be born in St. Petersburg. It is much better for them to live in a city that bears the name of a saint than that of a devil."[130]

The referendum, however, was still nonbinding. An official decision on the fate of the city's name could be made only by the Soviet parliament. Given its makeup, it could not be expected to act anytime soon. But history acted in its own way. In August 1991 the hardliners in Moscow attempted an anti-Gorbachev coup. The attempt failed, but as a result, the Soviet Union, already creaking at the seams, collapsed completely. The isolated Gorbachev lost power, and the leader of the new independent Russia became its recently elected first president, Boris Yeltsin. Russia was free of Communist Party rule after more than seventy years. Yeltsin replaced the Communist symbol, the red flag and star, for the prerevolutionary tricolor flag. Leningrad, which had supported the new leader, was granted its wish this time. It became St. Petersburg once again. The wheel of history had made a complete revolution.

This was a dizzying moment for the city of five million. During the August coup attempt, Mayor Sobchak managed to organize the biggest pro-Yeltsin demonstration in the country; this decisive act brought Petersburg back, after a long hiatus, into the political arena. The courageous, dignified speech, before 250,000 attentive listeners on Palace Square, of the eighty-four-year-old academician Dmitri Likhachev, a noted Christian scholar and soon after the first honorary citizen of the new St. Petersburg, gave the demonstration a cultural and symbolic focus characteristic of the city.

Far-reaching and interesting experiments in privatization soon began. The economic importance of the city as a major port grew sharply after the Baltic republics broke off from the new Russian nation. Alluding to the traditional description of Petersburg as "the window into Europe," Sobchak said pointedly, "In connection with the changes in the borders, our city is now taking on special significance. It is the only Russian door to Europe."

As seldom before, ties with Europe became a political priority. Even before the ruble became a convertible currency, post-Communist Petersburg was prepared to restore to circulation the "golden coin of the European humanistic legacy" (in Mandelstam's phrase). Predictably, this movement created an acute polarization of the city's political forces.

Opposing the pro-Western and promarket reformers was a small but extremely vocal nationalist movement that flourished in Petersburg. In the fall of 1991 it held a demonstration on Palace Square. Orators assured the crowd that the country was in the grip of a "terror of democrats, faithful servants of world Zionism," and they declared, "Do you think that St. Petersburg was given its old name in honor of a Russian tsar? No, it is in honor of the Jewish Apostle Peter!"

A witness described a similar gathering: "A woman stood in a crowd, with tight curls, mean eyes, and a squeaky voice—but she spoke and the crowd listened. 'I am a biologist, I work at the University. We did an analysis in our university laboratory of Jewish blood and listen, it all has a gene of hatred for the Russian people!"[131] Attacks on other "foreigners" became more frequent, particularly on cultural matters. Petersburg's ultranationalistic element was displeased that the new conductor of the Philharmonic after Mravinsky's death was Yuri Temirkanov, a Kabardian, and that the artistic director of the Maryinsky Theater was the Ossetian Valery Gergiev.

One leading proponent of nationalist thought was Lev Gumilyov, the son of Nikolai Gumilyov and Anna Akhmatova. When his historical studies began appearing, they found an interested audience. Gumilyov's thesis was that the Russian Empire had not been a "prison of nations," as the liberals had traditionally maintained, but a natural and voluntary association of European and Asian peoples under the benign protection of the tsars. According to Gumilyov, "a united Eurasia headed by Russia was traditionally opposed by Europe in the West, China in the Far East, and the Muslim world in the South."[132] Russia, he thought, did not share a path with Europe, since Russian ideology was based on standards of behavior that were alien to Europeans and borrowed significantly from the Mongols—absolute discipline, ethnic tolerance, and religious fervor.

Paradoxically, the views of Gumilyov, who died in 1992 before his eightieth birthday, restored the line of Slavophile philosophy broken by the Soviets and transplanted it onto Petersburg soil. The fact that his anti-European theories found such sympathy in Petersburg showed how volatile the intellectual atmosphere had become even in so traditionally pro-Western and cosmopolitan a city. A sensation was caused by the premiere in Petersburg of *Bell Chimes*, a nationalistic "symphony-ritual" (as the composer called it) by Valery Gavrilin, a follower of Georgy Sviridov, a leading Slavophile musician (and former student of Shostakovich) and composer of the *Petersburg Songs*, set to the poetry of Blok.

To be sure, the imperial theme was always strongly present in Petersburg culture, going back to the first panegyrists of Peter the Great. But bearing in mind Russia's geographic situation, its size, its multiethnic populations, and its relations with its neighbors, such a circumstance is hardly surprising. Russia has always striven for imperial position. The question is whether this imperial principle is manifested through crude force or cultural influence. As Lev Gumilyov put it, "Every nation has the right to be itself."[133]

Brodsky countered, "You can try to save yourself from imperial excesses only through culture, because culture alone transforms us into civilized men who subsequently give rise to the democratic system." Bitov addressed the same issue: "Democracy is work and freedom is work. It is the work of everyone. Skepticism is the cheapest trick possible, especially for the intelligentsia."[134]

The role of Petersburg and the Petersburg mythos in this process is potentially enormous. One of the city's ambitions, which can again be spoken aloud, is its desire to be the spiritual capital or, at least, the cultural arbiter of the new Russia. The foundation for such an aspiration is the city's brilliant past and its tragic mythological aura.

But the spiritual impulses of Petersburg, a city that appeared at a tyrant's whim and developed haphazardly, are in the end unpredictable. Many Petersburgers would like to see it as the anchor of a Western-oriented Russia, but in certain circumstances, the city could easily become lost and bewildered, as it did in the tumultuous years of the revolution.

The search for the new may end in the loss of the past, in isolation from reality and civilization. Built on the line separating order from chaos, Petersburg has always been on the edge of the abyss. Any reader of the Petersburg texts is familiar with the view. The émigré philosopher Georgy Fedotov, who died in New York in 1951, proposed an original interpretation of one of the central images of *The Bronze Horseman*—the flood threatening to swallow Petersburg. Fedotov noted that Pushkin depicts the flood as almost a living force. He drew a parallel between the flood and the snake that Peter the Great's horse tramples in the middle of the city. "The snake and the flood represent the irrational, the blind aspects of Russian life, that which was shackled by Apollo and was always ready to break out: into sects, nihilism, anti-Semitism, rebellion. Russian life and Russian statehood are constant and tortuous mastery of chaos through reason and will."[135]

This confused and not always progressive movement to a distant goal cannot hope to succeed without drawing on the tradition of Petersburg culture, at least on that line whose principles were enumerated by Brodsky: "Sobriety of consciousness and sobriety of form; a desire for freedom inspired by the spirit of the place and the architecture of the place; aesthetic stoicism and the thought that order is more important than disorder, no matter how much the latter is congenial to our perception of the world. . . . This is a case where the sets determine the actor's repertoire. The problem lies only in who the actor is and how prepared he is for those sets and, therefore, for his role."[136]

Public opinion polls have consistently shown that up to 20 percent of the inhabitants of Petersburg are prepared to go to the West—either for work or permanent resettlement—showing that even such an unusual city can lose its attraction for a substantial number of its residents. The ostensibly victorious Petersburg mythos is still threatened.

First of all, the very physical existence of Petersburg is in danger, its fifteen thousand historic mansions and palaces falling apart. "Hundreds of old Petersburg buildings are dead . . . the colors are fading before your very eyes and the gilt is peeling," sighs an observer.[137] Decades of neglect have damaged the city's beauty, its loveliness is wearing thin.

The authorities cannot afford major restoration work, and there is no certainty that the hoped-for investment from the West will go to preserve the city's landmarks. Everyone is aware of crumbling Venice, but Petersburg probably faces a graver crisis, one worsened by economic and political instability.

No less troubling are the signs of spiritual malaise. The Petersburg mythos is no longer underground, but this very circumstance predictably is depriving it of its inner dynamic. Praising persecuted geniuses of the past and celebrating their posthumous anniversaries do not of themselves add vitality to modern Petersburg culture. Bitov admits that "we are now speaking the truth looking backwards. And as a result, we are standing in place."[138]

Is the Petersburg mythos dead? "We can and must study Petersburg culture, but we will not be able to resurrect it. At best, we will be able to put its defiled cemetery back in order."[139] But even this modest goal could be years away or turn out to be too much for an impoverished Petersburg.

The metaphorical cemetery has already been taken over by the entrepreneurs of mass culture, shamelessly manipulating the potent symbols to suit the needs of commerce. Thus, a recent pop hit was one of Mandelstam's most tragic texts set cynically to disco music:

> Petersburg! I do not yet want to die:
> You have my telephone numbers.

Having survived repression, the Petersburg mythos is now in danger of becoming a contentless shell. A contemplative Brodsky expressed an idea about the periodic regeneration of Petersburg culture. It occurs every twenty-five or thirty years, he said, drawing a line from Derzhavin to Pushkin and the poets of his circle and then to Nekrasov and Dostoyevsky; from them to the early symbolists and, through Mandelstam, Vaginov, and Akhmatova, to Brodsky's own contemporaries. This periodic renewal of creative generations is bound to recur, since "the city's landscape and ecology are fundamentally unchanged."[140]

This particular prediction may turn out to be too optimistic. On the other hand, the history of the city's culture and its mythos gives reason to harbor hope. Petersburg has been buried over and over in folk legends and books. Its demise has been prophesied, and the city truly was on the brink of destruction more than once. But even its most intransigent critics often had ambivalent feelings about it.

When Petersburg's cultural fortunes seemed to be declining, Tchaikovsky mourned its fate in his music, inspiring a generation of Russian aesthetes. Exiles on distant shores—Diaghilev, Stravinsky, Nabokov, and Balanchine—dreamed about Petersburg, and their homesickness nourished the legend of a lost paradise.

Gumilyov, Mandelstam, and Kharms paid with their lives for their adherence to the idea of a unique Petersburg culture. Blok, Akhmatova, Shostakovich, Zabolotsky, Zoshchenko, and later Brodsky brought sacrifices to its altar. The sacrifices were not in vain: the blood revived the mythos to a new and richer life.

Legend has it that as long as the Bronze Horsemen is in its place, Petersburg will not perish. In the shade of that monument, miracles seem possible. The new incarnation of the Petersburg mythos may be a surprise even for its devotees and scholars, let alone for general audiences. Brodsky readily accepted the possibility that a new renaissance, if he lived to see it, might be totally alien to him.[141]

Tradition and stability were always intertwined in Petersburg culture with spiritual ambivalence and creative unpredictability. This unpredictability, pregnant with new achievement, is enshrined in the most dramatic and enduring of Petersburg's visual symbols—the Bronze Horseman, at once dashing into the sky and rooted in stone. Most people desire to look beyond the line separating today from tomorrow. Very few manage to do so; even a genius like Pushkin stopped at the line to ponder.

But geniuses can at least give utterance to inchoate feelings, to anxieties and cares of confronting the unpredictable, and to secret hopes—as Pushkin did in the lines that seem cast in bronze, which anyone who has ever read the greatest Russian narrative poem feels impelled to repeat when standing, by design or by happenstance, at the equestrian statue of Peter the Great, thinking about the past, present, and future of the magnificent and long-suffering city founded by the legendary emperor and yearning to be immortal:

> *Where are you galloping, proud steed,*
> *And where will you plant your hoofs?*

NOTES

PREFACE

1. Anna Akhmatova, *Sochineniia* (Works), 2 vols., vol. 2 (Moscow, 1986), p. 205.

2. *A. S. Pushkin v vospominaniiakh sovremennikov* (A. S. Pushkin in Reminiscences of Contemporaries), 2 vols., vol. 1 (Moscow, 1974), p. 468.

3. *Semiotika goroda i gorodskoi kul'tury (Peterburg). Trudy po znakovym systemam* (Semiotics of the City and of Urban Culture (Petersburg), vol. 18 (Tartu, 1984), p. 6.

4. Ibid., p. 28.

5. *Doklad t. Zhdanova o zhurnalakh "Zvezda" i "Leningrad"* (Comrade Zhdanov's Report on the Journals *Zvezda* and *Leningrad*) (Moscow, 1946), p. 16.

6. Daniil Granin, *O nabolevshem* (About What Has Been Hurting) (Leningrad, 1988), p. 73.

7. *Peterburgskii zhurnal* (Petersburg Journal), 1–2 (1993), p. 9.

CHAPTER 1

1. A. S. Pushkin, *Polnoe sobranie sochinenii* (Complete Collected Works), vol. 10 (Moscow, 1951), pp. 453–54.

2. Ibid., p. 454.

3. Ibid., p. 109.

4. The history of the founding of Petersburg and the legends surrounding it are related, in particular, in P. N. Petrov, *Istoriia Sankt-Peterburga s osnovaniia goroda do vvedeniia v deistvie vybornogo gorodskogo upravleniia po Uchrezhdeniiam o guberniiakh, 1703–1782* (The History of St. Peterburg from the Founding of the City to the Implementation of the Elected City Government According to Administrations of Provinces, 1703–1782) (St. Petersburg, 1885); P. N. Stolpyanskii, *Kak voznik, osnovalsia i ros Sanktpiterburkh* (How St. Petersburg Arose, Was Founded, and Grew) (Petrograd, 1918); M. I. Pyliaev, *Staryi Peterburg* (Old Petersburg), 2nd ed. (St. Petersburg, 1889); *Ocherki istorii Leningrada* (Sketches of the History of Leningrad), vol. 1 (Moscow and Leningrad, 1955); V. Mavrodin, *Osnovanie Peterburga* (The Founding of Petersburg) (Leningrad, 1983).

5. The basic sources for the description of Peter the Great were V. O. Klyuchevsky, *Sochineniia* (Works), 9 vols., vol. 4 (Moscow, 1989); S. M. Solovyov, *Chteniia i rasskazy po istorii Rossii* (Readings and Stories in Russian History) (Moscow, 1990); K. Shmurlo, *Petr Velikii v otsenke sovremennikov i potomstva* (Peter the Great in the Evaluation of His Contemporaries and Descendants) (St. Petersburg, 1912); M. Ustryalov, *Istoriia tsarstvovaniia Petra Velikogo* (History of the Reign of Peter the Great) (St. Petersburg, 1859–1863); N. I. Pavlenko, *Petr Velikii* (Peter the Great) (Moscow, 1994); V. V. Mavrodin, *Rozhdeniie novoi Rossii* (Birth of the New Russia) (Leningrad, 1988); E. V. Anisimov, *Vremia petrovskikh reform* (The Time of Petrine Reforms) (Leningrad, 1989).

6. Klyuchevsky, *Sochineniia* (Works), vol. 4, p. 196.

7. Ibid., p. 115.

8. M. I. Semevskii, *Slovo i delo! 1700–1725* (Word and Deed! 1700–1725) (St. Petersburg, 1884), p. 88.

9. Ibid., pp. 87–90.

10. The description of Catherine the Great used, in particular, A. G. Brikner, *Istoriia Ekateriny Vtoroi* (History of Catherine the Second) (St. Petersburg, 1885); *Zapiski imperatritsy Ekateriny Vtoroi* (Notes of Empress Catherine the Second) (St. Petersburg, 1907); E. R. Dashkova, *Zapiski* (Notes) (Leningrad, 1985); E. V. Anisimov, *Rossiia v seredine XVIII veka: Bor'ba za nasledie Petra* (Russia in the Middle of the Eighteenth Century: The Struggle for Peter's Inheritance) (Moscow, 1986); A. Kamenskii, *"Pod seniiu Ekateriny . . ."* ("Under Catherine's Protection") (St. Petersburg, 1992).

11. Quoted in A. Kaganovich, *"Mednyi Vsadnik": Istoriia sozdaniia monumenta* (The Bronze Horseman: The History of the Creation of a Monument) (Leningrad, 1975), p. 42.

12. Ibid., p. 88.

13. Ibid., p. 90.

14. Ibid., p. 164.

15. Anna Akhmatova, in conversation with the author, Komarovo, 1965.

16. In the description of the personality and reign of Emperor Nicholas I, sources were N. K. Shil'der, *Imperator Nikolai Pervyi: Ego zhizn' i tsarstvovanie* (Emperor Nicholas I: His Life and Reign), 2 vols. (St. Petersburg, 1903), as well as numerous notes and memoirs by contemporaries, particularly Marquis de Custine,

Zapiski o Rossii (Notes on Russia) (Moscow, 1910); A. I. Herzen, *Sobranie sochinenii* (Collected Works), 30 vols., vol. 14 (Moscow, 1958); A. F. Tyutcheva, *Pri dvore dvukh imperatorov: Vospominaniia i fragmenty dnevnikov freiliny dvora Nikolaiia I i Aleksandra II* (At the Court of Two Emperors: Memoirs and Diary Fragments of a Lady-in-Waiting of the Court of Nicholas I and Alexander II) (Moscow, 1990).

17. N. V. Gogol, *Sobranie sochinenii* (Collected Works), 7 vols., vol. 7 (Moscow, 1967), p. 62.

18. Ibid., p. 207.

19. Vladimir Nabokov, *Nikolai Gogol* (New York, 1961), p. 12.

20. I. I. Panaev, *Literaturnye vospominaniia* (Literary Reminiscences) (Moscow, 1988), p. 281.

21. Vladimir Nabokov, *Lectures on Russian Literature* (New York and London, 1981), p. 313.

22. V. A. Sollogub, *Povesti. Vospominaniia* (Novellas. Reminiscences) (Leningrad, 1988), p. 667.

23. Quoted in Kornei Chukovsky, *Sobranie sochinenii* (Collected Works), 6 vols., vol. 5 (Moscow, 1967), p. 14.

24. Quoted in P. A. Zaionchkovskii, *Pravitel'stvennyi apparat samoderzhavnoi Rossii v XIX v.* (State Apparat of Sovereign Russia in the Nineteenth Century) (Moscow, 1978), pp. 181–82.

25. Ibid., p. 186.

26. *Ocherki istorii Leningrada* (Sketches of the History of Leningrad), vol. 2 (Moscow and Leningrad, 1957), pp. 170, 173.

27. S. V. Belov, *Roman F. M. Dostoevskogo "Prestuplenie i nakazanie": Kommentarii* (F. M. Dostoyevsky's Novel *Crime and Punishment:* Commentaries) (Leningrad, 1979), p. 38.

28. Ibid., p. 50.

29. Richard Stites, *The Women's Liberation Movement in Russia: Feminism, Nihilism and Bolshevism, 1860–1930* (Princeton, 1978), pp. 60–61.

30. See N. V. Yukhnyova, *Etnicheskii sostav i etnosotsial'naia struktura naseleniia Peterburga: Statisticheskii analiz* (Ethnic Composition and Ethnosocial Structure of the Population of Petersburg: Statistical Analysis) (Leningrad, 1984).

31. A. Ya. Panaeva (Golovacheva), *Vospominaniia* (Reminiscences) (Moscow, 1986), p. 335.

32. Quoted in *F. M. Dostoevskii v vospominaniiakh sovremennikov* (F. M. Dostoyevsky in the Reminiscences of Contemporaries), vol. 1 (Moscow, 1964), p. 294.

33. *N. G. Chernyshevskii v vospominaniiakh sovremennikov* (N. G. Chernyshevsky in the Reminiscences of Contemporaries) (Moscow, 1982), p. 248.

34. Quoted in *Literaturnoe nasledstvo* (Literary Heritage), vol. 86, *F. M. Dostoevskii: Novye materialy i issledovaniia* (F. M. Dostoyevsky: New Materials and Research) (Moscow, 1973), p. 26.

35. *Dostoevskii v vospominaniiakh sovremennikov* (Dostoyevsky in Reminiscences), vol. 1, p. 319.

36. *Literaturnoe nasledstvo* (Literary Heritage), vol. 86, p. 48.

37. Quoted in *Vremia i sud'by russkikh pisatelei* (The Times and Fates of Russian Writers) (Moscow, 1981), p. 193.

38. *Literaturnoe nasledstvo* (Literary Heritage), vol. 86, p. 622.

CHAPTER 2

1. Alexander Benois, *Moi vospominaniia (My Reminiscences)*, 2 vols. (Moscow, 1980), vol. 1 (bks. 1–3), p. 16.

2. B. Asafyev, *Simfonicheskie etiudy* (Symphonic Etudes) (Leningrad, 1970), p. 160.

3. Quoted in P. N. Stolpianskii, *Staryi Peterburg i Obshchestvo pooshchreniia khudozhestv* (Old Petersburg and the Society for the Advancement of the Arts) (Leningrad, 1928), p. 71.

4. Quoted in A. V. Kornilova, *Karl Briullov v Peterburge* (Karl Briullov in Petersburg) (Leningrad, 1976), p. 51.

5. Panaev, *Literaturnye vospominaniia* (Literary Reminiscences), pp. 131–32.

6. Igor Stravinsky and Robert Craft, *Expositions and Developments* (Berkeley and Los Angeles, 1981), p. 86. Reprint.

7. Benois, *Moi vospominaniia* (My Reminiscences), vol. 1 (bks. 1–3), p. 641.

8. Quoted in L. V. Korotkina, *Rerikh v Peterburge-Petrograde* (Roerich in Petersburg-Petrograd) (Leningrad, 1985), p. 11.

9. I. Remezov, *M. I. Glinka* (Moscow and Leningrad, 1951), pp. 3, 35.

10. Igor Stravinsky, *Khronika moei zhizni* (Chronicle of My Life) (Leningrad, 1963), p. 40.

11. M. Glinka, *Polnoe sobranie sochinenii: Literaturnye proizvedeniia i perepiska* (Complete Collected Works: Literary Works and Correspondence), vol. 1 (Moscow, 1973), pp. 248, 249.

12. *Dorozhnyi dnevnik M. Pogodina* (Travel Diary of M. Pogodin), part 1 (Moscow, 1844), pp. 9–10.

13. Quoted in T. Livanova, Vl. Protopopov, *Glinka*, 2 vols., vol. 2 (Moscow, 1955), pp. 228–29.

14. Glinka, *Literaturnye proizvedeniia* (Literary Works), vol. 1, p. 310.

15. A. N. Serov, *Stat'i o muzyke* (Articles on Music), 7 issues, issue 4, 1859–1860 (Moscow, 1988), p. 341.

16. Glinka, *Literaturnye proizvedeniia* (Literary Works), vol. 2B, p. 93.

17. Sollogub, *Vospominaniia* (Reminiscences), p. 615.

18. George Balanchine, in conversation with the author, New York, 1981.

19. Robert Craft, *Present Perspectives: Critical Writings* (New York, 1984), p. 280.

20. *New York Times*, January 7, 1953.

21. Sollogub, *Vospominaniia* (Reminiscences), p. 615.

22. Ibid., pp. 593–94.

23. A. G. Rubinstein, *Literaturnoe nasledie* (Literary Heritage), 3 vols., vol. 1 (Moscow, 1983), p. 87.

24. Sollogub, *Vospominaniia* (Reminiscences), p. 593.

25. Quoted in L. Raaben, *Zhizn' zamechatel'nykh skripachei: Biograficheskie ocherki* (The Lives of Outstanding Violinists: Biographical Sketches) (Moscow and Leningrad, 1967), p. 107.

26. Rubinstein, *Literaturnoe nasledie* (Literary Heritage), vol. 1, p. 70.

27. Ibid.

28. Ibid., p. 76.

29. V. V. Stasov, *Stat'i o muzyke* (Articles on Music), 5 issues, issue 2, 1861–1879 (Moscow, 1976), p. 9.

30. A. P. Borodin, *Kriticheskie stat'i* (Critical Articles) (Moscow, 1982), p. 60.

31. F. I. Chaliapin, *Maska i dusha: Moi sorok let na teatrakh* (Mask and Soul: My Forty Years in the Theater) (Paris, 1932), pp. 157–58.

32. Dmitri Shostakovich, in conversation with the author, Moscow, 1972.

33. Stasov, *Stat'i o muzyke* (Articles on Music), issue 3, 1880–1886 (Moscow, 1977), pp. 73–74.

34. Quoted in A. Gozenpud, *Russkii opernyi teatr XIX veka, 1857–1872* (Russian Opera Theater of the Nineteenth Century, 1857–1872) (Leningrad, 1971), p. 286.

35. M. P. Mussorgsky, *Literaturnoe nasledie. Pis'ma. Biograficheskie materialy i dokumenty* (Literary Heritage. Letters. Biographical Materials and Documents) (Moscow, 1971), p. 100.

36. Ibid.

37. Quoted in L. Barenboim, *Anton Grigor'evich Rubinshtein. Zhizn', artisticheskii put', tvorchestvo, muzykal'no-obshchestvennaia deiatel'nost'* (Anton Grigoryevich Rubinstein. Life, Artistic Path, Work, and Musical and Public Activity), vol. 2, 1867–1894 (Leningrad, 1962), pp. 251–52.

38. Joseph Brodsky, in conversation with the author, New York, 1978.

39. Quoted in Mussorgsky, *Literaturnoe nasledie* (Literary Heritage), p. 17.

40. Ibid., p. 20.

41. N. Rimsky-Korsakov, *Letopis' moei muzykal'noi zhizni* (Annals of My Musical Life) (Moscow, 1980), p. 183.

42. Quoted in *Sovetskaia muzyka* (Soviet Music), 9 (1980), p. 104.

43. *M. P. Musorgskii v vospominaniiakh sovremennikov* (M. P. Mussorgsky in the Reminiscences of Contemporaries) (Moscow, 1989), p. 204.

44. Ibid., p. 168.

45. P. Tchaikovsky, *Polnoe sobranie sochinenii. Literaturnye proizvedeniia i perepiska* (Complete Collected Works. Literary Works and Correspondence), vol. 5 (Moscow, 1959), p. 105.

46. Quoted in N. A. Troitskii, *Tsarskie sudy protiv revoliutsionnoi Rossii: Politicheskie protsessy 1871–1880 gg.* (Tsarist Courts Against Revolutionary Russia: Political Trials 1871–1880) (Saratov, 1976), p. 73.

47. Ibid., p. 79.

48. Ibid., p. 95.

49. Tchaikovsky, *Polnoe sobranie sochinenii* (Complete Collected Works), vol. 10 (Moscow, 1966), p. 54.

50. See Troitskii, *Tsarskie sudy* (Tsarist Courts), p. 311.

51. A. Gozenpud, *Russkii opernyi teatr XIX veka, 1873–1889* (Russian Opera Theater of the Nineteenth Century, 1873–1889) (Leningrad, 1973), p. 222.

52. A. Gozenpud, *Russkii opernyi teatr na rubezhe XIX–XX vekov i F. I. Shaliapin, 1890–1904* (Russian Opera Theater at the Turn of the Century and F. I. Chaliapin, 1890–1904) (Leningrad, 1974), p. 6.

53. I. E. Repin, *Dalekoe blizkoe* (Distant Closeness) (Leningrad, 1982), p. 211.

54. *Perepiska I. S. Turgeneva* (Correspondence of I. S. Turgenev), 2 vols., vol. 2 (Moscow, 1986), pp. 318–19.

55. P. I. Tchaikovsky, *Pis'ma rodnym* (Letters to Family) (Moscow, 1940), p. 667.

56. Rimsky-Korsakov, *Letopis'* (Annals), p. 66.

57. Tchaikovsky, *Perepiska* (Correspondence), vol. 5, p. 372.

58. Quoted in A. Orlova, *Trudy i dni M. P. Musorgskogo. Letopis' zhizni i tvorchestva* (Works and Days of M. P. Mussorgsky: Annals of His Life and Work) (Moscow, 1963), p. 405.

59. Ibid., p. 500.

60. Quoted in A. N. Kriukov, *"Moguchaia kuchka": Stranitsy istorii peterburgskogo kruzhka muzykantov* ("The Mighty Handful": Pages from the History of a Petersburg Circle of Musicians) (Leningrad, 1977), p. 183.

61. Ibid., p. 184.

62. Quoted in *Sovetskaia muzyka* (Soviet Music), 3 (1989), p. 113.

63. Benois, *Moi vospominaniia* (My Reminiscences), vol. 1 (bks. 1–3), p. 371.

64. Ibid., p. 366.

65. Orlova, *Trudy i dni Musorgskogo* (Works and Days of Mussorgsky), p. 354.

66. Rimsky-Korsakov, *Letopis'* (Annals), p. 160.

67. Benois, *Moi vospominaniia* (My Reminiscences), vol. 1 (bks. 1–3), p. 650.

68. Tchaikovsky, *Perepiska* (Correspondence), vol. 5, p. 70.

69. Quoted in A. Dolzhanskii, *Simfonicheskaia muzyka Chaikovskogo* (Tchaikovsky's Symphonic Music) (Moscow and Leningrad, 1965), p. 94.

70. Ibid., p. 99.

71. Igor Glebov [B. V. Asafyev], *Chaikovskii* (Tchaikovsky) (Petersburg and Berlin, 1923), p. 34.

72. A. V. Ossovskii, *Muzykal'no-kriticheskie stat'i, 1894–1912* (Musical Criticism Articles, 1894–1912) (Leningrad, 1971), p. 171.

73. P. Tchaikovsky, *Polnoe sobranie sochinenii. Literaturnye proizvedeniia i perepiska* (Complete Collected Works. Literary Works and Correspondence), vol. 8 (Moscow, 1963), p. 226.

74. Tchaikovsky, *Perepiska* (Correspondence), vol. 10, p. 202.

75. Quoted in *Muzykal'noe nasledie Chaikovskogo: Iz istorii ego proizvedenii* (Tchaikovsky's Musical Heritage: From the History of His Works) (Moscow, 1958), p. 239.

76. Glebov [Asafyev], *Chaikovskii*, pp. 43–44.

77. Quoted in L. M. Konisskaya, *Chaikovskii v Peterburge* (Tchaikovsky in Petersburg) (Leningrad, 1969), p. 240.

78. Benois, *Moi vospominaniia* (My Reminiscences), vol. 1 (bks. 1–3), p. 640.

79. Ibid., p. 644.

80. Ibid., p. 646.

81. Ibid., p. 603.

82. Ibid.

83. Ibid., p. 654.

84. Ibid., p. 653.

85. P. Tchaikovsky, *Polnoe sobranie sochinenii. Literaturnye proizvedeniia i perepiska* (Complete Collected Works. Literary Works and Correspondence), vol. 13 (Moscow, 1971), p. 349.

86. Quoted in *Russkaia literatura kontsa XIX–nachala XX v. Devianostye gody* (Russian Literature of the Late Nineteenth and Early Twentieth Centuries: The Nineties) (Moscow, 1968), p. 276.

87. Alexander Benois, *Moi vospominaniia* (My Reminiscences), 2 vols. (Moscow, 1980), vol. 2 (bks. 4–5), p. 48.

88. Benois, *Moi vospominaniia* (My Reminiscences), vol. 1 (bks. 1–3), p. 592.

89. Ibid., pp. 697–98.

90. Quoted in Yu. B. Solovyov, *Samoderzhavie i dvorianstvo v kontse XIX veka* (Sovereignty and the Nobility in the Late Nineteenth Century) (Leningrad, 1973), p. 121.

91. Quoted in *Russkaia khudozhestvennaia kul'tura kontsa XIX–nachala XX veka, 1895–1907* (Russian Art Culture of the Late Nineteenth and Early Twentieth Centuries, 1895–1907), vol. 2 (Moscow, 1969), p. 133.

92. Ibid., p. 18.

93. V. V. Stasov, *Pis'ma k deiateliam russkoi kul'tury* (Letters to People in Russian Culture), vol. 1 (Moscow, 1962), p. 80.

94. Benois, *Moi vospominaniia* (My Reminiscences), vol. 1 (bks. 1–3), p. 16.

95. *Mir iskusstva*, 1 (1902), p. 1 ("Khronika" [Chronicle]).

96. Ibid., p. 4.

97. M. V. Dobuzhinsky, *Vospominaniia* (Reminiscences) (Moscow, 1987), p. 188.

98. A. Fedorov-Davydov, *Russkoe i sovetskoe iskusstvo: Stat'i i ocherki* (Russian and Soviet Art: Articles and Sketches) (Moscow, 1975), p. 333.

99. Quoted in A. L. Ospovat and R. D. Timenchik, *"Pechal'nu povest' sokhranit' . . ."* ("To Preserve the Sorrowful Tale . . .") (Moscow, 1987), p. 229.

100. Ibid., p. 232.

101. Ibid., p. 231.

102. Dobuzhinsky, *Vospominaniia* (Reminiscences), p. 188.

CHAPTER 3

1. *Ocherki istorii Leningrada* (Sketches of the History of Leningrad), vol. 3 (Moscow and Leningrad, 1956), p. 104.

2. Benois, *Moi vospominaniia* (My Reminiscences), vol. 2 (bks. 4–5), p. 412.

3. Quoted in *Panorama iskusstv* (Panorama of the Arts), issue 4 (Moscow, 1981), p. 32.

4. Akhmatova, *Sochineniia* (Works), 2 vols., vol. 2, p. 253.

5. Nathan Milstein, in conversation with the author, New York, 1987.

6. Sergei Prokofiev, *Avtobiografiia* (Autobiography) (Moscow, 1973), p. 538.

7. M. F. Gnesin, *Stat'i. Vospominaniia. Materialy* (Articles. Reminiscences. Materials) (Moscow, 1961), p. 141.

8. Prokofiev, *Avtobiografiia* (Autobiography), pp. 503–4.

9. I. F. Stravinsky, *Stat'i i materialy* (Articles and Materials) (Moscow, 1973), p. 445.

10. N. A. Berdyaev, *Samopoznanie (opyt filosofskoi biografii)* (Self-Cognition [An Attempt at a Philosophical Biography]) (Moscow, 1991), p. 144.

11. Alexander Blok, *Zapisnye knizhki, 1901–1920* (Notebooks, 1901–1920) (Moscow, 1965), p. 126.

12. Ibid., p. 118.

13. Kornei Chukovsky, *Sobranie sochinenii* (Collected Works), 6 vols., vol. 6 (Moscow, 1969), pp. 122, 124.

14. Quoted in N. M. Zorkaia, *Na rubezhe stoletii. U istokov massovogo iskusstva v Rossii 1900–1910 godov* (At the Turn of the Century: At the Source of Mass Art in Russia 1900–1910) (Moscow, 1976), p. 94.

15. Quoted in A. N. Bokhanov, *Burzhuaznaia pressa Rossii i krupnyi kapital: Konets XIX v–1914 g.* (The Bourgeois Press in Russia and Major Capital: The Late Nineteenth Century–1914) (Moscow, 1984), p. 40.

16. Quoted in Chukovsky, *Sochineniia* (Works), vol. 6, p. 146.

17. Quoted in *Voprosy literatury* (Issues of Literature), 2 (1977), p. 198.

18. Quoted in A. Turkov, *A. P. Chekhov i ego vremia* (A. P. Chekhov and His Times) (Moscow, 1980), p. 73.

19. Ibid., p. 60.

20. Ibid., p. 54.

21. I. I. Yasinsky, *Roman moei zhizni* (The Novel of My Life) (Moscow and Leningrad, 1926), p. 280.

22. Nathan Milstein, in conversation with the author, New York, 1980.

23. Quoted in E. A. Dinershtein, *"Fabrikant" chitatelei: A. F. Marks* ("Manufacturer" of Readers: A. F. Marx) (Moscow, 1986), p. 77.

24. V. V. Vorovskii, *Estetika. Literatura. Iskusstvo* (Aesthetics. Literature. Art) (Moscow, 1975), p. 255.

25. Chukovsky, *Sochineniia* (Works), vol. 6, pp. 370–71.

26. Vorovskii, *Estetika* (Aesthetics), pp. 530–31.

27. D. S. Mirsky, *Contemporary Russian Literature, 1881–1925* (London, 1926), p. 151.

28. Anna Akhmatova, in conversation with the author, Komarovo, 1965.

29. Kornei Chukovsky, *Iz vospominanii* (From Reminiscences) (Moscow, 1959), p. 373.

30. Ibid., p. 371.

31. Quoted in D. Maksimov, *Poeziia i proza A. Bloka* (Poetry and Prose of A. Blok) (Leningrad, 1975), p. 507.

32. *Literaturnoe nasledstvo* (Literary Heritage), vol. 92 (in four books), *Aleksandr Blok: Novye materialy i issledovaniia* (Alexander Blok: New Materials and Research), book 3 (Moscow, 1982), p. 438.

33. V. E. Meyerhold, *Stat'i. Pis'ma. Rechi. Besedy* (Articles. Letters. Speeches. Conversations), part 1, 1891–1917 (Moscow, 1968), p. 103.

34. Georgii Chulkov, *Gody stranstvii. Iz knigi vospominanii* (Years of Wanderings: From the Book of Reminiscences) (Moscow, 1930), p. 221.

35. Amanda Haight, *Anna Akhmatova: Poeticheskoe stranstvie. Dnevniki,*

vospominaniia, pis'ma A. Akhmatovoi (Anna Akhmatova: A Poetic Pilgrimage. Diaries, Reminiscences, Letters of A. Akhmatova) (Moscow, 1991), pp. 323, 324–25.

36. *Ob Anne Akhmatovoi. Stikhi. Esse. Vospominaniia. Pis'ma* (About Anna Akhmatova. Poems. Essays. Reminiscences. Letters) (Leningrad, 1990), p. 33.

37. Joseph Brodsky and Solomon Volkov, *Vspominaiia Akhmatovu: Dialogi* (Remembering Akhmatova: Dialogues) (Moscow, 1992), p. 35.

38. Quoted in G. A. Tishkin, *Zhenskii vopros v Rossii, 50–60-e gody XIX v.* (The Women's Question in Russia, 1850–1860s) (Leningrad, 1984), p. 202.

39. Quoted in E. V. Letenkov, *"Literaturnaiia promyshlennost'" Rossii kontsa XIX–nachala XX veka* ("Literary Industry" of Russia in the Late Nineteenth and Early Twentieth Centuries) (Leningrad, 1988), p. 114.

40. *Rech'* (Speech), February 21, 1910.

41. Tamara Ivanova, *Moi sovremenniki, kakimi ia ikh znala* (My Contemporaries As I Knew Them) (Moscow, 1984), p. 424.

42. V. I. Nemirovich-Danchenko, *Na kladbishchakh* (In Cemeteries) (Revel, 1922), p. 135.

43. I. A. Bunin, *Sobranie sochinenii* (Collected Works), 9 vols., vol. 9 (Moscow, 1967), p. 289.

44. Ibid., p. 281.

45. Quoted in *Literaturnoe nasledstvo* (Literary Heritage), vol. 85, *Valerii Briusov* (Valery Briusov) (Moscow, 1976), p. 691.

46. Anna Akhmatova, in conversation with the author, Komarovo, 1965.

47. Ibid.

48. Quoted in *Pamiatniki kul'tury: novye otkrytiia. Pis'mennost'. Iskusstvo. Arkheologiia. Ezhegodnik– 1988* (Cultural Monuments: New Discoveries. Literacy. Art. Archaeology. Annual for 1988) (Moscow, 1989), p. 58.

49. Ibid.

50. Ibid., p. 54.

51. Ibid., p. 59.

52. Quoted in *Druzhba narodov* (Friendship of the Peoples), 6 (1989), p. 250.

53. Quoted in Anna Saakyants, *Marina Tsvetayeva. Stranitsy zhizni i tvorchestva, 1910–1922* (Marina Tsvetayeva: Pages of Her Life and Work, 1910–1922) (Moscow, 1986), p. 88.

54. Valery Briusov, *Sobranie sochinenii* (Collected Works), 7 vols., vol. 6 (Moscow, 1975), p. 365.

55. N. Gumilyov, *Sobranie sochinenii* (Collected Works), 4 vols., vol. 4 (Washington, D.C., 1968), p. 262.

56. R. D. Timenchik, *Khudozhestvennye printsipy predrevoliutsionnoi poezii Anny Akhmatovoi* (Artistic Principles of Anna Akhmatova's Prerevolutionary Poetry) [Synopsis of dissertation] (Tartu State University, 1982), p. 6.

57. B. Eikhenbaum, *O poezii* (On Poetry) (Leningrad, 1969), p. 75.

58. Osip Mandelstam, *Sochineniia* (Works), 2 vols., vol. 2 (Moscow, 1990), pp. 265–66.

59. V. Piast, *Vstrechi* (Encounters) (Moscow, 1929), p. 157.

60. *Aleksandr Blok v vospominaniiakh sovremennikov* (Alexander Blok in the Reminiscences of Contemporaries), vol. 2 (Moscow, 1980), pp. 62–63.

61. Quoted in Anatoly Nayman, *Rasskazy o Anne Akhmatovoi* (Stories About Anna Akhmatova) (Moscow, 1989), p. 200.

62. *Blok v vospominaniiakh sovremennikov* (Blok in Reminiscences), vol. 2, p. 66.

63. Piast, *Vstrechi* (Encounters), p. 156.

64. *Ob Anne Akhmatovoi* (About Anna Akhmatova), p. 74.

65. V. F. Khodasevich, *Nekropol'* (Necropolis) (Paris, 1976), p. 10. Reprint.

66. Yu. N. Tynyanov, *Poetika. Istoriia literatury. Kino* (Poetics. History of Literature. Film) (Moscow, 1977), pp. 118–19.

67. Khodasevich, *Nekropol' (Necropolis)*, p. 14.

68. *Literaturnoe nasledstvo* (Literary Heritage), vol. 92, book 4 (Moscow, 1987), p. 572.

69. *Ob Anne Akhmatovoi* (About Anna Akhmatova), p. 35.

70. Nathan Milstein, in conversation with the author, New York, 1984.

71. V. V. Rozanov, *Mysli o literature* (Thoughts on Literature) (Moscow, 1989), p. 402.

72. *Panorama iskusstv* (Panorama of the Arts), issue 12 (Moscow, 1989), p. 192.

73. Ibid.

74. N. N. Punin, *Russkoe i sovetskoe iskusstvo* (Russian and Soviet Art) (Moscow, 1976), p. 147.

75. Benedikt Livshits, *Polutoraglazyi strelets* (One-and-a-Half-Eyed Archer) (Leningrad, 1989), p. 538.

76. Punin, *Russkoe i sovetskoe iskusstvo* (Russian and Soviet Art), p. 150.

77. *Panorama iskusstv* (Panorama of the Arts), issue 12, p. 183.

78. Nathan Altman, in conversation with the author, Leningrad, 1966.

79. V. P. Verigina, *Vospominaniia* (Reminiscences) (Leningrad, 1974), p. 173.

80. *Il'ia Sats* (Ilya Sats) (collection) (Moscow and Leningrad, 1923), p. 20.

81. Livshits, *Polutoraglazyi strelets* (One-and-a-Half-Eyed Archer), p. 465.

82. *Teatr i iskusstvo* (Theater and Art), 10 (1913), p. 232.

83. Irina Odoevtseva, *Na beregakh Nevy* (On the Banks of the Neva) (Washington, D.C., 1967), p. 144.

84. Ibid.

85. Quoted in B. Kats and R. Timenchik, *Anna Akhmatova i muzyka. Issledovatel'skie ocherki* (Anna Akhmatova and Music. Research Articles) (Leningrad, 1989), p. 39.

86. *V. G. Karatygin* (collection) (Leningrad, 1927), p. 73.

87. *Apollon*, 1 (1913), p. 66.

88. Fyodor Lopukhov, in conversation with the author, Leningrad, 1967.

89. *Vozdushnye puti* (Aerial Paths), issue 5 (New York, 1967), p. 139.

90. Vera Stravinsky, in conversation wtih the author, New York, 1976.

91. *Vozdushnye puti* (Aerial Paths), issue 5, p. 141.

92. Ibid., pp. 142–43.

93. Nadezhda Mandelstam, *Vtoraia kniga* (Second Book) (Paris, 1972), p. 510.

94. Quoted in V. Krasovskaia, *Russkii baletnyi teatr nachala XX veka* (Russian Ballet Theater of the Early Twentieth Century), part 2 (Leningrad, 1972), p. 35.

95. Ibid., p. 47.

96. Ibid., p. 55.

97. Ibid., p. 54.

98. Quoted in *Zinaida Serebryakova* (collection) (Moscow, 1987), p. 245.

99. Fyodor Lopukhov, *Shest'desiat let v balete* (Sixty Years in Ballet) (Moscow, 1966), p. 182.

100. Piast, *Vstrechi* (Encounters), p. 275.

101. Viktor Shklovsky, *Zhili-byli* (Once upon a Time) (Moscow, 1966), p. 115.

102. Blok, *Zapisnye knizhki* (Notebooks), p. 237.

103. N. P. Antsiferov, *Dusha Peterburga* (The Soul of Petersburg) (Petersburg, 1922), pp. 218–19.

104. Livshits, *Polutoraglazyi strelets* (One-and-a-Half-Eyed Archer), p. 544.

105. *Nikolai Gumilyov v vospominaniiakh sovremennikov* (Nikolai Gumilyov in the Reminiscences of Contemporaries) (collection) (Paris, New York, and Düsseldorf, 1989), p. 215.

106. N. Wrangel, *Vospominaniia* (Reminiscences) (Berlin, 1924), p. 210.

107. *Sovremennye zapiski* (Contemporary Notes), 18 (1924), p. 235.

108. Quoted in K. Rudnitskii, *Meierhol'd* (Meyerhold) (Moscow, 1981), p. 216.

109. Leonid Dolgopolov, in conversation with the author, New York, 1990.

110. Yu. M. Yuryev, *Zapiski* (Notes), vol. 2 (Leningrad and Moscow, 1963), p. 194.

111. Quoted in K. Rudnitskii, *Rezhisser Meierhol'd* (Meyerhold the Director) (Moscow, 1969), pp. 200–202.

112. Viktor Shklovsky, in conversation with the author, Moscow, 1975.

113. Quoted in *Avangard, ostanovlennyi na begu* (The Avant-Garde, Halted in Mid-Run) (Leningrad, 1989), p. 2.

114. *Literaturnoe nasledstvo* (Literary Heritage), vol. 80, *V. I. Lenin i A. V. Lunacharskii. Perepiska, doklady, dokumenty* (V. I. Lenin and A. V. Lunacharsky. Correspondence, Speeches, Documents) (Moscow, 1971), p. 260.

115. A. Blok, *Dnevnik* (Diary) (Moscow, 1989), pp. 267–68.

116. *Dekrety Sovetskoi vlasti o Petrograde, 25 oktiabria [7 noiabria] 1917 g.–29 dekabria 1918* (Soviet Decrees Regarding Petrograd, 25 October [7 November] 1917–29 December 1918) (Leningrad, 1986), pp. 126–27.

117. Nikolai Martyanov, in conversation with the author, New York, 1976,

118. D. L. Golinkov, *Krushenie antisovetskogo podpol'ia v SSSR* (The Collapse of the Anti-Soviet Underground in the USSR), book 1 (Moscow, 1978), p. 186.

119. *Dekrety Sovetskoi vlasti o Petrograde* (Soviet Decrees on Petrograd), pp. 149–50.

120. *Literaturnoe nasledstvo* (Literary Heritage), vol. 80, p. 58.

121. Quoted in S. Varshavskii, B. Rest, *Bilet na vsiu vechnost'* (Ticket to All Eternity), parts 1–2 (Leningrad, 1986), p. 149.

122. Ibid., p. 160.

123. Antsiferov, *Dusha Peterburga* (Soul of Petersburg), p. 219.

124. *Maksim Gor'kii v vospominaniiakh sovremennikov* (Maxim Gorky in Reminiscences of Contemporaries), 2 vols., vol. 2 (Moscow, 1981), p. 23.

125. *V. I. Lenin o literature* (V. I. Lenin on Literature) (Moscow, 1971), p. 160.

126. Quoted in *Kontinent*, 55 (1988), p. 195.

127. S. N. Semanov, *Likvidatsiia antisovetskogo Kronshtadskogo miatezha 1921 goda* (The Liquidation of the Anti-Soviet Kronstadt Rebellion of 1921) (Moscow, 1973), p. 25.

128. Yuri Annenkov, *Dnevnik moikh vstrech* (Diary of My Encounters), vol. 1 (New York, 1966), p. 34.

129. A. P. Ostroumova-Lebedeva, *Avtobiograficheskie zapiski* (Autobiographical Notes), vol. 3 (Moscow, 1974), p. 22.

130. A. V. Lunacharsky, *Vospominaniia i vpechatleniia* (Reminiscences and Impressions) (Moscow, 1968), p. 210.

131. Nathan Altman, in conversation with the author, Leningrad, 1966.

132. A. I. Piotrovsky, *Za sovetskii teatr!* (For the Soviet Theater!) (Leningrad, 1925), pp. 51–52.

133. M. Gorky, *V. I. Lenin* (Moscow, 1974), p. 37.

134. Quoted in Andrei Bely, *Peterburg* (Moscow, 1981), p. 528.

135. Alexander Bakhrakh, *Bunin v khalate. Po pamiati, po zapisiam* (Bunin in a Robe. From Memory, From Notes) (New Jersey, 1979), p. 109.

136. Blok, *Dnevnik* (Diary), p. 186.

137. Alexander Blok, *Sobranie sochinenii* (Collected Works), 8 vols., vol. 8, *Pis'ma, 1898–1921* (Moscow and Leningrad, 1963), pp. 130–31.

138. Blok, *Dnevnik* (Diary), p. 121.

139. *Literaturnoe nasledstvo* (Literary Heritage), vol. 92, book 3, p. 478.

140. Blok, *Zapisnye knizhki* (Notebooks), p. 406.

141. V. M. Zhirmunsky, *Tvorchestvo Anny Akhmatovoi* (The Work of Anna Akhmatova) (Leningrad, 1973), p. 97.

142. Quoted in Osip Mandelstam, *Sochineniia* (Works), 2 vols., vol. 1 (Moscow, 1990), p. 42.

143. V. Milashevsky, *Vchera, pozavchera . . .* (Yesterday, Day Before Yesterday . . .) (Moscow, 1989), p. 239.

144. Dobuzhinsky, *Vospominanya* (Reminiscences), p. 23.

145. Ibid.

146. N. N. Evreinov, *Original o portretistakh* (A Model About His Portraitists) (Petrograd, 1922), p. 55.

147. Milashevsky, *Vchera, pozavchera* (Yesterday, Day Before Yesterday), p. 180.

148. Semanov, *Likvidatsiia antisovetskogo Kronshtadskogo miatezha* (Liquidation of the Anti-Soviet Kronstadt Rebellion), p. 69.

149. Annenkov, *Dnevnik moikh vstrech* (Diary of my Encounters), vol. 1, pp. 75–78.

150. *Literaturnoe nasledstvo* (Literary Heritage), vol. 92, book 4, p. 273.

151. Quoted in *Nikolai Gumilyov v vospominaniiakh sovremennikov* (Gumilyov in the Reminiscences of Contemporaries), p. 216.

152. Georgii Ivanov, *Stikhotvoreniia. Tretii Rim. Peterburgskie zimy. Kitaiskie teni* (Poems. Third Rome. Petersburg Winters. Chinese Shadows) (Moscow, 1989), p. 440.

153. *Literaturnoe nasledstvo* (Literary Heritage), vol. 92, book 3, p. 478.

154. Quoted in Anna Akhmatova, *Requiem* (Moscow, 1989), p. 31.
155. *Ob Anne Akhmatovoi* (About Anna Akhmatova), p. 135.
156. Odoevtseva, *Na beregakh Nevy* (On the Banks of the Neva), pp. 477–78.
157. Quoted in *Daugava*, 8 (1990), p. 118.
158. Blok, *Dnevnik* (Diary), p. 321.
159. Annenkov, *Dnevnik moikh vstrech* (Diary of My Encounters), vol. 1, p. 74.
160. Chaliapin, *Maska i dusha* (Mask and Soul), p. 288.
161. Ibid., p. 294.
162. Alexander Blok, *Sobranie sochinenii* (Collected Works), 8 vols., vol. 6 (Moscow and Leningrad, 1962), p. 167.
163. *Literaturnoe nasledstvo* (Literary Heritage), vol. 80, p. 261.
164. Blok, *Sobranie sochinenii* (Collected Works), vol. 8, p. 537.
165. Ibid., p. 539.
166. *Literaturnoe nasledstvo* (Literary Heritage), vol. 92, book 2 (Moscow, 1981), p. 164.
167. *Daugava*, 11 (1990), pp. 91–93.
168. Khodasevich, *Nekropol'* (Necropolis), p. 122.
169. *Ogonyok*, 18 (1990), p. 14.
170. Ibid., p. 15.
171. *Daugava*, 8 (1990), pp. 120, 122.
172. Victor Serge, *Memoirs of a Revolutionary* (London, 1984), p. 150.
173. *Vozvrashchennye imena* (Returned Names) [anthology], book 1 (Moscow, 1989), p. 191.
174. Nina Bruni-Balmont, in conversation with the author, Moscow, 1974.
175. *Ob Anne Akhmatovoi* (About Anna Akhmatova), pp. 197–98.
176. Quoted in Anna Akhmatova, *Poema bez geroiia* (Poem Without a Hero) (Moscow, 1989), p. 11.
177. K. Chukovsky, *Dnevnik, 1901–1929* (Diary, 1901–1929) (Moscow, 1991), p. 143.
178. Ibid., p. 194.
179. *Literaturnoe nasledstvo* (Literary Heritage), vol. 92, book 3, p. 816.
180. Quoted in Saakyants, *Marina Tsvetaeva*, p. 310.
181. Odoevtseva, *Na beregakh Nevy* (On the Banks of the Neva), p. 480.
182. Ibid., p. 473.
183. Ibid., pp. 480–81.

CHAPTER 4

1. George Balanchine, in conversation with the author, New York, 1981.
2. Ibid.
3. Marquis de Custine, *Empire of the Czar* (New York, 1989), p. 106.
4. M. M. Zagoskin, *Roslavlev, ili Russkie v 1812 godu* (Roslavlev; or, Russians in 1812) (Moscow, 1955), p. 48.
5. Quoted in Ospovat and Timenchik, *"Pechal'nu povest' sokhranit' . . ."* ("To Preserve the Sorrowful Tale"), p. 263.
6. Ibid.

7. Igor Stravinsky and Robert Craft, *Memories and Commentaries* (Berkeley and Los Angeles, 1981), p. 30. Reprint.

8. Benois, *Moi vospominaniia* (My Reminiscences), vol. 1 (bks. 1–3), p. 13.

9. Quoted in V. Krasovskaia, *Istoriia russkogo baleta* (History of Russian Ballet) (Leningrad, 1978), p. 15.

10. Quoted in A. Gozenpud, *Russkii opernyi teatr XIX veka, 1836–1856* (Russian Opera Theater of the Nineteenth Century, 1836–1856) (Leningrad, 1969), p. 77.

11. Ibid.

12. Quoted in V. Krasovskaia, *Istoriia russkogo baleta* (History of Russian Ballet), pp. 64–65.

13. Quoted in O. Petrov, *Russkaia baletnaia kritika kontsa XVIII–pervoi poloviny XIX veka* (Russian Ballet Criticism of the Late Eighteenth–First Half of the Nineteenth Centuries) (Moscow, 1982), p. 146.

14. Yu. M. Lotman, *Stat'i po tipologii kul'tury* (Articles on the Typology of Culture), issue 2 (Tartu, 1973), p. 64.

15. Quoted in Mikheil Gorgidze, *Gruziny v Peterburge* (Georgians in Petersburg) (Tbilisi, 1976), p. 104.

16. George Balanchine, in conversation with the author, New York, 1982.

17. Ibid.

18. Marius Petipa, *Materialy. Vospominaniia. Stat'i* (Materials. Reminiscences. Articles) (Leningrad, 1971), p. 90.

19. Ibid.

20. V. Gayevsky, *Divertisment* (Divertissement) (Moscow, 1981), p. 79.

21. Ibid., p. 70.

22. Petipa, *Materialy* (Materials), p. 68.

23. Quoted in Yu. Slonimsky, *P. I. Chaikovskii i baletnyi teatr ego vremeni* (P. I. Tchaikovsky and the Ballet Theater of His Times) (Moscow, 1956), p. 121.

24. Ibid., p. 9.

25. George Balanchine, in conversation with the author, New York, 1982.

26. Alexandra Danilova, in conversation with the author, New York, 1986.

27. *Sergei Diagilev i russkoe iskusstvo* (Sergei Diaghilev and Russian Art) [collection], 2 vols., vol. 2 (Moscow, 1982), p. 100.

28. Quoted in V. Krasovskaia, *Russkii baletnyi teatr nachala XX veka* (Russian Ballet Theater of the Early Twentieth Century), 2 vols., vol. 1 (Leningrad, 1971), p. 361.

29. Stravinsky and Craft, *Memories and Commentaries*, p. 36.

30. Stravinsky, *Stat'i i materialy* (Articles and Materials), p. 462.

31. Ibid.

32. *Apollon*, 6 (1911), p. 74.

33. Stravinsky and Craft, *Expositions and Developments*, p. 135.

34. Quoted in Nesta Macdonald, *Diaghilev Observed by Critics in England and the United States, 1911–1929* (New York, 1975), p. 76.

35. Ibid.

36. Fyodor Lopukhov, in conversation with the author, Leningrad, 1967.

37. M. Fokine, *Protiv techeniia. Vospominaniia baletmeistera. Stat'i, pis'ma* (Against the Current. Reminiscences of a Choreographer. Articles, Letters) (Leningrad and Moscow, 1962), p. 93.

38. Fyodor Lopukhov, in conversation with the author, Leningrad, 1967.

39. Alexandra Danilova, in conversation with the author, New York, 1991.

40. Quoted in Yurii Alianskii, *Teatral'nye legendy* (Theater Legends) (Moscow, 1973), p. 164.

41. Quoted in Samuil Alianskii, *Vstrechi s Aleksandrom Blokom* (Encounters with Alexander Blok) (Moscow, 1972), p. 11.

42. Quoted in *Voprosy literatury* (Issues of Literature), 2 (1974), p. 117.

43. Andrei Bely, *Simvolizm* (Symbolism) (Moscow, 1910), p. 212.

44. Ibid., p. 172.

45. Quoted in N. Khardzhiev and V. Trenin, *Poeticheskaia kul'tura Maiakovskogo* (Poetic Culture of Mayakovsky) (Moscow, 1970), p. 32.

46. Boris Pasternak, *Vozdushnye puti* (Aerial Paths) (Moscow, 1982), p. 264.

47. Shklovsky, *Zhili-Byli* (Once upon a Time), p. 301.

48. N. Evreinov, *Vvedenie v monodramu* (Introduction to Monodrama) (St. Petersburg, 1909), p. 8.

49. Livshits, *Polutoraglazyi strelets* (One-and-a-Half-Eyed Archer), p. 446.

50. Quoted in Pavel Nikolaevich Filonov, *Katalog vystavki* (Exhibit Catalogue) (Leningrad, 1988), p. 22.

51. Quoted in *V. Maiakovskii v vospominaniiakh sovremennikov* (Mayakovsky in Reminiscences of Contemporaries) (Moscow, 1963), p. 111.

52. Pasternak, *Vozdushnye puti* (Aerial Paths), p. 269.

53. *Maiakovskii v vospominaniiakh sovremennikov* (Mayakovsky in Reminiscences of Contemporaries), p. 625.

54. Quoted in A. Fevral'skii, *Pervaia sovetskaia p'esa: "Misteriia–buff" V. V. Maiakovskogo* (The First Soviet Play: Mayakovsky's *Mystery-Bouffe*) (Moscow, 1971), p. 11.

55. Milashevsky, *Vchera, pozavchera* (Yesterday, Day Before Yesterday), p. 84.

56. Ibid., pp. 121, 120.

57. Quoted in *Ezhegodnik rukopisnogo otdela Pushkinskogo Doma na 1974 god* (Yearbook of the Manuscript Department of Pushkin House for 1974) (Leningrad, 1976), p. 187.

58. Ibid., pp. 185–86.

59. Ibid., p. 192.

60. *Panorama iskusstv* (Panorama of the Arts), issue 12, p. 183.

61. Milashevsky, *Vchera, pozavchera* (Yesterday, Day Before Yesterday), p. 117.

62. *Panorama iskusstv* (Panorama of the Arts), issue 12, p. 193.

63. Ibid., p. 194.

64. Nina Bruni-Balmont, in conversation with the author, Moscow, 1974.

65. Quoted in *Ezhegodnik rukopisnogo otdela Pushkinskogo Doma na 1974 god* (Yearbook of the Manuscript Department of Pushkin House for 1974), p. 183.

66. A. N. Efros, *Mastera raznykh epokh* (Masters of Various Eras) (Moscow, 1979), p. 249.

67. Quoted in *Ezhegodnik rukopisnogo ordela Pushkinskogo Doma na 1974 god* (Yearbook of the Manuscript Department of Pushkin House for 1974), p. 183.

68. Ibid., p. 182.

69. Quoted in *Literaturnoe nasledstvo* (Literary Heritage), vol. 65, *Novoe o Maiiakovskom* (New Materials About Mayakovsky) (Moscow, 1958), p. 565.

70. Ibid., p. 586.

71. Annenkov, *Dnevnik moikh vstrech* (Diary of My Encounters), vol. 2, pp. 49–50.

72. Viktor Shklovsky, *Khod konia* (Knight Move) (Moscow and Berlin, 1923), p. 137.

73. Tamara Geva, in conversation with the author, New York, 1991.

74. P. M. Kerzhentsev, *Tvorcheskii teatr* (Creative Theater) (Petersburg, 1920), p. 137.

75. A. Lunacharsky, *Rasskazy o Lenine* (Stories About Lenin) (Moscow, 1971), p. 44.

76. *Literaturnoe nasledstvo* (Literary Heritage), vol. 80, p. 369.

77. Yu. Slonimsky, *Chudesnoe bylo riadom s nami* (The Marvelous Was Right next to Us) (Leningrad, 1984), p. 147.

78. George Balanchine, in conversation with the author, New York, 1981.

79. Viktor Shklovsky, *Gamburgskii schet. Stat'i-Vospominaniia–Esse, 1914–1933* (Hamburg Rules. Articles, Reminiscences, Essays, 1914–1933) (Moscow, 1990), p. 44.

80. Piast, *Vstrechi* (Encounters), p. 277.

81. Shklovsky, *Gamburgskii schet* (Hamburg Rules), p. 486.

82. Piast, *Vstrechi* (Encounters), p. 250.

83. Viktor Shklovsky, *O teorii prozy* (On a Theory of Prose) (Moscow, 1983), p. 72.

84. Shklovsky, *Zhili–byli* (Once upon a Time), p. 288.

85. Shklovsky, *Gamburgskii schet* (Hamburg Rules), p. 63.

86. D. S. Mirsky, *Uncollected Writings on Russian Literature* (Berkeley, 1989), p. 226.

87. Mandelstam, *Sochineniia* (Works), vol. 2, p. 273.

88. *Peterburg*, 2 (1922), p. 14.

89. George Balanchine, in conversation with the author, New York, 1982.

90. Konst. Fedin, *Sobranie sochinenii* (Collected Works), 10 vols., vol. 10 (Moscow, 1973), p. 128.

91. Slonimsky, *Chudesnoe bylo riadom s nami* (The Marvelous Was Right next to Us), p. 17.

92. Milashevsky, *Vchera, pozavchera* (Yesterday, Day Before Yesterday), p. 218.

93. Slonimsky, *Chudesnoe bylo riadom s nami* (The Marvelous Was Right next to Us), p. 135.

94. Valerian Bogdanov-Berezovsky, in conversation with the author, Leningrad, 1970.

95. Alexandra Danilova, in conversation with the author, New York, 1991.

96. George Balanchine, in conversation with the author, New York, 1982.

97. Quoted in *Muzyka i khoreografiia sovremennogo baleta* (Music and Choreography of Modern Ballet) [collection] (Leningrad, 1974), p. 165.

98. Alexandra Danilova, in conversation with the author, New York, 1991.

99. I. Sollertinsky, *Stat'i o balete* (Articles on Ballet) (Leningrad, 1973), pp. 18–19.

100. Slonimsky, *Chudesnoe bylo riadom s nami* (The Marvelous Was Right next to Us), p. 200.

101. Fyodor Lopukhov, *Shest'desiat let v balete* (Sixty Years in the Ballet) (Moscow, 1966), p. 14.

102. Ibid., p. 13.

103. Quoted in E. Ia. Surits, *Khoreograficheskoe iskusstvo dvadtsatykh godov* (The Art of Choreography of the Twenties) (Moscow, 1979), p. 284.

104. Sollertinsky, *Stat'i o balete* (Articles on Ballet), p. 29.

105. Ibid., p. 26.

106. Lopukhov, *Shest'desiat let v balete* (Sixty Years in the Ballet), p. 33.

107. Quoted in Surits, *Khoreograficheskoe iskusstvo dvadtsatykh godov* (The Art of Choreography of the Twenties), pp. 66–67.

108. *Teatr*, 13 (1923), p. 7.

109. *Teatr*, 1 (1924), pp. 6–7.

110. Quoted in M. Dolinskii, *Sviaz' vremen* (Connections of Times) (Moscow, 1976), p. 122.

111. Alexandra Danilova, in conversation with the author, New York, 1992.

112. Fyodor Lopukhov, in conversation with the author, Leningrad, 1967.

113. George Balanchine, in conversation with the author, New York, 1982.

114. V. Bogdanov-Berezovsky, *Vstrechi* (Encounters) (Moscow, 1967), p. 250.

115. M. Mikhailov, *Zhizn' v balete* (Life in the Ballet) (Leningrad and Moscow, 1966), p. 44.

116. Quoted in V. I. Berezkin, *V. V. Dmitriev* (Leningrad, 1981), p. 13.

117. George Balanchine, in conversation with the author, New York, 1981.

118. Alexandra Danilova, in conversation with the author, New York, 1992.

119. Quoted in Slonimsky, *Chudesnoe bylo riadom s nami* (The Marvelous Was Right next to Us), p. 214.

120. Mikhailov, *Zhizn' v balete* (Life in the Ballet), pp. 44–45.

121. Quoted in *U istokov* (At the Sources) [collection] (Moscow, 1960), p. 129.

122. Shklovsky, *Gamburgskii schet* (Hamburg Rules), p. 175.

123. George Balanchine, in conversation with the author, New York, 1982.

124. A. V. Lunacharsky, *Sobranie sochinenii* (Collected Works), 8 vols., vol. 7 (Moscow, 1967), p. 502.

125. George Balanchine, in conversation with the author, New York, 1981.

126. Ibid.

127. Quoted in Slonimsky, *Chudesnoe bylo riadom s nami* (The Marvelous Was Right next to Us), p. 182.

128. Ibid., p. 186.

129. Lopukhov, *Shest'desiat let v balete* (Sixty Years in the Ballet), p. 188.

130. Vladimir Mayakovsky, *Polnoe sobranie sochinenii* (Complete Collected Works), 13 vols., vol. 4 (Moscow, 1957), p. 253.

131. S. S. Prokofiev and N. Ya. Miaskovsky, *Perepiska* (Correspondence) (Moscow, 1977), p. 281.

132. Stravinsky and Craft, *Expositions and Developments*, p. 83.

133. Igor Stravinsky, *An Autobiography* (New York and London, 1962), p. 100.

134. Ibid., pp. 99–100.

135. Lincoln Kirstein, *Dance: A Short History of Classic Theatrical Dancing* (New York, 1969), p. 257.

136. Richard Buckle, *George Balanchine, Ballet Master* (New York, 1988), p. 68.

137. Stravinsky, *Stat'i i materialy* (Articles and Materials), p. 391.

138. Stravinsky and Craft, *Expositions and Developments*, pp. 34–35.

139. Ibid., p. 21.

140. Ibid., p. 32.

141. *Portrait of Mr. B: Photographs of George Balanchine, with an essay by Lincoln Kirstein* (New York, 1984), p. 16.

142. Igor Stravinsky, *Themes and Conclusions* (Berkeley and Los Angeles, 1982), p. 34. Reprint.

143. Arlene Croce, *Afterimages* (New York, 1977), p. 419.

144. Nathan Milstein, in conversation with the author, New York, 1984.

145. Nathan Milstein, in conversation with the author, New York, 1986.

CHAPTER 5

1. Galina Serebryakova, *O drugikh i o sebe* (About Others and Myself) (Moscow, 1971), p. 9.

2. Vera Inber, *Stranitsy dnei perebiraiia. . . .* (Going Through the Pages of the Days) (Moscow, 1977), p. 13.

3. Serebryakova, *O drugikh i o sebe* (About Others and Myself), p. 9.

4. Mikhail Bulgakov, *Chasha zhizni* (The Cup of Life) (Moscow, 1988), pp. 461–62.

5. Quoted in *Leningrad. Entsiklopedicheskii spravochnik* (Leningrad. Encyclopedic Guidebook) (Moscow and Leningrad, 1957), pp. 112–13.

6. Benois, *Moi vospominaniia* (My Reminiscences), vol. 1 (bks. 1–3), pp. 11–12.

7. Ibid., p. 12.

8. Boris Pasternak, *Perepiska s Ol'goi Freidenberg* (Correspondence with Olga Freidenberg) (New York and London, 1981), p. 68.

9. V. Kaverin, *Izbrannye proizvedeniia* (Selected Works), 2 vols., vol. 1 (Moscow, 1977), p. 370.

10. Quoted in *Vstrechi s proshlym* (Encounters with the Past), issue 5 (Moscow, 1984), p. 242.

11. Pasternak, *Perepiska s Freidenberg* (Correspondence with Freidenberg), p. 68.

12. *Stranitsy zhizni N.A. Rimskogo–Korsakova. Letopis' zhizni i tvorch-*

estva (Pages from the Life of N. A. Rimsky-Korsakov. The Chronicle of His Life and Work), issue 1 (Leningrad, 1969), p. 213.

13. Rimsky-Korsakov, *Letopis'* (Chronicle), p. 218.

14. Tynyanov, *Poetika. Istoriia literatury. Kino* (Poetics. History of Literature. Film), p. 198.

15. Ibid.

16. M. F. Gnessin, *Mysli i vospominaniia o N. A. Rimskom–Korsakove* (Thoughts and Reminiscences About N. A. Rimsky-Korsakov) (Moscow, 1956), p. 199.

17. Rimsky-Korsakov, *Letopis'* (Chronicle), p. 34.

18. N. A. Malko, *Vospominaniia. Stat'i. Pis'ma* (Reminiscences. Articles. Letters) (Leningrad, 1972), p. 49.

19. S. S. Prokofiev, *Materialy. Dokumenty. Vospominaniia* (Materials. Documents. Reminiscences) (Moscow, 1961), p. 138.

20. Anna Akhmatova, in conversation with the author, Komarovo, 1965.

21. Prokofiev, *Avtobiografiia* (Autobiography), p. 390.

22. Ibid.

23. Ibid., p. 503.

24. *Stranitsy zhizni N.A. Rimskogo-Korsakova. Letopis' zhizni i tvorchestva* (Pages from the Life of N. A. Rimsky-Korsakov. Chronicle of His Life and Work), issue 4 (Leningrad, 1973), p. 113.

25. Ibid., p. 114.

26. Rimsky-Korsakov, *Letopis'* (Chronicle), p. 191.

27. Malko, *Vospominaniia* (Reminiscences), p. 45.

28. Rimsky-Korsakov, *Letopis'* (Chronicle), pp. 211, 212.

29. B. Asafyev, *Kniga o Stravinskom* (Book About Stravinsky) (Leningrad, 1977), p. 30.

30. Prokofiev, *Materialy* (Materials), p. 138.

31. Quoted in *Vospominaniia o B. V. Asaf'eve* (Reminiscences of B. V. Asafyev) (Leningrad, 1974), p. 82.

32. A. K. Glazunov, *Pis'ma, stat'i, vospominaniia* (Letters, Articles, Reminiscences) (Moscow, 1958), p. 379.

33. Prokofiev, *Avtobiografiia* (Autobiography), p. 520.

34. Shklovsky, *Zhili-byli* (Once upon a Time), p. 164.

35. Glazunov, *Pis'ma* (Letters), pp. 367–68.

36. Asafyev, *Kniga o Stravinskom* (Book About Stravinsky), p. 28.

37. Rimsky-Korsakov, *Letopis'* (Chronicle), p. 215.

38. Valerian Bogdanov-Berezovsky, in conversation with the author, Leningrad, 1970.

39. *Novyi Amerikanets* (New American), June 22–28, 1982.

40. Ibid.

41. *Vstrechi s proshlym* (Encounters with the Past), issue 5, p. 257.

42. Berthe Malko, in conversation with the author, New York, 1982.

43. Berthe Malko, in conversation with the author, Hillsdale, 1987.

44. L. Anninskii, *Leskovskoe ozherel'e* (Leskov's Necklace) (Moscow, 1982), p. 80.

45. Yevgeny Zamyatin, *Sochineniia* (Works) (Moscow, 1988), p. 335.

46. Ibid.

47. Ibid.

48. Valerian Bogdanov-Berezovsky, in conversation with the author, Leningrad, 1970.

49. Ibid.

50. Nathan Milstein, in conversation with the author, London, 1987.

51. Yuri Shaporin, *Izbrannye stat'i* (Selected Articles) (Moscow, 1969), p. 101.

52. Nathan Milstein, in conversation with the author, New York, 1982.

53. Nathan Milstein, in conversation with the author, Vienna, 1976.

54. George Balanchine, in conversation with the author, New York, 1981.

55. *Muzyka i revoliutsiia* (Music and Revolution), 4 (1927), p. 31.

56. Vladimir Horowitz, in conversation with the author, New York, 1985.

57. Iosif Schwartz, in conversation with the author, Leningrad, 1961.

58. Valerian Bogdanov-Berezovsky, in conversation with the author, Leningrad, 1970.

59. Iosif Schwartz, in conversation with the author, Leningrad, 1961.

60. *Vospominaniia o Sofronitskom* (Reminiscences About Sofronitsky) (Moscow, 1970), p. 65.

61. Valerian Bogdanov-Berezovsky, in conversation with the author, Leningrad, 1970.

62. Berthe Malko, in conversation with the author, Hillsdale, 1989.

63. Maria Yudina, in conversation with the author, Moscow, 1970.

64. Quoted in *Vospominaniia o Asaf'eve* (Reminiscences About Asafyev), p. 83.

65. Quoted in *Protokoly Pervoi Vserossiiskoi konferentsii proletarskikh kul'-turno-prosvetitel'nykh organizatsii* (Transcripts of the First All-Russian Conference of Proletarian Cultural and Educational Organizations) (Moscow, 1918), p. 127.

66. Nikolai Otsup, *Sovremenniki* (Contemporaries) (New York, 1986), p. 100.

67. Quoted in Zamyatin, *Sochineniia* (Works), p. 543.

68. Viktor Shklovsky, in conversation with the author, Moscow, 1975.

69. Fedin, *Sobranie sochinenii* (Collected Works), vol. 10, p. 78.

70. Shklovsky, *Gamburgskii shchet* (Hamburg Rules), p. 413.

71. Chukovsky, *Dnevnik, 1901–1929* (Diary, 1901–1929), p. 407.

72. Ibid., p. 430.

73. Ibid., p. 406.

74. V. Kaverin, *Epilog* (Epilogue) (Moscow, 1989), p. 61.

75. *Novyi mir* (New World), 12 (1982), p. 131.

76. Annenkov, *Dnevnik moikh vstrech* (Diary of My Encounters), vol. 1, p. 310.

77. Quoted in Kaverin, *Epilog*, p. 501.

78. Mirsky, *Uncollected Writings*, p. 256.

79. Quoted in Kaverin, *Epilog*, p. 501.

80. Nikolai Chukovsky, *Literaturnye vospominaniia* (Literary Reminiscences) (Moscow, 1989), p. 320.

81. Ibid.

82. Grigory Kozintsev, *Sobranie sochinenii* (Collected Works), 5 vols., vol. 4 (Leningrad, 1984), p. 254.

83. *Sovetskaia muzyka* (Soviet Music), 6 (1983), p. 91.

84. Lydia Zhukova, in conversation with the author, New York, 1979.

85. Dmitri Shostakovich, in conversation with the author, Repino, 1972.

86. Ibid.

87. *Yunost* (Youth), 1 (1988), p. 56.

88. Maria Yudina, in conversation with the author, Moscow. 1970.

89. Fedin, *Sobranie sochinenii* (Collected Works), vol. 10, p. 105.

90. *Sovetskaia muzyka* (Soviet Music), 9 (1976), p. 50.

91. *Vospominaniia o Zabolotskom* (Reminiscences About Zabolotsky) (Moscow, 1977), pp. 86–87.

92. Quoted in *Sovetskoe iskusstvo 20–30-kh godov* (Soviet Art of the Twenties and Thirties) (Leningrad, 1988), p. 22.

93. Ibid., p. 16.

94. *Daugava*, 3 (1988), p. 109.

95. Yevgeny Shvarts, *Zhivu bespokoino . . .* (I Live Anxiously . . .) (Leningrad, 1990), p. 632.

96. Adrian Piotrovsky, *Teatr. Kino. Zhizn'* (Theater. Film. Life) (Leningrad, 1969), p. 93.

97. Ibid., p. 97.

98. Dmitri Shostakovich, in conversation with the author, Repino, 1972.

99. Ibid.

100. Pavel Vulfius, in conversation with the author, Leningrad, 1962.

101. Maria Yudina, in conversation with the author, Moscow, 1970.

102. Nikolai Chukovsky, *Literaturnye vospominaniia* (Literary Reminiscences), pp. 173, 172.

103. Kirill Kondrashin, in conversation with the author, Washington, D.C., 1980.

104. Yulian Vainkop, in conversation with the author, Leningrad, 1967.

105. George Balanchine, in conversation with the author, New York, 1981.

106. *Sovetskaia muzyka* (Soviet Music), 6 (1983), p. 92.

107. *Novoye Russkoye Slovo* (The New Russian Word), April 6, 1990.

108. Lydia Ginzburg, *Literatura v poiskakh real'nosti* (Literature in Search of Reality) (Leningrad, 1987), p. 242.

109. Anna Akhmatova, in conversation with the author, Komarovo, 1965.

110. Vyacheslav Zavalishin, in conversation with the author, New York, 1993.

111. Fyodor Lopukhov, in conversation with the author, Moscow, 1967.

112. Dmitri Shostakovich, in conversation with the author, Moscow, 1974.

113. Quoted in Anna Akhmatova, *Requiem* (Moscow, 1989), p. 105.

114. Shvarts, *Zhivu bespokoino* (I Live Anxiously), pp. 629–30.

115. Lydia Zhukova, *Epilogi* (Epilogues), book 1 (New York, 1983), p. 7.

116. *Voprosy literatury* (Issues of Literature), 9 (1974), p. 175.

117. Lydia Zhukova, in conversation with the author, New York, 1979.

118. Joseph Brodsky, in conversation with the author, New York, 1981.

119. Ibid.

120. Ibid.

121. Lydia Chukovskaya, *Zapiski ob Anne Akhmatovoi* (Notes About Anna Akhmatova), vol. 1 (Paris, 1976), p. 10.

122. Shvarts, *Zhivu bespokoino* (I Live Anxiously), p. 633.

123. *Sovetskaia muzyka* (Soviet Music), 9 (1989), p. 45.

124. Shvarts, *Zhivu bespokoino* (I Live Anxiously), p. 630.

125. Veniamin Sher, in conversation with the author, Leningrad, 1960.

126. *Novoye Russkoye Slovo* (The New Russian Word), May 10, 1991.

127. Quoted in Ales' Adamovich and Daniil Granin, *Blokadnaia kniga* (Blockade Book) (Leningrad, 1989), p. 28.

128. K. Kripton, *Osada Leningrada* (The Siege of Leningrad) (New York, 1952), p. 235.

129. Quoted in *900 geroicheskikh dnei* (900 Heroic Days) (Moscow and Leningrad, 1966), p. 56.

130. S. Khentova, *Shostakovich: Zhizn' i tvorchestvo* (Shostakovich: Life and Work), vol. 2 (Leningrad, 1986), p. 24.

131. Ilya Ehrenburg, *Liudi, gody, zhizn': Vospominaniia* (People, Years, Life: Reminiscences), 3 vols., vol. 2 (Moscow, 1990), p. 242.

132. *Novyi mir* (New World), 3 (1990), p. 267.

133. *Sovetskaia muzyka* (Soviet Music), 5 (1991), pp. 31–32.

134. *Sovetskoe iskusstvo* (Soviet Art), October 9, 1941.

135. A. Kriukov, *Muzyka v gorode-fronte* (Music in the Front City) (Leningrad, 1975), pp. 9–10.

136. *Kontinent*, 37 (1983), p. 363.

137. *Time*, July 20, 1942.

138. Embassy of the Union of Soviet Socialist Republics, *Information Bulletin*, Special Issue, Washington, D.C., August 10, 1942.

139. Antal Dorati, *Notes of Seven Decades* (Detroit, 1981), pp. 60–62.

140. Vera Stravinsky, in conversation with the author, New York, 1976.

141. Kripton, *Osada Leningrada* (Siege of Leningrad), p. 185.

142. Shvarts, *Zhivu bespokoino* (I Live Anxiously), p. 657.

143. *Minuvshee* (The Past), issue 3 (Paris, 1987), pp. 20–21.

144. Adamovich and Granin, *Blokadnaia kniga* (Blockade Book), p. 519.

145. Ibid., p. 370.

146. *Minuvshee* (The Past), issue 3, pp. 23, 38.

147. Kripton, *Osada Leningrada* (The Siege of Leningrad), p. 238.

148. Adamovich and Granin, *Blokadnaia kniga* (Blockade Book), pp. 273–74.

149. A. N. Kriukov, *Muzyka v kol'tse blokady* (Music Inside the Circle of the Blockade) (Moscow, 1973), p. 110.

150. A. Korol'kevich, *A muzy ne molchali* (But the Muses Were Not Silent) (Leningrad, 1965), pp. 141–42.

CHAPTER 6

1. Vsevolod Vishnevsky, *Sobranie sochinenii* (Collected Works), 5 vols., vol. 6 (additional) (Moscow, 1961), pp. 164–65.

2. Milashevsky, *Vchera, pozavchera* (Yesterday, Day Before Yesterday), p. 253.

3. Blair A. Ruble, *Leningrad: Shaping a Soviet City* (Berkeley and Los Angeles, 1990), p. 59.

4. Harrison Salisbury, in conversation with the author, New York, 1977.

5. *Doklad t. Zhdanova o zhurnalakh "Zvezda" i "Leningrad"* (Comrade Zhdanov's Report on the Journals *Zvezda* and *Leningrad*), pp. 32–33.

6. *Teatr*, 8 (1988), p. 143.

7. Quoted in Konstantin Simonov, *Glazami cheloveka moego pokoleniia* (Through the Eyes of a Man of My Generation) (Moscow, 1990), p. 111.

8. *Zvezda* (Star), 6 (1989), p. 167.

9. B. Eikhenbaum, *O literature* (On Literature) (Moscow, 1987), p. 28.

10. *Tynianovskii sbornik* (Tynyanov Anthology), issue 3 (Riga, 1988), p. 218.

11. Sergei Yutkevich, in conversation with the author, Moscow, 1976.

12. Quoted in *Iz istorii Lenfil'ma* (From the History of Lenfilm), issue 2 (Leningrad, 1970), p. 29.

13. Ibid.

14. L. Trauberg, *Fil'm nachinaetsia* . . . (The Film Is Beginning) (Moscow, 1977), p. 209.

15. Kozintsev, *Sobranie sochinenii* (Collected Works), vol. 4, pp. 253–54.

16. Sergei Yutkevich, in conversation with the author, Moscow, 1976.

17. *Iz istorii Lenfil'ma* (From the History of Lenfilm), issue 4 (Leningrad, 1975), p. 99.

18. Sergei Yutkevich, in conversation with the author, Moscow, 1976.

19. Trauberg, *Fil'm nachinaetsia* (The Film Is Beginning), p. 101.

20. G. Mar'iamov, *Kremlevskii tsenzor* (Kremlin Censor) (Moscow, 1992), p. 33.

21. Ibid., p. 35.

22. Lydia Chukovskaya, *Zapiski ob Anne Akhmatovoi* (Notes on Anna Akhmatova), vol. 2 (Paris, 1980), p. 215.

23. *Novyi mir* (New World), 3 (1990), p. 263.

24. Chukovskaya, *Zapiski of Akhmatovoi* (Notes on Akhmatova), vol. 1, p. 47.

25. Nathan Altman, in conversation with the author, Leningrad, 1966.

26. N. Ia. Berkovsky, *Literatura i teatr* (Literature and Theater) (Moscow, 1969), p. 446.

27. Nathan Altman, in conversation with the author, Leningrad, 1966.

28. Kozintsev, *Sobranie sochinenii* (Collected Works), vol. 4, p. 264.

29. Ibid., pp. 264–65.

30. Sergei Yutkevich, in conversation with the author, Moscow, 1976.

31. Nathan Altman, in conversation with the author, Leningrad, 1966.

32. *Akhmatovskii sbornik* (Akhmatova Anthology), issue 1 (Paris, 1989), p. 118.

33. Cf. V. N. Toporov, *Akhmatova i Blok* (Akhmatova and Blok) (Berkeley, 1981).

34. Cf. Brodsky and Volkov, *Vspominaiia Akhmatovu* (Remembering Akhmatova), pp. 36–38.

35. Irina Graham, in conversation with the author, New York, 1978.

36. Anna Akhmatova, in conversation with the author, Komarovo, 1965.
37. Dmitri Shostakovich, in conversation with the author, Moscow, 1973.
38. E. Dobin, *Siuzhet i deistvitel'nost'* (Plot and Reality) (Leningrad, 1976), p. 145.
39. Quoted in V. Vilenkin, *V sto pervom zerkale* (In the One Hundred and First Mirror) (Moscow, 1987), p. 237.
40. A. Afanas'ev, *Poeticheskie vozzreniia slavian na prirodu* (Poetic Visions of the Slavs on Nature), vol. 2 (Moscow, 1868), p. 85.
41. Quoted in *Vozdushnye puti* (Aerial Paths), issue 4 (New York, 1965), p. 280.
42. Joseph Brodsky, in conversation with the author, New York, 1982.
43. *Vozdushnye puti* (Aerial Paths), issue 4, p. 283.
44. Ibid., p. 303.
45. *Literaturnaya gazeta* (Literary Gazette), May 5, 1993.
46. Andrei Bitov, in conversation with the author, New York, 1988.
47. Yevgeny Rein, in conversation with the author, New York, 1988.
48. Joseph Brodsky, in conversation with the author, New York, 1981.
49. Joseph Brodsky, in conversation with the author, Washington, D.C., 1992.
50. Ibid.
51. Joseph Brodsky, in conversation with the author, New York, 1981.
52. *Iosif Brodskii razmerom podlinnika* (Joseph Brodsky in Original Meter) (Tallinn, 1990), p. 168.
53. Joseph Brodsky, in conversation with the author, New York, 1981.
54. Ibid.
55. Kirill Kondrashin, in conversation with the author, Washington, D.C., 1980.
56. George Balanchine, in conversation with the author, New York, 1982.
57. Maxim Shostakovich, in conversation with the author, New York, 1986.
58. Shvarts, *Zhivu bespokoino* (I Live Anxiously), p. 298.
59. Irina Kichanova-Lifshits, *Prosti menia za to, chto ia zhivu* (Forgive Me for Being Alive) (New York, 1982), p. 37.
60. *Novyi mir* (New World), 6 (1992), p. 101.
61. *Tynianovskii sbornik* (Tynyanov Anthology), issue 3, p. 210.
62. Shvarts, *Zhivu bespokoino* (I Live Anxiously), p. 630.
63. Kichanova-Lifshits, *Prosti menia* (Forgive Me), p. 49.
64. Shvarts, *Zhivu bespokoino* (I Live Anxiously), p. 117.
65. Berkovsky, *Literatura i teatr* (Literature and Theater), p. 566.
66. Sollertinsky, *Stat'i o balete* (Articles on Ballet), p. 90.
67. Ibid., p. 96.
68. Quoted in Konstantin Sergeyev, *Sbornik statei* (Collection of Articles) (Moscow, 1978), p. 154.
69. Rudolf Nureyev, in conversation with the author, New York, 1986.
70. Ibid.
71. George Balanchine, in conversation with the author, New York, 1982.
72. Ibid.
73. Joseph Brodsky, in conversation with the author, New York, 1981.

74. Yuri Grigorovich, in conversation with the author, New York, 1990.

75. *Literaturnaya gazeta* (Literary Gazette), May 5, 1993.

76. Brodsky and Volkov, *Vspominaia Akhmatovu* (Remembering Akhmatova), p. 49.

77. Ibid., p. 48.

78. Ibid.

79. Joseph Brodsky, in conversation with the author, New York, 1981.

80. Ibid.

81. Quoted in *Neva*, 2 (1989), p. 166.

82. Ibid.

83. Anatolii Afanas'ev, *Polyn' v chuzhikh poliakh* (Wormwood in Alien Fields) (Moscow, 1984), p. 248.

84. Joseph Brodsky, in conversation with the author, New York, 1981.

85. Solomon Volkov, *Iosif Broskii v N'iu-Iorke* (Joseph Brodsky in New York) (New York, 1990), p. 20.

86. Ibid., p. 50.

87. Joseph Brodsky, in conversation with the author, New York, 1988.

88. *New Criterion*, 1986, special summer issue, p. 11.

89. Joseph Brodsky, in conversation with the author, Washington, D.C., 1991.

90. *Literaturnaya gazeta* (Literary Gazette), May 5, 1993.

91. Nikolai Chukovsky, *Literaturnye vospominaniia* (Literary Reminiscences), p. 46,

92. *Iosif Brodskii razmerom podlinnika* (Joseph Brodsky in Original Meter), p. 179.

93. *Pushkin v vospominaniiakh sovremennikov* (Pushkin in Reminiscences of Contemporaries), vol. 1, p. 120.

94. Quoted in Vas. Bazanov, *Russkie revoliutsionnye demokraty i narodoznanie* (Russian Revolutionary Democrats and Knowing the People) (Leningrad, 1974), p. 316.

95. Ibid., p. 396.

96. *Knizhnoe obozrenie* (Book Review), June 16, 1989.

97. Ibid.

98. Andrei Bitov, in conversation with the author, New York, 1988.

99. Ibid.

100. Ibid.

101. Andrei Bitov, in conversation with the author, New York, 1992.

102. Ibid.

103. Ibid.

104. Andrei Bitov, in conversation with the author, New York, 1988.

105. Viktor Sosnora, in conversation with the author, New York, 1987.

106. Andrei Bitov, in conversation with the author, New York, 1992.

107. Ibid.

108. Joseph Brodsky, in conversation with the author, New York, 1981.

109. Konstantin Kuzminsky, in conversation with the author, New York, 1993.

110. Ibid.

111. Ibid.

112. Alexander Zhitinsky, *Puteshestvie rok-diletanta* (Travels of a Rock Dilettante) (Leningrad, 1990), p. 403.

113. Ibid.

114. Vladimir Rekshan, *Kaif polnyi* (Total High), (Leningrad, 1990), p. 23.

115. Ibid., p. 38.

116. Ibid., p. 125.

117. Anatoly Sobchak, *Khozhdenie vo vlast'* (Taking Power) (Moscow, 1991), p. 214.

118. Yu. Karyakin, *Dostoevskii i kanun XXI veka* (Dostoyevsky and the Eve of the Twenty-first Century) (Moscow, 1989), p. 606.

119. Sobchak, *Khozhdenie vo vlast'* (Taking Power), p. 65.

120. *Tsarstvennoe slovo: Akhmatovskie chteniia* (Royal Word: Akhmatova's Readings), issue 1 (Moscow, 1992), p. 41.

121. *Moskovskie novosti* (Moscow News), May 1, 1988.

122. *Literaturnaya gazeta* (Literary Gazette), August 17, 1988.

123. *Komsomolskaya pravda* (Komsomol Pravda), March 19, 1988.

124. *Nezavisimaia gazeta* (Independent Newspaper), July 16, 1992.

125. *Vechernii Minsk* (Evening Minsk), June 5, 1991.

126. Yegor Ligachev, in conversation with the author, New York, 1991.

127. *Sovetskaia Rossiia* (Soviet Russia), July 5, 1991.

128. *Novoye Russkoye Slovo* (New Russian Word), December 12, 1990.

129. Joseph Brodsky, in conversation with the author, Washington, D.C., 1991.

130. Ibid.

131. *Novoye Russkoye Slovo* (New Russian Word), October 22, 1993.

132. L. N. Gumilyov, *Ot Rusi do Rossii* (From Rus to Russia) (St. Petersburg, 1992), p. 255.

133. Ibid., p. 256.

134. Andrei Bitov, *My prosnulis' v neznakomoi strane* (We Awakened in an Unfamiliar Land) (Leningrad, 1991), p. 38.

135. G. P. Fedotov, *Sud'ba i grekhi Rossii: Izbrannye stat'i po filosofii russkoi istorii i kul'tury* (Russia's Fate and Sins: Selected Articles on the Philosophy of Russian History and Culture), vol. 2 (St. Petersburg, 1991), p. 146.

136. Joseph Brodsky, in conversation with the author, New York, 1988.

137. *Ogonyok* (Little Flame), 24 (1990), p. 10.

138. Bitov, *My prosnulis'* (We Awakened), p. 58.

139. *Iskusstvo Leningrada* (Art of Leningrad), 1 (1991), p. 53.

140. Joseph Brodsky, in conversation with the author, Washington, D.C., 1992.

141. Ibid.

A B O U T   T H E
A U T H O R

Solomon Volkov was born in the USSR in 1944 and studied violin at the Leningrad Conservatory, receiving his diploma with honors. He continued postgraduate work in musicology there, while serving as the artistic director of the Experimental Studio of Chamber Opera. In 1971 his book *Young Composers of Leningrad* appeared with a preface by Dmitri Shostakovich; he also published numerous articles on the subject of Russian culture. After Mr. Volkov came to the United States in 1976, he published *Testimony: The Memoirs of Dmitri Shostakovich,* which he had written in collaboration with the composer while in the USSR. *Testimony* became an international bestseller and received the coveted ASCAP-Deems Taylor Award for excellence in writing about music. Mr. Volkov's other collaborative books include memoirs of Nathan Milstein and interviews with George Balanchine and Joseph Brodsky. Now an American citizen, Mr. Volkov lives in New York City with his wife, Marianna, a pianist and photographer.

INDEX

Books, poetry, plays, operas, and other musical compositions are indexed under the authors' or composers' names. Films and ballets are indexed under the titles of the works.

Oblakov, Andrei, 303
Oborin, Lev, 340
Ogonyok (*Little Flame*), 155, 165
Oleinikov, Nikolai, 390–91, 397, 493, 539
Opera. *See* specific composers
Opoyaz, 288–90, 344, 371, 386, 453, 455, 482
Osipenko, Alla, 503
Ouspensky, P. D., 281
Overcoat, The, 455–56, 459

Palace Square, 22, 42, 92, 195, 213, 214, 545
Panov, Valery, 504
Paramonov, Boris, 513
Pasternak, Boris, 166, 273–74, 275, 339, 340, 366, 367, 405, 464, 469
Paul I, 21, 137
Pavlova, Anna, xv, 149, 258, 292, 471, 492, 501
PBO case, 234–36
People's Comedy, 284–85, 308
Perestroika, 411, 516, 535, 536
Perrot, Jules, 257
Peter and Paul Fortress, 12, 40–41, 47, 213, 541
Peter the Great: alcohol use by, 520; Brodsky on, 515–16; Chemiakin's monument to, 541–42; Dostoyevsky on, 51–52; founding of St. Petersburg by, xi, xiii-xiv, 6, 9–12, 195, 210, 249, 337; in literature, 215, 218, 397; as monarch, 7–16, 31, 32, 49, 125; and Moscow, 8, 9, 209, 210; Nicholas II on, 195; Pushkin on, 12; and railroads, 67; Stalin on, 452; Tchaikovsky's and Benois's interest in, 137; wax figure of, 388, 541. *See also* Bronze Horseman
Peterburgskaya gazeta, 153, 192
Petersburg. *See* Leningrad; Petrograd; St. Petersburg
Petersburg Conservatory, 74, 80, 111, 123, 149, 189, 253, 305–06, 343–45, 350–54, 360–66, 393. *See also* Leningrad Conservatory; Petrograd Conservatory

Petersburg Philharmonic, 546
Petersburg school of composition, 341–42, 352, 355–57, 363, 369, 487
Petipa, Marius, 124, 252, 256–60, 297–98, 305, 315, 317, 318–19, 327–28, 351
Petkevich, Inga, 531
Petrashevsky, Mikhail, 39–41, 43, 48
Petrograd: Akhmatova's identification with, xvii, 221–25, 240–43; Bolshevik Petrograd, 202–24, 336–37; after Bolshevik revolution, 211–14, 225–27; Bolshevik revolution in, 202–07, 336–37; as center of avant-garde movement, 369–71; first celebration of Bolshevik revolution in, 212–13; Lenin's move of capital to Moscow from, xvi, 207–11, 338, 339, 446; population of, 211; renaming of, to Leningrad, 336–40; St. Petersburg renamed as, 195–96, 337, 339; in World War I, 195–200, 206–09. *See also* Leningrad; St. Petersburg
Petrograd Conservatory, 305–06, 352–53. *See also* Petersburg Conservatory
Petrouchka, 137, 261, 263–66, 295, 316, 326, 348, 471, 489
Petrov, Andrei, 487
Petrov-Vodkin, Kuzma, 185, 293, 307, 395
Pilnyak, Boris, 431
Piotrovsky, Adrian, 399
Pisarev, Dmitri, 51, 81–82
Plisetskaya, Maya, 506–07
Polivanov, Yevgeny, 288
Polonsky, Yakov, 94
Ponomarev, Vladimir, 306
Popov, Valery, 526
Porcelain production, 282–83
Potemkin, Grigory, 17
Pravda, 157, 232, 410–11, 433, 434, 436, 496
Preobrazhenskaya, Olga, 258
Prokofiev, Sergei, 74, 79, 80, 149, 150, 296, 311, 315, 318, 341, 345–56, 360, 364, 369, 370, 422, 451, 453, 463, 489, 501, 511